D0213026

DICTIONARY OF AMERICAN CHILDREN'S FICTION, 1859–1959

DICTIONARY OF AMERICAN CHILDREN'S FICTION, 1859–1959

Books of Recognized Merit

ALETHEA K. HELBIG

AND

AGNES REGAN PERKINS

Greenwood Press
Westport, Connecticut • London, England

Library of Congress Cataloging in Publication Data

Helbig, Alethea.
Dictionary of American children's fiction, 1859-1959.

Bibliography: p.
Includes index.
1. Children's stories, American—Dictionaries.
2. American fiction—19th century—Dictionaries.
3. American fiction—20th century—Dictionaries.
4. Bibliography—Best books—Children's stories.
5. Authors, American—Biography—Dictionaries.
I. Perkins, Agnes. II. Title.
PS374.C454H45 1985 813'.009'9282 84-19278
ISBN 0-313-22590-7 (lib. bdg.)

Library of Congress Catalog Card Number: 84-19278
ISBN: 0-313-22590-7

First published in 1985

Greenwood Press
A division of Congressional Information Service, Inc.
88 Post Road West
Westport, Connecticut 06881

Printed in the United States of America

10 9 8 7 6 5 4 3 2 1

CONTENTS

PREFACE

The *Dictionary of American Children's Fiction, 1859–1959: Books of Recognized Merit* includes 1266 entries on such elements as titles, authors, characters, and settings based on 420 books of fiction for children and young people. It is intended for the use of everyone who is concerned with children's literature in any way: librarians, teachers, literary scholars, researchers in American studies, parents, book sellers, publishers, editors—those to whom literature for children is a vital interest professionally or personally.

We have long been aware of the need for such a reference work. In fact, just within a single week recently we had several experiences that demonstrated this forcefully. Puffing with indignation, a colleague dropped into a chair in our office. Neither the university nor the public library had been able to give him a list of novels for young people set in the eighteenth century. "Surely there is a standard reference they could consult?" he insisted. That same week we had been asked by students to suggest children's books with such diverse qualities as blind or sight-impaired characters, the theme of self-esteem, and a setting in Arizona or New Mexico. A graduate student writing a paper on the influence of Defoe consulted us for a list of Robinsonnades published for the juvenile market. A faculty wife called to ask for a critical opinion on the quality of a mystery novel requested as a Christmas gift by a young relative. Because of long interest in children's fiction, we were able to make a few suggestions in each case, as we had on numerous previous occasions, but we had to admit that no central reference source was available to answer such questions. This book is offered as the first of several to fill that need.

In planning this work, we encountered various problems. Of the thousands of books published for children, which should we include? Should we provide separate entries for all the major characters or rely on an extensive index? Should authors' biographies, the only part of our study already served widely by reference works, be included? How will this work differ from an annotated bibliography? Should we attempt critical evaluations?

It was immediately apparent that our own subjective judgment about which books are best or most important would produce a lopsided and idiosyncratic work. Since part of the value of this *Dictionary* would be to social historians and literary scholars tracing changes in subject matter, style, and attitudes, we realized that it would be necessary to include fiction which was once thought meritorious, even if changing values have dated it or made it unacceptable by modern standards. We decided to include those books which have won or been finalists for major awards in children's literature, using the award lists in *Children's Books: Awards & Prizes* issued by the Children's Book Council. We have not included translations or any strictly regional awards, nor those issued by organizations to their members only, nor those given to books chosen by children, since the selection of books made available to the children who are polled is necessarily limited. To get a larger representation, since award lists are comparatively brief, we added the fiction chosen annually by *Horn Book* magazine for its Fanfare list. Some books, however, that clearly have become important as literature for children were overlooked at the time of their publication by editors and award committees. Others, though perhaps of less than award quality, have become popular or have come to be considered standard novels that should be part of any representative collection for young people. To include these books, we added several other lists: the *Choice* magazine list of children's books for an academic library (1974 and 1978 editions); the Children's Classics list published by *Horn Book* magazine; May Hill Arbuthnot's choices in *Children's Books Too Good to Miss* (1959, 1963, 1966, and 1979 editions); and lists published by the Children's Literature Association of the Top Ten American Books for Children and the Children's Literature Association Touchstones. We have also included the Western Writers of America Spur award for westerns because this type has become increasingly significant and because westerns are seldom considered for other awards. A compilation of awards and citation lists appears in the front matter. These many inclusions have given us a broad spectrum of the literature recognized for merit by a wide variety of experts in children's literature over many years.

Because our study is of fiction and not of illustration, we have not included fiction in picture book form, because the texts of such books can seldom stand alone and their analysis requires a consideration also of the illustrations. Determining which brief books should be considered picture books, however, is not as simple as it seems. Different libraries, we discovered, catalogue highly illustrated books differently, and we could find no standard, reliable guide to decide whether or not to consider a highly illustrated book of fiction as picture book. After careful observation, we decided that for books to be stories in their own right, without pictures, most need at least five thousand words. We therefore set that as an arbitrary limit. Books with more than five thousand words, even if the illustrations are very prominent, are included; books with fewer than five thousand words are not.

Collections of short stories presented another problem. Although many of them are clearly fiction, plot summaries and critical analyses could not be done for them in the same way as for connected stories and novels. Again, our decision is arbitrary. Episodic books with the same characters in each chapter, like Eleanor Estes' Moffat books, are included. Books of stories each of which has a separate set of characters are not included. In a few cases stories which were originally parts of collections but have since been published as separate books, like Stockton's *The Griffin and the Minor Canon* and Irving's *Rip Van Winkle* and *The Legend of Sleepy Hollow*, are included if they have at least five thousand words.

A number of other books straddle the division between fiction and nonfiction. These are mostly novels based upon actual lives, realistic animal stories, fictionalized history, or retellings from oral tradition. Libraries we have consulted catalogue some of these with fiction, others with history, natural science, biography, or folk tale. In most cases we have been able to follow the Library of Congress classification for these books.

The time period to be covered was another consideration to be faced. Originally, we expected to cover all the books on our chosen lists with no time division. The starting point was obvious. None of the books on any of our lists was published before 1859, except for the stories of Washington Irving, and these were not issued as separate books until the 1860s. The ending point was more difficult to determine. When the manuscript became too long for a single book, we chose 1960 as the dividing line for two reasons. First, breaking between 1959 and 1960 divided our manuscript roughly in half. Second, and more significant, the type of fiction published for children changed radically about that date, with new and more controversial subject matter and more adult styles of writing being introduced into literature for children. A companion volume will cover fiction published after 1959. A later reference will deal with award-winning books in Canada, the British Isles, Australia, and New Zealand.

Since our study focuses on the fiction itself, we have not attempted primary research on authors in cases where this material is already available in published sources, of which there are several, but we have included brief author biographies for several reasons. Most important, since knowledge about the author may be of value to the researchers in considering a book, having such information in the same volume is convenient. This is particularly true for researchers in those areas where libraries are on limited budgets and do not own the other publications. Besides this, no other single publication includes all the authors whose books appear in our study. In some cases, even though the authors won awards, we could find only a few facts about their lives in spite of extensive and time-consuming detective work. Moreover, in our entries we have focused on what in the author's life is most relevant to children's literature and to the particular books in *Dictionary of American Children's Fiction*. In a few cases, we could find nothing published about an author's life and inquiries to the publishers and even to the authors produced no information. In those instances, the author entries list the books which the authors wrote and as much information as we could find out about them.

In presenting our entries we have tried to follow an arrangement that will be convenient for a variety of users. These entries are of several types:

A. Title entries, which consist of bibliographical information; the sub-genre of fiction to which the work belongs; the setting in time and place; a plot summary incorporating the plot problem, if any, essential characters with identifying features and how they function in the plot, significant episodes, and the denouement; a brief literary critical evaluation; sequels, if any; additional entries not mentioned in the summary, if any; and awards and citations in abbreviated form. A list of the complete names of the awards and citations appears in the front matter. Entries vary in length. Length does not indicate the importance or quality of a book, since plots can be summarized more briefly and critical judgments stated more succinctly for some books than for others. Most readers will be acquainted with the terms we have used for sub-genres, but a few terms may need some explanation. By realistic fiction, we mean books in which events could have happened some time in the world as we know it, as opposed to an imaginary or fantastic world, not necessarily that the action is convincing or plausible. Historical fiction includes those books in which actual historical events or figures function in the plot, as in *Johnny Tremain*, or in which the specific period is essential to the action and in which the story could not have occurred in any other time. Books merely set in past times we have called period fiction.

B. Author entries, which consist of dates and places of birth and death, when available; educational and vocational background; major contribution to children's literature; significant facts of the author's life which might have a bearing on the work; titles that have won awards; frequently titles of other publications, usually with brief information about them; and critical judgments where they can safely be made.

C. Character entries, which include physical and personality traits for important, memorable, or particularly unusual characters who are not covered sufficiently by the plot summary, and such aspects as how they function in the plot, how they relate to the major protagonist, and whether the characterization is credible and skillful. Characters are classified by the name by which they are most often referred to or by that by which the protagonist refers to them, for example, Aunt Debby Smith; Doctor Dolittle; Hopkins, John D. The name is also cross referenced in the index under the other most likely possibilities. If the plot summary gives all the significant information about a character, as with many protagonists, he or she is not discussed in a separate character entry. All major characters, however, are listed in the index.

D. Miscellaneous entries, which include particularly significant settings and elements that need explanation beyond the mention in the title entry.

Every book has title and author entries. Where character and other entries are provided, they contribute additional information to make the total picture of the book more complete.

Entries are in alphabetical order for convenience. An asterisk (*) indicates that the item has a separate entry elsewhere in the book. A dagger (†) indicates that the item appears in the companion volume covering American children's fiction from 1960 on. For names, the asterisk or dagger follows the word by which the entry is listed alphabetically; the asterisk or dagger follows the last word of a title. Publishers' names have been abbreviated; a full list appears in the front matter.

The index includes all the items for which there are entries and such items as cross-references, major characters for whom there are no separate entries, specific place settings, and settings by period, and such items as themes and subjects, books of first person narration, significant tone, authors' pseudonyms, illustrators, and genres.

It seemed essential to us to include some critical evaluation with the title and author entries. As university teachers of literature for children and young people for twenty years and as people trained in the study of literature *as literature*, we have noticed that up until recently literary judgments have seldom been made about books for children. This omission overlooks the fact that fiction for children is first of all *imaginative literature* and focuses attention instead on the utilitarian aspects of the books. We have attempted to bring literary judgments to bear upon the books, keeping in mind, of course, that children are the intended audience. Our inclusion of critical evaluation is in keeping with the national trend toward treating children's literature by the same critical standards as adult literature, as evidenced by the founding and growth of the Children's Literature Association International and sections in the Modern Language Association and its regional affiliates throughout the United States.

One of the purposes of this book is to provide springboards for further study. Subjects and interests changed during the period covered, and this book can assist scholars investigating these and similar topics. One conclusion, however, is too important not to be mentioned here. We have been struck by how much children's fiction has developed and expanded since its beginnings in the late nineteenth century, and how much more skillful the writers have become. Judged by late twentieth century standards of literary criticism, many of the early books appear naive, condescending, didactic, and clumsily written. The very best books measure up to modern standards and are rightly still read and enjoyed today. Authors of many books of secondary quality, however, even well into this century, show little awareness of how to plot, how to develop believable characters, how to use plot to reveal theme, and how to write with grace and vigor. Moreover, they frequently show little awareness of a child's literary capacities and interests. As a result, the books are often heavy with message and description, and while earnest, the tone is patronizing and the content shallow. Not all award-winning books written today measure up to critical standards either, but on the whole they are much more skillfully crafted.

While we ourselves have read every book included in *Dictionary of American Children's Fiction, 1859–1959* and have done all the research and writing in this volume, we have had some valuable assistance. We wish to acknowledge our debt to Eastern Michigan University and to the Josephine Nevins Keal Fund for leaves and grants and to the Eastern Michigan University Library and the Ann Arbor Public Library for the use of their extensive collections. Specifically, we wish to express our gratitude to Marcia Shafer of the Ann Arbor Public Library Youth Room and her staff for encouragement, for aid in research, and for their consistent cheerfulness; to Rita Bullard of the Interlibrary Loan Department of Eastern Michigan University Library for her invaluable help in obtaining obscure books; and to Christina Kuebler for typing the manuscript with good humor and competence.

ABBREVIATIONS

AWARDS AND CITATION LISTS

Addams	Jane Addams Peace Association Children's Book Award
Books Too Good	*Children's Books Too Good to Miss* (1959, 1963, 1966, and 1979 editions)
Children's Classics	Children's Classics list published by *Horn Book* magazine
Child Study	Child Study Children's Book Committee at Bank Street College Award (formerly called Wel-Met)
ChLA Top 10	Children's Literature Association Top Ten American Books for Children
ChLA Touchstones	Children's Literature Association Touchstones
Choice	*Choice* magazine list of suggested children's books for an academic library (1974 and 1978 editions)
Fanfare	*Horn Book* magazine Fanfare lists (including honor books for years when Fanfare lists were not compiled)
Lewis Carroll	Lewis Carroll Shelf Award
Newbery Honor	John Newbery Medal Honor Books and Runners-Up
Newbery Winner	John Newbery Medal Winners
Spur	Western Writers of America Spur Award
Stone	George G. Stone Center for Childrens' Books Recognition of Merit Award

PUBLISHERS

Abelard	Abelard-Schuman
Abingdon	Abingdon Press

American	The American Publishing Co.
Atheneum	Atheneum Publishers
Atlantic/Little	Atlantic Monthly Press in association with Little, Brown & Co.
Brewer	Brewer and Warren, Inc.
Bobbs	Bobbs-Merrill Co., Inc.
Bowen Merrill	The Bowen-Merrill Company
Caxton	Caxton
Century	Century House
Coward	Coward, McCann & Geoghegan, Inc.
Crowell	Thomas Y. Crowell Co.
Day	The John Day Co.
Dodd	Dodd, Mead & Co.
Doubleday	Doubleday & Co., Inc.
Duell	Duell, Sloan & Pearce
Dutton	E. P. Dutton & Co., Inc.
Farrar	Farrar, Straus & Giroux, Inc.
Fields Osgood	Fields Osgood & Co.
Follett	Follett Publishing Co.
Funk	Funk & Wagnalls, Inc.
Grosset	Grosset & Dunlap, Inc.
Hall	G. M. Hall Co.
Harcourt	Harcourt Brace Jovanovich, Inc.
Harper	Harper & Row, Publishers
Heinemann	W. Heinemann
Holiday	Holiday House, Inc.
Holt	Holt, Rinehart & Winston, Inc.
Houghton	Houghton Mifflin Co.
International	International Publishers Co., Inc.
Knopf	Alfred A. Knopf, Inc.
Lantern	Lantern Press
Lippincott	J. B. Lippincott Co.
Little	Little, Brown & Co.
Longmans	Longmans, Green & Co.
Lothrop	Lothrop, Lee & Shepard Co., Inc.
Macmillan	Macmillan Co.
McBride	R. M. McBride and Company
McGraw	McGraw-Hill Book Co.
McKay	David McKay Co., Inc.
McLeod	George J. McLeod, Ltd.
Messner	Julian Messner, Inc.
Morrow	William Morrow & Co., Inc.
Nelson	Thomas Nelson, Inc.
O'Kane	James O'Kane

Osgood	James R. Osgood & Co.
Oxford	Oxford University Press
Pantheon	Pantheon Books
Penn	The Penn Publishing Co.
Platt	The Platt & Munk Co.
Prentice-Hall	Prentice-Hall, Inc.
Putnam	G. P. Putnam's Sons
Rand	Rand McNally & Co.
Random	Random House, Inc.
Redpath	James Redpath
Reilly & Britton	The Reilly & Britton Co.
Reilly & Lee	The Reilly & Lee Co.
Reynal	Reynal & Hitchcock
Roberts	Roberts Brothers
Saalfield	The Saalfield Publishing Co.
Scribner's	Charles Scribner's Sons
Simon	Simon & Schuster, Inc.
Smith	Harrison Smith and Robert Haas, Publishers
Stokes	Frederick A. Stokes Company
Walck	Henry Z. Walck, Inc.
Walker	Walker and Company
Washburn	Ives Washburn, Inc.
Watts	Franklin Watts, Inc.
Way & Williams	Way and Williams
Webster	Charles L. Webster
Westminster	The Westminster Press
Whitman	Albert Whitman & Company
Whittlesey	Whittlesey House
Wilcox	Wilcox and Follett Co.
Winston	John C. Winston Co.
World	The World Publishing Co.

DICTIONARY OF AMERICAN CHILDREN'S FICTION, 1859–1959

A

ABDULLAH (*Little Boat Boy**), Hafiz's gentle, understanding, older brother. He is the only one in the family who can read. His father borrowed money to send him to school so that he would be able to communicate with potential tenants for the family houseboat. Abdullah would like to become a soldier. He takes Hafiz to see the boat races at his school, an outing the boy enjoys, fishes him out of the river when he falls in, and gives him a toy soldier and two copper coins as a gift. The coins give Hafiz the idea of saving money for his education. Hafiz admires Abdullah very much.

ABEL ZAKUTO (*Spice and the Devil's Cave**), wise, compassionate, respected Jewish banker in Lisbon who gives moral and monetary support to the search for the Way of the Spices to India, the sea route around the Devil's Cave, otherwise known as the Cape of Good Hope. Those interested in developing sea routes, among them Magellan and da Gama, gather in the workship where he makes maps and nautical instruments as a hobby, poring over maps and discussing various possibilities. He tricks King Manoel into declaring that Jews not be allowed to leave Portugal, thus rescinding an earlier edict of expulsion passed as part of the king's agreement with Spain when he married a Spanish princess. Abel and his wife provide a home and care tenderly for Nejmi* when she is fleeing from her captors. They treat her like a daughter.

ABRASHKIN, RAYMOND (1911-1960), born in Brooklyn, N.Y.; author, film producer, teacher. He attended New York City College and was in the United States Maritime Service during World War II. In addition to film scripts and magazine articles, he wrote, in collaboration with Jay Williams*, thirteen Danny Dunn books, a series of science fiction for middle readers, of which *Danny Dunn and the Homework Machine** (McGraw, 1958) is typical.

ADAM GORSKI (*Reunion in Poland**), engineer and member of the Union of Polish Patriots, father of Wanda. He directs the rebuilding of roads and bridges in Russia and eastern Poland after the Nazi retreat. He appears as a busy servant of the people and as a solicitous father, who is much too occupied with his work to give Wanda the attention and companionship he would like to. He appears reconciled to the expectation that they will eventually find that his wife, lost in the flight from Warsaw, is dead. He is an undeveloped character.

ADAM LADD (*Rebecca of Sunnybrook Farm**), handsome, wealthy young man to whom Rebecca* sells soap and who afterwards takes an interest in her and gives her (and her friend, Emma* Jane) gifts. Adam's mother died when he was ten years old, and he had a childhood in which he lacked food and clothes, but he is now well-to-do, having succeeded in some unexplained way. He follows Rebecca's progress in the school at Wareham, where he is conveniently a trustee, and falls in love with her, though he does not declare it before the book's end.

ADAM OF THE ROAD (Vining*†, Elizabeth Janet Gray, ill. Robert Lawson*, Viking, 1942), historical novel set in 1294 in England. As spring approaches, Adam* Quartermayne, 11, is getting restless at St. Alban's Abbey school where his father, Roger*, the minstrel, left him some months before while he went to France. Although Adam has a good friend, Perkin*, 12, and frequently sees his beloved red spaniel, Nick, who is boarded with a kindly widow, he longs to be back on the road with his father. When Roger, now in the employ of Sir Edmund de Lisle, reappears, Adam and Nick joyfully go with him to the de Lisle estate near London, where Adam makes friends with Margery de Lisle, the noble's younger daughter, and Hugh, his nephew, while Roger entertains at the wedding of an older daughter. Unfortunately, Roger gambles away to another minstrel named Jankin not only all his pay but even his war horse, Bayard, so they set off for Giles Fair in Winchester afoot. As they are staying at the inn at Burford Bridge, Jankin comes in with Bayard, having overridden and lamed him. The next morning the lame horse remains but Jankin and Nick are gone. Adam and Roger set out after him, and in Guildford Adam spots Jankin with Nick and runs after him, follows him to the River Wey, sees him get aboard the ferry, and, leaving his harp on the bank, impulsively dives in and swims across after the rascally minstrel. Almost overcome by the swift current, he crawls out on the other side and collapses and is taken in and nursed by Jill and John Ferryman, who also retrieve his harp. Recovered, Adam returns to Guildford to hunt for Roger, but hearing that his father has gone on toward Winchester hunting for him, he starts off on the road and on a series of adventures that include joining a merchant, Daun William, who is set upon by bandits, alerting the bailiff, who catches the robbers, hunting for Roger at St. Giles Fair in Winchester, falling from a wall during a miracle play, being taken in and nursed by the vicar, Master Walter, and his sister, Dame Prudence, joining a band of low-grade, thieving minstrels, being hunted in the hue and cry when the minstrels have been accused of house breaking, and finally, having lost his harp, returning to the de Lisle house for Christmas only to find that Roger and the family are away. The porter takes him in, and he spends a gloomy winter with the skeleton staff. When he runs into Jankin and learns that Nick has run away from the minstrel near St. Alban's, Adam sets off, hoping to find his dog has returned to the widow's house, but there learns that Perkin has taken Nick to his home at Ewelme. There he recovers his dog, helps with the plowing and planting, and is given badly needed clothes and shoes, and even a bagpipe. At Oxford, where Perkin has gone to study, Adam sings for the students at Merton College. The next day Roger shows up, having returned from Wales and traced Adam to Oxford, and the boy, though offered a chance to stay and study, goes happily back to the road with his father. Essentially a picaresque tale, a series of episodes strung on the thin thread of hunting the stolen dog, the novel has little tension and seems to be designed as a vehicle to show the character and variety of life in late thirteenth-century England. The pictures of the life, however, are entertaining, well researched, and detailed. Adam is a stout-hearted boy and, if the people he meets are inclined to be more kindly than is likely, his personal charm and his sweet voice make his good luck plausible. Choice; Fanfare; Newbery Winner.

ADAM QUARTERMAYNE (*Adam of the Road**), son of a late thirteenth-century minstrel who wanders for most of a year alone on roads in England hunting for his stolen dog and his father, from whom he has become separated. With a sweet singing voice and some ability at harp playing, Adam considers himself a minstrel and is able to earn his way. He is a rather cocky but good natured boy, boastful about his father but usually modest about himself.

ADAMS, JULIA DAVIS (1900-), born in Clarksburg, W. Va.; author of a number of novels, most of them with historical subjects and set in the Shenandoah Valley where she spent her childhood summers. This background also contributed to her non-fiction work, *The Shenandoah*, for the Rivers of America Series. Her college education at Wellesley was interrupted by a year in England. Later she was graduated from Barnard, married, and lived for two years in Denmark, an experience that inspired her best-known books, *Swords of the Vikings* (Dutton, 1927) and *Vaino** (Dutton, 1929). This book, a story of the Finnish revolution during World War I, and *Mountains Are Free** (Dutton, 1930), a fictional retelling of the William Tell legend, were both named Newbery honor books.

ADAMS, SAMUEL (*Early Thunder†; Johnny Tremain*; Mr. Revere and I**), American Revolutionary leader, an actual historical figure. In *Early Thunder*, Daniel views him as a shuffling, slack-faced man. He thinks he is a fortuneteller, until Jeremy Packer tells him otherwise. Adams directs activities after the government of Massachusetts colony is moved to Salem. In *Johnny Tremain*, he appears as one of the Patriots who meet in the attic of the *Boston Observer*. He organizes the Boston Tea Party. In *Mr. Revere and I* he is a very minor figure.

ADAMS, SAMUEL HOPKINS (1871-1958); authority on the Erie Canal, an interest reflected in his two books for young people, *Erie Canal* (Random, 1953) and the lively *Chingo Smith of the Erie Canal** (Random, 1958). He was graduated from Hamilton College, Clinton, N.Y., and lived near Auburn, N.Y.

THE ADVENTURES OF HUCKLEBERRY FINN (Twain*, Mark, Webster, 1885), sequel to *The Adventures of Tom Sawyer**, far deeper and more serious though with many humorous episodes, told in first person by Huck* in the unschooled dialect of Missouri in the 1840s. Having been taken in by the Widow Douglas, Huck, 14, suffers considerably from her efforts and those of her sister, Miss Watson, to ''sivilize'' him, but he sticks it out, with occasional relapses, until his brutal father turns up and takes him away to an isolated cabin three miles up the river on the Illinois side. There he keeps Huck a prisoner, drinking and beating the boy until Huck manages an ingenious escape, leaving clues that will make it seem he has been murdered and his body thrown in the river. He then floats down to Jackson's Island, where he camps for several lonesome days until he finds another runaway, Jim*, Miss Watson's slave, who has left to escape being sold down the river. When the water rises, they find various pieces of flotsam, including a part of a raft, 12′ x 16′. They explore a house washed out and floating by and find the body of a man shot in the back, but Jim, after secretly seeing that it is Pap* Finn, keeps Huck from looking at the face. One night Huck, dressed as a girl, goes to the Illinois side where he fails to fool a housewife but learns that the woman's husband is planning to hunt the runaway slave on Jackson's Island where he has seen a light. Huck and Jim push off on the raft and start a long odyssey down the Mississippi River, a trip idyllic while they are on the raft isolated from other people but containing episodes of barbarism whenever they go ashore or encounter other people. On a stranded steamboat they overhear two thieves planning to murder a third. When Huck is in the canoe, they get separated in a fog. After Huck finally gets back to the raft and finds Jim, exhausted by worry, asleep, he tries to convince the black man that their separation has been a dream and is ashamed when Jim points out the cruelty of the joke. Beyond Cairo, which they have passed unwittingly, having intended to turn there and go up the Ohio River, their raft is struck by an upbound steamboat, and Huck swims ashore. There he is taken in by the aristocratic Grangerford family, whose son Buck becomes Huck's good friend. Despite their polished manners and talk of honor, the Grangerfords are engaged in a senseless feud with a neighboring family, the Shepherdsons. In an outbreak of violence, all the Grangerford men are killed, including Buck, and Huck escapes with Jim, who has rescued and patched up the raft and hidden out in the swamp waiting for him. Further down the river, two rascally con men join them and take over the raft, saying that they are really a Duke* and a King*, fallen on hard times. At one small town Huck sees a cultivated man, Colonel Sherburn, coldly shoot a drunk named Boggs and then, just as coolly, face off a mob bent on lynching him. Huck attends a circus and is concerned for the drunk tightrope walker, not realizing it is an act. The Duke has been training the King in his garbled idea of Shakespeare, and they put on a show, ending with an evidently pornographic act called the Royal Nonesuch. On the third night, they escape with the door receipts before the show starts, knowing the audience is in a mood to attack them. Further downstream, the two con men pose as Harvey Wilkes and his deaf and dumb brother, William, come from England to visit their dying brother, Peter, with Huck as their servant, and Jim, painted blue, hiding out on a raft with a sign saying he is a "sick Arab." The Wilkes girls, Mary Jane and her two sisters, welcome their supposed uncles, and Huck feels so bad, knowing they are being cheated, that he takes the bag of money they have entrusted to the King and, unable to get it out of the house, hides it in the coffin. The whole scheme is jeopardized when the real uncles arrive, and the body is dug up to see which pair is correct in describing the mark tattooed on Peter Wilkes's breast. In the excitement the crowd forgets Huck, and he gets away, but just as he and Jim are pushing off, the Duke and the King come pelting after them. Blaming each other for the failure of the scam, the two rascals almost reach blows, but they are soon conspiring again, and before Huck realizes what they are up to, the King has sold Jim as a runaway slave for forty dollars. Learning that he is being held at Silas Phelps's farm, Huck goes there, hoping to help him escape. Mrs. Phelps, Aunt Sally, mistakes him for Tom* Sawyer, who is expected on a visit. Huck plays along, and when Tom does arrive, waylays him and explains the situation. Tom then poses as his half-brother, Sid*, pretending that he came along as a surprise. The boys see the King and the Duke, tarred and feathered and ridden out of town on a rail, having played the Royal Nonesuch once too often. Then Tom starts an elaborate series of contrivances to effect Jim's escape in a manner true to his idea of romantic literature. Huck, though unable to see the sense of most of it, cooperates with Tom's ideas, and Jim patiently suffers the torments and indignities that Tom's imagination imposes. When, at last, their schemes are exposed, Tom produces his trump card: Miss Watson has died and set Jim free in her will. At the end, Huck, about to be adopted and "sivilized" by Aunt Sally, decides to "light out for the territory." The depth of the book lies in its moral considerations which center on Huck's struggle with his conscience. Twice he decides that he must turn Jim in, since helping him escape is stealing, and both times is unable to go through with it, deciding finally that he would rather go to hell. The true naive goodness of Jim and Huck is contrasted to the hypocrisy and depravity they meet in both high and low status people during their journey. The natural speech rhythms are said to have influenced all subsequent American fiction. Although it was written as a boys' book, it is usually considered among the three or four greatest American novels for adults as well as children. Children's Classics; ChLA Top 10; Choice; Lewis Carroll.

THE ADVENTURES OF RINALDO (Holt*, Isabella, ill. Erik Blegvad, Little, 1959), lighthearted realistic novel set in the fifteenth century in a medieval European kingdom. Returning from the wars where he has fought for the Emperor

Sisimund and been rescued at a critical point by Colonel Gorchy, the famous but rather threadbare knight, Rinaldo di Paldo, is tired of blood and wants to settle down. Sewed into the waistband of his long red-flannel underdrawers he has a small treasure in jewels, and in his large boots he carries a supply of gold ducats. He fools a group of home-bound enemy soldiers into thinking he is crazy and entertains the country folk at the inn with his stories and the tricks of his great white charger, Wingfoot. Able to attract and train aminals of all kinds, he is soon joined by a squirrel, Pr-rwitt, a pig, Edward, a stag, Arthur, a bear, Chico, an elephant, Jummo, a dog, Bonzo, and various other animals. When the Duke of Hesse-Bonyard summons Rinaldo and his advance man, a boy called "Gooly," runs off, Rinaldo hires a young girl named Daffodil to collect the pennies for his show. Rather than give up all his gate receipts as the Duke demands, Rinaldo goes to prison, leaving his animals and his boots with Daffodil. As he is giving for the Duke a show of the rats and mice he has trained in his dungeon, Wingfoot appears and rescues him by leaping through the opening between the spiked top of the gate and the stone arch above. Rinaldo finds that Daffodil has kept all his animals well and that she refuses to take his gold as a reward. When Rinaldo saves the arrogant Countess de Goldilocks by stopping her runaway coach horses, he wins her gratitude but the enmity of her prissy fiancé, Count Considine. At the Countess's castle, Rinaldo puts on a show, but the Count trips Wingfoot with a cord he has rigged, and Rinaldo is thrown headfirst into a water butt. Daffodil leaps from the crowd to save him from drowning, and he marries her rather than the Countess, who had been about to switch her favors to him. Rinaldo and Daffodil buy an old castle and are fixing it up when a message comes from Colonel Gorchy saying he is being held captive by the tyrannical bandit, Grimius. Rinaldo leaves his animals and Daffodil, journeys to the emperor's court to get the ransom, finds the city crowded for the coronation and access to the emperor impossible. Seeing no other way to get his attention, Rinaldo changes places with the Spanish Knight in a tournament and fights off five other knights in turn, including the Count Nimpimm, only to find that the emperor has spent most of his money for the coronation and can give him only three thousand ducats. As Rinaldo sets off with this meagre ransom, he is joined by three squires, Tom, Dick, and Harry, who admire his performance and want adventure. On the way, they stumble during a snowstorm into a peasant's hut where a girl seems unable to understand their language, but Dick, speaking the language of young love, discovers she is Tamara, Count Gorchy's daughter, hiding from Grimius. In the bandit leader's country, they see his band of about fifty men riding off, but one turns around at Wingfoot's whinny. This proves to be a hunchbacked peddler named Jocko, who, though untrustworthy, joins their cause for a price. Rinaldo and the three squires pose as new recruits for Grimius, create weird sounds and spooky occurrences to terrify the superstitious bandits, and manage to rescue Colonel Gorchy from his dungeon. Jocko carries him out disguised as a bundle of hay for his horse and helps them make a getaway. Before they reach safety, however, Grimius's band nearly catches up, and they just make it across a bridge which the villagers have weakened by chopping almost through the supports. The charging horses of the bandit band make it break, and they and their riders are catapulted into the gorge. Tamara joins her father, marries Dick, and Rinaldo returns to Daffodil, who has presented him with an heir in his absence and has organized the animals to rock the cradle, keep the baby warm, and even knit him sweaters. Although mostly a farcical parody of the medieval hero novels, the story has a fast pace and clever enough adventures to keep it from becoming precious or dull. Rinaldo himself is an admirable hero and Daffodil a practical, competent heroine. Fanfare.

THE ADVENTURES OF TOM SAWYER (Twain*, Mark, American, 1876), humorous realistic novel of boyhood set in the village of St. Petersburg, a name the author gives to Hannibal, Mo., in the 1840s. Through the book run two main plots, one of love, one of murder. Tom learns of a new girl in town, Becky Thatcher, shows off outside her house and in Sunday school to get her attention, courts punishment at school by admitting he is tardy because he stopped to talk with disreputable Huckleberry* Finn, all so he will be sent to sit on the girls' side next to Becky, becomes "engaged" to her, is rejected when she learns that he was previously engaged to Amy Lawrence, and some time later wins her love again by falsely admitting he tore the anatomy book in the teacher's desk and thereby saves Becky, who actually tore the book, by taking the whipping she would have suffered. Near the end of the book he is lost in the cave with Becky when they wander off from the others at her picnic. The murder occurs in the graveyard when Tom and Huck take a dead cat there in a complicated ritual to get rid of warts. They see Dr. Robinson with the town drunk, Muff Potter, and the vicious half-breed, Injun* Joe, robbing a new grave of a body for anatomy studies. Quarreling over the pay, Injun Joe kills Dr. Robinson and blames it on Muff, who is too drunk to know. The two boys swear to each other not to tell, and guiltily befriend Muff as he waits in jail, but at the trial Tom testifies and then is terrified when Injun Joe escapes, knowing he will want vengeance. These two plots come together in the end when Tom finds in the cave the treasure he and Huck have earlier seen Injun Joe digging up from the haunted house and when the cave is sealed after Becky and Tom have found their way out and Injun Joe dies of starvation trying to hack his way out with his knife. Some of the best known episodes in the book, however, have only a tenuous connection with these plots. Tom, being punished for playing hookey and going swimming, is set to spend Saturday whitewashing the fence by Aunt* Polly, with whom he lives, and he cleverly persuades other boys to buy the right to work for him. Unlike his goody-goody half-brother, Sid*, and his kindly cousin, Mary, Tom never concentrates enough to learn his Bible verses, yet he manages to win a prize Bible by trading his whitewashing loot for tickets handed out as rewards for correct recitation of verses. During the tedious church service, Tom diverts himself by watching a dog stalking the pinch bug that he has brought and released. He plays pirate and Robin Hood, runs off to camp on Jackson's Island with Huck and Joe Harper, and arranges to come back to their own funeral. He feeds to the cat the painkiller with which Aunt Polly, an experimenter in patent medicines, has been dosing him and causes the animal to go into an amazing fit. At the school Examination Day, where the young ladies proudly read their pretentious poetry and purple prose, the boys get even with the schoolmaster by letting down from the loft a cat which claws off the master's wig, revealing his bald head gilded by the sign-painter's son as the teacher was dozing. Huck and Tom, trying to find the treasure, follow Injun Joe, now disguised as a deaf-and-dumb Spaniard, to a back room of the Temperance Tavern and find not treasure but a secret store of liquor. Huck follows Injun Joe another night and learns that he plans to disfigure the Widow Douglas as revenge for her husband's once having him publicly horse-whipped. Huck alerts a neighbor and the widow adopts Huck in gratitude and plans to bring him up properly. Tom's age is never clear and seems quite different in the various episodes, though the action spans less than a year. Such inconsistencies seem to matter little, however, in the exuberant spirit of the book. There is humor for all ages, from Tom's " 'tis-taint" fight with the new boy to the more adult passages satirizing small town religion and pretentions. Sequel is *The Adventures of Huckleberry Finn**. Books Too Good; Children's Classics; ChLA Touchtones; ChLA Top 10; Choice; Lewis Carroll.

AGBA (*King of the Wind**), stringy, sturdy, faithful, mute Arab stableboy, whose devotion to Sham, the colt he has raised and loves so much, takes him to France and then to England and through hunger, cold, rejection, and ridicule. Since he is mute, he cannot communicate to anyone what he knows about Sham's lineage—that the horse belongs to the line of Arabians descended from the mares of Mohammed the prophet. While still a child in Morocco, Agba promises the newborn colt that he will be a father ("Ba" means "father") to the motherless creature, and that when he is grown, the colt will be King of the Wind, bowed to by multitudes. Agba's prophecy comes true. Sham is acclaimed for the speed and stamina he transmits to his offspring. Two centuries later, the name of the Godolphin Arabian (Agba's Sham) is found in the pedigree of almost every superior thoroughbred racer.

A-GOING TO THE WESTWARD (Lenski*, Lois, ill. author, Stokes, 1937), historical novel of a trip from Connecticut to the Scioto River valley in southern Ohio in 1811. The Bartlett family—Reuben, a storekeeper, his wife, Roxana, and their children, Betsy, 12, and Thomas, 8—set out for "New Connecticut" in northeast Ohio at the urging of Reuben's footloose brother, James. With them are Aunt* Matilda Stebbins, an elderly lady intending to join a niece whose husband has left her in Portsmouth; Joel Blodgett, a cheerful shoemaker; Deacon Templeton, who wants to save souls in the godless West; Robert Phelps, Roxana's bookish younger brother, and the unwelcome Perkins family, shiftless Jedediah*, his feckless wife, Parthenia, and their unkempt children, Ezekiel (Zeke) and Florilla. On the way they have a variety of difficulties: most inns are dirty and primitive; roads are nearly impassible; a wagon wheel breaks and Betsy gets left behind, both events the results of Jed's skulduggery; at Pittsburgh, where Uncle James is to meet them, they get a message that he has gone to Illinois. Changing their destination to southern Ohio, they buy a boat on which the women, children, and livestock travel down the Ohio River, along with the Perkinses' boat, while Reuben drives overland a wagon loaded with goods to stock his store. They suffer further misfortunes: on the boat, which is set up as a store, wild Kentuckians select goods from Betsy, then start a fight and leave without paying; at a critical point in a rapids Jed fails to follow directions of the pilot, and the Bartlett boat is wrecked and most of the store goods lost; Reuben suffers a fever and nearly dies on his journey. On the trip they meet some fine people:three rough wagoneers, who soften before Aunt Matilda's pious exhortations; Johnny Appleseed, who gives Thomas a baby raccoon for a pet; the Ermintritts, a German family, whose younger daughter, Lotte, becomes a good friend of Betsy and whose destination in the Scioto River valley influences the Bartletts to head there from Pittsburgh; old Johannes, who is looking for his son lost years ago and who finally finds his grandson, young Johannes, adopted son and prospective son-in-law of the Ermintritts; and many others. When they arrive at the Scioto country, they are at first discouraged by the backwoods Scruggs clan, their closest neighbors, and the rough cabin where, temporarily, the Bartletts, the Perkinses, and their various hangers-on all live together. With hard work and enterprise they make good and start a thriving settlement. The author assures her readers in a foreword that she has studied diaries, letters, and records of the period, and a bibliography is given at the end. Inadvertently, she may be pointing out the weakness of the novel: the research predominates and almost every possible difficulty or piece of information is forced into the story. Characters are mostly underdeveloped. Betsy is pious but brave; Thomas is musical, sensitive, and sickly; Lotte is plump and complacent. Only Aunt Matilda comes alive. Jed is interesting in his rascality but unconvincing as a reformed citizen. Fanfare.

ALCOTT, LOUISA MAY (1832-1888), born in Germantown, Pa.; probably the most famous nineteenth-century author of realistic domestic novels for girls, the best and most widely known of which is *Little Women** (Roberts, 1868-1869). Daughter of the much-admired but improvident educator, Bronson Alcott, she lived as a child in Boston and at Fruitlands, an ill-fated experiment in communal living near Harvard, Mass., and at Concord, the town with which she is most closely associated. In 1862 she became a Civil War nurse in Washington, D.C., an experience related in *Hospital Sketches* (Redpath, 1863), and she wrote poetry and "thrillers," but her fame rests on her books for young people, including *Little Women*, based on her youth with her three sisters, its sequel, *Little Men*, (Roberts, 1871) and its sequel, *Jo's Boys and How They Turned Out* (Roberts, 1886); *An Old Fashioned Girl* (Roberts, 1870); *Eight Cousins* (Roberts, 1875), and its sequel, *Rose in Bloom* (Roberts, 1876); *Under the Lilacs* (Roberts, 1878), and six volumes of *Aunt Jo's Scrap Bag* (Roberts,

1872-1882). Never married, she frankly said she wrote for money to relieve her family's financial problems and to ease her parents' old age, a concern she never escaped since she died only two days after her father. Her books are noted for their honest portrayal of realistic life and characters, the favorite being the autobiographical Jo* March of *Little Women*. Compared with modern novels her books are somewhat sentimental and preachy, yet they were landmarks in their time and remain popular today, since they confront concerns that their readers recognize as universal: the problems of controlling temper and selfishness, the pressure for girls to become self-effacing and ladylike in a world that favors boys, the difficulty of having limited money in a society that equates worth with wealth.

ALDRICH, THOMAS BAILEY (1836-1907), born in Portsmouth, N.H.; prominent and highly acclaimed poet and writer in his day, who is now best remembered for his novel for young people, *The Story of a Bad Boy** (Fields Osgood, 1869), not literally autobiography but based on several adolescent years when he lived with his grandfather in Portsmouth. In 1846 he moved to New Orleans, but returned to Portsmouth to study for entrance to Harvard, a plan that was destroyed by his father's business failure and death. He worked as an editor and free-lance writer in New York, where he was part of both Bohemian and conventional literary groups, and returned to New England to edit *Every Saturday* and later the *Atlantic Monthly* in Boston. Such prominent literary figures as William D. Howells and Mark Twain considered his witty writing brilliant, but, though his short stories are clever and his poems competent, his popularity did not survive the change of taste in the twentieth century to realism and more experimental forms. His *The Story of a Bad Boy* was a landmark in its time, being a precursor of Twain*'s *The Adventures of Tom Sawyer** and probably the first realistic story for children whose hero was a normal boy, not always good, and it remains a lively and amusing series of episodes told with nostalgic affection.

ALEXANDER, WILLIAM P., collaborator with Maribelle Cormack on two books, *The Museum Comes to Life* (American, 1931) and *Last Clash of the Claymores** (Appleton, 1940). He also collaborated with Homer D. House in writing *Flora of the Allegany State Park Region* (University of the State of New York, 1927).

ALEXANDRINE (*Homespun**), beautiful, French-American daughter of Monsieur Foucher, planter who sells cotton to the Stillman firm. She has a good business head and helps Stephen* Greenman see the financial possibilities in cotton. The end of the book sees the two on their honeymoon to Paris.

ALEXIS DAHLBERG (*Swift Rivers**), Chris's* grandfather, who lives in the cabin built by the first settler in the area, his ancestor, at the head of the valley in a forest he owns. An old man, he cannot get along with dour, sharp-tongued Nels Anderson, his dead son's wife's brother, with whom he had lived for some time since his return from a life at sea. Chris is determined to provide for the old man.

ALICE-ALL-BY-HERSELF (Coatsworth*†, Elizabeth, ill. Marguerite de Angeli*, Macmillan, 1937), episodic novel of warm, close family life set in the early 1900s stressing the themes of cooperation and friendship. The third person narrative unfolds from the point of view of Alice, a little girl of perhaps ten, who lives with her mother and father in their eighteenth-century family home in a village on the Damariscotty River on the coast of Maine. Each chapter tells a separate story to take Alice through a year of adventures by herself, with her best friend, Marcia, and with her parents with whom she has an unusually close and loving relationship. Alice is an active, often impulsive, imaginative child who can find excitement in almost every situation, either in the events themselves or in her imaginings about those events. With Raymond, a Passamaquoddy youth who temporarily lives with her family, she visits the mounds of sea shells left by his ancestors along the coast. She attends the circus with Marcia, and, while the other girl enjoys the shows, Alice astonishes the pony keeper by riding without problem Brownie, the most unpredictable of his herd. She almost gets lost in a blizzard while ice skating at the farm of her next-to-best friend, Ellen, rejoices when the oxen of her family's new friend, Mr. Dunbar, win the pulling contest at the fair, and goes for a solitary rowboat ride down the Damariscotty, where she encounters a playful seal she names Calypso. She enjoys the antiques in an old mansion in which she and her parents take shelter during a rainstorm, helps to build an attic room in their house so they can listen to raindrops on the roof, and views a smelt run with her parents by moonlight. She makes friends with Miss Abby of the green thumb, Mr. Parsons, the last of the figurehead makers, and Simeon Hall, owner of the local junk shop. Her last adventure involves rescuing Polly, the wicked old parrot belonging to her next door neighbors, the Fairbanks, when their house catches fire. Alice's daydreams extend ordinary situations and add a dimension of interest to this affectionately told, unhurried, wholesome account of a spunky little girl's everyday, domestic adventures. Characters are flat but distinctively drawn, style is vigorous, and situations and events are described in clear, vivid details with much sensory appeal. Fanfare.

ALICE MOREAU (*Mademoiselle Misfortune**), eldest of the six Moreau sisters, who, when she learns that in their Paris *pension* they are regarded as the Six Misfortunes*, resolves to be a blessing, not a misfortune, to her family. She appears to have inherited the skill at diplomacy of her father, a former ambassador to Peru, and puts it to practice in, among other ways, mediating between her siblings. An imaginative child, she often makes up fairy stories for her younger sisters, particularly tales in which the characters wear beautiful clothes. Through becoming the companion of elderly, eccentric Miss* Weatherwax, she restores the fallen fortunes of her family.

ALICE WILDER (*Farmer Boy**), sister just older than Almanzo* and often his work- and playmate on the big farm in New York State in the 1860s. Although not a major character, she provides a contrast with bossy Eliza* Jane by being cheerful and lighthearted and far friendlier to Almanzo.

ALI LIVES IN IRAN ((Singer*, Caroline, and Cyrus LeRoy Baldridge*, Holiday, 1937), realistic story for young children set in the Iranian city of Shiraz in the 1930s. Ali, 10, the son of a professional letter writer, is a Moslem, or to use the term of the book, a "Muhammadan." In his close neighborhood live three other ten-year-old boys, Cyrus, a Zoroastrian, Isasac, a Jew, and Luke, an Armenian Christian. Although all four boys are lonely, they ignore or hurl epithets and sometimes rocks at each other, since adherents of each religion have no social contact with the others. One day, seeing a Kashgai, a nomad, with a wild kid for sale, Ali runs to his mother for a coin to buy it, since the meat of a young goat is a special treat. By the time she has given him a silver *kran*, the Kashgai has disappeared, and Ali hurries through the city, asking the water carrier, the charcoal seller, the policeman, the tea seller, the brick maker, the smith, and the harness maker whether they have seen the man, and at last finds him outside the South Door of the Great Bazaar. The Kashgai will not sell the kid for a single *kran* and tries to keep the one Ali has handed him, but gives it back when the boy insists. With difficulty Ali finds his way home. In the meantime, his little sister, Fatima, 5, wakes from her nap and, finding her mother busy weaving and Ali not there to watch after her, manages to open the door and run down the street. There Cyrus sees her fall down the Dangerous Unfenced Hole to the underground aqueduct, the *Kanat*. Luke, who has also seen the child fall, knows that this is the day the water is diverted into the pool in Isaac's yard. Ali, coming on the scene at this moment, runs with Cyrus and Luke to Isaac's yard. None of the boys can swim, but when Fatima is washed into the deep pool, Isaac bravely jumps in and pulls her out. She revives and is given a ride home on Luke's donkey. Ali's father plans to give a party, a Great Rejoicing for all his Moslem friends, to celebrate her surviving the Awful Calamity, but Ali, backed by his older cousin from the city, Muhammad, persuades him to invite only the boys who helped save Fatima and their parents. All three families hesitate to accept, but do, since they do not want to offend the dominant Moslem group, and the boys become fast friends. Most of the book is a discussion of life in Iran hung on a slight plot. The tone is didactic and condescending both to the young reader and to the Iranian culture. Strange customs and beliefs are described and the reader is cautioned, ". . . you must not laugh at the Iranis," because they have not had the advantage to learn how wrong they are. Since much of the information is no longer accurate, the book is mostly interesting as an example of the attitude frequent in literature for children in the 1930s. Fanfare.

ALL ALONE (Bishop*, Claire Huchet, ill. Feodor Rojankovsky, Viking, 1953), short, realistic problem novel set in the mid-1900s in a village in the French Alps of Savoie in which a boy's unselfish action helps his village to a new, better way of life. For generations the people of Monestier have kept aloof from one another, each family strictly minding their own business, afraid and suspicious of their neighbors. When his father sends Marcel Mabout, 10, up Little Giant Mountain to herd cows for the summer, he sternly admonishes him to have nothing to do with Pierre Pascal, who tends his cows across the ravine on Big Giant. Reluctantly and guiltily, Marcel relieves his loneliness and fear by returning Pierre's yodels at sundown. When Pierre's cows wander into Marcel's pasture, Marcel takes care of them and returns them to the boys' wateringplace. A sudden storm causes a landslide and maroons the boys on Big Giant where they remain for a week, sharing food and consoling each other. The villagers combine to dig them out and a jubilant reunion follows. All return home, grateful that the boys are safe and enjoying a new and very pleasurable sense of togetherness. A year sees the village celebrate their new spirit of cooperation. The people have decided to end their individualistic ways and combine for a community of work in which they will till their fields jointly. This is a slight but pleasant story, in which vigorous if awkward dialogue, the suspense of the storm and the rescue, and colorful and sensory descriptive passages relieve the obvious message. Rojankovsky's smudgy, folk-arty, black and white drawings clarify situations and setting and contribute to atmosphere. Their gentle humor tones down the didacticism of the story. Newbery Honor.

ALLEE, MARJORIE HILL (1890-1945), born in Carthage, Ind.; author best known for realistic books with contemporary settings for older girls, including *Jane's Island** (Houghton, 1931), and *The House** (Houghton, 1944), though she wrote some novels set in the past. A Quaker, she attended Earlham College and later the University of Chicago, where she met and married a professor of zoology, Warder Clyde Allee, with whom she wrote her first book, *Jungle Island* (Rand, 1925). With their three children, they spent most of their summers at the laboratory at Woods Hole, Mass., the setting for *Jane's Island*. Her only son was killed at ten in a traffic accident and her husband became an invalid in 1930, but she continued to write and to be prominent in pacifist and other civic and social causes, interests that are reflected in her novels. Because her subjects were contemporary, changing times and attitudes make her best-known novels seem bland and dated, but they are of particular interest to social historians.

ALLEN, ETHAN (*The Covered Bridge**), Vermont patriot and military leader during the American Revolution, an actual historical figure, whose concern for the well-being of his Vermont friends continues throughout his lifetime. In the novel, he visits schools and tells the children stories about their state and his adventures and helps the farmers with their problems. He organizes the neighbors to raise a barn for the down-on-their-luck MacGowans and obtains a really good price for Peter's* calf by cleverly getting two old skinflints, Ebenezer Hillton and Silas Simmons, to bid each other up for it. His story about how he escaped British soldiers at the covered bridge over Hebron Brook gives Peter the idea of how to save it during the spring flood.

ALLINDA (*Nino**), Nino's* pretty, young mother noted in their village for her ability to cook. She is a kind, solicitous woman, sensitive to her son's needs but firm about not indulging him. She, Nino, and Grandfather* have good times together. She leaves with Nino and Grandfather for America to join her husband.

ALL-OF-A-KIND FAMILY (Taylor*, Sydney, ill. Helen John, Follett, 1951), realistic, episodic family novel which takes place shortly before World War I, the first in the series about a close-knit Jewish family. Five sisters, Ella, Henny, Charlotte, Sarah, and Gertie, live on New York's Lower East Side with their parents, warm and loving Mama and practical Papa, a junk dealer. Although the novel's structure is episodic, the dozen chapters relate to one another, and events occur in chronological order. The episodes are linked by the same characters and by a little mystery involving Charlie, a young man who works for Papa, who has been estranged from his family since they objected to the girl he wished to marry, and who strangely disappears for short periods from time to time. The five girls have simple everyday adventures. They play dressups and visit the library, where they meet the new library lady, Miss Kathy Allen, and Sarah arranges to pay for the book she lost. They help about the house, and Mama makes dusting fun by hiding buttons and pennies for the girls to find as they work. They visit Papa's junk shop, chat with his peddlers, and poke through old books. They shop for candy, which they eat in bed at night, and for a birthday present for Papa. They go to the market with Mama and to Coney Island, where Henny gets lost. The girls help Mama prepare for the Sabbath, but all except Henny are ill with scarlet fever at Passover. They celebrate the Fourth of July with firecrackers and Roman candles that Charlie brings them. The last two episodes are particularly joyful. At Succos the girls prepare a booth with Charlie's help and invite Miss Allen to see it. To their surprise and delight, Miss Allen turns out to be Charlie's lost love, and the two are reunited. The final chapter sees the birth of Papa's long-awaited son, who is nicknamed Charlie after their family friend. The girls are delighted to have a brother, even though his birth means they are no longer an "all-of-a-kind" family. Charcterization is shallow, the girls are hard to keep separate, and the romance seems an unnecessary contrivance. Dialogue is extensive and genuine, language is easy, and tone is warm and affectionate. The book's strongest feature lies in its clear picture of Jewish family life and religious observances. Others in series include *More-All-of-a-Kind Family** and *All-of-a-Kind Family Uptown**. Choice; Fanfare.

ALL-OF-A-KIND FAMILY UPTOWN (Taylor*, Sydney, ill. Mary Stevens, Follett, 1958), realistic, episodic family novel, third in the series about the close-knit Jewish family. They have moved from the Lower East Side of New York and are now living in an uptown apartment. The book begins in 1917, one month after the United States has entered the war against Germany, and concludes in December of 1918 with the celebration of victory. Focus remains on the activities of the several daughters, the older three of whom are the best characterized. Indomitable, impetuous Henny borrows Ella's white party dress without her permission and wears it to a party, her first one with boys. After she spills tea on it, she resourcefully dyes it ecru, a color which, to Henny's relief, becomes Ella very much. While Mama is in the hospital recovering from an appendectomy, Ella runs the household and gets a taste of grownup responsibilities. The pleasant Sabbath she and the girls prepare for Papa ends on a dramatic note when Charlie plays with matches and sets fire to the hall curtains. Uncle Hyman and Aunt Lena invite the family to a *P'Idyon Ha-Ben*, the Jewish ceremony for redemption of the first-born son, and everyone welcomes their new baby into the family. After Charlotte forgets to pay for her ride on the El, her conscience bothers her so much she seeks out the trainman and pays him. Sarah, the student in the family, studies diligently, hoping to win the history prize when she graduates from grade school, but loses to a brilliant classmate whose exam is superior. Binding the episodes together is Ella's relationship with her sweetheart, Jules. He takes her out to dinner for an evening of amusingly awkward moments. Later he enlists, along with his friend Bill, who is the sweetheart of Grace, the daughter of Mrs. Healy, the girls' landlady, and Ella's good friend. Grace and Ella knit for the boys, worry about them, and eagerly await their letters. When Bill is reported missing in action, the family shares Grace's fears. In December, they all attend the victory parade and watch as Jules and his comrades march through the triumphal arch. Back home, they receive the grand news that Bill has been a prisoner of war and is safe. Like its predecessors, this is a warm story of a loving and happy family and their involvement with some friends and relatives. Their problems are only momentarily troublesome, there is little narrative tension, and the book projects a positive outlook on life. Choice.

ALL SAIL SET: A ROMANCE OF THE "FLYING CLOUD" (Sperry*, Armstrong, ill. author, Winston, 1935), historical novel of the first voyage of the famous clipper ship which sailed from 1851 to 1874. Told in his old age by Enoch* Thatcher, 97, it recounts his boyhood from the age of fourteen when, after his father's death, he goes to work for the famous shipbuilder, Donald McKay of Boston. Having fallen in love with a model of the *Flying* Cloud* and watched its building over the year in McKay's shop yard, Enoch is thrilled when

McKay arranges that he be taken as an apprentice on its maiden voyage and obtains his mother's permission. On board he meets the other apprentices, including red-haired, lively Archie "Brick" Warner, Tad "Lanny" Lancraft, and Jake "Whit" Whittlesy. He also gets to know the severe but admirable captain, Josiah Perkins "Perk" Creesy, the brutal first mate, Mr. Jones, and the gentler, efficient second mate, Mr. Andrews. Early in the voyage, which is scheduled to round Cape Horn to San Francisco and then go on to China, Enoch arouses the enmity of the troublemaker, Jeeter Sneed, who, after Enoch bests him in a fair fight, vows to get even. Enoch learns the duties of a seaman, is initiated when they cross the equator, and is nearly swept overboard in a storm off Cape Horn in which Brick is lost. Sneed leads an abortive mutiny and is clapped into irons but later escapes and waylays Enoch in the sail locker which he has set afire. Enoch knocks him out and gives the alarm, which saves the ship, but is so badly burned that he must be left in the hospital in San Francisco. The company representative, at the instigation of Captain Creesy, arranges to send him home as a passenger on another vessel when he has recovered. Both the pilot episodes and the characters are stock elements of sea stories, and the style is not consistently convincing as the first person recital by an old man. The strength of the book lies in its details of the construction and life aboard a historical clipper ship and in the frequent illustrations by Sperry, including some careful diagrams of sails and other parts of the ship. Newbery Honor.

ALMANZO WILDER (*Farmer Boy**, *On the Shores of Silver Lake**, *The Long Winter**, *Little Town on the Prairie**, *These Happy Golden Years**), protagonist of *Farmer Boy*, who, at nine years, does a great deal of the hard work on his father's big farm in New York State in the 1860s, and eventually courts and marries Laura* Ingalls in Dakota territory. As a child, Almanzo is an eager worker, a devoted admirer of his father's horses, which he is seldom allowed to touch, and a great appreciator of the good food which his mother and sisters prepare, and which he consumes with tremendous appetite. He reappears briefly as a homesteader in *On the Shores of Silver Lake*, but does not make a full appearance until *The Long Winter*, when he goes with Cap Garland on the desperate trek to find and bring wheat which saves the frontier town from starvation. In *Little Town on the Prairie* he begins to court Laura and continues in *These Happy Golden Years*, with rides home on weekends during her first, miserable teaching job, sleigh rides and buggy rides behind his beautiful but wild horses, and singing school. Although he is less strongly characterized in these later books, he remains a hard worker and a fine trainer of horses and is shown as patient but daring.

ALONG CAME A DOG (DeJong*†, Meindert, ill. Maurice Sendak, Harper, 1958), realistic animal story set on a farm in the United States in the mid-twentieth century. When a big black dog shows up at the old farm where Joe, hired hand for a neighboring farmer, lives and raises chickens, he is far from welcome. Although Joe loves animals, he doesn't want the threat to the chickens that a dog represents and repeatedly takes the animal off to lose him, and the dog repeatedly returns. Both of them have become protective toward a little red hen who has frozen her toes off. Joe tries to fit her with rubber flippers for feet, and the dog works out a system of avoiding Joe but sleeping beside the hen to protect her, although he is nearly starving. When the hen nests across the field near the swamp, Joe thinks she has been killed, but the dog sleeps close to the nest and even brings her a couple of eggs to add to her clutch. Joe's attitude toward the dog changes when the hen comes back across the field followed by five chicks and patrolled by the dog. The simple story is made striking by the unusual point of view, which shows the action from inside the minds of the dog and the hen, as well as Joe, without anthropomorphizing the animals. The characterization of both man and animals is realistic and convincing. Choice; Fanfare; Newbery Honor.

ALPHEUS OMEGUS (*At the Sign of the Golden Compass**), a magician and astrologer in sixteenth-century Antwerp, a man of mysterious abilities to read minds and predict future events. He is so enraged at the book by Gaspard Desjourdains, which debunks magic and astrology, that he leads a band to wreck the publishing house where it is to be printed and to destroy the manuscript. Taken a prisoner, he escapes in the streets when mutinying Spanish soldiers burn and loot Antwerp.

AMOS THOMPSON (*Flaming Arrows**), scout and Indian fighter, who owns the fort to which the Cumberland settlers flee when Indians raid. A frontier man, Amos leads the defense of the fort, and when it is clear that help is necessary, he climbs over the wall and goes afoot to the next fort to get help. He is a stock figure, wise in the ways of nature and man, a hero to the boys, a teller of tall tales.

AMY MARCH (*Little Women**), self-centered, artistic youngest sister in the New England family, who believes her greatest affliction is her flat nose. When Beth* has scarlet fever, Amy goes to stay with Aunt March and wins her favor so she is selected to go to Europe rather than Jo*. Amy's desire to be elegant backfires when she expends a good deal of effort and money on a party for the well-to-do girls in her art class and only one of the girls shows up. At first determined to marry for money, she refuses a very rich suitor only to marry slightly less wealthy Laurie* Laurence, their next-door neighbor.

ANDERSON (*Farm Boy**), Uncle* Gene's foreman, at O-at-ka farm. A tall, capable, demanding man of forty-five, Anderson had his own prosperous farm by the time he was twenty-five, which he sold for a handsome profit. Later he joined Mr. Warner, whose farm he has run for fifteen years. At first John rather fears him but works hard to earn Anderson's respect and approval. Anderson is an undeveloped character.

. . . ***AND NOW MIGUEL*** (Krumgold*†, Joseph, ill. Jean Charlot, Crowell, 1953), realistic problem novel in which a boy seeks to prove that he is capable of doing a man's work. The story is set on a New Mexican sheep ranch near the village of Los Cordovas at the foot of the Sangre* de Cristo Mountains about 1950. Miguel Chavez, 12, who tells the story, is the middle child in a large Spanish-American family of sheepherders. Grandfather* Chavez worked for a patron years ago, took his wages in sheep, and established what became the family business. Earnest Miguel has many wants. In particular, he longs to accompany his father, uncles, and older brothers (in his opinion, the greatest men in the world) to the summer pastures in the Sangre de Cristo, for him the symbol of manhood. During lambing season in the spring, Grandfather teaches Miguel how to paint identification numbers on ewes and lambs as the lambs are born, and Miguel, proud of compliments on his industry and accuracy, feels he is on his way to achieving his dream. When he rescues some sheep that have been lost in a sudden storm, he is certain that the mountains will be his reward. But his hopes are dashed when his father, Blas*, reproves him for skipping school, tells him bluntly that he is not yet ready for the mountains, and says he may care for an orphaned lamb of his own during the summer. Depressed, Miguel takes his problem in prayer to San Ysidro during the local saint's annual festival. He is certain the saint is intervening on his behalf when his father consults him about preparations for sheepshearing and when one of the shearers, Juan Marquez, praises him and asks that he be given a place at the dinner table with the men. After an unfortunate fall into the fleece bag, the boy resigns himself to not going to the mountains and to having made a fool of himself. In mid-June, he is surprised by the news that his older brother, Gabriel*, has been drafted and that he is to take Gabriel's place with the sheep. It is a bittersweet triumph for the boy; he has achieved his dream, but he is losing the brother he loves the most. His self-recrimination leads to a long discussion between the two brothers about the nature of prayer and life's existential problems. Somewhat wiser about the ironies, complexities, and ambiguities of life, Miguel journeys into the mountains and prepares to carve his name on a tree along with those of other Chavez men who have followed the flocks. The plot moves slowly, and the conclusion is impeded by the long, improbable conversation between the two brothers, which, like much of the extensive ironic humor, has greater appeal for adults than young readers. The characters are sympathetically and deftly drawn, Miguel's longings and reactions seem very real, and the point of view is unerringly true to Miguel's naive character. Equally appropriate are the conversational, introspective style, and simple, short sentences whose Spanish-American cadence is intensified by occasional Spanish words. The many occupational details and descriptions of the fiesta and the valley, mesa, and mountains, the importance of religion to the family, and the close family relationships contribute to the picture of a proud, hardworking people, close to one another, the soil, and their heritage. The novel is more complex and discursive than the rich, effective documentary film by the same name upon which it elaborates. First in Krumgold's series about modern American boys. (Faustina* Chavez; Pedro* Chavez) Books Too Good; Choice; Fanfare; Newbery Winner.

ANDOR (*And the Waters Prevailed**), fifteen-year-old youth about to embark on the wolf hunt to establish his manhood in the tribe when the book begins. Despised because he is little, Andor is intelligent and brave and yearns for glory, even after he earns the name Andor the Wolf Killer because he kills a wolf on his first hunt and one of the dreaded blacks from the south besides. He continues to feel a strong calling to do something great for his tribe and yearns to discover what lies on the other side of the mountains and at the end of the valley. The terrible irony of his life is that he is convinced that he is right about the impending flood, but his conviction leads to the deaths of the two people he loves most, Bardis*, and Kelan*. At the end, when the long-awaited flood finally comes, he is resigned to dreaming. He is vindicated, but there will be no one left of his generation to proclaim him a hero, nor does he any longer care about glory and honor.

AND THE WATERS PREVAILED (Barringer*, D. Moreau, ill. P. A. Hutchison, Dutton, 1956), historical novel about a prehistoric tribe in southern Europe at the end of the Ice Age, which offers an imaginative explanation for the origin of the Mediterranean Sea. The author builds the plot around the theory that the sea was formed when glacial melt-off caused the Atlantic to rise until it broke through the natural barrier at Gibraltar, inundating the valley behind. Events focus on a visionary tribesman who spends his life trying to convince his tribe that they will be destroyed by a flood from the great sea to the west if they do not vacate their valley home southeast of the Pyrenees and move to higher ground. The story begins when small Andor* is a plucky youth of fifteen and embarks on his manhood hunt. Even though he proves himself a skilled hunter by killing a wolf and a warrior by slaying one of the dreaded black men from the south, he never really wins the respect and confidence of his tribe. Stor* the Strong, in particular, seizes opportunities to disparage him. Only Kelan* the Merry, later slain by Stor, and Bardis*, Andor's bride, believe in him and recognize his intelligence and potential for heroism. When Talgar the Chief sends men out to determine where the black men are coming from, Andor and Kelan follow the valley for many days' walk westward to the coast. There, through observation and reasoning, Andor deduces that the ocean threatens the existence of the tribe. Kelan is killed on the return trip, and the people stubbornly refuse to believe Andor. When years pass without a flood, Andor becomes known as a dreamer of idle dreams. The plot moves quickly over his life; his two children grow to adulthood and have families of their own. Bardis continues to have faith in him, and his son, Mendi, accompanies him in his treks in search of a refuge from the danger that he remains confident will eventually come. In later years, he and Bardis travel to the cave he has discovered in the Pyrenees, a bear attacks, and Bardis dies from the shock of the event. Andor, ironically, now has lost the two people of his generation who have meant the most to him and who had believed steadfastly in his dream, both of them in pursuit of the dream itself. When the flood finally comes as Andor predicted, Mendi leads the family to the cave, but the other tribespeople perish in the rising waters. Andor, too old to flee and now ready to join Bardis in the afterlife, chooses to stay behind and drowns with them. Characters are types, dialogue is stilted and stiff, and style often plodding. The strongest aspects of this unevenly plotted novel, with its questionable but fascinating anthropological and geological hypotheses, are its sympathetic central character, a kind of prehistoric Noah, and the careful attention to details of the economic, political, social, and religious life of the tribe, which make the plot plausible. The author also suggests it may have been this event that touched off the flood stories of oral tradition. Fanfare.

ANDY MCPHALE (*The Cabin Faced West**), son of the squatters who live near the Hamiltons and eventual friend of Ann's. He teases her because he feels inferior to the Hamiltons. He is a complex little fellow who envies the successful Hamiltons, yet is loyal enough to his father to defend his roving ways. It is his idea that Ann teach him to read and write in return for his helping about the place. He then becomes more self-assured and often leaves notes. He hides Ann's diary when he is angry at her but later returns it with a handsome deerskin cover. Ann is delighted when she learns that the McPhales will homestead nearby when they return from the east in the spring.

ANDY RUSCH, JR. (*Onion John**), twelve-year-old schoolboy, son of the owner of the local hardware store in Serenity, N.J., whose father has planned that he attend the Massachusetts Institute of Technology to become a scientist and possibly some day go to the moon, thereby achieving his own unfulfilled ambitions. Andy is not yet ready to make such decisions about his future, preferring to help his father around the store and let things come as they may. Partly due to the conflict with his father, Andy becomes best friends with Onion* John, town character.

ANDY WESTBROOK (*Rifles for Washington**), black-haired farmer who becomes a York County rifleman. When he learns that his wife, Mary, has died in childbirth, he avoids going back to McCesson Town to see the baby, young Andy, for several years. Gradually, he recovers emotionally so that when he does return he is able to make an understanding of future marriage with beautiful Margaret Donelson, widow of one of his rifleman neighbors, who has been caring for his son.

ANGELO (*Red Sails to Capri**), regarded by the villagers as the laziest fisherman on Capri and a great blowhard but liked by the children because he takes time to talk and has a good sense of fun and adventure. He agrees to head up the expedition to the cove to find the source of the blue light because he says it will give him the chance to show that he is as good as he says he is.

ANGELO, VALENTI (1897-), illustrator and author; came to the United States from his native Tuscany in Italy when he was eight years old. His family settled in a small town in California where he went to school. Largely self-taught as an artist, he began illustrating in 1926 and has many times been honored by the American Institute of Graphic Arts. Among the more than two hundred books he illustrated for other authors are *Roller Skates** (Viking, 1936) by Ruth Sawyer*, a children's book which won the Newbery Award, and editions of Bret Harte, Elizabeth Barrett Browning, and Walt Whitman. At the age of forty he began writing books for children, based largely on his own childhood recollections. Of the sixteen books he wrote, the spirited *Nino** (Viking, 1938), a Newbery honor book, closely resembles his own youth in Italy at the turn of the century, while *The Golden Gate* (Viking, 1939) stems from his early experiences in America. *The Bells of Bleecker Street** (Viking, 1949) flavorfully recreates the Little Italy, in New York City, where his family lived briefly before leaving for the West. Several of his novels are set in San Francisco where he lived for many years, including *Hill of Little Miracles** (Viking, 1942) and *The Candy Basket* (Viking, 1960), while *The Marble Fountain** (Viking, 1951) involves the Italy of the reconstruction after World War II and conveys a strong anti-war theme. His writings are self-illustrated and exhibit a flowing, joyous style and an artist's keen eye for vivid and colorful details, feature working people in their ordinary everyday lives, and promote the ideals of hard work, neighborliness, brotherhood, faith in God, and respect for authority and the aged.

ANGIE WIGGINS (*The Boy Who Had No Birthday**), fat, cheerful, hard-working toll-keeper's daughter, about forty-eight years of age, who is raising David* Cring. Although she loves him very much, she disciplines him well and is concerned that he have a good sense of values and learn to work and apply himself. She loves to sing and would very much like to have an organ of her own. She is sometimes portrayed as a comic figure, a woman of tremendous physical bulk who is frightened of lightning and takes to her bed whenever a storm comes, because she believes that feathers will keep her from being struck. She is seldom cross, worries sometimes, but usually looks on the bright side of things. At the end, she is sad about giving Davy up but feels that he will have a better life with the family of Dr.* Carlisle.

ANN (*Knight's Castle**), Roger's* sister, and one of the four children who enter the fantasy world of *Ivanhoe*. She likes to read, preferring books about magic, and believes nearly everything she reads or is told. She is a follower, who, in the course of the story, learns to assume the initiative.

THE APPLE AND THE ARROW (Buff*, Mary, and Conrad Buff*, Houghton, 1951), an elaboration upon the familiar legend of the late thirteenth-century Swiss hero, William Tell, from the point of view of Walter, 11, Tell's elder son. After the authors have established setting and introduced Tell's two sons, Walter and little Rudi, and his wife, Hedwig, a cautious, but loyal and supportive woman, the mother describes to Walter how his father and grandfather have organized the men of their canton of Uri to revolt against the cruel tyrant, Gessler, who serves Albrecht, King of Austria. Shortly thereafter, Tell, a big, hearty man, outspoken, respected, if regarded as rash, decides to go to Altdorf, where Gessler has his headquarters, hoping to allay suspicions that rebellion is afoot. Walter happliy accompanies him. In the city he chats with his merry old grandfather and enjoys such sights as a caged bear and eagle. He understands why the town is deserted when he discovers that everyone is expected to bow to the Austrian king's hat, displayed on a pole by the town fountain. When William adamantly refuses, he is seized, but Gessler promises him freedom if he shoots an apple from Walter's head. Although an expert marksman, Tell fears failure, but Walter stoutly encourages his father, and the arrow splits the apple neatly in two. When Tell announces that he had intended a second arrow for the tyrant's heart had he slain his own son, Gessler in anger consigns him to the dungeon of a castle on the Lake of Forest Canton. On the way to the dungeon, a storm arises, and Tell escapes from the boat and later slays the hated tyrant from ambush. On the evening of the last day of 1290, Walter and Rudi tramp up the mountain to watch by firelight the Swiss patriots proclaim their freedom. The next day the Swiss learn their Austrian overlords have fled and realize that the nation of Switzerland has been born. Related in often cliched language but with an artist's eye for descriptive detail, this pleasing story moves quickly, fleshing out the legend with added episodes, characters, and details of place, characterization, much dialogue, and some calculated suspense. Misty full-page illustrations, some in black and white, others in color, help create setting and picture incidents. Choice; Newbery Honor.

THE APPRENTICE OF FLORENCE (Kyle*, Anne D., ill. Erick Berry*, Houghton, 1933), romantic historical novel intermingling real and fictitious figures and events set mainly in Florence, Italy, from about 1452 to 1454, just before and after the fall of Constantinople to the Turks. Sixteen-year-old Neno (Agenore di Giancavallo) leaves his farm home in Tuscany and travels to Florence, hoping to gain information about his long missing father from Messer Bardo (Bernardo) di Deo, importer and silk merchant, who once had employed Neno's father. Although Messer Bardo can tell him nothing about his father, he offers Neno an apprenticeship with his house, a position in which Neno makes friends with Vanni, an aspiring artist, Everardo, ne'er-do-well nephew of Bardo, and Clarice, Everardo's lively, pretty, and impulsive sister. Through Bardo, Neno comes into contact with the powerful and wealthy de' Medici bankers, is accepted in social and artistic worlds in Florence, and becomes aware of the efforts of such masters as Ghiberti and Pollaiuolo. One night Neno and Clarice observe Everardo kill a man in the street, one of the eminent Corsi family, but say nothing in order to protect him. When Neno is sent to Constantinople on business for the di Deo company, Everardo and Clarice accompany him, the latter two escaping just before the Turks take the city, when their "ships walked," that is, were transported overland on rollers. On his return to Italy, Neno chances to discover his father in an inn near Pisa. Ill and dying, his father tells Neno that he has journeyed to a strange and marvelous new world of great wealth and curious people who adorn themselves with feathers. When imprisoned later for murdering the Corsi, Neno gives Cosimo de' Medici a manuscript of the *Iliad* he had secured in Constantinople in return for Cosimo's arranging his release. Good details recreate the thinking, behavior, and attitudes of the arrogant, proud, materialistic, beauty-loving mid-fifteenth-century Florentines, who are just beginning to think about the need to develop new sources for trade. The plot, however, is predictable, not skillfully motivated, and lacks unity. The best drawn character is the shrewd, ambitious, calculating Cosimo; the others are shallow and seem purposely assembled for the story, especially little Christoforo Colombo, who makes a cameo appearance as Neno's guide while he is in Genoa. Newbery Honor.

ARLISS COATES (*Old Yeller**), five-year-old brother of the narrator. As described by his brother, Travis, Arliss is loud and lively, inclined to tell tall tales, to play, against orders, in the pool of drinking water, and to peg rocks, with great accuracy, at anyone who criticizes him. He is also full of curiosity, collecting snakes and frogs and lizards, and of affection, taking the ugly dog to his heart at first sight.

ARMACOST, MR. AND MRS. (*To Tell Your Love**), Anne's parents. Mr. Armacost at first appears to be only an often abstracted English teacher with a liking for hummingbirds, who is considered wise and knowledgeable, and she only an ordinary housewife, in short, stereotypes. But as the book proceeds, new dimensions of their personalities appear. Each interacts appropriately with other members of the family and often gives helpful but never pompous advice. Both parents are aware of Anne's rocky romance and make themselves available to her but never become directive.

ARMER, LAURA ADAMS (1874-1963), born in Sacramento, California; painter, illustrator, and writer of fiction and non-fiction for adults and children, best known for her works about the Navajo. Her first book, *Waterless Mountain** (Longmans, 1931), which tells about a boy who feels called to become a medicine man and is strong in its picture of Navajo life, won the Newbery Medal. Her historical novel, *Dark Circle of Branches* (Longmans, 1933), describes the removal of the Navajo from the Canyon de Chelly area in Arizona by Kit Carson and the Indians' long trek to Bosque Redondo in the late 1800s. She lived in

Navajo country in Arizona and studied Indian mythology and beliefs. *In Navajo Land* (McKay, 1962) is a book of personal experience for adults which describes in words and photographs her life among the Navajo. She studied at the California School of Design in San Francisco and married Sidney Armer, an artist. She was well known as a painter before she began writing books, and all her books are illustrated by herself or her husband. She painted pictures of Navajo life and produced a motion picture, "The Mountain Chant," about the Navajo. Books on other subjects include *The Forest Pool* (Longmans, 1938), a picture book about two small Mexican boys and the animals they encounter, which was a Caldecott Honor book, and *Farthest West* (Longmans, 1939), a story about the attempts of some California school children to save the redwoods. Her plots are weak and characterization unconvincing, but her style is poetic and mystical, and her recreations of Indian life in words and pictures are accomplished with sympathy, respect, and an artist's eye for details of setting, emotion, beliefs, and customs.

ARNOLD LAMONT (*The Great Quest**), Frenchman who has worked in Seth* Upham's New England store and who joins the adventurers on their quest for African treasure. Cool in the face of all dangers, he is responsible for saving Joe Woods several times and, in the end, confesses to being of noble birth, biding his time before he can reveal himself. His knowledge of Spanish and of fencing, both significant in the story, he has kept a secret, remarking cryptically to Joe, "A man does not tell all he knows."

ASA LAMB (*Call of the Mountain**), kindly, knowledgeable, elderly lawyer and farmer, who lives down the mountainside from Nathan and is Nathan's nearest neighbor. He advises Nathan in his problems with Hamilton* Bemis, in farming, and in how he might best conduct himself. For example, he and his wife, Anna, warn him about being so stubbornly proud and determined to make a go of the farm that he forgets to be neighborly. Asa and Anna are always ready to lend a hand.

AT THE PALACE GATES (Parish*, Helen Rand, ill. Leo Politi, Viking, 1949), brief realistic story set in Lima, Peru, in the mid-twentieth century. Paco, about nine, an orphan from the hills of Juliaca, has come to Lima with the latest of a series of "boss-men," a seller of hides. When his boss is hit by a truck and taken to the hospital, Paco runs away to escape the police who would take him to the Public Welfare Orphanage. He takes refuge in a church and comes out in the Plaza de Armas. He has almost decided to go back to the hills when he sees two vicuñas, the small, camel-like animals of his mountain home country, on the lawn of the presidential palace. He feeds them dried corn through the iron grillwork, and when the animals, tame and curious, seem to want to make friends, Paco decides to stay in the city. He becomes a bootblack, sleeping in a niche in one of the old buildings and making friends with the other urchins and with several adults: a flower seller named Señora Domitila, a fortuneteller with a monkey, a keeper of a food stand, and Don Tiburcio, the blind peddler. One Sunday, at the urging of Señora Domitila, Paco goes to church and meets a "little friar," actually an altar boy, who shows him the mummy of Don Francisco Pizarro, first Governor of Peru, and tells him the story of Pizarro's assassination. The soldiers, who have seen Paco visiting the vicuñas every day, warn him that he should not hang around the palace, and, fearing the Public Welfare, Paco decides that he should leave the city. In the evening, as he is ready to go, he stops to visit the vicuñas again and notices that they are nervous and upset. He also sees some men lurking inside the grounds. Hastily, he calls his friends, who throw stones; the blind man's dog gets through the grill and chases the men; the fortuneteller's monkey bites them; Paco climbs over the fence and hits and kicks them. When the guards appear, the men are taken into custody and Paco, surrounded by guards, is marched into the palace. To his astonishment, he is taken directly to the President, who thanks him for saving his life and asks if he would like to stay in the palace and become a guard. Paco sees that the fortune he bought on his first day has come true: "Seek no farther; your destiny is here." The story is slight, written in a simple style for young children, and tells of the wonders of Lima with considerable charm through the innocent point of view of the "little hillbilly." Fanfare.

AT THE SIGN OF THE GOLDEN COMPASS (Kelly*, Eric P., ill. Raymond Lufkin, Macmillan, 1938), historical novel set mainly in Antwerp in 1576. Led by his love of printing, young Godfrey Ingram, 19, has left Oxford and become estranged from his father to be an apprentice in the publishing house of Thomas Vautrollier in London. A jealous fellow apprentice, George Wykes, frames him by setting a treasonable leaflet on the press for which Godfrey is responsible. With the help of his older brother, Godfrey escapes, takes passage for Europe on a ship which is captured by the Spanish, and arrives in Antwerp a Spanish prisoner, destined for the galleys. Again he escapes, hoping to reach the English merchants, but collapses in a doorway and is hidden from the pursuing Spanish by a girl who wears a farthingale, a skirt with wide hoops at the side. Setting out again, he follows the smell of ink and collapses at the entrance to the printing house of Christopher Plantin, under the sign of the golden compass. There he is taken in, nursed to health, given a new name and identity, Pierre LaCour of Lille, and a job as apprentice, setting an edition of Horace. To his surprise, he finds the girl whose hoops saved him, Lucile Desjourdains, correcting proof, and learns that her grandfather, Gaspart, has written a book of free-thinking philosophic ideas being set by the press. At the Desjourdains' house he meets a sinister scholar, Alpheus* Omegus, an astrologer and magician. When two merchants from the English house question Godfrey in an eating house, Omegus rescues him and takes him to his mysterious study, full of strange incense and mirrors, where through hypnotism he extracts Godfrey's knowledge of the Desjourdains book and where the proofs are kept in Plantin's publishing house. On the night before the book is to go to press, the astrologer threatens the old man. Godfrey and Lucile follow him to a grotesque meeting of magicians, fortunetellers, astrologers, and other fakes who prey on the credulity of simple people, all of whom fear that the book, by spreading education, will put them out of business. There Godfrey and Lucile overhear plans to wreck the press and destroy the book. Although they are unable to prevent this disaster, Godfrey captures Omegus by trapping his hand in a press. The city of Antwerp then suffers an invasion by mutinying Spanish troops. In the midst of the looting and burning, Godfrey comes upon Wykes, whom he forces to confess and to clear his name. Shortly after, the gentlemen from the English house come with the news that Godfrey's father has died and left him a substantial sum, which he lends to Plantin to rebuild his business. Although the plot is heavily dependent upon coincidence and the characters are mostly stock types, the pace is fast and the historical pictures of Antwerp in a period of great ferment and change are vivid. Details of Plantin's publishing house, a historical place, are drawn from research in the museum which bears that name in Antwerp. (Justus* Lipsius) Fanfare.

ATWATER, FLORENCE (HASSELTINE CARROLL), co-author of the very popular fantasy, *Mr. Popper's Penguins** (Little, 1938), who completed the book when her husband became ill. She met Atwater when she was a student in his Greek class at the University of Chicago, later married him, and had two daughters.

ATWATER, RICHARD TUPPER (1892-1948), born in Chicago, Ill., originally named Frederick Mund Atwater; newspaperman whose column under the pseudonym of "Riq" ran in the Chicago *Evening Post* and the Chicago *Daily News*. He was a graduate of the University of Chicago in 1910 with honors in Greek, and he later taught Greek at that school and translated *The Secret History of Procopius* (1934). He wrote two children's books, *Doris and the Trolls* (Rand, 1931) and *Mr. Popper's Penguins** (Little, 1938). Before the second book was completed he became ill, and it was finished by his wife. *Mr. Popper's Penguins*, a simple, humorous fantasy, has been widley popular and has been translated into many languages.

AULUS CORNELIUS MARO (*The Forgotten Daughter**), highborn, idealistic Roman youth, a centurion newly returned from the service in Spain under Scipio Africanus who joins the partisans of Tiberius Gracchus, the champion of the poor and dispossessed and an actual historical figure. Aulus assists Tiberius in administering his program to break up the large estates and redistribute the land to the poor. After Tiberius is killed, Aulus returns to the Villa Cornelia in the Samnium hills, where he pursues his studies in law and Stoic philosophy and falls in love with Chloe*.

AUNT BELINDA PRIOR (*The Sea Is All Around**), Mab's aunt, a widow, her mother's elder sister. She is tall and stout like a tree and a very motherly sort of woman who has many friends on Pokenick* Island, where she has lived since a child. She and Mab get on well right away. She is lighthearted and open-minded, strong but not rigid, and shares her life with Mab.

AUNT COLMAN (*Away Goes Sally**), Sally* Smith's great-aunt, who lives in a big, comfortable, fashionable house in Quincy, Mass., with servants to wait on her. Sally finds her house and way of life fascinating because it is so different from her own life on the farm. Aunt Colman has a little black page boy, a parrot named Turk, and a monkey called Jackanapes with whom Sally plays. She gives Sally a necklace of coral and gold beads as a going-away-to-Maine gift. It is while the women are at Aunt Colman's that Uncle* Joseph finishes the house on runners as a surprise compromise for Aunt Nannie.

AUNT DEBORAH SMITH (*Away Goes Sally**; *Five Bushel Farm**; *The ''Fair American''**), shy, retiring, lighthearted aunt of Sally* Smith. In *Five Bushel Farm*, she unexpectedly and uncharacteristically asserts herself to stand up to Jennie Hallet when she is about to beat Andrew Patterson for smashing the ship he has carved. Deborah informally adopts the boy, and he becomes very fond of her. Later she marries Captain John Patterson of the *Fair American* and becomes Andrew's adored stepmother. When in *The ''Fair American''* the ship is stopped by French looking for Royalist refugees, Deborah boldly asserts, using for the first time the French she has been practicing, that Pierre is her eldest son, averting suspicion from him when he inadvertently speaks in French. She is a warm, calm, life-loving woman.

AUNT EMILY (*Roller Skates**), Lucinda's imperious, stuffy aunt on her mother's side, with four meek and ladylike daughters whom Lucinda dubs the gazelles because of their shy and demure ways. She keeps an eye on Lucinda's respectability during the year. Lucinda does not get on well with her. Near the end of the book, Lucinda persuades two of the gazelles to accompany her to a play that they all know Aunt Emily would not approve of. The girls have a fine time.

AUNT ESTHER SMITH (*Away Goes Sally**; *Five Bushel Farm**), Sally* Smith's aunt and younger sister of Uncle* Joseph and Nannie. In *Five Bushel Farm*, in May, 1790, she marries Sam Hallet, a distant cousin, after the Smiths emigrate to the Penobscot in Maine. The wedding takes place on the bank of the river and is a very exciting event for the family. A hard rain has washed away the ferry, and the minister is unable to cross the river. The wedding party gathers on one side of the river, and the minister conducts the service standing on the opposite bank. When unfeeling Jennie Hallet insists that Andrew Patterson give Esther the ship he has carved as a wedding gift, he smashes it in a fury. At that point Aunt Deborah*, intervenes and takes the boy home with her.

AUNT HILDA AND UNCLE CHARLIE (*In a Mirror**), Bessie's* nagging aunt and milktoast uncle, who epitomize for Til* what marriage should not be like. They contrast with Donald* Dunn and his wife.

AUNTIE KOBE (*The Promised Year**), whose real name is Mrs. Miyagawa, the elderly woman who is Keiko's* fellow passenger on the freighter from Japan. A mixture of shrewdness and simplicity, Auntie Kobe is able to understand Keiko's fear of spending a year with strange relatives in a new country and to play with her in a childlike way. Auntie Kobe is travelling to the United States to seek her son, Jiro, who went there twenty years before and from whom she has not heard in nearly that long. She has a naive faith that she will find him and in her home medications, which she dispenses liberally. Aboard ship, she attempts to keep her cat, Tama, hidden in her stateroom and solves her problem of getting the animal into the United States by giving it to Keiko, rightly supposing that a child is less likely to be challenged.

AUNT LOVESTA COFFYN (*Downright Dencey**), Dencey's aunt who is a Quaker preacher. She often goes on preaching trips or missions of care. Dencey feels close to her and admires her, but even Aunt Lovesta is too caught up in her own religious and personal affairs to sense that Dencey needs a confidant who will listen and advise her objectively. In one of the most memorable passages in the novel, Aunt Lovesta takes Dencey with her when she goes on "concern" to feed the hungry, a starving family whom in a mystical experience Lovesta discovers.

AUNT MATILDA STEBBINS (*A-going to the Westward**), actually second cousin to Roxana Bartlett's mother, lively and opinionated spinster who accompanies the Bartlett family on their journey to southern Ohio in 1811. A positive New Englander, Aunt Matilda is certain of the superiority of her heritage and her religion and, at first, is horrified by the Germans who sing and dance and enjoy life and whose language sounds to her like swearing. She also disapproves, with considerable reason, of Jedediah* Perkins, and she speaks her mind to him but nevertheless nurses his wife through her frequent "spells" and is properly grateful when Jed saves her from drowning. When she finds that the niece she hopes to join has died, she sensibly decides to stay with the Bartletts, and her energy and good sense help them through many misfortunes. By the book's end, she has overcome some of her prejudices, has become fast friends of the German Ermintritts, and has set up as a tailor for the frontier community.

AUNT POLLY (*The Adventures of Tom Sawyer**; *The Adventures of Huckleberry Finn**), elderly aunt who provides a home for Tom* Sawyer, her "dear dead sister's son." Sharp-tongued but warmhearted, she thinks it is her duty not to spare the rod and spoil the child, and she frequently uses a switch on Tom or raps his head with her thimble. In *Huckleberry Finn* she appears briefly at the end when she arrives at the Phelps farm some 1100 miles south of St. Petersburg to see for herself what that ''harem-scarem'' boy is up to.

THE AVION MY UNCLE FLEW (Fisher*, Cyrus, ill. Richard Floethe, Appleton, 1946), adventure story set in France shortly after World War II. Johnny Littlehorn, 12, somewhat spoiled after having injured his leg in a fall from his pony on his Wyoming ranch, is reluctant to accompany his parents to France, the native country of his mother, Yvonne Langres Littlehorn, where his father, Richard, is an officer in post-war liaison. In Paris, John is pushed in a wheelchair by the hotel doorman, Albert, who contrives several encounters with a tall, pale, sinister Monsieur Fischfasse, who also appears under the name of Simonis, trying to buy the family property near the village of St. Chamant. John, whose parents have gone to London, travels to St. Chamant in the French mountains with his Uncle Paul Langres, where Paul builds his ''avion,'' a very stable glider whose design he hopes to sell to an aircraft company so that he will have funds to rebuild the family home. In a fast-paced series of adventures, John finds a German pistol and other evidence that a Nazi has been hiding out in the ruins of the mansion, accidentally shoots the truffle-hunting pig of Mayor Capedulocque, and makes friends with the red-haired twins, Charles and Suzanne Meilhac. Together he and Charles discover that Simonis, really a Nazi, Albert disguised as a fisherman, and the Mayor, a wartime collaborator, are in league to dig up and abscond with embezzled French bank funds hidden at the Langres home's ruins. The youngsters are chased to the mountain home site where Suzanne unexpectedly launches the avion with John in the cockpit, so he is able to fly it to the village for help. Throughout the book, which is written in the first person, John reports the French words and phrases he learns, so that in the end he wins not only the three-speed bike promised by his father if he walks two miles but also the electric lighting dynamo promised by his mother if he will learn enough French to write a letter of six pages on any subject. The report on the Fete, given in honor of his uncle's successful avion, is given in French which the youthful reader can puzzle out if he has followed the story closely. While the plot is unlikely and the character development minimal, the story's fast pace and good nature make it attractive as a juvenile spy adventure. Fanfare; Newbery Honor.

AWAY GOES SALLY (Coatsworth*†, Elizabeth, ill. Helen Sewell, Macmillan, 1934), historical novel set at the end of the eighteenth century in Massachusetts and Maine, covering about a year's time. Little Sally* Smith lives with her three aunts and two uncles on a farm in Massachusetts. On the day in late summer when, for the first time, she is allowed to drive the gig to take lunch to her uncles while they are reaping salt hay by the ocean, she feels a keen sense of anticipation that something exciting is about to happen to the family. Later that day, hardworking, reliable Uncle* Joseph Smith receives a letter from Cousin

Ephraim Hallet in Maine urging the Smiths to emigrate. Everyone is excited about the prospect except prim, authoritarian Aunt Nannie, who asserts that she will never leave her own fire or sleep in any bed but her own. Days go by with the matter of Maine unsettled. Aunt* Esther and Sally visit Tuggie Noyes, the local "witch," who predicts that there will be a wedding before next fall and that both Uncle Joseph and Aunt Nannie shall have their ways. When in January the aunts and Sally return from visiting her great aunt, Aunt* Colman in Quincy, they are amazed to see that Uncle Joseph has cleverly circumvented Nannie's resolution by building a small house on runners. In this cozy, moveable dwelling, pulled by twelve oxen, Nannie can have her own fire and bed. For the most part, the trip is smooth and comfortable. At Kennebuc Ferry, Sally gets her portrait painted on Valentine's Day. Later jolly Uncle* Eben buys from an Indian a bear cub he names Hannibal, and Hannibal becomes a hero when he noses out of the snow a peddler buried during a blizzard, saving the man's life. When the Smiths reach the Penobscot River, Cousin Ephraim takes them to their one thousand acres of green and rolling pasture and woods in Pleasant Valley by the river. Aunt Esther and her sweetheart, Sam, are joyfully reunited, and a wedding is in the offing. A pleasing story for younger readers, the plot ambles with a few twists and some mild suspense to a satisfying conclusion. Sally and her big family are individualized and winning, and the narrative is rich with details of warm, close pioneer family life. (Sophronia* Hallet; Aunt* Deborah Smith) Books Too Good; Choice.

AYONBA (*Three Sides of Agiochook**), a Wabanaki Indian scout, who witnesses the massacre of the Indians at St. Francis on the St. Lawrence River by Rogers's Rangers. After the Rangers leave, he finds a blond, blue-eyed infant in the arms of its dead mother, a French-Indian girl named Louise Gill, who has married an English soldier held prisoner by the French. A truly noble savage, Ayonba has taken the child to a clergyman named Brewster in Montreal but has insisted that the child live with his Indian cousins during the summers. He has secretly kept track of the boy, known as Philip Brewster, but he does not reveal himself until he saves Philip from Mohawks in the early stages of Philip's journey north, and thereafter he escorts the boy and saves him a number of times. A Wabanaki of the Penobscot tribe, he inherits an enmity against the Mohawks but participates in a ceremony in which representatives of the two tribes literally and symbolically bury the hatchet.

B

BABCOCK, MRS. (*Homespun**), fussy wife of the blacksmith in Independence, Mo., at whose home Mark* and Sukey* stay while they are waiting for a wagon train to leave for Sante Fe. She keeps the cleanest house in town and is particularly proud of a century plant she brought west from her home in Rhode Island ten years earlier. She talks a lot about ''my-son-Henry,'' a trader in Santa Fe, and sends gifts to him via wagons leaving Independence. She almost goes west with Mark and Sukey, but changes her mind at the last minute, to their immense relief. It is to Henry, still after many years intimidated by his mother, that Mark and Sukey sell their calico.

BAILEY, CAROLYN SHERWIN (1875-1961), public school teacher, social worker, author and editor of books for children and of *Delineator* and *American Childhood*; born in Hoosick Falls, New York, and educated at Columbia University Teachers College, Montessori School in Rome, and the New York School of Social Work. She left a substantial body of stories, retellings, plays, verse, and books of pioneer arts and crafts that were based on meticulous research in town records, letters, and diaries. She fictionalized her informational books for interest, embodying in them her philosophy of teaching through entertainment. These works have little but antiquarian interest today, and her reputation as a writer for children now rests upon her Newbery Award-winning novel, *Miss Hickory** (Viking, 1946), also a *Choice* and Fanfare book. This episodic fantasy about the taciturn, stubborn doll with apple twig body and hickory nut head survives because of her creator's skill with characterization and talent for capturing in words the appearance and flavor of the New Hampshire countryside. This book had its origin in Bailey's own Victorian childhood. Her grandmother made for her the original Miss Hickory, with which Bailey played under a lilac bush, later broken and forgotten to be revived in the author's adulthood as the hard-headed spinster, whose adventures, if sentimental and didactic, have continued appeal for young girls. Among the most highly regarded of Bailey's other books are *Children of the Handcrafts* (Viking, 1935), stories of real children who became famous in their individual crafts, *Tops and Whistles* (Viking, 1937), true stories of historic early American toys, and *Pioneer Art in America* (Viking, 1944), stories about real American craftsmen. Bailey and her husband, Dr. Eben Clayton Hill, a radiologist, made their home in New Hampshire.

BAKER†, CHARLOTTE (1910-), born in Nacogdoches, Tex.; author-artist whose interest in animal welfare is reflected in her books, many of which, both fiction and non-fiction, concern care of pets and kindness to animals, including *Necessary Nellie** (Coward, 1945), a story of a dog in a Mexican-American family. She attended Stephen F. Austin State College in Nacogdoches, received her B.A. degree from Mills College in California and her M.A. at the University of California in Berkeley. She has taught art in Texas public schools, Ball State Teachers' College, and Texas College of Arts and Industries at Kingsville, Texas, and was at one time acting director of the Portland, Oregon, Art Museum. More recently she wrote *Cockleburr Quarters†* (Prentice Hall, 1972), a story of children and their pets set in a southern black neighborhood. With her attorney husband, Roger Montgomery, she has been active in the Humane Society at Nacogdoches, where they have made their home, and in similar state, national, and international organizations.

BALDRIDGE, CYRUS LEROY (1889-), born in Alton, N.Y.; author, illustrator. He studied at the Frank Holme School of Illustration and at the University of Chicago. During World War I he was a war correspondent. He married Caroline Singer* and collaborated with her on a number of books for young people including *Ali Lives in Iran** (Holiday, 1937) and *Boomba Lives in Africa* (Holiday, 1935), books designed to show the different customs of unfamiliar countries. He is author of *I Was There with the Yanks on the Western Front* (Putnam, 1919) and *Americanism: What Is It?* (Farrar, 1936).

BANNER IN THE SKY (Ullman*, James Ramsey, Lippincott, 1954), realistic adventure novel set in the Alpine Village of Kurtal in 1865 about a sixteen-year-old boy's determination to climb the Citadel, the highest mountain in Switzerland, now known as the Matterhorn. Since his father, a highly respected guide, froze to death in an attempt to scale the peak, Rudi Matt's mother wants him to become a hotel manager. Rudi is encouraged in his dreams to become a guide by Teo Zurbriggen, his father's good friend, who was crippled in the climb that claimed Mr. Matt's life, and Rudi often sneaks off for solitary climbs. While in the mountains one day, Rudi saves the life of a famous English mountain climber, Captain John Winter, who senses the boy's longing to emulate his father and to scale the peak. Since the guides in Kurtal are superstitious about the mountain, and Franz Lerner, Rudi's uncle and the ablest of them all, refuses to attempt the ascent, Winter engages as guide Emil Saxo, from the rival village of Broli. Rudi sneaks off by night to join them, and Franz and other Kurtalers search for him. Winter persuades them and Emil to rise above petty rivalry and cooperate in achieving their common objective. The other guides agree to form a support crew, Winter insists on Rudi's accompanying the assault team in spite of his inexperience, and the four, Winter, Emil, Franz, and Rudi, set out. When they are very near the top, Winter falls ill, and Emil strikes off on his own. Although he knows it is against the guide's code to leave his *Herr*, Rudi goes after Emil, determined that the glory of scaling the peak should not go to one from Broli. When Emil falls, Rudi is caught between the demands of ambition and propriety. He abandons his intention to be the first to scale the mountain in order to help the guide back to the camp, and both arrive wounded and exhausted. Uncle Franz and Winter manage to reach the top where Winter plants Rudi's rustic staff flying his father's red shirt as a victory banner. Although Rudi has not succeeded in reaching the top, he is hailed as a victor because his rescue of Emil exemplifies the code of the guides, and his mother agrees to let him become a guide. Rudi's personal problem is believable and interwoven well with the main details of the story, which is based on actual fact. But events are contrived and predictable, characterization is conventional, and the theme is obvious. The power of this stylistically pleasing book comes more from the description of inevitable tight spots and the rugged, forbidding terrain than from the emotions and personal problems of the characters. Books Too Good; Choice; Fanfare; Lewis Carroll; Newbery Honor.

BARDEAU, ETIENNE (*Clearing Weather**), mysterious, quick-thinking, well-dressed, daring adventurer and promoter of freedom, who encourages and assists Nicholas* Drury in his plan to build the sailing ship, *Jocasta**, save his uncle's financially troubled shipyards, and provide work for the people of Branscomb, Mass., during the hard times just after the Revolutionary War. Bardeau has a letter which proves that Darius Corland, who was the enemy of Nicholas's uncle and who wishes to take over the Drury shipyards, helped the British during the Revolution. Bardeau forces Corland to leave for England under threat of disclosure.

BARDIS (*And the Waters Prevailed**), Andor's* beloved wife, mother of his son and daughter. In their youth, she is as venturesome as he, and the two often roam the hills together until her first baby is born. Later, their son, Mendi, takes her place by Andor's side on his treks, equally as confident of his father's rightness as she. Bardis never loses confidence in her husband's heroic qualities and his cause.

BARNAC THE CAT (*The Quaint and Curious Quest of Johnny Longfoot, the Shoe King's Son**), Squire of Catnap, a city of cats comprised of many roofs built up and down the sides of a very steep hill. Barnac says he will give Johnny* three pounds of gold, half a pound of precious stones, and a short coat if Johnny will bring him the seven-league boots hidden on Coral Island. His request launches Johnny on a series of exciting and amazing adventures.

BARNES, NANCY (HELEN SIMMONS ADAMS) (1897-), author of *The Wonderful Year** (Messner, 1946), a Newbery honor book set in Colorado in the first decade of the twentieth century that has the ring of autobiography. She also wrote *Carlotta, American Empress* (Messner, 1943).

BARRINGER, D(ANIEL) MOREAU (1900-1962), born in Pennsylvania, graduate of Princeton, geologist, mining engineer, and investment counselor. His historical novel, *And the Waters Prevailed** (Dutton, 1956), set among a prehistoric tribe in southern Europe at the end of the Ice Age, projects an intriguing and plausible hypothesis for the origin of the Mediterranean Sea. In spite of its lumbering style and shallow characterization, it won critical acclaim and was selected for the Fanfare list by the editors of *Horn Book*.

BARTUSEK, LIBUSKA, author of two books for youngsters published in the early 1940s, *Happy Times in Czechoslovakia** (Knopf, 1940) and *Happy Times in Finland* (Knopf, 1941), both episodic fiction mainly designed to show traditional holidays and dress in the country of the title. She also was translator for a book of folk songs of old Vincennes.

BASIDIUM-X (*The Wonderful Flight to the Mushroom Planet**; *Stowaway to the Mushroom Planet**; *Time and Mr. Bass*†), small, previously unknown planet. It is thirty-five miles in diameter and 50,000 miles from Earth and is Tyco* Bass's homeland. The atmosphere is pale green, and its surface is covered with light green, spongy moss, fern trees, and myriads of grayish white and pinkish mushrooms of various sizes and shapes. It is inhabited by the Mushroom* People. Earth, which comes between it and the sun, called the Hot One, serves as its protector from the sun's heat.

BATES, YANCEY (*The Sea Is All Around**), Mab's Mr. Bates, the small, plump man with six-sided spectacles who owns the little curiosity shop on Pokenick* Island that Mab likes to visit. A dim, dark place with a pot-bellied stove, it is filled with old wares and oddities of every sort. Mab meets Mr. Bates when Aunt* Belinda takes an old set of china to him to sell, and they strike up a friendship. She spends her Christmas money on gifts for Aunt Belinda and others at his shop, and he presents her with the heirloom parrot cage that has a false bottom and that once belonged to his grandmother.

BATTY BARGLE (*Runaway Prentice**), lazy, bad-dispositioned son of Bartholomew Bargle, Lord* Timothy Dexter's gardener, who threatens to tell the authorities that Jeff is a runaway apprentice. To buy his silence, Jeff gives him the elegant brass buttons from the blue coat Mercy made for him when he ran away from home. The coat was torn when Jeff bravely went to the rescue of Lord Timothy's Mexican hairless dog.

BAUM, L(YMAN) FRANK (1856-1919), born in Chittenango, N.Y., died in Hollywood, where he had made his home for many years; prolific writer who is remembered almost entirely for his fantasy series for children, the Oz books. After being privately tutored at home and attending Peekskill Military Academy, he had a variety of careers—actor, producer, newspaperman, storekeeper—mostly unsuccessful, in New York, South Dakota, and Chicago. His first book for children, *Mother Goose in Prose* (Way & Williams, 1897), was illustrated by Maxfield Parrish and sold well, but it was *The Wonderful Wizard of Oz** (Hall, 1900) that started him on the road to success and Hollywood. Although he continued to write other children's books under his own name and the pseudonyms of Floyd Akers, Laura Bancroft, Capt. Hugh Fitzgerald, Suzanne Metcalf, Schuyler Staunton, and Edith Van Dyne, and published some novels, plays, and non-fiction for adults, and one of the first science-fiction novels for teenage boys, *The Master Key: An Electrical Fairy Tale* (Bowen Merrill, 1901), the Oz books were far and away the favorites and are the only ones much read now. In *The Emerald City of Oz* (Reilly & Britton, 1910), he tried to end the series but succumbed to requests that he continue, writing fourteen in all, the last two being *The Magic of Oz* (Reilly & Lee, 1919), and *Glinda of Oz* (Reilly & Lee, 1920). After his death, the series was continued by Ruth Plumly Thompson, who wrote nineteen, and others, until there were forty Oz books in all. *The Wizard of Oz* has been dramatized many times, the most famous screen adaptation starring Judy Garland. Although the series has its staunch defenders, most critics find Baum an inventive writer but a poor stylist whose books, after the happy concept of the first, deteriorated in quality.

THE BEARS ON HEMLOCK MOUNTAIN (Dalgliesh*, Alice, ill. Helen Sewell, Scribner's, 1952), very simple story based on a tall tale from the oral tradition. Jonathan, 8, has many aunts, uncles, and cousins, all of whom are coming together for the christening of a new cousin and are planning to stop for supper at Jonathan's home at the foot of Hemlock Mountain. His mother, who must make stew for twenty-three people, sends Jonathan over the mountain to borrow a large pot from Aunt Emma. He carries carrots, nuts, and bread crusts for the squirrels, rabbits, and birds. Although warned to start back early, he eats too many cookies at his aunt's and falls asleep, so finds it already getting dark as he makes his way back over the mountain. To keep up his courage, he repeats, "There are no bears on Hemlock Mountain," until he sees two bears approaching. He puts the large pot down, climbs under it, and waits while the bears sniff around the pot until his father and three uncles, carrying guns, come to find him. As a simple story of courage and ingenuity, the book has some appeal, but the theme of kindness to animals is somewhat obscured by the implication that the uncles will shoot the bears. Newbery Honor.

BEAVER (*Seven Stars for Catfish Bend**), one of the seven animals awarded a silver star for heroism in ridding the bayou of hunters. A comic figure, he is helpful in various ways on the trek northward and in routing the hunters. He has been rejected by the other beavers because he has trouble making trees fall where he wants them to. Doc Raccoon and his friends take him in.

BECAUSE OF MADELINE (Stolz*†, Mary, Harper, 1957), realistic novel of school and family life set in New York City one school year in the mid-1900s. Modestly reared, observant, articulate Dorothy Marks, 19 and a college art major, looks back on her fourteenth year, when flamboyant, garishly dressed, ungrammatical, gauche Madeline Portman enrolls as a scholarship student at exclusive Bramley School and changes the lives of Dorothy and her friends. At the beginning, the status-oriented Marks family live happily in their comfortable apartment, the lawyer father, homemaker mother, and dreamy, good-looking, idealistic Brian, 16, a Hotchkiss student of firm convictions and superior intelligence. Dorothy gossips about her family and her friends. She tells of taking a trip to Bonwits and making fudge with boy-crazy Madge Whittier, who brazenly chases Brian and commands a clique of pseudo-sophisticates at Bramley with whom Dorothy gets on variously; reports conversations with Celia Harris, her best friend at Bramley and a scholarship student, who contrasts with Madeline as a character, wisely avoids drawing attention to herself, and points out to Dorothy that Madeline needs to be tough to survive; describes the homecoming welcome at Christmas time for Brian and his Hotchkiss roommate, handsome Adam Fielding, with whom Dorothy later falls in love; tells of going skating in Central Park with Brian and Adam the time that Brian meets Madeline and of a party with Adam at which she learns about Madeline's working class background and the circumstances of her enrolling at Bramley; and reports how she takes Madeline on a tour of her beloved Bramley at the teacher's request. Conflict arises when Brian empathizes with Madeline in her aspirations for a better life, seeing as noble and brave behavior the other students consider brash and pushy. Although Dorothy maintains she is not snobbish, ironically she says she fears that Brian has lost his heart to a girl who is obviously unsuitable for him. Moved by loyalty to her brother and the pangs of conscience, she invites Madeline home, at the same time precluding friendship with her by her superior, snobbish attitude. Rejected by the girls at school, rushed by the boys who ogle her too-obvious charms, Madeline gradually learns to dress more suitably and becomes less brassy, although she maintains her aloofness for self-protection. The last chapter finds Dorothy reflecting on the changes that Madeline has brought to their lives. Brian has resolved the conflicts between position and altruism by going into the ministry; Lexy Carvel, whose mother persuaded the trustees of Bramley to admit Madeline, the daughter of her maid, and who promptly fell in love with the girl, has developed a warmth of personality that tempers his previously caustic intellectuality; and Dorothy sees herself as less smug, rigid, and complacent. A study in character and class, the book offers little in the way of story. The plot premise seems implausible, and the characters, though strongly drawn, are plaster figures. There is some humor, particularly of irony, and style is detailed, deft, and literary without being stuffy. The sense of setting is strong in this curiously unaware book; it presents an atmosphere innocent of sex, of the world of work, and of world issues. The worst thing that can happen, it seems, is for an outsider to intrude upon the secure, insulated microcosm of these wealthy New Yorkers. Fanfare.

BECKER, JOHN LEONARD (1901-), born in Chicago, Ill.; author, correspondent for the Chicago *Daily News*, director of the John Becker Art Gallery in New York. He was educated at Phillips Academy, Andover, Mass., and at Harvard University. During his varied career he was also associated with the Institute for Juvenile Research in Chicago, was Public Relations Advisor of the Council against Intolerance in America, and was owner of the Brattleboro Theater in Brattleboro, Vt. He worked with the American Red Cross field service in Italy in 1943-1944. Besides *Melindy's Medal** (Messner, 1945), written with Georgene Faulkner*, a simple story which treats a black protagonist sympathetically, he wrote a number of other children's books, including *Seven Little Rabbits* (Walker, 1973), illustrated by Barbara Cooney, and *Near-Tragedy at the Waterfall* (Pantheon, 1964).

BECKY LINVILLE (*The Jumping-Off Place**), plucky, courageous, hardworking seventeen-year-old who takes the major responsibility for establishing a home for herself and her younger brothers and sister on their dead uncle's claim in South Dakota. As the year progresses, she learns to give more responsibility to her brother Dick, 15, befriends neighboring homesteaders, the Wubbers and the Kennikers, whose daughter is bright but crippled, helps to lay out for burial the Oleson baby who has died of snakebite, teaches in the one-room school, saves the lives of the schoolchildren during a blizzard, and establishes a sense of community among the settlers of the area.

BECKY THATCHER (*The Adventures of Tom Sawyer**), schoolgirl friend of Tom*, to whom he becomes engaged and with whom he is lost in the cave. When she arrives as the new girl in town, he is immediately smitten and uses all his boyish wiles to win her attention. She rejects him, temporarily, when she learns he has been previously engaged to Amy Lawrence. When Becky has torn the teacher's anatomy book, Tom takes the blame, thereby saving her from a whipping before the school. Becky is pretty, blond, feminine, a boy's ideal girl, not characterized strongly as an individual.

THE BEEMAN (*The Windy Hill**), wise, kindly Thomas Brighton, cousin of the Peytons. Until near the end of the story, Oliver and Janet* do not know who he really is. They believe he is simply a kind man who keeps bees. Nor do they discover until later that his daughter, Polly, is really the Cousin Eleanor whom

Oliver has resisted meeting because he is sure she is priggish and lifeless. When the book begins, Oliver is running away to avoid meeting Cousin Eleanor. None of this is really convincing but suits the book's atmosphere of unreal realism.

BEEZUS AND RAMONA (Cleary*†, Beverly, ill. Louis Darling, Morrow, 1955), humorous episodic story set in an Oregon town in the mid-twentieth century. Beezus (Beatrice) Quimby, 9, is plagued by her little sister, Ramona, 4, who is a real pest and always gets her own way, by a tantrum if necessary. Hoping to distract her from a favorite book about a steam shovel, Beezus takes her little sister to the library, where Ramona finds another book about steam shovels, one she likes so well that she writes all over it with purple crayon so it will have to be paid for rather than returned to the library. She accompanies Beezus to her art class and creates considerable havoc. Determined to get Henry Huggins and Beezus to give up checkers for tiddely-winks, which she can join, Ramona crashes into their table and shuts Henry's dog, Ribsy, in the bathroom, where he manages to lock himself in. While Beezus is looking after her, she hides in the basement and eats apples, one bite from each apple because the first bite always tastes the best. She creates an even bigger problem when she invites her whole nursery school to a party without mentioning it, and her mother and Beezus cope all one rainy afternoon with fifteen nursery school children and one baby sister dropped off at the same time. Beezus organizes them into a continuous cellar to attic parade and her mother uses up the great surplus of applesauce (made from Ramona's bitten-into apples) for refreshments. For her tenth birthday, Beezus asks her favorite Aunt Beatrice, Mother's younger sister, to dinner, but it nearly turns into disaster when Ramona spoils one cake by dumping the eggs, shells and all, into the mixer and a second one by playing Hansel and Gretel and cooking her rubber doll as the witch in the oven with the cake. Aunt Beatrice brings a cake from the bakery, and when Beezus guiltily confesses that there are times she really doesn't love Ramona, her mother and aunt recount a hilarious series of times Beatrice was just as much of a trial to her big sister as Ramona is now. The girls are more individualized characters than Henry and his friends in the earlier books of the series, though Ramona is seen mostly through the perceptions of Beezus and therefore as a trial to the rest of her family. Sequels. Choice.

BEHN†, HARRY (1898-1973), poet and novelist; born in McCabe, Ariz. He spent his childhood in Prescott, Ariz., then attended Stanford University and Harvard, wrote scenarios for movies, and from 1938 to 1947 taught at the University of Arizona, Tucson. His translations of Japanese haiku make up two volumes published for children, *Cricket Songs* (Harcourt, 1964) and *More Cricket Songs* (Harcourt, 1971), and among volumes of his own poems for children are *The Little Hill* (Harcourt, 1949), *Windy Morning* (Harcourt, 1953), and *The Golden Hive* (Harcourt, 1966). He also wrote a book of comment and criticism, *Chrysalis: Concerning Children and Poetry* (Harcourt, 1968), which is considered one of the best introductions to poetry for young people. His novel, *The Two Uncles of Pablo** (Harcourt, 1959), is a lighthearted story of a Mexican boy whose affection and loyalty are sought by two great-uncles, one a conservative, respected scholar, the other a cheerful, irresponsible rogue. In a very different vein is *The Faraway Lurs*† (World, 1963), a poetic romance set in prehistoric Denmark. Both were chosen for the *Horn Book* Fanfare list and for the *Choice* list. At the time of his death, Behn was living in Greenwich, Conn.

THE BELLS OF BLEECKER STREET (Angelo*, Valenti, ill. author, Viking, 1949), realistic novel of family and community life set in New York City in 1945, relating the generally amusing adventures of Italian-American Joey Enrico, 12, his family, and friends. They live on Bleecker* Street near the Church of Our Lady of Pompeii, whose bells ring out the hours for the whole neighborhood. Joey's acquiring for luck the toe of St. John the Baptist, an old statue which is to be sent to China, provides tenuous unity for the highly episodic plot, which moves from spring to Christmas. Joey's good fortunes include hitting twelve home runs for his baseball team, playing the violin to lead the music in a grand parade to celebrate VE Day, and particularly his father's return from fighting in Italy to a big neighborhood party. Mother makes her excellent *gnocchi* for Father, and Professor* Dante, Joey's violin teacher who lives upstairs, provides a beautiful *pannetoni*. When Joey's conscience bothers him about having taken the toe, he and his best friend, Irish-American Peter Ryan, known as Pete* the Squeak for his high-pitched voice, ask advice of the priest. With his help they locate the old statue and glue the toe back on so that St. John will be whole and complete for the people in China. Other adventures include attempting to buy Peggy di Luca's cat in Sheridan Square and finding that birds have eaten the bakery-made cake Mother ordered for Father's homecoming. The end of the book sees the entire neighborhood joining in a special musical and puppet program in the school auditorium on Christmas Eve. Father manages the puppets, and Joey's rendition of ''Ave Maria'' on the violin provides just the right touch. Although dated by its uplifting attitude and earnest tone, this entertaining story of a simpler era in which all problems are capable of solution is affectionately told, stays true to the spirit of childhood, and projects a keen sense of the Italian-American community. Fanfare.

BEMELMANS, LUDWIG (1898-1962), born in Meran, Austria, in the Tyrol; artist, author and illustrator of books for adults and children. He is best known for his series of picture books about Madeline, the daring, irrepressible, perennially popular little French girl. Her slyly humorous adventures related in the catchy verses and expressive, unorthodox paintings of *Madeline's Rescue* (Viking, 1953) resulted in a Caldecott Medal for illustration. Most of his other books for children are also picture books, with texts sometimes in prose and sometimes in verse, but his novel *The Golden Basket**, also self-illustrated, (Viking, 1936) was a Newbery honor book and a Fanfare book. In engaging, understated humor and appropriately amusing, seemingly unsophisticated pictures, it improvises on his childhood. His home was in a hotel where he mingled with an assortment of exotic travelers and eccentric permanent residents. Other books, like *Hansi* (Viking, 1934) and *The High World* (Harper, 1954), reflect his youth in the Tyrol, and some grew out of his extensive travels in America, Europe, and South America, like *Quito Express* (Viking, 1938). He also wrote many humorous books of fiction and non-fiction for adults. He emigrated to the United States when he was sixteen and worked in a series of New York hotels and restaurants, later opening his own restaurant. In 1935, he married Madeline Freund, whose name he used for his winsome Parisian heroine, and devoted his full attention to writing and drawing.

BEN AND ME (Lawson*, Robert, ill. author, Little, 1939), fantasy biography subtitled, "A New and Astonishing Life of Benjamin Franklin As written by his Good Mouse Amos," and explained, in a foreword, as being a manuscript written in tiny script on pages the size of postage stamps found by workmen altering an old Philadelphia house. Amos, the first person narrator, relates many of the well-known incidents in Franklin's life in the late eighteenth century and usually explains how his own involvement produced the results considered genius by most biographers. Amos starts as one of a large family of poor church mice, who leaves home to seek his fortune and finds a cozy home in Franklin's fur cap. Using the analogy of how his family could get warm gathering around a hot chestnut dropped by a vendor, Amos persuades Franklin to move the fire into the middle of the room in a container, thereby creating the Franklin stove. Amos generously allows Franklin to take the credit but makes him sign an agreement to have regular supplies delivered to the church vestry for the mouse family and to give Amos a permanent home in the fur cap in exchange for continued advice. Once Franklin thinks he has lost his invaluable advisor when a dog carries off the cap while Ben is swimming; Amos, however, has escaped and hidden in some bushes. The mouse, who dislikes Franklin's frequent quoting of maxims and, in particular, dislikes "A cat in gloves catches no mice," edits it out of a new edition of *Poor Richard's Almanac* and takes liberties with various facts about tides. When irate shipmasters protest, Franklin disperses the mob by showing the book they have is a counterfeit, saying "Amos says" whenever the original says "Poor Richard says." During Franklin's period of infatuation with electricity, Amos, who has been sent up in a kite in a thunder storm, leaves, but after Franklin returns from an unsuccessful trip to London to set the grievances of the colonies before Parliament, Amos, for patriotic reasons, again takes up residence in the fur cap and contributes to the wording of the Declaration of Independence, actually a statement written by a fiery mouse named Red who has accompanied Thomas Jefferson to Philadelphia, a statement originally of the grievances of mice against men. Amos accompanies Franklin to Paris to seek financial aid for Washington's army. At the French court, Franklin is lionized and, at the war's end, hates to leave. Amos, in the meantime, has become acquainted with a beautiful white mouse named Sophia, who lives in Madam Brillon's towering headdress. Sophia has been the victim of court intrigue; her beloved husband has been banished to America, and her children are imprisoned in a cell beneath the Queen's throne. Amos organizes mice from the Swedish and Russian embassies; Red, who has arrived with Jefferson, organizes the street mice of Paris, and Amos sends word to the sailor rats of John Paul Jones's ships. Together they win a great battle against the court mice and free the prisoners, but the unseemly skirmish is blamed on Ben, and he is willing to go home, taking Amos, Sophia, and her children with him. In the interest of humor, the story plays fast and loose with historical facts, though the main outline of what happens is accurate. Franklin is pictured as a rather simple-minded putterer of whom Amos is scornful but fond. Choice; Fanfare; Lewis Carroll.

BEN DOBBS (*Hans Brinker; or, The Silver Skates**), Jacob* Poot's English cousin, to whom the boys show the sights on their skating trip down the canal to The Hague. He is able to contribute information about Thomas Higgs.

BENJ (*Mountain Born**), the kindly, capable, old shepherd who accompanies Peter to the hills with the flock, teaches him much about caring for the sheep, gives him practical advice about living, and kills the wolves which threaten the flock. He has served Peter's family for many years, enjoys their respect and affection, and is thought of almost as a member of the family. He helps Peter to accept the inevitability of Biddy's aging and directs his attention to her lamb which appears to have inherited her mother's intelligence and capacity for leadership.

BENJAMIN WEST AND HIS CAT GRIMALKIN (Henry*†, Marguerite, ill. Wesley Dennis, Bobbs, 1947), biographical novel about the boyhood of the famous eighteenth-century artist who became known as the father of American painting. Intense, conscientious Benjamin West, about seven when the story begins, is the tenth child of the prosperous owner of Door-Latch Inn in Chester County, Pennsylvania Province. He rescues a small, half-dead, black kitten, which he names Grimalkin*, little suspecting that the family favorite will help to launch him on his life's career. The kitten soon grows to be lively and independent, an energetic ratter and mouser of excellent manners, who becomes self-appointed supervisor of inn, yard, and barn. Benjamin has a secret wish to become a painter, a hope he fears will remain unrealized because Quakers regard painting as frivolous and unnecessary. His parents disapprove of the sketches he makes in his spare moments, and his stern father hopes he will soon outgrow this childhood foolishness. Benjamin is certain that Grimalkin approves and even encourages him, and he uses the cat's fur to make brushes. Humor results when he uses so much of the cat's hair that the cat begins to look quite mangy and the parents fear that the cat may be suffering from a disease. Local Indians teach the boy to make colored paints by mixing earth and bear's grease, and gradually he attracts attention among the neighbors for his colorful and apt paintings. A visit to Philadelphia with good-natured Uncle* Phineas Pennington, Grimalkin tucked away under his coat, brings Benjamin to the attention of painter William Williams and later an invitation to study at the Philadelphia Academy. Not convinced that such a vocation is suitable for their son, Mr.* and Mrs.* West take their problem to the Quakers in meeting, and, after viewing Benjamin's pictures and discussing the situation, the investigating committee votes to accept the invitation and send the boy to Philadelphia to study art. The last chapter describes a celebration 150 years hence in honor of the man who became President of the Royal Academy of England and Court Painter to George III of England and the first of the great American painters. This warm, affectionately told, often amusing story conveys some sense of the larger times, a good sense of the importance of painting to the boy, and a strong sense of Quaker ways. The bond between the child and the cat and their "conversations" ring true to the spirit of boyhood, and the family is close-knit, caring, and quite attractive as a group. Characters are clearly drawn and tinged with the comic. Vocabulary is easy and style is literate and pleasingly descriptive and employs Quaker speech. Events are arranged for mild suspense. The book succeeds admirably in its intention of showing in an interesting fashion how one of the greatest painters in American history got his start without sounding instructive, maudlin, or laudatory. Dennis's sketches depict incidents, help to visualize setting, and contribute to humor. (Sassoonan*; Jacob* Ditzer) Fanfare.

BENJIE (*The Railroad to Freedom**), Harriet Tubman's tall, unkempt, good-natured, older brother, who helps her escape from Cousin Susan's house and whom later she leads to freedom in the North. He is an unselfish, responsible man, who refuses to seek freedom for himself when Harriet flees, because his wife, Lily, is about to have a baby.

BENNETT, RICHARD (1899-   ), born in southern Ireland; artist, illustrator, and author of books for children. He came to the United States with his family when he was six. The family settled in Washington State about thirty miles from Seattle. After graduation from the University of Washington with a degree in art, he taught art for ten years, traveling in the summers to Europe and to his native Ireland, where he collected folk tales and absorbed atmosphere. After 1930, he turned his full attention to writing and illustration, subsequently illustrating about fifty books by other authors for both adults and children, including books for such writers as Ellis Credle, Padriac Colum*, and Evelyn Sibley Lampman†, a collection of Hans Christian Andersen's stories, and Harold Felton's book about Paul Bunyan. He wrote and illustrated seven books of his own, humorous stories set in either Ireland or the Pacific Northwest, the areas that have been the chief influences on his work. *Skookum and Sandy** (Doubleday, 1935), a Fanfare book, relates the comic adventures of a mischievous goat in an Indian village in the Northwest. The fantasy *Shawneen and the Gander*

(Doubleday, 1937) takes place in Ireland, while *Mr. Ole* (Doubleday, 1940) combines both settings when two boys emigrate from Ireland to the pioneer Northwest.

BERRY, ERICK (EVANGEL ALLENA CHAMPLIN BEST) (1892-1974), born in New Bedford, Mass.; very prolific author and illustrator mostly of books for young people and mostly under the pen name Erick Berry (her first married name), but she also used the pseudonym Anne Maxon. After attending the Pennsylvania Academy of Fine Arts and art schools in New York and Paris, she went into fashion drawing and illustrating greeting cards and juvenile books. She traveled extensively, and, while on a trip to Africa, she met and married Herbert Best*, an officer in the Nigerian Government Service. He eventually retired from the Service to write, and the couple made their home in England, and, after the outbreak of World War II, in the Adirondacks. With him she wrote and illustrated several books for young readers and illustrated a dozen of his books. She published about five dozen self-illustrated books, and she illustrated many books for other authors as well. She wrote informational books about other peoples and other countries, many as a result of her travels, while some of her books are biographies and collections of folk tales. Her many novels for older readers and young people include realistic career stories like *Illustrations of Cynthia* (Harcourt, 1931), based on her own experiences in art school in New York, or of family life, like *There Is the Land* (Oxford, 1943), about a hard-up family who settles on a farm in the Adirondacks in World War II. One of her historical novels was a Newbery honor book, *The Winged Girl of Knossos** (Appleton, 1933), a romantic adventure story set in Bronze Age Crete, which improvises upon the myths of Daedalus and Theseus. *Homespun** (Lothrop, 1937), a rich, ambitious story which follows the varying fortunes of the members of a New York State family in the 1830s, was a *Horn Book* Fanfare book.

BESSIE MULLER (*In a Mirror**), Elizabeth Muller; obese college girl, daughter of a mystery story writer, who in high school decided to devote herself to the "creative mind," since she was obviously too fat to get dates. Whether Bessie overeats to compensate for her inablility to get dates or because she is afraid to compete, even Bessie admits is unclear. Staunch friend of Til*, loving daughter, talented writer, who publishes a story while in high school, she is ambiguous about her feelings for Donald* Dunn and Johnny Todd. After her fight with Til, she begins to diet and by story's end is dating. The novel apparently suggests that being overweight repels and being slim attracts the opposite sex and a girl had better stay slim if she wants a man.

BEST, (OSWALD) HERBERT (1894-   ), born in Chester, Cheshire, England; author of many novels for children in the mid-twentieth century which, though he was British born, were published first in the United States where he lived for many years. He attended King's School, Chester, and Queen's College,

Cambridge, and, during World War I, was in the Royal Engineers in the British Army in the Sinai desert where he set up a system of communications by heliography. From 1919 to 1932, he was a district officer for the British Colonial Civil Service in Northern Nigeria. These experiences are employed in *Flag of the Desert** (Viking, 1936) and in *Garram the Hunter** (Doubleday, 1930), both of which treat the native characters with more respect than is usual in books of that period. He married American artist Erick Berry* (pseudonym for Evangel Allena Champlin), who illustrated a large number of his books and collaborated on the research and writing of some. They lived for many years in the Lake Champlain district of New York, an area employed as setting for *Gunsmith's Boy* (Winston, 1942), *Young 'un* (Macmillan, 1944), and *Border Iron* (Viking, 1945). In addition to his historical fiction and adventure stories for teenagers, in the 1960s he wrote a series about Desmond, a dog detective, for younger children and has published nine novels for adults.

BESTERMAN, CATHERINE (1908-), author of *The Quaint and Curious Quest of Johnny Longfoot, the Shoe King's Son** (Bobbs, 1947), comic fantasy of excitement and adventure with an array of eccentric and unusual characters based on the author's memories of European folklore from her Polish childhood. It was a Newbery honor book and was selected for Fanfare. Its sequel is *The Extraordinary Education of Johnny Longfoot in His Search for the Magic Hat* (Bobbs, 1949).

BETH MARCH (*Little Women**), shy and musical sister who is the soul of goodness and kindness and always seems destined for her early death. Although too bashful to meet strangers, she responds to the suggestion of old Mr. Lawrence who lives next door that she "keep his piano in tune" by playing it when no one is around, and she makes a warm friend of the old gentleman. Although her death is a favorite tear-jerker, it seems restrained and less sentimental when it is compared to similar scenes like Dickens's death of Little Nell.

BHIMSA: THE DANCING BEAR (Weston*, Christine, ill. Roger Duvoisin, Scribner's 1945), realistic adventure story set in northern India, probably just before World War II. Separated from his family by a torrential rainstorm which destroys their house in the mountains, Gopala, 10, and his pet dancing bear have been wandering around the countryside. To earn food and shelter, Gopala plays on his drum and clangs his cymbals while Bhimsa dances. He encounters young David, who is bored and longing for excitement, and takes him along with him. The three have various adventures before Gopala decides it is time to head north into the mountains and look for his family. Bhimsa's dancing attracts a great deal of attention, and, as the days pass, the bear becomes more and more skilled at catching rhythms and improvising steps. The three escape from the arrogant young Prince*, who covets the bear, are helped by a dealer in hides, are entertained by mystic Maana* Shah, and escape from robbers after Bhimsa defeats one in a dancing contest. In the hills Bhimsa saves them from a tiger and from drowning before Gopala is joyfully reunited with his family. Although David is tempted to stay with these cheerful hill-dwellers, he is persuaded by Gopala's compassionate and sensible mother to return home, lest his mother grieve for him as Gopala's mother has been grieving for him. Although the book is entertaining, David's departure and Gopala's wandering are not sufficiently motivated. Some scenes are vivid, but incidents, particularly in the last part of the book, happen too fast and are inadequately developed. The conclusion is didactic and sentimental, and tone is often patronizing. Characters are cardboard, and the author seems to be interested mainly in extolling the beauty of nature and in contrasting, if only superficiallly, the life and thought of peasants and ruling class. Fanfare; Newbery Honor.

BIANCO, MARGERY WILLIAMS (1881-1944), born in London, England, died in New York City; author who lived in both England and the United States but whose books for children were published first or simultaneously in this country. In her childhood she came to the United States and was educated in Philadelphia and Sharon Hill, Pa., schools. During World War I she lived in Italy. Her best-known book, *The Velveteen Rabbit* (Doubleday, 1922), though not highly illustrated, is picture-book length, only about 3000 words, and is criticized as sentimental; her doll story, *Poor Cecco* (Doran, 1925) is usually considered more successful. Besides five novels for adults, she wrote more than thirty books for children, among them *Tales from a Finnish Tupa* (Whitman, 1936), which she wrote with James Cloud Bowman, and a number with contemporary settings for older girls, including *Winterbound** (Viking, 1936) and *Other People's Houses** (Viking, 1939), both of which now seem quaintly dated but were praised at their publication for treating their subjects more realistically than the career-romance books current for this age group.

BIANCO, PAMELA (1906-), born in London, daughter of Margery Williams Bianco*; artist who both illustrated and wrote a number of books for younger children. Her childhood was divided between England, France, the United States, and Italy, where her family lived during World War I. When she was a child, Walter de la Mare saw some of her drawings and wrote a series of poems to go with them, published as *Flora* (Heinemann, 1921). In 1930, she married an American poet, Robert Schlick, and became a naturalized citizen, later was divorced and married again, to an artist, George Theodor Hartmann, who died in 1976. She has had a number of one-man art exhibits, and besides her own books, which include *Playtime in Cherry Street** (Oxford, 1948) and *Little Houses Far Away** (Oxford, 1951), she illustrated some of her mother's books for children.

THE BIGGEST BEAR ON EARTH (McCracken*, Harold, ill. Paul Bransom, Lippincott, 1943), realistic animal novel based on the author's observations, while on several trips to Alaska, of the daily life of the Great Brown Bears that live in the mountains and tundra along the Bering Sea. The story follows four years in the life of Little Roughneck from the time his mother, Old Lady, emerges with him and his twin, Little Sister, from the family cave on the side of the mountain overlooking Nursery* Valley. Little Roughneck is more adventurous and inquisitive than his mild-mannered twin, soon called Apron-Strings, because she always stays close to her mother. Old Lady takes her cubs down the valley to the river where she introduces them to gulls' eggs and salmon, where Little Roughneck sees Old Giant, the mighty monarch of the region, feasting on a caribou calf, where he has an unfortunate encounter with a porcupine, and where he meets others of his kind. He accepts challenges and battles young foes, always giving a good account of himself. After days of limited exploring and of much feasting in preparation for the coming hibernation, the little family return to Nursery Valley where Old Lady discovers a prospector's camp along the stream, and the bears leave hastily, their peaceful existence disturbed. Several days later the prospector, Swede, and his Aleut companion shoot Old Lady, and henceforth Little Roughneck takes responsibility for the well-being of his sister and himself, wintering, ironically, in the cave the men have dug on the mountainside below the nursery cave. The next spring Roughneck crashes out of the cave, bowling over Swede, and in doing so he realizes that Swede has less physical strength than he. The two bears move up-valley through a pass into another valley and after pleasant days decide to return to the Bering Sea for the annual salmon run. On the way Swede shoots and wounds Apron-Strings. Roughneck attacks him, but Swede escapes. The following spring, Apron-Strings leaves with a young male, Cotton Top, while Roughneck chooses Other Sister as his mate, only to lose her shortly to Giant after a brief and unsuccessful challenge to the old bear's authority. Roughneck then travels alone, aware of the prospectors and other bears but minding his own affairs. During his fourth year of life, he again has a chance to kill Swede, but as he stands over the helpless man, he realizes how powerless the human really is and lumbers away. Other bears defer to his size and strength, and this year he becomes acknowledged monarch of the area after battling and triumphing over Giant. This pleasing and emotionally engaging book of fictionalized natural science about a not-quite-typical bear of the largest species of bear on earth is told almost entirely from the animals' point of view. The author reports their probable thoughts and their activities but never puts words into their mouths or otherwise anthropomorphizes them. However, they are definitely individualized. Action scenes are lively and drawn for suspense, conflicts are distinct, as is appropriate for the wilds, and the sights, smells, and sounds of the tundra and mountains are clear and vivid. The author avoids an instructive or condescending tone. Fanfare.

BIG RED (Kjelgaard*, Jim, ill. Bob Kuhn, Holiday, 1945), realistic animal story set in a forested, mountainous area, the Wintapi, about three hundred miles from New York City in the mid-1900s. Danny Pickett, 17, and his father, Ross*, are trappers who live a simple life close to nature. Ross is particularly proud of his four hounds, and Danny has grown up loving dogs and helping Ross with them. Mr.* Haggin, the wealthy New York businessman who owns the estate on which stands the Picketts' rude cabin, hires Danny as handler for his champion setter, Red, paying him fifty dollars a month. In late spring, Danny joyfully accompanies Mr. Haggin to New York City to the dog show at which Red takes best of breed. When they return, dog and boy soon grow very close, as they tramp the wilderness and explore Old Smokey Mountain together. Although Ross would like to use Red to hunt "varmints," Danny insists on training the dog for partridges, and soon Red becomes a woods-wise and reliable bird dog. A brief threat to Danny's possession of the setter evaporates in an amusing scene when proud and beautiful Katherine Grennan, a business friend of Mr. Haggin from Philadelphia who has a yen for the dog, rejects Red after he encounters a skunk. The year that follows holds exciting adventures for Danny and Red. John Bailey, game warden, hires Danny to hunt and kill a wounded buck. Pinned down accidentally by the antlers of the buck after he has shot him, Danny lies helpless during the night, but Red refuses to fetch help when Danny orders him to. In the morning Danny discovers that the dog has been protecting him from a lynx. The two rescue Ross when he gets lost on the mountain during a sudden snowstorm, capture an escaped convict, and kill a vicious wolverine that has been raiding their traps. The biggest threat to their relationship comes when Mr. Haggin purchases Sheilah MacGuire, a champion female, as a mate for Red. Red jealously refuses her and rejects Danny (because Danny has brought home another dog) until he is reassured of the youth's affection and his own position of leadership within the Pickett household. Danny and Red's most dangerous adventure is slaying Old Majesty, the wise and crafty ancient black bear which has ruled Smokey Mt. and raided farms and cabins in the area for many years. The wound that Red receives in the battle spoils him for showing, and Mr. Haggin sells him to Danny on time. Spring sees Sheilah and Red the proud parents of five squirming puppies. Danny senses that one small male will become an even greater champion than Red. Although the story is clumsily plotted and poorly motivated, and characters and incidents are stock, the book moves along at a good pace with some humor and much excitement. The strong emotional attachment between boy and dog provides unity and charm, and the relationship between the father and son is warm, close, and understanding. (Bob Fraley*) Books Too Good; Choice.

THE BIG WAVE (Buck*, Pearl S., ill. with prints by Hiroshige and Hokusai, Day, 1947), short realistic novel set in Japan at an unspecified time. Kino is the son of a farmer whose land lies on the mountainside overlooking the sea. Kino's friend, Jiya, a fisherman's son, lives in the tiny village that lies on the narrow strand at the foot of the mountain. The villagers fear the sea, and their huts have no windows on the sides facing the water. When Kino asks his father why the fisherfolk fear the sea, his father replies that they have good reason to fear its power, but that the land holds dangers, too. He says, however, that it is the Japanese way to enjoy life and face with staunch heart whatever comes. Soon a huge tidal wave, caused by volcanic activity deep within the earth, destroys the village and most of the people in it, except for a few who take refuge with Old Gentleman, the wealthy man of the region whose castle rests on a high knoll outside the village, and Jiya, whose father has ordered him to flee up the mountainside. Orphaned Jiya grieves for his family, and Kino, his mother, father, and sister comfort the boy and give him a home. Old Gentleman offers to adopt Jiya, but the boy chooses to remain with the kind farmers, and Jiya and Kino grow up as brothers. Years pass, and one day some fisherfolk build houses on the beach. When Old Gentleman upbraids them and reminds them of the destructive force of the sea, Jiya comes to their defense, asserting that one cannot live in fear and that Old Gentleman will be kind and help them if need be, as he has done before. Jiya returns to the sea, saves money to buy a boat, marries Kino's sister, Setsu, and builds a house with a window that overlooks the water on the bit of land that had belonged to his father. He is prepared to face whatever life brings. The lack of a specified time, preoccupation with message, suggested symbolism, and the father's many aphoristic comments about life, death, fear, and courage give this brief story a strongly oriental folk-fable quality. The narrative is based upon an actual incident that Buck witnessed. Illustrations are reproductions of sea- and landscapes done by nineteenth-century Japanese artists. Child Study; Choice.

BIG WHISTLE (*They Came from Sweden**), Dakota (Sioux) Indian youth, whom Gustaf* encounters while gathering wood on the Minnesota claim and who is friendly and helpful to the Larssons. He is called Big Whistle because he can make a very loud, penetrating, shrill whistling sound. He has been to school and can speak English well and shows the children where to find honey and fish. He thinks the whites would not have to change the environment so much and could live quite well off the land as the Indians did. Later, when Gustaf is living in Red Wing, the boy discovers Big Whistle in the cabin near the river, where he takes Judge* Turner's horse after the fire. Since Indians are the target of prejudice and ill-feeling in the area, Big Whistle is certain that he will be blamed for the fire and leaves town quickly.

BILLY BUTTER (Hader*, Berta, and Elmer Hader*, ill. authors, Macmillan, 1936), highly illustrated realistic story about a little brown goat, set mostly on Telegraph Hill in San Francisco in the early 1930s. The goat is born on a farm south of the city and taken with other kids to an Italian butcher to be sold for Easter dinner. There he is purchased as a pet by Gabriel Marino, 10, his brother, Tony, 6, and their three sisters, Annie, Rosie, and little Gloria, for their entire combined savings, two dollars. They introduce him to their good-natured dog, Jack, and name him Billy Butter. Mrs. Flanagan, who keeps two goats on the eastern side of the hill, contributes milk until he outgrows the need. Billy gets into various scrapes: he climbs onto a ledge and has to be rescued by firemen; he travels with the Marino family to their summer fruit-picking job and encounters a wild cat; he gets into the feed room and samples corn, oats, and wheat. Gabriel makes a goat cart and trains him to pull it. Back on the hill, he follows the children to school and makes an enemy of Tuffy O'Toole, who owns a fierce goat named Buzz Saw. Later, when he wanders and encounters Buzz Saw, Billy Butter is saved by Bridget Flanagan. He has a part in the school Christmas play and disrupts things when he eats the scenery and jumps into the audience to find Gabriel. Having grown to a full-sized goat, he wanders to the foot of the hill one foggy day and is nearly hit by a train carrying workmen, including Papa Marino, on a flatcar. They take Billy to the yardmaster, who agrees to keep him and then is alerted to a fire in the yard by Billy's "Baaaaa." Another foggy day he wanders again and meets Buzz Saw and this time trounces him roundly. The pace of the story is leisurely and largely episodic. Billy is the only character developed. Full page illustrations for every three or four pages of text contribute greatly to the interest. For those who know Telegraph Hill in more recent decades, this is an interesting picture of a by-gone era. Fanfare.

BINNS, ARCHIE (FRED) (1899-), born in Port Ludlow, Wash.; novelist, journalist, and historian of the Northwest. He wrote fiction and non-fiction mainly for adults about the area in which he was born and grew up. His first two novels for children, which he wrote after he had established himself as a respected writer for adults, are amusing, fast-paced fantasies, *Radio Imp* (Winston, 1950) and *Secret of the Sleeping River* (Winston, 1952). *Sea Pup** (Duell, 1954) is a lively, pleasing, if concocted story set along the Washington coast about the adventures of a boy and the baby seal he finds and raises. It appears in *Children's Books Too Good to Miss*. Other juvenile novels include *Sea Pup Again* (Duell, 1965) and a family mystery-adventure on Puget Sound, *The Enchanted Islands* (Duell, 1956). He enlisted in the United States Army in 1918, graduated from Stanford University, where he studied philosophy, and was a correspondent with Scripps-Howard and editor at Leonard Scott Publishing Co. before accepting a position teaching creative writing at the University of Washington.

BIRUTA, MACIEJ (*Reunion in Poland**), elderly member of the Polish Peasant Party, often jailed before World War II for demanding that the government give the peasants land grants. At the New Year's party, he idealistically expresses the views of the assembled refugees that under the new democracy that will be established in Poland with Russian help all will have a fair share of the country's wealth. He appears from time to time throughout the novel to keep the reader apprised about the progress in land reform. He is a one-sided, undeveloped character.

"B" IS FOR BETSY (Haywood*, Carolyn, ill. author, Harcourt, 1939), episodic story of school and family life set in what appears to be a quiet, urban, residential neighborhood or small town in the mid-1900s. Although the stories of Old Ned, her grandfather's handyman, about switches and dunce caps have made Betsy apprehensive about beginning school, her year in first grade is filled with joy and excitement. Finding comfortable old Koala Bear, which Father has tucked lovingly into her new school bag, relieves Betsy's first day tensions. Koala also comforts Ellen, the classmate who becomes Betsy's best friend and for whom Betsy later gives a birthday party. During the year, Betsy's circle of friends gradually expands. The first time Betsy feels confident enough to walk to school by herself, she misses an important turn and gets lost. Fortunately, she encounters the wife of Mr. Kilpatrick, the crossing policeman, and stays at her house until he arrives. Then he takes Little Miss Red Ribbons (as he calls her) off to school in his red police car. Betsy and Ellen enjoy shopping for little items at the Good Lady's store after school, and at Thanksgiving Betsy and her classmates contribute generously to make up a large basket of food for Grandma Pretzie, the old woman who peddles pretzels at the school-yard gate. Later, Billy Porter brings to school two tadpoles, Wiggle and Waggle, which the children enjoy watching develop into frogs, and Betsy rescues Curly, the cocker spaniel belonging to Mr. Applebee, who lives near Betsy's school, when the dog runs away from home. In reward Betsy receives for her own one of Curly's puppies, little Thumpy. In the spring, the circus comes to town, and the class joyfully put on their own circus. Betsy is the bareback rider, and the children consume lots of peanuts and lemonade. The unexpected appearance of the organ grinder's runaway monkey provides the proper finishing touch to this very happy, end-of-the-school-year event. Book's end sees Betsy, Ellen, and Betsy's mother arriving at Betsy's grandfather's farm for their summer vacation. Betsy and Ellen happily inform Old Ned that first grade was filled with fun and tell him about the play farm the class has built in their schoolroom. The book is intended for those children who are reading just beyond primers. Vocabulary is easy, and sentences short and uncomplicated. Betsy's adventures are typical of children her age, her problems easily solved, and her life and activities pretty much those of the typical upper middle class, properly brought up, protected child of the period. Stressed are such qualities as sharing, family love, obedience, helpfulness, and generosity. Sequels. Choice.

BISHOP, CLAIRE HUCHET, librarian and author of books for adults and children; born in Brittany, France. After studying at the Sorbonne in Paris, in 1924 she helped to found L'Heure Joyeuse, the first children's library in France, and told stories to children there. When she married Frank Bishop, an American pianist, she came to the United States and joined the staff of the New York Public Library, where she also served as storyteller. She was children's book editor for *Commonweal*, traveled extensively in the United States, lecturing and storytelling, and became much involved in humanitarian efforts. Her storytelling led her into writing. Her first book, *The Five Chinese Brothers* (Coward, 1938), was a written version of a story she told in France and in New York. A picture book illustrated by Kurt Wiese, it is the best known of her books and is still very popular. While most of her children's books are picture books, she also published several short novels which reflect her humanitarian impulse. Two were Newbery honor books, *Pancakes-Paris** (Viking, 1947), also a Fanfare and *Choice* book, and *All Alone** (Viking, 1953). *Twenty and Ten** (Viking, 1952), also with a French setting, won the Child Study Award and a *Choice* listing. Although these novels are amusing and occasionally suspenseful and are related with verve and dry wit, they exhibit a strong strain of didacticism. They lift up the virtues of courage, cooperation, and personal and community responsibility and brotherhood. Her other novels include *Blue Spring Farm* (Viking, 1948) and *A Present for Petros* (Viking, 1961).

BLACK FOX OF LORNE (De Angeli*, Marguerite, ill. author, Doubleday, 1956), historical novel set in the tenth century of Vikings who leave the southern coast of Norway and are shipwrecked in Scotland. Brus and Jan, 13, twin sons of Harald Redbeard, accompany their father in *Raven of the Wind*, while their mother travels with the women and household goods in the *Hawk*, all bound to join the Danish settlements of the English coast. Separated in a storm, the ships all come to grief, with Harald's crew wrecked in the land belonging to Began Mor, whose men capture Jan, invite the other survivors to a feast, and slaughter them. Brus, at his father's orders, has remained hidden and is able to find the body of his father, discover that he is still alive, and drag him to a cave. When he returns after getting water, he finds his father murdered, his jeweled brooch of magic powers gone. Jan is given as a servant to Gavin Dhu, the Black Fox of Lorne, who reveals himself as the murderer by wearing the pin. Brus follows the expedition to Gavin's land, and he and Jan trade places at intervals, each doing what he does best—Brus handling animals and weapons well and Jan writing runes and making songs. Although they are often nearly caught, they manage to keep their dual nature secret, even from Alan MacDugal, nephew of Gavin, who hates his uncle for having murdered his father and for conspiring with the English. Less easily fooled is the blacksmith, Murdoch Gow, who also hates Gavin, but not until the clans are mustered to the service of King Malcolm and they have an opportunity to catch Gavin at his treachery do the twins reveal that they are two. They discover their mother alive and in the service of the queen, and they pledge themselves to King Malcolm and are rewarded with Began Mor's land and with having Alan returned to his rightful role as ruler of Lorne. A heavy dose of Christianity gives the book a pious tone, and, although there is a good deal of blood and thunder, the adventures and characters themselves are not very compelling. The illustrations by the author and the verbal descriptions of places and scenes are more interesting and convincing than the action itself. Newbery Honor.

BLACKIE (*Farm Boy**), the runaway delinquent of seventeen whom John persuades Uncle* Gene to take on as a probationer. Blackie has been in trouble with the law since he ran away from home some months before John meets him. He ran away from home because his father often beat him. Before the Work Farm, he hoped to go to agricultural school, but now he has grown hard and cynical and no longer has ambitions for an education. Uncle Gene arranges that he be paroled to work on O-at-ka so that he can learn to become a top farm hand. Blackie is an unconvincing character, whose only functions are to serve as a foil for John and to demonstrate the importance of a good home life.

BLACK MOSES (*Shuttered Windows**), great-great-great-grandfather of Harriet Freeman. A legendary figure on the sea islands of South Carolina, Moses was evidently an educated Moslem in Africa. He became a slave on the Taliaferro Plantation, where he was flogged to death.

THE BLACK STALLION (Farley*, Walter, ill. Keith Ward, Random, 1941), horse story set on an island in the Atlantic and a rural area near Flushing, New York, probably in the 1930s. Returning on the tramp steamer, *Drake*, from India where he has been visiting his uncle, red-haired Alec (Alexander) Ramsay, high school-aged, watches the loading of a beautiful, wild, black stallion at an Arabian port. In the following days he takes sugar lumps to the horse, leaving them on the window of the stall, but gradually becoming familiar to the wild animal. A storm makes it necessary to abandon ship, but Alec rushes first to release the stallion and is knocked overboard when the horse leaps into the sea. He grabs the rope and is towed through the sea for hours. They land on an almost barren island where there is a spring but little food or grass. Alec finds seaweed that he can wash and eat and that the stallion will also eat when he leaves it available. Gradually, he makes friends with the horse and even mounts him for wild rides. When sparks from his fire ignite his shelter one night and create a huge blaze, he is appalled, since there is little wood to replace it, but the light attracts a ship and the sailors take him aboard and, at his insistence and with difficulty, also take the black stallion. In South America, where they first land and again in New York, the horse is hard to control, but Alec persuades an elderly neighbor, Henry* Dailey, to keep the horse in his old barn, where Black becomes fond of Napoleon, the aging nag of an Italian fruit and vegetable vendor. Henry, who is a retired jockey and trainer, sees the great potential of Black as a race horse and helps Alec train him, getting a friend at the Belmont track to let them work out secretly in the middle of the night. Although they are unsuccessful in tracing Black's pedigree by letters to Arabia (a pedigree being necessary before he can race at a thoroughbred track), they get him listed, through the help of a newspaperman named Jim Neville, as the "Mystery Horse" in a three-way match with the two fastest horses in the country, Sun Raider, from the west coast, and Cyclone, Kentucky-bred and champion of the East. Henry, Alec, and Jim travel with the Black Stallion and Napoleon in a special train car to Chicago. Although the Black Stallion is injured in a conflict with Sun Raider at the beginning of the race and so gets a late start, he catches up and wins in a magnificent burst of speed. The most memorable part of the story, the period spent on the island, takes up about one-eighth of the total book's length. The rest is rather standard horse story in which the unknown animal triumphs. The book has been an unusually popular example of its sub-genre and has been followed by numerous sequels. Choice.

THE BLACK SYMBOL (Johnson*†, Annabel, and Edgar Johnson*†, Harper, 1959), realistic adventure novel set in Montana Territory in the late 1800s, in which the period plays some part in shaping events. Barney Morgan, perhaps fourteen, has been living with his Uncle George and Aunt Norah on their ranch while his father is away prospecting. When a year passes without word from John Morgan, his relatives decide to send Barney back East. Determined to find his father, Barney runs away and attaches himself to the traveling medicine show of glib, well-dressed Doc* Cathcart. Barney agrees to help with the show in return for keep and Doc's help in locating his father. Also traveling with the show are Doc's assistant, Prof. Charles Withrow, called Hoke*, Hoke's wife, Maddie, a mindreader, and Billy, timid black errand boy and juggler. Barney develops doubts about his new situation when Doc makes him responsible for Steve*, the sullen, long-haired, blind, strong man billed as Samson, whose wagon is always kept locked and whom Billy fears. Then Hoke appears overly fond of using his whip in encouraging Barney to learn to juggle, his part in the show's "bally" (the ballyhoo, or portion of the show in which the audience is "softened" for Doc's sales pitch), and Hoke's wife has a weird cast to her eye that disturbs Billy. It appears that only Doc can be trusted. But Steve turns out not to be the madman Barney is led to believe he is, and Barney's misgivings further increase when Billy warns Barney to get away while he can. Then Barney discovers a wanted poster tucked away in Hoke's trunk and learns slowly and painfully that he has misplaced his trust and that Doc is really a cruel, avaricious confidence man, whose miraculous Elixirs and Curatives are concocted of red pepper and molasses. In Virginia City, Doc tells Barney that he has learned that John Morgan is dead. When Barney goes into town to hear the bad news with his own ears, he discovers that Doc has again lied to him. When he confronts Doc with the fact and with his knowledge that Doc's medicine is worthless, Doc kidnaps him and forges papers making Barney his legal ward. Barney also discovers that Billy and Steve are prisoners, too. He and Steve escape one night through a hole that Steve has whittled in the floor of his wagon. Steve is captured, but Barney makes his way through the mountains to Butte, where he finds his father working a slim claim called the Misfortune. They return and set the others free by inciting the crowd into a "clem" (free-for-all) during a performance of the show. The tent is burned, and Doc and his accomplices are run out of town. Barney, Steve, Billy, and John return to the claim, which they subsequently discover is rich in copper, soon to be needed for the telegraph, rename it the Fortune, and look forward to a bright future. The plot grips quickly and moves at an even clip for a rousing adventure story in which a lad learns to think for himself pretty much as the reader expects he will. Incidents are contrived, underdone, and occasionally implausible, and characters, though flat, are an interesting combination. The most intriguing of them is Steve. The story has no great depth, but it does give some idea of what the traveling shows were like. The title refers to a Vigilante sign, 3-7-77, which Barney uses to help engineer their escape, giving the impression that Vigilantes are after Doc. Fanfare.

BLAHERIS (*The Hidden Treasure of Glaston**), half-crazy minstrel-hermit, called the Mad Master of Beckery, or Avalon, who removes the treasures from the cave and takes them to the Old Church. Convinced that only by giving can the Grail be regained, he steals the book of the Grail and takes it to the Old Church, where it is burned up in the fire which destroys the abbey. He is killed in the same fire.

BLAS CHAVEZ (*. . . And Now Miguel**), stern but loving and understanding father of Miguel. He is a strong authority figure, in the Spanish-American tradition, and Miguel has a great deal of respect for him. When he realizes that Miguel wants recognition for his efforts to help, he sets about raising the boy's ego by asking his opinion about various matters and his assistance with chores. His well-meaning efforts confuse the boy, however, since Miguel fears his father may only be making fun of him. A fair man, Mr. Chavez thanks Miguel for finding the sheep but reminds him forcefully that getting an education is the boy's first responsibility. Mr. Chavez is a well-drawn, sympathetic figure.

BLEECKER STREET (*The Bells of Bleecker Street**), the neighborhood in the Italian-American community in New York City where the novel takes place, vividly described with an artist's eye for color and detail. This is the Little Italy where the author, Valenti Angelo*, and his family lived briefly after they emigrated to America from Italy and before they left for California. Here live in the novel Joey Enrico, Pete* the Squeak, and their friends of the World War II era.

THE BLIND COLT (Rounds*, Glen, ill. author, Holiday, 1941), animal story set in the Badlands of South Dakota sometime in the twentieth century. A brown mustang mare gives birth to a gray and white spotted colt otherwise healthy except that he is blind. Uncle Torwal wants to shoot him, certain that the young horse will injure himself in a fall or be eaten by wolves, but young Whitey pleads for the colt's life. He assures his uncle that the colt is too smart to get hurt or killed. The colt soon proves Whitey's words true. He runs all summer with the range horses and grows fat and sassy. He learns to avoid gullies and outcroppings and survives a rattlesnake bite and a wolf attack. The following winter he and his mother follow the herd which alternates between the broken country of the Badlands, where they find some protection from the driving wind and snow, and the windswept prairie, where they can graze. A late spring snowstorm separates the colt from the band. The pony inches along the fences, carefully making his way to the shed where the ranch horses are stabled and where Whitey's own horse, Spot, befriends him. Whitey soon gentles the colt with oats and then hides him in a box canyon nearby, where he spends his spare time training him to halter and saddle. He even gets the pony to accept as passenger Confusion, the addleheaded old ranch dog. Whitey is certain that Uncle Torwal will let him keep the pony when he sees what the pony can do, and that indeed proves to be the case. This appealing, unsentimental, predictable story is based upon the author's own experiences and those of his father. Vocabulary is not difficult, and style is chatty and informal and flavored with cowboy dialect. Characterization is minimal, but there is a strong sense of place, and point of view moves variously from humans to animals. Many spot pencil sketches of horses in different situations and attitudes contribute to setting and situation. Sequel is *The Stolen Pony**. Choice; Lewis Carroll.

THE BLUE CAT OF CASTLE TOWN (Coblentz*, Catherine Cate, ill. Janice Holland, Longmans, 1949), fantasy based on the history of Castleton, Vermont, set at the end of the first third of the nineteenth century. A blue kitten, a rare and talented type, is destined to learn the river's song about the value of beauty and to pass it on to a human before he can find a hearth for a permanent home. After finding his way to Castle Town, he teaches his song to several—to Ebenezer Southmayd, a pewterer, who makes a last beautiful teapot before he dies, to John Gilroy, who weaves pictures of the town into fine linen tablecloths instead of the ugly wool in demand, to Thomas Royal Dake, a carpenter, who designs and builds with his savings a pulpit for the church, and finally to a girl, Zeruah Higley Guernsey, who is depressed by her homeliness and loneliness since her mother's death. The cat escapes being killed and stuffed by Arunah Hyde, who lives at Mansion House and wants progress for Castle Town in the form of cheap workmanship and fast coaches. With Zeruah, who is converted by his song and makes a rug which contains the cat's picture and hangs now in the Metropolitan Museum of Art, the blue cat finds his permanent home. The story is told in the style of a legend, rather slow moving and predictable. Newbery Honor.

BLUE RIDGE BILLY (Lenski*, Lois, ill. author, Lippincott, 1946), regional novel set in Ashe County, N.C., in the Blue Ridge mountains "before the coming of the automobile," presumably in the early twentieth century. Billy Honeycutt, 10, has one great desire: to own a banjo like the one in Jeb Dotson's store. Though his strict father, Rudolphus, keeps him hard at work most of the time, he occasionally gets away to the cabin of Old Man Posey, who teaches him to make baskets, lets him play his homemade dulcimer, and even helps him make one of his own. Billy sometimes satisfies his taste for music at the cabin halfway up the mountain where old Granny Trivett and her granddaughter, Sarey* Sue, 12, live by collecting and selling herbs, and Sarey Sue plays the accordion that once belonged to her father. On the way to Uncle Posey's, Billy runs into Granny and Sarey Sue, and they catch a glimpse of a man who looks like his father and see smoke coming from a thicket, a sure sign of a still. Granny makes him stay away and promise not to mention it. Pappy, who supposedly is off logging, says there's no need for him to bide at home when he has a son "most growed" to look after the crops. When Billy takes his baskets to Dotson's store, Jeb says he's stocked up and laughs at him but finally agrees to take them on consignment. After he leaves, a woman from Asheville buys all the baskets to resell in the city. When Billy's father learns of this, he claims the money and buys a hound puppy which he unkindly names "Banjo." Moreover, he burns Billy's dulcimer and punishes him sadistically for not keeping the water bucket filled. Worse, he sees the sheriff and plans to turn Granny and Sarey Sue out of their cabin, which he claims is on his land, and when Mammy protests, threatens to cut down the cowcumber tree that marks one corner. After he leaves, Mammy sends Billy up to warn Granny, and he finds her protecting the huge tree. She claims to have a paper proving it is her land, if only she can find it, and when Pappy turns her out of the cabin, she moves in, at Mammy's suggestion, with Billy's family. Tricked, Pappy endures them briefly, but when Granny produces her paper, which she finds hidden behind a stone in the collapsing chimney, he agrees that it substantiates her claim and offers to mend the roof and chimney if they will move back. Visiting his Uncle Jamie in Lost Hope Hollow, Billy learns a bit about playing his fiddle, which none of the uncle's own sons care about. With his cousins, Billy goes out on a panther hunt, and they see three men from tough Buckwheat Holler moving the still over the border into Tennessee. Billy's father admits that he knew about the still and tried to move Granny Trivett out for fear she would discover it before he could force them to move. Tipped off by Uncle Posey to Billy's genuine talent, Pappy gets him a real violin for Christmas and he plays at the next square dance. Some of the local customs and dialect are interesting, but the complete switch of Pappy from villain to good guy is too sudden and unmotivated to be believable, and since most of the tension in the plot comes from his opposition to Billy's music and from the suspicion that he may be a moonshiner, the resolution is a letdown and the story is unconvincing. Fanfare.

BLUE WILLOW (Gates*†, Doris, ill. Paul Lantz, Viking, 1940), realistic novel of family life among migrant workers set in the San Joaquin Valley of California during the Great Depression. The Larkins, Janey*, 10, and her father and stepmother, arrive in the valley and settle in a little chicken-coop-like shack on the cattle ranch belonging to Nils Anderson. The Larkins, who once had a ranch of their own in Texas, have been following the crops for many months, and Janey, from whose viewpoint events are seen, longs for a permanent home. She would like to go to a real school, not one just for the children of migrants, and to have lasting friends. Janey's prized possession is a blue willow plate that had once belonged to her real mother. For Janey the plate symbolizes home, family, love, beauty, and stability. She makes friends with Lupe* Romero, daughter of the

Mexican migrants who live across the road, to whom she shows the plate as a gesture of friendship. She and Lupe play and do chores together, and the Romeros take her to the Fresno fair with them. Father gets work in the cotton fields, and Janey goes to the camp school, where she becomes fond of Miss* Peterson, her warm, cheerful, and understanding teacher. Dad wins a cottonpicking contest, and the extra money that brings in soon goes to pay for necessities long postponed, such as tires and a new coat for Janey. With early winter, Dad is laid off, and Mom falls ill. When Bounce Reybourn, Mr. Anderson's shifty-eyed, arrogant foreman, comes for the monthly rent, Dad refuses to pay, asserting that he needs the money for Mom. To avoid a fight between the two men, Janey offers Reybourn the plate that she prizes so highly. When Mom is well enough to move, Dad prepares to shift the family northward, in hopes of getting work there. Janey goes to Mr. Anderson's house for just one more look at the plate she had cherished. When he hears her story, Anderson realizes that Reybourn has been grafting on the rent. He fires the man and offers Reybourn's job as foreman to Dad. At last, Janey and her parents have a home for as long as they want it, a cottage nestled under a willow near a bridge just like the one on the blue willow plate. The uneven, meager plot appears fabricated to show how difficult and uncertain the lives of migrant workers can be, the conclusion strains belief, and most characters are types. Janey's longings are vividly depicted, and the themes of courage to face everyday life, perseverance, and doing one's best come through strongly. Biblical imagery and allusions add texture. Books Too Good; Choice; Fanfare; Lewis Carroll; Newbery Honor.

BOLEK PIOTROWSKI (*Reunion in Poland**), foster brother of Wanda Gorska. He is a partisan in the Polish underground, who appears only at the end of the book, but who is often referred to in the novel. He came to live with the Gorskis after his parents were killed in an auto accident. Four years older than Wanda, he and Wanda were very close before the war started. He was left behind when the family fled from the Nazis.

BONNIE WEEMS (*Margaret**), the warm and loving servant who has raised Maggie (Margaret) from infancy. She and her husband, big, kind-hearted Prince Albert (P. A.), who is usually away on business, have a tiny cottage in Nichols Junction. Up to the time the book begins, this is the only home Maggie has known. Bonnie is a constant source of encouragement to the girl. Bonnie's child is Lois, a spoiled, demanding, bright, but still quite charming little girl of whom Maggie is very fond.

BONTEMPS, ARNA (1902-1973), born in Alexandria, La.; black educator, anthologist, poet, author of novels, plays, biographies, and children's fiction, who is remembered as part of the Harlem Renaissance literary movement. He grew up in California, received his B.A. from Pacific Union College and his M.A. from the University of Chicago. For much of his adult life he was associated with Fisk University, in Nashville, Tenn., where he was head librarian for twenty years, then public relations director, and where he returned, after teaching at the University of Chicago, as writer in residence. *Chariot in the Sky** (Winston, 1951) is about the founding and early days of Fisk and the Jubilee Singers from that school. His first children's book, *Popo and Fifina, Children of Haiti* (Macmillan, 1932) was written with Langston Hughes, and he collaborated with Jack Conroy on a number of books and with Countee Cullen on plays. His first novel for adults, *God Sends Sunday* (Harcourt, 1931) was dramatized as *St. Louis Woman* in 1946 with Pearl Bailey in her first Broadway role. His non-fiction for young people includes biographies of George Washington Carver and Frederick Douglass and *Story of the Negro* (Knopf, 1948), which, when reissued, won the Jane Addams Award of 1956. He compiled *Golden Slippers: An Anthology of Negro Poetry* (Harper, 1941) and *Hold Fast to Dreams: Poems Old and New* (Follett, 1969). His writings deal almost exclusively with black life and culture.

A BOOK FOR JENNIFER, A STORY OF LONDON CHILDREN IN THE EIGHTEENTH CENTURY AND OF MR NEWBERY'S JUVENILE LIBRARY (Dalgliesh*, Alice, ill. Katherine Milhous and with woodcuts from early books, Scribner's, 1940), book designed to look something like those published by Newbery and to tell children about his shop and times. Of the three Bannister children, Robert, Jennifer, and John, Jennifer is her mother's favorite and somewhat spoiled. When their pre-Christmas party is cancelled because Jennifer has a fever, her brothers go to Newbery's shop where Robert buys her *The History of Little Goody Two Shoes* and John, rather reluctantly, *A Little Pretty Pocket Book*, with which comes a black and red pin cushion with ten pins to be stuck, one each, in the red side for good deeds and in the black side for bad deeds. Jennifer appreciates the books but not the pin cushion since she already has a Valentine's ledger to record good and bad behavior, given her by her godmother, and finds it has too many entries on the bad side. Copying the burial of the dormouse in *Goody Two Shoes*, the children have a grand funeral for a mouse, for which Jennifer cuts two flower wreaths from the back of her mother's dress, an action which bothers her conscience and which she finally confesses. When they find the grave dug up and the mouse gone, she makes a formal call on Dr. Johnson, of dictionary fame, who lives across Gough Square from them, to complain of his cat, Hodge. Their most exciting experience occurs when, at Jennifer's instigation, they try to find the Peep-Show man who has a sick daughter, thinking they will give him their pocket money as a good deed. They lose their way, are set upon by rough boys, and are rescued by the Peep-Show man, whom their father promises to reward with a better job. The book has a quaintness that is interesting, but the events are not compelling nor the characterizations strong. Fanfare.

BOSTON OBSERVER (*Johnny Tremain**), the newspaper for which Johnny works as delivery boy after he hurts his hand and can no longer work as an apprentice silversmith. He and Rab* sleep upstairs in the attic of the print shop. Since the Patriots hold their meetings in the attic, Johnny soon becomes involved in revolutionary activities, among them the Boston Tea Party, and he sits in on meetings where he hears current issues and problems being discussed.

BOTHWELL, JEAN (-1977), born in Winside, Nebr.; teacher, missionary, and author of books for children and adolescents. After graduating from Nebraska Wesleyan, she taught high school history in Columbia, Nebr., for a year. In 1922, she went abroad and subsequently served the Methodist Church in India for twelve years as a missionary, where she was business manager of two boarding schools and of a tuberculosis sanitorium. On her return to the United States in 1936, she enrolled in a writer's workshop hoping to realize her long-held ambition to write, and in 1945, her first book, *Little Boat Boy** (Harcourt, 1945), came out to critical acclaim and was selected for Fanfare. It grew out of her own experiences on a houseboat in Kashmir. Other books set in India followed, including its sequel *River Boy of Kashmir* (Morrow, 1946). Over the next thirty years she published almost fifty mysteries and stories of family life and adventure, many based on India or the Far East, others set variously. Titles include *The Wishing Apple Tree* (Harcourt, 1953), *Golden Letter to Siam* (Abelard, 1953), *Parsonage Parrot* (Watts, 1969), *African Herdboy* (Harcourt, 1970), and *The Secret in the Wall* (Abelard, 1971). She also contributed several books to the Watts' First Book series on different countries.

BOWEN, WILLIAM (ALVIN) (1877-1937), born in Baltimore, Md.; lawyer and author for children of amusing, adventurous fantasies involving magic, fairies, and the like, including *The Enchanted Forest* (Macmillan, 1920); *The Old Tobacco Shop** (Macmillan, 1921), a Newbery honor book; *Solario the Tailor, His Tales of the Magic Doublet* (Macmillan, 1922); and *Philip and the Faun* (Little, 1926). Critics of the period praised his books as vivid and filled with exciting and mysterious happenings but complained about the loose plots and commonplace style. His books did not survive their time. He made his home in California.

THE BOY JONES (Gordon*, Patricia, ill. Adrienne Adams, Viking, 1943), period adventure novel set in London among the poor of Cheapside and in Buckingham Palace during the early part of the mid-1800s, while Victoria is queen. The greatest ambition of Jones, an orphaned London waif who gets by on his wits, is to live in Buckingham Palace. The unlikely events that lead to a rise in fortunes for this cheerful, resourceful, independent lad begin on the day of his twelfth birthday. While running an errand for a confectioner to Lady Sandwich's house, Jones meets the lady herself, who kindly takes him home in her carriage. Shortly thereafter, Jones disregards the reproving remarks of his Cheapside friends about knowing his place and is persuaded by the teacher to enroll at a Ragged School where he becomes an avid reader. This leads to a job with Mrs. Rogers, a bookseller, and jaunts about London, during which he has opportunity to survey the palace and make plans to realize his ambition. Disguised as a chimney sweep, he tours the palace grounds and some public and private rooms, gazing in awe and appreciation at the lavish and exotic appointments and has conversations with servants and overhears dialogue that convince him that affairs within the royal house are generally in such confusion that if he employs caution, good sense, and knowledge of human nature he can live there undetected. Several days later he exuberantly returns to Cheapside where he eagerly relates his adventures to his chum, Willie the potboy, who dismisses them as fancies of Jones's overactive imagination. A return foray several months later, during which he observes Sir Robert Peel, the prime minister, paying his respects to the infant princess, Victoria, and sits on the queen's throne, results in discovery. Dour and disapproving Prince Albert turns the boy over to the law, and Jones is sentenced to four months in a house of correction. The kindly keeper takes him into his own home and teaches him the rudiments of domestic service. The escapade receives broad coverage in the press, and Jones returns home to Cheapside to find himself a celebrity. Each of two subsequent visits finds him again apprehended and sentenced, first to jail and then to a ship in the Royal Navy. After learning to swim, Jones disappears overboard on a dark, moonless night while the ship is moored off Tunis, and he is presumed drowned, to the great disappointment of his now large and loyal British following. Two years later, Lady Sandwich is pleased to recommend to the palace a footman who has proved himself in her service. The new man, Johnson, who spends his off-days in Cheapside and loves to read, is soon at home in the palace and becomes a paragon among Victoria's servants. The author handles the *tour de force* of Jones's adventures with a light, objective, never patronizing or maudlin touch and always from Jones's point of view though using third person. The lad is a solidly realized protagonist, one who early wins and easily retains the reader's sympathies in spite of his morally questionable behavior. Other characters, too, are deftly sketched with bold but controlled strokes, among them, Mrs. Murrit, the eloquent vendor who is "superior to her station in her manner of speaking"; Willie, the cautious potboy whom Jones lures into such escapades as scaling the Bow Church steeple and crashing Madame Tussaud's Waxworks; Mrs. Hawkins, the charwoman who mothers him and who, together with Mrs. Murrit, devours details about royalty; and the prim, proper, both formidable and slightly pathetic royal couple. Jones's unlikely adventures are totally believable in the context of his character as presented. The sights, sounds, tastes, and smells of London, the palace, the courtiers, the ethics of the poor and the outlook of the wealthy—all are graphically drawn for a solid and convincing picture of the period. Fanfare.

BOY OF BABYLON (Gere*, Frances Kent, ill. author, Longmans, 1941), historical novel for younger children set in the Middle East about 200 B.C. Rimmani, a school boy of Babylon who is almost twelve, gets word from his merchant father in Asshur that he has found the large, perfect piece of lapis lazuli sought by King Sesostris of Egypt and wishes the boy to bring him the money for its purchase, to be raised by his wife from mortgaging some of their land to the temple. With a trusted servant, Rimmani fulfills this mission, then, to his delight, is included in his father's party to deliver the stone to Egypt. In the caravan they join is an Assyrian boy named Zukaliya. On the way they see, incidentally, the people of the Biblical Terah and his son Abram near Haran. In the mountains of Syria they are captured by bandits. In their forced march to an outlaw stronghold of caves, Rimmani's father hurts his leg, but the boys explore the caves, hunting for the chest containing the lapis, and find it, also discovering a natural shaft leading up to the mountain top. They work their way up the shaft at night and get to the camp of followers of Sinuhe, a former Egyptian court official, now a leader of Bedouins. These tribesmen rescue the rest of the captured caravan and take them to the headquarters camp of Sinuhe, where Rimmani's father remains to recover, sending the boy on to deliver the stone. He travels with a caravan to Egypt and takes a boat up the Nile to Lisht, but there he learns that the king is away. Asking directions, he runs into Khety, the son of his father's friend, Mentuhotep, and goes to his home in the palace. Mentuhotep welcomes him and locks the stone in a chest, but in the morning they find the lapis and a servant both missing. The boys travel upriver to Hebnu to alert the police there and stay at the villa of a friend whose son, Khnumhotep, takes them to visit the tomb being built for his father. There they fall into a shaft, and Khnumhotep, seeking help, sees a man running away. When they have been rescued, Rimmani searches the area and finds the lapis lazuli still in its sheepskin bag. He is allowed an audience with the king, who has conveniently returned, and presents the stone. The king provides an escort back to his father. Throughout the book, conversations are introduced about the natural features and products of the regions passed through, in barely disguised geography lessons. Events are predictable and characters are wooden. Although a great deal of research is evident, there is no sense of all this occurring in a distant time and place. Fanfare.

BOY OF THE SOUTH SEAS (Tietjens*, Eunice, ill. Myrtle Sheldon, Coward, 1931), realistic novel set in the Marquesas and Society islands of the South Pacific in the first third of the twentieth century. Teiki, 10, motherless son of the chief of a small Marquesas island, climbs aboard an English schooner that stops at his island and falls asleep in a life boat, only to find when he wakes that the ship has set sail. He is befriended by the ship's native carpenter but, afraid of what he has heard of Tahiti, their destination, drops off ship at the nearby island of Moorea, swims to shore, and hides out. Although life is not hard and food is abundant, he is lonesome and so eventually makes friends with a kind-faced woman who takes him into her largely adopted family and sends him to school. He makes friends and develops skills but finds something lacking in the ambitionless life. In attempting to rescue his fighting cock which has fallen over a cliff, he comes upon an old Marquesan man living like a hermit on a ledge, making his home in a hollow banyan tree. The old man teaches him to carve and tells him the stories and chants of the ancient Polynesian people. At the hermit's insistence they go to visit the burial place of the Moorean kings, a cave which Teiki can reach only by being let down on a rope. The sights fill him with terror, and, attempting to climb out, he falls and breaks his leg. When it is healed but not yet strong, he seems to hear the hermit calling him, makes his way to the ledge and finds the old man who, before dying, has him smash his personal god, his *tiki*, tells Teiki that he leaves him his valuable carvings, and directs him to find the anthropologist who will make a museum worker of him in Hawaii. Teiki hides in a cave through a hurricane that destroys the banyan tree, then does as the hermit directs and at the end is about to leave the island, having reconciled the two cultures. The story has a curious mixture of respect for the Polynesian culture and condescension toward it. "If [the people] had really understood the new civilization which the white man had brought them from Europe and America and could learn to live the white man's life and think his thoughts, all would have been well. But they couldn't do this. The new ideas were too hard for them to understand." There are also occasional asides to the child reader which date the book. In describing the life of the Polynesians and the beauty of the islands, however, the book shows appreciation and has interest. Newbery Honor.

THE BOY WHO HAD NO BIRTHDAY (Hunt*, Mabel Leigh, ill. Cameron Wright, Stokes, 1935), period novel with family and mystery story aspects set in 1875-1876 in a farming area near Marbury, Ind., not far from Indianapolis. Since the death of his parents and the loss of the entire family fortune of six hundred dollars (a goodly sum in those days) in the flood of 1867, David* Cring, now about ten, has been living with middle-aged Angie* (Angelina) Wiggins and her father, Pa (Lem) Wiggins, who operate the toll gate on the Marbury and Lanesville Turnpike just outside of Marbury. David loves the Wigginses and appreciates what they are doing for him, but the house is small, pennies are scarce, and the boy is convinced his parents were gentry and often longs for better things. He has two great ambitions in life: to become a doctor and to have a real birthday, since no one knows exactly when he was born. The year is filled with exciting events: a trip to Indianapolis for a New Year's party; a weekend with the family of Bob Carlisle, his pal, whose doctor father encourages David's ambition; a rousing revival service at which Davy learns that Angie yearns for an organ of her own; trips about the countryside helping Dr.* Carlisle tend patients; escapades with Daredevil* Jim Kelso, dashing young horse trader who is in love with Rose Carlisle, Bob's elder sister; and attending the graduation of Rose from the local Female Seminary before which Daredevil delegates David to deliver to Rose a charm necklace made of buttons, the latest fad. After school is out, David, Bob, Eddie* Howe, and Dovey Snow (stereotyped, slow-witted black) plan to search the river by raft for David's fortune and use part of the money to go to Philadelphia for the World's Fair. A bout with typhoid puts an end to that scheme. David recovers at the Carlisle house, and when he is well, the Carlisles offer to adopt him. Davy accepts, delighted to be part of a real family and to have the chance for an education. Then the doctor and Davy discover that Ol'* Patches (Elijah Demdike), dour farmer, has Davy's money, recovered from the river years ago and sewn under the patches of his ancient suit. While Ol' Patches is sick, his wife gives the suit away to John D. Hopkins*, itinerant eccentric. With Daredevil's help, Davy recovers the suit and uses part of the money to buy an organ for Angie. Ol' Patches also has a picture of Davy as a baby, underneath which is Davy's birthdate. In one year's time David has gained a family, a small fortune, an opportunity to achieve his ambition of becoming a doctor, and most important to him, a birthday. Earnest, sometimes mischievous David is a real boy, who grows and changes because of events. The slim plot is spun out to its overforeshadowed, fairytale ending, which is the most exciting part of the book. Upon the plot the author hangs entertaining episodes that reveal the thinking and attitudes of the period, and therein lies the strength of the book. It gives a good sense of what it must have been like in central Indiana just after the Civil War. Many characters are types, and the author occasionally patronizes Davy and her audience. Individual episodes are well drawn, and dialogue is lively and extensive. Though dated in attitude and narrative technique, the story is true to the spirit of childhood, and the scenes in which the children converse, play, and plan are very good. Fanfare.

THE BOY WHO WAS (Hallock*, Grace Taber, ill. Harrie Wood, Dutton, 1928), historical fiction with fantasy elements presenting ten stories about major events in the history of the Sorrento peninsula in Italy from ancient times to the mid-nineteenth century. They focus mostly on the towns of Amalfi and Ravello and are connected by the device of a storyteller who himself often takes part in them. In 1927, while the Fascists are in power in Italy, an artist who has climbed to the town of Ravello in the mountains overlooking the Bay of Naples for the Feast of Corpus Christi encounters a honey-skinned, black-haired young goatherd named Nino*, who agrees to pose for him. While he is being sketched, Nino tells the artist stories of mythical, legendary, and actual happenings that took place in the area, events of bravery, daring, and cleverness. He begins with the sirens who three thousand years earlier sing for him of the voyages of the Phoenicians to find tin with which to tip their spears and who die when Odysseus manages to elude the spell of their song by putting wax in his ears. He describes the building of the great temple of Poseidon on the coast during Greek times and the escape later under the Romans of a Jewish slave girl from Pompeii just before Vesuvius erupts. In other stories, he relates how children go on a crusade to the Holy Land, and how a wounded Goth escapes from the Byzantines who have captured him, how the Normans triumph against the Saracens through the cleverness of Robert the Wise, how the Turkish fleet under Barbarossa is destroyed by a storm during their attempt to sack Amalfi, and how Garibaldi captures a haughty prince to demonstrate that his *carbonari* are not ordinary bandits but are sincere in wanting to drive out the French and unite Italy under an Italian king. The stories are told in good style, the many interesting details making them lively and giving some sense of how that part of Italy changed from a simple, pastoral economy to a more complex one based upon trade and the paper industry. Nino, however, is little more than a literary device, the means by which the stories are conveyed to the reader and are given some unity as fiction. Tone is patronizing, and intent is didactic: to teach about the history of the area of Naples by fictionalizing upon it. Newbery Honor.

BOY WITH A PACK (Meader*, Stephen W., ill. Edward Shenton, Harcourt, 1939), historical adventure story of a journey from Fairfield, N.H., to Ohio in 1837. Having saved forty dollars to buy a stock of Yankee notions, Bill Crawford, 17, sets off afoot, hoping to peddle them in the newly settled territories to the west. On his trip he runs into a variety of situations: he spends a night in a deserted brickyard only to find that the berserk cook is lurking in the woods nearby; he frees a pup from a trap, adopts him, and names him Jody; he narrowly escapes being robbed and possibly murdered by a fancy-talking horse dealer, Alonzo Peel; he works on an Erie Canal boat all the way to Buffalo and helps the cook, Mary Ann Bennett, a girl about his age, escape from the drunken boatman, Buck Hoyle. Having come upon an auction of the horses left by Peel (newly hanged for horse theft), he gives evidence that one team was stolen from a canal boatman, and as reward the boatman buys him an old mare, Martha. When Mary Ann leaves him to travel alone to her sister's home at Buck Run, Ohio, Bill heads south and into another series of adventures: he is saved from an attacking bear by a backwoodsman, Simon Baker; Martha drops a colt and they camp for several days until it is strong enough to travel; Bill is almost robbed and killed by a couple of toughs but is saved in the nick of time. His greatest adventure occurs in Quaker country of southern Ohio, where he agrees to carry a slave, a boy of about ten named Banjo, in a bag of green corn from one station to the next on the Underground Railroad. He arrives safely only to find that there is no one to take Banjo on and he must risk another long day before finally putting the boy aboard a canal boat as a "package from Wm. Penn." All along the way Bill trades, using considerable Yankee shrewdness, and ends up united with Mary Ann at Buck Run, with evidence that his colt, Bub, was sired by a fine New York trotter, Tomahawk. Strung together in almost picaresque style, the episodes do not build to a climax, but each incident is interesting and suspenseful in itself. Bill is an attractive but not memorable hero. The book is most notable for its lively action and its descriptions of canal boating and the Quakers' aid to escaping slaves. Fanfare; Newbery Honor.

BRAUNE, ANNA, illustrator and author of *Honey Chile** (Doubleday, 1937), a story for younger children set on a southern plantation. This book, her first and apparently only published work, was widely praised when it appeared and was named on the *Horn Book* Fanfare list but now seems condescending in its attitude toward blacks.

BRIGHT APRIL (De Angeli*, Marguerite, ill. author, Doubleday, 1946), realistic story of a little black girl in Germantown, Pa., in the mid-twentieth century. April Bright, nearly ten, lives with her postman father, her homemaker mother, and her rhythmic older brother, Tom, in a well-kept home in a rundown neighborhood. Older sister, Chris, a nursing student, comes home occasionally, and older brother, Ken, a former architecture student now in the armed forces, checks in by letter. April's chief interest is her integrated Brownie Scout troop, and she is unaware of anti-black prejudice until, on a visit to a farm where she represents her troop, a white girl, Phyllis, refuses to sit next to her. The leader urges April to be understanding and forgiving, and that night, when they have to stay at the farm because of a storm, her forebearance pays off when Phyllis climbs into bed with her and they become friends. In the illustrations, all the black characters have features of white people tinted light brown; the virtues of patience, cleanliness, and hard work are extolled by all the adult characters. It is hard to believe that April has never before come up against any anti-black feeling, but the idealized protective family life supposedly accounts for this. The attitude toward racial prejudice seems now very dated and naive, but in historical perspective the book has some importance in being an early novel with a middle-class, educated black family, in which discrimination is treated. Since so little happens and the tone is so moralistic and didactic, the book is not likely to interest today's youngsters. Fanfare.

BRIGHT ISLAND (Robinson*, Mabel L., ill. Lynd Ward, Random, 1937), realistic novel about a girl's growing up and school story set on an island off the coast of Maine in the early 1930s. Free-spirited, lively, outdoorish Thankful Curtis has grown up on Bright Island with her father, Jonathan, a farmer, her mother, Mary*, and four older brothers, now married and living on the mainland. Taught by her stern, Scotsborn mother and close to her sea-captain Gramp until his recent death, she has never attended school or associated with youth her own age, except for Dave* Allen, a half-orphan who lived with the Curtises for a year. When told that she is to take her senior year of high school on the mainland to "learn what a girl's for," Thankful is reluctant at first to give up the freedom and beauty of Bright Island. When she arrives at the Academy, she feels intimidated by the confusion of voices and faces and soon becomes conscious that her clothes are inappropriate. She and her popular roommate, Selina*, get on grudgingly for a while but eventually become friends. Thankful invites Selina home for Thanksgiving, and Selina later helps her choose more fashionable clothes. Thankful is good in her classes and becomes recognized for her scholastic ability. Her Latin teacher, Orin Fletcher, befriends her in various ways. Thankful spends Saturdays on the beach with a lobsterman, goes to dances and parties, and invites home for Christmas a spoiled, rich youth, Robert*, on whom she has a small crush. Independent and self-possessed, Thankful gradually learns how to get along among youth her own age and to sort sheep from goats. Although she passes her finals with high grades, she decides not to continue her formal education, preferring to remain on Bright Island where she feels wanted and secure and where values, ways, and faces are familiar and trusted. She rejects a proposal of marriage from Orin Fletcher and looks forward to sharing life on the island with Dave Allen. The book exhibits typical conventions of the school story, in characters and plot, but style is graceful and winning with sensory details about the island and the sea and unexpected twists of phrase and Scots expressions. A sympathetic figure with believable thoughts, fears, and hopes, Thankful changes and matures realistically, and Mary Curtis, the mother, is an especially well-drawn figure. Newbery Honor.

BRIGHTY OF THE GRAND CANYON (Henry*†, Marguerite, ill. Wesley Dennis, Rand, 1953), realistic animal novel which takes place in the early 1900s and in which most of the characters are real and some of the events actually occurred. Brighty is a nondescript gray lump of a burro, of free and high spirits, who makes his home in the Grand Canyon of Arizona near Bright Angel Creek for which he is named. Although independent by nature, he enjoys the company of Hezekiah Appleyard, the Old Timer, a jaunty, talkative, goodhearted prospector who once pulled porcupine quills from the little burro's face and who indulges Brighty's taste for flapjacks. The murder of Old Timer provides some unity for this highly episodic novel. The old man unwittingly confides in a beaver trapper, Jake Irons, information about a copper vein he has discovered, and Irons murders him. Uncle* Jimmy Owen, the government mountain lion hunter, whose camp is on the North Rim of the canyon, and the sheriff discover that Old Timer has disappeared and suspect foul play but are unable to find the killer. Uncle Jimmy replaces Old Timer in Brighty's affections when he nurses Brighty back to health after he has been wounded by a mountain lion and later when he suffers lung congestion after being drenched in the Colorado River. He has fallen from the cable cage over the river in which Irons is forcing him to cross. Brighty helps Uncle Jimmy take visitors on lion hunts, among them President Theodore Roosevelt and his son, Quentin, and he takes pleasure in giving gentle rides to children at the summer camp where another friend, animal-loving Homer Hobbs, 11, works as waterboy. Years pass as Brighty winters in the canyon and summers on the North Rim with his friends. The biggest event of Brighty's life occurs when a new swinging bridge is built across the Colorado, replacing the cable cage and linking the North and South Rims. President Roosevelt gives the dedication address, but "T. R." suggests that Uncle Jimmy and Brighty should be the first to cross the bridge because they are the foremost outdoorsmen of the region. Brighty sports the chief engineer's helmet, to which are affixed the letters, B and A, Brighty's honorary Bachelor of Arts degree, and his mane and tail are twined with colorful ribbons. After that, Brighty leads a wild burro pack for a while on the South Rim, until he is deposed by a powerful, determined, young jack. Quite unintentionally the aging burro is the means of bringing Jake Irons to justice. Irons decides to move to Utah and impresses Brighty into carrying his packs. The two head up to the North Rim in a blizzard and take shelter in a cabin to which Brighty instinctively heads. Uncle Jimmy and Homer Hobbs arrive, the storm worsens, and food runs low. Uncle Jimmy identifies Jake as the killer and takes him captive, but not before shots are fired and Brighty is wounded. All are rescued when searchers blast their way through the drifts. Brighty continues to pursue his individualistic way of life in the canyon and becomes a legend in his time. The plot ambles along, and there is never much doubt that the villainous Irons will eventually be brought to account for his crime. The setting and atmosphere of the canyon are keenly perceived. Tone is warm and affectionate, there are touches of humor, and the style is simple and unmelodramatic, with only occasional lapses into sentimentality. The human characters are types, but Brighty is a lovable and memorable hero. T. R. displays those qualities for which he has become known: rugged outdoorsmanship, powerful interest in wildlife and magnificent nature, and a fondness for words. The realistic, slightly comic black and white sketches, in particular, support setting. Choice.

BRIGID (*The Cottage at Bantry Bay**; *Francie on the Run**; *Pegeen**), only daughter in the close-knit and loving O'Sullivan family, a motherly little girl, warm and generous, with a strong sense of responsibility. She helps Michael* explore the cave where Bran finds the box. At the fair, she gives a penny to a beggar instead of spending it on herself and suggests that she and Michael spend the rest of their pennies on balloons for the twins, Francie* and Liam. She becomes annoyed and jealous when the rest of the family excuses and puts up with Pegeen's disobedience and irresponsibility, but mother-daughter discussions help her sort out her feelings and come to terms with the situation.

BRIGITTE (*The Happy Orpheline**; *A Brother for the Orphelines**; *A Pet for the Orphelines†*), one of twenty little girls who are orphans in a French village. She is accidentally separated from the others and has a strange adventure with a couple who think they are the rightful king and queen of France. In the second and third book she is a supporting character, although in *A Pet for the Orphelines* it is her choice of a cat which finally prevails.

BRINK, CAROL RYRIE (1895-1981), free-lance writer, noted for her classic period novel for the young, *Caddie Woodlawn** (Macmillan, 1935). She was born in Moscow, Idaho, to descendants of pioneers. After the death of her parents when she was eight, she went to live with her maternal grandmother, who told her stories about her childhood in pioneer Wisconsin, and the remembered experiences of Caroline Woodhouse eventually emerged as those of the Caddie Woodlawn of the novel. The recipient of many honors, among them the John Newbery Medal and the Lewis Carroll Shelf Award, *Caddie Woodlawn* has been translated into a dozen languages and made into a play. *Magical Melons* (Macmillan, 1944) contains fourteen more stories about this real homesteading family and their neighbors. A versatile writer, Brink published about thirty books, mostly for children, among them, in addition to period pieces, several books of fantasy, including *Andy Buckram's Tin Men* (Viking, 1966), of family life and adventures, including *Family Grandstand* (Viking, 1952), *Family Sabbatical* (Viking, 1956), and *Mademoiselle Misfortune** (Macmillan, 1936), a *Horn Book* Fanfare book, and books of non-fiction, as well as novels for adults and many short stories, articles, poems, and plays. Much of her writing is autobiographical or based on remembered experiences or observation. Although her plots are often contrived, their endings predictable, and her books project an air of quaint archness, she has a graceful leisurely style, the ability to capture the atmosphere and appearance of places, a good sense of humor, and an obvious affection for her characters and life. After attending the University of Idaho, she graduated from the University of California at Berkeley. She married Raymond Brink, a professor of mathematics, and they made their home in Minnesota, where he taught, in Scotland and France briefly, and later in California.

BRONSON, WILFRID SWANCOURT (1894-), born in Morgan Park, Ill.; illustrator and author whose books reflect his deep interest in nature. At fifteen he went to a north woods camp and after that tried always to work with animals and other natural life. For two years he studied at the Chicago Art Institute and served in the army during World War I. As staff artist he went on an expedition to collect oceanic animals for the Peabody Museum at Yale and a later expedition to the Galapagos Islands. *Fingerfins* (Macmillan, 1930) is the result of the first trip, *Paddlewings* (Macmillan, 1931) of the second. All his books are about nature, including *Pollywiggle's Progress* (Macmillan, 1932), concerned with a bullfrog in a Catskill mountain pond, and *Children of the Sea** (Harcourt, 1940), about a dolphin. Others are about ants, rodents, the deer family, grasshoppers, and coyotes.

A BROTHER FOR THE ORPHELINES (Carlson*†, Natalie Savage, ill. Garth Williams, Harper, 1959), realistic story set in a village near Paris, sequel to *The Happy Orpheline**. Josine*, youngest and most stubborn of the twenty orphan girls under the care of Madame* Flattot and Genevieve, tells the Arab workers who are repairing the pipes of their decrepit home about the good and happy life they lead. Soon after, she discovers a dark-skinned baby left in the bread basket at the bottom of the steps. When they find that the baby is a boy, even Madame stretches the truth in reporting their find so the police will assume it is a girl, and they invent a name "Napoleon Lepetit," to register him with the mayor so he will be considered an orphan rather than a foundling. Josine, however, insists on calling him Coucky, and the name sticks. She feels he especially belongs to her and on outings insists on pushing his carriage, a *poussette*, or low basket on wheels with a lamp shade for an awning, and holds him on the merry-go-round when they are given a free ride. Monsieur de Goupil, director of the orphanage, says he must go to the boys' home, and Josine, who has been told tall tales of the horrors of that home by some of the boys, sets out to save him. She believes the kindly merry-go-round man will adopt Coucky, but he has moved on, and in trying to find him she is almost run down by a bicycle race and tells her story to a reporter who, with a picture of Josine and the baby and suitable exaggeration, makes a heart-rending story. Madame is distraught, thinking she will be fired, but Monsieur de Goupil is delighted, since it forces the board of directors to condemn both the boys' and the girls' buildings and to purchase his brother-in-law's castle for their new, combined home, where Madame will be in charge. Like the earlier Orpheline book, the amusing story has charming simplicity and is greatly enhanced by the illustrations. Sequels. Choice.

BROTHER JOHN (*The Hidden Treasure of Glaston**), kindly, lenient master of the library at Glaston abbey who is in charge of novice Hugh* de Morville. He finds overwritten parchment pages in the monastery which are similar to those Hugh has found in Dickon's* cave and shows Hugh the precious old book about the Grail, which is the abbey's most valuable possession. When Hugh saves his life in the Great Fire at the abbey, Hugh sees the Grail in a vision and his lame leg is healed.

BROTHER JOHN (*Otto of the Silver Hand**), simple-minded monk who cares for baby Otto and is his constant companion for the boy's first ten years. Brother John has visions of bright-faced angels who often speak with him, visions which he describes to Otto. His naive sincerity and simple goodness affect the delicate boy and give him a sort of quiet dignity that impresses hard-bitten and worldly men.

BROWDOWSKI, SERGE (*Roller Skates**), the father of the family that lives upstairs in the house where Lucinda is staying. He is a struggling violinist, and the family is very poor. When Trinket becomes ill, he and his wife do not call a doctor because they have no money to pay one. Lucinda becomes great friends with Trinket, whom she "borrows" regularly for outings.

BROWN, PAUL (1893-   ), born in Mapleton, Minn.; author-illustrator who has specialized in books about horses. He left school in high school and served in France in World War I. Although he never rode horses or groomed or trained them, he enjoyed drawing them from an early age and has been an illustrator for advertising agencies and magazines with horses as his main subject. Besides his *War Paint, an Indian Pony** (Scribner's, 1936), his children's books about horses include *Piper's Pony* (Scribner's, 1935), *Silver Heels* (Scribner's, 1951), and *Your Pony's Trek around the World* (Scribner's, 1956).

BUCK, PEARL S(YDENSTRICKER) (1892-1973), born in Hillsboro, W. Va., daughter of Presbyterian missionaries; distinguished American educator, philanthropist, and author of novels, biographies, essays, and juvenile fiction predominately about China. Her parents were stationed in China, where she grew up, and she attended boarding school in Shanghai. She returned to the United States to graduate from Randolph-Macon College and received her M.A. degree from Cornell University. Before she became a writer, she was a teacher of psychology at Randolph-Macon and later taught English literature in China at the University of Nanking and at Chung Yang University. After 1930, she turned to writing and humanitarian efforts. She became very active in promoting international understanding and in child welfare work, founding Welcome House, Inc., an agency to find homes for Asian-American children. *The Good Earth* (Day, 1931), was her best known book, and for it she received the Pulitzer Prize in 1932. She also received the Nobel Prize for Literature in 1938. Although chiefly remembered for her many books for adults, she also wrote more than twenty books of fiction and non-fiction for children. Some are *The Dragon Fish* (Day, 1944), *Fairy Tales of the Orient* (Simon, 1965), *Man Who Changed China* (Random, 1953), a book in the World Landmark series about Sun Yat Sen, *Matthew, Mark, Luke, and John* (Day, 1967), about children of Korean mothers and American fathers abandoned by their families and known as "Those," and *The Big Wave** (Day, 1947), which received the Child Study Award in 1948 and is cited in *Choice*. She was married to publisher John Day, with whom she put out *Asia* magazine.

BUCK FORRESTER (*The Yearling**), most decent of the six big, rough, black-bearded older sons in the backwoods family, the one most devastated by the death of their crippled little brother, Fodderwing*. When Penny* Baxter is bitten by a rattlesnake, Buck rides to pick him up and carry him home and stays at Baxter's Island to help with the farm work until his recovery is certain. Although Buck joins in the fight against Oliver Hutto, he is the least antagonistic toward the Baxters for their support of Oliver.

BUFF, CONRAD (1886-1975), artist, author and illustrator of books for children concerned with other cultures, particularly Indians, animals, and the out-of-doors. He was born in Speicher, Switzerland, came to the United States in 1904, and became a citizen in 1933. He attended the School of Arts and Crafts in Switzerland and private art school in Munich. He held a variety of odd jobs and was a sheepherder and house painter, until his art work won acceptance. Eventually his paintings were widely exhibited and included in the collections of the British Museum and the Metropolitan, among others. He wrote with Mary Buff*, his wife, fourteen books for which he did the illustrations, including *Magic Maize** (Houghton, 1953), a Newbery honor book, *Kobi** (Viking, 1939), a Fanfare book, and *The Apple and the Arrow** (Houghton, 1951), a Newbery honor book.

BUFF, MARY (MARSH) (1890-1970), born in Cincinnati, Ohio; teacher and author of children's books concerned with animals, nature, and other cultures, particularly Indians. She graduated from Bethany College in Kansas and studied painting in Cincinnati and Chicago. After teaching in elementary school in Montana and at a teachers' college in Idaho, she became assistant curator of the Los Angeles Museum of History and taught art in Hollywood. In 1937, she began writing children's books with her husband, Conrad Buff*, a happy collaboration that produced fourteen books over the next thirty-one years. Their short novels, *Magic Maize** (Houghton, 1953) and *Kobi** (Viking, 1939), were a Newbery honor book and a Fanfare book, respectively. The first deals with Guatemalan Indians, and the second, about a Swiss boy, developed out of a visit to Mr. Buff's native Switzerland, which brought back memories of things that happened to him in his childhood. Although their books are filled with incidents and are informative, the plots are predictable, characters shallow, and tone instructive. *The Apple and the Arrow** (Houghton, 1951), a fictionalization of the William Tell legend that is listed in *Choice*, and *The Big Tree* (Viking, 1946), a book of non-fiction about a giant redwood tree considered by many critics as their best work, both were Newbery honor books. Their picture book about two fawns, *Dash and Dart* (Viking, 1942), was a runner-up for the Caldecott Medal.

BULLA†, CLYDE ROBERT (1914-   ), born on a farm near King City, Mo.; author of many books, mostly for early readers. He attended King City High School, has lived in California, and has traveled extensively. Among his books for younger children are *The Sword in the Tree** (Crowell, 1956), which has a medieval setting, and *John Billington, Friend of Squanto** (Crowell, 1956), a story of the Pilgrims' trip to Plymouth, Mass., and their first months there. His other recognized books for children include *Viking Adventure†* (Crowell, 1963) and *White Bird†* (Crowell, 1967). He has also published one novel for adults, *These Bright Young Dreams* (Penn, 1941), a book about opera for older children, and a large number of books for younger children to read to themselves, and has written the music for a number of plays. His books are noted for simple, direct language and uncomplicated though interesting plots.

BUMPO KAHBOOBOO (*The Story of Doctor Dolittle*; The Voyages of Doctor Dolittle**), Crown Prince of Jolliginki, who leaves his African kingdom to attend Oxford and leaves Oxford to accompany Doctor* Dolittle to Spidermonkey Island. When Bumpo's father has imprisoned the doctor and his friends, Bumpo allows them to escape in return for being made white (temporarily) so that he can win the affections of a Sleeping Beauty, whom he afterwards makes the first of his many wives. In the second book he is less ridiculous, though his malapropisms make his ornate language amusing and his bare feet contrast with his otherwise impeccable dress. In the many trials of the voyage, he is a hard worker, loyal, and a formidable fighter when necessary.

BUNDY, HIRAM (*Magic or Not?**), doughty banker, who at first refuses to take seriously the children's intervention on behalf of Miss Isabella King, but who changes his mind about foreclosing when he learns that Lydia* is Mrs. Green's granddaughter. He has a great deal of admiration for Mrs. Green's paintings. He and Miss Isabella then resume their interrupted friendship.

BURGLON, NORA, born in Minnesota of Scandinavian parents. She lived in Everett, Wash., and wrote a number of books for children, many of them about Scandinavian countries, including *Children of the Soil** (Doubleday, 1932), which was a Newbery honor book. Before writing this story she went back to Norrland, the part of Sweden from which her father came. Among her other books are *Sticks across the Chimney* (Holiday, 1938), set in Denmark, *Cookoo Calls: A Story of Finland* (Winston, 1940), and *Ghost Ship: A Story of Norway* (Little, 1936).

BURMAN, BEN LUCIEN (1896-), born in Covington, Ky., American regional novelist, reporter, and war correspondent. After service in World War I and graduation from Harvard University, he became in 1920 a reporter for the Boston *Herald*, and later assistant editor of the Cincinnati *Times Star* and special writer for the New York *Sunday World*. He worked with Scripps-Howard for a while and then returned to Kentucky to devote himself to fiction. He became prominent for his stories of the Mississippi Valley and the Kentucky hills. World War II interrupted his writing career briefly, and he saw service as a war correspondent in the Middle East and Africa. He was the first reporter to reach the Free French in Africa after the fall of France. For his work there he received the French Legion of Honor. Most popular with adults and children have been his amusing stories about the anthropomorphized animals of Catfish Bend, filled with the local color and homespun humor of the Old Mississippi. The first of these was *Steamboat Round the Bend* (Farrar, 1933), which was made into a movie starring Will Rogers. Its five successors include *High Water at Catfish Bend* (Messner, 1953) and *Seven Stars for Catfish Bend** (Funk, 1956), which was a Fanfare book. The Catfish Bend books have sold over a million copies and have been translated into a dozen languages. *High Water at Catfish Bend* received the German Young People's Book Festival Prize. His wife, Alice Caddy, illustrated many of his books.

BURNETT, FRANCES HODGSON (1849-1924), born in Manchester, England; prolific and very popular novelist for both children and adults, now remembered mainly for a few of her children's books. She was educated in Manchester schools, came to the United States in 1865, and became a naturalized citizen in 1905. She married Swan Burnett, had two sons (the eldest of whom died of tuberculosis at sixteen), was divorced and briefly married again, to Stephen Townesend. Altogether, she wrote twenty-three novels and four plays for adults and twenty books for children, her great popularity coming from *Little*

Lord Fauntleroy, published serially in *St. Nicholas* magazine and later in book form (Scribner's, 1886). Although often misrepresented as being a foppish sissy, the protagonist is a sturdy, straightforward American boy who is heir to an English fortune and who takes his democratic principles with him, eventually converting his autocratic grandfather. Her other best-known books are *A Little Princess** (Scribner's, 1905), first published in a shorter form as *Sara Crewe* in *St. Nicholas* and then dramatized, and *The Secret Garden** (Stokes, 1911), usually thought to be her best work.

BURNS, THOMAS, author of *Terrence O'Hara** (Harcourt, 1939), rollicking Irish fantasy peopled by fairies, a traveling harper and his pretty daughter, and a simple country boy whose honesty and enterprise bring him both luck and a chance for love.

BUTTERWORTH†, OLIVER (1915-   ), born in Hartford, Conn.; educator and author of comic science fantasies for children. He received his B.A. degree from Dartmouth College, did graduate work at Harvard, and took his M.A. from Middlebury College. He has been a teacher of Latin and English to boys, an elementary school teacher, and a teacher of English at Hartford College for women. He began to write for children after teaching in elementary school for two years, his intention being to provide for the young imaginative and literate reading that would also be informative. His amusing stories involve outrageous incidents related in a dry and witty style and convey information without sounding instructive. His books take off on his own family's experiences. *The Enormous Egg** (Little, 1956), a Lewis Carroll Shelf selection and a *Choice* citation, rose out of an incident with backyard hens. His third book, *The Narrow Passage* (Little, 1973), again stars Nate Twitchell of *The Enormous Egg*. It resulted from a family visit to the famous cave of Lascaux in France. He also wrote *The Trouble with Jenny's Ear†* (Little, 1960), a *Choice* book.

BY SECRET RAILWAY (Meadowcroft*, Enid LaMonte, ill. Henry C. Pitz, Crowell, 1948), historical novel set in Chicago in 1860. David Morgan, 12, tired of school, tries unsuccessfully to get a job and meets a black boy a little older named Jim Clayton, who has come from the South because his father in Chicago has sent money to buy him out of slavery. David takes Jim to the hotel where the father works, the Tremont House, and they learn that his father died as the result of an accident ten days before. David takes Jim home, where his mother, his twin sister, Nancy, their two younger brothers, Peter and Robbie, and even Grandfather Morgan make him welcome and fix a place in the shed for him to sleep. Grandfather gets the two boys jobs in the construction of the big convention hall called the Wigwam, where the Republicans later nominate Lincoln. Mother, who runs a candy and baked goods store in the front of the house, sews Jim's freedom papers inside his jacket. All goes well until Robbie goes out in a boat alone and falls into the lake and Jim jumps in to save him, thereby ruining his papers. Mother writes to Jim's former owner, but before duplicate papers come, the Morgans' roomer, Adelbert Snively, learns of the loss and steals Jim in the night. One evening an escaping slave couple come to the door, bringing word that Jim is in Greenfield, Missouri, on a tobacco farm, and that he injured his foot trying to escape with them. Grandfather arranges with Allan Pinkerton, the detective and abolitionist, to send the couple on to Canada, and the family makes a plan for David to go to St. Louis, where relatives will help him reach Jim and somehow arrange his escape. When David arrives in St. Louis, however, the relatives are out of town. In a restaurant he meets a man, Simon* Perkins, who offers to take him on to Greenfield, yet, when he later meets Perkins as arranged, he is amazed to see the man disguised as a peddler and wearing a false beard. On the trip he learns that Perkins is dedicated to helping slaves escape and will get a message to Jim and even start the boys on their way to Chicago via the Underground Railway. With Jim dressed as a woman, the boys start on the stage coach, but a fellow passenger, greedy for the reward, sees through the disguise. The boys manage to get away and after being captured and escaping again, to cross the Mississippi into Illinois and to make their way home. All this time David has been carrying a pocket dictionary earlier left by Lincoln in their shop. Finding on the morning Jim leaves for Canada that Lincoln is visiting the Wigwam, he and Nancy take the book to the now president-elect, and Lincoln lets David keep it, encouraging him to return to school. That night Jim returns, having decided to brave it out in Illinois instead of Canada. The various elements in the story—the candy store, Lincoln's campaign and election, Jim's problems, David's dislike of school—give a good deal of information about Chicago in 1860 but are not well integrated. The trip north of David and Jim resembles many other slave-escape stories but is still the most interesting part of the novel. Choice.

C

THE CABIN FACED WEST (Fritz*†, Jean, ill. Feodor Rojankovsky, Coward, 1958), short historical novel set among pioneer farmers in Washington County in western Pennsylvania shortly after the American Revolution. It tells of a few weeks in the life of Ann Hamilton, 10, during which she decides she really prefers life in the free and untamed West. Since her brother Daniel, 19, established the Rule—whoever disparages the West gets drenched with a bucket of water—Ann is careful not to complain, but she has been lonesome since the family moved five months earlier from Gettysburg to the farm they are homesteading at Hamilton Hill. There is no girl her age with whom to play, and the whole family is always busy with tasks in the fields, in the cabin, and about the clearing. Not even when handsome, fun-loving Arthur Scott visits, while he looks for a place of his own, will her mother relent and use the lavender china and linen tablecloth in a party spirit. Ann forms a friendship of sorts with Andy* McPhale, 11, son of the squatters nearby, when Andy's ne'er-do-well father hires out to Mr. Hamilton. While Andy works as handyboy for the Hamiltons, Ann teaches him to read and write. When Uncle John Hamilton and the McPhales decide to go east for the winter, Ann is tempted to go along. One day when Ann is feeling especially restless and discontented, General George Washington and some friends ride up and ask to take dinner with the Hamiltons. To Ann's delight, mother makes the occasion festive with the lavender plates and linen cloth. Then Ann recalls that Arthur Scott had said that at Valley Forge Washington always appeared just when the men's courage was petering out. She learns that Washington feels there is great potential in this western country in which he also owns land. At last she realizes that she loves Hamilton Hill and really wants to continue to live there. Although the story is fiction, it is based upon an entry in Washington's diary and a story the real Ann Hamilton, who was the author's great-great-grandmother, told about her childhood. Most of the other characters were also real. The plot seems contrived, but scenes stand out, including that in which Arthur Scott helps Ann rekindle her fire, and a particularly tender one where Ann and her mother have a little tea party in the woods with

Semanthie, Ann's doll, using the cherished lavender plates. Language is mature, but the author's storytelling style carries the reader along, and the result is a pleasing account of pioneer life for young readers. Choice.

CADDIE WOODLAWN (Brink*, Carol Ryrie, ill. Kate Seredy*, Macmillan, 1935), loosely plotted historical novel set in the woods of Western Wisconsin during the Civil War and based upon the memories of Brink's grandmother. A story both of pioneer family life and of a girl's growing up, the novel focuses upon the lively adventures of eleven-year-old, spunky, red-headed Caddie (Caroline) on her own and with her brothers, Tom, 13, and Warren, 9, the middle children in the large Woodlawn family. Although Caddie's wildness offends her Boston-reared mother and her proper older sister, Clara, Mr.* Woodlawn insists that for her health Caddie be allowed to run freely with the boys. Caddie and her brothers roam the farm, the woods, and the banks of the Menomonie River, often with little sister, Hetty, tagging along and tattling to Mother about what they are doing. Some of their adventures are amusing, some embarrassing, some mischievous, some even dangerous, but all reflect the inclinations of imaginative and uninhibited youngsters. The three steal across the river to watch Indian* John's band build birch bark canoes, encounter rattlesnakes while picking wild berries, hold a show for neighbor children in their barn at which the chief attraction is Indian John's scalp belt. Caddie battles the school bully, Obediah Jones, and generously spends the silver dollar given her by Uncle* Edmund on gifts for three motherless, despised, half-breed Indian children. Her most exciting exploit is her daring ride through the night to warn Indian John that nervous settlers are planning to attack his people. Caddie's growing awareness that her behavior is considered improper for a well-bred girl and the gradual unraveling of Father's English background unify the several episodes. Such events as the visit of the Circuit Rider, the annual migration of the passenger pigeons, and the speaking program at the last day of school, conversations about Lincoln, the Civil War, slavery, and the Indians, and details of everyday life fill in the historical background and give the story depth. The book closes with the family receiving news of an inheritance in England and their decision to remain in Wisconsin. Although the novel has provoked criticism for the way it portrays Indians and women, its abundance of action and humor and its well-drawn heroine have endeared it to two generations and made it a classic of its kind. Further adventures of the Woodlawns appear in *Magical Melons* (Cousin* Annabelle) Books Too Good; Choice; Lewis Carroll; Newbery Winner.

CALICO BUSH (Field*, Rachel, ill. Allen Lewis, Macmillan, 1931), historical novel set on Penobscot Bay in Maine in 1743. Marguerite Ledoux, 12, a French girl of some refinement and education, has become, after the death of her uncle and grandmother, a bound-out girl for the Sargent family, required to serve them until she is eighteen in return for food and clothes. The Sargent family, which includes Joel and his second wife, Dolly, Joel's red-haired son, Caleb, 13, the six-year-old twins, Becky and Susan, Patty, 4, Jacob, 3, Debby, 8 months, and Joel's brother, Ira, are hard working and not unkind, but they have no sympathy for the fine needle work, singing, and dancing in which Marguerite has been trained, insist on calling her "Maggie," and try to repress her "Frenchified" ways. On the *Isabella B.*, they voyage from Marblehead to the frontier farm Joel has purchased, only to find when they arrive that Indians have burned the house. Neighbors warn them against resettling on the point which has been a ceremonial place for the Tarratine Indians, but when Joel stubbornly persists, they help him raise a cabin. Old Hepsa*, aunt of Seth Jordan and his son, Ethan, their nearest neighbors, who live on Sunday Island, takes to Marguerite, shows her the yarns and dye-pots and looms with which she makes beautiful cloth, points out the sheep laurel or calico bush, and sings her the sad ballad of that name while Seth plays his fiddle. At the house raising, Marguerite sees the other neighbors, all of whom come by boat, including Abbey Wells, 18, whose charms attract both Ethan and Ira. In the fall, Marguerite comes upon a cave where she finds bones, a blond scalp lock, and a buckle from a child's shoe, and while they are at a cornshelling bee at Jordans, Indians take their cow and calf, as well as their dog, Pumpkin, who later escapes and returns. At Christmas, which the Sargents do not celebrate, Marguerite goes into the woods alone, sings a carol in French to cheer herself, and is startled when a tall Indian appears, wishes her "Noel," talks broken French with her, and receives from her a gift, a gold button she has saved from her uncle's jacket. She keeps this meeting a secret, knowing the Sargents will not understand. In the depth of winter, Debby crawls into the fire and is badly burned. Marguerite and Caleb make the terrible trip across the frozen channel to get Aunt Hepsa, but the child dies despite her nursing. This joint experience makes Caleb less scornful of Marguerite. When a trading vessel, the *Fortunate Star*, puts in to their harbor for water, Ira and Caleb go with her to replace an injured crewman and to get much needed supplies, mainly ammunition, from Boston. While they are gone Joel, overworking, breaks his leg. As he lies suffering, Indians come. Marguerite takes charge, carries out all the corn and maple syrup they have left and distributes it to them. Then, to distract them when they seem to grow ugly, she tears a piece of red cloth Abby has given her and Dolly's best sheet into strips, nails them to the top of a pole in the yard, and organizes a Maypole dance for the children and the Indians. While the Indians are scrambling for bits of the cloth, the tall Indian she met at Christmas appears, says "Noel," motions to the button he wears, and leads the others off. When Ira and Caleb return, the grateful Sargents offer to free Marguerite from her bond and let her sail north on the *Fortunate Star* to French occupied territory where there is a convent that will take her in. Though tempted, Marguerite decides to stay with the family in the place that has become her home. Marguerite is a memorable character, sensitive but plucky, and the story has many exciting moments. The style is vivid, giving a strong feeling for the beauty of the region as seen through Marguerite's eyes. The tone of the telling is somewhat more refined than one would expect in a recent novel, and, for that reason, may seem to be for younger children, though the length and complexity would indicate older readers. Choice; Newbery Honor.

CALICO CAPTIVE (Speare*†, Elizabeth George, Houghton, 1957), historical novel set in New England and Montreal, Canada, just before the French and Indian War. The story starts at a fort in New Hampshire in August 1754, when Abenaki Indians capture James Johnson, a colonial captain, his wife, Susanna*, their three children, a neighbor, and Susanna's younger sister, Miriam Willard, about sixteen. The captives are forced to march overland through the forest to the Indian camp at St. Francis, where they live for a short time with Indian families. Then the Indians take them to Montreal and sell them to the French, where they remain for about a year. Miriam, from whose viewpoint the story is told, becomes a servant in the home of the wealthy and influential Du Quesnes. She works in the kitchen and also teaches English to the Du Quesne daughter, vain and giddy Felicité. But she worries about her family, and her quick tongue, rashness, and pride sometimes bring her trouble. Later Susanna joins her, and while James journeys to Massachusetts for ransom money, the two live as poor relatives with the Du Quesnes. When James fails to return in the specified length of time, the Du Quesnes throw them out, and they live briefly with the family of Hortense*, kitchen maid for the Du Quesnes, and then in a one-room shop, where Miriam, who has demonstrated skill with the needle, earns them a meager living as a seamstress. When James returns, the new governor casts him and Susanna into prison. They remain there until Miriam persuades the governor's wife, for whom she sews, to prevail upon her husband to release them. When last seen, the little family is partially reunited and preparing to set sail for England where they will be exchanged for French prisoners. Miriam refuses an offer of marriage from Pierre* Laroche, a handsome, dashing, wealthy young *coureur de bois*, and looks forward to marrying Phineas Whitney, a divinity student. The novel fictionalizes upon *A Narrative of the Captivity of Mrs. Johnson*, the personal account of Susanna's actual experiences during the war. Speare seems overly conscious of her audience, and most of the characters are types. Miriam emerges as a strong and likeable protagonist, whose experiences change her believably. She grows less rash and self-indulgent, and more aware of the effect that her actions can have on those around her. She learns tolerance toward people whose ways and values differ from those of her Puritan, colonial upbringing. The author draws clear pictures of life in the Indian camp and among various segments of the society in Montreal. An especially good feature of the book is the way the Indians are presented, realistically and without bias and sensationalism. Fanfare.

CALL IT COURAGE (Sperry*, Armstrong, ill. author, Macmillan, 1940), legend-like tale of a Polynesian boy of the far past, "before the traders and missionaries first came into the South Seas." Terrified by a storm which killed his mother when he was three, Mafatu has grown up to be known as The Boy Who Is Afraid, making a mockery of his name which means "Stout Heart." In a culture which worships courage, he endures the scorn of his peers and accepts woman's work of making tools and mending nets, but he suffers under the disapproval of his father, Tavana Nui. Realizing that he must prove himself, he leaves his home island of Hikueru with his dog, Uri, and guided by Kivi, an albatross he has tamed. His canoe is caught by a storm, blown a great distance, and wrecked on a distant mountainous island which he soon discovers is a ceremonial spot for the black Eaters of Men. From their sacred place he takes a spear, and from a whale's skeleton he makes a knife and other tools. When a shark wrecks his fish trap and then threatens Uri, Mafatu kills it with his knife. He also kills a wild boar and makes a necklace of its tusks, kills an octopus, makes a canoe, and prepares to travel homeward. As he is about to start, he encounters the cannibals, who chase him and nearly catch him before a trick of wind takes his canoe beyond their reach. Almost succumbing to the heat and need for water, he prays, as he has throughout his trip, to Maui, god of the fisherman, to protect him from the sea god, Moana, who destroyed his mother, and he reaches Hikueru safely. There he is accepted by his father and considered a hero by his people. The story is told with the tone of the oral tradition but with the detail and intensity of modern fiction. Mafatu's feats are unusual but not incredible, and, by telling this tale as a legend, Sperry makes the incidents plausible in their setting and makes the obvious theme of achievement through bravery and self-reliance acceptable. Mafatu, the only developed character in the book, is courageous and determined despite his fears. Newbery Winner.

CALL ME CHARLEY (Jackson*, Jesse, ill. Doris Spiegel, Harper, 1945), realistic problem novel set in Ohio in the mid-1900s. Being the first and only black youth in Arlington Heights is hard for Charley Moss, 12, who encounters prejudice on all hands. His parents are cook and chauffeur for Dr. Cunningham, over whose garage they live. Charley is an earnest, hardworking boy who wants to become an engineer and has a paper route to earn money for college. His mother encourages his ambitions, but his unsupportive father thinks he should go to work rather than continue his education. George Reed, a schoolmate and leader of the Tigers, a neighborhood boy's club, calls him Sambo, tells him the club doesn't accept blacks, and says that blacks don't enter professions. The local school accepts Charley as a student with the proviso that he behave and prove himself academically. The drama teacher excludes him from the school play, and his only friend is earnest, fun-loving Tom Hamilton, who lives on Charley's paper route. Charley teaches Tom how to deliver papers, and Tom shares his basement workshop with Charley, brings home assignments for him when he is sick, and encourages him to join school activities and speak up for his rights. Tom and Charley win season passes to the local pool in a model contest, but the pool manager takes away Charley's pass, informing him that blacks are not allowed to swim there. When Charley almost drowns in a quarry because he has not told Tom he is unable to swim, Tom grows disgusted with him. He declares that Charley must communicate his needs and stand up for himself. Overwhelmed by problems, Charley grows despondent and refuses to go to school. Word gets around about Charley's mishap, and the Hamiltons rally support for him in the PTA. Charley receives a part in the school play and returns to school. Contrived characters, situations, and dialogue combine with an earnest, instructive tone to inform young readers about prejudice against blacks. To late twentieth century readers, the book seems dated and projects a certain quaintness, the product of the era that was prologue to the big push for black rights. Very obviously written to thesis, it offers ready solutions to complex problems. Choice.

CALL OF THE MOUNTAIN (Meigs*, Cornelia, ill. James Daugherty, Little, 1940), realistic period novel set over a year's time in the Vermont Mountains overlooking the Champlain Valley in the 1830s. On his death, generous, respected Captain Jonathan Bemis, a lawyer and farmer, leaves to his ward, orphan Nathan Lindsay, 19, the family homestead, Rolling Willows farm, in the village of Forestdale, and Height* of Land farm on the mountainside, and a generous stipend to elderly Miss Eliza Thomas, a distant relative, whom he had also taken into his household. His younger brother, sharp-minded lawyer Hamilton* Bemis, threatens to contest the will, claiming Nathan and Miss Eliza exerted undue influence on his too-kindhearted brother. Impelled by a strong sense of justice and a good deal of pride, Nathan agrees, in writing, that the family farm should go to Hamilton but claims Height of Land as his own. With dogged determination, stubborn individualism, resource, energy, luck, and the assistance of neighbors Asa* Lamb, who advises him in points of law as well as in farming, and Simon* Harding, another farmer, over the winter months Nathan labors to turn the long-abandoned farm into a home and livelihood. He works so hard he neglects his own needs and social obligations as well and almost misses the wedding of his close friend, blacksmith and inventor Tom* Davenport, who seeks to harness electrical energy to the wheel. In the village, Nathan is amazed and hurt to discover that Hamilton Bemis has been stirring up people against him with malicious lies about Jonathan's death to strengthen his case at law. Charitably, however, the youth advises Hamilton's hired man, Stillman Choate, about operating Rolling Willows, and he in return apprises the youth of Hamilton's apparent intentions. At the town meeting, the boy offers to take in without fee Miss Eliza and her young relative, Joan, now wards of the town. While gathering spruce for their beds, Nathan and Canute, the wild dog he has tamed, tangle with a wild boar and in the process discover the stand of mighty oaks the farm has been reputed to hold, thus ensuring a continuing source of money by selling the logs for ships' timbers. Shortly thereafter Hamilton arrives with the sheriff to serve papers on Nathan. A terrible storm comes up, and on his way home the lawyer is injured in a fall when the bridge over the river gives way. Nathan rescues him and brings him back to the cabin, where, after being nursed back to health by Miss Eliza and Joan in the following weeks, the lawyer experiences a change of heart and drops his scheme. Nathan, who has learned the importance of controlling his pride and of being a good neighbor, looks forward to good years on Height of Land, with Miss Eliza to keep house, Asa Lamb to teach him the rudiments of law and to advise him, and Joan to share his love of the hills and valleys. Though filled with convenient happenings, the plot moves dramatically through clearly developed conflicts of man against self, another man, community, and nature. Characters, if types, are strongly realized, and the subplot about Tom Davenport, a real historical figure, if not well-knit with Nathan's own story, adds interest, but the most memorable aspects of this book lie in its graceful style and clearly drawn picture of the mountain setting and of Vermont village life. (Oliver* Davenport) Fanfare.

THE CALL OF THE WILD (London*, Jack, Macmillan, 1903), one of the most famous dog stories of all time, set in the Klondike during the Alaskan gold rush of the 1890s. Buck, half St. Bernard and half Scotch shepherd, is living a favored and leisurely existence on Judge Miller's estate in the Santa Clara valley of California when Manuel, the gardener's helper, acquires gambling debts and secretly sells him to men who make quick money transporting stolen dogs to Alaska for gold hunters. He is badly beaten with a club, a treatment which makes him wary but does not break his spirit. At Seattle he is sold to Perrault, a French-Canadian who carries Canadian government dispatches by dog sled, and his partner, the half-breed Francois, and they take him and a Newfoundland, Curly, north aboard the *Norwhal*. Buck learns the brutal law of the pack when a dog named Spitz attacks Curly and the onlooking dogs finish the kill. He also learns from Francois to pull in his place in the team and from experience to dig a hole in the snow for sleeping, to exist on little food, and to steal more when there is an opportunity. His dormant instincts also begin to wake. He challenges the authority of Spitz, who is lead dog, and eventually kills him, and insists on being made lead dog himself. At Dawson they change drivers and head for Skagway with a load of mail; when they arrive, exhausted and footsore, they are sold to a Greenhorn named Charles, who, with his wife, Mercedes, and her younger brother, Hal, head for Dawson with an overloaded sled, no system of camping, and not enough food for the dogs. The outfit is in terrible shape when they reach John Thornton's camp. Thornton warns them of the weak ice ahead, but they pay no attention and when Hal is brutal to exhausted Buck, Thornton cuts him out of the traces, so it happens that when the sled goes through the ice, Buck is not drowned with the others. Thornton nurses Buck back to health, and Buck adores him. He almost kills a man who attacks Thronton in a bar and later saves his life again when his boat overturns in the rapids. The next winter he wins a bet for Thornton by breaking out and pulling a sled with a thousand-pound load. For some time they travel happily while Thornton prospects and Buck occasionally goes off hunting moose for days, returning when he thinks of Thornton. One day he returns to find a party of Yeehat Indians dancing about the camp, having massacred Thornton. Buck kills some, drives off the rest, and, after mourning for a couple of days, runs off and joins the wolf pack he has heard howling at night. Originally published for adults, this book has been adopted into children's literature. The picture of life in the rough mining communities and the grueling days on the trail is vivid and compelling. Buck is a suitable hero for this macho, masculine society, and his conversion to a wild creature is convincing. Choice.

CAMERON†, ELEANOR (BUTLER) (1912-), born in Winnipeg, Canada; librarian, critic, author of novels for children and young people. Her family moved to Ohio when she was three and three years later to Berkeley, Calif., where she grew up. She attended the University of California and the Art Center School in Los Angeles. She has held various positions, including research librarian. The Mushroom Planet books launched her career as a children's writer. The first in the popular series was written in answer to her son's request for a story about boys his own age who build a space ship and fly away to discover a planet. For him she wrote *The Wonderful Flight to the Mushroom Planet** (Little, 1954) and the other Mr. Bass stories, a series of entertaining, briskly told, if rather conventional, science fiction for younger readers. The first of these and two of several sequels, *Stowaway to the Mushroom Planet** (Little, 1956) and *Time and Mr. Bass†* (Little, 1967), are cited in *Choice*. While these evidences of her inventiveness and storytelling ability continue to be well liked, her later books for older readers and young people are more highly regarded by critics. These novels show a greater sophistication in subject, treatment, and theme. *A Room Made of Windows†* (Little, 1971), and *Julia and the Hand of God†* (Dutton, 1977), loosely autobiographical novels about a budding writer, and *To the Green Mountains†* (Dutton, 1975), set in Ohio, have all won awards or citations. *The Court of the Stone Children†* (Dutton, 1973) a mystery-fantasy won the National Book Award. Another mystery, *A Spell is Cast†* (Little, 1964), was a nominee for the Edgar Allan Poe Award, and *The Green and Burning Tree: On the Writing and Enjoyment of Children's Books* (Little, 1969) stands as a major critical work about literature for the young. She has also written a novel for adults, *The Unheard Music* (Little, 1950), which was her first published book and the initial result of her early ambition to become a writer. Now considered a leading authority on books for the young, she frequently speaks before professional organizations. She makes her home in California.

CANDY CROCKER (*The Sea Is All Around**), Mab's best friend on Pokenick*. She has wild, curly, red hair and freckles and is never dull company. The daughter of the publisher of the Pokenick *Morning Star*, she is an inventive child and a leader. She, Mab, and her brothers play together, exploring the attic of the Crocker house and tearing wildly as cowboys and Indians through the house.

CAPTAIN CAT (*The Quaint and Curious Quest of Johnny Longfoot, the Shoe King's Son**), commander of the barge on Johnny* Longfoot's trip to Coral

Island. He was instructed by Barnac* the Cat to take care of Johnny on pain of his life. When Johnny is lost during the storm, he decides that he must commit hara-kiri, but Johnny turns up before he does. He stands up to Uncle* Lucas, but Uncle Lucas tricks him into disclosing the location of the treasure cave on Coral Island.

CAPTAIN COOK (*Mr. Popper's Penguins**), the penguin sent to Mr. Popper by Admiral Drake, the explorer. The bird mopes until the Mammoth City Aquarium sends a lonely female, Greta, to join him. They produce ten young penguins—Nelson, Columbus, Louisa, Jenny, Scott, Magellan, Adelina, Isabella, Ferdinand, and Victor—who are trained by the Poppers into a hit stage act. Captain Cook's main characteristic is curiosity.

CAPTAIN CRANDALL (*Miss Pickerell Goes to Mars**), commander of the space ship on which Miss Pickerell travels to Mars. Since he is a scientist, not a technician, he knows little about running the ship. When he discovers that Mr.* Haggerty has been left behind, he worries about the safety of his crew. He is impatient, curt, and bossy, and Miss Pickerell thinks he is very hard to talk to. After she saves Wilbur's* life, "nothing is too good for her" among her crewmates, and Captain Crandall and the others give her proper credit for her part in making the voyage a success.

CAPTAIN KURT VON KUHLENDORF (*Heart of Danger**), Nazi officer who appears repeatedly in the novel as the villain. He is polite and cultured, but he is ruthless in his determination to fulfill his duties. He plays the piano passably and first "performs" Rudy's* composition, "The Prisoners' Song," on the piano of the inn where Rudy had scribbled the song on paper and then carelessly crumpled it up and cast it into a drawer. The song leads von Kuhlendorf to see that Madame* Moreau has been attempting to subvert the Germans. When he learns that she has been working for the underground, he does not turn her in. Instead he seizes the opportunity to feather his nest and insists she deposit money in his Swiss bank account in return for freedom. He is almost a stereotyped character.

CARL LARSSON (*They Came from Sweden**), Gustaf's* father and head of the Larsson family of Swedish immigrants to Minnesota Territory in 1856-1857. A planner and a doer, he is determined to be a landowner. He seizes the opportunity to stake a large claim in Minnesota so there will be enough land for his brother and his two sons, as well as himself. He tends to make all the important decisions, but he is never authoritarian. Sometimes his enthusiasm for making a go of the farm carries him away. In Minnesota he focuses his attention on the crops and the barn, forgetting to build the cabin that Anna Marie, his wife, wants, until she forcefully reminds him that the family has lived long enough in the sod house. In the same way, he does not see the importance of learning English until he loses the two piglets that he had promised to Gustaf*.

CARL SCHUMMEL (*Hans Brinker; or, The Silver Skates**), bitter, cynical, selfish youth, who thinks Hans* and Gretel* are not good enough to skate in the Broek race. He is one of the youths who participate in the skating journey to The Hague. He almost wins the silver skates.

CARLSON†, NATALIE SAVAGE (1906-), born in Winchester, Va.; author of several distinct types of books for children, each reflecting a different part of her experience. She grew up in a large family of girls with just one younger brother, worked on newspapers in California, married a naval officer and lived for three years in France, where he was stationed, and has more recently made her home partly in Newport, R.I., and partly in Florida. Her collections of French-Canadian stories are mostly tales she first heard from her mother's visiting relatives. Her books set in France have been her most popular: *The Family Under the Bridge** (Harper, 1958) was a Newbery honor book and her Orpheline stories (about twenty little orphan girls and their one orphan "brother") have become a series, the first three of which are *The Happy Orpheline** (Harper, 1957), *A Brother for the Orphelines** (Harper, 1959), and *A Pet for the Orphelines†* (Harper, 1962). Her novels of social consciousness focus on questions of racial equality and integration and include *Ann Aurelia and Dorothy†* (Harper, 1968), *The Empty Schoolhouse†* (Harper, 1969), and *Marchers for the Dream†* (Harper, 1969). Her two books based directly on autobiographical experience are *The Half-Sisters* (Harper, 1970) and *Lurvy and the Girls* (Harper, 1971). In 1966 she was named the United States' candidate for the international Hans Christian Andersen Award.

CARMER, CARL (LAMSON) (1893-1976), born in Cortland, New York; professor of English, journalist, folklorist, historian of upstate New York, and novelist. He graduated from Hamilton College and Harvard and taught English and public speaking at colleges in New York State and Alabama. He then became a columnist for the New Orleans *Morning Tribune*, assistant editor of *Vanity Fair*, and associate editor for *Theater Arts Monthly*. A distinguished folklorist, he became well known as a regional writer and collector of American folksongs, legends, and ballads, and the bulk of his work was for adults. For young readers he wrote a dozen books of fiction and non-fiction, many of them also high in local color. His novels include *Wildcat Furs to China** (Knopf, 1945) a fictionalized account of a real voyage to China in 1785, *Windfall Fiddle** (Knopf, 1950), a diverting story of a boy's efforts to earn a violin, and *Too Many Cherries** (Viking, 1949), an amusing account of how a family gets rid of their excess cherry crop, all Fanfare books, while *Henry Hudson, Captain of the Ice-bound Seas* (Garrard, 1960) and *The Hudson River* (Holt, 1962) are two of his books of non-fiction for the young.

CAROLINE INGALLS (*Little House in the Big Woods**; *Little House on the Prairie**; *On the Banks of Plum Creek**; *On the Shores of Silver Lake**; *The Long Winter**; *Little Town on the Prairie**; *These Happy Golden Years**), ''Ma'' to Laura* and her three sisters in the series of seven autobiographical novels. Though firmly bound by her own ideas of propriety, especially for growing girls, she is a loving wife and mother and is hard-working and steadfast in the face of continued hardships which the family encounters. Religious and prim, she occasionally shows flashes of humor and fun that lighten her ladylike personality. Though she follows her husband across frontier America in the 1870s and 1880s, she sets her foot down against going west again beyond eastern Dakota, and she makes her decision stick.

CARR, MARY JANE (1899-), born in Portland, Oreg.; author best known for historical fiction. She attended St. Mary's College, now called Maryhurst, in Maryhurst, Oreg., and worked on newspapers in Portland, where she has made her home. Her interest in history stems, ironically, from an early dislike for the subject which she counteracted by making up stories of the characters and exciting events. Her *Children of the Covered Wagon* (Crowell, 1934) was made into a motion picture and television series called *Westward Ho, the Wagons*. *Young Mac of Fort Vancouver** (Crowell, 1940) a historical novel of one year in the life of a half-Indian boy at the fort school on the Columbia River, was named a Newbery honor book.

CARRIE INGALLS (*Little House in the Big Woods**; *Little House on the Prairie**; *On the Banks of Plum Creek**; *On the Shores of Silver Lake**; *The Long Winter**; *Little Town on the Prairie**; *These Happy Golden Years**), younger sister of Laura* in all seven of the ''Little House'' books, the baby when Laura is five. Until *Little Town on the Prairie*, Carrie does not figure much as an individual personality, but in that book she emerges as a frail child with a peaked face, much dependent upon Laura and admiring of Laura's sturdy determination. As they grow older, she several times volunteers to do the chores so that Laura can earn money toward their sister Mary's* schooling, and she is rather touchingly supportive in Laura's romance with Almanzo* Wilder.

CARROLL, (ARCHER) LATROBE (1894-), born in Washington, D.C.; journalist, editor, translator from the French, and author of books for children, most of them about animals. He grew up in Denver, attended schools in Lausanne, Switzerland, and Munich, Germany, graduated from Harvard, and sold a story while still in college. After service in World War I, he joined the editorial staff of *Century* in New York, served briefly with the Foreign Press Service, and then for nine years was an editor and writer for *Liberty*. After marrying Ruth Carroll*, he resigned his editorial position and devoted his time to writing fiction. With his wife he published *Luck of the "Roll and Go"** (Macmillan, 1935), a Fanfare book, and many other novels and picture books.

CARROLL, RUTH (ROBINSON) (1899-), born in Lancaster, N.Y.; landscape artist, portrait painter, author and illustrator of books mostly about animals. A graduate of Vassar, she attended the Art Students League and Cecelia Beaux's School of Portrait Painting in New York City. She wrote and illustrated many picture books of her own, such as *Where's the Bunny?* (Walck, 1950), *Where's the Kitty?* (Walck, 1962), and *Chimp and Chump* (Reynal, 1933), and her *What Whiskers Did* (Walck, 1932) was a story told entirely in pictures. With her husband, Latrobe Carroll*, she wrote and illustrated over a dozen and a half picture books and novels. *Luck of the "Roll and Go"** (Macmillan, 1935), about a daring and resourceful kitten that stows away aboard a ship and has many adventures, the first novel they did together, was a Fanfare book. The models for their animal books were their own pets or animals they met in their extensive travels. She and her husband lived in the Smoky Mountains and in New York City.

CARTER, THOMAS (*Harry in England**), gardener at Silverthorne and a great friend of Harry. He has bright, dark, twinkling eyes and a pleasant smile and chats in a good-natured way with the boy as he goes about his work in the potting shed, lawn, and garden. He helps Harry see the importance of obedience and not whining to get his way. He introduces Harry to Henry, the hedgehog under the holly bush, and promises to take good care of Henry's babies when Harry is reluctant to visit Cherry Lodge because of them. He makes a little box house for Tom, the dormouse, which he has given Harry as a pet. His mother is the Honey* Woman. He is one of the strongest and most likeable characters in the book.

CASH EVANS (*Good-bye, My Lady**), Alpheus, storekeeper in the nearest Mississippi village. Described as a hard man but a fair one, he never gives credit except to old Jesse Jackson, and from him he demands payment in cord wood. His great weakness is his love for dogs, particularly his registered English setter, Millard Fillmore. Through his influence, Jesse has been allowed to keep and raise his nephew, Skeeter, and it is he who has insisted that Skeeter go to school, though the attendance has been so irregular that the boy is barely literate.

CATAMOUNT (*Homespun**), real name, Ebenezer Smith; surly, malicious renegade white trapper and trader, who stirs up the Indians against the whites. He takes a dislike to Luke* Greenman, raids Luke's cache of valuable pelts, and finally kills him from ambush. When pursued by Dard* Rae, he is slain, ironically, by some sort of cat-like animal just as Dard is about to shoot him.

A CAT OF PARIS (Hoffman*, Eleanor, Stokes, 1940), lighthearted, talking animal fantasy set in a Paris artists' colony in the 1930s, in which events are told from the viewpoint of, but not by, Thom*, a handsome young Siamese cat. Born on the Right Bank of the Seine, vain, disobedient Thom yearns to live on the exciting, glamourous Left Bank and to have his portrait painted by a proper artist. Fed up with his mischief, his mistress, a concierge, disposes of him in the Bird Market, where luckily he is purchased by the family of an American artist, whose daughter has taken a fancy to him. The Belmonts carry him home to their small, comfortable studio apartment in the Rue de la Cigale on the Left Bank. Adventurous times follow for the perky kitten as Mrs. Belmont provides him with his favorite foods, chopped beef, eggs, and cream, Mr. Belmont allows him to loll about the studio, and young Polly and her friend, Jane Manning, take him for walks on his red leash and collar about the neighborhood and to the Luxembourg Gardens where he views a puppet show featuring a Siamese, to the studio of struggling young Maurice* Pascal, where Thom almost gets his portrait done in charcoal, and to the sweet shop, where Polly accepts the offer of affable Madam Pinard to one day sculpt Thom in marzipan. When Mr. Belmont decides to paint Jane Manning's handsome hyacinth Brazilian macaw, Thom takes offense and runs away. He intends to go to Madame Pinard's for the long-delayed marzipan sitting, but downstairs in the apartment building he encounters the concierge's vicious watchdog, Leo, who chases him out the door and through the streets. After harrowing experiences, Thom is captured by a surly street youth, Charles*, who peddles him in the cafes. Maurice recognizes Thom, reported lost by the vacationing Belmonts, spends his last francs to buy back the cat, takes him home, paints him, and eventually restores him to his family. Thom has finally been painted and has also grown to appreciate his loving family and comfortable home. Although characters are flat or types, an appropriately Parisian flavor, well-fleshed, if too fortuitous, incidents, straightforward and affectionate tone, upbeat view of life, some humor and sufficient suspense unite for pleasingly diverting reading. Thom has the power of speech, though he never so communicates with humans, and is otherwise somewhat anthropomorphized, but the author skillfully refrains from making him either grotesque or comic. Fanfare.

THE CAT WHO WENT TO HEAVEN (Coatsworth*†, Elizabeth, ill. Lynd Ward, Macmillan, 1930), short fantasy set in Japan. The earnest housekeeper of a virtuous, struggling, young artist brings home from the market a small, white, black, and yellow cat, which the two name Good Fortune. Meek, modest, and respectful, the cat often sits in reverent meditation before the statue of the Buddha, and even once mercifully releases a sparrow she has caught. Shortly after her arrival, the artist accepts a commission to do a painting of the death of the Buddha for the temple. If he succeeds in pleasing the priests, his reputation as an artist will be made. Realizing he needs to understand the Buddha before he can paint him, the artist positions himself before the statue, cat by his side, and meditates upon the life and experiences of the prince, letting scene after scene from the Buddha's life flow through his mind and touch his heart. After painting the designated scene, he paints the various gods of earth and sky and the disciples who came to bid farewell to the Buddha. He paints the various animals in whose form the Buddha came to earth to practice mercy and teach those around him, among them the elephant, the horse, the water buffalo, the Banyan deer, the monkey, and the tiger. He does not paint a cat because, of all animals, only the cat refused to accept the teachings of the Buddha and was not blessed by him. Remembering how sweetly his little cat has behaved and how admiring she has been of his work, the artist nevertheless adds a cat to his painting. Too happy to live any longer, Good Fortune falls dead at his feet. The finished painting is then given to the priests who reject it as inaccurate and plan to burn it the next day. At dawn, however, they see what they regard as a miracle: the Buddha in the picture has extended his hand over the cat, indicating his acceptance and approval of that creature, too. The many stories about the Buddha and a richly descriptive style strengthen this slight, sentimental, didactic story. The numerous illustrations picture scenes and contribute much to atmosphere and setting. Many are full page, some are free spots, some recall delicately detailed silk screen, and some show animals in striking full-page portraits. Choice; Newbery Winner.

CAUDILL†, REBECCA (1899–1985), born in Poor Fork in Harlan County, Ky.; author best known for her regional short stories and historical novels for children and young people. She grew up in Tennessee, one of eleven children whose parents were teachers. She graduated from Wesleyan College in Georgia and later took her M.A. degree from Vanderbilt. After teaching English in a girls' school in Rio de Janiero, she edited a Methodist church paper in Nashville. She married James Ayars, an editor, and lived in Urbana, Ill. She wrote short stories, novels, and verse for children and young people, eventually publishing about two dozen books, most of which drew upon the history of the Appalachians and her own memories of her childhood for subjects and settings. Her historical novels show extensive research and skillfully integrate personal conflicts with the concerns and aspirations of the times. A Newbery honor book and a Fanfare selection, *Tree of Freedom** (Viking, 1949), related from the standpoint of a thirteen-year-old girl, tells of the experiences of a North Carolina pioneer family who emigrate to Kentucky during the land rush of 1780. The colloquial, down-home style and abundant detail of everyday life create a substantial and enlightening picture of the period. *The Far-Off Land†* (Viking, 1964), also a Fanfare book, takes another group of pioneers westward to Tennessee in the same year. She wrote for younger readers *A Certain Small Shepherd†* (Holt, 1965) and *Did You Carry the Flag Today, Charley?†* (Holt, 1966). Both are highly illustrated and are Fanfare and *Choice* selections, and the second also appears in *Children's Books Too Good to Miss*. They reveal the author's deep sensitivity to the needs and yearnings of children and strong understanding of the problems of rural mountain life.

CEDRIC THE FORESTER (Marshall*, Bernard, Appleton, 1921), romantic, historical novel set in the days of chivalry in England during the reigns of Henry II, Richard I Lion-Hearted, and John and ending with the signing of the Magna Charta (Great Charter) at Runnymede. Richard (Dickon) of Mountjoy near the Welsh Marches tells of the steadily rising fortunes of a youth his own age, brave, stouthearted Cedric of Pelham, the son of a forester. Cedric attracts the attention of Lord Mountjoy, Dickon's father, when, through his skill with the crossbow, he saves Richard from being killed by Lionel, churlish scion of Carleton, a neighboring manor with whom the Mountjoys are on bad terms. Cedric is made Richard's man-in-arms and becomes regarded as one of the family. Dickon's mother, Lady Katherine, sees that he is taught his letters, and he soon becomes an avid reader of the writings of the foremost thinkers. He is particularly admired for his skill with the crossbow, for his daring and inventiveness, and for his courtesy and gentle manners. In spite of his rise in circumstances, he never becomes arrogant or proud but exhibits a steady and increasing concern for the rights of commoners, a matter that on one occasion leads to an angry confrontation with Lord Mountjoy and a brief exile from the manor. Cedric and Dickon share many adventures, in which Cedric is usually the leader. Among others, they rescue young Geoffrey of Carleton from Greenwood outlaws, healing the long-standing breach between their two houses; they rescue Geoffrey's mother, Lady Elizabeth, from the same outlaws; both deport themselves most creditably against the Welsh and are knighted, Cedric being henceforth known as Sir Cedric de la Roche and given the manor of Grimsby for his own; and they set free a slave who is about to be hanged by haughty Lord Gilroy for killing a dog. Years pass, and when the nobles combine against King John, both are made members of the committee to draft the Magna Charta. Cedric distinguishes himself by championing the rights of the common people by insisting that appropriate language be included in the several articles. Characters are types and the stock ones for this kind of novel, as are the romantic, swashbuckling episodes where "gadzookery," posturing, and sieges and confrontations in arms abound. Cedric is the only character one gets to know well, and his is a plaster figure, while Richard is merely the device by which Cedric's fortunes are made known. Language is stiltedly archaic, scenes and characters are described in conventional phrases, and the view of the period is mostly that of the nobles, with family rivalry, tournaments, warfare, and entourages. Individual episodes are well drawn and exciting if predictable, but the dramatic potential of Cedric's rise to fame and fortune is never properly exploited, and the novel lacks climax. Newbery Honor.

CENTERBURG TALES (McCloskey*, Robert, ill. author, Viking, 1951), episodic realistic fiction. Here in seven chapters are further adventures of Homer Price and his friends of Centerburg, Ohio. These episodes focus mainly on Homer's Grampa Hercules, called by the townspeople Grampa Herc. He is an old-timer of forceful personality and quick wit, who likes to entertain his friends with tall tales about events of his youth when Ohio was being settled. He tells how his quick eye and nimble intellect discern that the sparrows in the town of Sparrow Courthouse cause the town clock to run slow, until it is "daytime nightwards and nightside daymost," and the people get up when the sun goes down and retire at dawn. He rigs up a contraption called a Hide-a-Ride, something like a modern carnival thrill ride, on which the Indians are so eager to ride that they pay him in hides and furs for the privilege. He once supports on his back a rickety plank bridge so that his partner can drive across it their market wagon loaded with salt. He tells how he pans for gold with Hopper McThud in California, where he saw yellow stuff scattered all over the map like the spots on a speckled hen. He describes how he once hops up a three-hundred-foot-high cliff to rescue Hopper and gives Mr. Gabby, the advertising man, an idea for promoting a product he is selling, a breakfast cereal called Gravitty-Bitties, which are guaranteed to make the eater into a champion jumper. The last three episodes in the book concern other townspeople. Dulcy Dooner, the town handyman, inherits from his uncle, scientist Durpee Dooner, the seedman, a jar of what turns out to be very special ragweed seeds. After Dulcy plants them, they grow to such immense proportions that they threaten the well-being of the entire nation. A peddler, Professor Atmos P. H. Ear, sells Homer's Uncle* Ulysses and his friends cans of Eversomuch More-So, a product no one can see, feel, taste, smell, or hear, that is guaranteed to make whatever it is applied to ever so much more so than it is. The final chapter finds a stranger walking into Uncle Ulysses' lunchroom and putting on the gaudy jukebox an unbreakable record, whose tune proves to be so catchy that the entire town picks it up and sings it endlessly. These episodes, like those in the previous book, *Homer Price**, are all plot. Exaggerated yarns, they move fast and are quite comic. McCloskey's realistic cartoons contribute to the fun. Choice; Fanfare.

CHARIOT IN THE SKY: A STORY OF THE JUBILEE SINGERS (Bontemps*, Arna, ill. Cyrus LeRoy Baldridge*, Winston, 1951), fictionalized telling of the group of young blacks who became world famous singing "slave songs" to raise money for Fisk school in the years directly after the Civil War. Caleb, a young slave belonging to Colonel Williams, tries to run away, is whipped, and then is rented out to a tailor in Charleston, where his parents, who are also rented, live. Unusually bright and ambitious, Caleb teaches himself to read by memorizing the measurements the tailor calls out, then salvaging the scraps of paper on which they are written. A free Negro, Phillip Sazon, about his own age, lends him a book and later is helped to escape from Charleston by Caleb's father, who works on the docks. Just before the Emancipation Proclamation, Col. Williams appears and sells Caleb to a man from Chattanooga, where he takes Caleb to work in his dry-goods store. As the owner and the white clerks leave for the army, Caleb runs the store, once saving a pretty, free black girl, Precious Jewel Thomas, from harassment. At the war's end, he returns to Charleston, can't find his parents, and goes back to Tennessee, but when he learns that

Precious Jewel is attending the Fisk school for blacks, started by some Yankees, he heads for Nashville. To earn his tuition Caleb teaches in a little country school, which is broken up by Ku Klux Klan riders. At Fisk he becomes part of a singing group of eleven students, most of them ex-slaves, directed by George L. White, the school's treasurer. To earn money for the school, they start a tour, an enterprise at first discouraging, but when they are down to their last penny and hungry, they sing a spiritual for the National Council of Congregational Churches meeting in Oberlin, and they receive enthusiastic help. Switching from conventional music to slave songs, they become very popular as the Jubilee Singers. When they return from the tour, Caleb finds Phillip Sazon at Fisk, and together they go back to restart the little school. On the road they are set upon by two renegade blacks, and later Phillip is shot and killed by Klansmen and the schoolhouse is burned. Deeply remorseful, Caleb continues the school, foregoing the chance to go on a second Jubilee tour, meeting his students in the open, in barns, in cabins, moving frequently to throw off the scent. At the end of the term, the people determine to build a church which just might be used for a school. Caleb joins the Jubilee Singers in New York for an overseas tour and is seen off by his parents, who have recognized his picture in the paper. The book includes an introduction about the singers and the Fisk school, but gives no indication of whether Caleb and the other young people mentioned in the group are fictional. The portrayal of the blacks is earnest and, to modern readers, may seem stereotyped in the "good Negro" image of the 1950s. Although a great deal happens, the action is slow and the structure more like biography than like a novel, with various important elements, Precious Jewel, for example, simply dropped. Fanfare.

CHARLES (*A Cat of Paris**), unpleasant Parisian street boy, who grabs Thom*, the Siamese cat, after the policeman rescues the animal from the tree in which he has taken refuge. Charles feeds Thom very little, and the proud cat is soon a bag of bones. A surly lad, whose tailor grandfather often beats him for laziness, Charles peddles Tom in the open air cafes, hoping to realize a little spending money. He is unsuccessful until he encounters Maurice* Pascal, who recognizes the lost cat and spends his last francs to free him. Charles is a stereotyped character.

CHARLES DOAK (*"Hello, the Boat!"**), father who arranges and directs the trip down the Ohio from Pittsburgh to Cincinnati. Once a schoolteacher, he has been working as a trader on a flatboat on the Ohio and Mississippi to get money to buy a farm. Since land has become too dear in Pennsylvania, he decides to move his family westward. He is lighthearted, loyal, efficient, wise, knowledgeable, steadfast, and brave—the stereotypical pioneering father.

CHARLES INGALLS (*Little House in the Big Woods**; *Little House on the Prairie**; *On the Banks of Plum Creek**; *On the Shores of Silver Lake**; *The*

*Long Winter**; *Little Town on the Prairie**; *These Happy Golden Years**), ''Pa'' to Laura* and her three sisters in a series of seven autobiographical novels. Strong, cheerful, fun-loving, he is a contrast to his prim wife, though he is devoted to her and their daughters. He is amazingly competent, able to raise or build almost anything, to track and hunt, to play the fiddle, to sing, to lead meetings, and to stand up to angry crowds. Through a long series of hardships, he remains optimistic and communicates this spirit to Laura, along with his love of music and his itchy foot, which he controls to please his wife, though he longs to continue moving westward.

CHARLOTTE A. CAVATICA (*Charlotte's Web**), clever, resourceful spider who saves the life of Wilbur*, the runt pig, by spinning into her web words that convince the humans on the Zuckerman* farm and at the fair that Wilbur is a remarkable animal. Charlotte is, as only Mrs. Zuckerman notes, ''no ordinary *spider*.'' Although Wilbur finds her bloodthirsty at first, he comes to appreciate that she is both ''a true friend and a good writer.''

CHARLOTTE'S WEB (White*†, E. B., ill. Garth Williams, Harper, 1952), fantasy set on an American farm in the mid-twentieth century. When her father intends to kill a newly born runt pig, Wilbur*, Fern* Arable protests and is allowed to raise him on a bottle. Later he is sold to Fern's uncle, Homer Zuckerman*, and lives in the basement of his barn. When Wilbur learns from a sheep that he is to be slaughtered for Christmas, his friend, Charlotte*, a spider, sets out to save his life by spinning words in her web—Some Pig, Terrific, Radiant, and Humble—intended to convince the humans that he is a very special animal. She is reluctantly assisted by Templeton, the surly, self-seeking rat, who fetches scraps of paper on which appear words she can copy. In the fall, at the county fair, Wilbur wins a prize for attracting so many visitors to the fair, and Charlotte spins an egg sac and dies. With the help of Templeton, Wilbur brings the sac back to the Zuckerman's barn after the fair, and the next spring, the eggs hatch, releasing hundreds of baby spiders, three of which remain to become new friends of Wilbur. Strong charcterizations, important themes involving death, friendship, and the continuity of life, and a charming, amusing style skillfully combine to make this one of the outstanding twentieth-century books for children. Books Too Good; Children's Classics; ChLA Top 10; ChLA Touchtones; Choice; Lewis Carroll; Newbery Honor; Stone.

CHEE-CHEE (*The Story of Doctor Dolittle**; *The Voyages of Doctor Dolittle**), a monkey whom Doctor Dolittle* rescues from an unkind organ grinder. A message from Chee-Chee's cousin telling of an illness among the monkeys triggers the doctor's first voyage to Africa, where Chee-Chee remains when Doctor Dolittle goes home. He becomes so homesick, however, that he dresses like a woman, stows away on a ship to England, and makes his way across the country to Puddleby, still dressed in women's clothes. He accompanies the doctor on the voyage to Spidermonkey Island.

THE CHEERFUL HEART (Vining*†, Elizabeth Janet Gray, ill. Kazue Mizumura, Viking, 1959), realistic domestic novel set in Japan in 1946, one year after the end of World War II. The Tamaki family, including the parents, the Grandfather, Tomi, 11, and her little brother, Ken, 6, return to Tokyo to a newly built house after several years at Uncle Saburo's farm, where they have been living since bombing destroyed their old home. Because of lumber shortages, the new house is small and poorly built, but Tomi, who has, her Grandfather says, a "cheerful heart," is happy to be back. She greatly admires the room her cousin, Emi Kimura, 13, has all to herself when they visit the Kimuras on New Year's Day, but she doesn't envy her cousin. Her own New Year's gift of a bicycle makes her ecstatically happy until it is stolen by a burglar. A second theft prompts the family to think of a large watchdog, but instead they adopt a little black stray puppy and name him Moken, "fierce dog," only to call him Blackie. The family observes various customs of interest: they celebrate the birthday of older sister Mariko, who died during the war; they visit the farm and join in the ceremony of preparing the rice for the New Year; Tomi and Ken both distinguish themselves at Sports Day for the school children; they go to the mountains with the Kimuras and celebrate O Bon, the mid-summer festival honoring relatives who have died. Tomi discovers her bicycle among the secondhand merchandise at the curio shop, and the kind salesman, Sato, promises to hold it for her while she tries to get enough money to buy it back. Knowing her parents are putting all their money toward a better house, she decides that her only possibility is to win the calligraphy contest prize and is disappointed when her entry wins honorable mention but no money. Sato suggests that she might trade the lovely kimono she has inherited from Mariko, but the idea seems to her to desecrate her dead sister's memory. Finally she asks her mother, who gives her a silver medicine case with a toggle, called a *netsuke*, of ivory carved in the shape of a monkey, an antique piece of no sentimental value, to trade instead. When their new house is built, Tomi has a room of her own, small but delightful to her. The next day they are astonished by the return of Elder Brother, Ichiro, believed dead in a prison camp in Siberia. While he is bathing, Tomi quickly gathers all her things and cheerfully moves back in with Grandfather and Ken, not waiting to be told that Ichiro must have the room. The book is obviously designed to introduce children to the Japanese culture, not only their customs and immediate post-war living conditions but also the self-effacing temperament that is admired in Japanese girls. Although the story is attractively written, such a personality does not make a compelling heroine, and the virtual lack of plot tension keeps the book from being more than mildly interesting. Fanfare.

THE CHESTRY OAK (Seredy*, Kate, ill. author, Viking, 1948), historical novel set in World War II, which begins in a medieval castle in the remote valley of Chestry in Hungary and ends on a farm in the United States. The story spans four years in the life of young Michael, Prince of Chestry, who is six when the novel begins. Through flashbacks the reader learns that, before the Nazis occupy Hungary, Michael lives happily with his aloof, beautiful mother and his much-respected father, Prince Alexander, who has deeded the Chestry lands to his peasants. Michael dearly loves his Nana, Mari Vitez, the wise and sturdy peasant girl who was chosen at his birth to be his nurse. From her, he has learned love of homeland, parents, and soil. He enjoys his lessons with his French and English tutors and learns to ride with skill and perception the noble horses for which Chestry is renowned. After the war begins, Michael's way of life changes drastically. His new tutor, a harsh German whom the boy calls Professor War, emphasizes facts, a method of teaching that puzzles the boy, and Michael soon sees the need for watching both his movements and his tongue. Nana, however, continues to tell him stories of the old days about his country and family and keeps alive in him respect for the old ways and peasant values. When the Russians arrive, the castle is bombed, and Michael's father is killed. Alexander, ostensibly pro-Nazi but secretly allied with the underground, had arranged for Nana, also an underground worker, to smuggle Michael out of the valley. Plans go awry, and while the boy is on his way to Nana's house in the village, his horse, the fractious stallion, Midnight, runs away and throws the boy. An old charcoal burner finds him unconscious from a blow to the head. He is cared for by a succession of medical people, none of whom takes his assertions of identity seriously. An American soldier, Tom Brown, discovers him in a home for refugee children and arranges for him to be taken to the United States, where as Michael Prince he lives on the Brown family farm with two brothers, Bruce and Charlie, and their Mom and Pop. After Tom returns home, with, coincidentally, Midnight, among other horses the other soldiers found straying in the valley, the boy's identity comes out. Michael, however, chooses to live as a son of the Browns, whom he has come to love. As a symbol of his loyalty to his new homeland, Michael plants an acorn from the ancient Chestry oak, destroyed in the bombing, on the Brown farm. This grim, slow-moving, rather unconvincing story is told from Michael's point of view but not by the boy. Descriptive in style and rhythmical and euphonious in language, the story contains many details about life in the castle and the upbringing of a prince, altogether the most engaging part of the book. Characters are types, and the American family lacks credibility. Love for the earth, the importance of simple people and peasant values, the horror of war, and family love and loyalty are themes that are stressed. Fanfare.

CHICO (*The Silver Fawn**), Mexican youth who realizes his dream of becoming a respected silversmith. He has adventures by himself and with his employer, Señor* Bill, some humorous, some serious, and a few potentially dangerous. He can be something of a scamp and a mischief, particularly to get Señor Bill's attention or to get his way. Sometimes he is quite naive, as he forgets to size up the birds properly and apparently buys as a gift for his mother two parrots who cannot talk. He gets lost in Mexico City, persuades Bill to rent the rickety shop, accompanies him to the mountains to hire weavers, and reacts with fear and apprehension when the *vaquero* (cowboy) visits their camp. He becomes more serious in attitude and more responsible as the months pass. He is given an orphaned baby fawn to raise. In a humorous episode, Señor Bill buys a nanny goat to suckle it. It is this fawn that gives Chico the idea for the fawn design on the pitcher that receives so much acclaim in Taxco and Mexico City and gives Bill's shop its name.

CHILDREN OF THE SEA (Bronson*, Wilfrid S., ill. author, Harcourt, 1940), story of a dolphin and a boy set in southern Florida, the Bahama Islands, and the sea, mainly that surrounding these areas. The first of three parts, taking up nearly half of the long book, is about the birth and early life of Tursiops, a dolphin born in a tidal river of southern Florida. He meets a variety of river and sea creatures, eventually joins, with his mother, a herd of dolphins which make their leisurely and joyful way up the Atlantic coast, then back down, following the food supply. When they are attacked by a large number of sharks, Tursiops is wounded and makes his way to rest beside an old pier in Nassau harbor. The second section tells of a black infant abandoned on a fishing sloop, then re-abandoned on the doorstep of kindly Jeremiah Jones, who drives a tourist carriage when cruise ships are in port. He names the baby Ishmael but calls him Smudgy. Neglected by the old woman Jones has hired to look after him, Smudgy teaches himself to swim and learns about the sea from constant observation. When he is almost ten, he finds a boat washed up in a hurricane, names it *None-So-Prity*, and he and his friend, Pennycash, start a business of fishing and selling their catch in the market. Returning home alone one day, Smudgy sees the wounded dolphin, tries unsuccessfully to feed it fish, later returns with a squid, and makes friends with the convalescing animal. They enjoy swims together, and when Smudgy plays his harmonica, Tursiops performs with leaps and somersaults. The third section tells of their companionship until Jones finds Smudgy a position on a sponging boat as cabin boy, where he plays his harmonica until Tursiops, attracted by the music, follows the boat to sea. While the men are out sponging one day, Smudgy goes for a swim with Tursiops, finds some enormous sponges, and while trying to get one to take to Jones, is attacked by an octopus. The dolphin saves him and lifts the senseless boy to the surface where the cook pulls him aboard. Although we know what goes on in the dolphin's mind, the book is realistic and so full of factual information that the thin thread of story is overpowered. Drawings of much of the flora and fauna which the characters encounter illustrate the pages. As an informational book, however, it is badly dated by the "mammy" dialect of the human characters, which is likely to be offensive to readers today. Fanfare.

CHILDREN OF THE SOIL (Burglon*, Nora, ill. E. Parin D'Aulaire, Doubleday, 1932), realistic novel for younger children set in rural Norway, presumably in the nineteenth century. Guldklumpen Salstad, a second grader, and his slightly older sister, Nicolina, are poor crofter folk, though their mother, Olina, was daughter of a rich farmer. Since their father, a sailor, has evidently been lost at sea, the family scrapes by on the potatoes they grow and the cheese Olina makes and sells from their goats' milk, while she does weaving and spinning as partial rent for the Colonel, who owns Malmostrand, their home. Guldklumpen fixes a home for a tomte man, a good elf, and attributes to his help all the good fortune that comes from the children's hard work and cleverness: the wild duck they find, the chickens for which they trade ducklings, the grain they glean from the Colonel's field, the cup Guldklumpen wins for skiing skill, the new clothes and five-bladed knife he gets at Christmas as a reward for saving cry-baby Aspen, a gentry child, from an angry sow, the commercial demand for the figures he carves, Nicolina's prize at the fair for fine weaving with which she buys their first cow, and their good luck at the auction where their savings buy a second cow and a lamb. They have a few setbacks: the prize for weaving at school goes to a gentry girl, not to Nicolina, though her weaving is the best; their crab trap, for which they have weeded a potato patch, is swept away in a storm; the gentry mother, who commissions Nicolina to weave a tapestry to be submitted as her daughter's, rejects it. But most of their advances are acquired rather too easily to seem convincing. The style and characterization are simple and the tone earnest. Customs, foods, and social stratification of an unfamiliar time and place are made clear and believable. Newbery Honor.

CHINGO SMITH OF THE ERIE CANAL (Adams*, Samuel Hopkins, ill. Leonard Vosburgh, Random, 1958), lively historical novel set in 1816-1825 in New York State on the roads and canals from Albany to Buffalo. When a traveling higgler, or peddler, is arrested and escapes in Rochesterville in the bitter-cold August of 1816, he leaves behind a boy possibly seven or older who calls himself Chingo Smith, having traded an Indian a broken-blade knife for his name. Chingo becomes ort-boy at the Renolds Inn, running errands and doing all odd jobs under the watchful eye of the cinderwench, Horner's Betty, who impresses upon him the importance of saving money and getting an education. At the inn he hears Captain Fortescue Lumm telling of plans for the Erie Canal, and, impressed by the captain's magnificent appearance, acquires a great desire to become a canalboat captain. Before he achieves that position at the end of the book, he is kidnapped by runagates (wandering young hoodlums), is arrested and auctioned off as a county pauper, joins Isaac Mendham, the learned tinker, who teaches him to read and figure, and arranges for Tigy the Terrible, an Agonistes, to teach him boxing. Returning to the canal, he is surprised to find it no longer a muddy ditch but actually carrying boats. He becomes, in turn, a green grocer's helper, a traveling merchant in his little boat, *Cash Down*, then a hoggee, who drives the towhorses, and a powder monkey for the blasters. The miserable conditions in which the hoggees sleep with the horses prompts him to invent and install a sleep-shelf, an idea that he perfects during a winter as a carpenter's helper in Rochester and sells to Captain Lumm for the new passenger packet he is having built, the *Sleepwell*. Although booked solid, the *Sleepwell* is almost prevented from starting by the canal boat runners in a section of Schenectady called the Battleground, where they start a wild ruckus which the canalers narrowly win with the help of a variety of friends Chingo has made over the years. Chingo, however, is knocked out and only days later wakes to discover Captain Lumm has promoted himself to Admiral and has made Chingo what he has always hoped to be, captain of a canal boat. Although only Chingo is fully developed, the book is full of a long parade of characters of interest and gives a vivid picture of the rough life on and around the Erie Canal in its early years. Fanfare.

CHI-WEE (*The Runaway Papoose**), a little girl of the big mesa. She is rather fat but very active and manages to capture a wild burro colt when her friend, Loki, misses a chance to lasso a burro for himself. At the big festival she is given the honor of wearing the Butterfly Katchina mask in the dance because she has unselfishly given a jar she made to a friend who broke her own jar and feared that her mother would beat her.

CHLOE (*The Forgotten Daughter**), daughter of Laevinus, Roman centurion, and a Greek woman he captured in Lesbos. Abandoned by her father to a life of slavery on his Villa Caracinia in the hills near Rome, she grows up in a wretched hut, cared for by Melissa, her dead mother's Greek friend. She hates her father for condemning her to a lonely life of unending labor, hunger, and whippings. In her free moments she dreams of Lesbos, the island from which her mother and Melissa had been torn by the Romans, and sings with Melissa songs from such Greek poets as Sappho. Because she rescues from an animal trap young, highborn Aulus* Cornelius Maro, whose family owns the nearby Villa Cornelia, she is reunited with her father. She eventually forgives her father and marries Aulus.

CHOATE, FLORENCE, author-illustrator; born in Elizabeth, N.J. She studied at the Art Students League, where she became friends with Elizabeth Curtis*. The two went to Paris to study painting and illustrating and then returned to New York City to open a studio together. They first collaborated on illustrating for various publishers, doing, among others, several books in the Stokes's Wonder Books Series, including *Stokes' Wonder Book of the Bible* (1918), *Stokes' Wonder Book of Mother Goose* (1919), and *Treasury of Heroes and Heroines* (Stokes, 1920). They then turned to preparing books of their own, first compiling and illustrating a collection of myths and tales from Europe, *The Little People of the Hills* (Harcourt, 1928). Later they collaborated in writing and illustrating eight novels. Some are career stories, like *Dance of the Hours* (Harcourt, 1934) and *Absolute Pitch* (Harcourt, 1939), but most are somewhat romantic historical novels with didactic intent. Their first of this type, *The Crimson Shawl** (Stokes, 1941), about Acadian refugees relocated in a New England town during the French and Indian War, was selected by the editors of *Horn Book* as a Fanfare book. Others include *The Five Gold Sovereigns, A Story of Thomas Jefferson's Time* (Stokes, 1943), and *Lysbet: A Story of Old New York* (Lippincott, 1947), about an English girl captured by Indians who lives with a Dutch family.

CHRIS BRABSON (*The Perilous Road**), eleven-year-old Confederate who resents his older brother's enlistment in the Union army and starts a one-man campaign to help the Southern cause. Chris is first enraged at the Yankees because his friend, Silas* Agee, has been accosted and robbed by Union soldiers on his way back from town and, besides his supplies, has lost the hunting shirt Chris had cut out from deer skins he shot and cured himself and which a sister of Silas in town has sewn for him. Before the end of the story, Chris has seen the Yankee soldier who gave him ginger snaps killed and has interrupted his flight home to bring water to a badly wounded young Yankee soldier who had given him an apple the night before.

CHRIS DAHLBERG (*Swift Rivers**), youth with a very strong sense of honor and responsibility. Because his dead father had arranged that he work for Uncle Nels in return for keep, he continues to work for the man even though Uncle Nels exploits him and never shows him any affection. Chris has a seeking, questing mind and yearns for more education. Most people in Goose Wing Valley are skeptical about his scheme for getting his logs to market in St. Louis, but he stubbornly sticks with the job. He learns to have confidence in himself and to have greater self-assurance in dealing with other people.

THE CHRISTMAS ANNA ANGEL (Sawyer*, Ruth, ill. Kate Seredy*, Viking, 1944), short story of family life set in Hungary in World War I. Little Anna longs for a cake of her own for Christmas, but her father, Matyas Rado, explains that no one has any wheat to make one. When St. Nicholas comes in his sleigh drawn by a prancing white horse for his traditional visit on St. Nicholas Eve to usher in the Christmas season, Anna first asks for a Christmas cake shaped like a clock, then in response to admonishing looks from her mother, Mari, alters her request to a little white muff with a hot potato to keep her hands warm. While she and her younger brother, Miklos, and their parents decorate the family tree, her mother cautions her to put thoughts of a cake from her mind. Anna is confident that the bright sunset that night indicates that the angels will be baking Christmas cakes for people that year. On St. Lucy's Day, Anna and Miklos play with the hens, as is the custom, to insure that they will continue laying the year round. Anna finds eggs, which she interprets as a good omen. She is certain, too, that, even though the army officers take all her father's wheat at harvest's end, the angels have plenty up in heaven, and that there is a special angel among them who will see to a cake just for Anna. On Christmas Eve, the children dress in their finest, the Christmas story is told, and there is a sumptuous feast of goose. That night Anna dreams that her little dog, Ferko, wakes her and ushers her downstairs to the kitchen. There she sees her Christmas Anna Angel, an angel girl who looks just like Anna herself, busily making Christmas cakes in the exact shapes each member of the family prefers—a manger for Mari, shepherds for Matyas, three kings for Miklos, a clock-cake for Anna, and even a bone-cake for Ferko. The next morning, to their delight, the children see the cakes hanging from the family tree. Only Mari and Matyas know that the soldiers did not get quite all the Rado wheat when they came collecting that fall. This pleasing story of childlike faith, dreams come true, and vividly described old customs grew out of an actual experience described to the author. The many, mostly full-color illustrations in decorative folk-art style elaborate on the story with Central European ethnic details. Fanfare.

CHÚCARO: WILD PONY OF THE PAMPA (Kalnay*, Francis, ill. Julian de Miskey, Harcourt, 1958), realistic problem story set on an *estancia*, a large ranch on the Argentine Pampa not long ago. Juan, a *gaucho* (cowboy), captures a spirited, wild pony found by twelve-year-old Pedro, his ward. Juan names the pony, ''a shade between yellow, brown, and pink,'' Chúcaro, after one he had when he was a boy, and helps Pedro to break him and ride him. When the mayordomo of the *estancia* orders them to give the pony to Armando, the spoiled son of the *patrón*, the owner of the ranch, Pedro's father, the old *vaquero*, suggests letting Chúcaro decide for himself whether Armando or Pedro should be his master. The horse kicks Armando, who, unable to lasso him, uses a *bolas*, a throwing weapon made of cowhide and heavy balls, against him. When Juan reprimands the youth severely for so ill-treating the horse, the *patrón* fires him. He and Pedro leave the *estancia* and strike out on their horses for the falls, Iguazu, which Juan has long yearned to visit. The plot is slight, contrived, and predictable, and the characters stereotypes, the rich too idle and vacuous, and the workers too virtuous and clever. The book is most notable for its details of the everyday life of those who live and work on the Argentine ranches. Fanfare; Newbery Honor.

CHUCK MASTERSON (*The Wonderful Flight to the Mushroom Planet**; *Stowaway to the Mushroom Planet**; *Time and Mr. Bass†*), David* Topman's best friend. Chuck is short and square with brown skin and dark hair. While David is the planner and thinker, Chuck likes to do things. His grandfather, Cap'n Tom, gives the boys the materials to make the space ship with which they travel to Basidium-X*, the Mushroom Planet. Although likeable, Chuck is a flat character, almost indistinguishable from David.

CHUTE, MARCHETTE (GAYLORD) (1909-), born in Wayzata, Minn,; specialist on the medieval period and the sixteenth century, who has written and illustrated a number of books of verse for younger children. She grew up in Minnesota, the middle of three sisters, all of whom became writers, and received her B.A. degree from the University of Minnesota. Her *The Innocent Wayfaring* (Scribner, 1943) is set in the period of Chaucer and *The Wonderful Winter** (Dutton, 1954) is in the Shakespearian period. In addition, she has published an introduction to Shakespeare, a book of songs from Shakespeare, and a number of books on religion for children, and two plays for adults.

CHUTO (*Secret of the Andes**), Cusi's aged teacher, the preserver of the sacred llama herds of the Incas. Periodically he takes strong, young beasts down the mountain and gives them to deserving families. He deliberately withholds from Cusi information about the boy's identity and about his mission in life. Because his previous herdboy, Cusi's father, chose to return to civilization, Chuto wishes to ground the boy thoroughly in Inca culture before allowing him to go to Cuzco.

CILLA LAPHAM (*Johnny Tremain**), Priscilla, 14, granddaughter of the owner of the Lapham silver house. A spunky, gentle girl, she is faithful and solicitous in caring for her spoiled, pretty little sister, Isannah*. Since Johnny trusts her, he shows her the Lyte cup. She helps to free him of the charge of theft. At first Johnny treats her casually but later begins to think of her as a sweetheart. She is a strongly drawn, dynamic character, who grows and changes quite realistically in the course of the novel.

CINDERS (Gibson*, Katharine, ill. Vera Bock, Longmans, 1939), fantasy of Cinderella's coachman, set in the timeless unspecified kingdom of the märchen. Having hidden behind a bush when the Fairy Godmother waved her wand, the coachman, a small man in a gray velvet suit, is the only part of the enchantment not returned to its original condition at midnight. Finding himself before the castle steps with no memory of any earlier life, he makes his way to the king's stables and hires on to polish harness in exchange for a place to sleep and a little cheese. Challenged to give his name, he says the first thing that comes into his head, Cinders, and asked what he can do, he modestly replies that he's "a good hand with horses." His polite manners win him the good will of the stable man, Tim, and of the cook, and his cleverness helps him evade the ill will of the stable boys. When Flash, the king's favorite horse, goes lame and even the king's own surgeon can't treat him, Cinders makes a poultice of leaves, tends him devotedly, and eventually walks, then rides him to the astonishment of Tim and the other stable hands who can't get near the fiery animal. War comes to the kingdom and the stable boys go off into the army but Flash is too light for a war horse and Cinders too small for a soldier. One night an exhausted rider comes with a message that must be carried on to the Prince, telling him that he is between the armies of Count Tor and Count Hoof. The messenger also carries a token, a diamond cut in the shape of a tiny glass slipper, which will bring the bearer directly to the Prince. Before Tim and the other men can finish making excuses for not taking the message on, Cinders, with the token, is off on Flash. When morning comes, they find a little house in the forest where an old herb woman lets them stay and gets them hay, oats, and a little cheese in exchange for money to buy her heart's desire, a cow. When he leaves, the old woman promises him one wish, but he cannot remember what he wishes. To reach the Prince, they must go past Count Hoof's sentry, which they do by convincing him that he has seen a ghost rider. Cinders gives the message to the Prince, who has to come to the stable for it, since Cinders won't leave Flash until he is rubbed down and fed. The Prince attacks first one army, then the other, beats them both, and announces that his father, Old King Cole, is abdicating in his favor. Then Cinders remembers his wish—to see Cinderella. He is not only granted that wish but is also made her coachman and given Flash for his own. The language of the story is deft and distinguishes it from more ordinary modern fairy tales. Cinder emerges as a definite and appealing little character. His adventure, in the context of the tale, is altogether plausible. Fanfare.

THE CITADEL OF A HUNDRED STAIRWAYS (Malkus*, Alida Sims, ill. Henry C. Pitz, Winston, 1941), realistic novel set in the early 1900s near the ancient Inca city of Macchu Picchu in the Andes Mountains of Peru among the Quechuan Indians. Enterprising Titu, 13, lives with his hardworking, widower father, his superstitious grandmother, and his two younger sisters on a tiny farm which clings precariously to the terraced hillside overlooking the Urubamba River. The boy is delighted when Don Martin Ladrón, a rich landowner, hires him as guide for the American John Selden and his son, Tony, for he hopes to learn about "Yankee-landia" from his new friends. John Selden, a mining engineer, displays a keen interest in the technical accomplishments of the ancient Incas. His company has an agreement with the Echeandia family, to which Ladrón belongs, to develop a mine once worked by the Incas in that region. For Selden the days pass with little success, and there are hints of purposeful obstructions, but shy, awkward Tony develops muscles and a better self-image as the two youths hike the mountains and fish. Titu takes Tony to visit the Old One, the wise hermit who has shared with him stories of the Indians' proud past. The Old One shows Titu and Tony how Selden can secure enough gold to maintain operations until the rich vein known to be inside the mountain can be located. He also sends the boys on a quest into the Valley of Kings for the treasure of the last King of the Incas. He orders the boys to bring back whatever the king holds beneath his arm. The boys discover the king's body and release the golden urn clutched under his arm, and, after a harrowing journey over the ancient Incan trail through the mountains, they arrive home to learn that Selden has figured out how to reach the mother lode inside the mountain. The Old One is pleased with the *quipu*, or counting cord, inside the urn, which he is sure will reveal secrets of Inca history and wealth. The last legitimate heir to the Inca throne, his name José Tupac Amaru the Fourth, the Old One had hoped to find the Inca treasure himself and had intended to use it to improve life for the

Indians. Now aged, he sees, in Titu, hope for the future of his people. John Selden gives the boy a share of the proceeds of the mine to pay for his education, but recovery of the king's treasure awaits a later trip. This ambitious book never fulfills its potential for suspense. It suffers from uneven pacing and a confusion of details about mining. Tony changes too abruptly, and the Old One is too remote and all-wise to be believable, nor are his reasons for helping the Seldens clear. The book is doubly didactic: to illustrate the trouble that gold can cause and to teach about the way of life of the Andean Indians and their rich heritage. Mountain life is overidealized, and the writer generally does too much telling and not enough showing. Fanfare.

CLARK, ANN NOLAN (1898-), born in Las Vegas, Nev.; teacher and writer best known for her children's books about Indians. She attended New Mexico Highlands University, planning to teach English and history in high school. World War I found her in a one-room school teaching German immigrants, and through that experience she acquired an interest in minorities that changed the course of her life. She accepted a position with the Bureau of Indian Affairs as a junior high school teacher in 1930, and since then she has taught Indian children in the Southwest, has served as an educational specialist with the BIA, and has trained teachers in Latin America. For her work among the Indians in the Southwest and Latin America, she received a Distinguished Service Award from the United States government. Her first books were textbooks published by the BIA for Indian children. She wrote them to provide reading material that would reflect the Indian children's own interests, environment, and way of life. One of these for Navajos, *In My Mother's House*, a book of verse, was picked up by Viking in 1941 and gained wide recognition. Many other short stories, texts, novels, and books of verse followed during her long and distinguished career. Of her novels, *Secret of the Andes** (Viking, 1952) received the Newbery Award; *Magic Money** (Viking, 1950) and *Santiago** (Viking, 1955) were Fanfare books. *Little Navajo Bluebird** (Viking, 1943) was also a Fanfare book, and it and *Secret of the Andes* are cited in *Choice*. Although artlessly plotted, her novels show that she understands the Indians and has great sympathy for them. The books are shallowly characterized and tend toward message but are high in atmosphere and mood and employ a simple, poetic style. Her more recent novels have moved in a different direction, relating the experiences of immigrants to this country, among them, *All This Wild Land* (Viking, 1976) about Finns, and *To Stand Against the Wind* (Viking, 1978) about Vietnamese.

CLARK, MARGERY (MARY E. CLARK [1887-1958] and MARGERY QUIGLEY [1886-1968]), librarians who collaborated on *The Poppy Seed Cakes** (Doubleday, 1924), episodic story for young children. Its simple, lively humor and bright, primary-colored illustrations marked a departure in the picture-story book category. Clark was born in New York City, attended Columbia University, and worked in the public library in Montclair, N.J., becoming assistant librarian in 1927. Quigley was born in Los Angeles, graduated from Vassar College, took her library work in St. Louis and worked there in the public library until 1922, when she was appointed chief librarian at the Montclair, N.J., public library. Both women also published independently.

CLEARING WEATHER (Meigs*, Cornelia, ill. Frank Dobias, Little, 1928), historical novel of domestic problems and adventure set in Massachusetts and on the high seas against the economic difficulties of the American states and the development of the China sea trade just after the American Revolution. Nicholas* Drury, 19, of the port of Branscomb, Mass., seeks to save the once-prosperous shipbuilding business of his uncle and mentor, Thomas Drury, from falling into the hands of Thomas's unscrupulous creditor, Darius Corland, and Corland's rascally lawyer, Joseph Ryall. Goodhearted, conscientious Nicholas impulsively hides a stranger whom Corland wishes to have arrested, Etienne Bardeau*. This French adventurer and promoter of freedom expresses his gratitude to Nicholas by giving him a letter of Corland's that indicates that Corland had been secretly helping the British during the Revolutionary War. With the aid of Michael* Slade, winsome young adventurer from South Carolina who has been traveling with Bardeau, Nicholas decides to build a stout sailing ship and offers to make the people of Branscomb partners in its profits from sea-trade in return for their labor in building it. The townspeople readily agree to his plan, grateful for his leadership and courage, since keeping the shipyards in operation during this economically depressed period will give them work and save their homes. Nicholas believes that, if the trading venture is successful, all the Drury debts can be paid and the shipyards saved. The *Jocasta** sets sail for the West Indies, where successful sales suggest to Captain Douglas and Michael that still greater profits can be made by trading with American Indians and the Chinese. They round Cape Horn, sail up the coast of the Western Hemisphere, where they are attacked by Indians in the Pacific Northwest while bartering for furs, and then make for Hawaii and China. After enduring storms and pirate attacks, they take on a rich cargo in Canton and then sail home across the Atlantic. Two years after her departure, given up for lost, the *Jocasta* returns just in time to save the Drury shipyards from foreclosure. Etienne Bardeau forces the traitorous Corland, who has been obstructing Nicholas's efforts, to go to England, and a prosperous future lies ahead for the town. Although the plot is predictable, the characters stock, and the author's voice obvious, the many details of story and setting sustain interest and produce a good sense of what it must have been like for the people of the Massachusetts coast when the new United States struggled for economic independence (political independence having been won) and began trading with the world on its own. Newbery Honor.

CLEARY†, BEVERLY (BUNN) (1916-), born in McMinnville, Oreg.; author of many books, most of them humorous episodic stories for the eight-to-ten-year-old reader. She attended the University of California in Berkeley and received a degree in librarianship from the University of Washington in Seattle. After serving in the public library in Yakima, Wash., and as post librarian in an army hospital during World War II, she started writing books for children, her most popular being in two series, those of *Henry Huggins** (Morrow, 1950) and its many successors, and those about *Ellen Tebbits** (Morrow, 1951) and her friends. These books are mildly humorous stories of a typical boy and a typical girl, written in simple language accessible to readers just beyond the primer stage. Henry has a dog of uncertain ancestry which is featured in *Henry and Ribsy** (Morrow, 1954) and *Ribsy†* (Morrow, 1964). The series takes on a new dimension, however, when it shifts to Henry's neighbors in *Beezus and Ramona** (Morrow, 1955) and develops far more interest in such books as *Ramona the Pest†* (Morrow, 1968), *Ramona and Her Father†* (Morrow, 1977), and *Ramona Quimby, Age 8†* (Morrow, 1981). Ramona, and, to some extent, her sister, Beezus, are individuals rather than types and their stories incorporate subtler humor and more complex language, though still written for an audience of early readers. Cleary has also written light, down-to-earth fantasy in *The Mouse and the Motorcycle†* (Morrow, 1965) and its sequel, *Runaway Ralph†* (Morrow, 1970), and a number of novels for young teenagers, among them *Fifteen* (Morrow, 1956) and *Sister of the Bride* (Morrow, 1963). She has received many honors, the most prestigious being, in 1975, the Laura Ingalls Wilder Award for total contribution to children's literature, the 1983 George G. Stone Recognition of Merit Award for her body of work, and the Newbery Medal for *Dear Mr. Henshaw†* (Morrow, 1983).

COATSWORTH†, ELIZABETH (JANE) (1893-), born in Buffalo, N.Y.; poet and novelist. She graduated from Vassar and received her master's degree from Columbia University, studied further at Radcliffe, and traveled widely in Europe, Africa, and the Orient. She married Henry Beston, a writer and naturalist, and they made their home in Maine. She became known for her stories and poems for adults before she began writing for children. She published her first book for the young in 1927, and in 1930 she received the Newbery Award for *The Cat Who Went to Heaven** (Macmillan, 1930), a short fantasy set in Japan that reflects her knowledge of the Orient and its lore. During her long writing career, she wrote over ninety books for children and young people, mostly fiction and ranging widely in subject, period, and place. She received high critical acclaim for her historical novels and period pieces set in New England featuring little Sally, *Away Goes Sally** (Macmillan, 1934), *Five Bushel Farm** (Macmillan, 1939), and *The "Fair American"** (Macmillan, 1940), the last two of which were Fanfare books, while the first is cited in both *Choice* and *Children's Books Too Good to Miss*. Although the plots are uneven and suggest contrivance, characters weak or stereotyped, and tone sometimes too cozy, her style is poetic and vivid, scenes have life, and the books carry the conviction that comes from knowledge and love of subject and place, and affection for the reader. Also on the Fanfare list are the less convincing *The Golden*

*Horseshoe** (Macmillan, 1935), with a background in Colonial Virginia, *Alice-All-By-Herself** (Macmillan, 1937), an episodic story of a little girl's adventures on the Maine coast, *Door to the North** (Winston, 1950), a substantial, didactic, uneven novel about a Viking expedition to Greenland in the fourteenth century, and *The Princess and the Lion*† (Pantheon, 1963), a short, not very convincing adventure novel set in Abyssinia. She received honorary degrees from the University of Maine and New England College.

COBLENTZ, CATHERINE (1897-1951), born in Vermont. She grew up in a small town there, in ninth grade becoming the town librarian when the incumbent eloped and in high school acting as reporter for the village newspaper. During World War I, she worked at the Bureau of Standards in Washington and attended university classes at night. She married a physicist and spent several summers at an astronomical observatory in the Southwest. Her interest in local Vermont history is reflected in *The Blue Cat of Castle Town** (Longmans, 1949), a fantasy which concerns the value of true craftsmanship.

THE CODFISH MUSKET (Hewes*, Agnes Danforth, Doubleday, 1936), historical adventure novel set around 1803, the time of the Louisiana Purchase, in Boston, Washington, and the Ohio-Mississippi frontier and dealing with the development of trade with the Pacific Northwest. Inspired by the profitable voyage of the *Columbia*, the first American ship to sail around the world, and by his Granddad's* stories about explorer John Ledyard's* efforts to develop trade between the Northwest and the Far East, young Dan Boit takes a position with Israel Cotton, Boston dealer in firearms. When a shipment of muskets bearing the codfish brand is stolen, Dan suspects Tom Gentry*, personable, enigmatic, young Englishman. When war with Spain appears imminent, Mr. Cotton sends Dan to Washington to gather information about the political climate and to seek a source for the new Kentucky rifles, now much in demand on the frontier. While walking near the White House, Dan finds a diary lost by Thomas Jefferson* and, by returning it, strikes up an acquaintance with the president, which leads to his being made Jefferson's secretary, replacing Meriwether Lewis. Lewis and William Clark have just been commissioned to lead an expedition of exploration to the Northwest, newly claimed for the United States. After the transfer of Louisiana to the United States, Dan bears a message to Lewis instructing him to consult the Indians about locations for forts in the Louisiana territory. Amidst threats to secede from the frontiersmen, attempts by the British to stir up the Indians against the Americans, and uncertainty over the intentions of Spain and France, Dan travels by stage, horseback, wagon, and flatboat to the Missouri, encountering traders, trappers, shippers, and various other frontierspeople. Along the way he intercepts a shipment of rifles Tom Gentry is running to the British who hope to obstruct the Lewis and Clark expedition. When Dan finds a musket with a codfish brand in a cabin near the Mississippi, his suspicions about the extent of Gentry's illegal activities are confirmed. Dan delivers Jefferson's message to Lewis, finally confident that Ledyard's dream of a transcontinental American route will be realized and his spirit of adventure satisfied. The richly delineated period of this ambitious book compensates for the inept plot that is too convoluted and too dependent on coincidence. Main characters in the first half of the book are distinctively drawn, but there are too many in the last part to keep straight, and while Dan provides unity, he is not a strong character in his own right. Fanfare; Newbery Honor.

COLIN CRAVEN (*The Secret Garden**), invalid cousin of Mary* Lennox. Having been born when his mother fell as a result of a breaking tree branch, he has been considered by his father the cause of her subsequent death. An intelligent boy, he has understood very young that the doctor and servants expect him to die and that his father fears he will inherit his hunched back. Colin has deliberately stayed hidden in his room so that people will not stare at him and whisper. He has tyrannized the servants and nurses by going into hysterical tantrums when his will is crossed, and it is only when he clashes with Mary, herself a strong-willed, spoiled child, that he is able to break the habit. In the secret garden, he is fascinated by the idea of magic and gives little lectures to the others about his plans to investigate it by scientific method.

COLLIN, HEDVIG, born in Naksskov, Denmark; artist, and author and illustrator of children's books. She grew up in Denmark and studied at the Royal Academy of Art in Copenhagen and the École des Beaux-Arts in Paris. She traveled widely throughout the world and in the United States and taught for a time at a girls' school in Maine and in New Mexico. She was well known as an artist before she wrote children's books, and her pictures were exhibited in Paris and Copenhagen and in galleries in the American West. She began to write for children in answer to their requests for stories about the places she lived in and visited. *Wind Island** (Viking, 1945), a pleasing, cozy, somewhat suspenseful self-illustrated novel set among the fisherfolk of the island of Fanoe off Denmark, where she spent many summers, was a Fanfare book and praised at the time as a worthy dividend of World War II. Her other books of fiction, also self-illustrated, also grew out of her Scandinavian background, among them, *Cyclone Goes A-Viking* (Whitman, 1939), *The Good-Luck Tree* (Viking, 1954) and *Nils, the Island Boy* (Viking, 1951). She illustrated numerous books for other authors, some published in Germany and in France, including an edition of Hans Christian Andersen's stories and a collection of Norwegian folktales, *East of the Sun and West of the Moon* (Macmillan, 1928).

COLUM, PADRAIC (1881-1972), born in Longford, Ireland; poet, playwright, teacher, and author. When he was a young man, the Celtic Revival affected Irish life and thought. He was part of the group that founded the Dublin Abbey Theatre, for which he wrote three plays, and he also helped found the *Irish Review*. After he moved to the United States in 1914, he began writing for children, eventually publishing over two dozen books of fiction, plays, information, and retellings of myths, legends, and folktales for a young audience. He was most successful with his retellings of old stories, drawing from several cultures, in particular with those he had heard as a child in his native land, and his novels and stories are also full of the flavor of old Ireland. His talking animal novel, *Where the Winds Never Blew and the Cocks Never Crew** (Macmillan, 1940), a Fanfare selection, exudes typical Irish twinkle-eyed whimsey and air of mystery. This and his other stories of fiction seem dated and quaint today, though typically euphonious and imaginative, but, unlike them, his retellings have survived. They are still enjoyed, particularly *The Adventures of Odysseus and the Tale of Troy* (Macmillan, 1920), *The Children of Odin: A Book of Northern Myths* (Macmillan, 1920), *The Golden Fleece and the Heroes Who Lived before Achilles* (Macmillan, 1921), and *Orpheus: Myths of the World* (Macmillan, 1930). A distinguished man of letters, he taught comparative literature at Columbia University.

CONN KILROY (*The Great Wheel**), Cornelius Terence, Irish boy who works on the first Ferris Wheel, constructed as an attraction for the Chicago World's Columbian Exposition in 1893. In this way he fulfills his Aunt Honora's prophecy: "Keep your face to the sunset and follow the evening star and one day you'll ride the greatest wheel in all the world." Naive but intelligent, Conn learns quickly and, although his cousin Agnes sets her cap for him, continues to yearn for the German immigrant girl, Trudy, whom he has met on the boat but whose last name he has failed to learn and whose destination he knows only as Wisconsin.

CORBIN†, WILLIAM (WM. CORBIN MCGRAW), (1916-   ), born in Des Moines, Iowa; newspaperman turned free-lance writer of novels for young people, many of them horse and dog stories. He was graduated from Drake University, did graduate work at Harvard, and worked on the Athens (Ohio) *Messenger*, the Cleveland *Plain Dealer*, the Oklahoma City *Times*, and the San Diego *Union-Tribune*. Because he is married to Eloise Jarvis McGraw*†, with whom he has made his home in the Willamette Valley south of Portland, he uses his middle name to avoid confusion. His newspaper background is employed in *Deadline* (Coward, 1952) and to a lesser extent in *High Road Home** (Coward, 1954), which concerns a cross-country search for a columnist by a refugee and an aspiring reporter. *Smoke†* (Coward, 1967) is a good example of his dog stories.

CORMACK, MARIBELLE (1902-   ), born in Buffalo, N.Y.; scientist who has written non-fiction nature books and also novels for young people, which often reflect her Scottish ancestry. She received her B.A. degree from Cornell University in English, her M.A. from Brown University in botany, and did graduate work at the University of Vienna and the University of Geneva. She worked at the Buffalo Museum of Science and at Park Museum in Providence, R.I., and has traveled widely to participate in gatherings of people interested in astronomy. When she was twelve years old, she went to Scotland and visited her grandfather's old home in the Orkney Islands, a setting she used for *Wind of the Vikings** (Appleton, 1937), a teenage novel concerned with sailing and the finding of archeological relics by a pair of twentieth-century young people. *Last Clash of the Claymores** (Appleton, 1940), on which she collaborated with Wm. P. Alexander*, concerns the rising of the Scottish clans to support the Young Pretender, Bonnie Prince Charlie.

CORNELIUS GLEASON (*The Great Quest**), villainous con man who returns to Topham pretending to have made a fortune and who, with tales of a treasure they will share, talks Seth* Upham into selling his store and putting all his money into the brig *Adventure*. Gleason has left town under a cloud years earlier and, before the time set for sailing, reverts to his old riotous ways and kills a drinking companion, forcing all those involved in the expedition to flee in the middle of the night. In the course of the story, he is revealed as a slave trader and a thoroughly unscrupulous man, but he has the courage to try to get water when the natives hold the adventurers by siege in a jungle hut and, after they have given him up for dead, manages to crawl back to the hut. He is drowned off the South American coast.

THE CORN GROWS RIPE (Rhoads*, Dorothy, ill. Jean Charlot, Viking, 1956), short, realistic problem novel told from the point of view of a twelve-year-old Maya boy in the Yucatan of eastern Mexico about the time the book was written. Just as he is starting to burn the bush (forest) for the family's *milpa* (cornfield), the father of Tigre (real name Dionisio) breaks his leg. Although the boy is lazy and often shirks his responsibilities and likes to lie in his hammock until late in the morning, Tigre makes up his mind that he must do his father's work so that his mother, father, great-grandmother, little sister, and new baby brother will not starve. He turns over a new leaf, and, all by himself, he cuts, burns the felled trees after they have dried, and then plants the family's *milpa*, even clearing a little more bush and sowing squash and beans for good measure. When the village holds a Chac Chac, the ceremony for bringing rain, in hopes of ending a prolonged drought, Tigre helps by playing the part of one of the frogs. The rains come, and the family plot bears abundantly. Simple descriptions of such Maya practices as the making of the *milpa*, the fiesta, the hip ceremony for the new baby, and the ceremony to gain the good will of Chac, the rain god, uplift the slight and predictable plot. Although the basic premise seems implausible, and characters are types, the book does show how important corn is to the modern Maya, who still live much as did their ancient ancestors and whose religion combines pagan and Christian beliefs and practices. Jean Charlot's many strongly composed, stylized drawings with their green and brown tones recall ancient Maya art and contribute to the sense of setting. Fanfare; Newbery Honor.

CORYELL, HUBERT VANSANT (1889-   ), born in Cornwall, N.Y.; educator, novelist. He received his A.B. degree from Harvard University and wrote educational articles and books as well as fiction. *Indian Brother** (Harcourt, 1935) and its sequel, *The Scalp Hunters** (Harcourt, 1936), are both historical novels set in pre–Revolutionary New England and are supplied with notes to identify characters and incidents based on fact. He also wrote *Lives of Danger and Daring* (Wilde, 1936) with his son, Vansant Coryell.

THE COTTAGE AT BANTRY BAY (Van Stockum*†, Hilda, ill. author, Viking, 1938), realistic novel of family life set in Ireland in 1930. The O'Sullivans are a peasant family who live in a tiny peatburning cottage on Bantry Bay. They include hardworking, understanding Father and Mother, bright Michael*, 11, earnest Brigid*, 9, and the twins, gentlehearted Liam and feisty Francie*, about five. The family is very close and loving, and their chief problem, other than the continuing one of making a living, concerns Francie's crippled foot, a congenital deformity that his mother has been assured can be repaired if the family can accumulate enough money to pay for the operation. On the way to Kenmare to sell their donkey, Michael and Brigid rescue a nondescript mongrel pup from a gypsy who is beating him and who ironically becomes instrumental in elevating the family fortunes. Bran, the pup, soon becomes a family favorite, even though his antics cause many a concern. Among other misdemeanors, he disrupts school, smashing the teacher's flowerpot. While in the hills picking blackberries to pay for the damage, the children discover a once-inhabited cave, in which Bran digs up a flat, old box containing layers of vellum inscribed with ancient Irish writing. The children share their discovery with Paddy* the Piper, itinerant musician and storyteller, who offers to take the sheets to Dublin. A picnic and fair intervene before Paddy leaves again for the road. That winter he returns to Bantry Bay with the joyful news that the National Library is offering the children fifty pounds for the vellums, which contain valuable Gaelic poems. The news elates the family, for now there is enough money to repair Francie's foot and to buy a cow besides. The characters are the best part of this artless formula story of a worthy family come into a needed small fortune. Narrative tension is minimal, and there is not much in the way of climax. The author's warm and affectionate tone earns her forgiveness for her occasional lapses into sentimentality. There are many scenes and much dialogue and activity. Descriptions of everyday life and the cadence of Irish speech evoke setting, and old stories about the Irish struggle for independence and from Irish folklore add to the entertainment value as well as contribute to atmosphere. Books Too Good; Fanfare.

COTTON IN MY SACK (Lenski*, Lois, ill. author, Lippincott, 1949), regional novel set in the cotton-growing country of Arkansas in the 1940s. On their sharecrop farm, Joanda Hutley, 10, and the rest of the family, Mavis, 14, Steve, 12, Ricky, 5, red-haired Lolly, 2, and their parents, Neva and Dave, all work in the cotton, chopping weeds and picking, according to the seasons, and spending all the money they have every Saturday in town. When Ricky is run over by the boss's tractor, Big Charley Shands seems to want to help, but his wife drags him away, and a neighbor, J. T. Burgess, takes the boy to the doctor and loans Dave the money. By Christmas there are no groceries left in the house. Mrs. Shands brings a goose and lots of unwanted advice, Neva's Uncle Shine Morse turns up for dinner, and J. T. brings money contributed by all the neighbors to pay Ricky's hospital bills. When Joanda returns Mrs. Shand's basket, she learns that the Shands are also in debt and that they want the Hutleys to stay and will help them. At school, the Hutleys resist the hot lunch program, because they do not want charity, until cockroaches are found in the bag lunches. Only Joanda knows that the teacher, Miss Fenton, has deliberately put the insects there as an excuse to give the children better nutrition. Joanda loves school until she drops the library book she has borrowed in the mud and is ashamed to return it. Uncle Shine buys a little bungalow and shows Dave how to put his odd-job money into a bank account. Uncle Shine gives them a front door with a glass window, and they begin to clean up the trashy yard to match it. Their hope of better fortune seems ruined when Neva has a heart attack and can no longer work in the cotton. The children all pick cotton, and one night a load of cotton is stolen. Dave blames Neva, who had put a lamp in the window to scare away the thieves. Joanda discovers the missing pick sacks and scales with Uncle Shine's coat, and she covers up the evidence, believing that he is the thief. Later they learn that he has hijacked the load, held it until prices are higher, and bought a pair of mules so that Dave can start work as a tenant, not a share-cropper. They have further troubles: as they move to a tenant house their furniture catches fire, and Lolly, neglected briefly by Joanda, falls through a rotten bridge but is rescued by some fishing Negroes. In the end, the family goes to town for another Saturday evening, but by now they have learned to buy more long-term purchases, and they start for home before they have spent or drunk up all their earnings. The story is written to present facts about cotton growing and the life of the share-cropping poor whites. The didactic message is obvious and the characters predictable. Even though some of the hardships facing the family are detailed, the assumption that upward mobility is possible by hard work and will power is simplistic. Books Too Good; Choice.

THE COURAGE OF SARAH NOBLE (Dalgliesh*, Alice, ill. Leonard Weisgard, Scribner's, 1954), historical story for young readers set in 1707 in what became New Milford, Conn. Based on a real incident, it tells how Sarah Noble, 8, travels with her father, John, from Westfield, Mass., to Connecticut to cook for him because her mother has a baby too young to travel and her older sisters will not undertake the trip. After building a house, John goes back to Massachusetts to get his wife and other children, leaving Sarah with the family of Tall John, a friendly Indian who has helped raise the logs. Throughout the experience, Sarah remembers her mother's exhortation, "Keep up your courage, Sarah Noble!" and quiets her fears by wrapping her warm red cloak about herself. Written in a very simple style, the book idealizes the early settlers and the Indians and lacks any realistic details of the hardships and rough life they led. John's decision to leave Sarah among strangers seems improbable in a loving father pictured as sensitive and concerned. Books Too Good; Choice; Fanfare; Lewis Carroll; Newbery Honor.

COUSIN ANNABELLE (*Caddie Woodlawn**), style- and status-conscious cousin from Boston, of about Caddie's age, who visits the Woodlawns on their farm in Wisconsin. Caddie, Tom, and Warren conspire to "take her down a peg." They encourage her to ride unreliable old Pete, who swings in under a low shed and scrapes her off his back into the dust, and to salt the sheep, which nibble the buttons from her dress. Later, while the children are somersaulting in the hay mow, Caddie slips an egg down the back of Annabelle's dress. These escapades prompt Mr.* Woodlawn to discuss with Caddie the propriety of her behavior.

COUSIN CEPHAS (*The Covered Bridge**), kindly relative of Sarah Macomber, who lives down the mountain from Sarah and who generally keeps an eye on her to give advice and help when needed. He gives Connie the sheepdog puppy, Jock, so that she will not be lonely while with Sarah. The dog proves invaluable in herding cattle and sheep during the year. Cousin Cephas tells the children about the contributions of Ethan Allen* to Vermont and about his continuing concern for the well-being particularly of the farmer, whose lot is very hard, and sees to it that Peter is not cheated by grasping Sam Breen.

THE COVERED BRIDGE (Meigs*, Cornelia, ill. Marguerite de Angeli*, Macmillan, 1936), period novel set in 1788 in the Green Mountains of Vermont from fall to early spring, which excels in showing how hard it was for the farm people to get along in that demanding region. While her sea-captain father and mother sail to the West Indies, Constance Anderson, 9, goes to live with elderly, warmhearted Sarah Macomber, a friend of the family, and her orphaned grandson, Peter*, 12, who run a small farm near Hebron. As the days pass, Connie learns to assume her share of the tasks around the farm and the pleasure that comes from hard work and helping others. Cousin* Cephas, a nearby farmer, gives her a sheepdog puppy, Jock, for her very own. Industrious Peter treats her as an equal, and she enjoys the Guyer youngsters, the six orphaned foster children all of an age she calls the "brownies." When churlish Sam Breen presses Sarah for the money she owes him for winter food supplies, Peter sells one of his calves with the help of Ethan Allen*, and Cousin Cephas instructs him to give Breen the proceeds and to ask for a spring lamb to boot. After maple sugar time, the spring rains set in and Sarah, the children, and the Guyers work frantically to help Sam Breen save his flock of Cheviots during a landslide. Peter claims a small orphan lamb they have found and Sarah has nursed. Later Sarah and the children save the covered bridge over Hebron Brook from being swept away by the spring floods. While the family's struggles to get through the winter on their limited resources unify the novel structurally, other highlights of the year include Ethan Allen's visit to the small country school, his overnight visit to the farm, during which Jock chews a hole in Allen's featherbed, and a birthday party for the Guyer children. In the spring, Connie's father comes for her, and she bids farewell to her mountain friends. Dated in tone, this occasionally moralistic and sometimes sentimental book exalts such old-fashioned virtues as hard work, patience, and neighborliness and presents living close to the land as hard but good. The loose, unfocused plot ambles along with fine views of farm life during the changing seasons. The barn raising for the poverty-stricken MacGowans and the rescue of Breen's sheep are especially well-drawn scenes, and Ethan Allen, an actual historical figure, is incorporated skillfully into the plot. This is a serious, mildly suspenseful, but never grim or solemn story, and one never doubts that things will turn out all right for Sarah. Fanfare.

COWARDLY LION (*The Wonderful Wizard of Oz**), the lion who joins Dorothy*, Toto*, the Scarecrow*, and the Tin* Woodman on their journey to the Emerald City of Oz*. There he plans to ask the Wizard* for courage, but when the Wizard appears to him as a ball of fire, he is told that they must first kill the Wicked Witch of the West. As they approach her land, the lion scares away her slave Winkies, but with Dorothy and Toto is captured and carried to her castle by the flying monkeys. After they have destroyed the witch and exposed the Wizard as a humbug, he gives the Lion a drink which he says is Courage, although the Lion has been exhibiting bravery throughout the adventures. In the end Glinda, the Good Witch of the South, has the Lion transported to the forest where the animals make him their king.

CRANBURY, CONN. (*The Moffats**; *The Middle Moffat**; *Rufus M.**; *Ginger Pye**), the small town in New England just before and during World War I in which the warm, close-knit Moffat family lives and in which their episodic family stories take place. The family lives there first in the yellow house on New Dollar Street, in *The Moffats**, and later in the house on Ashbellows Place with the barn in the back. It is also the town where the Pye family lives, but it is most famous in children's literature for its connection with the Moffats.

CRAWFORD, PHYLLIS (1899-   ), born in Little Rock, Ark.; editor and author of books for adults and young people in their early teens. After graduating from Randolph-Macon Woman's College, she took a degree in library science at the University of Illinois. She was an editorial assistant for the H. W. Wilson Co. and associate editor for Holt and for William Sloane Associates before serving as head of the children's division of the New Mexico State Library at Santa Fe. She wrote humorous books for adults under the pseudonym, Josie Turner, and contributed to the *New Yorker*. Known mainly for her several books of fiction for young readers, she received a Ford Foundation Prize of three thousand dollars for *''Hello, the Boat!''** (Holt, 1938), also a Newbery honor book, about a flatboat trip down the Ohio from Pittsburgh to Cincinnati in 1817. She also wrote *Walking on Gold* (Messner, 1940), about a covered wagon journey west, *Secret Brother* (Holt, 1941), a story of everyday life, *Let's Go!* (Holt, 1949), a fantasy for younger readers, and *Last Semester* (Holt, 1942), a school story for older girls.

CRESSY PIDGEN (*Penelope Ellen and Her Friends: Three Little Girls of 1840**), Lucretia, friend of Penelope Ellen, probably about eleven, a very responsible child who helps her widowed mother, a dressmaker, and acts as a foil for the more lively Penny.

CRIMSON SHAWL (*The Crimson Shawl**), the garment, from which the title derives. It belongs to Mary's mother, who gives it to Mary when she leaves for the Cogswell house. Woven from the wool of the family's prize sheep and dyed with beets from their garden, it has been their proudest possession. Her mother reminds Mary that the red stands for loyalty and courage, qualities which Mary reveals during the long ordeal.

THE CRIMSON SHAWL (Choate*, Florence, and Elizabeth Curtis*, ill. authors, Stokes, 1941), historical novel set in Ipswich, Mass., following the events of the French and Indian War as ''they affected that proud New England town'' and some Acadian refugees relocated there. Cold, frightened, and hungry, the Landreys and the Breaus (actual historical figures) arrive in midwinter in the New England shipbuilding town to the jeers and scorn of the townspeople. The older children of the despised ''Frenchies'' are placed with local families, among them, spunky, quick-tempered Mary Landrey, 13. She is bound out to William Cogswell, a wealthy farmer and horse breeder, to be the companion of his spoiled and willfull only daughter, Susan. Although Mary is grateful for a home where people are good to her, and indeed Mr. Cogswell and his sister, Miss Sarah, treat her like a child of the family, she resents the removal, having to leave behind a fine house, and being brought to a place where even the Neutral French are hated. Gradually, however, she gets involved in the life of the Cogswells and receives reports of the progress of the war with mixed emotions. She helps Susan stitch a quilt as a wedding present for John and his bride, is upset when the wedding is called off because John has decided to join up, is distressed when he is reported missing in action, and is saddened by the departure for the war of Chris, a Harvard student, for both John and Chris have been very kind to her. Her relations with the stand-offish Susan take a turn for the better, when both are marooned on an offshore island by the tide while cutting salt hay, and the two subsequently become good friends. Some suspense and mystery are introduced into the plot when a French soldier is washed up on the shore. Mary's suspicions that he is a spy are confimed later when she is captured by French privateers while she is searching the sea marshes for her lost Uncle Charlot, who is mentally handicapped. She escapes and warns the town that its newest ship is in danger, earning the gratitude of the community. After the fall of Quebec and the French surrender, the Breaus and Mary's Uncle Francois, a respected, young priest, elect to return to France, but the other Landreys decide to remain in Ipswich. Her bondedness over, Mary chooses to continue living with the Cogswells. The French have earned the respect and acceptance of the community. Throughout the novel, reports of military encounters reach the Cogswells by word of mouth, and the names of such real historical figures as Montcalm, Pitt, Howe, and Wolfe occur often in conversation, while among the events discussed are the encounters at Ticonderoga, Louisburg, and Frontenac. Some scenes have power (the arrival, the school, the quilting, the haying), but on the whole the story is more an outline of historical and personal events than a proper novel and never lives up to the potential for emotional involvement promised by the opening chapters. The numerous, insufficiently developed characters are hard to keep straight, the authors appear obliged to introduce the unlikely and unnecessary element of Mary's capture, and, curiously, the matter of religious differences is never dealt with. (Crimson* Shawl) Fanfare.

CROSS FACE (*Wolf Brother**), he leads a small band of Apaches who refuse to be herded onto reservations. His name comes from the peculiar facial scar that resulted from a wound a cavalryman gave him. For many months, he and his band elude the army's efforts to catch them and continue to live by hunting and raiding as the Apaches have traditionally done. To cover up for their failure to catch him, the army officers deliberately release false information about the number of men he leads, reporting that his band is many times the size it really is. Cross Face comes to see the futility of his cause but resists until forced by circumstances to surrender. While on the way to prison in Florida, he puts on shows of defiance and savagery to please newspapermen and photographers, purposefully playing the clown. At an opportune time, he uses a toy knife to help Jonathan escape. He is the most interesting character in the book.

CROWDER, JULIA MAUDE (*Shadow across the Campus**), elderly Zeta Nu member whose influence with the local and national Zeta Nus results in the sorority deciding to admit Jewish girls to membership. It is quite by luck that Marjorie finds out about her and about her interest in social causes. Miss Crowder foretells great changes in the Greek system on campuses and suggests that such societies may have outlived their usefulness.

CRYSTAL MOUNTAIN (Rugh*, Belle Dorman, ill. Ernest H. Shepard, Houghton, 1955), realistic novel set in the mountains above Beirut, Lebanon, in the mid-twentieth century. Escaping from the prospect of an afternoon playing with a little English girl named Dorothy Wilcox, 10, Gerald and Harry Sawyer, American boys (apparently about ten and twelve), climb to their favorite spot on the mountain above their home and run into a lively red-haired girl who tells them she is Boadicea, or Boadie, and with whom they find common imaginative interests. By the time they realize that Boadie is really the Dorothy they were avoiding, they are committed to meet her the next day, and with her, start cleaning out a small deserted house which has lost its roof. Boadie is accompanied by her governess, Miss Dunbar, a prim-looking woman who calmly climbs trees and lets her charge run quite free while she sketches or lies on her back meditating. The boys have with them their brother, Danny, 5, who charms both Boadie and Miss Dunbar and who discovers a cave, well hidden by the house which backs onto the hill and has a large rear window which looks out on the apparently blank hillside. Exploring the cave, they find a large jar buried in the floor which contains an old coat, a pair of shoes, a bottle of olive oil, and what seems to be the remains of Arab bread. In the meantime they have met two other boys: Braheem, an Arab goatherd who has a pet bird, a bulbul, which rides on his hat and listens while he plays his pipes, and Edmund Bixton, a disagreeable American boy who enrages them by mistreating his puppy. Boadie enlists Danny in a scheme to lure the puppy to run away, then to save it. When Edmund and his mother arrive and accuse Danny of having the puppy, he imitates Edmund's technique of howling and sobbing to get his way, and Mrs. Bixton hastily gives him the dog. The next day Danny's parents, who were not home for the big scene, make the boys apologize and offer to give the puppy back. Edmund, however, begins his reform by. insisting that the dog stay with Danny, who renames him Argos. They let Edmund in on the work of the house they are fixing up, and he begins to shape up further. One day they find Danny talking to a Mr. Haddad, whom they have met with their father, and they find that he was Butrus, the young freedom worker who built the house some twenty years previously, as a place to live after he "disappeared," so he could continue to oppose the Turkish rulers. His old mother seemed to be living there alone, and he simply escaped to the cave whenever anyone approached. They celebrate with a picnic at the house which includes all the major characters, plus the Sheik and the parents. Though set in an exotic place, the story could well be transferred to almost any country or location. The boys speak Arabic and like the food of the country, but otherwise seem to be typical colonial types, acting like children a generation or so earlier than the setting of the story. The action moves well but is never particularly compelling, seeming more like a Ransome holiday adventure than a modern American novel. Books Too Good; Fanfare.

CUFFY (*The Saturdays**), the Melendy "housekeeper, nurse, cook, and substitute mother, grandmother, and aunt" since the death of the children's mother. Her full name is Mrs. Evangeline Cuthbert-Stanley, but at eighteen months Mona* dubbed her Cuffy, and the name stuck. She is warm and loving with the children, and though she tries to be strict, is really quite indulgent. The ideal housekeeper, she is "fat in a comfortable way," and the children love her very much. She accompanies the children on their visit to Mrs.* Oliphant's lighthouse by the sea and moves with the family to the country.

CURLEY GREEN (*The Gammage Cup**; *The Whisper of Glocken*†), Minnipin painter, who flouts tradition by wearing a scarlet cloak instead of the customary green one and by painting scenes instead of diagrams. Considered one of "Them," and therefore not quite respectable, she is one of the "outlaws" who discover that the Mushrooms have invaded the Minnipin valley. In the second book, she is one of the Old* Heroes who helps to rescue the New Heroes.

CURTIS, ELIZABETH, born in New York City; illustrator-author whose books were in collaboration with Florence Choate*. For over a quarter of a century they worked together, doing, among others, books in the Stokes's Wonder Book Series, career novels, and romantic historical novels. The two women met as students at the Art Students League in New York City, subsequently studying art together in Paris and then opening their own studio in New York City. They first illustrated for various publishers and then worked together on writing and illustrating their own books. *The Crimson Shawl** (Stokes, 1941), a substantial historical novel about Acadian refugees in a New England town during the French and Indian War, was a Fanfare selection.

D

DAB-DAB (*The Story of Doctor Dolittle**; *The Voyages of Doctor Dolittle**), motherly duck who acts as housekeeper for Doctor* Dolittle. On his first voyage to Africa she accompanies him, but when he leaves for Spidermonkey Island, she stays home to care for his house.

DALGLIESH, ALICE (1893–1979), born in Trinidad, West Indies; teacher, editor, author of a large number of books, both fiction and non-fiction, for children. She came to the United States in 1902, studied kindergarten teaching at Pratt Institute, N.Y., and received her M.A. in English and education from Teachers College, Columbia University. For seventeen years she taught kindergarten and elementary school, and from 1934 to 1960 was editor of books for young readers at Charles Scribner's Sons publishers. She also reviewed children's books for *Saturday Review* and *Parents' Magazine* and taught children's literature at Teachers College. Among her many critically acclaimed works of fiction are such simple stories as *The Bears on Hemlock Mountain** (Scribner's, 1952), *The Courage of Sarah Noble** (Scribner's, 1954), both Newbery honor books, and *The Little Angel** (Scribner's, 1943). *A Book for Jennifer** (Scribner's, 1940) is based on what is known of John Newbery's shop, The Bible and the Sun, in eighteenth-century London. *The Silver Pencil** (Scribner's 1944), also a Newbery honor book, and *Along Janet's Road* (Scribner's 1946) are autobiographical novels for older children. Although in much of her fiction the educator seems to predominate, her best books show that she understood children's love of story and was herself a skillful storyteller.

DALLAS TYLER (*Teeny Gay**), boy whose father has just died and whom Teeny's* parents take in and plan to adopt. He and Teeny try to make money, but they do not make enough to attend the circus. They meet Larry* Bill in back of the big tent. He puts on a clown show just for them. When Dallas hears the organ at church, he decides to accept the townsman's offer to pay for sending him to school. He is an interesting but not very convincing character.

DALY, MAUREEN (1921–), born in Castle Caulfield, County Tyrone, Ireland; reporter, editor, and free-lance writer of fiction and non-fiction for adults and children. She grew up in Fond du Lac, Wis., on the shores of Lake Winnebago, the locale for her first and best-known novel, *Seventeenth Summer** (Dodd, 1942), and her many other stories. This innovative, moving, curiously unaware account of first love became an instant hit. It has remained popular, and, a Lewis Carroll Shelf Book, it is now considered a classic of its kind. Written when she was twenty and a college sophomore, it won the first Dodd, Mead Intercollegiate Literary Fellowship. Her other books of juvenile fiction are for younger readers, including *Patrick Visits the Farm* (Dodd, 1959), *Patrick Visits the Library* (Dodd, 1961), and *The Small War of Sergeant Donkey* (Dodd, 1966). She has also written travel books, a high school career series, and edited collections of mystery and suspense stories for young readers. A woman of a varied and active career, she has been editor of the sub-deb department of *Ladies Home Journal* and consultant to editors for *Saturday Evening Post*, and before that was police reporter for the Chicago *Tribune*. She graduated from Rosary College in River Forest, Ill., and married writer William McGivern. With him she wrote *Twelve around the World* (Dodd, 1957), about teenagers in several foreign countries which the McGiverns visited in order to complete the book.

DANNY DUNN AND THE HOMEWORK MACHINE (Williams*†, Jay, and Raymond Abrashkin*, ill. Ezra Jack Keats, McGraw, 1958), one of a long series of humorous novels for middle readers set in a university town in the United States in the mid-twentieth century. Danny Dunn, who lives at the home of Professor Euclid Bullfinch, for whom his mother is housekeeper, and his best friend, Joe Pearson, have constructed a machine that will write two assignments at once, thereby cutting down on the time they must spend on their upper-elementary-school homework. Danny plans to do the arithmetic and Joe the English, and they are soon joined by Irene Miller, the new girl next door, who knows as much science as Danny, or more. When Professor Bullfinch goes to a conference, he leaves the care of Miniac, his miniature automatic computer, to Danny. The possibilities for further reducing homework time occur to Danny, and soon the three are programing Miniac to take care of all their assignments. The problem comes when Eddie Philips, who is attracted to Irene and jealous of her friendship with Danny, follows them home, peeks in the window, and realizes what they are doing. He tells their teacher, Miss Arnold, who calls to forbid the use of the computer but is convinced by Danny's defense of its use and also by a quiet suggestion from Danny's mother, and lets them continue. She changes the assignments for the three of them, however, insisting that they start on high school math, which requires intense study before they can program Miniac. To get even with Eddie, Irene pretends to like him, leads him on to confess that he tattled, and then pushes him into a mud puddle. When Miniac types out Irene's report in gibberish, they know something is wrong, and when the professor returns early with two scientists who want to inspect Miniac for the government, the youngsters have no time to fix the computer. Dan discovers a knife covered with mud on the floor, realizes that Eddie has sabotaged the machine, and readjusts the temperature control that has caused the computer to malfunction. The government man is impressed, and the professor gives the young people permission to continue using Miniac for their homework. At the end of the school year, the three get special honors for doing more homework than any others since they have had to study so hard to program Miniac correctly. Told mostly in dialogue, the story is obvious, with no subtle shadings or character development. The miniature computer is about the size of a large sideboard, a development that seemed futuristic in the 1950s but would not impress readers today used to home computers nearer the size of a typewriter. The humor coming from Joe's scorn of girls, until he, like Danny, is impressed by Irene's knowledge, also seems outdated. Choice.

DANNY O'REILLY (*Hill of Little Miracles**), chum of Tony* and Ricco* Santo. Although the son of a rigorously honest policeman, Danny has a tendency to cut corners on what he knows is right. At Uncle Luigi's wedding, he and Tony get into a fight over whether Italian-Americans or Irish-Americans can dance better.

DARD RAE (*Homespun**), Scots-Indian trapper whose father is factor with the Hudson's Bay Company at Fort Vancouver in Oregon Territory. Sent to Scotland for schooling, he runs away and works passage home, where he casts in his lot with the Indians, with whom he feels more at home than with the white community. He becomes Luke* Greenman's trading partner and is respected and liked by Indians and whites of the woods. He sets out to avenge Luke's death at the hands of the renegade Catamount*.

DAREDEVIL JIM KELSO (*The Boy Who Had No Birthday**), shrewd, successful young horse trader who plays practical jokes. A rough-cut gem, he is a good-looking man who likes nice clothes. He is too proud and shy to declare his love for dainty, elegant, pretty Rose Carlisle, and uses Davy (David* Cring) as a go-between. When Rose spends New Year's in Chicago with her cousin, Daredevil attends the party, dressed in the highest fashion and pretending to be a gentleman from Chicago. Daredevil enjoys trying to get past Pa Wiggins's tollgate and once lifts the gate high with the old man sitting on it. He takes Davy for rides, teases him sometimes, and even paddles him if he thinks Davy needs it.

THE DARK FRIGATE (Hawes*, Charles Boardman, Atlantic, 1923), sea adventure novel which starts and ends in seventeenth-century England, with a voyage to the Caribbean between. Philip* Marsham, 19, a boy of good birth but rough upbringing, falls in with two suspicious seafaring characters, Martin Barwick and Tom Jordan, known as The Old One, and after Jordan leaves them, makes his way with Martin to Bideford, where they ship aboard *The Rose of Devon** under Captain Candle. Some weeks out, they find a storm-damaged ship and rescue part of its crew, which is led by Jordan. Shortly, the rescued seamen seize the ship, murder Candle, and set off pirating. Philip reluctantly becomes part of the group as does Will Canty, a well-born fellow who has become his friend, but when, after several unsuccessful ventures, the pirates discover that their designs to raid a Caribbean town have been given away by Canty, Jordan has him killed, and Phil escapes. He wanders across the mosquito-infested island, sights a vessel in a secluded harbor, swims to it, and is taken prisoner in what proves to be a disguised man-of-war. When the men from *The Rose of Devon* attack, they are defeated, taken back to England to stand trial, and are all condemned to be hanged, except Philip, who is released mainly because of Jordan's testimony that he was forced to serve. The story makes no romantic heroes of the pirates, but details their violent life with grim realism in a series of exciting and believable adventures. Lewis Carroll; Newbery Winner.

THE DARK STAR OF ITZA: THE STORY OF A PAGAN PRINCESS (Malkus*, Alida Sims, ill. Lowell House, Harcourt, 1930), historical novel set in 1250 A.D. in the Maya city of Chichen Itza in the Yucatan peninsula, which mixes real and fictitious characters and happenings to improvise upon the Toltec conquest of the city as related in the *Books of Chilam Balam*, the history of the Maya. Nicte is the beautiful and dutiful daughter of the high priest of the Itza people, Hol Chan, a lonely old man, whose two loves are his daughter and Maya learning. Herself a respected priestess, Nicte hopes eventually to marry Itzam Pesh, the earnest young priest, who is her father's brightest student, is skilled in building, and is adept at administration. At the May festival, Nicte predicts doom for the Itza if their king, Chac Zib Chac, accepts the invitation of King Hunac Ceel of Mayapan to visit his city and celebrate with him the festival of the god Kukulkan. Restless, ambitious, self-willed, Chac Zib Chac disregards her advice, and while there, he sees Kantol, the proud and beautiful princess, who is betrothed to the Mayapan king, falls in love with her, abducts her after dinner on the evening of the festival, and carries her back to Chichen Itza, intending to make her his bride. Hunac Ceel attacks Chichen Itza, burning the corn fields and laying siege to the city until it falls. His ally is Pantemit, a Toltec prince, who has visited Chichen and fallen in love with Nicte. Pantemit asks for and receives the city of Chichen as his reward for tipping the scales in Hunac Ceel's favor. During the sack of the city, Itzam Pesh fights valiantly and also hides Nicte, Hol Chan, and Kantol in an underground room in the temple that Chac Zib Chac was building for Kantol. Itzam barters Kantol for the release of Chac Zib Chac but cannot save Nicte and her father. He himself is taken captive to Mayapan. A proud and enterprising man, Pantemit sets about rebuilding the city, and he introduces some Toltec ways, among them, the bloody human sacrifice involving cutting out the heart and dismemberment, a practice abhorrent to Nicte. A year passes, during which Pantemit wisely bides his time, but Nicte continues to hope that Itzam Pesh will be set free. When a severe drought results in famine, Nicte is cast into the Sacred Well (the *cenote*) to appease the rain god but is rescued by Itzam who has escaped from Mayapan and who grabs her body as she falls into its dark waters. The two leave Chichen for some city beyond Pantemit's control. The plot is interesting and fairly well sustained, though some incidents, such as the rescue of Nicte, seem absurdly made to order. Characters are one-dimensional. Setting is the strongest element, with vivid scenes of festivals, religious ceremonies, dances, the construction of buildings, banquets, the women's quarters, and warfare that give a good sense of the life and thinking of the nobles at the height of the empire. Newbery Honor.

DAUDI (*Lion Boy**), earnest, loyal Wanyamlima warrior, who, to earn money to pay off his grandmother's brideprice, hires himself out to white hunters. After serving them for several years, he returns to the village, pays off the family debt, and marries the woman who has faithfully waited for him. About a year later he is killed while attempting to protect the village against raiding elephants. His story is particularly poignant and suspenseful and shows much about the relationships between blacks and whites in Africa at the time.

DAUGHTER OF THE MOUNTAINS (Rankin*, Louise, ill. Kurt Wiese, Viking, 1948), realistic novel of Momo, a ten-year-old Tibetan girl from the village of Longram near the top of Jelep La pass, who travels alone all the way to Calcutta to retrieve her stolen Lhasa terrier, Pempa, presumably in the mid-twentieth century. Having desired above all else one of the red-gold terriers when she saw one at the Kargayu monastery years before, she is delighted when a passing trader gives her a puppy whose mother has died, and even her father, Nema, a mail carrier over the steep mountain pass, is impressed when the astrologer predicts that the dog will bring the girl adventure and the family good fortune. A trader traveling with a passing mule caravan which stops at Momo's mother's tea shop steals the dog, and Momo sets out without hesitation to follow, sure she will get Pempa back. Undeterred by the steep mountains, she follows the Great Trade Route, getting aid from some friendly tea shop women and almost being made a slave by an unfriendly one, being accused of thieving in the market at Rongli, and making her way to the railway station at Kalimpong. When she realizes that she cannot board the train with no money, her wails and sobs attract the attention of an Englishman, whom she afterwards learns is ''Lat Sahib,'' Christopher Bates, who speaks her language and not only buys her a ticket but gives her money to get along in Calcutta and return, and tells the sullen trader, Big Dorje, to look after her. Although he grudgingly attempts to do so, she is robbed and separated from him in the city yet finds her way to the shop of Wing Fong, the Chinese merchant who trades with Tibetans and who is persuaded to tell her that the dog has been purchased by Sir Hugh and Lady Paton. When, through a series of chances, she actually gets to the Paton home and calls Pempa and the dog shows his joy at seeing her, the English not only give her the dog but also send her back with aid for Tsu Foo, an abused girl who has aided her on the trip, and a new, safer job for her father as caretaker of one of the new dak bungalows being built along the Great Trade Route. The book gives a great deal of description of the countryside and the people Momo encounters on her journey, and the incidents are lively enough to hold the interest, despite minimal characterization and a highly unlikely conclusion. Choice; Fanfare; Lewis Carroll; Newbery Honor.

DAVE ALLEN (*Bright Island**), steady, hardworking youth whose ambition is to follow the sea by working with the government shore patrol. During the year he lives with the Curtises, he and Thankful develop a brother-sister relationship, but later he asks her to marry him. Thankful comes to appreciate his reliability, generosity, and patience and looks forward to their life together.

DAVE TOLLIVER (*Far from Marlborough Street**), youth who is pretending to be the notorious horse thief, Tom Bell. When he is being chased, he tears the brim off his hat, dons a peddler's pack, and almost gets away with the change, but Nancy's sharp eyes detect that he is the outlaw she saw in the inn the night before. Given into the custody of the old gentleman, Dave makes a sudden and unlikely moral reformation and becomes an honest peddler, selling the toys he cleverly makes. At a crucial point in the story, he rides cross-country with Nancy behind him on the horse to find the will hidden in the blue teapot before a wicked cousin can find and destroy it.

DAVID CRING (*The Boy Who Had No Birthday**), impetuous and lively, he is a many-faceted character. He blurts out to Daredevil* Jim his secret ambition to marry Jenny Carlisle and suffers torments about it until Dr.* Carlisle puts his mind at ease. He is competitive and overly concerned about appearance. He wants people to think well of him and looks down somewhat on Angie* Wiggins and her father, because he is sure that his own parents came from a higher station in life. Yet he is almost always very kind and loving toward them, appreciates their generosity and love, and dreams of repaying them. He fantasizes, procrastinates, is lazy and industrious by turns, is usually polite, and sometimes saucy—a real boy, likeable and convincing as a character. The only really sour note in his characterization is the readiness with which he accepts the Carlisle's offer of adoption. His action here seems uncharacteristic, or if in character, then very callous and self-seeking.

DAVID MALCOLM (*Meggy MacIntosh**), steady, somewhat shy and awkward son of North Carolina Scots planters who tells Meggy where Flora MacDonald*, the Highland heroine whom she seeks, is living. A thoughtful youth, David helps Meggy to understand the puzzling, contradictory political alignments among the Highlanders at the beginning of the American Revolution. He leaves for the war as Meggy comes to help his mother run the Malcolm plantation, and at the end of the novel the expectation is that some day the two will marry.

DAVID TOPMAN (*The Wonderful Flight to the Mushroom Planet**; *Stowaway to the Mushroom Planet**; *Time and Mr. Bass*†), youth of about ten, who lives with his parents in Pacific Grove, California. He and his best friend, Chuck* Masterson, build a space ship with which Mr. Tyco* Bass helps them fly to Basidium-X*, the Mushroom Planet, and to Lepton. His father calls his attention to the ad in the paper for a space ship that starts the adventures out. He is freckled, tall, and quick, likes to plan things and worries a lot. He is a courageous, persevering boy who has doubts about the morality of taking scientists to Basidium. Although likeable, he is a flat character almost indistinguishable from Chuck. Sometimes he and Chuck influence the action. Most of the time Mr. Tyco Bass is the real hero, although David and Chuck are characters with whom young readers can more readily identify.

DAVID WILLIAMS (*South Town**; *Whose Town?*†), protagonist of four novels that trace the development of a black boy in the segregated South through his experiences in high school and work in a northern city to his return as a doctor to the southern town where he started. Through his story the problems of the blacks and the changes wrought by the early civil rights movement are illustrated. David is honest, hardworking, and dedicated, but he gets into trouble with the law through no fault of his own.

DAVIE (*Shadrach**), six-year-old Dutch boy who owns and loves his first pet, a little black rabbit. Intense and imaginative, Davie agonizes over the incredibly long week he must wait for Shadrach, over his plan to fill three large bags of clover and the amusement it causes the adults, and over his pet's continued skinniness. When he grabs a barn rat, thinking it is Shadrach, he is unable to let go, and, after Grandpa has pried his finger off, he is sick at his stomach. Although the adults seem unpredictable to him, he perceptively realizes that, because he has recently been seriously ill, his Mother and Grandma want to keep him a baby, while Father and Grandpa want him to be suddenly grown up.

DAVIS, ROBERT (1881–1949), born in Beverly, Mass.; journalist and free-lance writer of novels for young people. He graduated from Union Theological Seminary in New York City, and after serving as assistant to Henry Van Dyke, was for ten years pastor of a suburban New York church. During the First World War, he was commissioner of the American Red Cross in Europe. After the war he made his home on a farm in southwestern France. He began to write during his long convalescence from a near-fatal accident in 1929, contributing first to the Paris edition of the New York *Herald Tribune*. He subsequently became a correspondent in thirty-one countries. His first juvenile book was *Padre Porko*, *the Gentlemanly Pig* (Holiday, 1939), a book of Spanish stories he heard while serving in Spain. *Pepperfoot of Thursday Market** (Holiday, 1941), a Fanfare book, deals with Berbers of North Africa, where he also was stationed for a time. He wrote altogether a half-dozen novels of adventure and suspense for older readers, including *That Girl of Pierre's** (Holiday, 1948), a Fanfare book set in a village in southwestern France right after World War II, *Hudson Bay Express* (Holiday, 1942), *Partners of Powder Hole* (Holiday, 1947), and a nonfiction book about France. During World War II he was forced to leave France, and in the hasty departure, he lost everything he owned. He came to the United States and, at the age of sixty, took a position as professor of history at Middlebury College in Vermont. His stories are graphic and have dignity and charm, but they suffer from inadequate plotting.

A DAY ON SKATES: THE STORY OF A DUTCH PICNIC (Van Stockum*†, Hilda, ill. author, Harper, 1934), amusing story intended for younger children, set about the time the book was written, concerning the adventures of a group of Dutch schoolchildren while skating on a canal the first real day of winter. Nine-year-old twins, Evert and Afke, and their third form schoolmates of the village of Elst are delighted when Teacher announces that he will take them on a skating picnic the next day. They skate alone and in groups, sampling hot chocolate and little cakes from vendors along the way, stopping to watch an artist at work, and enjoying an exciting snowball fight with the children of Snaek. Evert has more adventures than his sister, who is less daring. He falls through a hole in the ice, joins with two close friends, Jan and Okke, to form the Three Columbians, an explorers' club, and with them and a new boy in school, orphaned Simon, gets locked in the historic old church the class visits. Simon, usually withdrawn and shy, suggests the four climb to the top of the church tower to try to find a way out and rings the church bells to attract attention. As a result of their experience in the tower, the three become friends with Simon and admit him to the Columbians. The children's activities are described in charming and vivid detail, if a little patronizing in tone, and the book is typical of the period in its treatment of the girls as weak homebodies in the making. The numerous, full-page, detailed paintings and black and white sketches extend the story and project an old-fashioned air. Newbery Honor.

DE ANGELI, MARGUERITE (LOFFT) (1891–   ), born in Lapeer, Mich.; illustrator who wrote at least nineteen books of fiction, among them the Newbery-winning historical novel, *The Door in the Wall** (Doubleday, 1949). She was educated in schools in Lapeer and Philadelphia and was a talented singer, giving up an opportunity to go to London in an opera by Oscar Hammerstein to be married and have four sons and one daughter. In art she was mostly self-educated but did a good deal to support the family by illustration during the Depression. Her family's struggles and triumphs are told in her autobiography, *Butter at the Old Price* (Doubleday, 1971). Many of her books are concerned with minorities or foreign born, among them *Bright April** (Doubleday, 1946) about a middle-class black family, *Elin's Amerika** (Doubleday, 1941) about Swedish immigrants in the 1640s, *Henner's Lydia** (Doubleday, 1936) and *Yonie Wondernose** (Doubleday, 1944) about Amish children, *Skippack School** (Doubleday, 1939) about Mennonites in eighteenth-century Germantown, Pa., *Thee, Hannah!** (Doubleday, 1940) about nineteenth-century Quakers, and *Up the Hill** (Doubleday, 1942) about a Polish-American family in a Pennsylvania mining town. She has been said to ''make the exotic seem unthreatening'' and to ''celebrate the universality of happy childhood,'' qualities that work better in her books for younger children than they do in historical adventures like *Black Fox of Lorne** (Doubleday, 1956), where even very exciting action is tamed by her style. The artist is apparent in the descriptions, which are often more vivid than the scenes of action. In 1968 she was awarded the Regina Medal by the Catholic Library Association. Even if she had written none of her fiction or illustrated, as she did, many books by other writers, she would earn a place in children's literature with her large *Book of Nursery and Mother Goose Rhymes* (Doubleday, 1954), beautifully illustrated with warm and gentle pencil drawings and muted full-color pages.

THE DEFENDER (Kalashnikoff*, Nicholas, ill. Clair Louden and George Louden, Jr., Scribner's, 1951), realistic novel set in northern Siberia, probably in the early part of the twentieth century. Turgen, a Lamut, one of a dying people, lives in the mountains near the Yakut people and has been known for his skill in folk medicine, but he is now avoided because the jealous shamanist has spread rumors that he is a sorcerer. One winter day he comes upon the *yurta*, or hut, of Marfa, a widow, where he finds her son, Timofey, 5, caring for his baby sister, Assa, 2, but unable to relight the fire which has gone out while he slept. Turgen aids the children and, realizing the desperate need that has made their mother leave them alone, returns with supplies which he trades for milk from their cow. They become friends, but Turgen's main interest is the *chubuki*, the wild mountain rams, which he feeds in the hard winter as he has been directed to do in a dream in which his dead wife and child lead him to the Great Spirit. When a baby ram is injured, Turgen rescues it, names it Lad, and having nursed it back to health, is rewarded by a dream in which the Great Spirit visits him and suggests that he marry Marfa. While she is willing and the children delighted, Turgen worries that the enmity of the villagers will now be directed against them, but the merchant Kamov, who trades with him for hides, solves the problem by arranging that the priest travel the sixty miles to the village to marry them in a Christian ceremony, which will prove that Turgen is not a tool of the devil. Although the plot is extremely simple and the characterization is minimal, the book has a legend-like tone that holds a reader's interest, and it gives a sympathetic picture of a very different way of life and shows deep appreciation of natural wild life. Fanfare; Newbery Honor.

DE JONG†, DOLA (1911–), born in Arnhem, Holland; writer and language specialist who reads and judges manuscripts for publishers in English, French, German, Dutch, Flemish, and South African. She was educated in the Netherlands and England and worked on a newspaper in Amsterdam. In 1940 she escaped from the Netherlands to North Africa, from there coming to the United States and becoming a citizen in 1946. Her novel, *The Level Land** (Scribner's, 1943), while not autobiographical, employs many incidents and scenes from her childhood and the immediate pre-war period in the Netherlands. *The House on Charlton Street†* (Scribner's, 1962), a mystery set in Greenwich Village, New York City, shows her versatility as a writer. She also writes for adults and has worked for the U.S. Information Agency. In 1947 she won the Literature Prize of the City of Amsterdam and in 1955 was elected to the Dutch Academy of Arts and Letters.

DEJONG†, MEINDERT (1906–), born in Wierum, Netherlands; author whose unusual ability to express the point of view of animals and young children has won him a special place among writers for young people. When he was eight, he came with his family to the United States and settled in Grand Rapids, Mich., where he was graduated from Calvin College. During World War II he served in the U.S. Army Air Force, where he was historian of the Chinese-American Wing, 14th Air Force, an experience employed in *The House of Sixty Fathers** (Harper, 1956), about a Chinese boy adopted by American flyers. Among his other books two types predominate, those about animals, usually seen wholly or partly through the point of view of the animal characters, including *Hurry Home, Candy** (Harper, 1953), *Shadrach** (Harper, 1953), *Along Came a Dog** (Harper, 1958), and *The Last Little Cat†* (Harper, 1961), and those set in the Netherlands of his childhood, usually featuring young children, including *The Tower by the Sea** (Harper, 1950), *The Wheel on the School** (Harper, 1954), *Far Out the Long Canal†* (Harper, 1964), and *Journey from Peppermint Street** (Harper, 1968). He has won many honors including the Newbery Medal, the National Book Award, the Hans Christian Andersen International Medal, the Regina Medal from the Catholic Library Association, and the Aurianne Award for books which tend to develop humane attitudes toward animal life. His books have been translated into twenty languages and published in Europe, Australia, Japan, and South Africa.

DENMARK CARAVAN (Owen*, Ruth Bryan, ill. Hedvig Collin*, Dodd, 1936), travelogue thinly disguised as a novel set in Denmark in 1935. A family group, consisting of Mother-in-Chief, two older boys, Ben and Barney, who do the driving, and two younger girls, Peggy and Nancy, take their blue car and house trailer to Denmark by tramp steamer and tour the country. They visit Frederiksborg Castle, Kronberg Castle at Elsinore (setting for Hamlet), the Tivoli, an amusement park in Copenhagen, Rosenborg Castle, Roskilde Cathedral, and Højerup Kirke, a smaller church. At Svenborg, they talk about Saint Jørgen and the dragon, and at Odense, birthplace of Hans Christian Andersen, they talk about the ugly duckling and dogs with eyes as big as windmills. On the fourth of July, they attend a celebration at Rebild Park in Jutland, a park built by Danish Americans. Twice they see the king, Christian the Tenth. By ferry they cross to the island of Fanø where they find people wearing native dress and engaging in crafts like amber carving. The story is plotless and themeless, and the characters are scarcely differentiated; their ages are undetermined, and, except that Ben likes information and Nancy likes fairy tales, they are not individualized. Each place the family visits has a story or anecdote that they discover, but the description is not vivid enough to interest readers unless they have been in Denmark or, perhaps, expect to visit the country. Fanfare.

DIANA-KATE (*Hitty: Her First Hundred Years**), the whaling ship on which the Preble family sail. Since Mrs. Preble objects to the ''heathen'' name Diana, Captain Preble adds her name, Kate. After a difficult trip round the Horn, they are well started on a good season when the vessel catches fire, presumably through some skulduggery of the disgruntled mate, Patch. The mate and all but three faithful sailors abandon the ship, leaving the Preble family who stick to it until the last possible moment, then make their way to a nearby island.

DIANE ROTHBERG (*Heart of Danger**), Jewish girl whom Madame* Moreau hides during the war and for whom Rudy* Behrens writes a waltz, which is pirated during his imprisonment and later becomes a hit song. She encourages him to resume his composing, and her letters to Tod* Moran after Germany falls inform the reader of Rudy's despondency and inability to compose. She is a flat, colorless character.

DICKON (*The Hidden Treasure of Glaston**), son of a peasant, oblate at Glaston abbey, who discovers the cave in which treasures and parchments are buried. Adventurous, kind, occasionally frivolous, he longs for miracles but does not have the staying power to produce them. He eventually is released from his office and becomes Sir Hugh de Morville's squire. He is obviously a foil character for the serious, bright Hugh*.

DICKON SOWERBY (*The Secret Garden**), twelve-year-old brother of the housemaid, Martha, at Misslethwaite Manor. A nature lover, he has spent most of his life wandering the moor, coming to know the habitat and customs of all the birds and animals. When Mary* Lennox becomes interested in the locked garden, she and Martha compose a note to Dickon asking him to buy seeds and garden tools for her. When he brings them, Mary shares the secret of the garden with him, and he works with her and later with Colin* Craven there. Red-haired, blue-eyed, round-faced, he is an unspoiled child of nature and acts as foil and guide to the two unhappy, spoiled youngsters, though he is of a lower class and education.

DICKS, DICKY (*Downright Dencey**), tavernkeeper on the docks who feels some concern for Sam Jetsam. He tells Sam that a certain Bill, a survivor of a shipwreck, had brought him as a baby to Injun* Jill to raise. Dicks thinks that Sam may be Bill's own son. What happened to Bill is unknown. Dicks is otherwise unimportant in the story.

DIETRICH (*The Sword and the Scythe**), smith of the village in which Martin Biemler lives. He organizes the peasants' revolt in that area with the help and encouragement of Konrad. He is killed in the fighting. The organization of peasants called the Union Boot, with its symbol the inverted peasant boot, is his idea.

DILLAL BEN ABBES (*Pepperfoot of Thursday Market**), cunning, ill-tempered thief, who has trained his dog to steal from the tradespeople in the *souks* (marketplaces). He steals Pepperfoot when the donkey is tethered in the village of Ali Taza during the barley harvest. When last seen, he is on his way to prison, captured by the French Legion for stealing from their camp. Driss trades him a pair of sandals and a knife for his smart, sandy-colored, skinny dog.

DOBRY (*Dobry**), the young Bulgarian peasant boy who likes to draw, carve, and mold figures in clay. He lives with his mother and grandfather, is described as bright-eyed and full of life, and, when he is older, the huskiest boy in the village. As a young boy he plays with Neda, the shoemaker's daughter, and at the book's end, when he is leaving for art school in Sofia, he plans to return to marry her.

DOBRY (Shannon*, Monica, ill. Atanas Katchamakoff, Viking, 1934), realistic novel set in a village of Bulgaria, presumably in the early twentieth century. Divided into two books, *Childhood—The Gypsy Bear*, and *Youth*, the book is essentially plotless, consisting of day-to-day village happenings interrupted by stories told either by Dobry or his grandfather. These two with Dobry's mother, Roda, live in a typical peasant home with their oxen on the first floor and family quarters above, the oven in the yard, and the house heated by a tile fireplace or *jamal*. At the first snow, Dobry digs tomatoes for himself and his grandfather from the storage mound and gets a stomachache from overeating. He and Neda, the shoemaker's daughter, go to the mill with Grandfather, on the way helping Bekir, the gypsy, polish pots. Dobry watches the village storks leave, makes a stork kite for Neda, and draws her a picture of her pig. The gypsy bear, which walks on the village men to massage them, comes, and they all have a party. Book II starts at least four years later when Dobry has taken over the duties of Asan, the village herdboy, and spends his long solitary days happily drawing and carving. He meets the Macedonian, Maestro Kolu, the *jamal* maker, who shows him where to get clay so he can model. Grandfather wins the snow-melting contest, in which the men lie on the deep snow and vie to see whose body heat will make him sink far enough to disappear first. On Christmas morning, Dobry makes the nativity scene in snow sculpture which peasants come for miles to see, and later is the only boy brave enough to dive for a cross dropped through a hole in the river ice, thereby bringing good fortune to the village, and is rewarded by coins ripped from the peasant wedding dresses and contributed so he can go to Sofia to study art. The book ends after the gypsy bear has returned, the event which signals time for the spring bath of all the villagers in the river, and Dobry is about to set off for Sofia but promises to return to marry Neda. Although Roda worries that Dobry prefers drawing to farming, there is little tension in the book and the interruption of the narrative with stories is clumsy. Dobry is strong, brave, and full of life, as is also his grandfather, but none of the characters is memorable. The book is notable mainly for its details of the living arrangements, clothes, and ethnic customs of the Bulgarian villagers. Newbery Winner.

DOC CATHCART (*The Black Symbol**), Dr. Primus D. Cathcart; the cruel, ambitious, greedy confidence man who runs the traveling medicine show with which Barney travels while hunting for his father. A tall man with an air of grace and grandeur, he dresses well and speaks smoothly and authoritatively. Barney immediately trusts him, to the boy's later dismay. Doc wants Barney in his company so that Barney can give him information about the territory through which they are traveling and because his youth and clean-cut appearance make him particularly useful as a shill.

DOCTOR DOLITTLE (*The Story of Doctor Dolittle**; *The Voyages of Doctor Dolittle**), John Dolittle, M.D., originally a physician for people, who learns the languages of animals and becomes a great naturalist. A rotund little man who always wears a top hat, Doctor Dolittle is brilliant, an accomplished flautist, and has many other unusual talents, but is impractical about money and undisturbed by such trifles as his ship being wrecked or his dinner burned. He is friendly, unpretentious, and cheerful, being aroused to fury only by such institutionalized cruelty as bullfighting.

DOCTOR MACRAE (*Red Planet**), elderly, wise friend of the boys from the Martian colony. When Mr. Marlowe's reasonable approach to the Company officials' tyranny fails, MacRae leads a group which charges the Company headquarters and captures the Resident Agent General. Better at native languages than any other colonist, MacRae negotiates with the Martians, who want to wipe out the colony, and learns a little of their greatly advanced development including the fact that they once engaged in space travel but have since given it up.

DODGE, MARY (ELIZABETH) MAPES (1831–1905), born in New York City; editor and author of books for children. She achieved a position of eminence in the world of literature for children and young people for two main contributions, her novel about family life in Holland, *Hans Brinker; or, The Silver Skates** (O'Kane, 1865), one of the first books to portray life in a foreign country realistically, and her long and distinguished service as editor of the most influential magazine in the history of children's literature, the *St. Nicholas*, which she helped to found, for which she persuaded the best authors of the period to write, and which, therefore, set standards in taste in children's literature for all time. She came of a well-off and book-loving family. When she was sixteen, she helped her father, a horticultural expert, run his experimental farm and wrote articles for his magazine, *The Working Farmer*. After the death of her husband, she returned to the family farm in New Jersey, where she began writing down the stories she made up for her two small sons. After the publication of *Irvington Stories* in 1864 (O'Kane), her publisher asked her to write a novel, and the result was *Hans Brinker*, which went to one hundred editions within thirty years, was translated into six languages, has never yet been out of print in its over one hundred years of existence, and is listed in *Choice* and Children's Classics. In 1870, she became associate editor of *Hearth and Home*, of which Harriet Beecher Stowe was editor. She was then asked by Roswell Smith of the Century Company to start a children's magazine, and, in 1873, she became founder-editor of the *St. Nicholas*, which ran for almost seventy years and did much to raise people's expectations about literature for the young. She retained the editorship until her death, in the thirty-two years of her tenure compiling an impressive list of contributors, which no other magazine for the young has yet been able to approach in quality. Her other books for children include *Rhymes and Jingles* (Scribner's, 1874), *Along the Way* (Scribner's, 1879), both books of verse, and *The Land of Pluck* (Century, 1894), also about Holland. She also contributed articles to *Atlantic Monthly*, *Harper's*, and other well-known magazines.

DOLBIER, MAURICE (WYMAN) (1912–), born in Skowhegan, Maine; actor, columnist, radio news editor and announcer, playwright, and author of books for adults and children. After attending Whitehouse Academy of Dramatic Arts in Boston, he toured as an actor with Shakespearean companies. He worked for radio stations in Maine and Rhode Island, became literary editor for the Providence *Journal*, and in 1956, joined the New York *Herald Tribune* to write the column, "Books and Authors." Subsequently he was book critic for the New York *World*, rejoining the Providence *Journal* in 1967 as literary critic. Among his several plays, a fantasy for children, *Jenny: The Bus that Nobody Loved*, was broadcast by Columbia Workshop and the BBC in England and then rewritten as a book, *The Magic Bus* (Wonder, 1948). His other books for children include the fantasies *The Magic Shop** (Random, 1946), a fast-moving, diverting, if insubstantial and condescending, short novel typical of its time that received *Horn Book* honor status; *The Half-Pint Jinni and Other Stories* (Random, 1948), a collection of humorous stories of magic; *Torten's Christmas Secret* (Little, 1951), about a gnome who works for Santa Claus; *A Lion in the Woods* (Little,

1955), a comic fantasy that satirizes the newspaper world; and a book in the Legacy series of American heroes, *Paul Bunyan* (Random, 1959). A resident of Providence, he has also written books of humor and fiction for adults.

DONALD DUNN (*In a Mirror**), Bessie* Muller's literature teacher, with whom she disagrees over the Romantic poets and whose class she eventually drops in favor of one in mythology and folklore, an interest sparked by Til* Carey's desire to create a dance around the basilisk. About thirty, Dunn served in World War II and Korea, then finished his course work, and now is in his first teaching position. He is a very warm, happy, and loving father and husband, at home quite different from the cool, aloof, distant instructor Bessie sees in class. His feelings for Til are left in doubt.

DONALD ROGER CABOT (*Kildee House**), mean son of neighbors of Jerome Kildee, who takes pleasure in instructing his dog, Strong Heart, to worry small animals, a practice which earns him the enmity of Emma* Lou Eppys. He reports Jerome to the game warden, hoping thereby to get revenge on Emma Lou for bean-shooting his dog with a marble. He eventually becomes intrigued by Jerome's menagerie and comes up with the idea of advertising for homes for the creatures.

DON BECKER (*Shadow across the Campus**), pre-law student, who becomes Marjorie's steady boyfriend. He is president of the student council. He listens carefully and sympathetically when she solicits his advice about bringing before the council the issue of sororities excluding Jews from membership but makes the point that it is very difficult to legislate emotional issues. He does, however, encourage her to pursue the matter, and, after she is successful in persuading the Zeta Nus to accept Jewish girls, he informs her that it was her concern for this social injustice that first attracted him to her. Don is too exemplary to be convincing. His foil is the even more phony Leslie Burke, a freshman who also dates Margie, and who tells her emphatically that men do not like women who take up causes.

A DONKEY FOR THE KING (Price*, Olive, ill. Valenti Angelo*, Whittlesey, 1945), short animal novel in which events from history play an important role. It fictionalizes upon Christ's triumphal entry into Jerusalem. Lame Joshua, 12, serves kind, just Benjamin, a wealthy Lebanese farmer. While they are going through the village of Bethany on their way to Jerusalem to buy supplies, Joshua, Benjamin, and Benjamin's son, domineering, insolent Philip, observe two of Jesus' disciples fetch a little, gray-white donkey, named Dusty, for their master to ride upon as he enters the capital city. Benjamin later buys the small, sturdy beast, who to Philip's disappointment shows a decided preference for gentle Joshua. The little donkey soon reveals special powers. He saves a blind child from being trodden down by Philip's horse, and, back at Benjamin's villa, Dusty wins the hearts of the family and servants by his sweet and docile ways. As the year passes, Philip remains resentful and tries several times to cause trouble for Joshua and Dusty. The next spring, Dusty and Joshua are chosen to lead the annual Spring Procession in the village. Philip instructs a servant to dig a pit on the parade route and to disguise it with branches and flowers. Dusty is aware of the danger and stops short. Philip's small cousin runs over to see why the plucky beast is balking and falls into the pit, severely injuring himself. Philip flees into the hills, and a diligent search fails to locate him. That night, in a driving rain, Joshua and Dusty undertake the treacherous mountain paths to look for their master. Dusty unerringly leads Joshua to the shepherd's hut where Philip is hiding. Philip is impressed and chastened by their loving act and experiences a change of heart. This pleasing, if sentimental, didactic story of the power of love holds few surprises. Characters are flat, but generous use of details make setting and incidents vivid and distinct, and the reader learns something about life in that era. Occasionally the narrative echoes the King James Version in style and tone, and some dialogue is taken directly from the Bible. Fanfare.

THE DOOR IN THE WALL (De Angeli*, Marguerite, ill. author, Doubleday, 1949), historical novel set in fourteenth-century England. Robin de Bureford, 10, expects to go to the castle of Sir Peter de Lindsay on the Welsh border to be trained as a page after his parents leave to go into royal service, but before his escort arrives, he is stricken with a crippling disease. When the servants succumb to the plague sweeping London, Robin is abandoned and rescued by Brother Luke, who takes him to the nearby monastery, nurses him, teaches him to use crutches and to swim, awakens his interest in carving, and encourages him to overcome his handicap, saying that there is always "a door in the wall" if one but looks for it. A letter from Robin's father directs him to travel to Sir Peter's accompanied by Brother Luke and a minstrel, John-go-in-the-Wynd, an eventful trip during which they visit St. John's College at Oxford, enjoy a country fair, and narrowly escape being robbed by thugs at a wayside inn. At Lindsay they are welcomed by Sir Peter and Lady Constance, but the castle is soon attacked and besieged by the Welsh. When the water supply gets low, Robin sneaks out, swims the river, and, disguised as "Crookshanks," a simple shepherd boy, makes his way through enemy lines to the home of John-go-in-the-Wynd's mother, so that John can go for help. The Welsh are defeated and Robin's parents arrive in the company of the king, Edward III, who knights Robin for his bravery. Perhaps because the author is an artist, the descriptions in the book are full and pictorial and give a good deal of information about life in the late medieval period. The characters, however, are stock types never fully developed and, although much happens, the action is never exciting so that the book has the static quality of a tapestry. The message that there is always a way of achieving despite handicaps is presented directly and in the "door in the wall" metaphor so often as to be inescapable even to the least perceptive reader. Fanfare; Newbery Winner.

DOOR TO THE NORTH (Coatsworth*†, Elizabeth, ill. Frederick T. Chapman, Winston, 1950), historical novel which builds a story around the sudden and nonviolent disappearance of an entire colony of about nine hundred people from Greenland in the late 1350s. The story starts in Norway in the spring of 1360, when King Magnus Eirickson authorizes Paul Knutson to sail to Greenland to find out what happened to the Western Colony. Among the forty men Paul chooses to accompany him are young Olav Sigurdson, who demands the right under God to go on the voyage in order to vindicate the memory of his dead father, branded a coward by Knutson, and whom Knutson's daughter loves, and Eirik, Olav's father's Lapp steward. At Greenland, Olav acquires a huge hound, which often proves helpful during the journey, and a woman soothsayer makes an obscure pronouncement, which Olav later recalls and which affects the entire venture. The travelers learn that the Greenlanders greatly fear the small, dark, aggressive people of the North called Skraelings. The voyagers sail westward to Helluland and then to Vinland, where they winter in the houses built by Leif the Lucky. In the spring, when Paul decides to return home, Olav recalls the soothsayer's obscure comment about a place ''behind Vinland,'' which triggers the pilot's memory about a voyage some Norse once made to a place called ''Hóp'' far inland. After storms and an encounter with treacherous Skraelings, they arrive at Hóp, where a runic inscription informs them that the Greenlanders left Hóp in the spring of 1359 to make for Vinland. Paul leads a group, including Olav and Eirik, that takes the small boats and continues in pursuit. Their hard journey sees Olav and others lost and attacked by wolves while hunting, and ten of the Norse, among them Eirik, slain by hostile Skraelings. Olav avenges Eirik's death and wins a statement of approval from Paul that vindicates his father's honor. Farther on, they suddenly encounter a Greenlander, Thorfinn, who tells how the Western Colony was helped by friendly Skraelings, really some Mandan Indians. To get away from other Skraelings, hostile Ojibwa, the Mandans are migrating westward, taking the Norse with them. Some of Paul's party elect to join them, but most, Paul and Olav among them, return home to Norway. The author seems primarily interested in informing her readers. Characters are one-dimensional and never engage the emotions. Potential for excitement is not exploited, and the novel lacks a telling climax and really satisfying conclusion. The story finds its source in such historical and archaeological evidence as Magnus's charge to Knutson and a runic stone found in Minnesota. Fanfare.

DORCAS LAIDLAW (*Kaga's Brother**), daughter of a white settler at La Pointe on the south shore of Lake Superior, with whose family Mat (Matthew* Steele) and Captain Lewis stay while in the area. Dorcas is one of ten children, and, according to Mat, she is nice looking and sensible. She is also capable about the house, good at playing games, and quick-thinking. Since her stepmother is Indian and she has lived among Indians all her life, she knows well their ways and beliefs. Through a trick with a mourning dove, a bird of significance to the Chippewa, she enables Mat to convince the Indians that Mr. Laidlaw can heal Kaga's* wounds.

DOROTHY (*The Wonderful Wizard of Oz**), Kansas girl blown in a cyclone to the magical land of Oz*, where she meets strange characters and seeks continually to get back to her grim Aunt Em and Uncle Henry. When she is captured and enslaved by the Wicked Witch of the West, Dorothy kills the witch by throwing water on her. Eventually Dorothy is able to return to Kansas by clicking together three times the heels of the silver shoes that belonged to the Wicked Witch of the East. Dorothy is a girl of the 1890s, somewhat younger than Judy Garland was in the popular movie version of the story.

DOVE (*Johnny Tremain**), lazy, sulky, surly apprentice in the Lapham silver establishment, who, out of resentment at Johnny's bossiness, employs a cracked crucible, which breaks and burns Johnny's hand. Later he becomes a stableboy for the British soldiers, and Johnny picks up valuable information about British plans through him.

DOWNRIGHT DENCEY (Snedeker*, Caroline Dale, ill. Maginel Wright Barney, Doubleday, 1927), historical novel set among the seafaring Quakers of Nantucket Island shortly after the War of 1812, spanning several years in the life of young Quaker girl, Dencey (Dionis) Coffyn, schoolgirl daughter of a ship's captain, Thomas* Coffyn. When he taunts her on the way home from school, earnest, pious, assertive Dencey thoughtlessly throws a stone and wounds Sam Jetsam, waif and foster son of drunken outcast Injun* Jill. When conscience-stricken Dencey tries to make amends by presenting him with her cherished copy of *Pilgrim's Progress*, Sam demands that she teach him to read. Although Dencey knows that her stern and proper mother would disapprove, she complies anyway. She finds Sam an apt pupil, and, moved by his hard and bitter circumstances, steals food and even her cousin's castoff jacket for him, deeds which cause her considerable anguish of mind. Horrified when she discovers that her daughter is associating with a half-breed outcast, Mrs. Coffyn locks Dencey in her room to repent on a diet of bread and water. Nevertheless, Dencey staunchly remains "under concern" for Sam, and, while attempting to keep him from leaving the island with a vagabond ventriloquist, loses her way in a blinding snowstorm. Sam saves her life and is taken in by her family in gratitude. He blossoms into a likeable, industrious young man, who becomes a Quaker and then puts himself "under concern" to the unfortunate Jill. Impressed by the youth's diligence and self-sacrifice, Captain Coffyn finds a berth for him as cabin boy, and as Sam Seaman (a name Dencey suggests), Sam looks forward to a good life on the sea. Judged by late twentieth-century standards, the plot seems contrived and sentimental and the tone self-conscious. The author often intrudes with information about Nantucket and Quakers and moralistic and melodramatic statements. The story depicts Dencey's emotions vividly, and her conflict with herself and her remote, introverted mother and her warm relationship with her less rigid father are quite convincing. Point of view shifts from Dencey to Sam about two-thirds of the way through the book, but the mystery of Sam's parentage remains unsolved. The main characters are distinctively drawn, and the setting carries conviction, being indeed the book's best aspect. Flashbacks concerning the courtship and earlier lives of Dencey's parents, Thomas Coffyn, Presbyterian, and Lydia Severance, a Quaker who marries "out of meeting," provide depth and contribute to an understanding of Dencey's relationships with them and her conflict with herself. The dialogue is extensive and employs Quaker idiom. Further adventures of the Coffyns and Sam appear in *The Beckoning Road*. (Aunt* Lovesta Coffyn; Dicky Dicks*) Newbery Honor.

DOWN RYTON WATER (Gaggin*, E. R., ill. Elmer Hader*, Viking, 1941), historical novel which mixes real and fictitious characters and events, set in England, the Netherlands, and the New World from 1608 to about 1630 and dealing with the founding of Plymouth Colony by the Pilgrims. Young Matthew Over, five years old when the book begins, tells how the Overs and some of their neighbors in Scrooby, Nottinghamshire, England, notice that agents of King James Stuart are visiting their village more frequently. They are afraid that the king will no longer let them continue their Separatist way of worship. Led by William Brewster and William Bradford, they flee by night, the men plodding through the marshes and the women and children floating by boat down Ryton Water to the sea where they take a ship to the Netherlands. Matthew Over, a farmer, Orris, his wife, baby 'Memby, fiery Winover, an orphan foster child of eight, Uncle John Brode, also eight, and young Matt take with them only the barest essentials and starts from Orris's cherished herb garden. They settle first in Amsterdam, where they share a house with Separatists who had emigrated earlier and where Orris plants her herbs in small kegs, since there is no space for a proper garden. But the men cannot find work, and the children begin to forget their English ways and speech, and, after a year, many of the Separatists, now calling themselves Pilgrims, move to Bell Alley in Leyden. The Overs, however, choose a little cottage on the Weddestag by the dike, where Orris can have a real herb garden. Ten years pass happily with Matthew becoming a partner in a lumber business and taking Dutch citizenship, the children attending school, and the addition of young Nicolas to the family. When war breaks out on the continent and the Pilgrims learn that King James has discovered their whereabouts, many, among them the Overs, decide to emigrate to the New World to Virginia Colony. In July, 1620, they leave on the *Mayflower* and the *Speedwell*, stopping in England to add to their company John Alden, a cooper, and Miles Standish, a soldier, both men who possess needed skills. When the *Speedwell* proves unseaworthy, the Over women are left behind in England with others, while Matthew and young Matt sail on with the *Mayflower*. After a taxing voyage, during which the ship is blown off course, they land on Cape Cod in November.

Young Matt describes the hardships of the first winter in letters home to his mother. The next year the women arrive, and after that things go better for the settlers, with the help of such Indians as Squanto and Samoset, and they hold a thanksgiving celebration. Eight years see the Overs prosper and grow in numbers until, through marriages and births, they total thirty-one persons. The book ends with young Matt and his mother discussing how grateful they are for their hard-won peace and freedom. Dialogue is extensive and vigorous, but characterization is minimal, and the only story there is simply provides a line on which to hang the familiar account of the Pilgrim migration. There is little attempt at suspense or at exploiting the dramatic potential of significant events. Some important related historical happenings, such as the signing of the Mayflower Compact, are omitted entirely. Although the book gives a good picture of everyday life during the period, the author seems less interested in telling a good story well than in conveying to the young readers of World War II some sense of what motivated the Pilgrims and how they met their challenges. Fanfare; Newbery Honor.

DOWRY FIELD (*That Girl of Pierre's**), the small piece of farm land that goes down through the women in the Dufour family. Danielle and Mathilde* are hurt and angry when they discover that the field is no longer theirs, because they had counted on planting a late crop of vegetables to tide them over the winter. The Dowry Field is especially desirable because it is one of the most fertile pieces of land in the area.

DR. CARLISLE (*The Boy Who Had No Birthday**), a deliberate, thoughtful, kind man, he helps David* Cring see that the important part of being a doctor is not the visible signs of the profession but the work of making sick people well. He takes David on his rounds, gives the boy opportunities to help him, and praises him for his quick thinking and capable actions. He delights the boy by calling him his colleague. He takes an interest in David's education and loans him a book so he can study Latin in preparation for medical school. David trusts him and confides in him, even telling him that he hopes some day to marry Jenny, the doctor's daughter.

THE DREAM COACH (Parrish*, Anne, and Dillwyn Parrish*, ill. authors, Macmillan, 1924), group of four fantasy stories held together loosely by a frame of the coach which travels from heaven bringing dreams to sleeping children. The first concerns the seven white dreams of a much-abused little princess, who ends by becoming a playmate of the little angels. In the second a Norwegian boy named Goran bravely stays alone through a snowstorm while his grandmother sails off with a neighbor for supplies. In the third a bored little Chinese emperor naughtily cages a bird until the dream shows him the misery of losing one's freedom. In the last a small French boy, Philippe, goes to visit his grandparents and meets his uncle and dreams that his grandmother becomes Grandmother

Rain, his uncle the wind, his grandfather the snow, his cousin the spring, and in a didactic allegory they together produce the flowers. The arch tone and the stereotyped settings and characterizations, particularly in the Chinese story, date the book and though the style may appeal to adult lovers of Hans Christian Andersen's tales, it is doubtful that young children would understand them or that older children would find them interesting. Newbery Honor.

DR. EDGERTON (*Talking Drums**), British physician in Kumasi, Gold Coast, whose diagnosis of the illness of Dagoumba, Ashanti laborer, as sleeping sickness sets Philip Baring on the trail of deciphering the language of the drums. He leaves the city and sets up a camp in Ashanti country where he treats the ill and encourages Philip to use the drums to order the natives to stay away from the river where the tsetse flies are thickest.

DR. HITCHCOCK (*Roller Skates**), the Wyman family doctor, whom Lucinda summons to treat little Trinket Browdowski*. Skillful and determined as he is, he cannot save the golden-haired four-year-old, and she dies. When Lucinda sees the empty bed, she assumes that the little girl has recovered, but later on a walk by the river, Dr. Hitchcock breaks the bad news to her. Lucinda takes it with equanimity, especially when he tells her of the Eskimo belief that the soul of the departed becomes a white gull. This romantic notion catches her imagination and gives the sad event beauty for her.

DR. ZIEMER (*The Enormous Egg**), a paleontologist, who takes an interest in the huge egg even before it hatches. He tells Nate* that the hatchling is a dinosaur, gives Nate information about dinosaurs, tells him how to take care of the creature, convinces him to move Uncle Beazley to Washington, and, finally, when the dinosaur is threatened by the Senate bill, gets Nate to take his case to the people on national television. He replaces the speech that the radio station commentator had prepared for Nate with a blank sheet so that Nate is forced to tell his story in his own, much more convincing fashion.

DU BOIS†, WILLIAM PÈNE (1916–   ), born in Nutley, N.J.; artist who has been author and illustrator for more than twenty books for children and who has illustrated many books written by others. The son of a painter and an art critic, at eight he went to France with his parents and was educated in a French boarding school and later in Morristown School, N.J. From 1941 to 1945 he served in the U.S. Army, most of the time as a correspondent for *Yank*. His books range from picture books through picture-stories, like *The Flying Locomotive** (Viking, 1941) to longer works like *The 21 Balloons** (Viking, 1947), a fantasy which won the Newbery Medal. One of his great enthusiasms is the circus, an interest reflected in *The Alligator Case†* (Harper, 1965), a spoof of mystery novels. A number of his stories concern characters of unusual size, among them several about Otto, a Bunyanesque otterhound, and *The Giant**

(Viking, 1954), a story about an enormous eight-year-old boy. All his books concern bizarre or eccentric characters and situations, told in straight-faced, mock-serious style. Action is fast paced with little description, elaboration being left to the precise and detailed illustrations.

DUDE QUINLAN (*Trigger John's Son**), 12, ragged president of the Goosetown Gang, who befriend Trigger* when he arrives in Beechwood in a boxcar. Dude and his friends from the tough Irish Catholic section of town are considered disreputable by the town's respectable Protestant element but are secretly envied by their sons. Dude cusses, fights, and plays hookey but is tactfully sensitive in his relations with the old Englishman and lets Trigger commit the gang to giving all the money they can raise toward the old man's operation. Though Trigger actually begins to lead the gang, Dude does not object because Trigger is careful to defer to Dude's position in letter if not in spirit.

THE DUKE OF BRIDGEWATER (*The Adventures of Huckleberry Finn**), younger (around thirty) of the two drifting con men who invade and take over the raft on which Huckleberry* Finn and the runaway slave, Jim*, are floating down the Mississippi River. Although he and the King* have not been previously acquainted, they each recognize the other for what he is and soon become partners in fraud. Claiming to be the rightful Duke of Bridgewater (called Bilgewater by the King), he insists that the others wait upon him and call him "Your Grace" and "Your Lordship." A journeyman printer, among other things, he takes over a print shop while the owner is at a camp meeting and prints up a wanted notice offering $200 for Jim, planning that they will tie Jim up when anyone approaches and pose as slave hunters returning a runaway. This handbill eventually leads to Jim's being held at Phelpses' farm. Though the most outrageous schemes are suggested by the King, the Duke seems somehow more ruthless and dangerous, perhaps because he is younger and more vigorous.

E

EAGER†, EDWARD (MCMAKEN) (1911–1964), born in Toledo, Ohio; playwright, lyricist, and author of books for later elementary-aged children. After growing up in Toledo, he went to school in Maryland and Massachusetts and attended Harvard. He wrote plays and songs for the Broadway stage, radio, and television before turning his attention to writing books for the young. He was motivated to work for children by reading stories to his own son, Fritz, and *Red Head* (Houghton, 1951), a picture book in verse, was his first book for a young audience. His admiration for the fantasies of E. Nesbit led him to write his magic books, several episodic novels that openly imitate the work of that turn-of-the-century English author. The first of these, *Half Magic** (Harcourt, 1954), gained immediate popularity, was a Fanfare book, and is listed in *Choice*. Although some critics thought it self-conscious and overdrawn, it won general praise. Clever in concept, it describes the misadventures of some children who find a magical coin that grants only half a wish. In a similar vein, and also rather cute, contrived, and overextended, are *Knight's Castle** (Harcourt, 1956), which takes several children back to Ivanhoe's time; *Magic or Not?** (Harcourt, 1959), which relates extraordinary happenings connected with an old well that stands in the yard of a house in Connecticut where George Washington reputedly had his headquarters; and *Seven-Day Magic†* (Harcourt, 1962), a *Choice* selection that describes the adventures of several children in literary lands. All these books employ essentially the same formula as a vehicle for inventive but rather repetitive adventures. Among his other books are *The Time Garden* (Harcourt, 1958) and *The Well-Wishers* (Harcourt, 1960).

AN EAR FOR UNCLE EMIL (Gaggin*, E. R., ill. Kate Seredy*, Viking, 1939), realistic novel of family and community life set in the mountains of Switzerland at an unspecified time, perhaps the 1920s or 1930s, to judge from the illustrations, and, indeed, in the story, motor cars are still rare enough to arouse comment. Energetic, warmhearted, quick-tongued Resi Witt is a little girl who lives in a house with a pink door with her father, who sings a lot, her grandmother, and her mother, who are both also named Resi. Peter Kirchli, who takes care of Edelweiss, the mischievous Kirchli family goat, informs Resi that the children are expected to give something they value highly to little Angela Roggi, who was lamed and orphaned in an avalanche, when she leaves the mountain for the city to live with an aunt. He says that Resi is to give Angela her herdsman doll, Uncle Emil. But Uncle Emil has been battered and tattered by age, love, and Gigi, the family goose, and over the next several months, Resi has her doll completely remade with the advice and help of her grandmother. She first goes to Mr. Oberegg on Toymaker Street to get a new ear for Uncle Emil, but when she sees the beautiful doll's head with long golden curls that he has fashioned to send to America, she chooses to have it installed on Uncle Emil's body, though everyone remonstrates with her about it. Succeeding trips to craftsmen in Toymaker Street result in two new ladies' arms with rings on the fingers and a woman's body, legs, and clothes for Uncle Emil. At the end of the story, Resi suddenly realizes to what getting a new ear for Uncle Emil has led. She no longer has a herdsman doll; she now has a mountain maid doll, which she names Emilie. While all this is happening, Sepp Gutzberger, a local youth who emigrated to America and became successful in business there, has returned on a toy-buying trip. To commemorate his own happy Swiss childhood, he pays for the operation to correct Angela's lame legs, and, when Angela returns to the village from the hospital, the Witts offer her a home. Resi is delighted. She now has a little sister and her Uncle Emil, too, for this new sister, to whom she gives Emilie, agrees to share the beautiful mountain maid doll with Resi. Interspersed among Resi's trips to Toymaker Street are adventures with Peter, Margit, who herds ducks, and other Alpine friends, and stories Grandmother Resi tells of her youth. The plot ambles along for a pleasant, innocuous story which appears to be intended to provide diverting reading and at the same time inform young readers, particularly girls, about the Swiss people. Events often seem contrived or overdone, and much of the dialogue, which is extensive, seems pointless. The view of mountain life is idealized. Fanfare.

EARL OF MACKWORTH (*Men of Iron**), powerful lord of Castle Delven, who becomes sponsor for young Myles Falworth and has him trained as a champion and knighted for his own ends. A kinsman and old friend of Myles's blind and impoverished father, he takes the boy for training reluctantly and has him entered as a squire at arms rather than a page of his household, so that it will not be noticed that he has in his entourage the son of a man out of favor, but when he sees the possibility of using the daring youth to further his own cause against Falworth's enemy, the Duke of Alban, he takes an interest, arranges special training, and maneuvers to have Myles knighted by King Henry IV himself. Mackworth is called "Gaffer Fox" by Prince Hal, who treats him ironically, recognizing the need for this Machiavellian noble in his cause at the same time he is making it clear that the Earl is not to be fully trusted.

EDDIE HOWE (*The Boy Who Had No Birthday**), friend and playmate of David* Cring. He is a take-charge sort of boy who likes to boss the other boys around and often assumes superior attitudes. He is the self-appointed pilot for the raft trip and directs the building of the raft. After his grandfather takes him to the World's Fair, he loses interest in searching for the money. The Sunday afternoon that Davy and some other boys head for the swimming hole instead of going to Sunday School, Eddie reports to class, less out of virtue than necessity, for his grandfather is the Sunday School superintendent.

AN EDGE OF THE FOREST (Smith*, Agnes, ill. J. Sharkey Thomas, Viking, 1959), fable-like fantasy set at an unspecified time in an ancient forest called, enigmatically, "The Young Woods" or "The Children's Grove." A ewe and her female black lamb are harried away from the flock by a half-trained, half-mad dog that used to be a pet of the shepherd's daughter. After he kills the ewe, a black leopardess, disturbed by the smell of blood and madness, kills the dog and drags its body away. Partly from curiosity and partly because she herself was orphaned young by a falling tree that killed her mother and wounded her paw, the leopardess is attracted to the lamb and takes on its care. To provide it milk she attacks a faun and agrees to free it if the doe will nurse the lamb, too. A pedantic owl, living above the leopardess's den, observes, offers advice and comment, and eventually becomes involved in the protection of the lamb. The leopardess fights off a tiger and gives the lamb a choice of staying with her or going off with the doe to join the deer herd. At the owl's suggestion, the lamb chooses to try living with the deer herd and seems at first to like it. She is favored by the old one, the senior doe of the herd, who helps save her when the herd is attacked by wild dogs. She in turn saves the old one by keeping her from drinking too much of the drugged water in the "singing valley." The life of the deer proves too hard for the lamb, however—too restless and quick moving. As they return to the hillside where the leopardess makes her home, the bucks corner a leopard in a thicket, and the lamb, who sees that he has a wounded eye, persuades them to let it go free. Then she tries to get the owl and the leopardess to catch a hummingbird, the only creature which can pull the thorn from the leopard's eyelid. They both fail, but the hummingbird volunteers, and the leopard is treated; later, two leopards fighting for the leopardess are killed, but the wounded leopard is accepted. The lamb adopts a mouse and protects him from the other creatures, and a small brown owl also joins the group. The lamb realizes that her innocence and love have made the other animals afraid of her, and she decides to return to man. In a parallel story, the shepherd's third son represents a sort of misunderstood innocence and love, particularly love of his grandmother. They are together looking for the black lamb when she appears, escorted by all the animals. The grandmother wants him to kill the lamb and throw it to the leopards to distract them and give the humans time to escape, but the boy instead moves trustingly toward the animals, and they vanish. The theme of the power and fearsome quality of innocent love is handled with some subtlety, but the dreamy quality and the absence of names for the characters give the story an abstractness that keeps a reader emotionally at a distance. Lewis Carroll.

EDIE CARES (*A Lemon and a Star**; *Terrible, Horrible Edie*†; *Edie on the Warpath*†), Edith, youngest of the four original Cares children in the episodic family novels set in the early 1900s. Seen through the viewpoint of her siblings in the first book, Edie, then five, is a pest, spoiled by the servants, tattling to Father*, tolerated by the others mostly as a source of news she picks up in the kitchen and from Nurse's gossip with Gander, the parlor maid. In the second book, *The Wild Angel* (Harcourt, 1957), she has much the same role, but in the last two books, both told from Edie's viewpoint, she is different, a sensitive, forthright child of ten and eleven, filled with rage at the unfairness of women's lot and hers in particular and uninhibited and clever at getting revenge. The object of disparaging remarks from birth (''Everybody knew that Edie had killed Mother by having to be born,'' Ted* points out), Edie fights back with vitality and ingenuity.

EDMONDS†, WALTER DUMAUX (1903–), born on a farm near Boonville, N.Y., not far from the Erie Canal; author best known for his adult novels about the history of upstate New York, including *Drums along the Mohawk* (Little, 1936) and *Rome Haul* (Little, 1929). Of his several books of fiction for children and youth that draw upon the history and life of the same area, the two for which he received major awards are separated by more than thirty years. He won the Newbery Award for his first novel for children, *The Matchlock Gun** (Dodd, 1941), which was also named to the *Horn Book* Fanfare list and the Lewis Carroll Shelf. This essentially single-incident story about an actual Indian attack on a Dutch family when New York was still a British Colony captures the moment with color and excitement for a limited and decidedly white viewpoint of a crucial event. He won the National Book Award, another prestigious prize, for his longer and considerably more substantial period novel, *Bert Breen's Barn*† (Little, 1975), based on remembered scenes from his own upstate boyhood. His second book for young readers, *Tom Whipple** (Dodd, 1942), which retells with droll humor and colloquial language the true story of a resourceful Yankee youth who gains an audience with the Emperor of Russia in 1837, was also a Fanfare book. His writing for the young is generously detailed but avoids unnecessary embellishments, combining a Yankee tendency for understatement with a vividly pictorial style. He also contributed many stories to such leading magazines as *Harper's*, *Atlantic Monthly*, and *Saturday Evening Post*. He graduated from Choate School and Harvard University.

EDWARD TUDOR (*The Prince and the Pauper**; *The Oak Tree House**), son of Henry VIII and Jane Seymour, king of England as Edward VI from 1547 to his death in 1553. In *The Prince and the Pauper*, he becomes mistaken for a slum boy with whom he has exchanged clothes after noticing their striking resemblance and has a series of adventures among the thieves and beggars who inhabit London's most poverty-stricken sections. Mark Twain* pictures him as a boy with imperious manners but a strong sense of justice and staunch courage that withstands the terrible experience. He profits from it to be a king who better understands the suffering and needs of his people. In *The Oak Tree House*, he hears about the house through his squire, Jock, and grants the Goodman title to the tree and the island in the highway where it stands. Katharine Gibson* inaccurately pictures him as already king at eight years old, a boy who is so fascinated with the idea of visiting a tree house that he agrees to a trip that he previously resisted.

ED WILLIAMS (*South Town**, *Whose Town?†*), father of David* in the series. Although raised in the segregated South and used to holding his tongue with white people, Ed has a strong sense of self-worth and resents being expected to do the work of a skilled mechanic at laborers' wages. When he speaks up for his rights, Mr. Boyd, the wealthy owner of the Ford agency, has him arrested for disturbing the peace. In jail he is beaten and his injuries later necessitate brain surgery, from which he eventually recovers though he is never as strong again. As a father, he is a firm support to his son, standing behind him in his various scrapes with the law and counselling nonviolence but determination. His own self-image is damaged when he is laid off and, unable to get a job, must watch his wife going out to clean for white families, and he begins to stay away from home and drink. By the fourth book, he has died.

ED WINTERS (*Jennifer**), foil to Griff* Nolan, steady youth, who works at a gas station to help support his widowed mother and his sister, Diane, who is Jennifer's friend. When Jennifer invites him to her party, he presents her with a small replica of her house to hang in the tree out front, which he knows symbolizes the permanence and security she longs for.

ELIN'S AMERIKA (De Angeli*, Marguerite, ill. author, Doubleday, 1941), story of the New Sweden colony on the Delaware River in the 1640s. Elin Sigstedt is lonely, though she lives with her parents and her two older brothers, Knute, 14, and Bror, grown up, because there are no girls her age in the pioneer community. Her only friend is a young Indian herb woman, Lamefoot, who treats her when she is bitten by a snake. Elin pretends to talk to the tomte, the house elf, who she is sure has followed them to America. When her mother has gone to make soap with the other women, Lamefoot brings word that Indians, excited by rum traded them by the English and Dutch, plan to attack, but Elin is able to warn the women in time, and they drive off the attackers by pouring boiling soap on them. On Lucia Day, Elin wears the traditional white gown and crown of candles and carries breakfast to the family in bed. For Christmas, Lamefoot gives her doeskin stockings, they make a suit for the tomte, and they all attend service in the new church. The whole community is waiting for the arrival of the ship from Old Sweden, since they need news and supplies, but Elin's family are particularly anxious because her brother, Alex, 16, is cabin boy and Bror's intended bride, Britta, is expected to be on board. After one false alarm when the ship sighted turns out to be a Dutch vessel, the Swedish ship finally arrives, and Britta has brought her orphaned niece, Gudrun, to live with them so Elin at last has a girl her own age for a friend. Although there are some exciting events like the Indian attack, the book gives little feeling of the hardships and dangers of life in the early colony, most of the emphasis being upon the chores Elin is expected to do and the moral lessons her mother draws about hard work and a shiny-clean house. De Angeli's illustrations add to the story, particularly the initial letters for each chapter showing the tomte in a different pose. Fanfare.

ELIZA (*Knight's Castle**), eleven-year-old cousin of Roger* and Ann*, and one of the four children to enter the world of *Ivanhoe*. She is quite bossy and wants things her way. Predictably, she learns to defer more to the wishes of others.

ELIZA JANE WILDER (*Farmer Boy**; *Little Town on the Prairie**), bossy older sister of Almanzo*, who later reappears as the unsuccessful teacher in Dakota territory. Never a sympathetic character, she does, however, save Almanzo by covering with scrap wallpaper the spot where he threw the stove blacking brush against the parlor wall. As a school teacher, she cannot manage the youngsters, uses poor judgment in listening to Nellie* Oleson's twisted stories, and accuses Laura* unjustly of causing trouble.

ELLEN TEBBITS (Cleary*†, Beverly, ill. Louis Darling, Morrow, 1951), episodic story set in an Oregon town in the mid-twentieth century. At the Spofford School of Dance, Ellen Tebbits, third grader, hides in the broom closet to change clothes so that no one will learn her humiliating secret: her mother makes her wear woolen underwear. With the garment rolled down and bunched around her waist, she hopes to keep the other girls from knowing, but it keeps slipping, and as she clutches and tugs, between leaps, Otis Spofford, the teacher's son, dropping by to get a dime from his mother, mimics her. The new girl, Austine Allen, distracts the attention by complaining aloud, something the other girls would not dare to do, and later reveals that she, too, wears woolen underwear, thereby becoming Ellen's best friend. In an effort to please the teacher so that she will be allowed to clap the erasers, Ellen offers to bring to school a beet that has gone to seed, a project that turns out to be much more exhausting than she anticipated. A careless remark that she has ridden horses "several times" gets exaggerated by the other children, and when she and Austine, who is crazy about horses, rent a couple from a riding stable, her horse wades into the middle of a stream and stops, and it takes a passing man to lead the animal out and head it home. Ellen's big problem occurs when she and Austine decide to dress like twins, but Austine's mother is not clever at sewing, and their dresses turn out to be quite different. This leads to a quarrel which lasts through a performance of "The Pied Piper of Hamelin," in which Ellen, as a substitute rat, can't find the eyes of her costume and gets lost on stage. When they are both chosen to clap erasers, they make up and all is well again. The style is simple and the events humorous, though only the woolen underwear incident has the ring of authenticity that makes it memorable. While disagreements between best friends are of major importance to eight-year-olds, they do not make particularly interesting subjects for fiction. Choice.

ELLIOT, KATHLEEN MORROW (1897–1940), born in Illinois; author of regional stories of family life for younger readers. The daughter of a minister, she graduated from Wooster College and married Arthur Elliot, an executive of the Standard-Vacuum Oil Co., who was stationed in the Dutch East Indies. The couple spent most of their life in the Far East in the Straits Settlements and in Java. She published poetry in magazines, and her three books all deal with the East Indian area and its people. *Jo-yo's Idea** (Knopf, 1939), an amusing story about the everyday adventure of a Javanese boy, was selected by the editors of *Horn Book* for their Fanfare list. She also wrote *Riema, Little Brown Girl of Java* (Knopf, 1937), a picture book about a little girl who summons a white doctor for her ill mother, and *Soomoom, Boy of Bali* (Knopf, 1938), a short novel about a mischievous ten-year-old boy. Although critics of the time spoke highly of her books, terming them charming, appealing, genuine, and good reading for adults as well as children, they seem dated, quaint, and instructive to late twentieth-century tastes.

EMBURY, LUCY (1883–), born in Englewood, N.J.; writer, editor, expert on architecture and home decoration. She attended Barnard College and Columbia University and taught history and Latin for two years, then worked at the Art Students League and the New York School of Applied Design for Women, where she won four awards. For eight years she was on the editorial staff of Doubleday, Page and Co. as associate, then managing editor of *Garden and Home Builder*. She traveled widely and contributed articles to many journals on architecture and home decoration, some with the advice of her architect brother. She wrote one novel for adults, *Persis: Pilgrim of Tomorrow* (Moray Press, 1936) and edited, under the name Lucy Embury Hubbell, *The Book of Little Houses* (Doubleday, 1927). Her book for children, *Painted Saints** (Viking, 1938), was inspired by the Fair of the Little Saints in Provence, where she purchased the little carved figures used by Guy Alexander as his models for the illustrations.

EMMA JANE PERKINS (*Rebecca of Sunnybrook Farm**), unimaginative friend of Rebecca* Randall, who follows her far more lively friend slavishly and acts as a foil for her character. Plump and a bit dull, Emma Jane is considered far better looking than Rebecca. Being very matter-of-fact, she is often uncomfortable with Rebecca's acting and vivid imagination, but she is nonetheless devoted to her and insists on attending the academy in Wareham, though she dislikes school, just so she can be with Rebecca for three more years.

EMMA LOU EPPYS (*Kildee House**), highly assertive, energetic tomboy, only daughter and youngest child of the large Eppys family who live down the hill from Jerome Kildee's cabin. A crack shot with a bean shooter, she vows vengeance when Donald* Roger Cabot's dog kills the female of Old Grouch, Jerome's raccoon. She helps Jerome organize his animals, get rid of the game warden, and share Christmas with her own family. She is the first human with whom Jerome is able to converse with some degree of freedom.

THE ENCHANTED SCHOOLHOUSE (Sawyer*, Ruth, ill. Hugh Troy, Viking, 1956), fantasy set first in Ireland and then in the United States in the mid-1900s. Before he leaves to visit his Uncle Seamus, who has emigrated to Lobster Bay, Maine, Brian Boru Gallagher, 11, of Donegal captures on May Eve a small, red-capped fairyman*. He wishes to show the children of the richest country on earth that Ireland is a grand country, too, and promises to release the wee fellow after he has done some enchantment for them. Brian Boru takes the fairyman with him to the United States in his grandmother's old, brown, earthenware teapot. After Uncle Seamus shows Brian Boru the sights of New York, they travel to Lobster Bay on the Atlantic where the boy meets his new aunt, Delia, admires Uncle Seamus's comfortable house, and learns to help with the lobsters. The school is a great disappointment to him, for the building is shabby and rundown and not nearly as pleasant as the whitewashed, fuchsia-covered one he attended back home. His teacher, Peter Haskins*, tells him that for years they have been trying to get the town council to build a new one. Brian Boru takes the problem to the fairyman, and, for a while, the little fellow just plays tricks on the townspeople. Settling down, finally, to the task, the fairyman enlists the aid of the birds, who transport the old schoolhouse filled with children to Egg Rock in the bay, where the children remain happy hostages until the council agrees to build a new school. The task accomplished, both Brian Boru and the fairyman return to the Ireland they love so much. This amusing story improvises skillfully on folklore motifs. Slight in plot and shallow in characterization, it is filled with action and moves fast, and the lilt of Irish speech adds considerable charm. Many black and white realistic comic sketches contribute to setting, picture situations, and add to the humor. (Thomas* Teeney; Old* Timothy) Choice.

ENDERS, NAOMI (*Homer Price**), the great-great-great-granddaughter of Ezekiel Enders, the first settler of Centerburg. She builds houses on the Enderses' homestead to rent cheaply to needy families. Problems arise when residents cannot tell one mass-produced house from another.

ENOCH THATCHER (*All Sail Set**), Boston boy who goes to work at fourteen for the ship builder, Donald McKay, in 1850, and the next year sails as an apprentice aboard the *Flying Cloud**, a clipper designed and built by McKay. Enoch has always been fascinated by the sea and has learned a great deal about it from his old seaman friend, Messina Clarke, and from his year at McKay's, but he finds life aboard ship full of unexpected challenges. In the story narrated by Enoch as an old man, he is depicted as an earnest and courageous boy, adequate to be convincing in his role in the adventure but not a particularly memorable character.

THE ENORMOUS EGG (Butterworth*†, Oliver, ill. Louis Darling, Little, 1956), science fantasy set in the small town of Freedom, N.H., and then in Washington, D.C., in the mid-1900s, in which Nate* Twitchell, 12, tells about his experiences over three months' time with Uncle Beazley, his pet dinosaur, who brings him both embarrassment and joy. Nate's hen lays an egg of tremendous size from which, after six weeks of setting, she hatches a baby Triceratops dinosaur, which creates a sensation in the scientific world and puts Freedom on the map. Dr.* Ziemer, a paleontologist, tells Nate how to feed and care for the tame and friendly creature, who soon outgrows the little town of his hatching. Dr. Ziemer advises Nate to donate the dinosaur to the National Museum in Washington, D.C. There Nate continues to take care of his still growing pet. By the end of September, Uncle Beazley is almost twenty feet long and weighs about three thousand pounds, and while Nate is taking him for his morning exercise walk, Uncle Beazley accidentally overturns a truck. When the police insist that Uncle Beazley must be moved, Dr. Ziemer finds a place for him in the Elephant House in the Washington Zoo. The next threat to Uncle Beazley's well-being comes from the United States Senate. Senator* Granderson, a pompous exploiter of specious causes, introduces a bill in the Senate to outlaw dinosaurs from the United States, on the grounds that keeping Uncle Beazley is a waste of money. Nate tells his story on national television with such simple sincerity that bushels of telegrams pour in, vociferous demonstrations take place against the bill, and over $200,000 in donations are contributed for the dinosaur's care. Nate returns to Freedom to a hero's welcome and then writes down the history of his life with Uncle Beazley, confident that his unique American pet will be well taken care of henceforth. Careful attention to the small details of Uncle Beazley's hatching, appearance, care, and behavior and a matter-of-fact, occasionally tongue-in-cheek style make this preposterous story believable. Mild suspense, lively and extensive dialogue, humor of conversation and situation, some gentle satire, originality of concept, and the strong appeal to the emotions of a boy's love for his pet outweigh the stereotyped characters and add up to light, diverting reading. Occasional "newspaper stories" contribute to credibility, while Louis Darling's black and white representational, comic sketches chronicle Nate's experiences and enhance the comedy. (Albert Morrison*) Choice; Lewis Carroll.

ENRIGHT†, ELIZABETH (1909–1968), born in Oak Park, Ill., daughter of a political cartoonist and illustrator and niece of architect Frank Lloyd Wright; illustrator and author best known for her amusing episodic family stories for children. She studied at the Art Students League in New York City, in Paris, and at Parsons School of Design, and worked as an illustrator for magazines before she began writing stories and books for children. An influential writer of her time, she published twelve books of fiction for young readers, mostly episodic novels and some short stories in picture book form. Her second book, *Thimble Summer** (Farrar, 1938), a story of rural life one hot summer in Wisconsin during the Great Depression, received the Newbery Award, was a Fanfare book, and is listed in *Choice*. *Gone-Away Lake** (Harcourt, 1957), about adventures in what was once a popular resort, and *The Sea Is All Around** (Farrar, 1940), about a little girl who goes to live on an island off Massachusetts, both realistic, and the short fantasy *Tatsinda†* (Harcourt, 1963), were Fanfare books, and the first of these was also a Newbery honor book. Although it won no major award at the time, *The Saturdays** (Farrar, 1941), about the escapades of the Melendy children in New York City, has remained the most popular of her books and is cited in *Choice* and *Children's Books Too Good to Miss*. The Melendys' story is continued in *The Four-Story Mistake* (Farrar, 1942), and in *And Then There Were Five* (Farrar, 1944), also published later with the first book in a combined volume, *The Melendy Family* (Farrar, 1947). Her other titles include *Return to Gone-Away* (Harcourt, 1961) and *Spiderweb for Two* (Rinehart, 1951), which also concerns the Melendys. Her family stories combine keen characterization, pictorial style, and trueness to the child's point of view. She illustrated most of her own books and wrote for adults books and short stories that were published in nationally circulated magazines. She lectured in creative writing at Barnard College and conducted writing seminars at Indiana University, the University of Connecticut, and the University of Utah.

ENRIQUE ROLDAN (*Homespun**), casually graceful, effervescent, Creole youth, lover of beautiful things. A generous sort, he introduces Stephen* Greenman to the city of New Orleans and to such diversions as horseracing, and loans him his horse Yanqui, a white Arab, on which Stephen competes admirably.

ERIC (*Thimble Summer**), thirteen-year-old orphan who, hungry and friendless, is attracted by the fire of the Lindens' lime kiln. Orphaned son of Swedish immigrants, he has been hitchhiking around the country doing odd jobs to survive. He is taken in by the Lindens for whom he becomes a hired man. He develops a special fondness for Garnet, who comes to regard him as a brother. He hopes to some day have a farm of his own.

ESTES†, ELEANOR (1906–), born in West Haven, Conn.; librarian and author best known for her first three books about the close-knit Moffat family set in Cranbury, Conn., a community much like the town she herself grew up in, *The Moffats** (Harcourt, 1941), *The Middle Moffat** (Harcourt, 1942), and *Rufus M.** (Harcourt, 1943). Episodic in structure, each is held together by a slight theme, but all are most appealing for their keen characterization, quiet humor, sincere warmth, and accuracy to the child's point of view. All highly acclaimed critically, the first was elected to the Lewis Carroll Shelf and the other two were Newbery honor books, among other awards and citations. She has written over a dozen other books about children in family and neighborhood situations, including *The Hundred Dresses** (Harcourt, 1944), a message story about a little Polish-American girl who is shunned by classmates for her strange-sounding name, which was a Newbery honor book; *Ginger Pye** (Harcourt, 1951), an engaging novel about a lost dog, which won the Newbery Medal and was a Fanfare book; *The Alley*† (Harcourt, 1964), cited in *Choice*; and *The Witch Family*† (Harcourt, 1960), a fantasy selected for Fanfare. After high school she took a position as children's librarian in the New Haven Public Library. She subsequently attended Pratt Institute Library School and became children's librarian at the New York Public Library. She married Rice Estes, professor of library science and director of the Institute, and lived in a little faculty house on campus, the prototype of the alley houses that appear in her books. After *The Moffats* came out, she devoted full time to writing. She also wrote a novel for adults and magazine articles. Her other titles for children include *The Tunnel of Hugsy Goode* (Harcourt, 1972), *The Lost Umbrella of Kim Chu* (Atheneum, 1978), and *The Moffat Museum* (Harcourt, 1983), in which Jane opens a museum in the old barn behind the house on Ashbellows Place, that is less convincing than the earlier Moffat books.

ETS, MARIE HALL (1893–   ), born in Milwaukee, Wis., illustrator, author of many picture books. She attended Lawrence College, the New York School of Fine and Applied Art, and the Chicago School of Civics and Philanthropy, now part of the University of Chicago; she also has done graduate work at the University of Chicago, the Art Institute of Chicago, and Columbia University. After a career in organizations devoted to social welfare, including organizing American Red Cross foreign service in Pilsen, Czechoslovakia, after World War I, she became primarily an author-illustrator in 1935. Her *Play with Me* (Viking, 1955) was the American nominee for the Hans Christian Andersen Award, and *Nine Days to Christmas* (Viking, 1959) won the Caldecott Medal. With Ellen Tarry* she wrote *My Dog Rinty** (Viking, 1946), a story illustrated with photographs taken in Harlem.

EVERNDEN, MARGERY (1916–   ), born in Okeechobee, Fla.; free-lance writer and playwright for children. The daughter of a research chemist, she attended Williams Junior College in Berkeley, Calif., and took her A.B. degree from the University of Pittsburgh in theater arts. She has also been an instructor in English at the University of Pittsburgh. She is author of eight books of adventure and historical fiction for older children and young people. Two were

Fanfare books, *The Secret of the Porcelain Fish** (Random, 1947) and *The Runaway Apprentice** (Random, 1949), instructive introductions to life in Old China filled with action and vivid detail for young readers. Her other titles include *Knight of Florence* (Random, 1950), about an apprentice to the painter Giotto, and *Lyncoya* (Walck, 1973), about Andrew Jackson's adopted Indian son. More recently she has devoted her attention to writing plays for children's theater, often adapting folk tales and legends to the dramatic form. She has also contributed articles and stories to national magazines.

EWAN MACNEILL (*Meggy MacIntosh**), blond, debonaire, handsome, and confident young Scot, who treats Meggy as a meek, timid, poor relation of Veronica, the girl he adores and hopes to marry. When, one day out to sea, Meggy appears, instead of Veronica, to be married by the shipboard minister, Ewan is humiliated and furious, but her solicitous nursing when he is seasick makes him begin to forgive her. In Wilmington, the beginning of the revolution dashes his hopes of making his fortune in trade, and he falls into a depression that Meggy helps him overcome. He makes contact for her with Captain MacLeod so that she can ride with him into the back country to find Flora MacDonald*, and he even trades his fine horse for her lazy old Whitey. After the start of the revolution, he rides all the way to Cross Creek to tell her that the death of his older brother makes it necessary that he return to Edinburgh as family heir and to ask her to marry and return with him, an offer she appreciates but refuses.

EYRE, KATHERINE WIGMORE (1901–1970), born in Los Angeles, Calif.; author whose best known books for children, *Spurs for Antonia* (Oxford, 1943), *Star in the Willows* (Oxford, 1946), and *Rosa and Randy* (Oxford, 1948), have a ranch setting. She was educated at the Marlborough School for Girls. Besides her fiction for children, which includes *Lottie's Valentine** (Oxford, 1941), set in New Orleans, and *Susan's Safe Harbor** (Oxford, 1942), set in San Francisco, both named to the *Horn Book* Fanfare list, she wrote several adult novels and for young people both biography—*Another Spring: The Story of Lady Jane Grey* (Little, 1949)—and fictionalized history—*Children of Light* (Lippincott, 1957), the story of the discovery of the Dead Sea scrolls.

F

THE "FAIR AMERICAN" (Coatsworth*†, Elizabeth, ill. Helen Sewell, Macmillan, 1940), historical novel, set first in France and then on a sailing ship on the Atlantic bound for New England during the French Revolution, which continues events begun in *Away Goes Sally** and *Five Bushel Farm**. When village Revolutionists come to burn his family's chateau, Pierre de la Tour, about thirteen, escapes from the place with the help of his executed father's loyal valet, Jean. The village eccentric, Mad Marie, dresses them as beggars, and the two make for Brest on the coast of Brittany. Jean hopes to secure for Pierre a position as cabin boy on an American ship so that he can join his uncle and aunt who have already emigrated to Boston. Their journey of about a month leads them through territory rife with revolutionary fervor, and they have close calls with both Republicans and Royalists. In Brest, Captain John Patterson of the *Fair American*, ashore with Andrew, his son of about eleven, and his niece, Sally* Smith, about ten, takes Pierre on as cook's helper. During the voyage to New England, Aunt* Debby, now Mrs. Patterson, conducts lessons in English and French, and the children soon become fond of their new friend. Tense moments occur when the *Fair American* rescues an English deserter, who after being cruelly treated has jumped overboard from his ship; when a storm severely buffets the ship and causes considerable damage; and when the *Fair American* is boarded by an officer from a French Republican frigate looking for Royalist refugees. The travelers arrive safely in New England and sail up the Penobscot to Winterport, where they are met by the Smiths and taken home to Five Bushel Farm. Pierre continues with Captain Patterson to Boston where he expects to join his relatives. Characters, if flat, are distinctively drawn. Language is easy and capably handled, and the descriptive passages are often poetic. The author sustains a mild amount of narrative tension and creates a limited sense of the revolution in France and of life on the high seas in a sailing ship during a turbulent period. Fanfare.

THE FAIRY CIRCUS (Lathrop*, Dorothy P., ill. author, Macmillan, 1931), fanciful tale of how the fairies, having seen the real circus whose tent was set up in the meadow, stage a circus of their own. In it the red efts act as seals, the shrews as trained dogs, the turtles as elephants, the chipmunks as tigers, the mice as horses, the weasels as camels, and the toad as a hippopotamus. The show rings are lit by fireflies; fairy acrobats, trapeze artists and tightrope walkers perform on equipment made of cobwebs, fairies riding frogs dive into the pond; and when the Queen appears, they all put on a parade for her. Virtually plotless, the book consists mainly of whimsical description, without any developed characters, and the style seems condescending by modern standards. Although the book has more text than a picture book, it is most notable for its rather misty, imaginative illustrations. Newbery Honor.

FAIRYMAN (*The Enchanted Schoolhouse**), stalwart little chap that Brian Boru captures and who to earn release contrives to get the council to build a new schoolhouse. The fairyman is an amusing character, who puts up with the inconveniences of imprisonment well and who comes to enjoy greatly ice cream and other modern American dishes. As proof that if Brian Boru returns his cap he will not immediately leave for Ireland, the fairyman suggests that they become blood brothers. He delights in playing tricks on the children and on the townspeople. For example, he causes all the pages of the children's school books to go blank as the teacher is teaching the lesson.

THE FAMILY UNDER THE BRIDGE (Carlson*†, Natalie Savage, ill. Garth Williams, Harper, 1958), story of an old hobo of Paris who befriends a homeless family in the mid-twentieth century. Until he finds the red-haired Calcet children, Suzy, Paul, and little Evelyne, and their dog, Jojo, in the spot under the bridge which he claims as his, old Armand has been a contented tramp, carrying his worldly goods in a baby buggy and living for himself, particularly disliking children, whom he calls "starlings." When he grumblingly shares his food with the hungry youngsters, he starts a train of events in which he reluctantly helps them and their mother, first entertaining the children while their mother works by taking them to see Father Christmas, played in a department store by a friend, Camille, then, when they are discovered by do-gooders who would separate them from their mother, taking the family to stay with his friends, the gypsies. The children, who have asked Father Christmas to bring them a home, are enchanted with the gypsy wagon and decide it should be a home on wheels, but the gypsies leave when a policeman appears. At first it seems that Paul has left with the gypsies, but he has only been off trying to get a job. Shamed, Armand decides to try for a job he has heard of as night watchman, and, with help from Madame Calcet, he gets cleaned up to apply. He discovers it is really a job as caretaker for apartments, with family living quarters. Claiming to be the Calcet's grandfather, he accepts the job and plans to move them in for New Year's Day. Though somewhat sentimental, the simple story is lively and appealing for the pictures it gives of Paris. Fanfare; Newbery Honor.

FAR FROM MARLBOROUGH STREET (Philbrook*, Elizabeth, ill. Marjorie Torrey, Viking, 1944), realistic novel set in Massachusetts in 1793. When an urgent request from Uncle Jonathan Quincey arrives at the Wadsworth home while her older brother, Tom, has a badly sprained ankle and the rest of the family are unable to leave Boston, Nancy Lee, 10, is sent to take a very important box all the way to Springfield. For this, her first trip alone, Mother fastens the key to the box to a chain around her neck, bookish Tom tells her it is a "quest," her father tells her to use her head, and Grandfather deplores his gout, which keeps him from accompanying her. In the care of the stage driver, Nancy, an adventurous child, has a marvelous time though she almost forgets her box at the inn where they eat dinner, and it is found and returned by an old gentleman fellow traveler. When the coach leaves without the old gentleman, Nancy is concerned, and, later, when she sees him trying to catch up in a chaise driven by the innkeeper, she lets her bonnet fly off so the stage driver must stop and let him aboard. At the inn that night, Nancy watches as a swaggering, dashingly dressed guest reads a handbill which offers a reward for a notorious horse thief, Tom Bell, and then suddenly leaves. The next day the coach is overtaken by men chasing the thief, and shortly thereafter they meet a boy peddling toys he has made. Only Nancy recognizes him as the thief from the inn the night before. The boy, named Dave* Tolliver, confesses that he has been playing at being Tom Bell, tells them where to find the real thief, and is given into the care of the old gentleman, who arranges to set him up with a cart as an honest peddler. In the meantime, Nancy has caused confusion the first night at the inn by wandering out to see a pet moose, and, enchanted by the creature, "buying" it from the little black boy named Jezebel*, who cares for it. The next morning, when she discovers her mistake, she tries to make it up to the boy for his punishment by showing him the box and the key, not noticing that the key has slipped off its chain. Later they learn that Jezebel has disappeared, and the old gentleman, whose name is Reuben* Sparks and who turns out to be a friend of Grandfather, sends Dave to help look for him. Before reaching Springfield, Nancy discovers her key is lost. At Springfield, she learns that Uncle Jonathan has gone to a trial at Windsor. She decides to go on to Windsor and catches sight of Jezebel, who runs off, but leaves his red cap, with the key which he was trying to return to her, inside it. At Windsor the trial is proceeding, with a cousin, Silas Newcomb, trying to get rights to the house that Great-grandmother Quincey left to Jonathan, since the will cannot be found. Nancy produces the box, which contains Great-grandmother Quincey's diary in which she has written about making the will and hiding it in the blue teapot. Nancy is able to tell the court where the teapot is, since she herself hid it in a trunk four years before. Dave shows up with his peddler cart, and taking Nancy on his horse behind him, rides across fields, over fences, and through a deep stream to reach the house before Silas. Nancy finds the teapot before Silas can get it and destroy the will. Back at Windsor, Nancy finds her father has come to help and will take her home, that Jezebel has been found and returned to the kindly innkeeper, and, at home, that Reuben Sparks has come for a visit to her Grandfather. Considering the very proper household of the Wadsworth family, the opportunity for the adventure Nancy has is highly improbable, as are the many coincidences of the plot. The attitude toward Jezebel, tolerant in the literary style of the white liberal 1940s, now seems embarrassingly condescending. The story, however does show a good deal about travel, inns, and life of the period, though all as through a rosy glass, far cleaner, safer, and friendlier than it probably was in reality. Fanfare.

FARLEY, WALTER (LORIMER) (1920–), born in Syracuse, N.Y.; author of the all-time most popular series of horse stories. Though a city boy, he always longed for horses and started writing *The Black Stallion** (Random, 1941) when he was attending Erasmus Hall High in Brooklyn, continued it at Mercersberg Academy in Pennsylvania, and at Columbia University. It was published before he entered the 4th Armored Division in 1942 and served there and on the staff of *Yank* until 1946. During that time he wrote the first sequel, which has been followed by more than twenty others. He breeds and races horses and lives in Pennsylvania and Florida. In addition to the many Black Stallion novels, he has written a biography of *Man O' War* (Random, 1962) seen through the eyes of a fictional stableboy.

FARM BOY (Gorsline*, Douglas, ill. author, Viking, 1950), realistic novel of family life with problem story qualities set in western New York State at an unspecified time that appears to be just prior to World War II. Fifteen-year-old John Warner, expelled from the latest in a series of private schools, is sent to live with his great-uncle, Gene Warner, who operates O-at-ka, a large and successful mixed farm. Under his uncle's wise and firm guidance, John changes from a bitter, fearful, self-centered child to a young man who takes pleasure in responsibility, hard work, and getting along with his co-workers. John arrives in March, to be welcomed by his maiden aunts, Martha and Kate, Gene's sisters, and elderly Nora, the demonstrative, eccentric black cook, whose kitchen is her kingdom and who loves to prepare sumptuous feasts. Uncle* Gene, a genial, cigar-smoking, dignified man of about seventy, advises John never to feel sorry for himself, but rather to transfer that energy into observing people and searching for facts to live by, a philosophy that returns time and again to the boy's mind and which he sincerely endeavors to practice. Uncle Gene shows John about the place and then turns him over to Anderson*, his stern, no-nonsense foreman, for instructions. Manuring the barn, feeding the cows, and caring for the calves become John's chief responsibilities, for which he must rise each day at 5:30. John soon gains a new sense of self-esteem from being able to perform these duties to Anderson's satisfaction. Spring, summer, and fall bring their particular duties, and John helps wherever he is needed. He assists Paddy*, the old Irish handyman, to make the garden, makes hay, and once even helps Ernie, the milkman, deliver milk to the Warner cutomers on his pre-dawn run. John earns a stern lecture from Uncle Gene when he refuses to fill in for George*, the unreliable milkhouse man. Uncle Gene impresses upon the youth the need to do whatever must be done to keep the farm running smoothly. In mid-summer, John has a scary adventure. He goes for a walk in the countryside, where he sees an idling freight train, climbs into an open car, and soon finds himself going for an unexpected ride. After walking and hitchhiking the fifty miles back to the farm, John reflects that the experience and the farm labor have given him a new and welcome sense of self-sufficiency. Grateful for what Uncle Gene has done for him, he persuades the old man to offer a home to Blackie*, a runaway from the local county Work Farm, who has sought refuge in the willows by the Warner pond. John tells Uncle Gene how much he has come to enjoy life on the farm, and Uncle Gene confides that some day he would like to turn the operation of the farm over to John completely. Late September brings a bountiful harvest and Uncle Gene's annual Harvest Dinner for neighbors and relatives. John's mother and father drive out from New York City to attend and take the boy back to the city for school. John is a plaster figure, too acquiescent to be credible. He accepts his situation too readily and changes too quickly. The remaining characters are stock, and, of them, Blackie is the least convincing. The bland, episodic plot showcases life on a well-run farm; the book's strength lies in such details. Themes are obvious; stressed are respect for nature, the beauty of the seasons, doing one's best, cooperation, unselfishness, knowing one's trade, and respect for authority. Attitudes and activities date this instructive book. Fanfare.

FARMER BOY (Wilder*, Laura Ingalls, ill. Helen Sewell, Harper, 1933), biographical novel recording a little more than a year in the childhood of the author's husband on the prosperous family farm near Malone, in northern New York State, in the years 1866–1868. Almanzo* Wilder, nearly nine when the story starts, has one brother, Royal*, 13, and two sisters, bossy Eliza* Jane, 12, and lively Alice*, 10. Together they trudge through the snow the mile and a half to the schoolhouse at the foot of Hardscrabble Hill, and before and after school the boys help with the chores and the girls help with the housework, though sometimes Alice works in the fields and Almanzo is pressed into service for housecleaning, churning, candle-making, and other women's work. Most of the book details the day-to-day and seasonal work of the big farm, feeding stock, cutting ice, loading and hauling potatoes, planting, harrowing, hoeing the crops, washing and shearing sheep, harvesting, threshing, hauling wood, baling hay for sale, building and repairing the equipment—all told with remarkable clarity and interest in third person but consistently from the point of view of Almanzo. Most of the work is done by the family members with occasional help from French Joe and Lazy John, trappers who live in cabins nearby. There are special joyful times: the whole family goes berrying in the late summer, and Alice and Almanzo help with gathering beech nuts in the fall; the traveling tinsmith visits and the jolly cobbler, who makes Almanzo's first pair of boots to replace his moccasins; relatives come for Christmas, and Almanzo gets a store-bought cap and a pocket knife; they attend the Malone celebration of Independence Day, when Almanzo, egged on by his cousin Frank, asks Father for a nickel and gets a half-dollar and a lesson in saving and investment; they spend three days at the county fair where Almanzo's milk-fed pumpkin wins a blue ribbon. There are also problems: while cutting ice, Almanzo nearly slips into the open water hole and narrowly escapes a whipping for carelessness; his inexperienced oxen flounder in deep snow while he's hauling wood, but he persists though injured; when Father sells colts to a strange buyer, Mother worries all night at keeping $200 in the house, but a stray dog which Alice has fed drives off thieves; a late spring freeze threatens the young corn and the whole family spends the night pouring water on the plants to save them. Special episodes include the day the tough Hardscrabble Settlement boys decide to break up the school and mild Mr. Corse, the teacher, cows them and beats them with Mr. Wilder's fifteen-foot-long ox whip. On Almanzo's ninth birthday, Father gives him a little yoke for his ox calves, Star and Bright, and lets him start to train them. He also gets a sled Father has made. Father and Mother must visit relatives for a week, leaving the children on their own. They make ice cream, cake, and candy until they almost use up the sugar, and they neglect the garden and housework until the last day. Then in the mad scramble to finish all the work, Eliza Jane gets so bossy that Almanzo throws the stove-blacking brush at her, misses, and hits the parlor wall. Terrified and expecting a whipping, Almanzo hides in the hay but learns that Eliza Jane has so cleverly patched the spot with scraps of wallpaper that their parents never know. Riding to town on the wagon of baled hay, Almanzo spots a pocketbook containing $1500. His father suspects that it belongs to miserly Mr. Thompson and sends Almanzo to return it. He tracks the man down in the shop of Mr. Paddock, the wheelwright, and is insulted when he is suspected of stealing some of the money and given a nickel reward. Paddock furiously forces Thompson to give Almanzo two hundred dollars, then offers to make the boy his apprentice. Almanzo opts to be a farmer, and his father gives him Starlight, the beautiful colt he has coveted so long. The book gives a remarkable sense of life on a prosperous, well-managed farm and provides a strong contrast to the stories of Laura* Ingalls's childhood on marginal frontier homesteads. Though a fascinating picture of farming in that period, the book is most remarkable for its descriptions of food. On almost every page something good to eat is lovingly described with enthusiasm that surpasses even Almanzo's love of horses. A later edition is illustrated by Garth Williams. Choice.

FATHER (*A Lemon and a Star**; *Terrible, Horrible Edie†*; *Edie on the Warpath†*), John Cares, in a series of episodic amusing novels set in Massachusetts in the early twentieth century. Explosive and dictatorial, he is respected but avoided as much as possible by his four children and only partially tamed by Madam*, his second wife. Although he works at "business" in Charlottesville, they live on a large estate-like farm adjoining the dairy farms of relatives—his sister Charlotte, his father, his brother Charlie. Occasionally he decides the children need discipline or hardening, and he sets up rules or organizes them with a sort of Teddy Roosevelt spirit, but much of the time, if they can manage it, he has little idea of what they are doing.

FATHER AMBROSE (*That Girl of Pierre's**), the priest in the village of Arsac-le-Petit, France. An old man who has served the village for many years, he is highly regarded, and people come to him for advice. Since he knows everyone in the village well, he is able to make sage suggestions. Danielle goes to him for advice about how to support her family. He suffers from asthma, and everyone is careful to keep him from exerting himself.

FATHER BELLACOSA (*The Marble Fountain**), beloved priest in the village of Rosa. During the village clean-up campaign, he discovers in the church a long-lost diary written by a priest of the church in 1510. The diary indicates that the priest ordered that the statue of St. Francis and other treasures of the church be buried in a particular place in the hills overlooking the village so that they would not fall into the hands of the invaders who were about to attack the village.

FAULKNER, GEORGENE (1873–1958), born in Chicago, Ill.; storyteller, author of *White Elephant, and Other Tales from Old India* (Wise-Parslov, 1929). She was educated at Kenworth Institute, National Kindergarten College, and the University of Chicago. She was an editor for *Ladies' Home Journal* and, with John Becker*, wrote *Melindy's Medal** (Messner, 1945), an early book for younger readers with a seriously treated black protagonist.

FAUSTINA CHAVEZ (*. . . And Now Miguel**), Miguel's little sister, whose habit of repeating nonsense words over and over again sometimes annoys Miguel, but he is very fond of her. Like Pedro*, she understands Miguel's longing to go to the mountains. She brings him the news, while he is fishing at the stream near the house, that a letter has come for Gabriel*, and that because of the letter Miguel must go to the mountains this year. Miguel takes the letter and hides it, in a naive effort to keep Gabriel from being drafted. This action leads to the long conversation between the two brothers, Miguel's acceptance of the inevitable, and his longed-for trip to the mountains.

FERN ARABLE (*Charlotte's Web**), tender-hearted, imaginative farm girl who persuades her father not to kill the runt pig, Wilbur*. After he has been sold to her uncle, Homer Zuckerman*, she visits him and sits by his pen, understanding the animals' conversation but never joining in. At the fair, her attention is diverted from the pig when she rides the Ferris wheel with Henry Fussy, and it is apparent that Fern is growing out of her fascination with pets.

FERRIS, ELMER (1861–1951), author of three books for young people based on his own early life in Wisconsin, *Jerry of Seven Mile Creek** (Doubleday, 1938), *Jerry at the Academy* (Doubleday, 1940), about the Wayland Academy in Beaver Dam, Wis., which he attended from 1878 to 1881, and . . . *Jerry Foster, Salesman* (Doubleday, 1942). His other books are nonfiction, mostly about business, including a text, *Salesmanship* (Roland, 1924), which went into many editions.

FIELD, RACHEL (LYMAN) (1894–1942), born in New York City; dramatist, poet, widely popular novelist. She attended Springfield High School and Radcliffe College and was a member of the editorial department of Famous Players-Lasky film company in Hollywood, 1918–1923. In 1918 she was recipient of the Drama League of America Prize. For children her interest in drama resulted in ten books of plays; she also wrote six books of verse and thirteen works of fiction for children, and for adults plays, verse, and novels, including the best-selling romantic biography, *All This and Heaven, Too* (Macmillan, 1938). A wooden doll which both she and artist Dorothy Lathrop* admired in an antique dealer's window was the inspiration for her Newbery-winning *Hitty: Her First Hundred Years** (Macmillan, 1929), illustrated by Lathrop. The Maine coast where she spent the summer for most of her adult life is the setting for perhaps her best novel for young people, *Calico Bush** (Macmillan, 1931).

FIERCE-FACE: THE STORY OF A TIGER (Mukerji*, Dhan Gopal, ill. Dorothy P. Lathrop*, Dutton, 1936), short animal novel with fantasy aspects that purports to be the "biography of a tiger." It is set in India at an indeterminate time and presents "some information about the jungle through the life of a tiger." The narrative follows Fierce-Face from birth to first mating, presenting him as typical of young males of the species. When he is only a few months old, Bagni, his mother, fights his father to save her cub's life after Fierce-Face has inadvertently incurred the elder tiger's anger by getting between him and his prey. After she drives the male away, Bagni begins her cub's education, teaching him how to select and stalk prey, to defend himself against animals and human enemies, and to drive away those who might challenge his territory. During the dry season, a man-eating tiger poses a threat to the mother and son by attracting the attention of the humans who live near by. The two tigers cleverly arrange his capture. Food becomes very scarce as the drought advances, and the two are disappointed when they fail to down a buffalo. They wander the jungle in their quest for food, passing through the place where tigers go to die, and survive the forest fire brought on by the drought. They escape by immersing themselves in a river, where Bagni both saves her son's life and secures food for them by killing a python. After the rainy season begins, Bagni takes another mate, and Fierce-Face leaves for a life of his own. He soon encounters a young female, which he calls Light-Leap because she is so graceful, and fights another young male to win her. The last paragraph of the novel leaps ahead one year to the birth of their cubs. Sometimes the point of view is that of the author, sometimes that of the tigers. The author anthropomorphizes the animals, but neither grotesquely nor sentimentally. He reports their thoughts, attributes to them powers of logical reasoning and the ability to live by definite rules and to plan, though the system by which they are governed never approaches the complexity of Kipling's Law of the Jungle, and only occasionally does he give the animals human speech. The book is mostly summarized narrative, with short, simple sentences that heighten the drama of the action scenes. Some language is quite mature, but the storytelling atmosphere carries readers along. Descriptive passages are rich and vivid with sensory imagery and figures of speech. Black and white drawings contribute to the setting and atmosphere. Fanfare.

FISCHER, MARJORIE (1903–1961), author of a number of novels including *Street Fair** (Smith, 1935), a lighthearted story of two youngsters in a series of misadventures that carry them through France. With the poet, Rolfe Humphries, she edited two books of stories of the marvelous, mysterious, and strange, *Pause to Wonder* (Messner, 1944) and *Strange to Tell* (Messner, 1946). Among her other books are *Palaces on Monday* (Random House, 1936), *Red Feather* (McLeod, 1937), *Embarrassment of Riches* (Random House, 1944), and *Mrs. Sherman's Summer* (Lippincott, 1960).

FISHER, CYRUS (DARWIN TEILHET) (1904–   ), born in Wyanette, Ill.; mystery writer and novelist. He attended Drake University, Stanford University, the University of Paris, and Heidelberg University, and has worked in consumer marketing. Starting in the 1930s, he has written a great many books under his own name and, for young people, under the pseudonym of Cyrus Fisher, wrote *The Avion My Uncle Flew** (Appleton, 1946) and *Ab Carmody's Treasure* (Holt, 1948). His hobby is flying, an interest reflected in several of his books, including *Murder in the Air* (Grosset, 1932) and *Death Flew High* (Morrow, 1931).

FIVE BUSHEL FARM (Coatsworth*†, Elizabeth, ill. Helen Sewell, Macmillan, 1939), historical novel set in New England in 1790, continuing events begun in *Away Goes Sally**. When Mrs. Titcomb dreams that Captain Patterson of the *Fair American* has been lost at sea, she and her husband leave Philadelphia for New England, taking with them their ward, the Captain's son, unhappy, lonely Andrew, about eleven. In Happy Valley, Maine, on the Penobscot River, they leave Andrew with the Hallets in what proves to be a long, bitter winter for the boy. Spring brings the arrival of the Hallets' cousins, the Smiths, who have emigrated from Hingham, Mass. Among the numerous group are lighthearted, ten-year-old Sally*, and her kind, pretty Aunt* Deborah, who rescues Andrew from unfeeling Mrs. Hallet and sends out notices for information about Andrew's father. The summer is filled with joyful adventures for Sally and Andrew with berry picking, Indians, a wedding by the river, and housebuilding for Sally's family. Through one of Aunt Debby's notices, Captain Patterson is reunited with his son, and subsequently he and Aunt Debby fall in love and get married. The story concludes with a great houseraising celebration at which Sally names her new home "Five Bushel Farm" in memory of the purchase of the land from the local Indians for five bushels of cornmeal. This book, the second in the series about the Smiths, authentically portrays pioneer life for younger readers. The simple, occasionally sentimental story is plausible and well sustained. It is sometimes hard to keep the many characters straight, but the main ones are drawn with insight. Fanfare.

5 THALLO STREET (*The Wonderful Flight to the Mushroom Planet**; *Stowaway to the Mushroom Planet**; *Time and Mr. Bass*†), where Mr. Tyco* Bass lives in Pacific Grove, California. His house is dome-shaped like a mushroom, with a telescope jutting out from the dome. Within the dome is a perfectly outfitted laboratory, and Tyco has a workroom in the basement. The house becomes the headquarters for the Society of Young Astronomers and Students of Space Travel. The Mushroom Planet Books start and conclude on Thallo Street.

FLAG OF THE DESERT (Best*, Herbert, ill. Erick Berry*, Viking, 1936), adventure novel set in the early 1930s in Nigeria, then British-held territory in West Africa, mostly in the northern area near the edge of the Sahara Desert. Two British boys of high-school age, Bill Griffiths and Terry Cordell, become involved in three adventures which are nearly unrelated: the recapturing of a stolen white racing camel, the Pearl, owned by the Emir of Kornu; the deposition of Moyi*, chief priest of the Jukon tribe, who has seized power, and the reestablishment of the rightful Aku or local chief; and the capture of Mallam Fuskaddare*, The Face at Nightfall, a mysterious agitator who is preaching for a *Jihad*, a Holy War of Islam against the white rulers. Terry, whose father is the District Officer, is a hyperactive type, continually dragging the more sedentary Bill, son of the Superintendent of Education, into his activities and adventures. At Terry's insistence, they have learned Morse Code and practiced sending messages with flags. When the camel disappears, Terry, left behind when Bill and his father visit a northern outpost, sees with powerful binoculars that a camel, obviously the Pearl, is easily outdistancing its pursuers and will reach French-held territory if not stopped first. He rigs a makeshift heliograph with a mirror and sends a message in Morse. Although Bill does not interpret the entire message correctly, he does intercept the fleeing camel. The second adventure occurs in the Benue River area where Terry's father has been posted to clear up some mysterious political problems and where Bill's father is transferred. In the bush country of the Jukon tribe, the last Aku has been dead for three years, and the head priest, Moyi, has not called the elders to elect a new one, as he should, but has instead set up a rule of terror in which most of those eligible for the position have been murdered. There are left only three, a madman, a woman, and a boy, Tamna*, who realizes that his days are numbered. Pressed by Terry's father, Moyi finally calls the elders to the sacred spot, the Pujé, hoping to elect the madman so he can rule, using him as a puppet. Terry and Bill, however have rigged a loud speaker in the sacred tree and get Tamna to impersonate the voice of his ancestors, saying that only Tamna should be chosen. The rejoicing villagers then throw off the rule of Moyi, and Tamna becomes Aku. The third adventure occurs back in a village near Kornu, where Terry, disguised as a native boy, overhears Fuskaddare inciting a group to *Jihad*. Since Terry's father has been called away on a wild goose chase, Bill's father sends a message to the Emir, but the messenger is found murdered. Terry and Bill undertake to ride with the message to Kornu. There the Emir enlists their help to intercept Fuskaddare, who is on foot, by sending them on the Pearl and another racing camel, with his eldest son disguised as their baggage boy, hoping they can entice the terrorist to shoot at them in French-held territory so the French will arrest him. On the camels they travel a longer route, hitting Fuskaddare's trail beyond where he is. Terry, however, collapses from the heat, and the Emir's son backtracks to get help, only to have Fuskaddare steal his camel. When the terrorist approaches, the boys pretend to be praying and when he joins them in prayer, they capture him. Fuskaddare is executed, and the boys, who have dreaded going back to England for college, are invited to enter the college at the Gold Coast as the first white pupils. Though the connection between the three parts is too loose to give the book much unity, the pace of the adventure makes the story lively. Modern readers may have trouble with the fact that the continual and preferred sport of the boys is shooting—at almost any game available. Also, the boys seem untouched by any doubts about the rightness of colonial rule, though they have a strong interest in and respect for the natives and their cultures. Mothers are conveniently never mentioned, and the fathers are stock figures, but as an adventure story of the period there is enough action for three books. Fanfare.

FLAMING ARROWS (Steele*, William O., ill. Paul Galdone, Harcourt, 1957), historical novel for middle readers set in the Cumberland settlements in the 1780s. At eleven, Chad Rabun is proud to do a good day's work clearing land with his father and to be old enough to carry a musket. In the middle of the night, warned by a neighbor, the Rabun family—Chad, his parents, his sister, Sarah, 9, and brother Ambrose, 5—flee to the fort with the other nearby families to escape raiding Chickamauga Indians. There they are organized by Colonel Abijah Boyd, an officious ex-militia officer. When the family of "Traitor" Logan, a no-good suspected of working with the Indians, show up, Boyd tries to deny the woman, her two sons and baby, entrance, but Mr. Rabun insists that they be allowed to stay and offers to feed them from his supplies. All the children are set to carry water from the stream, since the spring in the fort is almost dry, and before they dip up much, shots ring out and they must run for the fort. Amos* Thompson, owner of the block house, a scout and Indian fighter, reports that there are some fifty Indians, evidently tipped off that this is the weakest fort, defended by only nine men and a dozen boys with guns. Led by Boyd, the settlers start to vote to turn the Logans out, thinking that Traitor is to blame, but Amos reminds the Colonel that it is his fort and says that the Logans stay. The other boys Chad's age shun him for his father's stand, and he directs his anger toward Josiah Logan, a boy about his age. When the men set out to get water, Indians attack, and Chad shoots one down in time to save his father but is shamed by having left his powder horn behind so he can't reload. That night one young man sets off to ride to the next fort for help. In the morning his body is seen, headless, propped against a stump. As the settlers get thirstier and testier, a couple try to force Josiah and his mother from the fort. Chad protests, kicks and bites the man, and is interrupted by Amos's shot of an Indian climbing over the walls. They fight off the attack and wait, tense, for worse. That night Amos goes off afoot to get help, and the Indians attack with flaming arrows. With no water to quench fires, the defenders are hard pressed to subdue the blazes. At the worst of the attack, some dry, rotted logs in the section Chad is defending catch fire. He chops them out, while Boyd, feverish and illogical, protests. A burning log falls on Boyd, and Chad beats the flames out with his hands. Later, he and Josiah hear someone at the wall and discover Mrs. Boyd, sneaking out to try to get water for her delirious husband. Josiah takes her bucket and goes for her. This act, on top of what Chad has learned of Josiah's supporting his family after Traitor has left them, confirms the boy's bravery to Chad, and when Amos returns with men, drives off the Indians, and they can all start for home, the two boys are friends. The action is fast paced and believable, characters well delineated, and the central conflict of blame by family association is clear but not overly didactic. No attempt, however, is made to see the Indians' point of view, and their portrayal as simply evil dates the novel. Choice.

FLEMING, WALDO (THAMES ROSS WILLIAMSON) (1894–), born on an Indian reservation near Genessee, Idaho, where his father, a former scout, was a trader; professor and author of many novels for adults and young people. A man of varied interests and extensive travel, he has had an extremely colorful career. He ran away from home in his teens and lived as a tramp for a while. He was a railroad worker, shepherd, circus roustabout, and newspaper reporter and traveled throughout the West, to Peru, and to Alaska. He became fluent in ten languages and once served as interpreter at Hull House in Chicago in Italian, Spanish, and Greek. After receiving his B.A. degree from the University of Iowa and his M.A. from Harvard, he taught economics at Simmons College and economics and sociology at Smith. The proceeds from the several texts he published enabled him to devote his full time to writing fiction. He published over four dozen books of fiction, period novels, mysteries, adventure stories, and non-fiction for adults and teenagers. He wrote for young people under several pseudonyms, including S. S. Smith, Edward Dagonet, Gregory Trent, and De Wolfe Morgan. As Waldo Fleming he wrote fast-moving mystery-adventures for boys, among them *The Lost Caravan* (Doubleday, 1935), a story of the Sahara; *Talking Drums** (Doubleday, 1936), a story set in the Gold Coast that was selected by the editors of *Horn Book* for their Fanfare list; *A Riddle in Fez* (Doubleday, 1937), set in Morocco; and *The Pygmy's Arrow* (Lothrop,1938), set in the Belgian Congo.

FLOATING ISLAND (Parrish*, Anne, ill. author, Harper, 1930), doll fantasy set mainly on a tropical island where a doll house has been washed ashore after a shipwreck. The characters, Mr. and Mrs. Doll, their children, William, Annabel, and Baby, Dinah the black cook, and an assortment of plaster food items on plates—Finny, a fish, Lobby, a lobster, Chicky, a chicken, and Pudding—have been separated in the wreck and the story consists of their efforts and eventual success in finding each other. By setting the story where there are no humans, except for the sailors who eventually find and rescue the doll house, the author avoids the usual illogic of doll stories in which the characters have self-will but must be maneuvered by humans. The story is full of asides to youngsters. (It starts: "Children, I need your help. Somewhere in the world is a Doll House, with a family of Dolls living in it. Can any of you tell me where?") It is about one-third footnotes, also in the same cozy tone, giving further information about the flora and fauna, the shipwreck, and other elements of the action. The characterization of Dinah, who finds she has a great deal in common with the monkeys and chooses to stay with them, would make the book unacceptable to modern audiences even if the tone and the relatively slow action did not date it. Newbery Honor.

FLYING CLOUD (*All Sail Set**), historical clipper ship designed and built by Donald McKay of Boston and launched April 15, 1851, on which Enoch* Thatcher is an apprentice. In the fictional story, Enoch saves the ship from a fire set by a hate-crazed mutineer. In both fact and fiction the ship makes a record run from Boston to San Francisco in eighty-nine days. In fact, the ship continued to sail until 1874, a relatively long life for the hard-driven clippers.

THE FLYING LOCOMOTIVE (Du Bois*†, William Pène, ill. author, Viking, 1941), brief fantasy set in 1909 in Switzerland. When two identical locomotives are completed in the railway yards at Basil, the workmen spin them on the turntable to decide which shall become one of the famous Swiss Flyers and which shall be sent to Gruyères to deliver cheese. The story follows the fortunes of the cheese engine, later known as Toto No. 2. This locomotive is even further humiliated to share its shed with Madame Susie, a prize cow, who arrives with much fanfare on the same day. At first he ignores his neighbor, but, needing an audience, he soon encourages evening visits from Madame Susie, during which he boasts about his punctual service on the route and confides his great desire to be a flyer. Madame Susie, who has a sweet, understanding nature, encourages him and promises to pray that his wish be fulfilled, and that very evening, a beautiful gold locomotive appears to him, announces that it is his fairy godmother, and grants his wish to be a flyer, without waiting to hear that he means one of the trains called Swiss Flyers. That evening Madame Susie clambers into his coal tender to guide him, and they take off on their flight. Toto No. 2 finds it difficult to direct himself without tracks, and the cow, unable to see clearly, guides him into a lake, and a tree, and onto the dome of a large building. To get a better look, she climbs down the rope ladder and falls off. Disconsolately, Toto No. 2 makes his way back to his shed but is delighted when he hears the townspeople cheering for Madame Susie the Flying Cow. He learns that she fell into a big snow drift and was able to carry an exhausted mountain climber to safety. Reunited, they both do their jobs happily. The story is told with illustrations on every page in the mock-serious tone of a report, which adds humor to a rather simple plot. Fanfare.

FODDERWING FORRESTER (*The Yearling**), crippled, addle-witted youngest son in the rough, backwoods family. As Penny* Baxter says, ''He's the second settin' and he ain't to blame for hatchin' out peculiar.'' Fodderwing got his name from attaching cow-pea hay to his arms, thinking something so light and airy could make him fly, and jumping from the barn roof. Though deformed and ''witless,'' he is sweetly gentle among the six large, hard-drinking older brothers, and has a way with animals that makes them trust him. His death devastates the noisy, quarrelsome family. It is he who has given the name ''Flag'' to Jody's fawn.

FOG MAGIC (Sauer*, Julia, ill. Lynd Ward, Viking, 1943), time fantasy set in Nova Scotia in the mid-twentieth century. Greta Addington, 11, is the only child in the village of Little Valley who loves the fog, a fascination that worries her mother but that her father seems to understand. She discovers that when she goes over the mountain to Blue Cove on foggy days, she goes back in time to Victorian days, when a thriving village existed there. She meets Retha Morrill, about her own age, and Retha's mother, Laura, who seems to understand that she comes from a different time. Greta is drawn in, though mainly as an observer, to the stories of Blue Cove, of the legless foreign sailor marooned there, of the servant girl, Ann, who flees after wrongly being accused of theft, of the widow who walks to Halifax and contrives to meet the Duke of Kent and get justice against the man who usurped her land, of the captain's bride who seizes the ship when he dies so she can bring his body back for burial. On her twelfth birthday, Greta realizes that she will not be able to return again but that her father has had a similar experience, presumably when Laura Morrill was young. The story has a sweet charm, but the fantasy is never convincing and the action lacks tension. Characterization is minimal. The best quality is the evocative mood of the setting. Newbery Honor.

FOG SMITH (*The Iron Duke**), J. Faugeres Smith, the roommate of Jim Wellington and Mickey* McGuire at Harvard. He is wealthy, a good student, and highly involved in extracurricular activities. From Groton and Long Island, impeccably well mannered, he knows everyone worth knowing socially at Harvard, but he is no snob, and Jim regards him as a "darn good guy." Fun-loving, gregarious, and energetic, he comes up with the ideas for such escapades as reporting the proceedings of the Fly Club meeting in an amplified broadcast and publishing a hoax account of the selection of a new Harvard president.

FORBES, ESTHER (1891–1967), born in Westborough, Mass.; historical novelist, short story writer, and biographer. She grew up in New England, her father a judge and her mother a historian. Her reputation in the area of children's literature rests solidly on her only book of fiction for young readers, *Johnny Tremain** (Houghton, 1943), considered by many critics and others as the classic novel of American historical fiction for the young. About an apprentice silversmith in Boston who becomes involved in the Revolutionary movement, this now highly familiar novel has been praised for its excellent blend of story and research. It received the Newbery Medal, was chosen for Fanfare, and is cited in *Choice, Children's Books Too Good to Miss,* and Children's Classics. A graduate of Bradford Junior College, Forbes also studied at the University of Wisconsin, and from 1920 until her marriage in 1926 she served with the editorial staff of Houghton Mifflin Publishing Co. Author of six historical and period novels and four books of non-fiction for adults, she received the Pulitzer Prize in history in 1942 for her adult biography, *Paul Revere and the World He Lived In* (Houghton, 1942). While researching and writing this book, she became interested in the lives of apprentices of the period, and her investigations plus the concern for freedom and the rights of ordinary human beings occasioned by World War II resulted in *Johnny Tremain*. The biography *America's Paul Revere* (Houghton, 1946), intended for younger readers and her only other book for children, summarizes the main achievements of the Revolutionary hero's life in an edition evocatively illustrated by Lynd Ward. Her best-known adult novels are *The Running of the Tide* (Houghton, 1948), which was filmed, *Rainbow on the Road* (Houghton, 1954), which was made into a musical, and the very ambitious *Paradise* (Harcourt, 1937), which is about Massachusetts at the time of King Philip's War. She made her home in Worcester, Mass.

THE FORGOTTEN DAUGHTER (Snedeker*, Caroline Dale, ill. Dorothy Lathrop*, Doubleday, 1933), historical novel set in the city of Rome and the hills near Rome in the second century B.C. Chloe*, daughter of Laevinus, Roman centurion, is born into slavery on the villa Caracinia in the Samnium Hills after her father mysteriously abandons her Greek-born mother after two years of marriage. She grows up in a wretched hut, cared for by the faithful Melissa, her dead mother's dear friend, and hating her father for condemning her to a miserable life of unending labor, hunger, and whippings. In her free moments, she dreams of Lesbos, the island from which her mother and Melissa were torn by the Romans, sings with Melissa songs from Greek poets, and wanders the hills from where she observes the expert horsemanship of young, highborn Aulus* Cornelius Maro, whose family owns the Villa Cornelia next door. After a period of service in Spain, Aulus, a centurion, returns to Rome, becoming a partisan of Tiberius Gracchus, tribune of the people, who has embarked on a program of land reform involving redistribution of land to the poor. When Tiberius is murdered by his political enemies, his mother, the gentle, practical Cornelia, helps Aulus escape from the city to the Villa Cornelia. He and Chloe meet when she rescues him from an animal trap into which he has fallen. The two fall in love, and he learns later her true identity. After a plague devastates Rome and carries off Laevinus's wife and two children, he returns to his villa for solace. He becomes reconciled with Chloe, of whose existence he had been unaware, and the story of why he abandoned his daughter comes out. Since his father had opposed his marriage to Chloe's mother, he had been led to believe that both mother and child were dead. He happily arranges a marriage between Chloe and Aulus. Careful, extensive research into the period strengthens this sentimental romance, and the brief appearances of Tiberius Gracchus and his mother, Cornelia, provide substance. The plights of Chloe and Melissa and Aulus's involvement with Tiberius capture interest if strain credibility occasionally, but the potential for character development remains unrealized and many moralistic statements, didactic passages about Roman customs and the nature of life among the ancients, and the author's personal judgments about things inhibit the flow of the narrative. Newbery Honor.

FOX, J. C. (*Seven Stars for Catfish Bend**), one of the seven animals awarded a silver star for heroism in ridding the bayou of hunters. Smart alecky and a show off, he talks a lot and makes much noise but can always be counted upon in a pinch. When Old Joe, the hunting alligator, is tried *in absentia*, J. C. acts his part during the trial. He helps Doc Raccoon make Old Joe swallow the jug, that is, actually swallow a jug, which prevents him from submerging and sneaking up on the animals to catch them.

FRALEY, BOB (*Big Red**), impatient, unpleasant dog handler who works for Mr.* Haggin on his Wintapi estate. He lacks sensitivity for the animals with which he works and would have beaten Red for straying if Danny and Mr. Haggin had not intervened. He does not have the ability to bring out the best in the dogs.

FRANCIE AND LIAM O'SULLIVAN (*The Cottage at Bantry Bay**; *Pegeen**; *Francie on the Run**), twins, they amuse and sometimes distress the family with their antics, some of which are merely mischievous, some well-intentioned efforts gone awry. They sometimes pretend to be Irish heroes whose thrilling stories they have heard by the fireside. One night they get lost in a terrible thunderstorm, in which they think the thunder is the sound of the guns during the conflict for Irish independence, and during the picnic on the island they give the family a terrific scare when they set out to explore by themselves in the rowboat. They remain steadfastly loyal to Pegeen and defend her when she gets into trouble. Of the two, Francie is the spunkier and the more memorable as a character. He is sometimes stubborn and willful, a little spoiled because of his disability, clearly the family favorite. Liam is the more tenderhearted and has a special fondness for animals and birds that have been injured or are sick.

FRANCIE ON THE RUN (Van Stockum*†, Hilda, ill. author, Viking, 1939), realistic adventure story set in Ireland, the second in the series about the O'Sullivans, following *The Cottage at Bantry Bay**. Spunky, individualistic Francie*, 5, tired of the hospital routine and lonely for his family, escapes from the Dublin hospital, where he has been staying for seven months while the doctors operate on his club foot, and has a series of adventures in the Irish countryside before he reaches County Cork again. He wanders through Dublin, sits in on a lecture in Trinity College, and unwittingly boards the wrong train. A fellow passenger, grizzle-headed Tim Gallagher, takes him home for the night and the next day puts him on a bus. Francie thinks the bus is going wrong, gets off, and trudges along the country road until he is picked up by kind, wistful Captain McDermott, who lives in a castle in the forest with his crotchety old mother. That night Francie has a dream about little people which leads to a reconciliation between Mrs. McDermott and White Lady, the blooded horse which caused her husband's death and which she and her son now anticipate may restore the family fortunes. Captain McDermott's rickety old car breaks down on the next leg of Francie's journey. While the Captain seeks help, fiery Pegeen Murphy, about Francie's age, comes by, chasing the Murphys' runaway pig. Francie leaves to help her, and the two children get lost in a sudden mountain mist. Father Kelly comes upon them, restores Pegeen to her grandmother, and takes Francie to his home and then with him on a visit to parishioners on the Aran Isles. There Francie makes friends with formidable, heavy-fisted Murteen O'Shea, whom Francie first thinks is a girl because he wears skirts, in the local fashion. A steamer ride takes Francie and the priest to Galway and a *feis* (storytelling and musical contest), where Francie encounters Paddy* the Piper, who takes him back to the welcoming arms of his family. Characters are well drawn, and the well-paced plot moves along with plenty of action and dialogue and just enough episodes to satisfy a later elementary reader. As readers follow Francie they see different sides of Irish life. Old stories and poems contribute to setting. Companion book is *Pegeen**. Fanfare.

FRITZ†, JEAN (GUTTERY) (1915–   ), born in Hankow, China; author noted in children's literature for her well-researched American historical novels for older children and her amusing, authentic biographies of early American figures for younger readers. Her parents were missionaries, and she lived in

China until she was thirteen, attending a British school and *in absentia* developing a deep curiosity and affection for America. She graduated from Wheaton College in Massachusetts and continued her studies at Columbia. She married Michael Fritz, who has been affiliated with the Hudson Laboratory at Columbia, and the couple has made their home in Dobbs Ferry, N.Y. In 1952, she started a children's room in the Dobbs Ferry library, and working there sparked her interest in writing children's books of her own. Since 1954, she has published over two dozen books for children and young adults, including picture books, animal stories, and books of non-fiction, as well as the historical novels and period pieces and lively, humorous biographies for which she is most acclaimed by critics. For younger readers, *The Cabin Faced West** (Coward, 1958) tells what happens when a little pioneer girl meets George Washington. Based on an incident in the life of Fritz's own pioneer great-great-grandmother, this book is listed in *Choice*. More substantial are her novels for older readers, *Brady*† (Coward, 1960), *I, Adam*† (Coward, 1963), and *Early Thunder*† (Coward, 1967), all involving boy protagonists, all set before the Civil War, and all the recipients of critical citations. Her popular, highly regarded, authentic picture-book biographies, intended to give children realistic views of historical figures, include *Why Don't You Get a Horse, Sam Adams?* (Coward, 1974) and *What's the Big Idea, Ben Franklin?* (Coward, 1976). She has written for Silver Burdett Co., been a research librarian, directed several writing workshops, and taught at Appalachian State University in South Carolina. She is often asked to speak on children's literature and has contributed short stories to national magazines and written a non-fiction book for adults, *Cast for a Revolution: Some American Friends and Enemies, 1728–1814* (Houghton, 1972). Her autobiography is *Homesick: My Own Story*† (Putnam, 1982), and she was nominated for the Laura Ingalls Wilder Award in 1983.

FROG (*Seven Stars for Catfish Bend**), one of the seven animals awarded a silver star for heroism in ridding the bayou of hunters. He is a talented old fellow who trains the young frogs for the Indian Bayou Glee Club concerts at Catfish Bend.

FU BE BE (*Young Fu of the Upper Yangtze**), mother of Young* Fu, a scolding, worried, penny-pinching, hardworking widow tied to the superstitions of the past. Although she hates and fears the city, she is willing to live there and put in long hours at sorting pig bristles so that her son can have a chance to learn a skilled trade. With her bound feet and her belief that dragons of fire, flood, and disease cause human suffering, she represents the old ways being challenged and changed by the foreigners and the natives of her son's generation.

FUSKADDARE (*Flag of the Desert**), the Face at Nightfall, the mysterious preacher who is inciting the natives to a *Jihad*, a Holy War of Islam against the British and French colonial rulers. When captured by Terry and Bill, who pretend to be devout Moslems praying until he joins them in prayer, he believes they are professional spies and therefore brothers in the international game. He admits to being a white man in the employ of a "distant power," and, riding behind Terry on his camel, spends the night telling him stories of his exploits, stories that Terry, terrified by his temporary blindness from sunstroke, scarcely understands. Knowing that he will be executed, Fuskaddare requests only that a white man will be present so he will remain proud enough not to flinch, a request fulfilled by Terry's father.

G

GABRIEL CHAVEZ (*. . . And Now Miguel**), Miguel's nineteen-year-old brother and, according to Miguel, the greatest man in the world, next to his father, grandfather, and uncles. Miguel says that Gabriel excels at everything he sets his hand to and has no wants because he gets everything he wants. Miguel sees Gabriel as a kind and loving big brother, who tries with patience and without condescension to help Miguel understand that his being drafted is not the result of Miguel's prayer. He says he too has had unsatisfied longings, yearnings that Miguel has not known about. He too has prayed for the opportunity to leave the valley and see something of the world. Ironically, his being drafted fulfills his wish. Although the long conversation between the two brothers holds up the story and goes on too long, it does reveal the brothers well.

GAGGIN, EVA (ROE) (1879–   ), novelist for children, whose books reveal the author's varied interests and narrative techniques. Two books are spirited stories of family life, *An Ear for Uncle Emil** (Viking, 1939), a flavorful account of a little Swiss girl and her herdsman doll, quite highly praised by critics of the period and selected for Fanfare, and *All Those Buckles* (Viking, 1945), an entertaining story set on the St. Lawrence during World War II, about how the Buckle family moves when the army needs their land for an airfield. *Down Ryton Water** (Viking, 1941), a substantial, highly detailed historical novel for young people dealing with the emigration of the Pilgrims to Plymouth Colony, was both a Newbery honor book and a Fanfare Selection.

GAMMAGE CUP (*The Gammage Cup**), the precious Cup of Wisdom that the Minnipin leader, Gammage, carried, wrapped in silk and slung over his shoulder, when the Minnipins fled from their enemies, the Mushrooms, and entered the valley of the Land-Between-the-Mountains. It is to be given as a prize to the village judged most worthy of having the precious heirloom. This leads to the outlawing of "Them," the five nonconformists, who refuse to paint their doors green, and to the discovery that Mushrooms have invaded their valley.

THE GAMMAGE CUP (Kendall*†, Carol, ill. Erik Blegvad, Harcourt, 1959), Tolkienesque fantasy-adventure about how the Minnipins, or Small Ones, of the village of Slipper-on-the-Water* repel their ancient enemies, the Mushrooms, or Hairless Ones, who have invaded their valley of the Land-Between-the-Mountains. The Minnipins are a sober, peaceable, homeloving, industrious people, who live along the banks of the Watercress River where they settled hundreds of years before. The twelve villages decide to have a contest in which the Gammage* Cup, priceless Minnipin heirloom, is to be given to the village judged most worthy of the honor. When several Minnipins question the decisions of their leaders, the Periods, about the contest, and among other things refuse to conform to established practice and paint their doors green, these nonconformists—Curley* Green, painter, Gummy*, poet, Walter* the Earl, lover of antiquities (called "Them" because they are considered not quite respectable), Muggles*, museum curator, and Mingy*, town treasurer—are outlawed and go to live on the slope of a nearby mountain, taking with them the treasure of swords and armor which Walter the Earl has recently unearthed. The swords have the special quality of glowing when danger is near. The Exiles discover that the Mushrooms are planning to invade, and Walter the Earl succeeds with difficulty in persuading the villagers to put on his armor and advance against them. After a mighty battle, the Minnipins triumph, and the five outlaws are welcomed back into the village. The villagers bedeck Slipper-on-the-Water, paint their doors many colors in their joy and gratitude, and win the cup for the strong sense of unity and well-being that pervades their town, an honor which is anticlimactic, considering events. The land and ways of the Minnipins are ingeniously worked out, and the plot is inventive, with fast-moving, amusing incidents, but it is never really clear why the Mushrooms are invading, some scenes seem overdrawn, and the book is heavy with message. Except for Muggles, who becomes recognized as a capable leader, rising to her friends' need for direction, the characters are static and one-dimensional but likeable. Style is detailed, dialogue extensive, and pacing is good. Sequel is *The Whisper of Glocken†*. (Old* Heroes) Choice; Fanfare; Newbery Honor.

GANNETT, RUTH (STILES) (1923–), born in New York City, daughter of a book reviewer; author of books for younger readers. She grew up in New York City, attended a Quaker boarding school in Pennsylvania, and graduated from Vassar with a degree in chemistry. During World War II she worked as a medical researcher in Boston and in radar research at Massachusetts Institute of Technology. After the war, and between positions, she wrote *My Father's Dragon** (Random, 1948) for her own pleasure. This talking animal fantasy about Elmer Elevator's adventures in rescuing a baby dragon was a Newbery honor book and was named to the Fanfare, Lewis Carroll Shelf, and *Choice* lists. Very popular, it has been translated into Japanese, Danish, and Swedish. Sequels are *Elmer and the Dragon* (Random, 1950) and *The Dragons of Blueland* (Random, 1951). Much less well known are *The Wonderful House-Boat-Train* (Random, 1949) and *Katie and the Sad Noise* (Random, 1961). In searching for an illustrator for *My Father's Dragon*, she met her husband, artist Peter Kahn, who helped with the book's design, but her stepmother, illustrator Ruth Chrisman Gannett, did the pictures. She and her husband, a faculty member at Cornell University, have lived in New York City, Louisiana, Canada, and New York State, and she has also taught in elementary school.

GARRAM THE HUNTER: A BOY OF THE HILL TRIBES (Best*, Herbert, ill. Erick Berry*, Doubleday, 1930), adventure story set in tropical Africa in an unspecified time, presumably before the coming of white men, certainly before the natives had gunpowder. Garram, son of Warok, chief of Kwallak village, is known as ''The Hunter'' because of his skill and because he prefers to hunt alone with his great dog, Kon, rather than with the crowd led by loutish Menud. After thwarting an attempt by Menud to frame him and have him executed for theft of goats, Garram takes the advice of the village priest, The Rainmaker, to leave before Menud and his wealthy father, Sura, murder both Garram and his father and seize power. Garram travels to Yelwa, walled city of the Fulani of the West, a Moslem people, where through chance, quick action, and the help of Kon, he saves the Emir from assassination by a relative, Ibrahim. He becomes a favorite at court, warns the Emir of the Grand Vizier's scheme to murder him, and as a reward asks that Ibrahim's life be spared, thereby gaining a valuable friend. Sensing that something is wrong at home, he leaves Yelwa and meets a messenger from The Rainmaker who tells him that Warok is being held prisoner, to be executed in the morning. Having handily killed a leopard, Garram enters the prison hut through the roof, frees Warok, and, wearing chain mail, which was a parting gift from the Emir, under his leopard skin, he scares off the guards who take him for a ghost-leopard whose hide wards off arrows. No sooner is Warok restored to power than a new threat appears in the form of an army of Fulani of the East attacking the hill villages for slaves. Warok leads his men and the bands from other villages in a brilliant victory against the much larger Fulani army, a victory almost ruined by the treachery of Menud, who has revealed to the enemy the narrow secret pass into the hills from the east. The Rainmaker saves the day by burning a bridge across the chasm, and Warok destroys another bridge, trapping the Fulani on a narrow cliffside path, easy prey for the village women who roll stones down on them from above. After they return to Kwallak, an army of Fulani appear from the west, but it turns out to be a group coming to their aid, led by Ibrahim. Although full of action and local color, the story has many stock characters and some inconsistencies of plot. How do the hillmen, for instance, get back to their village so rapidly with loot and prisoners when the bridges on the only path have been destroyed? Newbery Honor.

GATES†, DORIS (1901–), born in Mountain View, Calif.; librarian and author of novels of family and community life for children. She was educated at Fresno State College, Los Angeles Library School, and Western Reserve

University and for ten years was head of the children's department in the Fresno County Library in California, then taught library science and children's literature at San Jose State College, the University of California at Berkeley, and the University of San Francisco. She grew up on a prune ranch, where she had a little gray donkey like the one in her first novel, *Sarah's Idea** (Viking, 1938). This Fanfare selection tells how little Sarah achieves her long-held desire to own a burro of her very own by picking enough prunes to buy Jinny, a little gray-brown one that has captured her heart. Out of Gates's library work with migrant children in the San Joaquin Valley rose her most highly regarded novel, *Blue Willow** (Viking, 1940), in which her dead mother's blue willow plate symbolizes for young migrant Janey Larkin the beauty and security of a permanent home. It was a Newbery honor book, was selected for Fanfare and the Lewis Carroll Bookshelf, and is cited in *Children's Books Too Good to Miss* and in *Choice*. She also wrote a mystery-fantasy, *The Cat and Mrs. Cary*† (Viking, 1962) and *The Elderberry Bush* (Viking, 1967), a novel that tells the story of her childhood. Her books on other subjects include *North Fork* (Viking, 1945), a story for older boys set in the lumbering area of the Sierra Nevada which also involves Indians, *River Ranch* (Viking, 1949), about rustling on a western cattle ranch, and *Little Vic* (Viking, 1951), about a race horse, while *Trouble for Jerry* (Viking, 1944) follows on *Sarah's Idea*. More recently she has published a well-received series of retellings of stories from Greek myth and hero tale and the novels *A Morgan for Melinda* (Viking, 1980) and its sequel *A Filly for Melinda* (Viking, 1984). She married William Hall, an attorney, and has made her home in southern California. She has also been associate editor for Ginn and Company, co-authoring several readers in their Enrichment Series, has contributed to professional journals, and has written a book about children's literature for adults.

GATTI, ATTILIO (1896–   ), born in northern Italy; commander of exploring expeditions and authority on Africa in the early twentieth century. After suffering illness as the result of his service in World War I, he went to Egypt to recover and there joined a big game hunting safari. Becoming fascinated with Africa, he organized and led eleven scientific expeditions in the next fourteen years. He married an American woman who helped him with his first book, *The King of the Gorillas* (Doubleday, 1932), written before he knew English. He later became an American citizen and lived literally on the Quebec-Vermont border, in a house partly in the United States and partly in Canada. His books about animals and peoples of Africa, like *Saranga the Pygmy** (Scribner's, 1939), show far more accurate understanding of and respect for the natives of the continent than was usual in children's books of the period.

GAY-NECK: THE STORY OF A PIGEON (Mukerji*, Dhan Gopal, ill. Boris Artzybasheff, Dutton, 1927), realistic animal novel with fantasy elements set in Calcutta, the Himalayas, and France just before and at the beginning of World War I. The book is divided into two sections: the first is mainly concerned with the early life and training of Gay-Neck, a carrier pigeon, while the second tells of Gay-Neck's service in France for the Allies in 1914 and 1915, his bravery under fire, and his recovery from serious wounds. Based upon the author's own experiences with pigeons when a boy, Gay-Neck's story is told in first person, mostly by a youth of about fifteen who watches the bird hatch and grow to become a strong and steady flier with brilliant, glowing neck feathers which give him his name, and partly by Gay-Neck himself. While he and his family are spending the summer in the Himalayas, the narrator is joined by his friend Radja and by Ghond*, a skillful hunter and their mutual teacher in jungle lore. After Gay-Neck's mother is slain by a hawk, the young pigeon disappears. In searching for him, the three have various adventures while traveling through the jungle that introduce the reader to the terrain and atmosphere of the area and the beliefs of the monks. Among others, they visit a lamasery, where a monk tells them that he has healed the bird of the fear which has caused him to flee. Later, the narrator acquires a flock of about fifty carriers which he trains for war work and of which Gay-Neck, now mature and mated, becomes the leader. Ghond and Gay-Neck sail to Flanders, where Gay-Neck carries important messages between the front and headquarters, earning the respect and gratitude of the Allied Commander-in-Chief. Gay-Neck is shocked and distressed by what appears to him to be wanton and excessive destruction of life and property. Both Gay-Neck and Ghond are wounded while on a mission to locate a German ammunition depot. Gay-Neck valiantly bears essential information through the German lines in spite of heavy enemy fire. After both suffer severe emotional depression from their experiences, they are invalided back to India and taken to the lamasery where they are restored to health in body and tranquility of spirit through the kind attention and devout prayers of the monks. This slow-moving, quiet story of courage and serenity engages the emotions even though the strong anti-war theme, the detailed descriptions of the pigeons, and philosophical discussions make the novel heavily didactic. Language is formal and sometimes flowery, but the tone is intimate and warm. The many details about Gay-Neck's life and his kind reveal careful observation and make him seem real and alive, but the passages in which he picks up the story startle the reader and fail to convince in context. Choice; Newbery Winner.

GEKKO (*Red Planet**), a Martian rather small for his type, only twelve feet high, with three legs and a warm, good-natured personality. When he gets to know Jim Marlowe, he goes through the Water Ceremony with him, becoming a water friend or true comrade, and later is instrumental in saving Jim and the whole Earth colony. The Martians are pictured as unhurried, highly evolved people, who keep largely to themselves and do not reveal their advanced technology and attitudes to the colonists.

GENTRY, TOM (*The Codfish Musket**), personable, devil-may-care, young English adventurer engaged in running guns from East coast sources to the British and Indians on the Mississippi-Missouri frontier to be used against American settlers. He steals Mr. Cotton's shipment of codfish-marked muskets. He is killed, accidentally shot by his own gun, when Dan Boit intercepts his shipment of Kentucky rifles near St. Louis.

GEORGE (*Farm Boy**), the milkhouse hand at O-at-ka farm who resents orders and sloughs off responsibility whenever he can. For a brief time his attitude rubs off on John. John is also influenced slightly by the attitudes of the other hands. When George leaves his chores and John is assigned them, John picks up on the grumbling of the other hands and simply overlooks George's tasks. The result is that Anderson*, the foreman, must do George's work. Uncle* Gene then points out to John how unfair it was of him to think only of himself and not to consider the effect upon others of leaving George's tasks undone. The boy later apologizes to Anderson. George is obviously a character who exists for the purpose of conveying a lesson about the importance of responsibility.

GEORGE†, JEAN CRAIGHEAD (1919–), born in Washington, D.C.; naturalist, author of novels concerned with animals and natural science, mostly self-illustrated. She grew up in the Washington area, often out of doors with her twin brothers, both of whom became wildlife ecologists. She received her B.A. degree from Pennsylvania State College and studied further at Louisiana State University, Baton Rouge, and at the University of Michigan in Ann Arbor. In 1942 she became a reporter for the International News Service and from 1944 to 1946 wrote for the Washington *Post*. For many years she has been connected with *Pageant* magazine. In 1944 she married John L. George*, with whom she wrote her first book, *Vulpes the Red Fox** (Dutton, 1948) and five others. They were later divorced, but she continued to write, publishing more than twenty novels for young people, frequently employing scientific study of nature, as in *Gull Number 737†* (Crowell, 1964) and *Who Really Killed Cock Robin? An Ecological Mystery†* (Dutton, 1971). Her most popular books are both stories of survival away from civilization, *My Side of the Mountain** (Dutton, 1959), about a boy who lives alone in the Catskills, and *Julie of the Wolves†* (Harper, 1972), about a girl on the north slope of Alaska. Although her research is always meticulous and her natural science fascinating, her novels often suffer from weakness in plotting.

GEORGE, JOHN L(OTHAR) (1916–), born in Milwaukee, Wis.; conservationist and college professor, who wrote six books with his wife, Jean Craighead George*†, the first being *Vulpes the Red Fox** (Dutton, 1948). He received his Ph.D. degree from the University of Michigan School of Forestry and Conservation and later taught at Vassar College. During World War II he served in the U.S. Navy.

GEORGE SMITH (*Trigger John's Son**), chief clerk of the Beechwood dry goods store, deacon in the Union Church, and adoptive father to Trigger*. George looks at life with quiet humor and has the understanding and tolerance to get along with his stiff wife, Myrtle*, his pompous boss, Mr. Woodruff, and Trigger's disreputable friends, who elect George honorary member of the Goosetown Gang. In spite of his wife's over-active conscience and the town's stuffiness, George usually manages to get his way with patience and good humor. When he volunteers to skip church to show Trigger around town and Myrtle reminds him that it is his duty to go to church, he replies, "It's my duty to think of others, too, isn't it, even on Sunday? And I'm thinking of Trigger."

GERE, FRANCES KENT, illustrator, author of two books about the eastern Mediterranean area, *Boy of Babylon** (Longmans, 1941), a historical novel set about 200 B.C., and *Once Upon a Time in Egypt* (Longmans, 1937), a book of non-fiction which follows the life of a boy named Jaty in ancient Egypt. Her illustrations, based on her observation of original sources in Egyptian tombs, were praised for their accuracy by the curator of the Department of Egyptian Art in the Museum of Fine Arts in Boston.

GHOND (*Gay-Neck: The Story of a Pigeon**), wise and skillful Asian Indian hunter, learned in jungle lore, who advises the narrator in training Gay-Neck, the carrier pigeon with iridescent neck feathers. Gay-Neck accompanies Ghond to Europe in World War I, and both are wounded in action in France. Ghond has been ordered to find where the German ammunition depot is located and to send that information back to headquarters via Gay-Neck. He does so, but before he can leave the area, Gay-Neck arrives at headquarters, and when the Allies bomb the depot, Ghond is wounded. Although he recovers from his bodily injuries, he suffers severe emotional trauma from his experiences and is sent back to India to recover. There he and Gay-Neck, also wounded, are restored to health in a Himalayan monastery.

THE GHOST OF FOLLONSBEE'S FOLLY (Hightower*†, Florence, ill. Ati Forberg, Houghton, 1958), realistic novel of family life set about 1950 in rural Massachusetts. The Stackpoles—ebullient, undaunted father, loving mother, clever Elsie, 12, rowdy Tom, 11, twin baby sons, and Angela, their imperious, devoted, hymn-singing black cook, who adopted the family after the death of her son in Italy in World War II—look forward to moving from Boston to the big, old house in the country that father has bought for them. It is away from the bustle of city life, has a room big enough to hold mother's piano, and has space enough for them to spread out in. They set out eagerly to renovate it, but problems soon crop up. The family hears strange noises at night, the repairs turn out to be more expensive than they expected, and they realize that they have been victimized by the real estate agent, unscrupulous Mr. Creel, who has lied about the house and about not intending to develop the vacant land next door along the river.

The family settle in, though, and try to make the best of things. Elsie spends most of her time fixing up a doll house which she has discovered on the third floor and which is a replica of the big one they live in. It has secret doors, closets, and passageways which the children discover duplicate those in the big house. At the library Elsie learns that the doll house used to belong to the daughter of Old Mr. Follonsbee, who built the big house, called locally Follonsbee's Folly, and which had been a station on the Underground Railroad. Tom explores the river, where he makes friends with a capable and adventure-loving black youth, Joe, with whom he fishes, camps, and has outings on the river but who is vague about his home and family. Events come to a head when a terrific storm causes the river to rise, breaking the dam at the very time Tom and Elsie are exploring a passageway beneath the house. Joe, who has been living there and whose activities have provided the ghostly noises that have disquieted the family, helps them to escape the flood. He and Angela recognize each other. He is her son, presumed dead, but really an amnesiac, unable to remember anything about himself. The storm changes the course of the river and puts an end to Mr. Creel's plans for developing the land next to the Follonsbee property. Twists and turns on stock incidents and characters and a light, whimsical, occasionally tongue-in-cheek tone produce a mildly Gothic story, which, if implausible and predictable, is consistently entertaining. Fanfare.

THE GIANT (Du Bois*†, William Pène, ill. author, Viking, 1954), fantasy, a straight-faced farce set in an unidentified European city in 1950. The narrator, known as Bill (or Señor Beel) is touring Europe writing a guidebook for children with Teddy Bear characters, to be titled *A Bear's Guide to the World's Pleasure Spots*. When he arrives at the small hotel where he has reserved an apartment, he finds a note from *El Muchacho y Cia*, The Boy and Co., warning him to leave at once. Annoyed, rather than intimidated, he determines to stay and notices a strange building under construction across the street with a single window looking directly at his balcony. During the night a practice air raid and blackout is obviously covering some movement into the building, and the next morning he sees an enormous eye peering at him through the single window. When an effort by a dapper Spanish-speaking gentleman named Fernando to bribe him to leave fails, he is told the truth: the building across the street houses an eight and a half-year-old boy from Argentina who, because of an ability to assimilate his food completely, has grown seven stories high. At two he had been brought to see a specialist in Vienna but had grown so greatly before his examination was completed that he couldn't be returned to his native country. A syndicate of good friends of the family was formed to cope with his problems and keep his existence secret so he will not be exploited as a freak. He is kept in special buildings, moved frequently via a specially designed trailer, and provided with real lions, elephants, trucks, and automobiles to play with. When the narrator insists on visiting the boy, he has some hair-raising experiences of being balanced on an elephant's head, having the car he is in kicked across the room, and being placed on a high window sill, but he finds the boy good-natured and friendly, if a bit heedless like other boys his age. Bill undertakes to train the boy to make an appearance in public, teaching him to walk carefully, even to dance, and warning him severely not to pick up people without permission. On the fateful day the boy at first obeys but soon finds the automobiles and trolley cars too great a temptation, and starts playing with them. He is lured back into his building by a band playing his favorite dance, the samba, and is again spirited away in the middle of the night. The next morning Bill and Fernando discover that the boy has made a real hit with the people of the city, who admire his gentle ways, his cheerfulness, his genuine boyishness. He is called back and returns in triumph, welcomed by the people. This tall tale has charm mainly because it is told with complete seriousness and is accompanied by skillful illustrations. Choice.

GIBSON, KATHARINE (1893–   ), born in Indianapolis, Ind. She was a member of the staff of the Cleveland Museum of Art and was associated with the Artists and Writers Guild of New York City. She married a Unitarian minister and traveled widely. She wrote a number of books for young children which, despite their simplicity, show a sly cleverness of language and idea, including *The Oak Tree House** (Longmans, 1936), *Cinders** (Longmans, 1939), and *Jock's Castle** (Longmans, 1940), all three named to the *Horn Book* Fanfare list.

GINGER PYE (Estes*†, Eleanor, Harcourt, 1951), realistic family novel set in the sleepy little town of Cranbury*, Conn., in the early 1920s. Jerry*, 10, and Rachel* Pye, 9, live with their mother and father, an eminent ornithologist. Jerry longs for a dog of his very own. Just before school starts in the fall, he, Rachel, and their energetic, earnest Uncle Bennie, 3, earn a dollar dusting church pews for tall, basketball star, Sam Doody. With it, they buy one of Mrs. Speedy's fox terrier puppies, and, after a family disussion, name it Ginger. On several occasions after that, the children hear footsteps behind them and glimpse a shadowy figure wearing a yellow hat lurking in the neighborhood. They become convinced that an "unsavory character" wishes to steal Ginger. On Thanksgiving Day, Jerry discovers that Ginger has disappeared from the Pye backyard. The children search diligently for their pet and enlist the help of almost the entire town, including Police Chief Larrimer, for the greatest search in Cranbury history, with no success. Months pass with no sign of Ginger. The children keep their eyes and ears open for him, however, wherever they go, and oddly, whenever they are on Second Avenue near the home of surly, unfriendly Wally Bullwinkle, a classmate of Jerry's who once ordered them away from his house, they have a strong sense of Ginger's presence. On the twenty-ninth of May, Jerry's birthday, the children are at the train station watching when, to their amazement, Wally Bullwinkle boards, wearing an old, yellow felt hat. They report immediately to Chief Larrimer, who investigates the Bullwinkle house and finds signs that Ginger was there. When the children return home, they discover that Uncle Bennie is a hero. He insisted that a dog which had been following him and Gramma was Ginger, and thus the family pet is found. The whole town rejoices in Ginger Pye's recovery. Wally had stolen Ginger to train him to perform in a circus act with Wally and his father. The Pye children are well drawn, and Uncle Bennie is a winsome lad. The conclusion is predictable, nor is there much suspense. Gentle humor abounds, and most of the reading interest stems from the author's skill at catching the details of everyday life and the thoughts and ways of children. The point of view is mostly Rachel's, sometimes Jerry's or both, and in one very entertaining chapter, Ginger's. Though it earned the prestigious Newbery award, the book lacks the charm and staying power of the author's Moffat books. Choice; Fanfare; Newbery Winner.

GIPSON, FRED(ERICK BENJAMIN) (1903–1973), born in Mason, Tex.; reporter and magazine editor, novelist, and screenwriter. He was a graduate of the University of Texas at Austin and became a reporter for several Texas newspapers. He was an editor of *True West* magazine and editorial director of *Frontier Times*, Bandera, Tex. Besides his three novels for children, he wrote three for adults, and a number of screenplays and books of non-fiction. Though *Old Yeller** (Harper, 1956), a story of an ugly stray dog with one ear chewed off, is by far his best known book, its sequel, *Savage Sam* (Harper, 1962), about the son of Old Yeller, was also popular. Before his death he lived on a small stockfarm near Mason, Tex., the area in which his favorite books are set.

GLEIT, MARIA (HERTHA GLEITSMANN), author of books in both German and English, including *Pierre Keeps Watch* (Scribner's, 1944), set in the French mountains during World War II, and *Niko's Mountains* (Scribner's, 1946), about a group of French children suffering from malnutrition immediately after the war who are taken to Switzerland for a two-month summer vacation. Her *Paul Tiber** (Scribner's, 1949), based on the life of a real man, Stanley Mesavage, who started reforestation efforts in Pennsylvania's coal mining district, won the Child Study Award.

GLORY OF THE REPUBLIC (*The House of Sixty Fathers**), the pig belonging to the family of Tien* Pao. Together he and the boy are swept in their sampan down river from Hengyang into Japanese-held territory during World War II. Glory of the Republic roots among the leaves and finds caves in which they can hide from both the soldiers and the starving civilian population. Later the pig is used as bait by the guerillas to catch Japanese at night and, during the last portion of the journey, must be carried, trussed and stuffed into a false-bottomed bucket, by Tien Pao, then is given a bed of straw in a barrel by the "sixty fathers," the American airmen who take them in.

GLORY OF THE SEAS (Hewes*, Agnes Danforth, Knopf, 1933), historical novel set in Boston about 1855 involving the Fugitive Slave Law and the use of clipper ships to carry passengers and goods to California around Cape Horn. Young John Seagrave, chief clerk in the Boston counting house of Pinckney and Fay, lives with his uncle, Asa Wentworth, a judge. While John's main concerns revolve around his conservative employers' refusal to invest in the clippers, their insistence that the Fugitive Slave Law be enforced, and his romantic attraction to Mr. Fay's daughter, Sue, Asa looks at larger issues. He sees the clippers, which he calls Messengers of Destiny, as a way of keeping California in the Union, a circumstance he sees endangered by the passage of the law. An ardent Abolitionist, he resigns his position rather than face the possibility of having to decide a case based upon what he considers a bad law. John is also puzzled by the strange association between Mr. Fay and Benny Paradiso, an orphaned youth newly returned from California, who keeps pigeons. When John attempts to help Jasper, an escaped slave, evade authorities, Benny is wounded. John then discovers that Benny's pigeons have been carrying messages for Mr. Fay. He takes one of the messages to Asa, who learns from it that Mr. Fay has been engaging in the illegal importation of slaves and that he has contracted to use Donald McKay's *Great Republic*, the largest clipper ship afloat, for his next shipment. While in New York harbor, the *Republic* catches fire, and Mr. Fay is killed attempting to save the ship. Accompanied by Benny, Asa and John leave for California on the rebuilt *Republic*, in part of whose cargo, the iron* houses, Mr. Pinckney has invested. Asa gives up his work with the Abolitionists because he feels their efforts are harming rather than helping the Union. He feels that California will need strong leaders like himself in order to keep her in the Union, while John sees going to California and becoming involved in business there as a way of contributing to his country's future. He is encouraged by Sue, who says she will join him when he is established there. The plot seems overly complicated and too heavily foreshadowed, and the point of view shifts unnecessarily and disconcertingly. While the book gives a good sense of the problems, concerns, and thinking of the period, incidents and characters are stock and underdeveloped, and both John and Asa, while sympathetic, are one dimensionally drawn. Notable but confusing are the many references to clippers, their building, builders, and to the sailing charts of Matthew Maury. Newbery Honor.

GOBO (*The Marble Fountain**), old man who lives in a cave in the hills above Rosa near the stone quarry where Uncle* Gigi works. At first he refuses to come down to the village, he is so afraid of another war. The music of his clarinet can often be heard in the village, and in spite of what he has heard about the man's reclusiveness, Piccolo* climbs up to meet him because he can play so beautifully. He finds Gobo merry and mischievous and very comforting to be with, and the two become friends. Gobo finds Piccolo an apt student on the clarinet, and Piccolo decides he would like to become a musician when he grows up. When Piccolo is ill, Gobo makes his first trip down from the hills to bring the boy a clarinet upon which to play while he recovers.

GODOLPHIN, EARL OF (*King of the Wind**), kindly English aristocrat who frees Agba* from Newgate and purchases Sham. He confides in Agba, telling him that his estate, Gog Magog, has fallen on hard times and that his hope of saving his stables lies in one of Sham's sons winning the Queen's Purse at Newmarket Races. Godolphin means "God's Downs."

GODWIN, EDWARD F(ELL) (1912–), born in London, England; author-illustrator. He grew up in England and on the continent and attended art schools in London and Oxford. He emigrated to the United States in 1948 and subsequently lived in Woodstock, N.Y. He illustrated a great many books, both alone and with his first wife, Stephani Godwin*, and with her he wrote and illustrated four, among them, *Warrior Bard: The Life of William Morris* (Harrap, 1947), a biography of the poet in whose house the Godwins lived for a time while still in England and with whose sister they became friends, *The Greenwood Tree: A Portrait of William Shakespeare* (Dutton, 1950), *Out of the Strong* (Oxford, 1955), a book of fiction, and *Roman Eagle** (Oxford, 1951), a historical novel set in the first century A.D., which was a Fanfare book. In 1956, he married Elizabeth Bridges, a poet and artist, whose *A Child's Book of Butterflies* (Maxton, 1956) he illustrated.

GODWIN, STEPHANI (MARY ALLFREE), born in London, England; author-illustrator. After her father, a landscape painter, died, her mother traveled extensively, and she lived in Switzerland, Italy, and Canada, as well as England. She attended art schools in London and Oxford, and after graduation, tried unsuccessfully to break into commercial art and also painted for private exhibitions. She came to the United States in 1948 and subsequently illustrated alone, or in collaboration with her husband, Edward Godwin*, a large number of books, and with him wrote and illustrated four. Their historical romance *Roman Eagle** (Oxford, 1951) was a Fanfare book. Set in ancient Palestine in Jesus' time, it tells how the Apostle Peter brings together two estranged young lovers, a Roman noble and his beautiful Hebrew wife.

THE GOLDEN BASKET (Bemelmans*, Ludwig, Viking, 1936), amusing episodic family story set in Bruges, Belgium, in 1925. Accompanied by his two little daughters, Melisande and Celeste, Mr. Coggeshall of London makes a business trip to Bruges where the three stay at the Golden Basket Inn. Several days of excitement follow for the two girls as they make friends with the hotel keeper, his wife, and son, Jan, the *maître d'hôtel*, Monsieur Carnewal, and other travelers, and visit the Bruges tower with the carillon and museum. They catch flies for Jan's pet frog, and play submarine in their room with Jan, drenching the carpet with water. When they go for a ride in Jan's new rowboat which capsizes, they are rescued by the Mayor of Bruges. While visiting a cathedral, they encounter a teacher with a dozen little girls from a girls' school, the smallest of whom is red-haired Madeleine. This is a pleasant story of the delights and misdeeds of two children, decorated with stylized, distorted, black and white sketches and full-color paintings. Fanfare; Newbery Honor.

THE GOLDEN HORSESHOE (Coatsworth*†, Elizabeth, ill. Robert Lawson*, Macmillan, 1935), historical novel set in colonial Virginia in the early 1700s. Tamar, and Roger, 13, live with their father, prosperous Colonel Antony Stafford on his plantation along the James River, Stafford Green. Although Colonel Antony is very proud of his pretty, intelligent, warm-hearted, half-Indian daughter, her half-brother, Roger, is ashamed of her Indian ancestry. When Governor Spotswood visits Stafford Green, Tamar's Uncle Opechancanough, chief of the Weyanokes, presents him with the Indians' annual tribute of a deer. Opechancanough informs Tamar that the French are stirring up trouble on the other side of the mountains and are building forts along the great river to the west. Tamar relays the news to her father who passes it along to the Governor who immediately organizes an expedition to see what is going on in the West. Tamar wagers Roger her Indian grandmother's crown against his cherished mount, Rambler, that she will accompany the expedition. When her father refuses her request, she appeals to her Indian uncle, whose people stain her skin and dress her as a boy. As Raccoon, she joins the company's Indian guides. The journey proceeds uneventfully into the uplands of Virginia. As a diversion, the group decides to have horse races. Raccoon (Tamar) foils a scheme by which the Governor's proud and arrogant English secretary, Mr. Bridge, would have lamed Roger's mount so that his own horse, Grenadier, could have defeated Rambler. The expedition crosses the mountains, views the Shenandoah valley, names the highest peak Mount George after the king, and returns to the coast. When the story of how Tamar accompanied the expedition comes out, Roger is grateful to his Indian sister for her help, and the Governor commends her for her courage. He bestows upon each member of the expedition, including Tamar, a golden horseshoe, dubbing his traveling companions the Knights of the Golden Horseshoe. The theme of acceptance and tolerance is laid on, most characters are flat or stock, and the plot is underdone and contrived. Tamar is a paragon of virtues, and Roger changes predictably. The Indians are idealized, and passages describing their treatment by the whites are obtrusively didactic. The first part of the book, which tells of life and events on the plantation, is far more interesting than the expedition, which is bland and obviously a vehicle for theme. John Dummer, the Quaker indentured servant whose freedom Tamar persuades her father to buy, is a potentially interesting character, as is Mr. Reid, the children's new schoolmaster, but neither character is developed. Style is graceful and often sharp with imagery. Fanfare.

THE GOLDEN NAME DAY (Lindquist*, Jennie D., ill. Garth Williams, Harper, 1955), realistic story of everyday life in the early twentieth century set in New England. Because her mother must be in the hospital for a year, Nancy

Bruce, 9, comes to live with adopted grandparents, Albertina and Erik Benson, Swedish immigrants, whose household is full of animals, including Theodore Roosevelt (Teddy), a cat which drinks coffee, Oscar, a dog, and Karl the Twelfth, a horse. The Bensons make Nancy welcome, as do their granddaughters, who live nearby—the three Carlson girls, Elsa, a bookworm Nancy's age, practical Sigrid, and Helga, the youngest—and Aunt Anna, the girls' mother, and Aunt Martha, who keeps house at the farm of Erik's older brother, Sven. A loose series of episodes, the book is held together by Nancy's love of the color yellow and her desire to have a "nameday" of her own as the Swedish people all do, even though neither Nancy nor her middle name, Wanda, appears in the almanac. Nancy chooses wallpaper of yellow roses for her room, attends several parties among the sociable Swedes, is allowed to have her own *efter-Kalas*, the traditional after-party to use up the leftover refreshments, drives Aunt Martha's horse, Whoa-Emma, when she visits the farm, helps make flower decorations for the anniversary party at the country school, and finds a kitten which the girls officially name Lady Griselda Gray from *Cuckoo Clock*, a book the girls all like, but always call by the book's title. When she is lonely and out of sorts, Grandma Benson sends Nancy off to find someone worse off than she is, and she discovers and makes friends with Alex Brown, a crippled boy confined to a wheelchair. When a new girl named Wanda moves near to Aunt Martha's farm, Nancy learns that she celebrates her name day from the Polish tradition, so they have a summertime joint name day picnic celebration for both girls, with everything decorated in yellow. Then Grandpa comes up with the real solution for Nancy's name-day problem by noting that Jan. 1 has no name listed in the Swedish almanac, and they all agree to write Nancy's name in there. The story is written very largely in simple and rather unrealistic dialogue and seems dated with eipsodes about things presumed to be of interest to little girls—cake making, flowers, parties, new dresses, etc. Although the name-day question is too slight to make a compelling plot and none of the characters is memorable, the tone is warm and the details of ethnic customs are interesting. Newbery Honor.

GONE-AWAY LAKE (Enright*†, Elizabeth, ill. Beth and Joe Krush, Harcourt, 1957), amusing, realistic family novel set in the fifties in a rural area in northeastern United States. While on a butterfly hunting expedition, Julian* Jarman, 12, and his visiting cousin, Portia* Blake, 11, come upon a swamp about which stand several large, dilapidated, turn-of-the-century houses, once evidently fairly elegant, now abandoned. They discover two of them occupied by an elderly brother and sister, Pindar Payton and Minnehaha Cheever, who inform the children that the swamp was once Tarrigo Lake, a popular resort and the focus of summer vacations for a number of families until drained by the construction of a dam. Late in life and fallen on hard times, Minnie and Pindar have returned to what is now known as Gone-Away Lake, where they have fitted out homes for themselves with furniture garnered from the various houses. They dress in old-fashioned clothes, keep bees and goats and raise and preserve their own food, drive an antique Franklin, which they call the "Machine," and live a simple life close to nature and each other with a radio their only modern convenience. Portia and Julian become close friends with Minnie and Pindar, who help them make a clubhouse to play in and tell them stories about the people who once lived at Gone-Away. Portia and Julian keep their new friends a secret until Foster, Portia's younger brother, is lost in the swamp and rescued by Pindar from the quicksand known as Gulper. At the end, Portia's father and mother hope to be able to buy and renovate one of the old houses so that the Blakes, who live in New York, can spend their summers at Gone-Away. The setting is inventive, the sharply descriptive style holds much sensory appeal, and the incongruous set of characters are engaging, if obviously assembled, and a trifle cute. The plot is bland and lacks unity and focus, and an air of innocence dates the book. Sequel is *Return to Gone-Away*. Choice; Fanfare; Lewis Carroll; Newbery Honor.

GOOD-BYE, MY LADY (Street*, James, Lippincott, 1954), realistic dog story set in Southern Mississippi, evidentally during the 1930s. Skeeter (Claude) Jackson, 14, has lived with his uncle, Old Jesse* Jackson, since his mother died when he was a baby. Their one-room cabin on the Pascagoula River is at the edge of the swamp, and they earn a little by fishing, trapping, and cutting wood. When Skeeter hears a strange yodeling cry from the swamp, they get the storekeeper, Cash* (Alpheus) Evans, to bring out his hunting dog, Gabe, and his two vicious "hog" dogs to track down the strange creature. When the animal outruns Gabe and fights off the hog dogs, they realize that it, too, is a dog, a breed they afterwards learn is a Basenji—a small, short-haired African hunting dog that does not bark. Skeeter determines to find it and carefully lures the Basenji, discovering it is a female which he names "Lady." At first he is shocked that Lady chases rats, a dangerous practice since it can lead her into snake- and alligator-infested pools, and chickens, a habit that would make her an outlaw in the countryside. With firmness and patience, he trains her, however, and finds she is highly intelligent and skilled. When she out-hunts Cash Evans's registered English setter, Millard Fillmore, Cash loses a bet and has to cancel Jesse's outstanding debt on his power saw. Word gets around the area and people come to see the wonder dog, but unfortunately one traveling man has seen a magazine ad for a Basenji lost in the area, and Cash tells Jesse. At first Skeeter says finders-keepers, but his conscience makes him go to Gates Watson, a black neighbor who has been to college, and Gates agrees to telegraph the kennel listed in the ad. A representative of the kennel flies to Mobile and comes to Jesse's cabin while Skeeter and Lady are out. Jesse gets him to go wait in Cash's store, where Skeeter brings Lady and gives her up with dignity but great pain. He gets a one hundred dollar reward, which he gives to Cash to get dentures, "Roebuckers," for toothless old Jesse. Cash gets Skeeter to agree to take his dog, Mill, to train. The characterization is strong, with the relationship between Jesse and the boy particularly moving and the minor characters, Cash and Gates and even the man from the kennel, rounded and believable. The swamp and the woods surrounding the remote cabin are beautifully realized, integral parts of the story. Although the situation, like many animal stories, has a degree of sentimentality, it is restrained and acceptable in context. Choice.

THE GOOD MASTER (Seredy*, Kate, ill. author, Viking, 1935), humorous, episodic, realistic novel of family life set just before World War I. Wild, spoiled, motherless Cousin Kate from Budapest goes to live with her uncle, Márton Nagy, called the Good Master for his wise and gentle ways, his wife, and earnest, hardworking son, Jancsi, 10, on their horse and sheep ranch on the Hungarian plains. As the year moves from Easter to Christmas, Kate gets caught up in the pleasures and responsibilities of farm life, calms down, and develops a sounder sense of values. Jancsi looks forward eagerly to Kate's arrival, since visitors at the remote and isolated ranch are few. Both he and Márton, his father, however, are taken aback when Kate runs off with their team of horses on the way home from the train station and, once home, climbs into the kitchen rafters to feast on the sausages stored there, her favorite food. Father takes her in hand, and under his patient and firm guidance, she changes. Soon she and Jancsi become partners in chores about the ranch and have many pleasant and exciting times together. Jancsi teaches her to ride, and she becomes adept enough on horseback to help him avert a stampede during horse round-up. Kate is very proud to have chickens of her own to raise. The two accompany Uncle Márton when he visits his shepherds and listen delightedly to their stories about Hungary's past. At Easter, they color eggs, dress up in their finest clothes for visiting, and exchange eggs with friends and neighbors, following the age-old Hungarian custom. They go to a fair and hunt crawfish. Jancsi rescues Kate when she is in danger of being swept away by the current while swimming in the stream near the range where the sheep graze. In a very exciting episode, Kate is kidnapped by gypsies. At Christmas, Kate's father, Sándor, a schoolteacher, arrives from Budapest. Dressed as Mikulás (St. Nicholas), he distributes gifts to the children of the village. Uncle Márton persuades his brother, who has grown dissatisfied with life so far from the soil, to accept the position of village schoolmaster, and the family is reunited on the land. Kate, no longer a hoyden, but not yet quite a lady, is delighted to be able to remain on the ranch. The writing has rich auditory and strong visual qualities. Colorfully described festivals and scenes of everyday life about the house and ranch, and the folk tales told by the peasants interspersed among them, set in relief the themes of the value of living close to the soil, hard work, love for neighbor, and faith in God. Dialogue is natural and contributes to character and plot. Situations often seem contrived to please a young audience and impress them with certain themes, but they are also filled with action and excitement and are often amusing. Jancsi is a static figure, the Good Master seems a trifle too patient and understanding, and Kate changes too readily for belief, but there is a wholesome charm about the book that pulls readers in and carries them along. Seredy's romantic and stylized illustrations contribute to action, setting, and understanding of character. Sequel is *The Singing Tree**. Books Too Good; Choice; Fanfare; Newbery Honor.

GOODWIFE CRUFF (*The Witch of Blackbird Pond**), mean-spirited, bigoted woman, who dominates her husband and verbally abuses their child, Prudence*. She tells Prudence she is too stupid to learn and refuses to let her go to school. She is one of the leaders in the witchhunt against Hannah* and lodges the charge of witchcraft against Kit. She is a one-sided character.

GOOSE (*Seven Stars for Catfish Bend**), one of the seven animals awarded a silver star for heroism in ridding the bayou of hunters. A comic figure, he has been hissed out of the flock because he fell asleep while on watch. He proves vigilant and very helpful in various ways.

GORDON, PATRICIA (1904–   ), author of books for children and young people; born in British Columbia, she lived in England, Alaska, and India, and later made her home on an island off the coast of Maine. Under this name or the pseudonym Joan Howard she has published some dozen picture books and novels for middle-graders and up. Among her realistic novels appears *The Boy Jones** (Viking, 1943), an amusing story of a London street waif who several times steals into Buckingham Palace while Victoria is queen, selected for the *Horn Book* Fanfare list, and *Rommany Luck* (Viking, 1946), about gypsies in England during the time of Queen Elizabeth I, while her fantasy novels include *Not-Mrs. Murphy* (Viking, 1942), about the adventures of some American school children with a substitute bus driver, and *The 13th Is Magic* (Lothrop, 1950) and its sequel, *The Summer Is Magic* (Lothrup, 1952), about New York City youngsters who have adventures in their apartment house. She also wrote biographies, including *The Story of Mark Twain* (Grosset, 1953) and *The Story of Louisa May Alcott* (Grosset, 1955).

GORSLINE, DOUGLAS WARNER (1913–   ), artist, illustrator, and writer of self-illustrated books for young readers; was born and grew up in Rochester, N.Y., and attended Yale University and the Art Students League in New York City. He has done commercial art and illustrating for many publishers and has worked in advertising. Once art instructor at the Art School of the National Academy, he has won many awards and honors for his paintings, and his fine art has been exhibited widely in eminent galleries and institutions. He wrote and illustrated a book of realistic fiction for young people, *Farm Boy** (Viking, 1950), selected for Fanfare, the story of a spoiled boy who develops a sounder sense of values under the wise guidance of his farmer uncle, and a book of non-fiction, *What People Wore: A Visual History of Dress from Ancient Times to Twentieth Century America* (Viking, 1952). The many books he has illustrated for other authors for the young include an edition of Louisa May Alcott's *Little Men* (Grosset, 1957) and books by Alida Malkus*, Frederick Monjo, Clyde Robert Bulla*, and John and Patricia Beatty.

GRACE INGALLS (*On the Shores of Silver Lake**; *The Long Winter**; *Little Town on the Prairie**; *These Happy Golden Years**), fourth daughter in the frontier family, a baby when Laura* is twelve. Golden-haired, blue-eyed, she is described as "almost spoiled," but except for the time when she is lost on the prairie and discovered by Laura sitting among the violets in an old buffalo wallow (*On the Shores of Silver Lake*), she does not figure much as an individualized personality.

GRAHAM†, LORENZ (BELL) (1902–), born in New Orleans, La.; teacher and social worker, whose stories of the black experience have been widely commended. He attended the University of Washington, Seattle, the University of California, Los Angeles, and received his B.A. degree from Virginia Union College, Richmond. He also did graduate work at Columbia University and New York University. From 1924 to 1929 he was a teacher in Monrovia College, Liberia, the setting for his novel, *I, Momolu†* (Crowell, 1966). From this experience he also wrote *How God Fix Jonah* (Reynolds and Hitchcock, 1946), a collection of Bible stories told as if by the African, which were more recently reprinted as picture books, *David He No Fear* (Crowell, 1971), *God Wash the World and Start Again* (Crowell, 1971), etc. Between 1930 and 1942 he worked for the Richmond Adult Schools and was Educational Director for the Civilian Conservation Corps in Virginia and Pennsylvania. Later he worked as a housing authority manager and a real estate salesman and building contractor, and in the 1950s and 1960s, was a social worker in Queens and a probation officer in Los Angeles County. Of at least ten novels, his best known are *South Town** (Follett, 1958), *North Town* (Crowell, 1965), *Whose Town†* (Crowell, 1969), and *Return to South Town* (Crowell, 1976), a series about a black family which copes with prejudice in the segregated South and the bigoted North, and whose son returns to a changed and hopeful but still imperfect South.

GRANDDAD (*The Codfish Musket**), stern, affectionate, occasionally explosive and impatient scholar, who heard John Ledyard* tell of his adventures with Captain Cook and explain his plan for opening trade with the Far East. Granddad believes that Ledyard was a truly great American, whose ideas were unappreciated and ignored. He encourages Dan Boit's sense of adventure.

GRANDFATHER (*Nino**), big, strong, laughing man of about sixty who works the small Italian farm on which he lives with Nino* and Nino's mother, Allinda*. He loves to tell stories, enjoys the company of his grandson and his neighbors, and is a stabilizing force in Nino's life. He decides to accompany the family to America.

GRANDFATHER CHAVEZ (*. . . And Now Miguel**), called Padre de Chavez (the father of the Chavez), Miguel's grandfather, regarded with much respect and deep affection by his family. Now that he is too old to follow the flocks, he helps with light tasks about the ranch. For him, a mystical relationship unites humans and sheep, and raising sheep is far more than the practical matter of making money to support the family. The close relationship between Miguel and his grandfather is one of the book's most attractive features. He has a great influence on Miguel.

GRANDMA BEEBE (*Misty of Chincoteague**; *Stormy, Misty's Foal†*), grandmother of Paul* and Maureen*. She is a homeloving lady, who protests, but never very strongly, interruptions to her normal routine of taking care of house and family. Although in *Stormy* she objects to being moved out of her kitchen so that Misty can stay there and dislikes the idea of being airlifted to the mainland, she takes all the inconveniences of the flood in good part when she realizes there is no acceptable alternative. She is a typical loving grandmother.

GRANDMA HUTTO (*The Yearling**), pretty, warm, flirtatious older woman, who is an old friend of Penny* Baxter and mother of Oliver, a handsome young seaman. Fun-loving and sociable, she is a foil for grim Ma* Baxter, with whom she has little patience. Her true grit shows when she blames herself for her house fire, really caused by the Forresters, so that Oliver will leave right away with her for Boston and not engage in a feud which would probably mean his death or imprisonment as a murderer, even though the move takes her away from the area and people she loves.

GRANDPA BEEBE (*Misty of Chincoteague**; *Stormy, Misty's Foal†*), one of the Chincoteague islanders, on whose horse farm Paul* and Maureen* Beebe are staying. He is their grandfather. He agrees reluctantly to their plan to buy Phantom, not because he does not want them to have the horse, but because he feels that they will be disappointed when Phantom, which always eludes pursuit, is not caught in this year's drive either. He is generally very supportive of their plans, however, and on the night of the big storm, he moves Phantom and her foal inside the truck, so they will stay warm and dry. Paul is very grateful when he discovers what Grandpa has done and spends the night there with the horses. Grandpa Beebe is a practical, plainspoken man. He has a strong sense of community, and, in *Stormy* particularly, he works very hard along with his neighbors and the Coast Guard to get the island back in shape after the storm. He often teases Grandma* Beebe and goodheartedly tries to please her. He is a good family man, a typical grandfather.

GRANDPAPA (*Magic Money**), Tony's* mother's father, a fiercely independent old man of very limited means who is determined to continue to live in his own home in spite of the urging of his daughter and her family that he move in with them. Tony is pleased to stay with him at night sometimes and watch over him. Grandpapa's last ox has died, and, since he no longer works, he is too poor to buy another. Yet he longs to enter the ox-cart contest in San José, where he once won first prize for the most beautifully painted cart and best-kept oxen. He feels especially close to Tony and is very patient with him, and he tries very hard to look at things from Tony's point of view. It is a ''knife in his heart'' to him that he does not have the money to give Tony what he longs for. He helps the boy with gentle advice and intercedes for him with his parents. He and Tony have a beautiful relationship, and he is a winning character.

GRAN'MA PIDGEN (*Penelope Ellen**), grandmother of Cressy, who lives with her widowed daughter-in-law and tells exciting stories to the little girls. Her husband and brother having been killed at Bunker Hill, she is interested in the campaign to finish the monument in Boston commemorating the battle, and she organizes the Newburyport women to make a quilt to be sold at the benefit fair. Despite being in her eighties, she is a spry and independent old lady who faces philosophically the storm that wrecks her house and who insists on riding the Iron Horse, the new railroad between Boston and Newburyport.

GREAT DAY IN THE MORNING (Means*, Florence Crannell, Houghton, 1946), realistic novel set during World War II, mostly on St. Helena Island off the Carolina coast and at Tuskegee Institute in Alabama. Having been graduated from Penn School on the Sea Islands, Lillybelle* Lawrence, 20, is determined to be somebody important and thinks her first step is teaching the shabby Moss Island school. Already she does most of the field work for her aging grandfather, Noah*, with whom she lives along with her superstitious grandmother, her ineffectual aunt, Ginny, Ginny's good-for-nothing husband, Ed, and Sanctify*, their five-year-old son. After scrubbing the schoolhouse and making friends with the ragged students, she is told that the board reversed their decision and replaced her with a barely literate island girl because of pressure from the whites, suspicious of her ideas of improving the school and lengthening the term. Disappointed but undaunted, Lillybelle sets out to earn enough to go to Tuskegee on a five-year work program. She takes in the washing for the white manager's family at the local plantation, continues her field work, and sets out a field of potatoes herself, hoping to earn tuition and railroad fare. A tall, dark girl with a face like an Egyptian sculpture, she is courted by her distant cousin, stubborn, slow-thinking Abner Jones and by Lonnie, a good-looking but ''light-headed'' schoolmate. Her teachers at Penn, who have tried to persuade her to take up nursing, help her to buy some smart clothes from those contributed to the school, and in the fall she sets out for Tuskegee with her neighbor and friend, Callie (Calendar) St. Francis and Lonnie. There she is chosen for a roommate by Trudy (Gertrudine) Sands, a black girl from Ohio of a sort she has never known, well-to-do, self-confident, and flirtatious. Trudy quickly appropriates Lonnie, but Lillybelle acquires a devoted beau in Dolphus Bascom, a small fellow who always acts the comedian. Lillybelle meets George Washington Carver, her hero, who is now an old man and ill, and she is annoyed when he suggests that she should choose a profession to help her people but is deeply grieved when he dies. To earn money for a brown velvet evening dress, Lillybelle starts baby-sitting for the Tollivers, the family of a black officer at the nearby airbase. Occasionally Trudy, who has met a young officer, fills in for her as a way to see him, since strict school rules forbid such dating. At term's end Lillybelle falls ill from overwork, and, fearing she may develop tuberculosis, the doctor sends her home, but soon the Tollivers, who have been transferred to Denver, ask her to go with them to the healthier climate, and she accepts. The morning they leave Tuskegee, Trudy and her young officer, who have been secretly married, whizz past the Tolliver car and have a serious accident minutes later. Because the local hospital won't take in blacks, Trudy must be taken back to Tuskegee and dies on the way. Bad fortune pursues Lillybelle when they get to Loury Field, and Major Tolliver finds he has been ordered overseas. On a picnic they have to celebrate their last day together, young Roland is injured, and Lillybelle acts promptly and competently. In appreciation, Major Tolliver pays her expenses to stay and live at the YWCA, where she meets some girls in nurse's training and Dakie Dave, a veteran who lost one arm early in the war. She falls in love with Dakie, stiffens his resolution to do well, and plans to start training as a nurse, having at last realized her true vocation. Although the simple life and the beauty of the sea islands is depicted with appreciation and the tragedy of discrimination in health service is shown with indignation, the standards to which the characters are expected to aspire are clearly those of the white middle class, and this dates the book. The variety of personalities on St. Helena Island and at Tuskegee is well presented, but the pace is slow and the romance seems antiseptic and innocent compared with more recent realistic novels. Fanfare.

THE GREAT QUEST (Hawes*, Charles Boardman, ill. George Varian, Little, 1921), rousing adventure novel set in 1826 in Topham, Mass., then aboard a sailing vessel to Cuba and the Gulf of Guinea, and in the African jungle. Since the death of his widowed mother, Joe Woods, now in his early twenties, has lived with his Uncle Seth* Upham and worked in his uncle's general store, along with simple, garrulous Sim Muzzy and Arnold* Lamont, a close-mouthed Frenchman with a mysterious past. Their quiet routine is disrupted by the return to town of Cornelius* Gleason, an old acquaintance of Seth's, who had left Topham a wild youth and now appears to have made a fortune. Cornelius insinuates himself into the confidence of the town and particularly of Seth, whom he persuades to sell his store, home, and other interests and purchase the brig *Adventure*, to sail on a mysterious quest in which Joe, Sim, Arnold, and Abe Guptil, a former sailor on whose farm mortgage Seth has foreclosed, are to share with Gleason and Seth in the profits. In Havana, Sim is shanghaied, but, because Arnold has a previously unrevealed knowledge of Spanish, he and Joe escape an ambush set by Gleason, and they sail for Africa after taking on a pal of

Cornelius, Molly* Matterson, as mate and supplies that show they expect to engage in the slave trade. The sides are soon clearly drawn, Cornelius and the huge, soft-voiced Molly against Joe, Arnold, Abe, and honest Captain Gideon North, with Seth alternating between his old imperious ways and a fearful subservience to Cornelius. Arriving on the Guinea shore, they stop at a settlement where the missionary repulses them, but his daughter, Faith Parmenter, makes a great impression on Joe. A third friend of Cornelius turns up, Bud O'Hara, who leads a party of those who will share in the profit from the mysterious quest into the jungle where throbbing drums, wails, and glimpses of black figures warn them they are in danger from the natives. With great difficulty they travel inland to where a fourth in the villainous plot, known as Bull, has been living, only to find him long dead, a native spear through his skeleton, but a treasure in jewels in the hut. Their presence, however, has roused the natives, and they are held in the hut in a siege, which completes the unhinging of the mind of Seth, who has deteriorated as he has realized how he has been defrauded. When he walks out the front, singing a hymn, the natives kill him but are distracted long enough so the others escape out the back, losing the gems on the way, and make their wild retreat to the coast where Parmenter refuses them shelter but is himself killed by the Africans. It is only through the skill in handling a canoe in the surf of Faith Parmenter and her black servant that Joe, Arnold, and Abe reach the waiting *Adventure*. There Joe, as Seth's heir and therefore owner of the vessel, challenges Cornelius's authority to load slaves. They duel, Joe is wounded, but Arnold finishes the fight, and they sail for South America where the ship is wrecked, Molly and Cornelius are drowned when they leave in the only boat, and the other main characters are washed ashore with the wreckage. Arnold reveals that he is really a French nobleman and lends the others enough money to get home to Topham, Faith and Joe having been married on the way. There Joe finds that Seth had held out some money from the *Adventure* enterprise, so he is able to buy the store back, repay Arnold, and set Abe up in a farm again. The pace of the novel, once the company has left Topham, is breathless and the sense of impending treachery by Cornelius and Molly keeps a strong tension throughout. Characters, even some of the minor ones, are vivid and memorable. Although the good characters in the book are strongly against the slave trade, the portrayal of the African natives as almost inhumanly savage and superstitious is dated, that of the white imperialist, not the modern anthropologist. Newbery Honor.

THE GREAT QUILLOW (Thurber* James, ill. Doris Lee, Harcourt, 1944), brief fantasy set in a far country of giants and craftsmen of somewhat medieval types. A giant named Hunder is terrorizing the area, travelling from village to village demanding huge meals until each town is impoverished. When he appears on the hill above the village, the councilors meet to discuss ways to avoid his demands but can think of none and begin serving up his daily three sheep, pie made of a thousand apples, chocolate as high and wide as a spinning wheel, and the huge clothes and candle he orders. Only the toy maker, Quillow, who volunteers to be the giant's storyteller, has an idea. He cleverly tricks the giant with a story of a former giant who fell ill of a curious malady, first hearing only the word "woddly," then perceiving all red chimneys as black, and finally seeing blue men. He enlists the town's help in answering all questions with "woddly" and in painting their chimneys black during the night. He himself makes a series of toy blue men, and the giant, terrified, runs off to try what Quillow has said is the only possible cure: to wash in the yellow water in the middle of the ocean. The story uses the pattern of a traditional fairy tale but differs in its use of clever language and the ingenuity of its humor. Fanfare.

THE GREAT WHEEL (Lawson*, Robert, ill. author, Viking, 1957), lighthearted historical novel about the construction of the first Ferris Wheel for the Chicago World's Columbian Exposition in 1893. The story opens in County Mayo, Ireland, where Mary Kate Kilroy receives a letter from her brother, Michael Gilbin, asking her to send her son, Conn* (Cornelius Terence) Kilroy, 18, to help him in his New York business of constructing sewers and sidewalks. On the steamship, *City of Bristol*, Conn, an attractive coppery-haired boy, meets an old sailor and ship rigger, Martin Brennan, and a German girl, Trudy Zillheimer, bound to join her Uncle Otto in Wisconsin, but he fails to learn Trudy's family name. After a successful start in New York, Conn is hired away by Uncle Patrick, a large, black-bearded man, who works as construction supervisor for a brilliant young engineer, George Washington Gale Ferris, who has contracted to build an enormous wheel as an attraction for the Exposition. With Martin Brennan, who has also been hired by Uncle Patrick, Conn works on the wheel from the digging of the enormous footings to the final hanging of the passenger cars and then stays on as a guard, partly because of his affection for the wheel but more because he hopes Trudy may visit the fair. When she finally does, he is astonished to find she is the niece of a wealthy man, not the simple immigrant girl he had been dreaming of, but, after some misunderstanding, they marry and start farming in Wisconsin. Written with a pleasant suggestion of Irish lilt, the book is notable for making the details of the actual construction of the wheel not only understandable but also exciting. While the characters are not drawn in depth, they are attractive and often amusing, and the tone of the story is so cheerful that coincidences in the plot seem deliberate rather than clumsy. Lawson's illustrations add both clarity and humor. Newbery Honor.

GRETEL BRINKER (*Hans Brinker; or, The Silver Skates**), a little blue-eyed girl of twelve, younger sister of Hans*. She is lithe and quick and is a very fine skater. Like Hans, she is patient and enduring and bears their poverty without complaint. She is sometimes left out of family decisions and sent away at critical moments because Meitje and Hans think she is too young to be consulted or allowed to see things that might upset her. She often feels left out of things. She is a Good Girl, a fairly well revealed character, but still a type figure.

THE GRIFFIN AND THE MINOR CANON (Stockton*, Frank R., ill. Maurice Sendak, Holt, 1963, originally in *The Bee Man of Orn and Other Fanciful Tales*, Scribner's, 1887), literary tale set in an imaginary country in an unspecified time. There, in a certain town, stood an old church with a sculpture of a griffin over the door. The last real griffin, living in the dreadful wilds far from this town, hears of the statue and takes a fancy to see it. He flies to a meadow near the town, terrifying the inhabitants. When two farm laborers hurry by, he accosts them and demands to know whether there is anyone in town brave enough to speak to him. The men suggest the Minor Canon, a church subordinate to whom most of the onerous chores fall. Feeling it is his duty to keep the creature from wrathful vengeance, the Minor Canon goes out to talk with him and persuades him to wait until morning to see the statue. The Canon tries to get all the people out of the way, but since some of them hope to keep the Griffin away by destroying the image, he spends the night protecting it from vandalism. The Griffin is so pleased with it that he stays and stays, much to the consternation of the people. The Minor Canon is relieved to learn that the Griffin eats only twice a year, at the vernal and autumnal equinoxes. Most of the important people leave town; the poor people and the workers get used to the Griffin following the Minor Canon around but begin to worry as the equinox approaches. They blame the Minor Canon and insist that he go off to the dreadful wilds, hoping the Griffin will follow. The Griffin, however, stays and begins to take over the Minor Canon's duties, visiting the sick and teaching the school for bad children. The townspeople suggest that they will cook a marvelous meal for the creature, and if that doesn't suit, he may try the orphan asylum in the next town. The Griffin refuses saying they are all too mean and selfish to prepare anything edible, that only for the Minor Canon would he have an appetite. When an old man tells him that they sent the Minor Canon away, he is enraged, makes them promise to place the Minor Canon in the position of highest honor when he returns, and tears the statue from the church front and flies back to the wilds. There he finds the Minor Canon close to starvation, nurses him, and returns him to the meadow near the town. The Griffin, finding nothing as suitable to eat as the Minor Canon, lies and gazes at his statue until he pines away. The story is told in mock-serious language, with a straight-faced humor, and is careful not to draw morals about the courage and dedication of the modest young man or the relative goodness of the Griffin compared with the townspeople. The modern edition with Sendak's illustrations brings the old story to life again after being nearly forgotten. Choice; Fanfare; Lewis Carroll.

GRIFF NOLAN (*Jennifer**), good-looking, self-satisfied, well-mannered high school junior, sometime boyfriend of Patsy Gordon, and later of Jennifer Martin. He has a reputation for rushing new girls, a practice of which Jennifer, new in town, is unaware, until after she begins going with him. He dropped Patsy, Jennifer's best friend, for Jennifer, and he then drops Jennifer for another new girl, Diane Winters. Jennifer's father is cool toward him when he calls to introduce himself to the family, regarding his politeness as pretense.

GRIMALKIN (*Benjamin West and His Cat Grimalkin**), orphaned, ailing, little black kitten adopted by Elmira, Benjamin West's mother cat, and named Grimalkin after the kitten's dead mother. Grimalkin grows like magic into a slick, black cat, with fluffy, soft, shining fur and with uncommonly thick, long hairs in his tail. Benjamin is sure the cat encourages him to paint, and he uses his pet's hairs to make brushes.

GUMMY (*The Gammage Cup**; *The Whisper of Glocken†*), Minnipin idler, roamer of the fields, and poet. He is fond of pranks and making up rhymes and often speaks in verse. When "They" (he and others considered not respectable because of their nonconforming behavior) are outlawed from Slipper-on-the-Water*, they live in his stone house on the Little Trickle River up in the mountains. He first sees the mysterious fires on the mountain, which the Minnipins later learn have been made by their traditional enemies, the Mushrooms, who are planning to attack the Minnipins. In the second book, he helps to rescue the New Heroes.

GUSTAF LARSSON (*They Came from Sweden**), son of Carl* and the character about whom the book mainly revolves. Earnest, hardworking boy, he early gets the idea that he wants to be a lawyer, an ambition his father doesn't clearly approve of but nevertheless encourages, because he sees how much the boy wants it and because he realizes that a lawyer who knows both Swedish and English is needed in the area. Gus is an inventive, resourceful boy, who often comes up with ideas that help the family out of difficulties. He teaches himself to read English by using newspapers that the stage driver gives him.

H

HADER, BERTA (HOERNER) (1890–1976), born in San Pedro, Coahuila, Mexico; artist-author, half of a very popular husband-wife illustrator team. When she was three, her parents returned to the United States, lived in Texas and later in New York. She was educated in New York schools and at Washington (State) School of Journalism, then worked in California as an apprentice fashion designer. From 1915 to 1918 she attended the California School of Design in San Franciso, where she met Elmer Hader*. They married in 1919 and worked together for the rest of their lives, writing and illustrating nearly fifty books, mostly about animals, like *Billy Butter** (Macmillan, 1936), starring a Telegraph Hill goat. Some, like *Jamaica Johnny** (Macmillan, 1935), are the result of their travels. Their work spans the development of the highly illustrated book in this country and shows an increasing skill and sophistication. In 1949 they won the Caldecott Medal for *The Big Snow* (Macmillan, 1948). She was a lifelong pacifist and conservationist.

HADER, ELMER (STANLEY) (1889–1973), born in Pajaro, Calif.; illustrator-author, whose published works for children are all in collaboration with his wife, Berta Hader*. He lived for most of his youth in San Francisco and attended the Julian Academy, Paris, working as a vaudevillian to pay his way. Later he attended the California School of Design in San Francisco, where he met his wife. During World War I he served in the Army Camouflage Corps in France. In 1927–1928, he and his wife wrote and illustrated seven "Happy Hours" books, a project that launched them on a lifetime career as an author-illustrator team. They lived near Nyack, N.Y., during much of their married life.

HADJ SIDI AHMED (*Pepperfoot of Thursday Market**), kind and supportive grandfather of Driss, respected headman of the Berbers of Ali Taza. He takes his responsibilities very seriously, consulting with the elders on matters of importance to the tribe and teaching the youth the history and wisdom of the people and instructing them in religious beliefs and practices on Fridays at his tent.

HALE, LUCRETIA P(EABODY) (1820–1900), born in Boston, Mass.; writer now remembered almost entirely for her episodic *The Peterkin Papers** (Osgood, 1880). She was educated at private schools, Susan Whitney's, Miss Peabody's, and George B. Emerson's, and later taught correspondence school and was a private tutor. Although she was well known as the sister of Edward Everett Hale and for her three novels and several works of non-fiction on religion and needlework for adults, and for her six books of fiction for children, it is her stories of the droll Peterkin family, first published in *Our Young Folks* and *St. Nicholas* magazines, which have kept her a place in the history of children's literature. In *The Last of the Peterkins* (Roberts, 1886), less popular than the simple, ludicrous early stories, she takes the family overseas and marries them off.

HALF MAGIC (Eager*†, Edward, ill. N. M. Bodecker, Harcourt, 1954), episodic family fantasy in which most of the adventures take place in Toledo, Ohio, in the early 1920s. After she and her younger brother, Mark, and her younger sisters, Katherine and Martha, have been reading the magic books of E. Nesbit and longing for adventures, young Jane discovers in a crack in the sidewalk a magical token that grants half of every wish. With it the children have adventures that make this summer vacation unique. Some of them take place near home, some in distant times and places. Some involve danger, while others are funny. The children first realize that the token is special when Jane accidentally sets a playhouse on fire with it. Then Martha inadvertently gives Carrie Chapman Cat, the household pet, the ability to speak a kind of pidgin English. Mother gets transported only halfway home from a visit to relatives. When they see the connection between the happenings and the token, the children agree to take turns using the charm. The children also come to see that the token does not grant full wishes, and to compensate they must be sure to ask for twice as much as they want. Mark then shifts them to the Sahara where they are captured by an Arab trader, and Katherine to the days of King Arthur where she defeats Sir Launcelot in jousting. An accidental wish causes Martha to become transparent while attending a movie and Jane to become the prissy daughter of a very ''proper'' family. A romance parallels the children's adventures: Mother and a local bookseller, Mr. Smith, who is a congenial and imaginative man whom the children have grown to like and who knows about their charm, become interested in each other. When Mother refuses Mr. Smith's proposal of marriage, the children help him win her. At the end, the children leave the charm on a sidewalk for a little girl who looks as though she needs some happy experiences. Characterization is shallow, and the children are almost indistinguishable from one another. The emphasis is on fun and adventure. Style is relaxed, playful, and sometimes tongue in cheek, with lots of natural dialogue. Though amusing, the fantasy portions of the novel are strained, particularly those that take place in the Sahara and England, and the whole thing simply goes on too long. Sequel is *Magic by the Lake*. Choice; Fanfare.

HALLOCK, GRACE TABER (1893–1967), author of books about health and hygiene for children, teachers, and parents; a series of biographies on figures who made important advances in medicine and public health; a book of verses and picture maps for children, *Bird in the Bush* (Dutton, 1930) and two novels for the young, *Petersham's Hill* (Dutton, 1927), a fantasy about a little girl and some fairies, and *The Boy Who Was** (Dutton, 1928), a Newbery honor book of historical fiction with fantasy elements describing in lively detail and didactic intent a series of real events that happened in Italy from ancient times to the mid-nineteenth century. She was a graduate of Mt. Holyoke College and in 1914 helped organize the Ulster County Division of the New York State Women's Suffrage Party. From 1933–1949, she directed the health and welfare bureau of Metropolitan Life Insurance Co. She also wrote promotional materials for the Quaker Oats Company.

HAMILTON BEMIS (*Call of the Mountain**), younger brother of Jonathan Bemis, Nathan Lindsay's benefactor; clever lawyer, untiring worker, sharp dealer, adroit manipulator of thoughts and actions, the villain of the novel. He angrily sets out to break Jonathan's will when he discovers that Jonathan has left Rolling Willows farm to his ward. Although he seems not to care for the family farm and indeed seldom spends time there and even hires shiftless Stillman Choate to run it, it is learned later in the novel that he really has looked forward to living on the farm in his old age and that his pride has been sorely hurt by his brother's decision to leave the land to the youth. At first Hamilton appears merely to be just another stock villain, but gradually his character is fleshed out and the reader sees other facets of his personality.

HANCOCK, JOHN (*Johnny Tremain**; *Mr. Revere and I**), actual historical figure, presented in *Johnny Tremain* as one of the revolutionary leaders who meet in the Lorne attic. He first appears in the novel at the Lapham establishment, where he orders a silver sugar bowl from Mr. Lapham. Later Johnny applies at his counting house for a job but is rejected because he cannot hold a pen to write. Hancock, a fastidious, gentlehearted man, averts his face to avoid looking at Johnny's crippled hand, yet sends his errand boy with a rich gift of money for Johnny immediately afterward. At the meetings in the Lorne attic he is seemingly in the hand of Sam Adams, shown as fervidly against compromise with the British and in favor of revolution. In *Mr. Revere and I* he is a minor character.

HANNAH TUPPER (*The Witch of Blackbird Pond**), gentle old Quaker who befriends Kit. She lives in the tiny cottage near Blackbird Pond which her husband built after they were branded and driven out of Massachusetts because they were Quakers. Unknown to anyone in town, Nat* Eaton looks after her. She also befriends Prudence* Cruff. Words of consolation and support come quickly to her tongue.

HANS BRINKER (*Hans Brinker; or, The Silver Skates**), fifteen-year-old only son and elder child in the family of Raff and Meitje Brinker, a poor, honest, working family of Broek, Holland. He has great square shoulders, and bushy yellow hair, and in height he towers over his little sister, Gretel*, whom he sometimes patronizes. He is a solid, hearty-looking lad, with honest eyes, who is consistently steadfast, respectful, obedient, and hardworking. Although fairly well revealed, he is the Good Boy upon whom his mother and father can always rely.

HANS BRINKER; OR, THE SILVER SKATES (Dodge*, Mary Mapes, O'Kane, 1865), realistic novel of family life set in Holland in the 1840s. One month's time brings significant changes in the lives of earnest, hardworking Hans* Brinker, 15, his loving, resilient sister, Gretel*, 12, their patient mother, Meitje, and mentally ill father, Raff, who occupy a broken-down hut in the village of Broek, not far from Amsterdam. Raff, a workingman, lost his mind in a fall from a scaffolding ten years before the story begins, and Meitje barely makes ends meet. Although Raff sometimes becomes violent, his family is devoted to him. The family savings of one thousand guilders mysteriously disappeared just before Raff became disabled. At that time Raff also gave Meitje a gold watch to keep for someone, a valuable timepiece which only loyalty to Raff has prevented her from selling to buy food and clothing for her family. Warmhearted Hilda van Gleck, daughter of a rich burgomaster, organizes a skating race for mid-December to celebrate her mother's birthday. The prizes will be silver skates. When Hilda sees that Gretel has only wooden skates, she gives Gretel money to buy a pair of metal ones in return for the necklace that Hansel has carved for his sister. Similarly, Peter van Holp, another kind, generous youth, provides Hansel with money for skates in return for a carved chain for his sister. On the way to buy the skates, Hansel encounters renowned Dr. Boekman, whom he bravely asks to come and examine his father. Dr. Boekman agrees to do so when next he returns to Broek. Peter and five other boys organize a skating journey to The Hague, during which Hans recovers the purse Peter loses. Peter agrees to carry a message to Dr. Boekman in Leyden that Mynheer Brinker has worsened. The doctor hurries to the village and operates on Raff. To everyone's joy, the operation is successful, and Raff recovers his mind. He tells Hans and Meitje that he buried the family savings and that the watch had been given him by a youth fleeing from prosecution for a crime he did not commit. Gretel handily wins the silver skates in the girls' competition in Hilda's race, and Hans graciously enables Peter to win by giving him a needed skate lace. The morocco case for Gretel's new skates bears the name of its maker, Thomas Higgs, a leatherworker, who turns out to be the owner of the watch and Dr. Boekman's long-lost son. After a joyful reunion, Dr. Boekman offers to send Hans to medical school, and his son hires Raff to supervise his leatherworks. The lean, predictable, contrived plot enables the author to accomplish her stated purpose for the novel: to inform readers about the history, geography, and culture of Holland. Characters are stock, tone is earnest, instructive, and often moralistic and sentimental. The book exerts a certain charm, however, that arises out of the abundance of carefully realized details and affectionate tone. One of the first novels of family life for young people, it enjoys the stature of a classic, and for years it influenced attitudes about the Dutch people. (Carl* Schummel; Jacob* Poot; Ben* Dobbs) Children's Classics; Choice.

THE HAPPY ORPHELINE (Carlson*†, Natalie Savage, ill. Garth Williams, Harper, 1957), realistic novel for younger children set in the village of Ste. Germaine near Paris in the mid-twentieth century. Brigitte* is one of the twenty little orphan girls cared for by Madame* Flattot and by Genevieve, who tells them stories of her godmother's poodle, Zezette. When Brigitte gets the bean in her piece of cake on the Feast of the Kings and so becomes Queen for the day, she commands that Genevieve take the orphelines, as they are known in the village, to the dog cemetery to see Zezette's grave. Accidentally, Brigitte is left behind when they board the return bus, because the youngest, Josine*, has been allowed to do the counting. Weeping loudly, Brigitte attracts sympathy and is taken in charge by eccentric Madame* Capet, who believes her husband is the true King of France, descended from the dauphin, son of Marie Antoinette. The pretender's "queen" has Brigitte clean her run-down room and do the dishes, then takes her back to the orphanage in a harrowing ride on her motor bike. Several days later, knowing that Madame Capet plans to adopt her for a drudge, Brigette determines to do something so bad that no one will want to adopt her. She lets out all the dogs from the yards which have signs saying "Wicked Dog." The dogs, none of which is really vicious, cause such a disturbance in the marketplace that Madame Capet, arriving on her motorbike, believes Brigitte is inciting a revolution and refuses to adopt her. In a switch on the usual orphan story, the book gets an amusing irony from the way the girls are happy in their institution and don't want to be adopted and in the mistaken sympathy of the people who call them "poor unhappy little orphelines." Although the story is simple, the characters are well defined and the setting gives a flavor of a French village. Sequels. Choice; Fanfare.

HAPPY TIMES IN CZECHOSLOVAKIA (Bartusek*, Libuska, ill. Yarka Burés, Knopf, 1940), simple, plotless series of episodes in the life of three children of Czechoslovakia, set probably in the early twentieth century. Maruska Horak, $6^1/_2$, lives with her two brothers, Tomash, 11, and Yura, 5, their parents and grandparents, and their hired girl, Anichka, in a village. The chapters mostly tell of the traditional happenings of holidays—Easter, the celebration of spring, Whitsuntide, the feast day of St. Mary, and Christmas. Other chapters tell of Yura's first day of school and of his first job, when he is set to watch the goose and its twelve goslings, and how he nearly suffocates them by carrying them home in his boots. At the end, Anichka is engaged to a young village worker, Yanko, who plans to take her to America, and the children go to sleep thinking of visiting her in that far off land. The book is exactly what its title promises, a series of pictures, in words and illustrations, of happy times in a traditional Czech culture, but since there is no plot and very little characterization, its literary value is minimal. Fanfare.

HAROLD BOYD (*South Town**), self-important, prejudiced white boy, who forces the black youngsters off the road with his fancy car. At the mill he orders the black boys out of the water but panics when his cousin, Little Red, is in danger and must be saved by David* Williams. When the night-riders, led by Harold's father, have terrorized the Williams family, Harold and Little Red walk to their house to say they are sorry. Fifteen years later, when David returns to South Town, Harold is a doctor running a fancy hospital built by his father (*Return to South Town*, Crowell, 1976). At first he welcomes David and suggests that he might join their hospital staff to work on black patients in a separate wing. When he finds that David plans to set up his own practice, he slows down the approval of his license and, when David has saved a woman's life after a plane crash, has him arrested for practicing without a license.

HARRIETT (McKinley*, Charles, Jr., ill. William Pène Du Bois*†, Viking, 1946), highly illustrated brief fantasy set in London and Surrey in an unspecified time, the mid-twentieth century to judge by the pictures. Harriett, a horse who pulls the delivery cart for Sedgerow, Ltd., is particularly fascinated by the hats in the window of a corner shop, arranged by a person she always refers to as "That Nice Young Man." Among Harriett's many friends are the two stone lions who live across from the British Museum, and who always have some flattering remark for her as she passes by. Her only brother, Gregory, is in the King's Guards, a very important position so he can't speak to her when they meet, but he always tosses his head and shakes it fiercely to say hello when he sees her. One day she sees the manager of the store, whom she believes is Mr. Sedgerow, Ltd., talking to That Nice Young Man, calling him "Edward," so she realizes that he must be Mr. Edward, Esquire. Shortly after that, Mr. Edward takes her, with her favorite belongings neatly packed in a small brown case, to a farm in Surrey. There Harriett immediately starts making friends of the White Ducks, the Rabbits, the Squirrel, the Fox, the young Meadowlark couple, and other inhabitants. On Harriett's birthday they all give her a surprise party, and Mr. Edward gives her a beautiful straw hat decorated with flowers. The very simple story has some rather clever small twists occasioned by Harriett's ladylike misinterpretations, and the illustrations are entertaining, but little of interest happens in the plot. Fanfare.

HARRY IN ENGLAND (Richards*, Laura E., ill. Reginald Birch, Appleton, 1937), episodic family novel set mostly in England, subtitled "being the partly true adventures of H. R. in the year 1857." Because his brother, Bob, has scarlet fever, Harry Grahame, a small boy of unspecified age, sails alone for Silverthorne, the English countryside estate of his wealthy Grandmother Grahame. The highlight of his pleasant voyage is making friends with Captain Barney Buncle, a merry, middle-aged fellow traveler, who teaches him to make sailors' knots and who gives him a flat, round sea-bean, which to Harry's impressionable mind holds the promise of a charm. His grandmother's large and rambling house, her unsmiling lady's maid, and even his staid and proper grandmother herself intimidate the homesick lad at first. But he likes his cheerful nurse, Anne, right away, and soon makes friends with the other servants with whom he becomes a great favorite, in particular, the cook, Mrs. Tadd, who supplies him generously with gingerbread "nuts" (ginger snaps). He soon comes to appreciate the comfortable well-appointed house and realizes that his grandmother, though stern and often rather aloof, really loves him and is his friend. He especially enjoys the company of Carter*, the gardener, whose potting shed exudes most agreeable odors and who introduces him to Henry, the female hedgehog, and Bones, the stable dog, and makes him a present of Tom, a dormouse. Weeks of good times follow, with a visit from his cousin, Jim* Marriott, during which the two share a substantial tea in the modest cottage of the Honey* Woman; with lessons from his youthful, unconventional tutor, Mr.* Dakyns; and with renewing his acquaintance with Captain Buncle, who pays a call, bringing with him an American robin for the local aviary. Harry spends a week with Jim at his home in Cherry Lodge where he enjoys getting to know the large and gregarious Marriott family. They all travel to North House, the home of Harry's six, chittery great-aunts. In the maze on the lawn, Harry pretends to be Theseus and rescues Jim's little twin sisters, Flopsy and Mopsy. Upon his return to Silverthorne, Harry learns with dismay that he must go to boarding school. Then to his joy he discovers that Jim will be his classmate and Mr. Dakyns his master in History and Latin. He attributes his good fortune to Captain Barney's sea-bean. Although the novel is episodic, events relate to one another, characters recur, and the themes of obedience and respect for authority are often reinforced. Everyone behaves extremely well. Harry is a likeable lad, Jim a lively counterpart. Adults are firm but always genial and sympathetic, and their occasional preachiness and emphasis on decorum seem typical of the period. One of the novel's best points, in fact, looked at from today's vantage point, is its revelation of middle-class English society of the period. Tone is affectionate and lighthearted (though sometimes arch), conversations are pleasant and revealing, and the many details of food and animals produce a strong sensory appeal. This story of a small boy's growing into a new home life is high in entertainment value and exerts a certain old-fashioned charm. Fanfare.

HARRY THE HERMIT (*Miracles on Maple Hill**), elderly man who lives alone with his goats and chickens and becomes a good friend of Marly and especially of her brother Joe*. Among his other skills he carves wooden chains of all sizes. A veteran of World War I, his story parallels Dale's in that he had difficulty adjusting afterwards, left his family, became a hobo, and settled on

Maple Hill through the influence of Mr.* Chris. Although he is unwashed and smells strongly of his goats, he is taken in by the family when he has hurt his leg, mostly because Dale backs Joe's desire to keep the old man over Christmas.

HASKINS, PETER (*The Enchanted Schoolhouse**), Brian Boru's pleasant, young teacher in the United States, who conducts a unit on Ireland which Brian Boru helps teach. Haskins's questions about Irish schools give Brian Boru the idea of helping the children of Lobster Bay, Maine, get a new school.

HAVE SPACE SUIT—WILL TRAVEL (Heinlein*, Robert A., Scribner's, 1958), science fiction novel set in an American town called Centerville and on the moon, on Pluto, and in various more distant parts of space in the future less than a generation from the 1950s. A lunar city having been established and regular earth-to-moon trips instituted, Kip (Clifford) Russell, a high school senior, has a great desire to visit the moon and in a slogan contest wins an obsolete model space suit. He names the suit Oscar and rerigs it with air bottles, radio gear, and other equipment it lacks. One evening as he is walking in a field near home, wearing the suit and testing the radio, he gets an answer. Two space ships land, a couple of creatures run from the first, and Kip, trying to help one who is obviously hurt, is knocked unconscious by someone from the second. He wakes to find himself aboard the ship, a prisoner in the company of an eleven-year-old girl named Peewee* (Patricia Synant) Reisfeld, a young genius who has been captured by space pirates while she was on a tourist trip to the moon. She has almost escaped by stealing a space ship and piloting it to earth, aided and directed by the "Mother* Thing," an advanced space creature with a vaguely feline body and maternal attitudes. Kip learns that they are being held hostage by horrible creatures he calls Wormfaces, who have established a secret base on the moon and have in their employ two unprincipled humans, Tim and Fats. When they arrive on the moon, Kip and Peewee manage to escape and, with Kip carrying the Mother Thing inside Oscar, make a grueling trip by foot over mountains to within sight of Lunar City, where they are ironically recaptured by the Wormfaces. They are taken to a major Wormface base on Pluto, and Kip is thrown into a pit dungeon, where later Tim and Fats join him, having fallen out of favor. After some time these two disappear, presumably eaten by the Wormfaces, who like human meat. The Mother Thing engineers a terrific explosion which destroys most of the Wormfaces, but she collapses trying to light a beacon to attract her people. Peewee rescues Kip, and he, in Oscar, risks the terrible Plutonian cold to activate the beacon and retrieve the body of the Mother Thing, who turns out not to be dead. They are taken by the Mother Thing to their home planet, Vega Five, where Kip's frozen extremities are regrown by their advanced medical techniques. They then are taken by the Mother Thing to the court of the Three Galaxies in the Lesser Megallanic Clouds, where they and the Wormfaces are to be tried. The Wormfaces are determined to be detrimental, and their planet is destroyed. Kip and Peewee, with a caveman and a

Roman legionnaire, must represent the human race which is being tried. The decision is to let the race continue with aid to help it keep from destroying itself and to reexamine it again in the future. Kip and Peewee are taken home where the information they bring back is of tremendous interest to Peewee's brilliant father and other major scientists. Kip gets a scholarship to MIT. Today's space enthusiasts will perhaps be amused at the discrepancies between the fictional projections and actual developments. Less well informed readers may be bored by the wealth of technical detail included. As an adventure story, the action is fast-paced and at times engrossing, but the characterization is shallow and some essential elements (the description of the Mother Thing, for instance) are not clearly imaged. Choice.

HAVIGHURST, MARION (BOYD) (–1974), born in Marietta, Ohio; author of novels and fictionalized history, who collaborated with her husband, Walter Havighurst*, on *Song of the Pines** (Winston, 1949), on *High Prairie* (Farrar, 1944), and on *Climb a Lofty Ladder: A Story of Swedish Settlement in Minnesota* (Winston, 1952). She was a graduate of Smith College and received her M.A. degree from Yale Universiy, and taught English at Western College and Miami University, both in Oxford, Ohio. Individually she published poetry, a mystery novel, and fiction for young people, including *The Sycamore Tree* (World, 1960).

HAVIGHURST, WALTER (1901–), born in Appleton, Wis.; writer of regional fiction, biography, and informal history, mostly about the Midwest. He received his A.B. degree from the University of Denver, attended Kings College, University of London, and got his M.A. degree from Columbia University. He worked as a deck hand on a Great Lakes freighter and spent one year in the merchant marine, and from 1928 on, taught at Miami University of Oxford, Ohio. Among his works for children are a number of "first" books: *First Book of Pioneers* (Watts, 1959); *First Book of the Oregon Trail* (Watts, 1960); *First Book of the Gold Rush* (Watts, 1962). He collaborated with his wife, Marion Havighurst*, in writing *Song of the Pines** (Winston, 1949), historical novel of the Norwegian lumbermen in Wisconsin, a Newbery honor book, *High Prairie* (Farrar, 1944), and *Climb a Lofty Ladder: A Story of Swedish Settlement in Minnesota* (Winston, 1952). He also wrote biographies of Annie Oakley and Buffalo Bill.

HAWES, CHARLES BOARDMAN (1889–1923), born in Clifton Springs, N.Y.; editor, author of stirring sea stories. He attended Bowdoin College and Harvard University graduate school. At one time he taught at Harrisburg Academy in Pennsylvania, and he became editor of *Youth's Companion* and *Open Road*, two prominent magazines of their day, in both of which some of his stories were published. His novel of the slave trade, *The Great Quest** (Little,

1921), was a Newbery honor book and *The Dark Frigate** (Atlantic, 1923) was a Newbery winner after his death. A story of sailing ships and piracy, it is still one of the strongest novels on that distinguished list.

HAYWOOD, CAROLYN (1898–   ), born in Philadelphia; author-illustrator of children's books; artist. She grew up in Philadelphia, graduated from Philadelphia Normal School, and attended the Pennsylvania Academy of Fine Arts. She studied with several of Howard Pyle's pupils, among them Jessie Wilcox Smith, and taught at the Friends Central School in Philadelphia. Since 1939, she has written over three dozen self-illustrated, humorous, episodic novels about ordinary children in everyday home, school, and neighborhood situations for readers of the eight-to-twelve age range, many featuring the very popular characters, Betsy and Eddie. She draws her ideas from her childhood memories, from observation, and from her travels. Though the plots are spun out and the characters types, the incidents are exciting, amusing, and typical, the language is easy enough for young children to read for themselves, and children can easily identify with what goes on. Both *"B" Is for Betsy** (Harcourt, 1939), her first book and the first of the several Betsy books, and *Little Eddie** (Morrow, 1947), also a series book, are listed in *Choice*. Other titles about these perennially popular, lively children, who might live next door, are *Betsy and the Boys* (Harcourt, 1945), *Eddie and the Fire Engine* (Morrow, 1949), *Eddie's Valuable Property* (Morrow, 1975), and *Betsy's Play School* (Morrow, 1977). Most of her books have been translated into the Scandinavian languages, and some into French, German, and Japanese. In addition to writing, she has been a muralist and portrait painter, specializing in portraits of children. Her artwork appears in the permanent collection of the Pennsylvania Academy of Fine Arts.

HEART OF DANGER (Pease*, Howard, Doubleday, 1946), historical adventure novel which takes place in France during the German occupation in World War II. In the fall of 1943, Tod* Moran, third mate on the American freighter *Araby*, and Rudy* Behrens, fireman and ex-music student on violin and piano, in convoy to the Mediterranean, are ferried to France by a French fishing boat. The two youths are to make their way to Paris where they are to contact a German officer known only as X 31* who will give them information about the location of German atomic bomb laboratories. There follows a harrowing, danger-filled journey as the two travel overland by train, on foot, by haywagon, and subway, assisted from one underground station to another by members of the French Resistance and by other German-hating French, even schoolchildren and nuns. They stay in private houses, inns, a local bath, and at the comfortable villa of Madame* Moreau, whose family shares Rudy's love of music. In Paris, the youths rendezvous with X 31, receive the information, and learn to their great surprise that Rudy's father, Professor* Behrens, formerly a professor of German at the University of New Mexico thought to have defected to the Germans, is actually a leader in the Jewish underground, now smuggling Jews out of France.

Shortly after Rudy and his father are reunited, the Gestapo closes in. Rudy is captured while helping his father to escape, but Tod reaches safety. Rudy is sent to Buchenwald, the German internment camp for Jews. Two years pass, and Germany falls. Rudy, now 21 and minus his left arm, is freed by the Americans and identified as a U.S. citizen. He travels to the Moreau country home at Auvergne, where Madame, her family, and Diane* Rothberg, a Jewish girl she sheltered, nurse Rudy back to health. He remains despondent and aloof, unable to compose, until, prodded by Diane, he writes a requiem for the war dead. The book skips a year and ends, as it began, by focusing on Tod. On the *Araby* in New York harbor, Tod catches a radio broadcast featuring a serenade by a young Albuquerque composer named Rudy Behrens and realizes that his friend has recovered from the physical and psychological wounds of war. Suspense, action, and conflict combine with detailed views of the activities of the French underground to produce a novel of many incidents and characters that is rich in plot and setting, if unfocused and shallow in characterization, and occasionally melodramatic. Such recurring motifs as Rudy's "The Prisoners' Song" and the Beethoven four-beats and flashbacks into Rudy's past provide color and texture and keep the book from being just another spy story set in World War II. The title comes from a comment by a Resistance worker: to conquer danger, one must go directly to its heart. Rudy recalls the man's words, not only when confronted with physical danger but also when attempting to deal with the guilt and anger he feels about his father's apparent treason. One in a series about Tod Moran. (Captain* Kurt von Kuhlendorf) Child Study.

THE HEAVENLY TENANTS (Maxwell*, William, ill. Ilonka Karasz, Harper, 1946), fantasy set on a farm in the northern United States in the mid-twentieth century. The Marvell family—Heather, 8, Roger, 11, the twins Tom and Tim, 5, and their parents—are leaving their farm for a three-week visit to the children's grandmother in Virginia. The night before they leave, Mr. Marvell shows the children the stars of the zodiac and explains the signs. In the morning they wait for the hired man, August, who lives across the swamp and will care for the house and animals while they are gone, and when they see a man coming who they assume is August, they leave hurriedly for the train station, not realizing that it is actually a neighbor and that August is suffering from a sore hip and not planning to come. In Virginia Mr. Marvell gets out the old telescope in the attic and is disturbed that he cannot find the Crab or other constellations of the zodiac. At home, the neighbors are amazed by a bright light that illuminates all the area at night and seems to come from the Marvell house. When firemen scorch their boots as they approach to investigate, they and the onlookers decide to leave well enough alone. August, recovering enough to limp close to the house, sees a white bull, a ram, a bowman, twins, a young girl (Virgo), two enormous fish, a new glowing weather vane in the shape of a lion, and other indications of unusual tenants at the house. When the Marvells return, they find that everything has been beautifully cared for, but there are some minor changes—

Mr. Marvell finds new shiny milk pails, Roger finds a silver arrow, Heather finds a patch of strange and beautiful flowers, the twins find sand in their toy pail that glitters like sparks, Mrs. Marvell finds that everything in the house gives off static electricity. Mr. Marvell sees that the constellations are back in the sky. Only Heather is individualized and she just slightly as a child who doesn't want change. Since there is really no attempt to create a believable fantasy and no compelling adventure, the book seems to be a thinly disguised, though nicely illustrated, lesson in astronomy for young children. Newbery Honor.

HEIGHT OF LAND (*Call of the Mountain**), the farm in the Vermont mountains overlooking Champlain Valley which Nathan Lindsay inherits from his benefactor, Jonathan Bemis. Once the property of the Armitage family, it had been a prosperous farm, but Kit Armitage, the last of the family, was a wanderer who did not wish to remain on the old place, took no care of it, and finally sold it to Jonathan. When Nathan decides to live there, the cabin has long been unused, the Armitage dog, Canute, has gone wild, and the family's breeded boar roams the hills, gone wild, too. The farm is reputed to have a large stand of mighty oaks of the kind much in demand for shipbuilding. After Nathan finds the trees, a chance remark of Joan's gives him the idea of transporting the logs down the mountain through the frozen stream bed. Selling the oaks to the sawmill provides Nathan with the cash he needs to get the farm going and to provide for Miss Eliza and Joan.

HEINLEIN, ROBERT (ANSON) (1907–   ), born in Butler, Mo.; prolific science fiction writer for both children and adults. He is a graduate of the U.S. Naval Academy at Annapolis, Md., served as a naval officer, and retired because of physical disability. He has written at least fifteen science fiction novels for young people and more than that for adults, winning the Hugo Award for science fiction four times. Some of his work was published under the pseudonyms of Anson MacDonald, Lyle Monroe, John Riverside, and Caleb Saunders. Typical of his novels for young people are *Red Planet** (Scribner's, 1949) and *Have Space Suit—Will Travel** (Scribner's, 1958), both written in terse, conversational style, with fast-paced plot and enough technical information and jargon included, without condescension, to be convincing.

"HELLO, THE BOAT!" (Crawford*, Phyllis, ill. Edward Laning, Holt, 1938), historical novel, episodic in structure, set on the Ohio River from February to July of 1817. Charles* Doak decides to move his family from Pittsburgh to a farm near Cincinnati. He arranges to transport them downriver on a storeboat—a flatboat which is a traveling store—in return for transportation and a share of the profits. He, Miss Biddy, his wife, pretty Susan*, 16, Steve*, about 14, who knows a lot about boats, and chubby David, 10, set out in March in high anticipation, along with their two dogs, their cow, Bessie, some chickens and geese, and sundry gear of their own, and dry goods, hardware, and food to sell. A pleasant fairly uneventful trip ensues as they drift with the current, flying their yellow storeboat flag. There are no great disasters, few troubles, and many happy moments, particularly after Pappy, a feisty old riverman, joins as crewman. He plays lively tunes on Katy, his worn fiddle, to which they often frolic, loves to yarn about the past, and spins tall tales about Mike Fink and colorful other river figures. Pappy provides comic relief and serves as a device for conveying information about the developing West. The family meets General William Henry Harrison, then in Congress, and Henry Shreve, an entrepreneur who is fighting the Fulton Company monopoly on steamboats in the western waters. The Doaks meet farmers and their wives, other travelers going both ways on the river, many of whom become their customers, friendly Indians, and other colorful river people. They attend a traveling show one evening and contend with rapids, storms, and floods. The boys hunt, fish, and swim in the river, while Miss Biddy and Susan take the responsibility for cooking and keeping the accounts. Much of the book describes the details of everyday life on the river, the preparation of the food, sleeping arrangements, doing the washing, and passing the time. The spirit of the river is very high, and much camaraderie exists among the people who live on and by the river. The book lacks narrative tension and meanders like the river most of the way. Near the end, the author interjects a note of suspense when cocky Pappy catches sight of an old river enemy and lights out after him. Susan discovers their cashbox of three thousand dollars empty, and the Doaks sadly assume Pappy absconded. The loss of the money means that Father will have to return to the river, but the setback dampens their spirits only slightly, and they arrive joyfully in Cincinnati. Father settles up for the trip, and the book concludes with a big Fourth of July celebration at which everyone has a fine time with games, races, and eats of all kinds. Pappy shows up unexpectedly, with the money, which they learn had been stolen by his enemy. Father accepts a position as manager of a newly formed manufacturing company, Pappy agrees to settle down and run the Doak farm, the children will go to school, and Susan looks forward to eventual marriage to Simon Winthrop, a young law student she has met on the way to Cincinnati. This action-filled story is amusing and informative with details of family life and flavored with much river talk and terms. It gives a rosy-toned look at the push westward. Newbery Honor.

HENNER'S LYDIA (De Angeli*, Marguerite, ill. author, Doubleday, 1936), simple story of the daily life of an Amish girl in Pennsylvania Dutch country between Lancaster and Reading in the mid-twentieth century. Written alternately in present and past tense, it tells of Lydia Stolzfus, known as Henner's Lydia to distinguish her from the other Lydia in a school where most of the children share the same surname. Lydia helps with the chores at home and with the care of her little sister, Nancy, 3, and goes to school with her younger brother, Yonie, 6. Together they visit the neighbor who is making apple butter and the friend who has a new baby, which Lydia is allowed to hold briefly. When Lydia finishes her "piece," a small rug, she is to be allowed to go to market in Lancaster with her father, but she has a hard time keeping her attention on her work and has problems: Nancy cuts into the edge when Lydia has failed to put the scissors away, and the rug gets wet and colors run when she leaves it outside, but since it is finished her father lets her go to market, an exciting experience for her. The details of Amish life and their patterns of speech must hold the interest in this almost plotless book. De Angeli's illustrations show the clothing and the horse-drawn vehicles, but Lydia is not a memorable character. Fanfare.

HENRI (*Out of the Flame**), historical second son of Francois I of France, who was held hostage and imprisoned in a dungeon along with his brother, Francois, by Charles V of Spain for three years. Frequently moody and sullen after his return, he resents Pierre de Bayard's leadership of the boys at court and often taunts and even strikes him. He is a political reactionary and regards the reformers and new philosophers as heretics. He marries Catherine de' Medici.

HENRY†, MARGUERITE (BREITHAUPT) (1902–), born in Milwaukee, Wis.; writer of fiction and non-fiction for children, best known for her popular horse stories. She attended schools in Milwaukee, where her father had a printing business, and graduated from Milwaukee State Teachers' College. After her marriage, she went to live in Chicago, where she wrote articles for trade journals and various other publications, and then moved to a farm near Wayne, Ill., where she began writing for children. She first wrote picture geographies for early elementary readers and then storybooks and biographies and other non-fiction for the eight-to-twelve-year-olds, compiling an impressive total of more than three dozen books. Among them is a Newbery Medal book, *King of the Wind** (Rand, 1948), a historical novel which tells how the Arabian horse came to England; two Newbery honor books, *Justin Morgan Had a Horse** (Wilcox, 1945), which makes a story out of the origin of the American line of horses named for a Vermont schoolmaster; a Fanfare and Lewis Carroll Shelf book, *Misty of Chincoteague** (Rand, 1947), which tells about the wild horses that roam Assateague and Chincoteague, islands off Virginia, and whose sequel is *Stormy, Misty's Foal†* (Rand, 1963); a *Choice* book, *Brighty of the Grand Canyon** (Rand, 1953), which tells of the turbulent life of a tough little burro; and another Fanfare book, *Benjamin West and His Cat Grimalkin** (Bobbs, 1947), a biographical novel about the man who became the father of American painting. Her novels combine action and drama with sound research and straightforward, nonpretentious, if undistinguished, writing. Not anthropomorphized or sentimentalized, her animals are invested with enough personality to make them seem real, individual, and memorable. The reader is kept aware that though the books are fiction the subjects and major events actually occurred. Other titles include *Mustang†* (Rand, 1966), which won the Western Heritage Award, and *White Stallion of Lipizza†* (Rand, 1964), *San Domingo: The Medicine Hat Stal-*

lion (Rand, 1972), *All about Horses* (Random, 1962), and *A Pictorial Life Story of Misty* (Rand, 1976). She has written for Bobbs-Merrill's Childhood of Famous Americans Series, contributed articles and stories to many magazines, and published several books in the Picture Geographies Series for Whitman. Several of her books were made into movies.

HENRY AND RIBSY (Cleary*†, Beverly, ill. Louis Darling, Morrow, 1954), episodic story set in an Oregon town in the mid-twentieth century, sequel to *Henry Huggins** (Morrow, 1950). Henry Huggins, about nine, is devoted to his mixed-breed dog, Ribsy, but has a hard time keeping him out of trouble. While Henry is sitting in the car on the service station grease rack as it is being lubed, he sees Ribsy steal a paper bag from a police car parked in the supermarket lot, and, before he can intervene, Ribsy has gobbled the policeman's lunch. Ribsy causes further problems when he guards the garbage can so faithfully that the garbage man fails to make the collection, and the whole neighborhood is soon aware of it. Henry's father promises to take him salmon fishing in the fall if he can keep Ribsy out of further trouble, but try as he will, Henry finds this difficult. When Ribsy gobbles down the ice cream cone that Ramona Quimby, Beezus's little sister, drops on the porch, Ramona grabs his bone and shuts it in her lunch box, then climbs the jungle gym and howls because she thinks Henry and Beezus are spelling something good to eat when they speak of the PTA meeting at the school. Finally Henry buys some potato chips, calling them PTA, but by the time he gets back, the ladies are accusing Ribsy, who still wants his bone, of terrifying poor little Ramona, who is still atop the jungle gym, howling for some PTA. Other episodes include the haircut Henry suffers when his mother buys an electric clippers, and his loss of his two canine teeth. At last Mr. Huggins, Henry, and Ribsy, along with Mr. Grumbie, a neighbor, go fishing. Ribsy, after knocking over the tackle box, shaking water all over the sandwiches and coffee, and causing Mr. Grumbie to lose a good-sized salmon, goes overboard and nearly gets swept out to sea. He and Henry are put ashore, and Henry manages to catch the biggest fish of the day by tackling it after Ribsy has spotted it heading up a small stream. Fortunately, Scooter McCarthy, Henry's old antagonist, is present to see Henry's catch weighed and admired. Like the other books about Henry, this is written in simple language and gets its humor from a combination of situation comedy and nostalgic recognition of the way children see the world differently from adults. Sequels. Choice.

HENRY DAILEY (*The Black Stallion**), elderly neighbor of Alec Ramsay who owns the run-down farm where Alec keeps his magnificent horse. Henry was a jockey in his youth and later a trainer, and his heart is still at the race track, even though his wife is determined that he has retired. Although only Alec can handle and ride the wild black stallion, Henry provides the know-how and the contacts that enable them to train the horse, and he shares Alec's enthusiasm and efforts.

HENRY HUGGINS (Cleary*†, Beverly, ill. Louis Darling, Morrow, 1950), realistic episodic story for early readers set in a town in the United States in the mid-twentieth century. Henry Huggins, who is in the third grade, finds an underfed "mixed breed" dog at the drug store and then has such a hard time getting him home on the bus that his worried mother calls the police, and Henry and his dog, whom he has named Ribsy, arrive in the patrol car, sirens blowing. Several of the episodes feature Ribsy: he climbs on the scaffold and knocks over a can of green paint onto Henry, thereby saving him from having to play the part of the little boy in pajamas that he dreads in the school operetta and letting him get the part of a somersaulting green elf instead; he wins the cup for the most unusual dog at the show, partly because, still damp from his bath, he gets dirty and Henry tries to cover the mud with pink talcum powder; when his original owner shows up he is delighted, but given a chance to choose between the two boys, he opts for Henry. Other episodes include Henry's attempt to keep up with the population explosion when he raises guppies, and his money-raising to pay for a football he has lost by collecting 1,331 night crawlers. Other neighborhood children include Scooter McCarthy and Beezus (Beatrice) Quimby and her little sister, Ramona. Although the events are only mildly humorous, they are livelier than most stories that children at this level can read for themselves. Sequels. Books Too Good; Choice.

HENRY REED (*Henry Reed, Inc.**; *Henry Reed's Journey†*; *Henry Reed's Baby-Sitting Service†*; *Henry Reed's Big Show†*), teenaged son of a diplomat stationed in Italy, who spends several summers with his aunt and uncle in Grover's Corner, N.J. An intelligent and inventive boy, Henry creates mild chaos with all his projects, though he never means to cause trouble, and being very literal-minded is usually surprised when people are annoyed or amused at the results of his ideas. According to his uncle, he resembles his mother in his ability to stir up unexpected action no matter what he undertakes, as well as in his interest in animals, insects, and other natural history. Henry is the first-person narrator of his adventures in the form of journal entries.

HENRY REED, INC. (Robertson*†, Keith, ill. Robert McCloskey*, Viking, 1958), humorous episodic novel set in Grover's Corner, near Princeton, N.J., in the mid-twentieth century. Henry* Reed, about fourteen, comes from Naples, Italy, where his father is in the diplomatic service, to spend the summer with his Uncle Al Harris, his mother's brother, and Uncle Al's wife, Aunt Mabel. Both are plump and good-natured. On their way home from the train station, they stop to avoid a beagle in the middle of the road, and when they try to get him to move, he climbs into the car. Henry names him Agony, because of his pained-sounding howl, and despite their efforts to find his owner, he is with them for the summer. The story is told first person as entries in a journal which Henry keeps so he can give a report on free enterprise when he returns to his school. To get firsthand experience, he starts "Henry Reed, Inc., Pure and

Applied Research,'' in an old barn on land that belongs to his mother. Soon he is joined by the only resident of Grover's Corner near his age, Midge* (Margaret) Glass, 12, who promises to contribute her two rabbits if she can join the firm. Because the male, Jedidiah, has escaped, Henry allows her to be a probationary partner until they can catch him. This is complicated, because the rabbit, when chased, runs to the yard next to the barn, which belongs to the disagreeable Apples, a fussy couple who will not allow children to enter their yard. The two youngsters have a number of adventures with the Apples as main antagonists: trying to net Jedidiah, they catch the Apples' white cat, Siegfried, by mistake and are accused of cat stealing; Mr. Apple accuses them of breaking the zoning law, so they change to ''Agricultural and Biological Research Supplies,'' since farm-related business is legal; Agony digs holes in the Apple yard, and Mr. Apple demands that he be tied up, but since Henry points out Siegfried killing a bird in their yard, Uncle Al suggests that neither dog nor cat be prosecuted; Henry and Aunt Mabel confuse their identical car with the Apples' car and shut Agony in the Apples' car at the fourth of July celebration; Henry and Midge catch Siegfried in a trap intended for Jedidiah, but, having seen Mr. Apple scaring deer off his yard with a shotgun, are able to dissuade him from reporting to the game warden; when they start to send a carrier pigeon in their homemade balloon (hoping to sell their idea to the space agency), Siegfried eats the pigeon and gets carried up instead, then leaps to the Apples' roof as the balloon passes over; when a neighbor's sheep get into the special fenced-off plot in Apple's lawn, Henry shuts them in to keep them from wandering, and they eat all of Mr. Apple's special curly grass which he has developed secretly, though Midge has been sure he has buried bodies in the well-guarded patch. The research firm makes money in both traditional and unusual ways: they sell earthworms; they try dousing, strike an old oil tank, and sell the oil; they paint flowers on the backs of the turtles Agony finds and sell them to the garden club; Henry tries to train Agony to hunt truffles and is paid for discovering the site of an old pottery instead; when Agony chases Jedidiah through a culvert and gets stuck, Henry persuades the road crew to dig the culvert and replace it with a larger size, for which Uncle Al, whose yard has been flooded in every storm, pays him a fee. They get free publicity from the local newspaper several times, as when Henry's garden tractor, pulling a wagon which carries the bathtub for raising earthworms, stalls and blocks the road during rush hour, and the paper runs a story about the group of professors and high-paid engineers pushing it off the road. In the end, Midge's female rabbit produces a litter, so she becomes a full partner in the firm. The episodes are all possible, though often highly improbable, and some of the humor comes from Henry's inability to see what is funny. Though most of the incidents are on the level of situation comedy, there are some comments and more subtle touches that raise the book above the average comic stories. The convention of the journal works well enough though entries are too long and detailed to be realistic. Choice; Fanfare.

HENRY'S LINCOLN (Neyhart*, Louise A., ill. Charles Banks Wilson, Holiday, 1945), short historical novel set on August 27, 1858, the day of the Lincoln-Douglas debate in Freeport, Ill., in which a youth who has been encouraged to listen to what candidates say before making up his mind switches his loyalty to a virtually unknown political aspirant because the man stands for freedom and morality. Young Henry Oaks rushes to finish his farm chores, excited to be going on his own to Freeport to hear Senator Douglas, whom he greatly admires. He stops his buggy to pick up talkative old Grandpa Higgins, who does not hesitate to state his views about slavery. Henry is convinced all Illinois has descended upon Freeport, which teems with jostling crowds and features a huge free barbecue. At the local hotel, Henry and his friend Rufus try on hats belonging to Lincoln and Douglas and then go to the grove where the debate is to take place and where they take seats in a front row. They watch the dapper, chunky Douglas and the lean, awkward Lincoln take their places on the bunting-bedecked platform and find interesting the comments they hear about the two candidates. Henry is sure that renowned Senator Douglas will easily outtalk his less experienced and virtually unknown rival. As the debate goes on, Henry finds very appealing Lincoln's earnestness, intensity, and emphasis on doing the right thing. When he shakes Lincoln's hand after the debate, he informs the kindly, homely railsplitter that he is now on Lincoln's side because he doesn't "want slavery to spread." In this well-paced reconstruction for younger readers of a memorable day, the two historical figures are vividly, if stereotypically, drawn, the essential issues are clearly presented, and many vivid details make the setting palpable. Numerous full-page, black-and-white, humorously realistic drawings show emotion, help create setting, and contribute believability. Fanfare.

HEPSA JORDAN (*Calico Bush**), past seventy, aunt to Seth and his son, Ethan, who live on Sunday Island across the channel from the Sargents and are their nearest neighbors. Spry and competent, Aunt Hepsa makes beautiful woolen cloth, nurses all the scattered neighbors, and can dance a light-footed jig. It is she who sings the "Ballad of Calico Bush" that gives the book its title. She has been making a quilt in the Delectable Mountains pattern, inspired by her view of the hills on Mount Desert Island. After Marguerite has given up her red cloth for the Indians' Maypole, Hepsa gives her the half-finished quilt to finish for her own dowry.

HESSIAN HILL (*Onion John**), hill overlooking the small town of Serenity, N.J., where town character Onion* John lives in a house built out of piled-up stones. It is here that the townspeople construct a new dwelling with modern conveniences for him. It symbolizes his inability to fit into their way of life.

HEWES, AGNES (DANFORTH), born in Tripoli, Syria; author of novels for young adults that blend history, adventure, and romance. She lived until she was twelve in Syria, where her father was a medical missionary and her grandmother was also a missionary. She grew up speaking Arabic more fluently than English, and until she came to America she was educated at home. After studying at Elmira College and Radcliffe, she married Laurence Ilsley Hewes, an engineer and writer of technical books and articles, and they made their home in San Francisco. From the 1920s through the 1940s, she published over a dozen books, many of which deal with the trade that drew together East and West and the expansion of knowledge during critical periods. Her first book grew out of her memories of her Syrian childhood, *A Boy of the Lost Crusade* (Houghton, 1923). She later wrote three Newbery honor books of historical fiction, *Spice and the Devil's Cave** (Knopf, 1930), set in Portugal at the time of Vasco da Gama and Magellan, *Glory of the Seas** (Knopf, 1933), about the introduction of clipper ship trade to California, and *The Codfish Musket** (Doubleday, 1936), about the opening of overland trade with the Pacific Northwest in the early 1800s, which was also a Fanfare book. *Swords on the Sea* (Knopf, 1928) and *The Sword of Roland Arnot* (Houghton, 1939) are also set in the past, but *A Hundred Bridges to Go* (Dodd, 1950) is a contemporary story about the building of the Alaskan highway. For thirty years her husband directed Federal road construction in the Western States, Alaska, and Hawaii, and was directly involved in building the Canadian-Alaskan route. Popular when published, her books are substantial in content and show extensive research, but characterization is shallow, and they lack wit and verve.

THE HIDDEN TREASURE OF GLASTON (Jewett*, Eleanore M., ill. Frederick T. Chapman, Viking, 1946), historical novel set in England during the time of King Henry II and Queen Eleanor from 1171–1172 which mixes real and fictitious characters and events in improvising upon the legends and historical discoveries about King Arthur and his knights and the Holy Grail. While on pilgrimage to the Holy Land to do penance for his part in the murder of Thomas à Becket, Sir Hugh de Morville leaves his lame son, Hugh*, 12, with the monks at Glastonbury Abbey. Since he can read and write, Hugh is assigned to kindly Brother* John, the librarian of the monastery, to help with the work of the scriptorium. He makes friends with Dickon*, an oblate, who shows him a cave containing rich treasures, among them, a sword and a small altar, and some overwritten parchment pages which he realizes might belong to a damaged, ancient book about the Grail, the abbey's most valued possession. The two encounter Blaheris*, a half-crazy old minstrel now living as a hermit in the marsh called Avalon near the Abbey, who tells them stories about Gawain and the Grail and who is convinced the sword is Excalibur and that the Grail lies somewhere in the area. The three embark on a quest for the Grail, which Blaheris says can only be found through sacrifice and not by deliberate searching. While lost in the fog-enshrouded marsh, Hugh has a vision of a funeral barge, which leads eventually to the recovery of the bones of Arthur and Guinevere. When a fire breaks out at the abbey, Hugh rushes into the Old Church to rescue Brother John. There he has a vision of the Grail and his leg is miraculously healed.

Blaheris is killed and the book about the Grail is destroyed by the fire. Hugh's father returns, but Hugh decides to remain at the abbey to write down what he has heard and read of the old legends about Arthur and the Grail so that they will not be lost. Although the legends, Hugh's visions, details about life in the abbey, and the appearance of Henry and Eleanor and their court contribute substance, this story of dedication to an ideal and personal sacrifice is unevenly paced and developed, spun out, and shallowly characterized. Fanfare; Newbery Honor.

HIGH ROAD HOME (Corbin*†, William, Coward, 1954), adventure novel set in the United States in the early 1950s. Having agreed to be adopted by an American family in order to get to the United States, streetwise French refugee Nico (Nicholas) LaFlamme, 14, jumps off the train in Cleveland. He is determined to find his father, who he believes is still alive despite official reports that he died in the French resistance movement in World War II. His hopes are based on a clipping given him by a GI in Paris from an American paper telling about a new French refugee professor whose first name is Achille as was Nico's father. The rest of the clipping is torn off, leaving no last name or the name or location of the newspaper, but there is a picture of the newspaperman in whose column the item appeared. With this slim set of clues, Nico begins his search, soon finding that police are searching for him. He stows away in a furniture truck heading for Columbus, nearly suffocating and suffering from heat prostration, but recovers and makes a friend, red-haired Dud Hamilton, who aspires to be a newspaperman and is fired from his lunch-counter job for giving Nico a cut-rate dinner. They team up, hitchhike to Cincinnati, then, on a freight train, to Chicago, where they work as pinsetters in a bowling alley. When Nico discovers that Dud has been making calls to newspapers planting stories about the travels of the run-away French boy, he feels betrayed and leaves, hitchhikes to Springfield, then stows away on a circus train on which he meets an old hobo, who tells him stories of his travels around the country. At the newspaper office in St. Louis, where Nico takes his clipping to see if anyone recognizes the picture of the columnist, he finds Dud, who has followed him by bus to apologize and explain that he was building the background for a human interest story that might get him a newspaper job. Reconciled, they travel west, but are apprehended by the police in Arizona and held there for Nico's foster father, Calvin Dennison, pilot, vice president of an airline company, who comes in a plane. Cal, an attractive, young, genuine, all-American type, takes Nico to Lake Tahoe, where his wife, Sally, an artist, is delighted with the boy and soon develops fine rapport. Nico, however, runs away to Dud in Los Angeles, and together they find the newspaperman in San Diego and learn that the French professor is at the State College. There Nico discovers that it is not his father, but a man who owes his freedom to Achille LaFlamme, who, he confirms, was killed by the Nazis. Through Dud's contrivance, Cal finds Nico, and they go back to San Francisco, where Dud gets a newspaper job on the strength of the story he writes about

Nico. Nico's original hatred and suspicion of Americans has changed to love and appreciation. While the picaresque adventures across the continent are interesting and Nico himself is an appealing character, a clever actor, cynical yet vulnerable, the other characters are types, particularly Cal and Sally. The patriotic and upbeat ending is not very believable. Child Study.

HIGHTOWER†, FLORENCE (COLE) (1916–1981), born in Boston, Mass.; author of good-natured mysteries, some of them period pieces, in a family context, based loosely on the activities of her own family. She grew up in Concord, Mass., attended Concord Academy, where her mother taught, and later graduated from Vassar College. Her husband was James Hightower, Professor of Chinese Literature at Harvard, and the couple lived in China both before and after World War II but made their permanent home in Massachusetts. Of her six novels for young readers, *The Ghost of Follonsbee's Folly** (Houghton, 1958), a mildly Gothic story about strange happenings after a large and lively family moves into and renovates a big, old, pre–Civil War house, and *Dark Horse of Woodfield†* (Houghton, 1962), a lighthearted mystery about the restoration of the Armistead family fortunes, were both chosen for Fanfare by the editors of *Horn Book*, and the latter is also listed in *Choice*. Her settings are vivid, her style deft, literary, and witty, the pace vigorous, and interpersonal relationships well conceived, but her characters are often stock or tend to be eccentric and her plots mechanical and overly intricate. She also wrote *Mrs. Wappinger's Secret* (Houghton, 1956), about an elderly lady and a ten-year-old boy who go treasure-seeking, *Fayerweather Forecast* (Houghton, 1967), about the strange disappearance of Aunt Lucy's fiancé, *The Secret of the Crazy Quilt* (Houghton, 1972), which involves rum-running and a coded message in a quilt, and *Dreamwold Castle* (Houghton, 1978), about a girl who becomes innocently involved in illegal activities.

HILL OF LITTLE MIRACLES (Angelo*, Valenti, ill. author, Viking, 1942), episodic novel of family and neighborhood life set in the bay area of San Francisco in the early 1940s. The story covers about a month in the lives of the Italian-American Santo family and is told mostly from the viewpoint of, but not by, twelve-year-old Ricco*. Ricco has a physical handicap; his left leg is shorter than his right. One Saturday, Mamma Santo takes him to Rinaldo Gamba, a shoemaker, who fits him with a new pair of shoes, the left one of which has an elevated sole. For the first time, Ricco can walk without crutches. The boy does not know that Gamba has put a miraculous medal under the sole of the left shoe in hopes that it will help to cure the boy's handicap. That night when he goes to bed, as on every other night, Ricco suspends a brick from his left leg, hoping to stretch it to match the right one in length. The next few weeks are full of activities and small miracles for Ricco, his friends, and his family. All the Santos, including wealthy winemaker Uncle Alessandro and his stuck-up daughter, Celeste, and jolly artist, Uncle Tito, whose car, Benito, is always breaking down, gather to celebrate baby Nina's baptism. Even Policeman O'Reilly joins the *festa* afterwards with its many rich Italian dishes, joyful singing, and often energetic dancing that goes on for many hours into the night. Ricco and his chums from the Irish and Spanish communities lug home, not without problems from a neighborhood gang, two old piano cases with which they build a clubhouse. Old Theresa, who has behaved oddly since her husband's death, wanders off and is struck by a car. The head injury restores her sanity, surely a miracle, Ricco and his friends believe. Family and neighbors celebrate the wedding of Uncle Luigi and Widow Flanigan. Everyone thinks Ricco has miraculously captured the likeness of the doughty old fisherman, Jonah, in the painting he gives them as his wedding gift. The novel concludes with three more little miracles: Gamba must remove part of the sole from Ricco's left shoe because it is too high, a clear indication that his leg has grown; Theresa gets new false teeth that delight her because they fit her so well; and the boys' mascot, Sunshine the kitten, escapes when their clubhouse burns down. This somewhat sentimental, often humorous novel projects a strong sense of the mixed ethnic community and the geography and atmosphere of San Francisco's bay area. Few of the many characters are roundly drawn, and none is dynamic, but all are warmly and affectionately presented. Here is no strong story, just a lively and richly detailed account of everyday things that happen to simple, hardworking people who are trying to live good lives and who are close to their church, relatives, and neighbors. (Danny* O'Reilly; Tony* Santo) Fanfare.

HITTY (*Hitty: Her First Hundred Years**), Mehitable, a very small doll carved by an old peddler from an ash stick he has brought from Ireland. She has joints at hip and shoulder, but not at knee and elbow. Throughout her many adventures she retains her chemise, on which her original owner has worked her name in cross-stitch, and her pleasant expression.

HITTY: HER FIRST HUNDRED YEARS (Field*, Rachel, ill. Dorothy Lathrop*, Macmillan, 1929), fantasy telling the adventures of a wooden doll carved from an ash stick by an old peddler for young Phoebe Preble, 7, in Maine in the early nineteenth century. The doll, Hitty* (Mehitable), writes her memoirs one hundred years later in an antique shop owned by a Miss Hunter in New York. Hitty's first adventures, being carried secretly to church in Phoebe's muff and lost there, and being left in a berry patch by Phoebe and her brother, Andy, then carried by crows back to the Preble house, are tame compared to the whaling voyage aboard the *Diana-Kate* on which Captain Preble takes his family and which ends with a burning ship and the Prebles cast up on a heathen island. When they are rescued and taken to India, Phoebe drops Hitty in the street, where she is found by a snake charmer, who sells her to a missionary's wife for her little daughter, Thankful. In Philadelphia, where Thankful is sent to live with her grandparents, she hides Hitty in an attic sofa, where Clarissa Pryce, 10, a Quaker child, later finds her. With Clarissa, Hitty hears the singer Adelina

Patti and meets the poet John Greenleaf Whittier. Later, after being packed in moth balls, delivered to a wrong address, and stored in an attic in Washington Square, N.Y., Hitty is found by a dressmaker, Milly Pinch, and used as a model but claimed by Isabella Van Rensselaer, 8, in whose presence she meets the author, Charles Dickens. After that she has a series of owners: Katie, an Irish child in Pawtucket, R.I., Mr. Farley, an artist who takes her to New Orleans, Miss Hortense and Miss Annette Larraby, who dress her beautifully for the Cotton Exhibition, Sally Loomis, from the riverboat *Morning Glory*, who steals her from the Exhibition, and Car'line, a little black girl. She lands in a dead letter office, from which she is sold at auction, only to be made into a pincushion, a fate from which she is rescued by Miss Pamela Wellington, a doll collector. She is purchased from Miss Wellington's estate for Miss Hunter's antique shop. In her first hundred years, Hitty sees many places and observes many historical events, but the characters and situations are all stock types, and except for the Preble episodes, they are not developed enough to be memorable. Hitty's tone is proper and often didactically informational, so that the book, despite having many events, is rather slow moving. Newbery Winner.

HOFFMANN, ELEANOR (1895–   ), born in Belmont, Mass.; author of novels of mystery and adventure and of animal stories for children. After receiving her bachelor of arts from Radcliffe, she studied further at Massachusetts Agricultural College and the University of North Carolina. She has contributed many stories and articles to magazines for children and for adults and has made her home in California. Her dozen and a half published books include *Melinka and Her Donkey* (Stokes, 1937), a picture book that was critically praised and was her first published book for the young; *A Cat of Paris** (Stokes, 1940), about a young Siamese kitten in the Left Bank artists' colony, which was a Fanfare selection; *Mischief in Fez* (Holiday, 1943), a fantasy set in Morocco; *The Four Friends* (Macmillan, 1945) and *Princess of the Channel Isles* (Nelson, 1947), both animal novels; *The Mystery of the Lion Ring* (Dodd, 1953); *Summer at Horseshoe Ranch* (Dodd, 1957); and *Feeding Our Armed Forces* (Nelson, 1943) and *Realm of the Evening Star: A History of Morocco and the Lands of the Moors* (Chilton, 1965), both non-fiction.

HOKE (*The Black Symbol**), also known as Professor Charles Withrow; real name, "Hokum" Charlie Wilson. His wife, called Maddie, is "Mad Mollie" Wilson. Hoke is the assistant to Doc* Cathcart, who operates a traveling medicine show, and Maddie is the show's mindreader. They are part of the show's "bally." Barney quite early realizes their act is a sham. Hoke and Maddie are wanted for fraud and extortion. Hoke has a sadistic streak; he enjoys using his long whip, with which he is very adept.

HOLD BACK THE HUNTER (White*, Dale, ill. Albert Orbaan, Day, 1959), historical novel set in the upper Yellowstone country in 1870. Sent by aging mountain-man Jim Bridger, who has been a foster father to him, young Gabe (George) Kirkpatrick has come by steamboat to Ft. Benton and walked from there to Helena, Montana territory, to join the Washburn-Langford-Doane Expedition to explore the as yet uncharted area that later became Yellowstone Park. Bridger's stories of the country he saw years before are widely thought to be tall tales, but Gabe believes in the two-hundred-foot spouters, the falls twice as high as Niagara, the boiling pools, the glass mountain, and other wonders. At the same time, his Indian heritage on his mother's side makes him wonder if it is a land of evil spirits. Since Bridger has "foxed a map in his head," Nathaniel Langford takes him as a cook's helper on the expedition, which starts in mid-August, made up of General Washburn, Surveyor General of Montana Territory, with an escort of Lieutenant Doane and five soldiers, a black cook named Nute, a few wranglers, a bragging hunter named Jake Smith, and an oddly assorted group of Helena businessmen, including Sam Hauser, a banker, Walter Trumbull, a greenhorn, Judge Hedges, and elderly, half-blind Mr. Everts. A rivalry grows up between loud-mouthed Jake, who thinks he is a great hunter and scoffs at all Bridger's tales, and Gabe, who wants very much to find that they are true and who is really a far superior hunter. The first proof is the magnificent canyon and falls of the Yellowstone, followed by Alum Creek and the hot springs basin, where Gabe conquers his fear of the spirits. The expedition, which enters what is now the Gardiner entrance, goes south around Yellowstone Lake, encountering a good deal of difficulty in the bad weather and dense timber. When they get to the place where the Yellowstone River runs into the lake, Gabe, who wants to find the source, gets permission to scout ahead. He climbs a mountain and sees the shore line but gets turned around and dark closes in before he finds his way back. In the night, a mountain lion scares his pony away and trees Gabe, but when he returns he finds that several others also have been lost and have come straggling in later. Mr. Everts, however, does not come in and an early snowstorm slows their search. After several days they finally give up searching and move on, discovering the larger geyser basins which include Old Faithful. Through the whole trip, Gabe has felt a special affinity for the beautiful, strange area, so undisturbed that the animals do not fear man, and he has been sickened at the talk of lumbering and staking claims for mining and homesteading. Just before they leave the area, Judge Hedges proposes trying to get it preserved by law. In Virginia City, he and Langford start their campaign and also send out an expedition to try to find Everts, who is discovered almost back to their starting point, having survived by huddling over hot springs and eating thistle roots. The next year, Gabe guides a group of scientists in the Hayden expedition, whose photographs of the wonders persuade Congress to make it the first National Park. A long note at the end traces the history of the area and the expeditions, which are historical, though Gabe is fictional. The story of the explorations of this unusual group is fascinating, but the fictional treatment is clumsy, with Gabe and Jake stock figures and the research dominating the story. Spur.

HOLLING, HOLLING C(LANCY) (1900–1973), born in Holling Corners, Mich.; artist-author of a series of books that mix well-researched fact and fiction with gorgeous full-page paintings and detail drawings and diagrams. He studied at the Art Institute of Chicago and privately under the anthropologist, Dr. Ralph Linton, and was a member of the zoology department of the Chicago Natural History Museum in the 1920s. With his wife, also an illustrator, he started working on children's books with *Book of Indians* (Platt, 1935), followed by *Book of Cowboys* (Platt, 1936), but the first in the style for which he is best remembered was *Paddle-to-the-Sea** (Houghton, 1941), the story of a toy wooden canoe carved and set in motion by an Indian boy in Nipigon country north of Lake Superior which eventually reaches France, telling the geography of the Great Lakes and the St. Lawrence Waterway as it traces its voyage. Others in similar style include *Tree in the Trail* (Houghton, 1942), the story of the history of the Southwest as it passes a cottonwood tree, *Seabird** (Houghton, 1948), telling the history of whaling and sailing ships, and *Minn of the Mississippi* (Houghton, 1951), about a river turtle.

HOLT, ISABELLA (1892–1962), born in Chicago, Ill.; novelist. Among a large number of books published from 1921 on is *The Adventures of Rinaldo** (Little, 1959), a lighthearted romp set in the Middle Ages which parodies heroic literature. This mock-chivalric adventure was invented for her children and put on paper for her grandchildren. Among her other books are *Golden Legend* (Bobbs, 1935), *My Son and Heir* (Bobbs, 1949), *Midpoint* (Bobbs, 1955), *Rampole Place* (Bobbs, 1952), and *The Golden Moment* (Random House, 1959).

HOMER PRICE (McCloskey*, Robert, ill. author, Viking, 1943), humorous, episodic novel of community life set in the fictitious town of Centerburg, Ohio, in the mid-1900s. Homer Price, about twelve, lives with his father and mother who operate a tourist camp just outside of town. Homer does odd jobs about the place and also for his Uncle* Ulysses, who runs the town lunchroom, and for the town barber. He is a fun-loving boy, well liked by his peers, thoroughly reliable, quite conscientious and resourceful, and he often helps his friends and relatives out of tight situations. The book relates in detailed, relaxed storytelling style six episodes about Homer and his Centerburg friends. Homer's pet skunk, Aroma, helps Homer capture the four robbers who have taken the two thousand dollars Mr. Blott won in a radio advertising contest. Homer, his pal, Freddy, and Freddy's little brother, Louis, meet their comic book hero, the Super-Duper, at a Saturday matinee and afterward help him get his car out of the ditch. When Homer fills in for Uncle Ulysses at the lunchroom, he is faced with the perplexing problem of a doughnut machine that refuses to stop producing doughnuts. In the contest to determine who has the biggest ball of string in town, the Sheriff* or Homer's Uncle Telemachus, Miss* Terwilliger resourcefully defeats both gentlemen and then chooses the one she wishes to marry. Homer cleverly prevents Mr.* Murphy from ''Pied-Piper-of-Hamlin-ing'' away with his musical mousetrap the children of Centerburg along with the town mice. The book concludes with a great historical pageant to celebrate one hundred fifty years of progress in Centerburg as exemplified by a big, new, housing project on the Enders* homestead. Characters are one-dimensional, easily recognizable types that approach caricature and are quite appropriate for the inventive situation comedies that McCloskey puts them in. McCloskey's amusing cartoons add to the entertainment value, which is very high. Books Too Good; Choice.

HOMESPUN (Berry*, Erick, ill. Harold von Schmidt, Lothrop, 1937), historical novel set in the 1830s in New York State, en route to and in Santa Fe, in New Orleans, and in the Far Northwest, which follows for about two years the varying fortunes of the four eldest children of John Greenman, who owns a farm near Friendship, N.Y. Although Jerusha Greenman loves all her brothers, she is particularly close to the eldest—earnest, patient, willing Luke*. She sympathizes with his longing to go to sea but sees little chance for him to realize his dream because, as the eldest son, he is obligated to help his father run the farm. The next two brothers, Mark* and Stephen*, leave on business ventures, and a large part of the book describes what happens to them. Mark has contracted with a cotton manufacturer from Connecticut to deliver a load of calico to Santa Fe for a half-share of the profits. He and his bride, Sukey* Cray, set out in their ox-drawn wagon for the West, and after a demanding journey by wagon train arrive safely at Santa Fe where they sell their goods at a fine profit. Stephen shows discretion and good judgment in dealing with his businessman uncle's customers in New Orleans and in getting to know the Creoles, particularly planter Monsieur Foucher, whose cotton gins are destroyed in a fire, and attracts the attention of and eventually marries his intelligent, farsighted daughter, Alexandrine*. When young Pepin Crandell, who lives nearby and eventually marries Jerusha, comes to live with the Greenmans after the death of his father, Mr. Greenman has the help he needs for the farm. Luke seizes the chance to leave home, forming a trapping partnership with mixed-blood Dard* Rae. Luke hopes to make enough money through the sale of furs to compensate his father for the loss of his labor. Ironically, he is killed near Fort Vancouver in Oregon by a renegade white, known as Catamount*, at the end of a successful trapping season, shortly before reaching the sea he yearned for. The book ends with Jerusha reading a letter in which Luke explains his extended absence, but the family has yet to learn of his death. This is a rich, ambitious, satisfying novel, in which scenes of Jerusha and the work on the farm bind together the separate story strands about the brothers to produce a panoramic tapestry of an exciting era. The book offers contrasting views of social and economic life on the eastern farm, in New Orleans, in Santa Fe, on the overland trail, and among the *voyageurs* of the northern forests. Although Jerusha's story is undeveloped compared to those of the boys, her hopes for all of them and especially her favorite, Luke, unify and set in relief the components of what might otherwise have been a disjointed, tenuous plot. The four Greenmans are strongly realized, conscientious, industrious, responsible, caring youths—"homespun" products for whom situations hold more than mere expediency. Even minor figures are drawn with depth and discernment, and, numerous as they are, there is no problem with keeping them straight. (Enrique* Roldan; Musa*, Mrs. Babcock*) Fanfare.

HONEY CHILE (Braune*, Anna, Doubleday, 1937), episodic story for young children of a single day at Magnolia Hills Plantation in Alabama. Although the book does not tell us the date or the age of Jane, the protagonist, internal evidence from both text and illustration (presumably by the author, since no other illustrator is listed) place the story in the early 1930s and Jane's age at six to eight. Visiting her Aunt Nellie and Uncle John, Jane is the darling of all the black servants: Lou, who helps dress her and put her to bed and takes her fishing; Marigold, the cook; Centennial and Aunt Cindy, the house servants, and Aunt Sara Belle, who was once nursemaid to Uncle John and now tells Jane stories as she boils laundry over an outdoor fire. Jane plays with the black children, Eloise and her Brother Blue and Lil' Sistah, on the grapevine swings and with the corn cob dolls that Lou has dressed for them. She talks to the farm animals and makes a clover-chain crown for the red bull. Although the plantation house is elegant, it is not modern; water is heated on the stove and carried to the bathtub. The tone of the book is nostalgic and detail seems to have come from actual observation, but the dialect of the black characters and the condescending attitude toward them would make it offensive to many modern readers. Since little happens in the story, it is unlikely to be of interest in the present period except as an example of how a book once praised for its acceptance of interracial mixing now appears biased in its portrayal of minority characters. Fanfare.

HONEY WOMAN (*Harry in England**), an elderly woman who has a little cottage not far from Silverthorne, mother of Carter*, the gardener. Harry and his cousin, Jim*, go to her house for tea. Their visit provides a very pleasant interlude in the account of Harry's adventures. The Honey Woman wears a blue dress and a white apron and has a funny little cap on her head and large, round spectacles on her eyes. Her kitchen fills the whole space of her tiny house, one side of which is taken up by a great open fireplace, with pots and kettles hanging about it. Harry loves the idea and smell of her open peat fire. She feeds the boys a great tea of eggs, bacon, honey, brown bread, and milk, a feast on which the two stuff themselves. Harry thinks her house is the "jolliest place" he has ever seen.

HONK: THE MOOSE (Stong*, Phil, ill. Kurt Wiese, Dodd, 1935), humorous story for younger children set in the iron range of Minnesota in the early twentieth century. Ivar Ketonen and Waino, two ten-year-old boys of Finnish descent, after a make-believe moose hunt with their skis and air rifle, return to Ivar's father's livery stable in Birora to find a real moose helping himself to the horses' hay. They tell Ivar's father, who at first is skeptical, and when he can't shoo the moose out, they alert in turn the policeman, the mayor, and the city council, who decide to pay for the hay and hope the moose will leave of its own accord. The next morning the boys find the moose gone and tell a new boy, Jim Barry, but when they take Jim to the stable they arrive just in time to see Honk, as they have begun to call the moose, returning. He and the boys are delighted to see each other. The next day, when he has been shut out, the boys lure him to the park with hay and shut him under the band stand, but he follows them back through town. He spends the winter in the livery stable but in the spring, after causing considerable trouble to vegetable dealers and gardeners, disappears. The next winter, however, Honk returns to the easy life at the livery stable. The highly illustrated story, only a little longer than a picture book, is lively but slight, and serves to show how much this genre has developed since its publication. Fanfare; Lewis Carroll; Newbery Honor.

HOPKINS, JOHN D. (*The Boy Who Had No Birthday**), itinerant eccentric, an actual historical figure, whose antics provoke merriment wherever he goes. He is a round, florid-faced little man of wandering wits, who pulls a two-wheeled cart, to which he has hitched himself, behaving like a horse. For years he has wandered through Ohio and Indiana, preaching to whoever will listen, selling his "ballads," and boasting of his deeds in the Civil War. Daredevil* Jim Kelso trades him a new suit for the one in which Ol'* Patches has sewn Davy* Cring's money.

THE HORSECATCHER (Sandoz*†, Mari, Westminister, 1957), historical novel set among the American Indians of the Great Plains in the middle 1800s after they have received the horse but before the push westward has destroyed their traditional nomadic way of life. Young Elk, Cheyenne, does not wish to become a warrior; he dislikes killing. He wishes to become a catcher of the wild mustangs that roam his native plains, and indeed he early shows a special gift for gentling horses by voice and touch. Even after he earns a warrior name, Kiowa Killer, for slaying an enemy, proving that he is capable of brave deeds, he is shunned by the youth of the tribe because he refuses to join in their exploits. After the elders censure him several times for stealing away to hunt horses, his father gives in and turns him over to Old Horsecatcher, renowned hunter of horses, who instructs him in the lore and secrets of horse catching. The remainder of the book describes the youth's growing ability to capture and tame horses. His efforts to acquire the best horses he can take him against enemy Kiowa, into the territory of his tribal cousins, the northern Cheyenne, who live along the Yellowstone, and deep into the country of the dreaded Comanche, where he observes how two skilled sisters handle the wild mustangs. On his solitary hunts, he endures hunger, thirst, cold, and constant danger. He shares the horses he catches with his parents and his mentor and is especially generous in distributing them to the needy of his tribe. He catches, among others, a colt with a bear pattern on his hide (on his first hunt), a great blue stallion, a mighty dun, a spotted Pelousy, like those of the Nez Perce, and on the last hunt described in the book, a ghost-white mustang, the desire of all the mounted Indians, which he releases to divert raiding Kiowa and save his people. In gratitude for his valor and sacrifice, the tribe honors him with the name of Horsecatcher in a special ceremony. A few scenes are exciting, but overall the book is dull, and even the chase scenes fall flat, laboring under an excess of descriptive detail. Plot and characterization are meager, and Young Elk remains a plaster protagonist. The novel's saving feature lies in its convincing picture of Cheyenne life with descriptions of rituals, dress, hunts, raids, women's work, everyday life, activities of elders, the contrary and other leaders, discipline, the vision quest, courting customs, and the like. Fanfare; Newbery Honor.

HORTENSE (*Calico Captive**), pretty, young French-Canadian servingwoman in the Du Quesne household who befriends Miriam and Susanna*, and of whom Miriam becomes fond. Hortense's fiancé, Jules, a *habitant*, secures information for Miriam about where James and the children are being held. When Hortense and Jules get married, Miriam makes a wedding dress for Hortense out of the flowered material the governor's wife has given Miriam for her own, an action which demonstrates that Miriam has become less selfish.

THE HOUSE (Allee*, Marjorie Hill, ill. Helen Blair, Houghton, 1944), realistic novel set in Chicago in the early 1940s, sequel to *The Great Tradition* (Houghton, 1937). Merritt Lane, having returned to the University after working as a biologist in the Caribbean, joins a group which rents an old house and lives cooperatively. Spark plug of the group is scatterbrain Nancy Allen. Danny Davidson, called "Uncle" because of his greying hair, is the most stable influence, while Janet Smith does most of the cooking and more than her share of the work to make up for her husband, Tom, who is too busy. The other married couple, Bill and Susie, are devoted, idealistic youngsters. Other prominent house members are cynical Stuart Jackman, sweet, inexperienced Clover Carter, and plain Beechy Lemke. When the group considers the application of a Chinese girl, Alice Chen, the gentleman who lives across the street, elderly Arthur Johnson, arranges to have their lease cancelled, fearing that racial mixing will harm the neighborhood, though his spirited sister, Bertha, likes the young people. Stuart discovers a better house for less rent in an already mixed neighborhood, to which they move. Clover loses her job in a bookstore, but Miss Johnson finds her a new one in a nursery school which her granddaughter, Jeannie, attends. Pearl Harbor shatters their lightheartedness and increases Merritt's worry about her fiancé, John Gordon, who is working near Java. When an old derelict known as Freddy takes a dislike to Clover, he abducts Jeannie, who is in her care, and Stuart, who has been attracted to Clover but is engaged to Beechy, finds and rescues the child. Severe flu turns to pneumonia for Susie, who is hospitalized, and also afflicts Stuart and Janet, who is pregnant. Merritt is worried that Stuart mooches from Beechy but doesn't love her. They are all shocked and grieved when Susie dies.

The Johnsons give Stuart a handsome reward for finding Jeannie, which he leaves for Beechy along with a letter ending their engagement when he departs secretly to join an ambulance corps. Although she has not heard from him for months, Merritt's John reappears, and they plan to marry soon. This slice-of-life narrative is long on descriptions of cooking meals, making bedsteads, arguing in house meetings, and other nondramatic activities. The idea of a group of both males and females keeping house together, novel in the 1940s, seems unusual today only in that they keep relationships so extremely proper. Child Study.

THE HOUSE OF SIXTY FATHERS (DeJong*†, Meindert, ill. Maurice Sendak, Harper, 1956), historical novel set in China during World War II. When the invading Japanese destroy his village, Tien* Pao, a young Chinese boy, flees upriver in a sampan with his parents and his baby sister, Beauty of the Republic. At Hengyang his parents go to seek work, carrying the baby and leaving Tien Pao at the sampan. A blond American airman, whom Tien Pao at first takes for a river god and later learns is Lieut. Hamsun, hires him to row across the river, then has to help with the rowing since the river is too strong for the boy. Angry at the risk Tien Pao has taken, his father next day leaves the oars with a neighbor, and when the boat is knocked loose and the swollen river washes it away, it is carried back into Japanese-held territory. Tien Pao manages to get to shore and, with only the family pig, Glory* of the Republic, for companion, starts to make his way back upriver, hiding from both the Japanese and the starving Chinese populace, who endanger the pig, and fearing the spirits that inhabit the mountains. From his hiding place he watches an airplane attack the Japanese troops and vehicles below, sees the plane crash and the airman escape, and when a Japanese soldier is about to kill the airman, Tien Pao yells a warning. The wounded man, who turns out to be Lieut. Hamsun, hides with Tien Pao and the pig, then at night they start out and are rescued by Chinese guerillas and taken, separately, upriver to Chinese-held territory. At Hengyang, however, the Japanese are taking the city, and Tien Pao's parents have fled. In a vivid scene of a city under shellfire, choked with a panicky populace, Tien Pao gets a precarious place on a crowded freight train and is knocked off in the night, still with his pig. He is found by two soldiers, who take him to their barracks, learn through an interpreter that he has helped save their squadron leader Hamsun, and all sixty flyers adopt him. Hamsun, who is recovering, takes him by low-flying plane to seek among the refugees for his parents, whom they spot working at the airfield. The whole adventure is seen through the mind of the naive boy, whose terror, weariness, and loneliness are convincingly portrayed. Even such unlikely coincidences as the three-time meeting with Hamsun and the finding of Tien Pao's parents among the sea of homeless Chinese are made acceptable by the boy's own acceptance of their possibility. Child Study; Choice; Fanfare; Newbery Honor.

HOWLAND, BARTON (*Swift Rivers**), settler upriver from St. Louis, an old man. Once wealthy, he moved to his little island after his wife and sons died in an epidemic of some sort and built a rude structure there for himself and his books. After the hut burns down, Chris* and Stuart* help him build another. He writes a letter to President Andrew Jackson, which Chris mails for him in St. Louis, urging that attention be given to the upper reaches of the Louisana Purchase, and a letter of introduction for Chris to David Payne, a minister in St. Louis who is starting a school.

HUBBARD, RALPH, specialist on American Indians who published in the early 1930s *Queer Person** (Doubleday, 1930), a Newbery honor book, and *The Wolf Song* (Doubleday, 1935). He also wrote a book on American Indian crafts published by a sales firm and was special instructor in Indian lore to the Boy Scouts of America in the late 1920s and early 1930s.

HUBERT CARES (*A Lemon and a Star**; *Terrible, Horrible Edie†*; *Edie on the Warpath†*), third child in the wealthy, motherless family of Summerton, Mass., in the early twentieth century. Neither concerned for his honor, like Ted*, nor worried about what is proper, like Jane*, Hubert concentrates on food and survival. Blond and, as a young child, solid, he reminds Jane of a sailor. Generally agreeable, he is a frequent companion in Jane's adventures and is less antagonistic to Edie* than is Ted, but he also has a mind of his own and can be stubborn and, on rare occasions, erupts with sudden spurts of bravery.

HUCKLEBERRY FINN (*The Adventures of Tom Sawyer**; *The Adventures of Huckleberry Finn**), disreputable friend of Tom* Sawyer, who with him witnesses a murder in the graveyard, and protagonist and narrator of the sequel. Son of a brutish drunk, Huck has lived by his wits and slept in empty hogsheads, doing much as he pleases, until he and Tom find the treasure and he is taken in by Widow Douglas. He finally escapes both the constraints of "civilized" small town living and the brutality of his father by floating down the Mississippi River on a raft with Jim*, the runaway slave. Huck is a mixture of naivete and sharp observation of human nature, impressed by status but seeing through sham, unsentimental but so kindhearted that he feels sorry even for the Duke* and the King* when they get their just deserts. Huck also is sensitive to the beauties of nature and genuinely poetic in his colloquial descriptions of the beauty of life on the river.

HUGH (*The Hidden Treasure of Glaston**), lame son of Sir Hugh de Morville, who is left by his father with the monks at Glaston Abbey while Sir Hugh is on pilgrimage to the Holy Land. Engrossed in his work of deciphering the overwritten parchments he has found in the cave and in his friendship with Blaheris* the hermit, Hugh forgets his hatred of the king and his anger toward his father for leaving him at the abbey. In an unconvincing passage, he travels to the court of Henry II seeking the book of the Grail, which he feels has been stolen by Henry's minstrel, Maurice, and archdeacon Sir Walter Mape.

HUGO, BARON (*The Sword and the Scythe**), Lord of Ritterswald in Swabia, known as "The Scowler" from the scar of an old swordcut on his forehead. Cruel, grasping, tyrannical, he organizes a movement among the knights of his area to improve their economic conditions against the peasants. Defeated in battle outside Memmingen by the revolting peasants, he agrees to become their military leader against the common foe, the princes, only to betray them for his own ends at the critical battle. Martin kills him just as the last, unsuccessful encounter against the princes begins. Hugh is a respected military commander but a much-hated lord.

HUMPHREY MARLOW (*The Prince and the Pauper**), whipping boy employed to take the punishment for Edward* Tudor, Prince of Wales, later Edward VI of England, who unwittingly provides much information to Tom* Canty under the guise of "reminding" him of names and customs his "madness" has made him forget. Although whipping boys may not have been employed in the court of Henry VIII, they were used by the time of James I and Charles II. Humphrey, whose father was a friend of Miles* Hendon, is instrumental in bringing Miles into the presence of Edward after he resumes his rightful identity.

THE HUNDRED DRESSES (Estes*†, Eleanor, ill. Louis Slobodkin*, Harcourt, 1944), short, realistic novel involving school classmates. Plain, poor, little Wanda Petronski has no friends. The children in her class tease her because she has a strange sounding name and because she always wears the same, ill-fitting, blue dress. Her classmate, Maddie, recalls how one day when the girls are admiring Cecile's new crimson dress, Wanda stuns them with her quiet assertion that she has one hundred dresses at home in her closet. The girls respond with hoots of derision and shouts of laughter. After that, Peggy, in particular, teases Wanda about her hundred dresses, but Maddie becomes increasingly uneasy about the way they treat her. Then Wanda wins first prize in the school drawing contest with her sketches of one hundred different dresses. The children now understand what Wanda was talking about, recognize her talent, and admire her creativity. Wanda's father writes the teacher that the Petronskis are leaving the neighborhood and chides the children for the way they have treated his daughter. Maddie is conscience-stricken because she had done nothing to defend Wanda. Peggy and Maddie go to Wanda's house, but find it empty, and Maddie resolves to speak up henceforth for justice. On Saturday, the two write to Wanda, congratulating her on her victory and asking her how she likes her new school. Christmas brings Wanda's reply which Miss Mason reads to the class. Wanda says she misses her old school and gives Peggy and Maddie each a sketch for a dress, those which they subsequently realize had been intended for them all along. Peggy and Maddie understand that Wanda has forgiven them for their behavior. This moralistic story is told mostly from Maddie's point of view. It is obviously an attempt to promote intercultural understanding and tolerance for the ways of those who are underprivileged or different. Slobodkin's humorous and gentle wash cartoons relieve the didacticism. Choice; Fanfare; Newbery Honor.

HUNT, MABEL LEIGH (1892–1971), born in Coatesville, Ind.; children's librarian and author for children. After a Quaker upbringing in Greencastle, Ind., she attended DePauw University and took her library degree from Western Reserve University. She was a children's librarian in Indianapolis for over ten years before she began writing for children. The author of thirty books, mostly for eight- to twelve-year-olds based on family relationships with historical or period settings, she drew her inspiration from her contacts with children, from their letters, from her childhood memories, and from research and reading. Although her books were well received and praised for authenticity and warmth, today they seem quaint and dated. Her first book, *Lucinda* (Stokes, 1934), grew out of her mother's stories about her Quaker childhood in Indiana during the Civil War. *Benjie's Hat* (Stokes, 1937) and *Little Grey Gown* (Stokes, 1939) also have Quaker backgrounds. Four of her novels were chosen by the editors of *Horn Book* for their Fanfare lists: *The Boy Who Had No Birthday** (Stokes, 1935), about an orphan in central Indiana just after the Civil War; *Little Girl with Seven Names** (Lippincott, 1936), about a little Amish girl who gives two of her names to her new baby twin sisters; *Michel's Island** (Lippincott, 1940), set on Mackinac Island off the lower peninsula of Michigan in the days of the fur trade; and *Sibby Botherbox** (Lippincott, 1945), an episodic novel set in the days of Theodore Roosevelt. Her biographies, *"Have You Seen Tom Thumb?"* (Stokes, 1942) and *Better Known as Johnny Appleseed* (Lippincott, 1950), were Newbery honor books and the latter was chosen for the White House Library. Her *Ladycake Farm* (Lippincott, 1952) was one of the first novels to treat blacks realistically and sympathetically, and she received the Indiana University Writers Conference Award for the best book by an Indiana author for *Stars for Cristy* (Lippincott, 1956), a story of the everyday life of a big-city tenement girl. She also wrote readers and contributed short stories, articles, and poems to anthologies, readers, and magazines for children.

HURRY HOME, CANDY (DeJong*†, Meindert, ill. Maurice Sendak, Harper, 1953), realistic animal story set in the mid-twentieth century United States. As a young puppy, Candy is bought and named by a girl, Catherine, 10, and her brother, George, 9. Their mother is unsympathetic, and their father has a macho, no-nonsense idea of raising dogs; between them, they terrify the puppy, especially when the woman punishes him with a broom. When they take the dog to see the children's grandparents, they have a flat tire and are caught in a storm, and they lose Candy. He becomes a stray, existing on scraps and other dogs' discarded bones. Chased by a pack, he takes refuge under a wagon of a pig-woman, who rescues him and plans to take him home, but when her horse strays off the road and her wagon overturns, she is taken to the hospital and Candy to the dog pound. Through a series of mischances, he strays onto a busy street and is rescued by a retired sea captain named Carlson, who adopts him. When they are walking at night to the bridge where Candy was originally lost, a bridge the artistic captain wants to paint, they blunder into some fleeing bank robbers who injure the captain, and Candy becomes a stray again. Catherine and George see the story and the offer of fifty dollars reward in the paper, go to their grandparents' neighborhood to search, and eventually their grandmother spots the dog sneaking through the brush behind them. This news wins them the reward (which they spend for bicycles), the captain lures the dog home with warm hamburger (a move almost thwarted because a cleaning woman has left a broom near the back door and Candy is afraid to approach), and Candy finally has a home with the captain. Although there is no fantasy dog conversation, the story is seen almost completely from the point of view of the dog, the only developed character. The emotions ascribed to him and the coincidences of the plot are all made plausible. As a character, however, he is so cringing that his adventures are not as compelling as some of DeJong's other animal characters. Newbery Honor.

I

IN A MIRROR (Stolz*†, Mary, Harper, 1953), realistic girls' novel set in an exclusive New England girls' college in the mid-1900s. Plain, overweight Bessie* Muller, aspiring writer, describes in her journal the three years she spends in Marion Shipley House as roommate of Til* Carey, beautiful, lively dance major. Ostensibly opposites, the two share love of the artistic and are essentially considerate and loyal. As the years pass, Bessie remains dateless, while Til flashes off to parties and goes through loves. When at the beginning of their junior year Bessie sees that handsome, serious Johnny Todd will also be dumped, she taxes Til with taking out on her boyfriends her disappointment in her unloving, self-absorbed father. In angry retaliation, Til announces that Bessie is simply jealous and that she too would attract boys if she only did not eat so much. Although both girls are hurt, they maintain their relationship, and Bessie finally manages to diet. An assignment to do a column for the school paper on Donald* Dunn, handsome young literature instructor new to the college, leads the girls into a friendship with him and his young family, his pretty, energetic wife, Audrey, and their two small children, fun-loving Josh and tiny Jennie, with whom they occasionally sit. Bessie is ambivalent about her feelings for Dunn, but Til falls head over heels in love with him, drawn by a relationship that contrasts so sharply with her own home experience. Her infatuation becomes common knowledge on campus. She performs especially for him the part of the child rescued by angry villagers in a dance about the basilisk, a production she and Bessie have created (and an obvious parallel to her own story), declares her love for Dunn, drops out of school, and joins her mother in Europe. Characters are well drawn, relationships are sensitively portrayed, style is literate and rich in imagery and allusion, and the look at the period is subtle and revealing, but the plot verges on the preposterous and moves very slowly. Bessie's journal is too much the product of a practiced pen to seem authentic, yet her inability to grasp what the reader can sense in the way of ambiguities and ironies of characters and situations gives strength to the form. (Mr. and Mrs. Muller*, Aunt* Hilda and Uncle Charlie.) Child Study.

INDIAN BROTHER (Coryell*, Hubert V., ill. Henry C. Pitz, Harcourt, 1935), historical novel set in the early eighteenth century near what is now Bristol, Maine. In continual danger from Indians stirred up to raid British settlements by the French, the family of Elias Hilton nevertheless moves north on the Kennebec River where he trades peacefully with them. Sam* Hilton, about 14, saves a young Indian, Sosepsis*, from an attacking moose, and they become blood brothers. Shortly afterwards Elias is forced to join, against his better judgment, an expedition to capture the Jesuit, Father Sebastian Râle, who is thought to be inciting most of the violence. Sam, accompanying the group to help hunt, has an opportunity to capture the fleeing Râle, but desists. Not long afterward, the Indians, in retaliation, kill and scalp Elias, then attack and burn the cabin of the family, who escape by hiding in the root cellar. After they reach the safety of Brunswick, Sam's twin sister, Martha, visiting a friend, is captured by the Indians, and Sam, rashly following to try to free her, is also captured. Sosepsis bargains with his captor and buys his freedom from being tortured to death, and when his tribe, the Penobscots, who have Martha, part company with the Norridgewocks, who have Sam, he promises to try to help Martha. Sam is ''playfully'' tortured but recovers and becomes a slave for many months. Eventually Sosepsis appears to tell him that Martha is to be married to brutal, drunken Sabatis and to suggest, obliquely, that Sam escape in the coming storm. This Sam does, following Sosepsis's trail, and comes to the Penobscot village, pretending to have been allowed a visit to see his sister married. Secretly they plan to escape to the mountain, K't-ahdin, which is shunned by the Indians who fear its spirit. Martha consults Mike* MacGregor, a Scotch-Irish boy who was captured earlier and has been adopted into the tribe. Mike decides to escape with them. They succeed nearly as planned, but Sabatis follows, and they confront and kill him. They are nearly recaptured, but Sosepsis outdistances the other Indians, bringing them a gun and some needed supplies, then insisting that they fight him and tie him up to avert suspicion. The twins and Mike spend a winter and most of the next summer high on the mountain, at first nearly starving but developing skills. At the season when the Indians go to the coast, they make a terribly difficult journey back to the British settlement, but just before they meet up with a group of soldiers, including Sam's brother John, Martha is captured again. Once more Sam follows to rescue her, this time hiding in the cabin of Father Râle at Norridgewock, where he is finally discovered and badly wounded by the priest, who is then killed in the massacre of the village by the British. The twins and Mike return to the settlement, and Sam recovers. Much of the action is historical, as a foreword, a postscript, and frequent footnotes tell us. The action, of which there is almost too much, proceeds at a lively pace, and the detail of both Indian life and that of the settlers is interesting, but the attitude is confusing. Although Sam, as first person narrator, and the author, in his notes, acknowledge the Indians' right to the country and their essential nobility, they are also described as cruel, ignorant, superstitious savages. Sequel is *The Scalp Hunters**. Fanfare.

INDIAN CAPTIVE: THE STORY OF MARY JEMISON (Lenski*, Lois, ill. author, Lippincott, 1941), biographical novel based on the life of a white girl captured by Seneca Indians in Eastern Pennsylvania on April 5, 1758. Encouraged by the French, then at war with the British in North America, the Indians of the Iroquois nation raid the settlements and farms, including that of Tom Jemison at March Creek Hollow, where they capture the Jemison family, except for two brothers who escape, and a neighbor, Widow Wheelock and her two children. A day's journey away, yellow-haired Molly (Mary) Jemison, 12, and Davy Wheelock, 9, are separated from the others who, Mary later learns, are killed immediately. The two children are taken on an arduous trip on foot to Fort Duquesne, at the junction of the Allegheny and Ohio rivers, where Mary is turned over to two Indian women, beautiful, kindly Shining Star and her cross sister, Squirrel Woman, who take her to Seneca Town and adopt her into their family in place of their brother, who was killed by whites. Mary gradually learns Indian ways and language, helped by the old man who has befriended her on the trip, Shagbark, and by a young boy, Little Turtle, who later earns the name of Turkey Feather. After several months, Mary, now called Corn Tassel, goes with her Indian sisters to trade at Fort Duquesne and attracts the attention of an officer and his lady, who propose to keep her. She is rushed away by her sisters, who take her on a long journey north to Genishau, on the Genesee River, the main Seneca settlement. There she fits better into Indian ways but twice is tantalized by hopes of rescue, once when the trader Fellenash comes through, and later when a young man, Josiah Johnson, who has been captured and, after running the gauntlet, adopted as the son of Earth Woman, escapes. Mary recognizes the genuine grief of Earth Woman, whom she loves. When Fellenash returns with the news that her family has been slaughtered, she gives up hope of return and turns her love to the Indians, including Blue Jay, later called Blue Trout, baby of Shining Star, whom Mary saves from a rattlesnake. When the Iroquois decide to side with the British, an officer offers to buy Mary and take her to Fort Niagara, but she chooses to stay with the Senecas. Like other Lenski books, this is stronger on research than on characterization or plot, but since this is based on a real life of dramatic events, the story itself has interest. The attitude toward the Indians and the brutality of the period are balanced. Fanfare; Newbery Honor.

INDIAN JOHN (*Caddie Woodlawn**), kindly Indian whose band lives near the Woodlawn farm and of whose friendliness Mr.* Woodlawn is certain in spite of rumors to the contrary among the settlers. John especially likes Caddie because of her spunk, candor, and red hair. He entrusts his valued scalp belt to her keeping and gives her his dog after Uncle* Edmund takes the Woodlawn dog, Nero, back to St. Louis with him.

INJUN JILL (*Downright Dencey**), cruel, half-crazy, old woman, who raises Sam Jetsam. She is apparently not Sam's mother, though she tells him and others that she is. She is the stereotype of the dirty, ignorant Indian.

INJUN JOE (*The Adventures of Tom Sawyer**), evil half-breed who kills Dr. Robinson in the graveyard and escapes at the trial after Tom has testified against him. Tom* Sawyer and Huck* Finn see him and an accomplice digging up the treasure in the haunted house and later glimpse him dead drunk in the Temperance Tavern back room, though he is by then masquerading as a deaf-and-dumb Spaniard. Presented as an unmitigated villain, he swears vengeance against the boys, attempts to disfigure the Widow Douglas, blames Muff Potter for the murder, and at last dies in the cave after the entrance has been sealed.

IRON DUKE (Tunis*†, John R., ill. Johan Bull, Harcourt, 1938), realistic problem novel set mostly at Harvard University in Cambridge, Mass., in the mid-1900s in which sports play an important part in the plot. Adjustment to the size and impersonality of a large university proves difficult for Jim Wellington, who comes from a small high school in Waterloo, Iowa. An honor student and star athlete at home, Jim finds college competition extremely keen. He fails to make the freshman football squad, and except for his determination not to disgrace his family and the help and encouragement of his roommates, Mickey* McGuire and Fog* Smith, he would have flunked out by the end of his first semester. Jim is made of tough stuff, however, and he decides that education must take precedence over athletics and socializing and devotes himself to his books, even giving up vacations to ensure that he will not remain on academic probation. Later, a running and kicking stunt earns him the attention of the track coach, who invites him to join the team, and Jim's junior year finds him both on the Dean's List for academic achievement and a campus athletic celebrity. His sprinting ability breaks both collegiate and intercollegiate records and earns him the captaincy of the squad for his senior year. Although he fails to gain membership in the exclusive Circle and his attitude remains serious, Jim finds some time for bull sessions, a trip to Boston for a show, and a few campus hijinks. He is early introduced to the power of the student mob through a riot in the Yard, and the Dunster Funsters (Jim and his two roommates in Dunster Hall) amusingly interpret the Fly Club meeting, for the campus, over a loudspeaker system Jim rigs up. At the end of his junior year, Jim returns to Waterloo, more sure of himself and of what he hopes to gain from life and proud to have achieved success after so shaky a start. Here are glimpses of both the fun and serious sides of college life before World War II. Events and characters are typical of school stories and appear deliberately assembled to promote Jim's maturation from a raw small-towner into a man worthy of the nickname given him by McGuire, who puts together Wellington and Waterloo and comes up with the "Iron Duke." Tunis's storytelling is vigorous and direct, and the extensive dialogue and details of sports carry conviction. Fanfare.

IRON HOUSES (*Glory of the Seas**), galvanized house frames all ready to use for offices and stores, made by a New York firm and shipped to San Francisco. John Seagrave and Mr. Pinckney invest in them.

IRVING, WASHINGTON (1783–1859), born in New York City; diplomat and writer of some of the earliest and best-loved American stories. He attended private schools, was employed in law offices, and was admitted to the New York Bar. He served as secretary of the United States legation in London and as United States Minister to Spain. Under his own name and the pseudonyms of Fray Antonia Agapida, Geoffrey Crayon, Diedrich Knickerbocker, Laurence Langstaff, and Jonathan Oldstyle, he wrote satire, essays, humor, and biography, including lives of Oliver Goldsmith, Mahomet, Washington, and Columbus. At fifteen he spent the summer in Westchester County in the region in which he later set *The Legend of Sleepy Hollow** (originally in *The Sketch Book of Geoffrey Crayon, Gent.*, C. S. Van Winkle, 1819–1820). In 1800 he traveled up the Hudson River to Albany, past the Catskill Mountains, the setting for his *Rip Van Winkle** (originally in *The Sketch Book*). His polished, leisurely prose style and witty, good-natured satire have kept these stories popular for more than a century and a half.

I.S.A.A.C. (*The Saturdays**), acronym for the Independent Saturday Afternoon Adventure Club that the Melendy children form. They enjoy using the term because no one else knows what it means. Rush* names his dog Isaac after the club.

ISANNAH LAPHAM (*Johnny Tremain**), exquisitely beautiful, blond, eight-year-old younger sister of Cilla*. Pampered, spoiled, parasitic, theatrical, she is the perfect offset to her unselfish older sister, who dotes on her. Her eloquent testimony frees Johnny of the charge of theft. She becomes the plaything of beautiful, fashionable Lavinia* Lyte and goes to England with the merchant's daughter.

J

JAC (*Out of the Flame**), Jacques, ugly, humpbacked dwarf whose life Pierre de Bayard saves while on a hunt. He becomes Pierre's loyal friend and adviser. He has prophetic dreams and the King's Touch, a remarkable ability to heal.

JACK (*Knight's Castle**), Roger* and Ann's* cousin, twelve-year-old brother of Eliza*, who is less imaginative than the other children but joins in their adventures. He is camera-crazy, and even takes his camera into the fantasy land, where of course, the pictures don't "take." He learns to believe in magic.

JACKSON, JESSE (1908-   ), born in Columbus, Ohio; author of novels and non-fiction about blacks. He writes out of his own experiences as a black growing up in white America and was one of the first writers to portray blacks realistically and sympathetically in books for children. He lived for part of his childhood in a ghetto in Columbus. After graduating from high school, he studied journalism at Ohio State University and later participated in the Breadloaf Writers' Conference in Vermont. He took up boxing in college and for a time considered making boxing his career. He has been a reporter, publisher of his own newspaper, a postal clerk, and a laborer and has worked in boys' camps and with youth agencies. While he was working as a probation officer, he decided that he would like to write for young people. *Call Me Charley** (Harper, 1945), about a black youth seeking respect and recognition as an individual in a predominately white community, was his first novel and is listed in *Choice*. Though simplistic and contrived, it remains read probably because of its plucky, earnest young hero, simple, straightforward writing, and honest tone. *Anchor Man* (Harper, 1947) and *Charley Starts from Scratch* (Harper, 1958) continue Charley's story. *The Sickest Don't Always Die the Quickest* (Doubleday, 1971), and *The Fourteenth Cadillac* (Doubleday, 1972) feature another hero, Stonewall Jackson, while *Tessie* (Harper, 1968) involves a black girl growing up in Harlem. He received the Carter G. Goodson Award of the National Council on Social Studies for *Make a Joyful Noise unto the Lord! The Life of Mahalia Jackson, Queen of Gospel Singers* (Crowell, 1974). He has also contributed to national magazines, and since 1974 he has taught at Appalachian State University in Boone, N.C.

JACOB DITZER (*Benjamin West and His Cat Grimalkin**), German immigrant boy whose family stays at the Wests' Door-Latch Inn and whose sick kitten Benjamin adopts and names Grimalkin*. The two boys confide to each other their life's ambitions, the author's way of orienting young readers about Benjamin's talent and hopes of becoming a painter. Later Jacob and his father give Benjamin a ride to Philadelphia when he leaves to study there.

JACOB POOT (*Hans Brinker; or, The Silver Skates**), jolly, rotund youth. A comic figure, he often comes to small griefs. The other children enjoy his company and watch out for him.

JACQUENCE (*Michel's Island**), real name Joseph, Michel's younger brother and his best playmate. The youngest son in the family, he is gullible and easily influenced. Sometimes Michel takes great advantage of him, though usually Jacquence manages to come out all right eventually. He gets his way about going out on the Arched Rock when the boys are playing the Gitche Manitou game. His subsequent fall from the rock provides Zhikag* with the opportunity to do the unselfish deed that breaks the sorceress's power over him.

JADIH YAZHI (*The Ordeal of the Young Hunter**), Navajo boy, usually obedient and reliable, who can run as swiftly as the antelope after whom he is named but is often moody and fierce as the bear, with whom he spent a night in a cave when he was very little. He would like to become a priest like Yellow* Nose, his uncle, but is confused by the conflict between his parents' support of new ways and his uncle's adherence to old customs. He offers to work for Trader* Jim Whitaker, to pay off his father's debts, and to earn the horse, Rawhide, known to him privately as Mr. Cloud.

JAMAICA JOHNNY (Hader*, Berta, and Elmer Hader* ill. authors, Macmillan, 1935), realistic story set on the island of Jamaica in the first third of the twentieth century. Since the death of his parents, little black Johnny Morgan, almost nine, has lived with his Uncle Solomon O'Connor, on his easy-going mountain farm, where Johnny takes care of Katy, the goat, Coco, the burro, Biddy, the dog, and the other animals, does the casual housework, and carves gourds to sell as rattle souvenirs to tourists. Uncle Solomon, who works sometimes on the nearby banana plantation, builds a new house with wattled walls made of sticks woven between poles, then plastered with mud made of red earth and wood ashes, and then brings home a wife, Aunt Millicent. Johnny likes his new aunt and has more time for carving but is discovered by the truant officer and marched off to school, where he has seldom bothered to show his face. When the teacher's back is turned, he slips off and goes to see his Aunt Caroline, who lives some distance away. There he plays with his three girl cousins. When he decides to return home after several days, Caroline gives him a book left for him by his mother, *The Story of Tommy, a Little Black Boy of Jamaica*, about an eighteenth-century boy. To be able to read the book, Johnny goes back to school and recruits his friend, Boswell, to go too. He does so well that the teacher encourages him to get more education, so he gets a job on the plantation, hoping to earn enough to go to some higher school. There he works hard and saves the sugar cane from a fire and also a little American girl, Elizabeth, by stopping her runaway horse. The overseer, Mr. Clarkson, arranges that Johnny can have lessons with Elizabeth (who turns out to be his visiting niece) and her brother, Ernest, from their English governess, Miss Babson. Johnny also becomes their guide to sights of the island. He takes them to the coastal village, White Horses, where he lived as a little child and where his Uncle Taddeus lives. There Elizabeth and Ernest go out to the reef on a canoe and are stranded as a storm comes up. Johnny swims out to the canoe, pushes it to the reef, and gets the children to shore just as a big storm hits. They later go to Port Royal to learn more about the famous pirate, Henry Morgan, from whom Johnny is descended. After Elizabeth and Ernest go home, they send Johnny a Christmas present: a scholarship to the parish school. The story is more a vehicle for a tour guide of Jamaica and to exhibit the pictures by the Haders than a realistic story. The coincidences are highly unlikely, and the promise of upward mobility through education dates the story. Fanfare.

JAMES (*Magic or Not?**), serious, practical boy who likes facts, but is never stodgy or judgmental. He is a bit condescending toward his sister, Laura*, but likes adventures and is willing to believe in magic. He is much slower to reach out to others than warm-hearted Laura.

JAMES, WILL(IAM RODERICK) (1892-1942), cowboy writer and artist, born, according to his autobiography, in the Judith Basin country near Great Falls, Mont., though some authorities say his real name was Joseph Ernest Nephtali Dufault, born in Quebec. His autobiography says he was orphaned at four and adopted by a French-Canadian trapper and prospector, Jean Beaupre, who was drowned while the boy was still in his early teens. He attended the California School of Fine Art and Yale University School of Fine Art and served in the U.S. Army during World War I. It is not disputed that he worked as a cowhand, a rodeo rider, and a stuntman for Hollywood studios, and wrote novels of cowboys and horses in a conversational dialect, nonsentimental stories with fine visual imagery. Besides some four novels, a collection of short stories, and a couple of non-fiction books for adults, he wrote five books of non-fiction and twelve novels for young people, the most famous among them being *Smoky, the Cowhorse** (Scribner's, 1926), an early Newbery winner. All his works were self-illustrated with line drawings that capture the horses and men of the working ranches. During his later years he owned and operated a ranch near Billings, Mont.

JANE CARES (*A Lemon and a Star**; *Terrible, Horrible Edie†; Edie on the Warpath†*), dreamy, worrying second child in the Cares family in a series of novels set in Summerton, Mass., in the early twentieth century. Plagued by her disparaging older brother, Ted*, and her own conscience, Jane nevertheless manages to assert herself and even to organize her younger brother, Hubert*, into various remarkable and unconventional activities. Sandy-haired and freckled, she resembles Ted. The first book (*A Lemon and a Star**), in which she is ten, is told mostly from her viewpoint, but in the other two she fades into a background figure, occasionally a supportive older sister to Edie* but not as important as either of the boys.

JANE MOFFAT (*The Moffats**; *The Middle Moffat**; *Rufus M.**), imaginative, good-hearted, energetic second daughter in the Moffat family of Cranbury*, Conn. *The Middle Moffat* is mainly about her, and much of *The Moffats* revolves around her, too. She is a strongly drawn character to whom it is easy to relate.

JANE SAWYER (*Rebecca of Sunnybrook Farm**), younger of the two aunts who take in Rebecca* Randall to educate her. Timid and dominated by her sister, Matilda*, Jane is gentle and kinder to Rebecca. Her past holds a lost love, a young man wounded in the Civil War who sent for her and died in her arms. It is Jane who patiently teaches Rebecca to sew, who persuades Matilda to let the girl trade the brown gingham for pink and blue, and who sews pretty trim on the dresses for her.

JANE'S ISLAND (Allee*, Marjorie Hill, ill. Maitland de Gogorza, Houghton, 1931), realistic novel set at Woods* Hole, Mass. Ellen McNeill, 17, has come from Chicago at the end of her freshman year in college to be companion-baby sitter for Jane Thomas, 12, whose father is a biologist at the Woods Hole marine laboratory. Ellen finds Jane a lively, tomboyish girl, more interested in science than in the pretty dresses and fine housekeeping her mother cherishes. In the community of the laboratory are a number of other young people including Jane's brother, Walter, about Ellen's age, who is employed as a collector of specimens; Jim Harrison, a graduate student from Chicago, who starts an antiseptic romance with Ellen; Miss Wareham, a retired biologist who remembers the early days of the lab; and Dr. Fritz Von Bergen, a crippled German biologist, who was a friend of Dr. Thomas in their student days. It soon becomes apparent that Von Bergen, a surly man, is attempting to disprove the conclusions Dr. Thomas has reached in his experiments with planaria, small aquatic creatures found on the underside of rocks. Although usually unsociable, Von Bergen joins one of the beach parties of the young people and attempts to swim the Gutter, a narrow channel between two islands through which the tides rush. When he is in difficulty because of his crippled leg, Jane dives in to aid him and Ellen, following, is instrumental in saving him, but her leg is injured in the attempt. Although he is ungracious in his acknowledgment, he later rescues the two girls when they are stranded on an island in the fog and, when Dr. Thomas has an emergency appendectomy and must abandon his experiment at a crucial stage, Von Bergen takes it over, even though the results run counter to his own conclusions. The title of the book refers to an imaginary island where Jane plans to live when she is old enough, a place where she can do as she pleases. Jane is pictured as a lively girl, but characterization and plot are subordinated to the Woods Hole setting and the information about marine biology, and the attitudes and incidents make the book seem very dated. Newbery Honor.

JANET, HENRY, DENISE, LOUIS, ARTHUR (*Twenty and Ten**), schoolchildren, the main characters in the novel. Arthur is one of the Jewish refugees that the French children hide in their midst during the Nazi occupation of France during World War II. When Henry shares his soup with Arthur, Arthur responds by giving him a piece of chocolate. Arthur is with the children when they discover the cave in which later the Jewish children are hidden. Denise falls into a hole while the children are playing, and the children soon realize it is the entrance to a cave. Janet is sweet on Henry and likes to play the part of Mary when the children act out the Nativity story. She sometimes regards Denise as a rival for his affections, thinks Henry is very good at make-believe, and tells the story.

JANET PEYTON (*The Windy Hills**), pleasant girl, Oliver's younger sister, usually content to allow him to lead and whom he usually patronizes. She influences the story, particularly when she finds the little lost boy who turns out to be Martin Crawford, Anthony's son, and returns him to his home. While helping Anthony's pathetic wife and her ill baby, Janet finds in the attic a miniature portrait which links the Peytons and the Crawfords and helps toward a solution of the mystery surrounding Cousin Jasper. When the children return the miniature, Oliver stands up to Anthony, asserting that he is no more substantial than his scarecrow. Oliver's words prick Anthony's conscience and, together with his realization of the possible effects on the community of his miserliness about keeping the dike in repair, produce his change of heart.

JANEY LARKIN (*Blue Willow**), ten, daughter of migrant workers Jim and Clara Larkin, once of Texas. Janey is small and thin for her age. At first she is lonely, dreamy, and defensive, but she gradually grows more outgoing as the story progresses. She is occasionally adventurous, as when she explores the river by herself, and she can be proud and quite assertive, as when she lights into Bounce Reybourn and flails him with her fists for calling her a thief. She enjoys books and reading, and her admiration for the courage of the knights in the King

Arthur stories precipitates a discussion between her and her father on the nature of bravery and nobility. Her father insists that she read at least two pages from the Bible every day when she is not going to school to keep up her reading skills. The stories she reads in the Bible influence her thinking, and she often likens her situations to those of Biblical figures. The Biblical language also affects her manner of speaking. At the end, she joins in the merry May dance with her schoolmates, delighted and grateful to have acquired roots and friends of her own. She has learned that real courage lies in meeting the everyday problems that life brings.

JANUS (*The Wheel on the School**), legless ex-fisherman who becomes a strong advocate of the children's effort to get storks for the village of Shora. Bad-tempered and reclusive, he has been mainly interested in keeping boys and birds from raiding his cherry tree, but once involved with the quest for the wheel, he displays his executive ability and regains the respect and friendship of the villagers. To please the children's appetite for adventure, he goes along with the story that a shark bit off his legs, which really have been amputated because of blood poisoning.

JAREB (Powell*, Miriam, ill. Marc Simont, Crowell, 1952), realistic novel set in south Georgia in the mid-twentieth century. Jeb (Jareb) Judson, about fourteen, has to admit that his lazy hound, Sawbuck, is not much of a hunter, but he is heartbroken when his parents let his married brother, Gabe, trade the dog in an effort to get a much-needed plow. Next morning, Dovey (Dovebird) Tatum, one of a new family in the area, brings him word that the dog is at their house, having escaped from Cal Calhoun, well-to-do farmer nearby, and been run over accidentally by her father. The dog recovers and is allowed to stay, with the agreement that Jeb will be more helpful, but trouble plagues the family. Gabe's wife, Melissy, dies giving birth to a daughter. The piney woods catch fire, and Jeb puts the blaze out with difficulty and with the help of Uncle* Thirsty (Thurston) Andrews, an old man reputed to be crazy, possibly an arsonist. Jeb's father can get no work, though Gabe goes to work for the new turpentine still, a business despised by Jeb's father and many of the old-timers because early turpentiners ruined the woods in the area. Gabe's baby is ailing and needs special care and medicines. Jeb, at the beach with the Tatums, witnesses a brutal fight in which Gabe beats Buck Yancey, one of the tough Slattery gang that Gabe ran with before his marriage. The hard times force Jeb's father to sell off the woods that the boy loves so, but the new tree farming methods promise to renew the land. Jeb works for Calhoun, planting trees, and he is given a bonus of the extra seedlings, which he shares with his friend, Little Lize Moody, planting his portion for a Christmas surprise for his father. During the Christmas Eve celebration, the newly built schoolhouse catches fire, and Jeb, on his way home, saves Uncle Thirsty, who is pinned by a falling timber, but then is accused by the Slatterys of having started the fire. Little Lize, who has seen one of the Slattery gang running from the scene, speaks up for him, and Uncle Thirsty recovers in time to confirm that the gang has set other fires and has been paid to ruin the new turpentine still, but has set fire to the schoolhouse by accident when the wind changed. Jeb's father makes him a full partner in the tree farming and convinces him that he should go back to school, with Dovey Tatum, to learn more about the business. The style gives a flavor of the backwoods Georgia dialect, and the descriptions of the beach and of the pine woods which Jeb loves are vivid. Jeb is convincing, as are his parents and some of the minor characters, but the plot is predictable and a bit clumsy. Child Study.

JARED AMIS (*Winter Danger**), a ''woodsy'' who would rather sleep in a hollow log or cave than a cabin and who assumes his eleven-year-old-son, Caje, has the same preferences. For days he will go without speaking, making no concessions for the boy's comfort or need for companionship. When the prospect of an unusually severe winter makes him take Caje to his dead wife's brother, he is restless and irritable, scornful when the boy enjoys sleeping under a quilt and annoyed when he accepts a gift of socks from his good-hearted aunt. Rather than be beholden to the family, he abandons his son, and there is no indication that he will return even if he survives the bitter winter.

JARED'S BLESSING (Woodward*, Hildegard, ill. author, Scribner's, 1942), short, highly illustrated story of a boy and his dog, set in Connecticut in 1762. Jared Sprague, a young schoolboy, is a minister's son, often taunted for his odd clothes and his wispy hair, and he still longs for England, where he lived until recently. Challenging the local boys' fear of the graveyard on Halloween, he goes there and finds a white puppy with black ears, which he names Blessing. At his father's insistence, he checks the notice board at the tavern to see if Blessing is a lost dog and learns that he was left behind by a family which moved away. Blessing is a problem, however. He chews up the slave boy's hat and Jared's new coat, scatters the shoemaker's shoes and the neighbor's newly made candles, eats the shopkeeper's caraway seed cakes, and falls into Granny Tibball's vat of blue dye. No longer white, he hides under the bed in Deacon Dering's fine house. He even arrives in church carrying Parson Sprague's yellow house slipper. When little Theodosia Dering is lost, however, he leads Jared to the cemetery where they find the child sleeping under a table-shaped tombstone. As the town celebrates Thanksgiving, particularly grateful that the little girl is safe, Jared decides that he likes life in Connecticut. The story is pleasant but slight, mostly a vehicle to accompany the pictures of life in an eighteenth-century New England community. Fanfare.

JARNAC, ALBERT (*Michel's Island**), successful fur trader at Mackinac, father of Michel, who is very proud of his French-Canadian heritage. He is a very practical man, who has learned how to get on with both government officials and with the Indians. His wife is Morning Star, the daughter of an Ottawa chief.

He is a vigorous, outgoing man whose booming laughter has earned him the nickname of Earthshaker. He enjoys fine clothes, elegant parties, and beautiful things. His most prized possession is an engraved brass standish (writing box). Although he rules his establishment with an iron hand and his sons are somewhat afraid of him, they also respect and love him for his generosity and appreciation of them as individuals. He teases Michel about his dark skin and about his ambition to become an herbalist, but he also understands the boy's need to be himself and to do what he feels is right. He accepts Michel's decision to remain on the island. He is the most fully developed character in the book.

JEDEDIAH PERKINS (*A-going to the Westward**), shiftless and malicious neighbor who travels with the Bartletts on their journey to Ohio in 1811. Jed is going west to escape Connecticut's strict religion and, he hopes, the hard work needed to make a living. Jealous of Reuben Bartlett, he plays a series of mean pranks to ensure that he and his family will get to Pittsburgh first, and because Betsy and Thomas Bartlett know he is responsible for their wagon wheel breaking, he terrorizes Thomas and gives deliberately misleading information that causes Betsy to be left behind. Thomas, however, keeps forgiving him because he offers to teach the boy to play his fiddle. Other people think less of his music, which usually accompanies his drunkenness. He causes the Bartlett's boat to crash by refusing to follow the pilot's instructions. Only his daughter, Florilla, whom he unaccountably fears, can control him. In Ohio he forsakes his wicked ways and becomes, unconvincingly, industrious and respectable.

JED GREEN (*The Singing Boones**), stalwart, intelligent, plainspoken young scout whose direction, advice, and hard work see Captain Jack's wagon train safely to California. He takes a special interest in the Boones during the trip, a concern that becomes more obvious as his romantic attraction for Ellen grows. She, in particular, comes to depend upon him. At the end of the journey, he is not yet ready to marry and settle down. He continues to work with relief trains and as a scout for some months before returning to California, searching for the Boones, and marrying Ellen.

JEFF BUSSEY (*Rifles for Watie**), Jefferson Davis Bussey, forthright, mannerly, steady, Kansas farm boy, who, after bushwhackers attack his father's farm, joins the Union army, filled with gallant spirit and convinced that the "war's just a breakfast spell." During his training at Fort Leavenworth, he inadvertently incurs the enmity of Captain Asa Clardy, the commander of his unit. Clardy's animosity unreasonably persists throughout the war, and he often assigns Jeff to such despised duties as digging latrines and burying the dead. Eager for battle, Jeff is terror-sticken during his first encounter with the enemy under fire, although he conducts himself well generally and later is decorated for outstanding conduct. While in Indian country, Jeff becomes acquainted with the Washbournes, a well-to-do Cherokee family, whose women Jeff helps by doing household chores. He falls in love with beautiful, self-assured Lucy, who at first is cool toward him, but, after he arranges for the body of her brother, Lee, executed by Clardy as a spy, to be brought home for burial, treats him more kindly. Later Jeff becomes a scout and falls in with Watie's* men, where, after contracting malaria, he is nursed by Heifer, a Rebel cook, and then by the Jackmans, a Southern family. Jeff discovers that the Indians are much more advanced in their way of life than he expected, is outraged by the way they have been treated by the government, and admires the brave and comradely behavior of the Watie men. After he learns that Clardy has been smuggling rifles to Watie, he flees to Fort Gibson with the information, hotly pursued by Rebel soldiers and bloodhounds. At the end of the book, he is mustered out and returns to his home in Linn County, Kansas, where he makes plans to fetch Lucy and marry her. During the four years of the war, Jeff has matured in mind and spirit, gaining in independence of thought as he has come to see the individuality of people and the danger of quick judgments.

JEFFERSON, THOMAS (*The Codfish Musket**), third president of the United States (1743-1826). In the novel he appears as a pleasant, gentle, mild, home- and family-loving man on the one hand and as a man of vision, daring, and political action on the other. Since Jefferson knew John Ledyard* in Europe, he is able to give Dan Boit many details about the life of the man who has become a hero in Dan's eyes.

JENNIFER (Sherburne*, Zoa, Morrow, 1959), realistic problem novel set in a small town in western Washington state in the mid-twentieth century, in which an adolescent girl learns that she must not let her mother's alcoholism control her life. The mother of sixteen-year-old Jennifer Martin has been in and out of hospitals and sanitariums for eight years, ever since the accidental death of her daughter, Molly, Jennifer's twin. Now with the help of Alcoholics Anonymous (AA), she appears on the road to recovery, and Jenny fervently hopes there will be no more drunken episodes so embarrassing to her and her father in the past. She welcomes life in the small town to which her father's work has brought the family, because no one here knows about her mother's disease. School becomes a very satisfying part of her life after a new friend, Patsy Gordon, introduces her to a lively circle of high school juniors whose companionship she enjoys at lunchtime and with whom she also socializes outside of school. A major problem develops when she dates handsome Griff* Nolan, who, unknown to Jenny, is Patsy's former boyfriend. Patsy proves exceptionally understanding and charitable, and later Jennifer is grateful for Patsy's commonsense support when she herself is dumped by Griff for another girl new in town, Diane Winters. Jennifer tries to take the experience as philosophically as did Patsy, and through befriending Diane she meets Diane's brother Ed*, a steadier, more serious-minded youth, more Jenny's type than the playboy Griff. Although her mother appears happy and has been accepted socially, Jennifer continues to worry about her.

She is startled and angry when she discovers a liquor bottle in the cupboard, hidden behind a box of crackers, and she worries about how her mother will handle her father's office cocktail parties. She is especially concerned when Mrs. Martin's application for a Christmas orphan is rejected because the agency discovers she has a history of alcoholism. But through Mrs.* Kirby, her friend in AA, Mrs. Martin keeps in touch with her support group and survives each crisis. When Jennifer's mother unexpectedly leaves the house just before Jennifer's big Thanksgiving party for her crowd, Jennifer fears the worst. To her immense relief, she discovers that her mother has been on an AA call, to help someone else who is in need of loving assistance. At story's end, Jennifer feels secure in her new friendships, proud of her mother for reaching out to others, and confident of her ability to cope with problems and to let the past take care of itself. A forerunner in the area of social problem stories for adolescents, the novel moves quickly with extensive, realistic dialogue through a series of contrived episodes to its predictable climax and simplistic and somewhat sentimental conclusion. A few flashbacks of Mrs. Martin's illness supply some family history, but Jennifer still seems unduly anxious. Characters are flat or types, except for Jennifer, who develops a more healthy attitude, and Patsy, whom the reader sees from several angles. Jennifer moves with a crowd of exceptionally socially mature young people. The author seems more concerned with sociology than story, and the novel gives a superficial look at the effect of alcoholism on the other members of the family, a sort of handbook of encouragement in fictionalized form for youths whose parents have the disease. Child Study.

JERRY OF SEVEN MILE CREEK (Ferris*, Elmer E., ill. Thomas J. Fogarty, Doubleday, 1938), quiet, almost episodic novel set near Fond du Lac, Wis., probably in the late decades of the nineteenth century. Jerry Foster, 12, has a great desire to be a drummer, perhaps to play in a circus band, as did his father, Hiram, a cornetist, and now a town clerk of the village of Seven Mile Creek. Most of the episodes are concerned with Jerry's efforts to acquire a drum—first making a tin can drum, then earning money by picking off potato bugs, acting as janitor in the Baptist church, and picking hops for a nearby farmer. Finally he organizes a fife and drum band that plays in the Republican torchlight parade in Fond du Lac. Other episodes include an evening when the boys, playing in the woods, find a tramp who sings and tells them of the wonderful life on the road, a town meeting at which the local "rassling" hero beats a challenger from Over North and Hiram beats challenger Peter V. Rousch, Jerry's step-grandfather, in the contest for town clerk, and one in which Grandma Rousch tells Jerry and his younger brother, Tommy, a "Slo Slocum" story about pioneer and Indian fights. Somewhat more exciting are chapters in which Jerry, in the family barn, confronts a local hired hand who has become a horse thief and in which he rides at night through a flooded stream to get the doctor for his sick father. Most memorable is the chapter in which Jerry and Tommy get up at three A.M. and watch the circus pass through town, hiding behind the picket fence as the great elephants loom out of the morning dusk and move noiselessly past along the village street. Although there is little plot, the incidents have the genuineness of remembered life, laced with mild, nostaglic humor, which gives a good feel of setting in both time and place. Fanfare.

JERRY PYE (*Ginger Pye**), Jared, 10, older brother of Rachel*, 9. Jerry's longing for a dog of his very own leads them to the adventures with the fox terrier puppy, Ginger. He is a pleasant boy, well liked by everybody, but not nearly as interesting a character as his younger sister, from whose point of view most of the story is told.

JESSE JACKSON (*Good-bye, My Lady**), old uncle with whom Skeeter lives. Illiterate, Jesse pretends he can read and write, a pretense both the boy and the storekeeper, Cash* Evans, help him keep up to save his pride. Since he has lost all his teeth, his big ambition is to get a set of dentures, "Roebuckers" as he calls them, but being far from industrious he never gets enough ahead to pay for more than essential groceries. He does, however, have a vast knowledge of the swamp and the creatures that live in it, information he passes on with love to Skeeter.

JEWETT, ELEANORE M(YERS) (1890-1967), born in New York City; author for adults and children. She grew up in New York City, where she attended Horace Mann School. After receiving her bachelor's degree from Barnard College, she taught in private school, and then took her master's from Columbia in comparative literature. Her growing interest in the medieval period resulted in her historical novels set in the Middle Ages, *The Hidden Treasure of Glaston** (Viking, 1946), an exciting and adventurous spin-off on the Glastonbury legend about King Arthur, vivid in the manners and customs of the times, that is her best-known book and received Newbery honor and Fanfare status, and *Big John's Secret* (Viking, 1962), about a youth sent away to become a page who goes on a crusade. Critics deemed these novels colorful and strong in period, but contrived in plot, melodramatic, and shallow in character. She also wrote mystery-adventure stories for later elementary and junior high girls, *Mystery at Boulder Point* (Viking, 1949), *Cobbler's Knob* (Viking, 1956), and *Friend among Strangers* (Viking, 1958). Her other titles include books of folktales retold, *Wonder Tales from Tibet* (Little, 1922), *Egyptian Tales of Magic* (Little, 1924), and *Which Was Witch?* (Viking, 1953), tales of ghosts and magic from Korea, and *Told on the King's Highway* (Viking, 1943), a collection of stories about knights, ladies, fairies, and sprites. She also wrote poems and short stories for magazines. She and her physician husband made their home in upstate New York.

JEZEBEL (*Far from Marlborough Street**), nine, the little black boy whom the innkeeper, Mr. Comfort, bought to save him from being sent south. One of Jezebel's duties at the inn is to care for the pet moose, Hiram, and, at Nancy's urging, he sells her the animal for her two gold pieces, then repents and hides the gold pieces under the syrup pitcher where he thinks she will find them. Ignorant and superstitious, he is easily tricked by Nancy into thinking that her key is a magic way to open her box, and when the key slips off her chain and he finds it, after her departure, he sets out to return it to her since he has promised Mr. Comfort never to keep anything that doesn't belong to him. Although technically free, he is the stereotype of the honest and devoted slave boy.

JIM (*The Adventures of Huckleberry Finn**), runaway slave who travels with Huck* Finn down the Mississippi River on a raft. Though ignorant and superstitious, Jim is shown to have natural good sense, loyalty and devotion to Huck, and true dignity when they are alone on the raft. He has run off only because Miss Watson, his long-time owner, has been dazzled by an offer of eight hundred dollars by a slave trader and plans to sell him down the river. One of the most poignant passages in the book is when Jim tells of how he discovered that his four-year-old daughter, little 'Lisbeth, has been deafened by scarlet fever. He shocks Huck, who has been raised in a society that thinks of slavery as natural, by stating that once he is free he will buy or even steal his wife and children. Once he has been captured, he seems to revert to slave mentality and to endure patiently the romantic nonsense Tom* Sawyer insists on going through for his release. When he actually has escaped, he nobly allows himself to be retaken so that Tom, who has been shot, can get medical treatment.

JIM KEATH (*Moccasin Trail**), nineteen-year-old mountain man who has been adopted at about twelve by Crow Indians and who joins his younger brother Jonathan, their sister Sally, and a younger brother, Dan'l, in their attempt to settle in the Willamette valley. Jim helps them take up land, being the only one old enough to homestead legally, but he has difficulty reconciling the very different ethics and values of the Indian culture he has grown up in and those of the settlers. He is haunted by the words which came to him in English in his "medicine dream" during the Crow initiation to manhood about green valleys and still waters, and only with Jonnie's help can he finally realize that he has been remembering the Twenty-third Psalm. Although he opts at last for the settlers' way of life, he has made them understand something of the values of the Indian lore.

JIM MARRIOTT (*Harry in England**), Harry's cousin, about his own age, red-haired and freckled, with a round and pleasant face. Jim likes to decide issues by fighting them out in a friendly way. His favorite expression is "fight for it." When Harry asks him why he always wants to fight, he says that he and his older brother, Phil, intend to be prizefighters when they grow up and that these skirmishes are for practice. He and Harry become great friends.

JIRO ITO (*The Moved-Outers**), handsome, popular, young Japanese-American, who is evacuated from his home and becomes a neighbor of the Ohara family in the internment camps. Although his family is of a somewhat lower class, Jiro himself is clever, artistic, and more levelheaded than the young Oharas and acts as a stabilizing influence. He falls in love with Sue* Ohara and hopes to marry her after he has served in the army and gone to medical school.

JOAN LOCKHARDT (*Shadow across the Campus**), tall, good-looking, outgoing, bright, congenial, serious-minded yet fun-loving roommate of Kate and good friend of Marjorie. She accepts invitations during rush but has no intention of accepting a bid to pledge because she cannot afford to belong to a social sorority. Well-liked and a good athlete, she is captain of almost every freshman team. She breaks her arm before the campus variety show, the Waa-Mu, but typically she and Kate make the most of the mishap. They cleverly work Joan's disability into their act and stop the show. Joan represents the new kind of college girl, one who can make her way without one particular support group.

JOCASTA (*Clearing Weather**), sailing ship built by the Drury shipyards. It is one of the first vessels to round Cape Horn, trade with the Indians of the Northwest Coast, take cargo to China, and return via the Atlantic. The ship's successful voyage saves the financially troubled Drury shipyards from bankruptcy and opens new economic opportunities for the sea-dependent residents of New England.

JOCK'S CASTLE (Gibson, Katharine*, ill. Vera Bock, Longmans, 1940), historical story for younger children set in England near the Welsh border, presumably in the early sixteenth century. Jock Howison, a massive young man nearly seven feet tall, buys a bit of land near Afton Town and sets up a mill, where he lives with his Skye terrier, Sniffer. The solitary life seems to suit him until, in the woods one night, he meets Tansy, granddaughter of Goody Mullins, who is gathering wild thyme by moonlight. He tries to buy her thyme, then offers her gold to come the next day and cook him a meal. Before she and her grandmother arrive, he has been visited by Tanner John, who is worried about his sons who play at jousting, by the Smith, who has just been evicted by the new lord, by the Hermit, who doesn't relish the abstemious life, and by the Tanner's sons, Tim and Michael, who fear they have just killed Tod, the sheriff's son, in their mock battle. Jock sends them to hide in the Hermit's cave, invites the Hermit to dinner, and allows the Smith to set up a sod house on his land. Tansy finds cooking with almost no pans or utensils impossible, but just then the Tinker's cart breaks down at the door, spilling out the Tinker's wife, eleven children, and all the pots, pans, spoons, and forks she needs. The Smith returns with his wife and twin infants, and they all have a fine feast, after which the Tinker children do the washing up. Tod recovers, bears no grudge against the Tanner's sons, and soon almost all the visitors have moved onto Jock's land. While the others are at the Afton Fair, Jock saves a hunter beset by three hoodlums, and this turns out to be the Prince. As a reward Jock is made a baron and given the old Castle, which has fallen into disrepair. He is doubtful about the honor, since he thinks he's a better miller than lord, but Tansy points out that he already has a large number of followers, and he moves them all to the castle. Tansy recruits local girls to clean and arranges all Jock's people in appropriate parts of the castle. Antonello, the guardian of the castle, becomes the captain of the guard, Jock diverts a stream to make a mill of the castle tower where he lives, and all seem happy except Tansy, who throws a hot pancake at Jock's face. This wakes him up to the fact that he should wed her, but she has disappeared. He finally finds her back at the old mill, they are married, and they have twins, Jock and Judy, who carry out the one requirement the king has made with his gift: whenever he visits or passes by, Jock's descendants must greet him with water and a cloth to wash with, as Jock did after he drove away the hoodlums. The pleasant story is written in simple language and has more the quality of a folktale than of historical fiction. The illustrations seem to indicate that the Prince is Henry VIII, but this is not specifically stated. Fanfare.

JODY BAXTER (*The Yearling**), eleven-year-old boy who lives a hardworking, lonely existence with his elderly parents in the Florida scrub. Through his love for his pet fawn and his grief at the need to destroy the animal, Jody grows up in one year to face the harshness of life. Jody has inherited his father's small frame and shares his father's love and sense of wonder at the beauty of nature.

JOE (*Miracles on Maple Hill**), twelve-year-old brother of Marly, who frequently asserts himself by snubbing her, criticizing her wonder over her discoveries, and going off to explore without her, only to show her, later, with proprietary interest, what he has found. Joe is inclined to an intellectual approach, looking things up and quoting books, in contrast to Marly, who is all emotion and enthusiasm.

JOE LANGFORD (*Swift Rivers**), pilot on the Mississippi. Widely respected as one of the best in his trade, he helps take Chris* Dahlberg's logs to St. Louis. He had been best friends with Pierre* Dumenille until they had a falling out. As easy going as Pierre is taciturn, unyielding, and stern, he suffers from a fever, which causes him to lose the raft above St. Louis at Lone Tree Crossing shoal. Pierre later helps to nurse him, and they make up their quarrel.

JOEL GOSS (*Justin Morgan Had a Horse**), Randolph, Vt., farm boy at the beginning of the 1800s, apprenticed to Miller Chase. He gentles Little Bub, learns to love the horse, and longs to have him for his own. A steady, uncomplaining boy, he follow Little Bub's progress from owner to owner and watches him grow and develop into an excellent puller and racer. After the horse falls on hard times, Joel buys him and restores him to health. Although the book is fictionalized, the basic facts are true, and Joel Goss really lived, as did the horse.

JOEY MOFFAT (*The Moffats**; *The Middle Moffat**; *Rufus M.**), 12, hard-working, serious-minded youth. Ever since Papa Moffat's death, Joey has become more and more important to the family. He fills coal scuttles, locks doors, checks shutters, goes to the store for coal, and does odd jobs to earn money. Several episodes in the three books about the Moffats revolve about him. He gets on very well with his younger brother, Rufus*, and sisters, Sylvie* and Jane*, and Mama can always rely on him.

JOEY NANDLE (*Vinny Applegay**), one of the large and noisy Nandle family that lives down the street from the Applegays. He is an impulsive boy who provides some comedy in the story through his tendency to get into trouble. The kitten he brings for the Applegays' inspection gets away and becomes the ghost in the basement that drives eccentric Zenobia away, and when found, is adopted by the Applegays and given the name of Lady Jane Grey. A sketch he makes results in the arrest of the burglar.

JOHANSEN, MARGARET (ALISON) (1896-), born in Alabama; author of novels and non-fiction. She lived in Texas after she married. Her husband's Danish ancestry aroused her interest in Vikings, and the result was the informational book, *Voyagers West* (Washburn, 1959). She also wrote *From Sea to Shining Sea: How Americans Have Lived* (Washburn, 1960), and previous to that a historical novel about Indians set in Texas before the coming of the whites, *Hawk of Hawk Clan* (Longmans, 1941). Most of her writing was in collaboration with her sister, Alice Lide*, with whom she wrote fifteen novels. Their adventure story, *Ood-le-uk the Wanderer** (Little, 1930), about an Eskimo youth swept away to Siberia on an ice floe and his harrowing experiences there, was a Newbery honor book.

JOHN BILLINGTON: FRIEND OF SQUANTO (Bulla*†, Clyde Robert, ill. Peter Burchard†, Crowell, 1956), historical novel for early readers concerned with the *Mayflower* voyage in 1620 and the first years of the Plymouth Colony. John Billington, one of the younger boys on the ship, is continually getting into trouble for fighting or being careless. His older brother, Francis, is better behaved. On board, John, showing Francis that he knows how to fire a musket, nearly sets the ship on fire. On shore, he is not believed when he says he saw an Indian moccasin track. After the first terrible winter, an Indian, Samoset, appears and later returns with Squanto, an Indian who has spent some time in England and who befriends the colony, teaching them many survival skills, and becomes a special friend to John. Later John is punished for pushing a girl on a vine swing, as she begs him, who then falls in the water, and for breaking through the roof thatch while playing bear with Francis. After he is punished again for carelessly breaking a corn stalk when playing, he decides to run away and is captured by the Indians of Cape Cod, who have been unfriendly. When he finds an Indian boy has taken his precious shoes, he attacks the boy and wins the respect of the Indians. Squanto comes looking for him, and although an Indian woman tries to hide him, he breaks out and is taken home. When the Pilgrims celebrate their first Thanksgiving, the Cape Cod Indians arrive to see John and offer friendship to the colony. The style is extremely simple, with short sentences and easy syntax: "The white men gave the Indians presents. They gave them knives and mirrors and hats and a compass. The Indians gave the white men animal skins. There was a present for John, too. It was a pair of Indian moccasins." Although there is no indication of how much is fiction, the story follows the well-known facts of the *Mayflower* colonists and many prominent Pilgrims appear as characters: John Alden, Priscilla Mullins, Edward Winslow, Miles Standish, Governor Carver. As a book for children who have just mastered the art of reading to themselves, it is a good example of its type. Choice.

JOHN CANTY (*The Prince and the Pauper**), brutal father of Tom* Canty, who mistreats Edward* Tudor, the Prince of Wales and later King Edward VI, thinking he is Tom, now completely mad from his learning and romantic notions. Because he has killed Tom's benefactor, Father Andrew, Canty must flee the city and becomes one of a band of thieves roaming the countryside, forcing Edward to accompany him. Though more than once Edward escapes from him, he recaptures the boy and expects him to steal or beg for the group.

JOHN HOLBROOK (*The Witch of Blackbird Pond**), sober divinity student who courts Judith but later marries Mercy*. He enlists in the militia to fight Indians and is captured. Released, he returns to Wethersfield and then marries Mercy, whom he has loved all along but was too shy to speak for.

JOHNNY ARMACOST (*To Tell Your Love**), Anne's younger brother, 14, almost a comic figure. Fairly typical of early teens in certain concerns, such as muscle building, and in constantly embarking on schemes of one sort or another, he is not particularly self-centered and has some appreciation for what Anne is going through. He also relates well to his parents and Theo*. He is a thoroughly likeable youth, though the emphasis on his ever-changing vocational objectives seems exaggerated for effect.

JOHNNY LONGFOOT (*The Quaint and Curious Quest of Johnny Longfoot, the Shoe King's Son**), son of Peter Longfoot the shoemaker, an expert leather and skin repairer, garrulous and fond of rich foods, who, wearing a tricorn and his father's coat, which is much too big for him, sets out to spend his vacation with his Uncle* Lucas but ends up on a voyage to Coral Island for seven-league boots. On the way, his shoe-making skills help him, for he makes clogs for bears and teaches them to dance, and repairs the torn hides of sea animals, in return for which they help him when he is in need.

JOHNNY TREMAIN (Forbes*, Esther, ill. Lynd Ward, Houghton, 1943), historical novel set in Boston in the years 1773-1775. Arrogant, brilliantly talented Johnny Tremain, envied and disliked by his co-apprentices, is the mainstay of the Lapham silver shop. As Johnny is rushing to finish an important silver piece commissioned by John Hancock*, mischievous, vengeful Dove*, another apprentice, puts into use a defective crucible, which breaks under the intense heat, badly burning and crippling Johnny's right hand. His dreams of becoming an eminent smith shattered, Johnny reacts with bitterness, deeply resenting his reduced position of shop errand boy. Despising all other trades, yet realizing the necessity of learning another for survival, Johnny wanders the city in loneliness and despair, finding a brief consolation in conversation with Rab* Silsbee in the printing office of the *Boston* Observer*. At the nadir of his fortunes, he recalls his genteel, dead mother's instructions to seek assistance of his rich relative, the merchant Jonathan Lyte, if in need, and to substantiate the kinship by displaying a silver cup, with a distinctive crest, she gives him before she dies. But the dishonest, cruel merchant declares Johnny a fraud and has him imprisoned as a thief. Proved innocent through the labors of Rab and Cilla* (Priscilla) Lapham, granddaughter of the silversmith, Johnny accepts employment as courier for the *Observer* and finds himself in the center of revolutionary activities, for not only is Mr. Lorne of the *Observer* the Patriots' printer, but the Patriots, including Sam Adams*, Paul Revere*, John Hancock*, and James Otis*, hold their secret meetings in the very attic where Rab and Johnny sleep. Henceforth Johnny's life is entwined with the political activities in Boston and excitement follows excitement. After participating in the Boston Tea Party, Johnny becomes "eyes and ears" for the Patriots among the British soldiers billeted in the city. As the days go by and tension mounts, Johnny significantly retains the friendship of Cilla, who with her little sister, Isannah*, now lives with the Lytes, for it is through this connection that Johnny learns from the merchant's daughter, Lavinia*, the true story of his parentage and that he has been acknowledged by Merchant Lyte as real kin. When fighting begins, Johnny learns of the planned British advance upon Lexington and Concord and relays the information to Paul Revere who accordingly warns the colonists. In disguise, Johnny makes his way to Lexington seeking Rab, who has joined the fighting, only to find his friend dying. But Johny's sadness is tempered by the good news that he will probably regain the use of his hand. A tense, dramatic style, excellent character portrayal, even of minor figures and especially of the historical leaders, a complex yet skillfully motivated and sustained plot, a carefully researched and generously detailed setting, and a capable blend of story and period results in a rich, substantial novel about maturity gained under stress and involvement and the struggle for freedom against oppression and tyranny. (Pumpkin*) Books Too Good; Children's Classics; ChLA Top 10; ChLA Touchstones; Choice; Fanfare; Newbery Winner.

JOHNSON†, ANNABEL (JONES) (1921-), born in Kansas City, Mo.; with Edgar Johnson*†, one-half of the husband-wife team that has written a dozen and a half novels of history and adventure set in the American West. She attended William and Mary College and the Art Students' League in New York and worked in publishing houses, as a librarian, and as a secretary previous to becoming a full-time writer in 1957. The Johnsons have traveled extensively absorbing atmosphere, information, and ideas for their novels, which develop such phases of the American past as the gold rush, medicine shows, the push westward, and the fur trade. By herself she published *As a Speckled Bird* (Crowell, 1956), her first book, a contemporary novel about life in an academy of fine arts. Four of the Johnsons' period and historical novels have been Fanfare books: *The Black Symbol** (Harper, 1959), about the adventures of a boy who is kidnapped by the unscrupulous proprietor of a traveling medicine show in old Montana, *Torrie*† (Harper, 1960), *Wilderness Bride*† (Harper, 1962), and *The Golden Touch*† (Harper, 1963); one received the Spur Award of Western Writers of America, *The Burning Glass*† (Harper, 1966); and one appears in *Choice*, *The Grizzly*† (Harper, 1964), a contemporary adventure story with problem aspects. Their hallmarks are research, sympathetic protagonists, excitement, and judicious use of detail. Other titles include *A Peculiar Magic* (Houghton, 1965), a companion to *The Golden Touch*, and *Count Me Gone* (Simon, 1968) and *The Last Knife* (Simon, 1971), both contemporary problem stories. The couple have also written under the name A. E. Johnson.

JOHNSON†, EDGAR (RAYMOND) (1912-   ), with his wife, Annabel Johnson*†, one-half of the team of writers best known for their several novels of history and adventure of the American West for older readers. He was born in Washoe, Mont., a coal mining town, when stagecoaches were still in vogue there. After various jobs on the railroad, as a baseball player, and as a musician in a dance band, he studied art at the Billings Polytechnic Institute, the Kansas City, Mo., Art Institute, the New York State College of Ceramics, and the Art Students' League in New York City. Before he became a full-time writer with the publication of the couple's first novel together, *The Big Rock Candy* (Crowell, 1957), about a young sculptor who comes from the Ozarks to New York City, he was a ceramicist, model maker, jeweler, and woodcarver, and was head of the department of ceramics at the Kansas City, Mo., Art Institute. He has served the Smithsonian Institution in Washington as a restorer. With his wife he has published a dozen and a half novels, including *The Black Symbol** (Harper, 1959), which tells of a kidnapped youth's involvement with the unscrupulous proprietor of a traveling medicine show in frontier Montana, *Torrie*† (Harper, 1960), *Wilderness Bride*† (Harper, 1962), *The Golden Touch*† (Harper, 1963), *The Burning Glass*† (Harper, 1966), and *The Grizzly*† (Harper, 1964), all of which have received awards or citations. The couple have also published under the name A. E. Johnson.

JOHN TREEGATE (*John Treegate's Musket**; *Peter Treegate's War*†; *Sea Captain from Salem*†; *Treegate's Raiders*†), Peter's father, a Boston importer, at first staunchly loyal to the king, because he believes the alternative to royal rule is anarchy under the Mob of Sam Adams*. A man to whom duty to country is vital, he travels to England to try to persuade the government to relax its oppressive rules against American trade. During his absence he apprentices Peter to Tom Fielding. His action causes Peter to lose confidence in him and to feel abandoned and betrayed by his own father. Even after he and Peter find each other again at the end of the first book, he remains loyal to the British crown, and there is tension between father and son, until the British action at Lexington and Concord causes John to cast his lot with the colonials. In *Peter Treegate's War* he appears as a fighter, and in it and in the later books also as a high colonial official. He becomes the colonial man of business, borrowing money for the army and finding provisions wherever he can for the soldiers. He also becomes the head of the Contintental Intelligence. He ages appreciably and realistically as the stories advance.

JOHN TREEGATE'S MUSKET (Wibberley*†, Leonard, Farrar, 1959), historical novel set just before the outbreak of the American Revolution, the first in a series. In 1769, John* Treegate, Boston merchant, sails for London to petition the Prime Minister, Lord North, to relax the restrictions on American trade. Before he leaves, he apprentices his son, Peter, 11, to Tom Fielding, a well-off maker of barrel staves with radical leanings. Small, fearful, protected Peter likes and respects Mr. Fielding, although he finds his anti-British sentiments somewhat unsettling compared to his father's strong Loyalist views. He finds life as an apprentice demanding, though he is conscientious and does well under Mr. Fielding's instruction. He is greatly intimidated by the threats of the eldest apprentice, a bullying youth named Blake, who commands the older Boston apprentices and comes and goes on mysterious errands of his own. Circumstances bring Peter into contact with Sam Adams*, Dr. Warren, James Otis*, and other Patriots with whom Mr. Fielding is acquainted. When a British soldier strikes Peter with a musket one day, the street mob comes to Peter's defense, and the unrest caused by unemployment and British policies toward the colonies results in the Boston Massacre, which Peter witnesses and feels he has been the cause of. When Blake kills and robs a man whom Peter is escorting home one night and Peter fears he will be blamed for the deed, Peter flees in a rowboat. Run down by a ship, he is rescued by the sailors and then serves as galley helper on the ship, the *Maid of Malden*. One of John Hancock's* fleet, it is bound for the West Indies on illegal trade. On its return voyage, the *Maid* is wrecked in a hurricane, and Peter is washed ashore on the Carolina coast. There he is found half dead by the Maclaren* of Spey, who takes him to his wilderness home in the mountains and raises him as his own son. Although the Maclaren is brutally demanding and often beats the boy, the two grow fond of each other. The Maclaren teaches Peter how to use a gun, to fight, to survive in the wilds, and to be self-sufficient, loyal and steadfast, all qualities that will stand the boy in good stead in the years to come. The boy has no memory of his life in Boston or how he came to be on board ship. Five years pass before a chance encounter with some woodsmen restores his memory. Accompanied by the Maclaren, he returns to Boston. He and his father are reunited, though tension builds between them because of their differing political views. Events that culminate at Lexington and Concord sway John Treegate to the side of the colonists and the end of the story finds the three, Peter, his father, and the Maclaren, preparing to fight the British at Breed's Hill in the encounter that will go down in history as the Battle of Bunker Hill. Although some events strain credulity, and the plot is uneven, characters are well drawn. Even such minor figures stick in the mind as the half-demented wife of Mr. Fielding and Goldie, Peter's sympathetic fellow apprentice, who leads the Suckling Babes (group of younger Boston apprentices) and comes to Peter's aid when the Blake-led group, the Pot Wallopers (older apprentices) brutally haze him. Peter himself grows and changes believably. The author aptly catches the temper of the times in Boston, showing well the reasons for the rising sentiment against Britain, and Peter's involvement with historical figures and events is believable. The author shows the life of apprentices and also economic conditions in cities through representative scenes in Boston, Fort de France in Martinique, and London, the latter passages involving John Treegate. Sequels include *Peter Treegate's War†*; *Sea Captain from Salem†*; *Treegate's Raiders†*. Choice; Fanfare.

JO MARCH (*Little Women**), Josephine March, hot-tempered, tomboyish, energetic, and loving chief protagonist in one of the earliest and most famous of all family novels. Impulsive and unruly, Jo is most typically seen in the attic, eating apples and "scribbling" on one of her early stories. She is also typically employed scolding Laurie* Laurence, the boy next door, or being gentle with Beth* her favorite sister. Although she sells her sensational stories, they are not treated as worthy of pride in the book, and she gives up writing in favor of marriage and caring for the "ragamuffins" in her husband's school.

JONATHAN COLEMAN (*Uncharted Ways**), Puritan youth who falls in love with Margaret* Stevenson, a staunch Quaker, when she, Marmaduke Stevenson, and William Robinson take shelter at his house during a sudden rainstorm. He enlists the aid of Governor John Winthrop of Connecticut Colony to plead with Governor Endicott of Massachusetts Bay Colony to spare Margaret's life when she is sentenced to hang. Although he loves her very much, he often has mixed emotions about her religious beliefs, knowing them to be potentially dangerous not only for her but also for himself and his family. At the end, moved by love for her and admiration for her courage, he declares himself a Quaker, too. He is presented as one of the first settlers of Nantucket Island. He is not entirely convincing as a character, appearing to be made to order to provide a romantic element for the novel.

JONES, ELIZABETH ORTON (1910-), born in Highland Park, Ill.; illustrator-author of a number of books for young children. She studied painting at the University of Chicago and in France, and when she returned wrote her first book, a series of episodes published as *Ragman of Paris and his Ragamuffins** (Oxford, 1937). Two Bohemian girls who worked for her family when she was a child were the inspiration for *Maminka's Children** (Macmillan, 1940). Among her other well-known books, some of which are written with her mother, Jessie Mae Jones, is a fantasy, *Twig** (Macmillan, 1942). For her illustrations in Rachel Field's* *Prayer for a Child* (Macmillan, 1944), she was awarded the Caldecott Medal.

JONES, IDWAL (1892-1964), was born in Wales, came to the United States as a child, and attended school in New York State. Writer, prospector, newspaperman, and teacher, he was a man of broad experience, many interests, and a deep and abiding appreciation for California, where he made his home for most of his life. He was drama editor and columnist for the San Franciso *Examiner*, later joined the New York *American* as an editorial writer, columnist, and editor of the Sunday book page, was book critic for *Life*, and lectured on writing at Claremont and Stanford. He was most widely known for his many books, stories, and articles of fiction and non-fiction about California, ranging from histories of grape growing, the wine industry, and old houses to stories about mining and Chinese and Japanese immigrants. His one juvenile novel, *Whistlers' Van** (Viking, 1936), a book about gypsy life in Wales for young people, drew upon his childhood memories of the moors of his native land and was a Newbery honor book and a Fanfare selection.

JOSEPH BRANT (*Three Sides of Agiochook**), Mohawk Indian, whose Indian name was Thayendanegea, a historical figure to whom Philip takes the message. Brant, who had been a student of Eleazar Wheelock*, founder of Dartmouth College, is a leader of Indians loyal to the Tories in the American Revolution.

JOSIAH LOGAN (*Flaming Arrows**), eleven or twelve, son of the ne'er-do-well who is thought by other settlers to be working with the Indians that raid the Cumberland area and burn their cabins. Although Josiah himself has no use for his father, who has deserted the family, some of the other settlers sheltering at the fort try to force him and his mother out. With his bow and arrows, since he has no gun, Josiah has been keeping his mother and siblings supplied with meat. At a crucial point, he sneaks down to the stream, despite the lurking Indians, to get water for the very man who tried to vote him out of the fort, now badly burned and desperately thirsty.

JOSINE (*The Happy Orpheline**, *A Brother for the Orphelines**, *A Pet for the Orphelines*†), the youngest of the twenty little orphan girls in a village near Paris. Because she is too young to attend school classes with the others, she is often on hand to become involved in incidents, as when she finds the baby boy in the bread basket. Curly-haired and sweet-looking, her strongest characteristic is stubbornness, and she is described as having a "strong character . . . with remarkable tenacity." She is a supporting character in the first book but the chief character in the two others.

JO-YO'S IDEA (Elliot*, Kathleen Morrow, ill. Roger Duvoisin, Knopf, 1939), realistic novel of family life set in the mid-1900s on the tiny South Sea island of Madura just off Java in the East Indies while the area is still a Dutch colony. Everyone in the Village of the Black Stone, his parents, his teacher, his neighbors, even the boy himself, considers Jo-yo, 13, stupid and lazy. He cannot keep his mind on the task at hand, curls up for a nap at the slightest inclination, and botches even the simplest of tasks. One day after school, Sastro, a youth from the nearby Village of the Great Turtle, tells Jo-yo that he fully expects to win the races with his family's pair of bulls at the island festival in a few weeks. Although he has never before been interested in races, Jo-yo is so proud of his family's bulls (carabao or water buffalo), Kembang and Boonie, that he decides to enter them, too. This is the first plan that he can ever remember making for himself. During the next few weeks, Jo-yo grooms the animals until they glisten, takes particular care with their diet so they lose weight and become sleek and trim, repairs the *klailis*, the driver's racing drag, and practices running the bulls with it. A series of misadventures seems destined to keep him from achieving his objective. He is sent to learn the trade of bamboo weaving, after he is expelled from school. The odor of the slain rooster he purchased for feathers to decorate the bulls drives teacher and pupils from the schoolhouse. After he inadvertently drinks mango juice, to which he is allergic, he spends several crucial days in bed. The last major threat to his plan occurs when his father sells the bulls, but luckily the purchaser is jailed for theft, and the bulls remain family property. Jo-yo's aspirations attract the attention of kindly neighbors who help him finish training the bulls. At the festival they decorate the bulls with paper wreaths, while Jo-yo himself sticks red peppers on their horns. Jo-yo's bulls win handily, with a tremendous burst of speed because, as Jo-yo soon discovers, a pepper seed has fallen into Kembang's eyes. Even so, Jo-yo is proud of the outcome of the first and only plan he has ever put into action. This amusing, anticipatory, occasionally exciting story of the despised youth who triumphs partly through effort and mostly by luck proceeds much like the familiar droll of folk tale. While Jo-yo is flushed with success at the end, he learns little from his experiences, leaving the reader to suspect that he will probably return to his sluggish habits. Characters are stick figures, and events spin out the meager plot to introduce the reader to island life. The setting is richly described with much mention of mangoes, sugar cane, sarongs, batik, banana trees, and similar elements, Malay words are worked into the conversation, and there are interesting scenes of school life, in the market, on a fishing boat, at the vendor's, in the weaver's hut, of the procession when the Dutch governor visits, and in the sparsely furnished family hut with its bare dirt floor. Fanfare.

JUBAL RINGO (*Whistlers' Van**), quiet, taciturn craftsman Rommany, twin of Natty*, who tells young Gwilym why the whistlers have appeared at Gwilym's grandfather's farm every spring. Since most of the Ringos were killed in World War I, the remaining three hope that Thomas Anwyl will rejoin them and assume the kingship, thereby ensuring that the horseman part of the tribe will remain in power.

JUDGE BLACK (*Seven Stars for Catfish Bend**), one of the animals awarded a silver star for heroism in ridding the bayou of hunters. He is a kindly, helpful blacksnake, a vegetarian, who serves the Catfish Bend residents as judge. He had once been a judge in Claiborne County, Miss. The animals regard him as wise and respect his judgment. His most pronounced characteristic is that he speaks in mottoes. He organizes the trial by which Old Joe, the ugly, prowling alligator, is tried *in absentia*, because, the Judge asserts, convicting a defendant first saves hunting for an innocent man.

JUDGE ELI TURNER (*They Came from Sweden**), lawyer who comes on the same boat as the Larssons up the Mississippi to Red Wing in Minnesota Territory and who opens an office in Red Wing. Gustaf* first attracts his attention when the boy rescues the judge's box of books that has fallen overboard during the unloading. He helps and advises the youth and the family and gives Gustaf a job as office helper. The reader is led to believe that because of him Gustaf will some day realize his ambition of becoming a lawyer.

JUDITH OF FRANCE (Leighton*, Margaret, ill. Henry C. Pitz, Houghton, 1948), historical and biographical novel set in France and England of the mid-ninth century. At fifteen, Judith, daughter of King Charles the Bald of France, great-granddaughter of Charlemagne, is married by her father to aging King Aethelwulf of Wessex, because quarrelsome Charles is in need of money for his wars against his brothers and nephews. Though dismayed at first, Judith soon comes to love the saintly man and is a great friend of his youngest son, Alfred (later Alfred the Great), about ten at the time of the wedding. She wins her husband's respect and gratitude by vowing that no strife will come between his sons through her actions. Aethelwulf's people, especially his eldest son, Aethelbald, resent the new marriage, and a revolt is already begun when they enter the country, but the old king, who has just made a year-long pilgrimage to Rome to pray for aid against raiding Danes, quells the rebellion by abdicating, giving Wessex to Aethelbald and Kent to his second son, Aethelbert, and bestowing some lands on Judith and his other sons. The strife and the journey, however, have taxed his strength, and he does not live long afterwards. Still in mourning, Judith is startled by the sudden appearance of a young man, and, thinking it is Baudoin Bras-de-Fer, one of her father's captains for whom she has a secret love, greets him warmly, only to discover that it is Aethelbald, who has come to force her into marriage with him. Although she protests and refuses to say her part of the vows, he goes ahead with the ceremony. When Alfred and Aethelbert come to protest, she remembers her vow and refuses to let them fight to defend her. Aethelbald's people, however, are displeased and although Judith, at times, falls under his charm, she sees him to be ambitious and cruel. His brutality causes her to miscarry her first child, and while she is still recovering, he sends word that he renounces his marriage for political reasons and will contract another marriage. Although her father demands that Judith sell her English lands and bring him the money, she is relieved until Aethelbald insists that their relationship continue outside marriage. She refuses with shock and fury, and in his anger he threatens to have her burned as a witch. Her urgent letter to her old tutor, John Scotus Erigena, brings not the religious advocate she has requested but Baudoin, who with his second in command, Othere, sweeps her away, with her maid Gisele, in a wild ride to the sea and a channel crossing in a storm. Just before they sight land, they pick up a shipwrecked Viking, a lucky find since they are blown into a camp of Viking raiders, and it is only because the rescued youth is son of the leader, and some added good luck, that they are allowed to get away. By now Judith and Baudoin have expressed their mutual love, but Charles is furious at the idea of a marriage and imprisons Judith. Baudoin rescues her, they ride to the territory of one of Charles's wrangling nephews, and are married. Then finding themselves pawns in the royal family conflict, they must escape and make their way disguised as pilgrims to Rome, where they plead their case before the Pope, and he declares their marriage valid. For political reasons Charles backs down and gives Baudoin Flanders, an area rich but hard to defend against the Vikings. The full tapestry of royalty and intriguing court figures includes many historical personages and seems to follow what is known of actual events, though romanticized and highly dramatized. Judith is a strong-willed girl, and the novel's action is fast-paced. Fanfare.

JUDSON, CLARA INGRAM (1879-1960), born in Logansport, Ind.; author best known in children's literature for her biographies of eminent Americans, but who also wrote fiction. She grew up in Indianapolis, where she attended elementary and high school and Girls' Classical School. After her marriage to an oil company official, she lived in the Chicago area. She began writing down the stories she made up for her two daughters, and her first book, *Flower Fairies* (Rand, 1915) was published when she was thirty-five. She then began writing a daily newspaper feature, "Bedtime Tales," for children in the Richmond, Ind., *Item*, which became nationally syndicated. During World War I, she was considered an authority on family finance, and she lectured widely at the invitation of the U.S. Treasury. She became a consultant to banks and, in 1928, pioneered in broadcasting, being one of the first women to have her own radio program. She published altogether more than eighty books, among them, four adult books on finance and money management. Her popular They Came From series of novels for young readers resulted from a conversation with an immigrant Iowa farm woman. The first of these, *They Came from Sweden** (Follett, 1942), was a *Horn book* Fanfare book. It tells of the challenges the resilient and resourceful Larssons face when they homestead in Wisconsin and Minnesota. Others in the series include *They Came from France* (Houghton, 1943), *Peter's Treasure* (Follett, 1945), about immigrants from Dalmatia, and *The Lost Violin* (Houghton, 1947), about Czechs. Her first, and still one of her most highly regarded biographies, was *Abraham Lincoln, Friend of the People* (Wilcox, 1950). She also wrote about Andrew Carnegie, Justice Holmes, Benjamin Franklin, Andrew Jackson, and Theodore Roosevelt. Among her many honors was the Laura Ingalls Wilder Award, which came to her posthumously.

JUDY'S JOURNEY (Lenski*, Lois, ill. author, Lippincott, 1947), realistic novel for middle-grade readers about migrant workers on the east coast of the United States in the mid-twentieth century. When they are evicted from the land they sharecrop in Alabama, the Drummond family pile into a jalopy with all they own in a trailer and head for Florida. At first leaving the cotton fields and camping out is an adventure to Judy, 10, and her little brother, Joe Bob, and sister, Cora Jane. Judy buys a Nanny goat for a dime, and with the milk the sick baby, Lonnie, perks up. At Beantown, they camp along a drainage ditch, where other migrants live in shanties. The parents both work in the packing house, and Judy, after one bad experience, goes to school and likes it. Judy is given a feed sack and makes a dress to go to a birthday party, only to discover that she isn't invited. When the beans run out, they head north, but before they get far Judy meets a woman who needs a picker for tomatoes while her husband is ill, so they stay for a happy time at the Gibson farm, only to have the crop ruined by hail so they have to move on. In Georgia they have car trouble, get separated when Judy and Joe Bob walk into town for a fan belt, but are happily reunited. In South Carolina they stop to pick beans and are made unwelcome by the local people until Judy, using a first-aid kit and knowledge given her by the school nurse in Florida, patches up a boy whose leg is cut. Judy also starts a school in an old boxcar, using a geography book she found in a dump. In Virginia, Joe Bob finds a puppy, but they have to give it to the Darnell family that travels in comparative luxury in a house trailer. In the potato fields there, Judy is knocked off the back of a crowded truck and is given a pair of shoes, her first, by the Darnells. In Delaware they stay in a tenant house at a farm where the foreman is a gypsy, Torresina. Judy and Angeleena Torresina are soon good friends. In a nearby town the children are taunted by town kids, and while Judy fights, her new shoes are stolen. In New Jersey they live in a barracks, and at school Judy takes charge when a girl is injured. It turns out to be a black girl she knew in Florida. Mama has a new baby and names it Jersiana. For the third time, they run into Madame Rosie, a carnival fat woman who told Judy's fortune back in Alabama. They head back south and trade the old jalopy for a truck, and Papa buys a fallen down tourist cabin and builds it onto the back for a camper. When they stop to see the Gibsons, they find that an old farm nearby is for sale cheap. They can live in the camper and settle down on their own farm. Judy's little schools which she conducts with her geography book all along the route give opportunity for didactic discussion of the products of the different states. There is also a didactic attitude toward the social condition of migrant workers, who, despite sympathy, are not made convincing characters. Although the family moves frequently, the story moves slowly. Child Study; Fanfare.

JULIAN JARMAN (*Gone-Away Lake**), twelve, adventurous, science-minded, "take charge" boy, the leader during the summer of adventure, when he and his cousin, Portia*, discover Gone-Away Lake and become good friends with Pindar Payton and Minniehaha Cheever, the elderly brother and sister who live there in turn-of-the-century style. It is Julian's idea to keep Pindar and Minnie secret, but later he generously opens the clubhouse he and Portia have created to the children who live nearby.

JULIO (*Nino**), spoiled only son of Signor* and Signora Ditto who live near Nino's* family. He shares Nino's birthdate and is his playmate from infancy. Indulged by his parents, he wants his wishes gratified immediately and loves to eat. Although not an unpleasant child, he is often thoughtless and rash and has not been taught to value beauty as has Nino. At the fair he angers his father by trading his goat for an alarm clock, but he recovers the goat when he wins at lotto. He is Nino's foil.

THE JUMPING-OFF PLACE (McNeely*, Marian Hurd, ill. William Siegel, Longmans, 1929), historical novel set in 1910 among the homesteaders on the prairie of the Rosebud Reservation in South Dakota. After the untimely death of their guardian, Uncle Jim, the four Linville orphans, Becky*, 17, Dick, 15, and Phil and Joan, both younger, travel from their comfortable but modest home in Platteville, Wis., to Omaha, Nebr., and then to Dallas, S.Dak., the "jumping-off place." Relying steadily on the detailed written instructions and admonitions Uncle Jim left them and on the advice of his friend, Mr. Cleaver, a kindly Dallas businessman, the children collect horses, wagon, cow, and necessities and set about putting in crops and making a home for themselves for the fourteen remaining months to get title to the land. Arriving in May, hardworking, plucky Becky and Dick fix up part of the barn for living quarters and plant vegetables, corn, and alfalfa to get the family and the animals through the coming winter. In addition to flies, scorching winds, drought, rattlesnakes, general weariness, and dwindling money, the children must contend with harassment from the ne'er-do-well Welps*, claim-jumpers who have erected a shanty over the hill and who are determined to drive the Linvilles away and get their land. Unable to establish good relations with the Welps, the children do become friends with and are helped by other homesteaders who exhibit frontier neighborliness. When it appears that the children will be unable to survive the winter because their crops have failed and their money is running out, Mr. Cleaver arranges for Becky to teach at the one-room prairie school, where in addition to performing her normal teaching responsibilities in a very satisfactory manner, she builds community spirit by persuading the settlers to establish a kind of lending library by sharing the few books they possess. After she gets the schoolchildren through a terrible late-winter blizzard, the settlers present her with a gift of appreciation and band together to drive away the troublesome Welps, insuring that the Linvilles will be able to prove their claim the coming July. The novel's didactic intent is indicated by the stock characters and incidents, and the numerous moralistic admonitions which are obviously designed to show the hardships endured by the pioneers and the courage, determination, and effort they needed to survive. Newbery Honor.

JUNKET (White*, Anne H., ill. Robert McCloskey*, Viking, 1955), amusing realistic story set on an American farm in the mid-twentieth century and subtitled "The Dog Who Liked Everything 'Just So.' " An intelligent and friendly Airedale, Junket is used to managing the farm for his family, making the lazy pony, Polyanna, exercise, driving the cow, Dorinda the Duchess of Dorset, to and from the pasture, checking on the hens, the "Fuss and Feathers Federation," and the pig, Clarissa, keeping the geese, Jack and Jill, from getting too uppity, and acting as surrogate parent for the frequent litters of kittens produced by the bored mother cat, Miss Milliken. After an extended visit to friends, he returns to find his family gone and the McDonegal family—Dougal, his wife, and their three children, Margaret, 13, Michael, 11, and Montgomery, 7—in the house. This does not disturb him, but he is concerned that the other animals are gone. The McDonegal youngsters, who have always lived in the city, also long for animals, but their father, a bookish man, has said firmly that he will have none. Their mother, a dreamy woman who thinks only of her painting, is no support for their position until she decides to paint Junket, thereby assuring his acceptance, at least temporarily. The children set out to get the animals of their choice, and Junket sets out to teach the family how to live in the country. Some of these things he does directly: when Margaret begs him to bring Polyanna back because she wants a horse, Junket simply goes to the woman who has taken the pony in, chews through her rope, and drives her back; when Dorinda, along with the other cows of a neighboring farmer, changes pasture, he helps her wander down the old lane to the barn. Some come more by round-about chance. Montgomery and Junket find a lost baby and as a reward are given two hens. Mrs. McDonegal finds the perfect subject for her pink painting in Clarissa and has Montgomery and Junket bring her home. Mr. McDonegal himself brings Miss Milliken home when mice begin to eat his snacks hidden behind the books in his study. Junket brings the kittens to their mother. At the local fair, Mr. McDonegal is so proud of his winning melon that he wants to keep on the handyman, Peter Paley, who really did all the work of the garden, and Peter will stay only if they have enough animals to keep him busy. Not only are all the animals kept after Labor Day, but plans are being made to get more. The story is light, with tongue-in-cheek humor about Junket's responsibilities in running the farm. The adults are all caricatures, and of the children only Montgomery is developed, but Junket is the main character and his personality is well defined without being anthropomorphized. Choice.

JUSTIN MORGAN HAD A HORSE (Henry*†, Marguerite, ill. Wesley Dennis, Wilcox, 1945), historical novel which makes a story out of the origin of the Morgan line of horses, an American breed originating in Vermont at the beginning of the 1800s. When Justin Morgan*, Vermont schoolteacher and singing master, sells the older of two colts he has received from Farmer Beane in payment of a debt, he is helped by Joel* Goss, a schoolboy, in gentling the younger of the two, a small, nondescript pony, considered by a horse expert to be too small ever to amount to anything. Apprenticed to Miller Chase down the road from his father's farm, Joel attends school after his daily labors are over and then hurries to Jenks's place where Morgan is boarding the colt to train Little Bub to the wagon. The boy develops a deep affection for the sturdy, plucky, little horse and yearns to have him for his own. In need of money, Morgan rents the horse out to a farmer who puts him to work clearing new ground, and in spite of his small size, Bub proves to be a crack puller. Though little, he is tough and light-footed and defeats all the horses around in pulling and running races until the prowess of "Morgan's horse" spreads throughout the valley. He even defeats two thoroughbred racers from New York, winning a tidy purse for the schoolmaster, while he is still barely more than a colt. After Morgan's death, Bub is sold at auction, then stolen, and Joel loses track of him. During the war of 1812, his apprenticeship ended, Joel serves in the United States cavalry and takes part in the battle of Plattsburg, with never a sign of Little Bub. After the war, he happens one night to see the Morgan, a bony workhorse hitched to a freight wagon, borrows from Miller Chase to buy him, and nurses him to good looks and health again. A living legend, Bub sires what becomes known as the Morgan horse line and has the distinction of carrying President Monroe in the anniversary celebration of Plattsburg. Although characterization is shallow and the research shows, the account is mildly suspenseful and unsentimental, and Joel's longing and affection for the pony are convincing. Bibliography of sources and individuals consulted is included. Choice; Newbery Honor.

JUSTUS LIPSIUS (*At the Sign of the Golden Compass**), historical scholar of the sixteenth century, who appears as a character among the Antwerp intellectuals. He was a representative of the Catholic Church but also a forward-thinking philosopher in a time of great intellectual ferment.

K

KAGA (*Kaga's Brother**), Kagayosh, sixteen-year-old Chippewa youth with whom Matthew* Steele becomes close friends on his trip to Fond du Lac at the west end of Lake Superior. Kaga is a stereotyped character, a composite of all the best traits romantically attributed to Indians, brave, fearless, strong, quick, resourceful, and knowledgeable about the terrain and its creatures, a true child of the forest.

KAGA'S BROTHER (Ross*, M. I., Harper, 1936), romantic historical novel combining real and fictional events and characters set in 1826 in the Upper Peninsula of Michigan and in what is now Minnesota and Wisconsin. Fourteen-year-old Matthew* Steele jubilantly joins the historic expedition of Thomas McKenney, United States Commissioner of Indian Affairs, and Gov. Lewis Cass of Michigan Territory to make a treaty with the Chippewa Indians at Fond du Lac at the west end of Lake Superior and gets involved in plots over the lucrative fur trade and mineral deposits there. He travels with Captain Lewis, an army comrade of his father for whom he has an adolescent crush. At Sault Ste. Marie, Henry Rowe Schoolcraft, U.S. Indian agent, introduces him to Kagayosh (Kaga*), the sixteen-year-old grandson of the renowned Chippewa chief, Myeengun. During the following weeks, Mat becomes very fond of the Indian youth, who teaches him to speak Chippewa, through whom he learns much about Indian ways and beliefs and for whose people he comes to have great respect and admiration. Although the captain fears for Mat's safety and has arranged for his ward to stay at the Soo, the two boys attach themselves to the expedition of soldiers, officials, voyageurs, and Indians which travels by barge and canoe following the southern shore of Lake Superior. The boys fancy themselves the special bodyguards of Captain Lewis, and, indeed, on several occasions they save his life. Along the way, Captain Lewis takes a side trip up the Ontanagon River to survey copper deposits. When two fur traders from the British Hudson Bay Co. plot to kill him by sending his canoe over a waterfall, the boys pull off a daring river rescue. During the week-long treaty councils on the St. Louis

River near Fond du Lac, the Indians pledge loyalty to the United States and the Chippewa make peace with their traditional enemies, the Sioux, insuring that the fur trade will continue. The Captain then is sent upriver to the American Fur Co. post to win to the American side those Indians still sympathetic to the British. When, on the way, Captain Lewis is captured by the two fur traders, Kaga rescues him singlehandedly in a daring dusk raid. After a hasty and hazardous canoe trip back across Lake Superior to La Pointe in the Apostle Islands, the party learns that Indians along the Upper Mississippi have become restive and are attacking white settlements. The boys are sent to the Soo for military reinforcements. After their return to La Pointe, Kaga is attacked and seriously wounded by a bear. On the advice of Myeengun and of the celebrated medicine woman, Ogeewyahnoquot Okwa, called the Prophetess, Mat travels westward with a party of Indians seeking the Captain. He catches up with him on the Sandy Lake River just in time to save his life again. Captain Lewis makes peace with the border chiefs, wins them to the U.S. cause, and negotiates a favorable fur trade agreement with them. He and Mat then return to La Pointe where the Captain intends to start a school with Mat's help. Mat, the Captain, and their friends at La Pointe, the Laidlaws, are fictitious, but Kaga is historical. The other historical characters make only cameo appearances. Although the author does not specify her sources, the narrative appears to rely upon such records as those of Schoolcraft and McKenney, fictionalizing upon them and other known historical facts for interest. Letters from Mat to his father appear in nearly every other chapter and carry about half the burden of the narrative. They contain much information about the customs of the whites and the Indians of the region and about political affairs. Abundant escapes, hazardous journeys, intrigues, and plots make for plenty of action and thrills, but research and plot are poorly blended and the research often shows. Tone is curiously condescending and playful toward both protagonist and audience, particularly in the first half of the book. Characters are flat, and only Mat changes as expected as a result of events. The author presents Native Americans in a sympathetic, but not always positive light. (Dorcas* Laidlaw) Fanfare.

KALASHNIKOFF, NICHOLAS (1888-1961), born in Minusinsk, Siberia, Russia; political refugee from Communist Russia whose books are set in his native country. For two years he studied at Moscow University and in 1905, at the age of sixteen, he participated in a rebellion against Czarist repression and was exiled to Siberia for four years, an area employed in his novel, *The Defender** (Scribner's, 1951). During World War I, he served in the Russian Army, then during the Russian Civil War commanded the People's Army of Siberia as a general. When the Bolsheviks dominated, he fled to China and thence in 1924 to the United States, becoming a naturalized citizen in 1930. His novel, *They That Take the Sword* (Harper, 1939), is autobiographical.

KALNAY, FRANCIS (1899-), born in Budapest, Hungary; author of fiction and non-fiction for adults and children. He came to the United States in

1919, after serving in the Hungarian army in World War I. He has been a teacher, farmer, journalist, and actor, and has worked in educational films. He served in the United States army in World War II. Among his novels, *Chúcaro: Wild Pony of the Pampa** (Harcourt, 1958) was a Newbery honor and a Fanfare book and was praised by critics of the time as a warm and colorful depiction of life on the pampa. *The Richest Boy in the World* (Harcourt, 1959) improvises on his own youth in a pre–World War I Hungarian boarding school, while *It Happened in Chichipica* (Harcourt, 1971) tells of life in a Mexican village and is based on his firsthand observations as a resident of Mexico. He also has written books for adults and contributed articles on gastronomy to *House Beautiful*. He has made his home in Carmel, Calif., where he has pursued interests in cooking and gardening.

KARSAVINA, JEAN (FATERSON) (1908-   ), born in Warsaw, Poland; librettist, editor, and free-lance writer. The daughter of a banker and pianist, she grew up in Poland, Moscow, and New York, spending her summers in France, Germany, and England and learning four languages fluently. After attending Smith College, she received her B.A. from Barnard College. She has been a member of the faculty at New York University and editor of *Soviet Review*, *Problems of Soviet Literature*, and *Reprints from the Soviet Press*. Writer of librettos for operas and translator of Tolstoi's *War and Peace*, she has also contributed many short stories to various magazines. Her first novel, *Reunion in Poland** (International, 1945), about the reconstruction of Poland after World War II, appears on the Fanfare list. *Tree by the Waters* (New World, 1948), also for older youth, tells of a present-day conflict between the owners of a New England factory and the townspeople which leads to a strike. *White Eagle, Dark Skies* (Scribner's, 1974), received the Jewish Book Council Prize. A book for adults, it tells the story of her own family's involvement in the Polish independence movement at the turn of the century.

KATE CALLAM (*Sandy**), sister of Sandy's father, who has raised the girl and plans that she will follow in her footsteps, graduate from the same exclusive women's college, become a teacher, and eventually take over as headmistress of Miss Callam's School for Girls. She is a woman of intelligence and high standards, not without humor, and she reasonably gives up her plans when Sandy decides to go to the University. Kate is clearly relieved that Sandy has declined the invitation of her Aunt Mimi* Edington to come live in Chicago, in Kate's eyes a cultural wasteland a great distance from New England where well-bred people live.

KEIKO (*The Promised Year**), ten-year-old Japanese girl who agrees to spend a year with her aunt and uncle, whom she has never met, in the United States to ease the financial problem for her widowed mother. A lively girl, Keiko makes friends easily aboard ship and in the United States but thinks her Uncle Henry does not like her, because he is preoccupied with his business of raising carnations, treats her abruptly, and has a bad allergic reaction to her cat. By the book's end, Keiko has proven herself a good daughter and has come to understand her uncle, and there is an assumption that she will stay on to live with them beyond the promised year.

KEITH†, HAROLD (VERNE) (1903-), born in Lambert, Okla.; sports publicist and author noted for his books of historical fiction for young people. He grew up in Kansas, Missouri, and Texas, as well as in Oklahoma, attended Northwestern State Teachers College, and took his bachelor's and master's degrees from the University of Oklahoma. He has taught school, been an assistant grain buyer, and for almost forty years, he was director of sports publicity at the University of Oklahoma in Norman. In 1961, he received the Arch Ward Memorial Trophy as outstanding sports publicist and has been president of College Sports Information Directors of America. Previously he received the Helms Foundation Sports Publicist of the Year Award (1950). He has written a dozen books mostly for older youth and mostly novels, some of them about sports, the most critically acclaimed being historical fiction. One of these received the Newbery Award, *Rifles for Watie** (Crowell, 1957), a rich and substantial novel, thoroughly researched and convincingly written, set during the Civil War, which takes a young Northern soldier behind the Southern lines as a scout to find out who is smuggling rifles to the Southern general, Stand Watie*, a Cherokee. It was elected to the Lewis Carroll Shelf, was a Fanfare book, and is cited in *Choice* and in *Children's Books Too Good to Miss*. Two of his novels received the Western Heritage Award, *Susy's Scoundrel†* (Crowell, 1974), a realistic animal novel which also won the Spur Award of Western Writers of America, and *The Obstinate Land†* (Crowell, 1977), about the land rush into northern Oklahoma in the 1890s. He also wrote *Komantcia* (Crowell, 1965), which fictionalizes upon the true story of a Spanish youth taken captive by Comanches. His other titles include *Shotgun Shaw: A Baseball Story* (Crowell, 1949), *The Runt of Rogers School* (Lippincott, 1971), a football story, *Boys' Life of Will Rogers* (Crowell, 1937), and *Sports and Games* (Crowell, 1941). He has also written fiction and non-fiction for many periodicals. A runner as an undergraduate, he has pursued this interest in later life, winning tropies in competition for his distance running.

KELAN THE MERRY (*And the Waters Prevailed**), the happy-go-lucky, always agreeable youth who goes on his manhood hunt at the same time as Andor* does. Because Kelan thinks so highly of Andor, he saves his friend's life when the wolf turns on him, even though helping a youth during the hunt is strictly forbidden by the rules of the tribe. Because he is somewhat of an iconoclast, he keeps the deed secret, and Andor gets full credit for the kill. Kelan accompanies Andor on the trek to the Atlantic coast in search of information about the black men from the south. Kelan understands the potential for destruction that the ocean represents, but he is unable to support Andor's story at the tribal council. On the way back home, an argument breaks out between Stor*, Andor's antagonist, and Stor's traveling companion and Andor and Kelan, and Stor kills Kelan. Andor never finds another friend as dear to him as Kelan.

KELLY, ERIC P(HILBROOK) (1884-1960), born in Amesbury, Mass.; professor of journalism and novelist, whose best-known books are set in Poland. As a child he lived in Denver but returned to New England and received his A.B. and M.A. degrees from Dartmouth College and worked as staff writer on various Massachusetts and New Jersey newspapers. During World War I, in France, he met Poles working with a relief organization, an experience that had a lifelong influence. From 1921 to 1954 he taught journalism and English at Dartmouth but took a year off in 1925–1926 to be a lecturer at the University of Krakow, Poland, and during World War II was sent by the government to Mexico to assist the Polish refugees there. He wrote two books on Poland for adults and for young people a biography of Countess Krasinka, a book of Polish legends and stories, and twelve novels, including a trilogy of Polish cities: *Trumpeter of Krakow** (Macmillan, 1928), a Newbery Award winner, *The Blacksmith of Vilno* (Macmillan, 1930), and *The Golden Star of Halich* (Macmillan, 1931). Among his other historical novels are *At the Sign of the Golden Compass** (Macmillan, 1938), which tells of the trials of early printing firms, and *Three Sides of Agiochook** (Macmillan, 1935), the story of the early days of Dartmouth College. Although their plots often depend on unlikely coincidence, his books are well researched and full of action.

KENDALL†, CAROL (SEEGER) (1917-   ), born in Bucyrus, Ohio; children's author, best known for her fantasies about the Minnipins. She graduated from Ohio University and married Paul Kendall, a writer and professor of English at Ohio University. She has traveled extensively, accompanying her husband on his trips abroad to collect material for his books, and speaks Chinese, German, French, and Russian. After publishing two novels for adults, she wrote a juvenile mystery, *The Other Side of the Tunnel* (Lane, 1956), and she has also published *The Big Splash* (Viking, 1960), a realistic story about what happens when six children decide to raise money for a hospital drive; *The Firelings* (Atheneum, 1982), a fantasy about little people who live in a land located on the slopes of a volcano; and a book of folktales, *Sweet and Sour: Tales from China* (Seabury, 1979). Most popular and critically acclaimed have been her fantasies about the strongly characterized little people of Minnipin Valley, Muggles* and her friends, and their conflicts with the Mushrooms and other enemies: *The Gammage Cup** (Harcourt, 1959), a Newbery honor book, a Fanfare book, and a *Choice* selection, and its sequel, *The Whisper of Glocken†* (Harcourt, 1965).

KEYSTONE KIDS (Tunis*†, John R., Harcourt, 1943), sports novel laid in the United States in the mid-twentieth century. Two brothers, Spike and Bob Russell, fast friends and a formidable doubleplay combination at the keystone slot of shortstop and second base, come up from the minors to join the Dodgers. At first impressed by major league perquisites and awed by rubbing elbows with heroes of the game, they come gradually to recognize the stars' weaknesses of character and performance as well as their strengths and to see them as men. Spike soon makes the regular squad, but manager Ginger Crane has decided to return Bob to the minors when the regular second baseman breaks his arm and Bob is given a chance for the position. Spike's clear head and solid bat and Bob's "holler and pepper" soon spark the team into contention for the pennant, and the brothers win deserved acclaim from fellow players and public. During the off-season, Spike coolly wangles a significant raise for them from Jack MacManus, the Dodger owner. Spike's self-control and calm assertiveness so impress the owner that MacManus makes Spike manager the next year when the team suffers a prolonged slump and Crane is fired. Spike has his work cut out for him, particularly when the team refuses to accept a new player, Jocko Klein, a rookie catcher on whom the teams' chances for a pennant ride. Bright, quick, good at hitting and at his position, Jocko is Jewish, and prejudice against him soon sunders the team. Even when Klein's brilliant play produces victory after victory the players ride him mercilessly, and he wilts under the ridicule. Emulating what he thinks his old Nashville manager, staunch disciplinarian Grouchy Devine, would have done, Spike tells the self-pitying Klein to buck up, stands up to Bob, who like his teammates maintains "Jews can't take it," and calmly addresses the team. In a lengthy speech, he asserts that Klein is engaged in a battle far bigger than that for the pennant—the centuries old prejudice against his people—and demands the team work together. Bob responds loyally, leading his mates in a free-for-all against a derisive fan (an interestingly ironic act), Klein and the brothers perform nobly, and the Dodgers defeat the Cards in a crucial game, giving them a chance at the pennant. Plenty of action and excitement and authentic inside views of the game produce an exciting and gripping sports story, even though the plot is implausible and characters and incidents are conventional. The story is strongly didactic, reflecting not only the mode of the genre, but also the prevailing attitude of the World War II era in which it was written. It supports the themes of sportsmanship, teamwork, standing up for principles, combatting prejudice, and loyalty to the common cause. Child Study; Choice.

KIBETI (*Lion Boy**), respected old storyteller of the Wanyamlima. He helps train Simba in a man's responsibilities. His stories perpetuate tribal traditions. A proud and admired warrior in his youth, he was bringing his old grandfather back to his ancestral village among the Wanyamlima when an elephant attacked. The grandfather was killed, and Kibeti was crippled. After that, he remained with the Wanyamlima.

KILDEE HOUSE (Montgomery*†, Rutherford, ill. Barbara Cooney, Doubleday, 1949), realistic animal novel of a year in the life of a shy, silent, elderly stonemason who makes friends for the first time in his life because of some animals with whom he shares his dwelling. When he retires, Jerome Kildee builds a tiny one-room cabin at the base of a giant redwood tree on a mountain in the Pacific Coast Range of California. Soon a pair of spotted skunks build a nest under his floor, and a raccoon, Old Grouch, who has lived for years in the tree, brings home a young bride. Gradually Jerome's tribe increases, until he has some twenty-five raccoons and twenty-seven skunks living with him. Through his animals he meets young Emma* Lou Eppys, the tomboy from down the hill, and her family, with all nine of whom he shares Christmas dinner in his little house, and Emma Lou's archenemy, Donald* Roger Cabot, whose dog chases and kills wild animals, among them, Jerome's Old Grouch's young bride. Emma Lou vows vengeance, but as she helps Jerome build a pen for a fawn she rescues, feed his animals, and keep his house clean, she and Donald become friends. Donald comes up with a plan for finding homes for the creatures so that Jerome will not be evicted from his own house by the animals he has befriended. When he advertises in sporting magazines, zoos and estates respond, providing homes for the animals and welcome relief for Jerome. Jerome comes out of himself realistically, but Emma Lou and Donald Roger are a trifle overdrawn and precious. This is a pleasing, unsentimental, if tailor-made, story in which the needs of the humans and animals are well integrated. Barbara Cooney's scratchboard illustrations contribute depth and texture to the story. Fanfare; Newbery Honor.

KILIAN (*The Sword and the Scythe**), peasant gunner of Memmingen who teaches Martin how to handle the cannon. He is tough and realistic and helps Martin to see things as they are and actually to enjoy the shock of battle. He helps Martin invent the "shell," a sort of grenade.

KIM OHARA (*The Moved-Outers**), Kimio, mercurial brother in the Japanese-American family evacuated and relocated after the attack on Pearl Harbor. Kim, more studious and sensitive than his sister, Sue*, is at first embittered by the experience and for a while joins the tough, trouble-making element in the camp but eventually decides to enlist in the all Japanese-American army unit being formed.

THE KING (*The Adventures of Huckleberry Finn**), the elder (seventy or more) and the more swinish of the two drifting rascals who join Huck* and Jim* on the raft floating down the Mississippi. When the younger man claims to be the rightful Duke* of Bridgewater, the "King" tops him by confessing that he is the long-lost Dauphin of France, son of Louis the Sixteenth and Marie Antoinette. A sometime preacher, lecturer, singing geography teacher, mesmerist, and faith-healer, the King specializes in dramatic productions and learns from the Duke a garbled version of Hamlet's soliloquy by Shakespeare. He poses as the brother from England arriving in time for Peter Wilkes's funeral and engineers the scheme to defraud the three Wilkes girls of their inheritance, a scheme that backfires because he is too greedy. He later sells Jim for forty dollars to locals who hope to collect the two hundred dollars offered in a fake handbill the Duke has printed. He is last seen tarred and feathered and being ridden on a rail, along with the Duke, by a crowd getting even for having been tricked by the indecent performance of the ''Royal Nonesuch.'' He is shown as typical of the glib confidence men preying on the ignorance and naivete of the small town people of the period.

KING OF SPAIN'S DAUGHTER (*Swift Rivers**), Barton Howland's* term for the Louisiana Purchase, which coincidentally is a line in the verse old Alexis* Dahlberg recites about his walnut tree, ''I had a little nut tree. . . . ''

KING OF THE WIND (Henry*†, Marguerite, ill. Wesley Dennis, Rand, 1948), animal novel based on history, set first in Morocco, briefly in France, and finally in England in the early 1700s during the reign of George II, which tells how the Arabian horse came to England. The novel begins in the twentieth century in Windsor, Canada, at a horse race where the renowned, red-gold stallion, Man o' War, handily defeats the pride of Canada, Sir Barton. His owner, Samuel Riddle, decides that this greatest of all race horses shall never compete again and then in his mind goes back two hundred years to review the story of the great Godolphin Arabian, the descendant of a mare belonging to Mohammed from which Man o' War descended. In Morocco, Agba*, the mute stableboy of Sultan Mulai Ismael, raises on camel's milk and honey a red-gold colt whose mother has died. Sham, meaning ''sun,'' soon grows to be the fleetest horse in the Sultan's stables. The Sultan ships to France as a gift for young King Louis XV six of his finest young horses and their stableboys, who are to care for the colts as long as they live. Boys and horses arrive in pitiful shape, and Sham becomes cart horse to the king's cook. Weeks of hard times follow for the spirited stallion and his faithful groom. Finding the horse unmanageable, the cook sells him to a cruel peddler of wood, who whips him. A kind-hearted English Quaker, Jethro Coke, rescues him and takes the horse back to England as a mount for his son-in-law, along with the boy and a cat, Grimalkin, which has attached himself to the horse, then turns the horse over to an innkeeper, who has Agba imprisoned in Newgate as a thief. When Coke's housekeeper, good-hearted Mistress* Cockburn, discovers that the boy is in prison, she enlists the sympathy of philanthropic Duchess of Marlborough and her son-in-law, the Earl of Godolphin*, who arranges for the boy's release and buys the horse. The Earl takes boy, horse, and cat to his estate, Gog Magog, where to Abga's intense disappointment the stuttering stablekeeper, Titus Twickerham, persuades the Earl that Sham will never be good for racing or breeding. When Agba violates orders and allows Sham to breed with Lady Roxanna, boy, horse, and their constant companion, the cat, are exiled from the estate to a rude hovel in the marshes. Two years pass, and Lath, Sham's colt, proves so fine a racer that the Earl sends for Sham, and horse, boy, and cat are reinstated at Gog Magog. Sham's colts win three major races at Newmarket, including the coveted Queen's Purse, which is presented to the Earl by Queen Caroline herself. Sham lives out his days in regal splendor in a stall marked "The Godolphin Arabian." Before he dies at twenty-nine, he sires a long line of high-crested racers, noted for speed and stamina and regarded as the pride of Newmarket. After Sham's death, loyal Agba returns to his native Morocco, his task completed. Characters are shallow and tinged with the comic, and incidents seem contrived, nor does the author exploit the novel's potential for suspense. Interest comes mainly from the emotional impact of the strong bond between the boy and the horse, the rapid succession of misfortunes that befall them, and their final vindication and elevation to success and comfort. Vocabulary is mature but not difficult, and style is simple and straightforward. Books Too Good; Choice, Fanfare; Newbery Winner.

KIP (*Magic or Not**), friendly neighbor boy, who loans James* his family's power mower on James's first day in the new house. Kip is consistently generous and adventurous and is the one who discovers that the little house in the woods really belongs to the movie star and her husband.

KIVIAT, ESTHER, author of *Paji** (Whittlesey, 1946), a Fanfare book. Set in modern Ceylon, the book resulted from a visit her husband, Charles, and his friend, Harold Price, made to Ceylon as merchant seamen in World War II. While there, they met a little boy like Paji, and on the way home Price drew pictures of him. From their stories and Price's pictures came the book. She was born and grew up in Grand Rapids, Mich.

KJELGAARD, JIM (JAMES ARTHUR KJELGAARD) (1910-1959), born in New York City; author chiefly known for his animal novels for children and young people. He grew up on a farm in Tioga County, Penn., and in the town of Galeton, Penn., where his father was a physician and where there was ample opportunity to fish, hunt, and trap. He held a variety of jobs, including trapper, teamster, surveyor, plumber's apprentice, and factory worker, but early decided on writing as a career, and he based his books on his own travels and experiences. After 1941, he published over forty books, including animal and historical novels, several books of non-fiction, and two collections of short stories that he edited for Western Writers of America. He is most remembered for his series about his favorite breed of dog, the Irish setter, *Big Red** (Holiday, 1945), later made into a movie of the same name, *Irish Red, Son of Big Red* (Holiday, 1951), and *Outlaw Red, Son of Big Red* (Holiday, 1953), but he wrote about collies, retrievers, hounds, and the Saint Bernard, as well as about such wild animals as polar bears and foxes. Among his historical novels is *Wolf Brother** (Holiday, 1957), about the last days of the free Apaches in the Southwest. *Big Red** is included in *Children's Books Too Good to Miss* and *Choice*, while *Wolf Brother** received the Western Writers of America Spur Award. A very prolific author, he also wrote several hundred short stories and articles.

KNIGHT, ERIC (MOWBRARY) (1897-1943), born in Menston, Yorkshire, England; novelist, cartoonist, illustrator. When he was a young child his father died and his mother took a job as governess for a family of Russian nobility, distributing her own three sons among relatives in England. Eric was fostered by an uncle who treated him well but died a few years later. At twelve the boy started working and in the next few years worked in a cotton mill, a worsted mill, and a glass-blowing factory. In 1912 his mother, now in the United States, sent for him to join her and his brothers, and he briefly attended various art schools in the United States but found it difficult to be treated as a child again and soon left to join the Canadian Light Infantry. Disillusioned and at loose ends, he returned from World War I and drifted for several years, then started to write. His *Lassie Come-Home** (Winston, 1940), famous story of a Yorkshire collie, was an immediate success and the filming of the book took him to Hollywood, a place he viewed with bewildered irony. In the following years he wrote a number of novels for adults, some about flying, the most successful being *This Above All* (Harper, 1941), a best-selling novel of World War II, which was also made into a popular movie. During the war he was in military service and died in a plane crash in 1943 in the Surinam jungle en route for Cairo. *Lassie* became a television series, widely popular but lacking the individuality and the genuine emotion of his book.

KNIGHT'S CASTLE (Eager*†, Edward, ill. N. M. Bodecker, Harcourt, 1956), humorous, episodic family fantasy in which the action begins, ends, and periodically returns to the real world of the mid-twentieth century. When their father needs an operation, Roger*, 11, Ann*, 8, and their parents travel to Baltimore, Md., where they stay with their Aunt Katharine (of *Half Magic**) and her two children, Jack* and Eliza*, about the same age. The first afternoon Aunt Katharine takes them to see the movie *Ivanhoe* and shortly thereafter they find themselves back with Ivanhoe, Rebecca, Robin Hood, Bois-Guilbert and others in the days of Scott's romance, taking part in the siege of Torquilstone. The oldest of Roger's large collection of toy soldiers, a paintless, weaponless antique he calls Old One, who speaks in Elizabethan language and grants wishes, a big, fancy doll house, and a castle, both from a special shop in New York, called the Knight's Castle, serve as vehicles to transport the children to the medieval dimension. Their trips occur on third nights, when they fall asleep, and each features one child. Roger, who enters the fantasy land first, helps Ivanhoe and Robin Hood against the villain Bois-Guilbert and at the critical moment terminates the scene by declaring his enemies nothing but lead soldiers. These become the "Words of Power" which subsequently end each adventure. After Ann and Eliza build a modern city around the play castle, the other children also enter the fantasy world, where they discover that modern life has disrupted the medieval setting with humorous incongruities and misadventures. For example, Ivanhoe lies around reading science fiction and the children employ a flying saucer to rescue Rebecca. The third time they enter the fantasy land the children find Normans and Saxons engaged in a tumultuous game of baseball and their storybook friends held captive in the doll's house by dolls grown to giant size. The final adventure restores King Richard to his rightful position and brings together Ivanhoe and Rebecca, concluding the novel to accommodate the children's romantic inclinations. This often absurd, tongue-in-cheek spoof built around the theme of magic blends elements from fairytale, romance, and science fiction. The four children are distinct, and there is plenty of action and humor, but episodes are so numerous and the pace so frenetic that it is often hard to keep track of what is going on. Judged by late twentieth-century standards the book seems condescending, strained, and stretched out. Choice.

KNOX, ROSE B(ELL) (1879-), born in Talladega, Ala.; teacher, author of educational texts and novels for children of family life and adventure mostly set in the South. She came of an old planter family and grew up in a small town and on a plantation in Alabama. Educated privately until college, she graduated from Agnes Scott College and Atlanta Kindergarten Normal. After teaching in a cottonmill village, she studied in Chicago and then taught at Mississippi State College for women. During World War II she was a free-lance writer in Washington. Her first storybook for children was *The Boys and Sally Down on a Plantation* (Doubleday, 1930), a reader based on her memories of her own childhood. Other period pieces followed, including *Miss Jimmy Deane and What Happened at Pleasant Meadows* (Doubleday, 1931) and *Gray Caps* (Doubleday, 1932), both stories of the pre–Civil War South which reflect tales she heard told at family gatherings when she was a child, and the Fanfare book *Patsy's Progress** (Dodd, 1935), an amusing school story of the gay nineties also set in the South. She also published *Marty and Company on a Carolina Farm* (Doubleday, 1933), *Marty and Company on a California Farm* (Doubleday, 1946), and *Cousins' Luck in the Louisiana Bayou Country* (Macmillan, 1940).

KOBI: A BOY OF SWITZERLAND (Buff*, Mary Marsh, and Conrad Buff*, ill. Conrad Buff, Viking, 1939), short realistic, episodic family novel set in the Swiss Alps perhaps in the early 1900s. Kobi Tobler, 11, lives in an old farmhouse with his parents, younger sister, and grandfather, helping with such daily chores as milking the cows and caring for the goats. His adventures with his Uncle Jacob provide some unity for the loosely plotted story. To Kobi's delight, Uncle Jacob invites the boy to join him in herding cows on Hoch Alp the coming summer. Since this will be the boy's first year in the mountain, Uncle Jacob gives him a herder's suit with a bright red, embroidered vest and yellow goatskin pants. Kobi and his friend Sepp sell Kobi's goat Whitie at the Zell Spring Fair, and Kobi uses part of the money to buy a pair of black leather braces (suspenders) decorated with brass cows to go with Uncle Jacob's present. He accompanies Uncle Jacob on a walking trip over the Alps to Wolfram's Castle in the Rhine River Valley, where he is thrilled to stay overnight in a room that has a suit of armor standing in a corner. After an exciting procession up the Alp with cows, pigs, and goats, Kobi lives with Uncle Jacob in his tiny hut on the mountain, every day helping to milk the cows, make cheese, chop wood, and clean out stables. Left in charge one night when a very severe storm unexpectedly rakes the mountain, Kobi manages with Sepp's help to get all the cows safely into shelter. When Kobi returns to his home in the valley in the fall, the surprise of a new baby brother awaits him. While individual scenes stand out, judged by late twentieth-century standards, characterization is slim, the potential for suspense remains unexploited, and tone is instructive and condescending. The purpose of the book appears didactic—to inform young readers about Alpine life from the viewpoint of a little boy. Rather smudgy full-color paintings and black and white drawings illuminate some episodes and depict setting. Fanfare.

KRAKATOA (*The 21 Balloons**), the volcanic island located in the Sunda Strait between Java and Sumatra, near which Prof. William Waterman Sherman crashes in his fantasy balloon trip across the Pacific and where he finds an elegant late-Victorian society living secretly in comfort and luxury because the island has incredibly rich diamond mines. In both the book and in history, Krakatoa was virtually destroyed by a tremendous volcanic eruption on Aug. 27, 1883, an explosion heard three thousand miles away and causing countless shipping disasters and casualties on coastlines and islands hundreds of miles distant.

KRUMGOLD†, JOSEPH (QUINCY) (1908-1980), born in Jersey City, N.J.; film writer, producer, and author noted in children's literature as the first writer to win the Newbery Award twice, for *. . . And Now Miguel** (Crowell, 1953) and for *Onion John** (Crowell, 1959). Among other honors, both were also Fanfare and *Choice* books; *. . . And Now Miguel* appears in *Children's Books Too Good to Miss*, and *Onion John* was named to the Lewis Carroll Shelf. Together with *Henry 3†* (Atheneum, 1967), also a *Choice* selection, these books form a trio about boys growing up in contemporary America and are unusually successful in employing the first person voice. The first is set on a sheep ranch in New Mexico in a society traditional in outlook and close to its Spanish heritage, the second involves the residents of a small town in New Jersey, and the third takes place in a big city suburb. Probably his best-known book, *. . . And Now Miguel* began as a documentary film, *Miguel Chavez*, prepared for overseas distribution by the United States Department of State. The novel was translated into fifteen languages and later made into a movie by Universal. Krumgold's father was a movie exhibitor who owned and operated movie houses, and the son early decided on a career in film. After graduating from New York University, he wrote and produced scripts for Metro-Goldwyn-Mayer and other major studios in Hollywood and New York City, then formed his own company, writing and producing motion pictures and television films for Columbia Broadcasting, National Broadcasting, and National Educational Television. His films won awards at the Venice, Prague, and Edinburgh film festivals. He traveled extensively in the United States, Europe, and the Middle East and made his home in Hope,

N.J., which provided the setting for *Onion John*. In addition to his numerous screenplays, he also wrote a novel for adults, *Thanks to Murder* (Vanguard, 1935). His first and last books for children were for younger readers, *Sweeney's Adventures* (Random, 1942), which takes place in the Bronx Zoo, and *The Most Terrible Turk* (Crowell, 1969), a short adventure story set in modern Turkey.

KYLE, ANNE D(EMPSTER) (1896-   ), born in Philadelphia, Pa.; author of novels for young people. She grew up in Frankford, Pa., the daughter of a Presbyterian minister who encouraged her interest in history. The family traveled to England, Italy, and Egypt during her childhood, and later, after she graduated from Smith College and World War I was over, she traveled to Japan, China, and India, and again to Italy, where she lived for some years in Florence. Her Italian experiences and studies of Italian history led to three novels laid in that country. *The Apprentice of Florence** (Houghton, 1933), which takes place during the time of the de' Medicis, was a Newbery honor book. The most critically acclaimed of her books, it was praised at publication for its accuracy of fact, panoramic view of the times, and sense of the period, though critics complained of its overcrowdedness and melodrama. Also set in Italy are *Prince of the Pale Mountains* (Houghton, 1929), about a village waif who travels with a gypsy, and *Red Sky over Rome* (Houghton, 1938), set during the Italian Revolution of 1849. She also wrote *Crusader's Gold* (Houghton, 1928), a mystery-adventure set in Palestine involving Colonel Lawrence, bandits, and excavations. Although her novels were fairly well received, they have not endured.

L

LANDERS SCHOOL (*Shuttered Windows**), the boarding school for black girls at Bosquet, S.C., which Harriet Freeman attends. Very inexpensive even for the 1930s (tuition, eight dollars, board and room, eighty-one dollars per year), it is even less for girls who wish to work their way and so has given an opportunity for some of the poorest girls of the area. The rules seem antiquated to Harriet, who has gone to public high school in Minneapolis: girls are allowed to correspond with young men only if parents write the names of those they approve; girls may write a total of three letters a week. The older buildings, constructed just after the Civil War, seem splendid to some of the local girls but dilapidated to Harriet. The book's dedication indicates that it is patterned on Mather School.

LARRY BILL (*Teeny Gay**), circus clown who is fired because he performs out in back of the big tent for Teeny* and Dallas*. He does this because he feels sorry for them since they do not have enough money to pay for tickets. Out of a job, he goes to live on the island in the river. The children find him there and take him and his things to the houseboat before the flood hits. He likes to read and shares his books with the Gays. He is not a very convincing character.

LASSIE COME-HOME (Knight*, Eric, ill. Marguerite Kirmse, Winston, 1940), realistic dog novel set in Scotland and Yorkshire, presumably in the 1920s or early 1930s. Sam Carraclough, Yorkshire miner, has a collie so consistent in going to the schoolyard to fetch home his son, Joe, almost twelve, that the wives of Greenall Bridge village can set their clocks by her. The closing of the mines and resulting hard times make it necessary to sell the dog, named Lassie, to the Duke of Rudling, a dog fancier who has long admired the animal. Joe is heart-broken, and Lassie is baffled but three times breaks out and comes home and is returned by the Carracloughs, though the insensitive, Cockney kennelman, Heynes, suspects that they have trained her to do this. Lassie is taken to the Duke's estate in northern Scotland to be trained as a show dog, where she languishes. Heynes, told to give her exercise, treats her with impatience, and she breaks away. She might have been confined on the estate and caught, but the Duke's favorite granddaughter, understanding Lassie's desire for freedom, deliberately opens the gate for her. The rest of the story consists of Lassie's return to her Yorkshire home, a journey of some four hundred miles as the crow flies, possibly one thousand miles as Lassie must go. She has some near escapes: she is shot for a sheepkiller; she is picked up by a dog catcher; she is nearly drowned in a rushing river. And she has some aids: an old couple take her in and nurse her back to health; kind people occasionally feed her; and she accompanies Rowlie* Palmer, a potter, and his trick dog, Toots, until he is attacked by thugs who kill Toots and are driven off by Lassie. At last she reaches her home village, nearly dead, and this time Sam Carraclough and his scolding but warm-hearted wife try to shield her. Sam "copes" the dog, disguising her as an ill-favored mutt, but doesn't fool the Duke, who nevertheless goes along with the story and hires Sam as his new kennelman to replace Heynes, who has been fired. As he explains to Priscilla, he gets the dog after all, though he has to buy the man to do it. The story has good characterization of the Yorkshire father and mother and gives a strong feeling for Joe's misery and sense of loss. Lassie is treated as a real dog, not an animal who talks or even thinks in English, and her difficult journey is made believable. The story is far more realistic, and, although like most animal stories it exploits emotion, it is far less sentimental than the television series which was based on the book's title character. Choice; Fanfare.

LAST CLASH OF THE CLAYMORES: A STORY OF SCOTLAND IN THE TIME OF PRINCE CHARLES (Cormack*, Maribelle, and William P. Alexander*, ill. Norman Prince, Appleton, 1940), historical novel set mainly in Scotland in the period from February 1744, to late summer of 1746, when Bonnie Prince Charlie, the young Stuart Pretender to the throne, raised the clans against the Hanoverian King George II. Young Marshall Cameron, 24, sent by his clan chief, Donald Cameron of Lochiel, to Brest to get news, meets Charles Stuart, known as Prince Charlie, in an inn on the night the great French fleet, which was to attack the English in his behalf, has been disastrously battered in a storm. Undaunted, Charles plans to enter Scotland virtually alone and rally the Jacobite sympathizers to his cause. The book follows history carefully through the gathering of the clans, the early victories, the march to within one hundred miles of London, the disputes between the rash Prince and blunt Lord George Murray, Commander-in-Chief, and the suspicions sowed by Broughton, the wily secretary. When the fortunes of the Scots begin to fail, Charles's disbelief, shock, and disappointment are catalogued, until the disastrous battle of Culloden Moor. The story, seen largely but not consistently through Marshall's eyes, leaves Prince Charles as Marshall and a handful of men of the Cameron Clan, led by Dr. Archibald Cameron, brother to Lochiel, struggle to get their wounded chief back to his own country in the highlands. When he recovers enough to understand what has happened, he berates Marshall for not deserting him to accompany

Charles and sends him off to find the Prince and bring him, if possible, to the safety of the highland hold. Marshall finds the Prince hiding, a hunted fugitive, on the island of Uist in the Hebrides, and through repeated close scrapes manages to help him back to the highlands and eventually, when a French ship is sent, to the coast of France. The book is good at showing the charisma of the Prince and the fierce loyalty of the highlanders, and it tells some rousing stories, among them that of Lady MacIntosh, known as Colonel Anne, who hides the Prince in her family hold even though her husband is an officer for the English and leads the ''Rout of Moy'' that turns back an army with a few well-placed servants and a fife and drum played by the Lady and her maid; of Jeannie Bailley, 13, who avoids sentries by crawling through a culvert which carries an icy stream, then runs eight miles to warn the Prince of the English plans; of Flora MacDonald*, who dresses the Prince as an Irish spinning woman and coolly leads him past soldiers to escape. But the excitement in the story is all in these historical events themselves. There is a great deal of swashbuckling action, but Marshall, presumably a fictional character, is never developed. The story ends with the return of Charles to France and does not go into his later bad fortune and deterioration. Fanfare.

THE LAST OF THE SEA OTTERS (McCracken*, Harold, ill. Paul Bransom, Stokes, 1942), realistic story of the life of a young sea otter in the Alaskan waters off the Aleutian islands in modern times. Medviedki (which is the Russian name for the otter baby) is born in a quiet cove surrounded by rock walls. There his mother, Matka, teaches him to swim and to avoid the dangers, including the octopus, which lives under a flat ledge near a small beach, and the eagle. Occasionally his father, Bobri Morski, visits the cove. When Medviedki becomes a good swimmer, he dives out the narrow opening through which he has seen his father enter and for the first time sees the open Pacific. His thrill at swimming in this great space turns to panic when he sees Aleutian natives hunting sea lions. At first he mistakes their skin boat for another animal, but when they shoot at him, he realizes his danger and flees to a jumble of broken rocks at the base of high cliffs. There he is battered by each wave and spends a miserable night. The next day, trying to return to his home island, he encounters a mother otter and her daughter, Little Matka, who allow him to join them. He sticks with them for a couple of days and is delighted when their male shows up accompanied by Bobri Morski. After escaping from killer whales, they swim for an island where Medviedki is reunited with his mother. They swim, rest on their backs in the water among kelp beds where it is quiet, and catch fish by clever teamwork. Their greatest enemy, man, returns and shoots Matka. Medviedki and Little Matka escape and from then on stay mostly together, although they are too young to mate. Eventually Little Matka's father is also shot, and a killer whale gets her mother. With Bobri Morski, Medviedki leads Little Matka to the Hidden Cove where he was born, sure that they will find security there. Although she seems happy, she disappears, and he finds her entangled in an Aleut net, spread to catch any otters who hope to winter there. With Little Matka drowned, Medviedki and Bobri Morski leave to find another wintering place. The book could be classified as non-fiction, since it is natural history told in the form of an engrossing story. Although emotions are ascribed to the animals, they are only such emotions as are observable by those who study otters closely. Fanfare.

LATHROP, DOROTHY P(ULIS) (1891-1980), born in Albany, N.Y.; artist whose illustrations for *Animals in the Bible* by Helen Dean Fish (Stokes, 1937) won the first Caldecott Medal. She was a graduate of Teachers College, Columbia University, and studied at Pennsylvania Academy of Fine Arts and the Art Students League in New York. For two years she taught art at Albany High School and began illustrating in 1918. Many of the distinguished books of the twentieth century were illustrated by Lathrop, and she wrote a number herself, the first being *The Fairy Circus** (Macmillan, 1931), a generally plotless fanciful story more interesting for its illustrations than its text.

LATTIMORE, ELEANOR FRANCES (1904-), born in Shanghai, China; artist, author and illustrator of children's books. She grew up in China, educated at home by her father who was a professor at a Chinese university. She lived also for a while in Switzerland when the older children of the family were in school there. When she was sixteen, the family returned to the United States, and, while they lived for two years in Berkeley, Calif., she attended the California School of Arts and Crafts. She later studied at the Art Students League and the Grand Central School of Art in New York. She worked as a free-lance artist until 1930, when she began to write and illustrate her own children's books. In her career that spans over half a century, she has published over fifty self-illustrated books predominately of family life and simple adventures. Although Japan, Denmark, England, and different parts of the United States have provided settings for her stories, it is those set in China and that reflect the China of her childhood that are the best known. *Little Pear** (Harcourt, 1931), which combines mildly exciting, if predictable and superficial, episodes, a winning five-year-old hero, and a strong picture of China remains a classic of its form and was selected for *Children's Books Too Good to Miss*. Sequels include *Little Pear and His Friends* (Harcourt, 1934), *Little Pear and His Rabbits* (Morrow, 1956), and *More About Little Pear* (Morrow, 1971). *Jerry and the Pusa* (Harcourt, 1932), her second book, describes the temple and the college of the city in China where she grew up. Other titles include *The Seven Crowns* (Harcourt, 1933), *The Story of Lee Ling* (Harcourt, 1940), *Bayou Boy* (Morrow, 1946), *Happiness for Kimi* (Morrow, 1958), and *The Taming of the Tiger* (Morrow, 1975). She has contributed many short stories to such national publications as *Jack and Jill*, *American Junior Red Cross Magazine*, and *Christian Science Monitor* and has illustrated books for other writers, and her art work appears in many galleries and permanent collections. She married Robert Armstrong Andrews, a free-lance writer, and has two sons. She has lived on Edisto Island, S.C., and in Kentucky.

LAURA (*Magic or Not?**), twin of James*. A dreamy girl who believes strongly in magic. She gets the idea that the magic of the well is an unselfish kind that works to help those who set out to help others. She is a warmhearted girl who continually reaches out to others.

LAURA INGALLS (*Little House in the Big Woods**; *Little House on the Prairie**; *On the Banks of Plum Creeek**; *On the Shores of Silver Lake**; *The Long Winter**; *Little Town on the Prairie**; *These Happy Golden Years**), protagonist in the series of seven autobiographical novels. A spirited child, Laura is usually well behaved but never the completely proper little girl her mother tries to make her. Small but sturdy, she is called by her father, "Half-Pint" and "strong as a little French horse." She shares his love of travel, of music, and of fun. As a little child, she loves to help her father by handing him tools. As she grows older, she helps with the haying and the milking. Although she much prefers to work out of doors, she takes jobs as a seamstress and becomes a school teacher in order to earn money to help pay college expenses for her blind sister, Mary*. Her romance which leads to her marriage with Almanzo* Wilder seems as much a love for his horses as for the young man himself.

LAURIE LAURENCE (*Little Women**), Theodore, spirited boy next door whose lonely life is cheered and whose character is formed by his association with the four March girls. Because his father ran off and married an Italian musician, his stern grandfather dislikes his piano playing and fears that he will waste himself on an artistic life. When he is in college, he does show signs of being spoiled by mild dissipation, but Jo sets him straight so that he graduates with honor. When Jo refuses his proposal, he again seems destined to amount to nothing, leading an idle existence in Europe until Amy tells him she despises him. He shapes up, marries her, and gives up music for business.

LAURITZEN, JONREED (1902-   ), born in Richfield, Utah; writer for adults and youth of novels about the history of the West, ranch life, and Indians. He grew up on a ranch in canyon country, absorbing atmosphere and ideas that would furnish material for his books. His father was a rancher who became involved in a scheme to irrigate the Arizona Strip and pioneered in that area with his family. While living in northern Arizona, Lauritzen became interested in the Navajo and Hopi Indians. His mother, who had been an actress and writer, encouraged his literary bent. He studied at the University of California at Berkeley and at Los Angeles and at Columbia University, and, after studying further in music, drama, and art, he pursued his ambition to write. He has held positions with the Department of the Interior as field representative concerned with parks, reclamation, fish, game, and public lands and has made his home in California. Of his several novels for young readers, his first, *The Ordeal of the Young Hunter** (Little, 1954), about Navajo family life in the twentieth century, received the Child Study Award. Among his historical novels, *The Legend of Billy Blue-*

sage (Little, 1961), an adventure story set in the Old West about a half-Spanish boy raised by Ute Indians, received the award of the Southern California Council on Children's Literature. Also for later elementary and junior high readers are *The Young Mustangers* (Little, 1957), *Treasure of the High Country* (Little, 1959), and *The Glitter-eyed Wouser* (Little, 1960), westerns of ranch life featuring the Marriner family. He has written novels of western history and adventure for adults, and his travel and descriptive articles have appeared in *Holiday*, *Westways*, and other national magazines.

LAVINIA LYTE (*Johnny Tremain**), haughty, idle, socialite daughter of merchant Jonathan Lyte, a kind of cousin of Johnny. She tells Johnny the story of his connection with the Lyte family just before she and her father, broken in health after the mob drives him out of Milton and back to Boston, leave for London for the duration of the war. Johnny's mother also was named Lavinia Lyte.

LAWSON, ROBERT (1882-1957), born in New York City; illustrator and author of warm, humorous stories with a particularly American quality. He grew up in Montclair, N.J., and attended the New York School of Fine and Applied Arts. During World War I he served in an engineers' camouflage section, then worked as a commercial artist until 1930 when he became a free-lance illustrator. His first prominent success was in the illustrations for Munro Leaf's *The Story of Ferdinand* (Viking, 1936). He is the only person to have won both the Caldecott and Newbery Medals, the Caldecott for his biographical picture story of his parents and grandparents, *They Were Strong and Good* (Viking, 1940), and the Newbery for his clever animal fantasy, *Rabbit Hill**, (Viking, 1944). This was followed by a sequel, *The Tough Winter** (Viking, 1954). Several of his books are fantasy biographies, told by the pets of famous people, including a story of Benjamin Franklin told by his mouse, *Ben and Me** (Little, 1939), and *Mr. Revere and I** (Little, 1953), told by Paul Revere's horse. Throughout his career he illustrated many books and wrote fifteen, all self-illustrated, including *The Great Wheel** (Viking, 1957), the story of the making of the first Ferris Wheel, which was published the year of his death.

LAY, MARION (MARION LAY DAVIS) (1903-), author of *Wooden Saddles** (Morrow, 1939), lively adventure story set in the Mexican deserts and mountains about a boy who runs away from gypsies and gains some fame for his ability to use the lariat. Although it was praised by critics at the time of publication, particularly for its evocation of the Mexican countryside, and was selected by the editors of *Horn Book* for the Fanfare list, it has not endured.

THE LEAST ONE (Sawyer*, Ruth, ill. Leo Politi, Viking, 1941), realistic animal story set near a village in Mexico in the middle 1900s. Ten-year-old Paco loves with all his heart Chiquitico, the "least one" and youngest of all the burros of his father, Vincente, a poor burden carrier with a large family. The two spend so much time idling in the hills and roaming the *barrancas* and plains that the father calls them good-for-nothings. Both enter the world of work on the same day, Paco as an apprentice to a sandalmaker and little Chiquitico as a bearer of heavy construction tiles. When Chiquitico balks at carrying Vicente's heavy load, Paco's father twists the little burro's tail, and the animal tumbles into a ditch and runs away. Sorry that he lost his temper, Vicente promises his son that, if Chiquitico returns, the boy may have him for his own. Paco searches for his friend unsuccessfully, noticing to his astonishment that the local photographer has a small gray-brown burro made of wood upon which patrons may sit to have their pictures taken. Concluding that Chiquitico has been bewitched into the photographer's dummy mount, Paco prays to the Virgin Mary to intercede with San Francisco, patron saint of animals, on behalf of his burro. He hires out in his spare time to the photographer, to watch over his bewitched friend, and does well also at his job with the sandalmaker, attracting so many customers to both shops that his employers share their profits with him. At the feast of the blessing of the animals, an old festival the local priest revives, Chiquitico mysteriously reappears. Paco joyfully spends his savings on baskets and wares to peddle with his friend in the villages throughout the countryside. His parents are proud of their merchant son, and Paco is grateful that Chiquitico is back and will never have to carry heavy burdens again. The story, if implausible, is warmly and affectionately told. It moves along well with a charming storytelling quality and without the sentimentality that mars many animal stories. Local customs, home life, religious beliefs and practices, and social attitudes are described in just enough detail for setting and interest. The author captures the cadence of Mexican speech, and the occasional use of Spanish words contributes authenticity. Leo Politi's stylized two-color illustrations extend the setting. Fanfare.

LEDYARD, JOHN (*The Codfish Musket**), actual historical figure (1751-1789), an explorer who traveled with Captain Cook. While at Nootka Sound in the Pacific Northwest of North America, he saw opportunities for great wealth through trade in furs with the Orient and envisioned a transcontinental route from Virginia to the West Coast. Although he never appears in the novel, his dreams form the historical background for the novel. Dan Boit's Granddad* knew him and first tells Dan about him.

THE LEGEND OF SLEEPY HOLLOW (Irving*, Washington, Putnam, 1864, originally in *The Sketch Book*, C. S. Van Winkle, 1819), humorous story set near Tarry Town, N.Y., on the eastern shore of the Hudson about 1790. To the quiet settlement of Sleepy Hollow comes the schoolteacher, Ichabod Crane, tall and loose-jointed, lank, with a long nose, big feet, and long arms, resembling ''some scarecrow, eloped from a cornfield.'' He fits into the credulous community by believing in the supernatural, Cotton Mather's *History of New England Witchcraft* being his favorite book. Among the local legends is the story of the ghost of a Hessian trooper whose head was shot off by a cannonball in the Revolution and who rides through the Hollow at night hunting for his head. Ichabod, who loves to eat, sets his sights on pretty, plump Katrina Van Tassel, as much for the marvelous meals promised by the livestock and produce on her father's substantial farm as for her own blooming charms. His chief rival is a large local fellow named Abraham Van Brunt and known as Brom Bones. He is a leader of a band of rowdies who play pranks throughout the neighborhood. At the quilting frolic given by Mynheer Van Tassel, to which Ichabod rides on an old horse named Gunpowder, Brom tells about an encounter he has had with the Headless Horseman. Ichabod, having lingered after the others in order to have a few private minutes with Katrina, is already apprehensive as a figure rides up beside him on his way home. When he sees from its outline against the sky that it is headless, he is so terrified that he prods Gunpowder into running at last, though the saddle slips and Ichabod clings to the mane. As Gunpowder thunders across the church bridge, the figure behind rises in his stirrups and hurls the head at him. The next day the villagers find the horse, the saddle, and a smashed pumpkin but no sign of the schoolmaster. Later he is reported to have been seen in a distant part of the country. Brom Bones marries Katrina. The tale, originally published for adults, is told in a leisurely, discursive style that spends as much time describing the local people and customs and poking mild fun at them as it does on Ichabod's story. Ichabod's ludicrous figure among the stout, substantial Dutch is one of the best known in American literature. Children's Classics.

LEIGHTON, MARGARET (1896-   ), born in Oberlin, Ohio; author of mysteries and historical fiction for young people. She studied at schools in Cambridge, Mass., in France and in Switzerland, and received her A.B. degree from Radcliffe College. After her husband's death in 1935, she moved to California and started writing books for older children. She has lived in Santa Monica and has written at least twenty books, among them *Judith of France** (Houghton, 1948), historical biography of the great-granddaughter of Charlemagne who became an early queen of England.

LEM FORRESTER (*The Yearling**), meanest of the six big sons in the hard-drinking, carousing, backwoods family. He fights Oliver Hutto over Twink Weatherby, a little blond who keeps company with Lem while Oliver is out to sea but follows Oliver to Jacksonville and returns his wife. It is Lem who is tricked by Penny* Baxter's honesty to trade a good gun for a dog that Penny frankly declares is worthless.

A LEMON AND A STAR (Spykman*†, E. C., Harcourt, 1955), episodic humorous novel set near Summerton Village, close to Charlottesville, Mass., in 1907. The four motherless Cares children—Ted*, 13, Jane*, 10, Hubert*, 8, and Edie*, 5—are well supplied with relatives whose estate-like farms adjoin theirs, and with servants—Cook, Gander, Nurse, Pat the coachman, Hobber the Gardner—and with formidable Father, but they are, nonetheless, frequently unsupervised and inclined to get into escapades mostly never reported in the Red House, their family home. The book starts with Jane's tenth birthday, when she pelts the imperious Ted with a mudpie on the back of his neck and he gets even at the family celebration at dinner by giving her a beautifully wrapped lemon. Nevertheless, at bedtime she gets a marvelous present, the sight of a star falling, sent, she is sure, just for her. On Nurse's day out, when Ted is supposed to be taking care of Edie (a duty he abhors), they track down on their bikes and attack big Will McCann to retrieve the sixty-five cents he has taken from Hubert. To their great embarrassment, they are rescued by the priest's houskeeper. On what she later thinks of as her lucky day, Jane, excluded when Father takes the boys to a prize fight, first visits Grandfather and joins him and a number of servants in a wild chase of a bat that has come into his living room, then, in an effort to outdo the boys in exciting adventures, she walks on the catwalk over the dam, falls in, is swept down, and miraculously is not drowned. Sometimes the incidents come out badly, as when the boys plan a steeple chase, Edie's horse joins in unexpectedly, and they just escape disaster, and the time when Jane and Hubert find the water out of the reservoirs and, playing on an island in a sea of mud, Hubert is stung by hornets, rescued when Jane summons Uncle Charlie's cook, Big Nora, and is in bed a week, swollen and feverish. Sometimes the adventures are satisfying, as when Jane and Hubert take Jane's gold piece and have a wonderful, independent day secretly in Charlottesville, going to the museum and the theater and eating "planked steak," and as when there is a robbery in the village, Will McCann is arrested, and they arrive home to find his old father threatening Father with a rifle in revenge. Ted, at Jane's urging, hurls himself against the back of McCann's legs, Jane retrieves the rifle, and when the whole affair is finally sorted out, Father actually thanks them! Their greatest surprise occurs when Father brings home a new wife, only to find them not standing for inspection but all disheveled from a fight the younger ones have been having in revolt against Ted's bossing. Ordered by Father to call his new wife, "Mother," Jane, loving the woman at first sight, calmly announces she will call her "Madam*." Most of the incidents are seen through Jane's eyes, with the insight and innocence of a bright ten-year-old. The antagonism between the children is strong and realistically conveyed, as is also the sense of period and place. The humor is far more subtle than the average amusing story for children, and the characters stand out as interesting individuals, even such minor figures as Grandfather and the Irish servants. Sequels. Choice.

LENSKI, LOIS (LENORE) (1893-1974), born in Springfield, Ohio; author of one hundred books for children, including sixteen books of verse, two collections of folk rhymes, three plays, non-fiction, picture books, and numerous novels for youngsters of the middle grades, most of them self-illustrated. She received her B.S. degree in education from Ohio State University and studied at the Art

Students League in New York and the Westminster School of Art, London. In 1920 she became a free-lance illustrator and produced a series of "Mr. Small" picture books that have been widely popular despite stiff, simplistic drawings and text. Her longer books fall into two general categories, the historical and the regional stories. Based on real instances or diaries and other records, the historical stories have pat plots and minimal characterization, like *Phebe Fairchild: Her Book** (Stokes, 1936), *A-going to the Westward** (Stokes, 1937), *Ocean-born Mary** (Stokes, 1939), and *Indian Captive: The Story of Mary Jemison** (Lippincott, 1941). For her regional novels she conscientiously traveled to different areas of the country and lived among her subjects to collect material. Although they were widely praised and do show differences in ways of life in different parts of the United States, the plots and characters are very similar, and they are about children who strive for the conventional values of the educated middle class. Typical are *Strawberry Girl** (Lippincott, 1945), *Blue Ridge Billy** (Lippincott, 1946), *Judy's Journey** (Lippincott, 1947), and *Cotton in My Sack** (Lippincott, 1949).

THE LEVEL LAND (De Jong*†, Dola, ill. Jan Hoowij, Scribner's, 1943), realistic family novel set in the Netherlands in the early days of World War II. Since Holland is officially neutral, none of the van Oordt family expects a Nazi invasion except sister Miep*, 18, who studies in the School for Social Work in Amsterdam. Vader, a doctor, thinks bomb shelters unnecessary for the village which he serves from their spreading, old-fashioned country home known as The Level Land. Jaap, 16, a musician, is planning a bicycle trip with a girlfriend. Jan, 13, is mostly concerned with his bad reports from school. He knows that he is lazy and that his hope of becoming a doctor will be dashed if he doesn't get recommended for high school. Ruth*, 11, is so concerned about Jan that she plays hookey and goes to Jan's school to talk to the principal and promises to make Jan work to catch up. Pieter Pim*, 4, an independent, enterprising child, gets into one scrape after another but, as he points out, always by mistake. Moeder, who helps her husband with his village practice, has just had another child, little Anne, when the book opens. The house is kept spotless and the family fed by Geesje, the tireless servant. After delivering a patient with a broken leg to the hospital, Dr. van Oordt brings home a German Jewish refugee boy, Werner, who has fled Germany with an uncle now seriously ill. The van Oordts take in the boy, but it is Jaap who is able to make him feel at home and who learns that Werner is a violinist. As is the custom, Sinterklaas (Saint Nicholas) arrives early in December in the form of Miep's fiance, Maarten, accompanied by Black Peter, who looks suspiciously like Jan. The gift giving is a warm family celebration which includes a violin for Werner. For Christmas itself, the whole family goes to Amsterdam, to stay with Moeder's mother and sister. Back at school, Ruth has a rivalry with Elly Verschuren. When Ruth becomes very ill, she is tormented by the memory of some hair ribbons she bought to try to outshine Elly. After a close brush with death, Ruth recovers and is sent to the seaside to recuperate, though Miep warns against getting the family separated. A German maid hired to care for Anne leaves without warning. Suddenly, German planes pass over in the night, and the next day bombs fall on the village itself. Vader turns the house into an infirmary; Elly, feeling guilty about her rivalry with Ruth, arrives and works diligently at all the most onerous tasks. The boys take turns helping at home and doing rescue work in the village. Vader's laboratory in the barn is destroyed by a bomb. A car horn wakes them in the night, and they discover Miep, with a leg injured by shooting, driving Maarten's car to bring Ruth home. Patched up by Vader, Miep leaves again with Werner, hoping to get him on a ship out of Rotterdam. Shortly afterwards, they hear that Rotterdam has been raided, hundreds have been killed, and the country has surrendered. Without knowing the fate of Werner and Miep, the family must turn its attention to the patients and carry on. Characters are well individualized and convincing. The book has an unusual structure. For about five-sixths of its length it is a warm, sometimes humorous family story, with only occasional ominous forebodings by Miep. Perhaps this gentleness makes the impact of the last sixth and the open ending more shocking. A 1961 edition is illustrated by Peter Spier. Fanfare.

LEWIS, ELIZABETH FOREMAN (1892-1958), born in Baltimore, Md.; Methodist missionary in China and author of several books set in that country. She attended Maryland Institute of Fine Arts, studied at secretarial school in Baltimore and at the Bible Seminary of New York. In 1917 she went to China with the Women's Foreign Missionary Society and taught in Shanghai, Chunking, and Nanking. In China she married the son of a missionary, but illness forced her to return to the United States in 1921. Her novel, *Young Fu of the Upper Yangtze** (Winston, 1932), won the Newbery Award. Both this book and *Ho-Ming, Girl of New China* (Winston, 1934), document the conflicts of young people in a transition period from the superstition-bound past to the opportunities and challenges of the early twentieth century.

LIDE, ALICE (ALISON) (1890-1956), born and lived in Alabama; author from the late 1920s to the mid-1950s of fifteen novels for later elementary and adolescent readers, most in collaboration with her sister, Margaret Johansen*. Several are adventure stories intended to inform readers about other cultures, among them, *Ood-le-uk the Wanderer** (Little, 1930), a rather spun-out and instructive Newbery honor book set among Eskimos in Alaska, and *Lapland Drum* (Abingdon, 1955), about a brother and sister who follow the reindeer herds. Others are historical novels, often of a romantic nature, including *Pearls of Fortune* (Little, 1931), featuring a princess of Russia at the time of Peter the Great who flees to the New World, and *Dark Possession* (Appleton, 1934), set in South Carolina in the early 1700s and presumably based on the sisters' own family's colonial experiences. Individually she did *Inemak, the Little Greenlander* (Rand, 1927),

Yinka-tu the Yak (Viking, 1938), *Aztec Drums* (Longmans, 1938), and *Princess of Yucatán* (Longmans, 1939). The books show extensive research and meticulous attention to detail of time and place.

THE LIGHT AT TERN ROCK (Sauer*, Julia L., ill. Georges Schreiber, Viking, 1951), Christmas story set at a lighthouse on the Atlantic coast near St. John, New Brunswick, presumably in the early twentieth century. When the keeper of the lighthouse at Tern Rock, Byron Flagg, wants a shore leave, he gets Martha Morse who lived at the Rock for fourteen years when her late husband was keeper, and her nephew, Ronnie, 11, to substitute for him for two weeks, promising to return on Dec. 15, so that Ronnie can take part in pre-Christmas activities at school. When he doesn't show up, Ronnie is outraged at his faithlessness, and when he finds a sea chest with his name on it marked "Christmas greetings," he rejects the gifts, angry to realize that the old man has planned to break his agreement. Aunt Martha accepts the situation, banishes the sulking boy to his room, cleans the house and makes what Christmas treats she can contrive from the lighthouse stores. When Ronnie reappears in a better mood, she reads him the letter from Flagg, explaining that he has tricked them because he has never had a family Christmas and wants to spend one with his niece's children. They agree that they have lit the biggest Christmas candle by keeping the lighthouse going and that they have the spirit of the holiday in their hearts. The moralism in the story is rather heavy-handed, but the setting makes it unusual, and practical Aunt Martha is an attractive character. Newbery Honor.

LILLYBELLE LAWRENCE (*Great Day in the Morning**), strong, tall, very hard-working black girl, who is impatient with her idler classmates, her listless aunt, and her bull-headed cousin Abner, and who has the reputation for being "hard." Her love for St. Helena Island where she grew up and for her grandfather, Noah*, who took her in when her parents died, proves she has a softer emotional side to match her ambition and drive.

LI LUN, LAD OF COURAGE (Treffinger*, Carolyn, ill. Kurt Wiese, Abingdon, 1947), brief tale set on Blue Shark Island off the coast of China at an unspecified time. Shamed and infuriated by the refusal of his son, Li Lun, 10, to join him on a fishing voyage, Teng Lun calls him a coward. When the mother, Wang Lun, points out with trepidation that the boy's grandfather did not go to sea but grew rice, Teng Lun gives his son seven grains of rice and insists that he must raise seven times that much at the barren top of Lao Shan, highest peak of the island, called The Sorrow Mountain, or agree to become a fisherman. Li Lun seeks the advice of wise old Sun Ling, the only one in the Village of Three Firs who remembers, from the time before a great storm destroyed agriculture on the island, how to grow rice. With his directions the boy carries soil, his food supplies, and the seven grains of rice to the mountaintop, finds a place sheltered from the winds to plant his garden, and tends his tiny crop for the three months it takes for the rice to mature. In a series of disasters he loses all but one plant to sea gulls and rats, but on that he grows far more than the required number of grains and wins his father's approval. Although he is alone and often afraid, he resists the impulse to take any of the ground dragon's bones his mother has given him as medicine against fear and therefore is recognized as a lad of courage by the priest of the temple and the villagers. More like a short story than a novel, this book makes no attempt at characterization beyond the minimal necessary to protray Li Lun as fearful but persistent, and while the mountaintop with its wind, rain, drought, sea gulls, rats, and rocks bare of earth is a well-developed setting, the rest of the book has the abstract quality of fable. Fanfare; Lewis Carroll; Newbery Honor.

LILY KORMOS (*The Singing Tree**), daughter of the respected and well-liked judge of the area in which the Nagy ranch lies. She is haughty and proud, considers herself too good to associate with the peasants, and even looks down on Kate and Jancsi as mere country folk. When she behaves badly and threatens to embarrass her father by her actions at Mari and Peter's wedding, Kate locks her in a shed. The judge asks Márton to take her in hand, and under his tutelage she soon improves. Lily influences the course of things most significantly when she insists that a cat get medical attention. The children take the cat to a military hospital and discover that Márton Nagy is a patient there. Lily is too much like Kate was in the first book and changes too readily to be convincing.

LINA (*The Wheel on the School**), the only girl in the school of Shora, who initiates the search for a wheel so that storks will return to the village. Bright but timid, Lina has been left out of the boys' games, but in the effort to get and install the wheel, she makes friends with Grandmother Sibble III, oldest woman in Shora, old Douwa, who long ago saved his fisherman father from his overturned boat after all others had given him up, and legless Janus, feared by the children for his temper. Lina finds the wheel, climbs to the rooftop of the school to test its installation, and rides out in the rowboat to rescue and carry back the exhausted storks which have become stuck on the sandbar.

LINDA (*Sarah's Idea**), Sarah's younger sister of seven. Linda is more quiet than Sarah, a decisive, assertive, pretty child with a mind of her own. She is much more feminine than Sarah, avoids getting dirty, and likes less active pursuits. She understands Sarah very well and is usually quite supportive of her sister's needs and wishes. For example, she chooses the bedroom away from the barn because she knows that Sarah would prefer the one facing the barn. She readily offers to help Sarah gather prunes and gives her her share of their earnings because she sincerely wishes to help Sarah achieve her objective of owning a burro. Sarah is continually amazed at how astute Linda is and really appreciates her generosity. One of the book's finest features is the close relationship between the two sisters, which grows and develops believably as the story advances. Unlike many sisters, these two do not compete and bicker, perhaps because they have quite different personalities and Sarah was ill for so long.

LINDQUIST, JENNIE D(OROTHEA) (1899-1977), born in Manchester, N.H.; librarian, editor, author. She was a children's librarian in Manchester and in Albany, N.Y., and taught classes in the appreciation of children's literature at the University of New Hampshire. For ten years, from 1948 to 1958, she was managing editor, then editor of *Horn Book* magazine. Memories of her grandparents, who were born in Sweden and passed Swedish customs on to her in her childhood, are incorporated into her three books, *The Golden Name Day** (Harper, 1955), *The Little Silver House** (Harper, 1959), and *The Crystal Tree* (Harper, 1966).

LION BOY: A STORY OF EAST AFRICA (Stevens*, Alden G., ill. E. A. Watson, Stokes, 1938), realistic, episodic novel of family and community life set in Tanganyika, East Africa, in the mid-1900s, among the Wanyamlima, tall, proud warriors and hunters of remote and beautiful Kandoa Irangi, ''The Land of Painted Sheep.'' For centuries the Wanyamlima have occupied this varied territory of veldts, forests, jungles, rivers, rugged uplands, and mountains, of mud-walled, grass-roofed huts, of lions, hyenas, and elephants, and of uncertain rain and few contacts with outsiders. The story is told mostly from the point of view of, but not by, eleven-year-old Simba (''lion''), the impetuous, earnest son of Kinanjui, a leading warrior in one of the Wanyamlima villages, and largely describes hair-raising encounters with wild animals near the village or while on the hunt. Most episodes focus on Simba, but some revolve about his father, Kinanjui, or Mucheri* and Daudi*, two warriors; Mche*, his little sister; Mganga, the witch doctor; and Kibeti*, the crippled, respected, old storyteller, and some include his best friend, Kimani. Simba bravely stands his ground when a lion attacks the family buffalo herd, and he accompanies his father to the crater of Ngoro Ngoro where he shouts and whoops with joy at seeing his beautiful country stretching out for miles below him. He is saved from a leopard when his puppy, the cowardly Runaway, unexpectedly disproves his name. While hunting, he comes upon the ruins of an ancient Assyrian temple, to the delight of a white explorer who has been seeking it. His greatest adventure involves saving a young white boy, Jack, from a bull buffalo. The most serious problems of the village involve predatory lions, dealt with through the ingenuity and bravery of Mucheri, and a prolonged drought, to which Mganga's rain-making spells put an end. The book concludes with Kibeti telling the villagers assembled around the campfire the story of how in his youth he was maimed by an elephant. Most characters are one-dimensional, and the author occasionally patronizes them and their culture and the audience as well. Episodes have great emotional appeal, but the strength of the book lies in its recreation of the everyday life and the physical environment of the Wanyamlima people. Occasional use of Kiswahili words adds to the sense of place. Fanfare.

LIPPINCOTT, JOSEPH WHARTON (1887-1976), born in Philadelphia, Pa.; publisher and naturalist. He studied at the Wharton School of Finance, which was founded by one of his grandfathers at the University of Pennsylvania, and entered the publishing firm of J. P. Lippincott, founded by his other grandfather, where he worked for fifty years from 1908 to 1958. He was also president of Frederick A. Stokes publishing company and of the Hibernia Mine Railroad. During World War I he served in the U.S. Naval Reserve. A very active sportsman, he engaged in polo playing, yacht racing, and big-game hunting, a pursuit that made him interested in the habits of wild animals and led him to the study of natural science. His seventeen books for young people are all about animals, most of them wild, with detailed characterization but no anthropomorphism or sentimentality. *The Wahoo Bobcat** (Lippincott, 1950), the story of a species endangered as the encroaching development ruins its habitat, and several others make a non-didactic plea for conservation.

THE LITTLE ANGEL: A STORY OF OLD RIO (Dalgliesh*, Alice, ill. Katherine Milhous, Scribner's, 1943), essentially plotless story set in Rio de Janeiro starting in 1819. Maria Luiza, about nine, is the eldest child and only daughter of Paulo da Silva, prominent and wealthy citizen and slave owner. Maria Luiza has four younger brothers, teasing Roberto, plump Paulo, contentious Pedro, and infant Miguel, but she prays to St. Antonio, their household saint, for a little sister. When her prayers don't seem to be answered, she throws the statue of the saint into the garden, then confesses to kind Father Sebastian, who helps her find and replace the statue. On the day that a daughter is born to Dom Pedro, crown prince (in exile) of Portugal, a baby sister is also born in the da Silva family, named Maria da Gloria, and baptized the same day as the royal baby. When the baby is three, Brazil declares its independence from Portugal and Dom Pedro becomes the Emperor of Brazil, news which Senhor da Silva announces to his family in the garden. When Maria Luiza is fifteen and her sister six, their father chooses a wealthy man to be husband to his elder daughter. Maria Luiza, summoned to see him for the first time, takes her little sister with her, but as they enter the garden, Gatinho, Maria da Gloria's kitten, annoys the man and he cruelly throws the animal away, a sign of callousness that makes Maria Luiza retreat weeping and refuse to marry him. Although this is unprecedented behavior, her kind father does not force her. They enjoy the carnival, and Gatinho is scared off by the pelting of wax lemons full of perfumed water, part of the celebration. Maria de Gloria has been chosen to be a little angel in the next day's Procession of Santo Antonio, but she goes out early in the morning hunting for her kitten and gets lost in the streets of Rio. She is found weeping and is brought home by a handsome young man who introduces himself as a pupil of the painter Debret.

Maria da Gloria is hurried by her mother and the black nurse, Carlotta, into her elaborate costume and is in time for the procession, and as they walk she sees and rescues her kitten, but she is so tired that both she and Gatinho must be carried by Father Sebastian. The young man calls to assure himself that she is all right, but it is at Maria Luiza that he looks, and when he treats Gatinho kindly, Maria da Gloria is sure he will be husband for her big sister. In an introductory note, the author tells something of the history of Brazil and of the paintings of the French artist, Jean Baptiste Debret, who thoroughly recorded life in Rio of the period, and she notes that the illustrations in the book follow his paintings. Unfortunately, so does the story. It has the tone of a narrative written to include events pictured rather than one with intrinsic interest in plot, character, or theme. Even as a description of Brazil in the early nineteenth century, it may be questionable, for the slaves are pictured as happy members of the household, and Maria Luiza's rebellion against her father's choice and the easy substitution of an artist's pupil for a wealthy landowner reflect twentieth-century values. Fanfare.

LITTLE BLACKNOSE: THE STORY OF A PIONEER (Swift*, Hildegarde Hoyt, ill. Lynd Ward, Harcourt, 1929), historical fantasy which anthropomorphizes the De Witt Clinton railroad locomotive, one of the first "iron horses" in the United States. Produced at the West Point Foundry in New York City in the spring of 1831, Little Blacknose, a four-wheeler with a "long black nose that stuck straight up in front of him, like an upsidedown elephant's trunk," is taken by his engineer, David Mathew, by steamboat up the Hudson River to Albany. He is surprised and disappointed when he is snubbed by a disdainful, rude, roan carriage horse, skeptical of his ability to pull the train, and he basks in the admiration of spectators who have never before seen a locomotive. On August 9, 1831, he is the center of the momentous and gala first excursion on the Mohawk and Hudson line from Albany to Schenectady, carrying high dignitaries and selected ticket-holders. He remains the center of attention as the only locomotive on the line for some time, until his position is threatened by John Bull, a larger locomotive newly arrived from England. When John Bull is unable to undertake an excursion because of a mechanical defect, Little Blacknose proudly and staunchly completes the other's run to Schenectady at the astonishing rate of nineteen miles per hour. The two form a firm friendship, and for years they make their scheduled runs with great reliability. Tired from his hard labor and replaced by larger, more powerful engines, Little Blacknose rests and dreams in the Albany stationhouse, until he is refurbished and displayed at the World's Fair in Chicago in 1893. He is delighted once again to be gazed at and termed a wonder, and he yearns for a little track in the country for his very own. Thirty-five more years of storage ensue, however, before he again proudly and joyfully makes the Schenectady run for the centennial celebration of the New York Central railroad. After this last trip, he is pleased to be put on permanent display in New York's Grand Central Station, where he enjoys the admiration of those who pass through the terminal. Simple in language, with much dialogue and descriptive portrayal of Little Blacknose's feelings and desires, this saccharine and overdrawn presentation of the facts of history is typical of the didactic and patronizing writing for children of its period. Newbery Honor.

LITTLE BOAT BOY: A STORY OF KASHMIR (Bothwell*, Jean, ill. Margaret Ayer, Harcourt, 1945), realistic novel of family life set on a river in a valley in Kashmir in the mid-1900s. Likeable, earnest, irrepressible Hafiz, 8, and his father, mother, older brother, Abdullah*, and big sister, Rafia, live on a *doonga*, a raft bearing a house made of mats. Behind the *doonga* trails a houseboat which the family rents for the summer to Sahib, an English artist, a fortunate occurrence since it insures that there will be enough money to get them through the coming winter. A happy child, Hafiz plays with his toy boats at the edge of the river, gets new shoes at the big market at Third Bridge, and enjoys the red ball he finds under the houseboat floor. But he has an unfortunate way of arousing the ire of the farmer next door. For example, he well-meaningly puts the farmer's baby on Sahib's bed because he thinks the child will be more comfortable there, and the child is assumed lost. Hafiz's greatest wish is to go to school, as Abdullah has done, to ''gain understanding'' of things in the world, a yearning likely to remain unfulfilled because Hafiz's father still owes the moneylender Sayyad* Khan for Abdullah's schooling. When the duck belonging to the farmer swims off with one of Hafiz's toy boats, Abdullah recovers it, but the farmer causes so much trouble over the incident that the Sahib offers to send Hafiz to school. With the lively child out of the way, Sahib hopes he will be able to continue his work in peace. The slim, almost suspenseless plot remains interesting, if contrived and marred by a too fortuitous conclusion. It serves as a vehicle for showing younger readers the everyday economic and social life of the river people in Kashmir from the viewpoint of a young child in a warm and loving family. Language is easy, sentences simple and direct, and characters mostly types. Fanfare.

LITTLE EDDIE (Haywood*, Carolyn, ill. author, Morrow, 1947), humorous, episodic novel of family and school life set in a small American city in the mid-1900s. This is the first in a series about Eddie Wilson, 7, youngest of four brothers that include Rudy, 11, and twins Joe and Frank, 9. Although the novel is set up with episodic chapters, events relate to one another, and the same characters recur, providing unity. Eddie is an average sort of boy, active and fun-loving, who clutters his room with crudely lettered signs and collects what the rest of the family calls junk. When father needs fireplace wood, Eddie hauls home an old telegraph pole, and as a reward acquires Grandpop's old desk, which he adds to his already rich collection of valuable refuse. He kindheartedly tries to find homes for the cats which trail him home from the fishstore and discovers to his joy that there is a reward of twenty-five dollars for the tortoise shell one. Betsy, his playmate and schoolmate, who always sticks up for him, joins him in striking against his brothers' baseball team, the Woodpeckers, who insist that the two are too young for the team. Mr. Kilpatrick, the fatherly policeman orders the Woodpeckers to let the two play, and Betsy hits a home run with the bases full to win the game. Eddie travels downtown by bus to buy cold cream for Mother and almost forgets what he came for. On the way back, he meets his namesake, who is running for mayor, and gets the idea of running for dogcatcher. When the children tease him about his ambitions, he decides to run away to Hollywood with banjo-playing Alexander Jones, for whom he will act as "hoofer." The two change their plans when they learn what fine dinners await them at home. The final episode finds Eddie visiting an antique shop with his parents. Although Father has decreed that Eddie can bring home absolutely no more junk, Eddie cannot resist buying a carriage lamp and a coffee grinder, both of which ironically so take his parents' fancy that they pay him three dollars for them. Eddie's attitudes and activities are typical of his age, and the episodes grow by accumulating complications, some of which seem strained and false, as the author strives to keep the comedy going. "Precious" comments occasionally interject a condescending note. The narrative is intended to provide light entertainment for "just readers," and stylistically is one step above the primer. Sequels; also see *"B" Is for Betsy**. Choice.

LITTLE GIRL WITH SEVEN NAMES (Hunt*, Mabel Leigh, ill. Grace Paull, Lippincott, 1936), short, realistic story of family life set in an Amish farming community somewhere in the United States at an undisclosed time. Melissa Louisa Amanda Miranda Cynthia Jane Farlow is pleased that she has been named after her two lively and loving grandmothers, her mother's pretty twin sisters, and her father's two sturdy sisters. She enjoys having Uncle Mark joke about her long name, as he often does in his gentle, affectionate way. But when she starts country school and the children tease her about how many names she has, she thinks it would be nice to get rid of some of them. She decides to offer two names, Cynthia and Jane, to the new baby of the young couple on the farm down the road, Susan and Dan Wheeler, and is very disappointed when the baby turns out to be a boy. Just before Melissa Louisa's second school year begins, Mama gives birth to twins. Melissa Louisa decides that the poetic names, Amanda and Miranda, would be more appropriate for her pretty, new twin sisters, and her parents agree. No longer is Melissa Louisa teased about her many names. This pleasant period story for little girls has easy vocabulary and gives some sense of Amish life. Melissa Louisa is a charming and resourceful protagonist, secure in the love of her family and the adults around her. Her feelings and ways seem accurately presented. Some black and white illustrations follow the story. Fanfare.

LITTLE HOUSE IN THE BIG WOODS (Wilder*, Laura Ingalls, ill. Helen Sewell, Harper, 1932), first of seven autobiographical, mostly episodic novels about the author's childhood in frontier America (*Little House on the Prairie**; *On the Banks of Plum Creek**; *On the Shores of Silver Lake**; *The Long Winter**; *Little Town on the Prairie**; *These Happy Golden Years**), this one set near Lake Pepin on the Mississippi in the western edge of Wisconsin about 1872. The point of view is consistently that of Laura* Ingalls, who has her fifth birthday in the winter in the isolated log house where she lives with her Ma, Caroline*, her Pa, Charles*, her sister Mary*, who is one year older than she, Baby Carrie*, and Jack, the brindle bulldog. Details of everyday life are meticulously recorded, with all the excitement and fascination they had for a perceptive child. They prepare food for winter, smoking wild game and butchering the hog, salting down fish, storing away pumpkins, squash, peppers, and herbs. The girls help Pa clean his rifle and make bullets and later help Ma make cheese. At Christmas an aunt and uncle and three cousins come for the holiday. The children make "pictures" by falling in the snow, and from Santa Laura gets a rag doll which she names Charlotte. During the long winter evenings Pa plays his fiddle and sings, and he tells them stories about Grandpa's narrow escape from a panther, about Pa as a boy being caught in the woods at night when he should have been bringing home the cows and how a screech owl scared him; of how Grandpa and his brothers broke the Sabbath by sneaking a ride on their new sled and were betrayed by the squealing of a pig which they hit and carried down the hill with them. Pa takes the furs he has trapped to town and is frightened to meet a bear on his way home, only to discover it is just a burnt stump. While he is gone, Ma and Laura go out to milk and meet a real bear, which Ma calmly slaps thinking it is Sukey. A late "sugar snow" is the occasion for a party and dance at Grandpa's, where they all have maple sugar candy, Laura meets a cousin also named Laura Ingalls, and she becomes fond of her wild Uncle George, who is outjigged by Grandma. In the spring they go into Pepin, the first town the girls have ever seen, where the storekeeper gives them each a candy heart and Laura collects so many pebbles on the beach that she rips out her pocket. When the girls quarrel about whether Mary's golden hair or Laura's brown hair is prettier and Laura slaps Mary, Pa whips her with a strap, then comforts her by pointing out that his hair is brown, too. At oat harvest, when Pa is helping Uncle Henry, their cousin Charley, 11, is lazy and troublesome and keeps distracting the men from work by screaming for help as a joke until they ignore him and discover he is terribly stung by hornets. For the wheat harvest, Pa hires a "separator," an early threshing machine with its crew that fascinates Laura and gets the work done in a fraction of the usual time. As winter approaches again, Pa goes out at night to hunt and later tells the girls how he watched deer and bear in the moonlight and found them too beautiful to shoot. The book gives a remarkably clear picture of how pioneers coped with the problems of daily living and how children were raised in a careful family. It also introduces bright, independent Laura and shows how her natural spirit vies with the conventions of what a proper little girl should do and how she is supported by a loving family. A later edition of all the books of the series is illustrated by Garth Williams. Books Too Good; ChLA Top 10; ChLA Touchstones; Choice; Lewis Carroll.

LITTLE HOUSE ON THE PRAIRIE (Wilder*, Laura Ingalls, ill. Helen Sewell, Harper, 1935), second in a series of seven autobiographical novels (*Little House in the Big Woods**; *On the Banks of Plum Creek**; *On the Shores of Silver Lake**; *The Long Winter**; *Little Town on the Prairie**; *These Happy Golden Years**), this one chronicling the Ingalls family's trip to Kansas and their year there. Restless because the Wisconsin big woods are filling up with settlers and game is scarce, Pa (Charles* Ingalls) loads Laura*, 6 or 7, Mary*, 7 or 8, Ma, (Caroline*) and baby Carrie* into a covered wagon, relatives come to say good-bye, and they cross the Mississippi at Lake Pepin just before the ice breaks in the early spring. On the long trip to Indian territory, which Pa has learned will be open for settlement, they camp each night. At one creek ford the water rises suddenly, Pa must jump out and swim at the heads of Pet and Patty, the mustang horses, and Jack the bulldog is swept downstream. That night, Pa almost shoots an animal approaching the camp, only to discover that it is Jack, muddy and weary but alive. Near the Verdrigris River they choose a site, on the high prairie but close enough to a creek to get logs, water, and game. Pa starts to build a cabin, and Ma helps until her ankle is sprained when a log rolls on it. A bachelor neighbor, Mr*. Edwards, who is settling two miles away, agrees to trade work, and the log house goes up quickly, followed by a stable. Laura helps as Pa makes doors and a fireplace, puts on a roof and a puncheon floor, and chinks the cracks between the logs. Another neighbor, Mr. Scott, helps Pa dig a well and is almost overcome by gas when he fails to send down a candle first, a precaution Pa always observes. Pa helps with a cattle drive going north to Fort Dodge and gets a longhorn cow and her new calf as well as some beef. The whole family comes down with malaria, "fever 'n' ague," and Laura, too weak to stand, crawls across the floor holding on to Jack to get water for Mary. A black doctor, Dr. Tan, who has been with the army, happens by, gives them quinine, nurses them, and alerts Mrs. Scott, who helps them until they can cope alone and assures them that the illness comes from eating watermelons. At Christmas time, Mr. Edwards goes to Independence, forty miles away, and swims the swollen creek to bring presents of tin cups and cakes and Christmas candy to Laura and Mary, gifts he says came from Santa Claus, for whom he was delivering them. Twice, fire threatens. When the stick and daub chimney catches fire, Laura saves Mary and Carrie by pulling the rocker where they sit back from the fireplace and throwing back the burning sticks which fall on the floor. In the spring, fire sweeps the prairie, but Pa plows a fire break and starts a back fire, and it misses the house. Indians scare them repeatedly. While Pa is gone, two Indians wearing fresh skunk skins come, insist that Ma make them cornbread, and take all Pa's pipe tobacco. Indians camp nearby, and later Laura and Mary find beads there, which Mary gives to Carrie, and Laura resentfully must follow suit. A tall, dignified Indian, whom they afterwards learn is the Osage chief, Soldat du Chêne, calls and tries to talk French to Pa. Later two Indians try to steal all the skins Pa is saving to trade for a plow and seeds. The biggest threat is the Indian jamboree that lasts for days, close enough so they can hear the songs and drums and eventually the war cries. Finally the Indians, thousands of them, leave, and Pa learns that du Chêne has prevented a massacre of the white settlers advocated by some of the tribes. As they go, Laura sees a papoose she wants to keep, more than anything she has coveted, more even than the marvelous Indian ponies she admires. Scott and Edwards bring word that soldiers are coming to drive settlers off the Indian territory, and Pa furiously decides to leave. They load what they can into the covered wagon again, leaving behind the new garden and crops, the little house with its glass windows which Pa brought all the way from Independence, and a whole year's hard labor. Since the story is told from Laura's point of view, this is not a tragedy, because the family is together and there is excitement in traveling. The year on the prairie gives this book more unity and form than some of the others in the series, but its strengths are the same, fascinating details of everyday life and a warm sense of family love. A later edition is illustrated by Garth Williams. ChLA Top 10; ChLA Touchstones; Choice.

LITTLE HOUSES FAR AWAY (Bianco*, Pamela, ill. author, Oxford, 1951), fantasy for young children set in modern times. Mark, 6, and his little sister Paula, almost five, are on a seven-hour train trip alone between their home of Laurelton and Magnolia, where their cousins live. Paula, who has never been on a train before, thinks the houses and people which look so small must be dolls and doll houses and won't believe Mark when he tries to explain about perspective. When Mark falls asleep, she gets off at the next station to investigate, and the train leaves without her. She meets a little girl, Jennifer, who seems to have been expecting her and who takes her to a strange house looking normal in the front but without any walls in the back. There she meets two more girls, Lavinia and Lucinda Lee, and realizes they are all dolls. They have a pretend tea and, refusing to listen to her story about having to get to Magnolia, take her up their ladder to bed. In the middle of the night, when the real visitor they were expecting shows up, Paula's doll Belinda, the dolls turn Paula out. On the hillside she meets Gabriel Robin, who gives her some real food and introduces her to Only Velvet, a musician doll who gets her an invitation to the ball to be given that evening by Miss Edwina Snow, an aristocratic wax doll. After the ball, Edwina sends Paula off to Magnolia in her coach, but they meet other dolls fleeing in terror from the wild bears, and the coachman joins those running away. Paula takes the lantern and wanders up the hill, eventually coming upon a cave where she finds Mark, who also left the train when he found her missing and has been hunting for her. They are surprised there by the bears, who turn out to be plush teddy bears. After a feast of raspberry wine, cake, cookies, and lollipops, the bears take them to the station where they catch the same train they were on originally. They decide not to tell their adventure to their cousins, who might think they had just made it up, or perhaps to tell them but pretend they had dreamed it. The story is consciously cute, coy, and without any tension in the plot. Dialogue is stiff and unlikely, characters are undeveloped and even the fantasy is inconsistent: dolls pretend to eat, but teddy bears eat real food, for instance. It is hard to imagine that a child of 1951 would not have traveled by car enough to understand that houses and people at a distance look small. Fanfare.

LITTLE NAVAJO BLUEBIRD (Clark*, Ann Nolan, ill. Paul Lantz, Viking, 1943), realistic novel of Navajo family life set in Arizona in the mid-1900s. The loosely plotted story follows one year in the life of little Doli, the Bluebird, almost six when the story begins, in which she comes to see that attending Boarding School will offer her important advantages. At first, Doli finds completely satisfying her life in the family hogan. She enjoys the family's occasional trips to the Trading Post to sell her mother's blankets and her father's silverwork, her father's songs in the evening, the frequent visits of Uncle, her mother's dashing and fun-loving brother, and herding sheep with Hobah, her big sister, who tells her stories about the gods. The decision of Big Brother to live like the whites pains her parents and strengthens Doli's resolve never to leave home. Certain events, however, help her to see the benefits of an education. Hobah very much wishes to attend school, and her parents decide to let her go. Uncle's Wife, who has been to school, has gained valuable skills: to sew with a machine and to care for the ill. Her ability to write even saves their lives when they are marooned in the mountains by a sudden, deep snow. When Doli meets the gods for the first time in the Night Chant coming-of-age ceremony, she gains the confidence to go to school when her time comes. Sentences are short and language easy. The loose, contrived plot moves without surprises to its expected conclusion. It serves as a device by which the author can present details of daily life among the Navajos as the seasons change. The sense of family comes through strongly, Doli changes believably, and Uncle and Trader are genial and likeable, but Uncle's Wife is too obviously a role model. The book's claim to memorability lies in its graphic picture of Navajo life, customs, and beliefs intended for the young. Verses from chants, stories about and many allusions to the gods, and descriptions of such activities as peach picking in Canyon de Chelly, the Sing for Hobah, the Night Chant for Doli, gathering pinon nuts in the mountains, weaving, silverworking, sheepherding, and games come together for a vivid depiction of Navajo life. Choice; Fanfare.

THE LITTLE OLD WOMAN WHO USED HER HEAD (Newell*, Hope, ill. Margaret Ruse, Nelson, 1935), story patterned on the droll, or simpleton folktale, with unspecified time and place. The little old woman meets a series of problems by tying a wet towel around her forehead and sitting with her eyes shut and her forefinger against her nose until a solution comes to her. In each case it is a ridiculous solution, but she is very pleased with herself. Because her blanket is wearing thin, she buys a dozen geese, but when she plucks them to make a feather bed, they are cold, so she cuts up the blanket to make them coats. When the new apron she has made is too short, she cuts a piece from the upper edge to make a ruffle on the bottom. When she wears her magnifying glasses, the meal she has prepared looks adequate, but when she removes the glasses she can scarcely find the food, so she puts the glasses back on to be sure she will have enough to satisfy her appetite. Although the book is divided into chapters, it is essentially an extended tale. There are more incidents than in a typical folktale, however, and there is more sense of contrivance by the author. The style is extremely simple, obviously designed for young children to read to themselves. Fanfare.

LITTLE PEAR (Lattimore*, Eleanor Frances, ill. author, Harcourt, 1931), realistic, episodic novel of family and community life set in China at an unspecified time but probably in the early years of the twentieth century. Spunky, adventurous, naughty Little Pear, 5, lives with his father, a farmer, his mother, and his two older sisters, Dagu and Ergu, in a small, pleasant house on the outskirts of a village not far from a large walled city. There is no clear plot problem to unify the book. Each chapter presents a separate adventure and is told from the viewpoint of but not by Little Pear. After big boys drive Little Pear away from the pond on which he has been sliding, he sets out on foot for the great walled city. A tall, thin, kind man gives him a ride on his shoulders, and Little Pear enjoys the exciting sights and the supper of dumplings the man buys him. He gets a cart ride back to the village, where his worried family welcomes him home. Later, Little Pear spends the four pennies his mother has given him on tang-hulur (candy), which he shares with his friend, Big Head, who in return shares his top with Little Pear. At New Year's, Little Pear sets off one of the firecracker man's firecrackers burning a hole in his handsome, brand-new, purple jacket, and is rescued by Ergu, when the wind threatens to carry him away while he is flying his new dragon-kite. In the spring, he and Big Head sail boats on an irrigation canal, and Little Pear eats green peaches, which give him bad dreams. He takes pity on the family canary and releases the bird from his cage and stows away in his father's wheelbarrow when his father takes his vegetables to market at the fair. In midsummer, Little Pear watches the boats sailing by on the river, falls in, and is rescued by a friendly houseboat man. Little Pear resolves to be good henceforth. The story seems intended to show how children are alike even though their circumstances may differ. Little Pear is a charming, strongly drawn character, his attitudes and activities typical of any lively child his age. Chinese family and village life seem idealized, and nobody has any problems that persist. Little Pear's parents are extremely indulgent, and his relations with his sisters seems consistently good-humored. Details are sufficient to make the setting and incidents vivid and distinct, and the reader gets some idea of the China of the period. The style is simple, with easy vocabulary and short, uncomplicated sentences that are within the reach of beginning readers. Books Too Good.

LITTLE PRINCESS (Burnett*, Frances Hodgson, Scribner's, 1905), realistic novel set in London in the late nineteenth century, a longer version of *Sara Crewe*, which was first published in 1887 in *St. Nicholas* magazine and turned into a play in 1902. At seven, Sara Crewe is brought from India by her doting father to Miss Minchin's* Select Seminary for Young Ladies, where she becomes a favored pupil because of her father's wealth. Despite the attention lavished upon her, she remains an unspoiled child, serious and intelligent, and is particularly loved by fat, simple Ermengarde St. John and four-year-old Lottie Legh, the youngest pupil, whom she is able to manage when severe Miss Minchin and her subservient sister, Amelia, are unable to. Her greatest admirer is Becky, the abused servant girl, to whom she kindly tells stories. Jealous Lavinia and her friend, Jessie, spitefully nickname her "the princess," but Sara calmly admits that she often imagines herself a princess and tries to act like one. During Sara's eleventh birthday celebration, word comes that Sara's father, who has invested all his money in diamond mines, has died when the mines failed, and Miss Minchin immediately demotes Sara to the role of a drudge who sleeps in an attic room next to Becky's. Sara endures her new hardships bravely, pretending she is a prisoner in the Bastille, and even making friends with a rat whom she calls Melchisedec. Into the house next door moves a gentleman from India and his Laskar servant, Ram Dass, whom Sara meets when the servant's monkey escapes across the roof into Sara's room and the Laskar follows to retrieve him. Unknown to Sara, the gentleman, Mr. Carrisford, is the diamond mine partner of her father, and, feeling guilty of causing his death, has been seeking her now that the fortune has been recovered. Because he has been ill and depressed, Ram Dass tells him about Sara's room and the stories he has overheard her telling Becky and Ermengarde. Together they contrive a surprise of transforming her room with a fire, warm blankets, and beautiful hangings, which Ram Dass carries across the roof and arranges while she sleeps on a particularly bleak night when Miss Minchin has discovered Becky and Ermengarde in her room and deprived her of food as punishment. She is also sent warm clothing, anonymously, and, sustained by the good food which appears in her room, she seems to blossom, a fact which worries Miss Minchin into treating her better. When she calls at the house next door to return the monkey, which has escaped to her room again, the whole story comes out, she is adopted by Mr. Carrisford, and she leaves the school, taking Becky to be her personal servant. Although the story is frankly sentimental and Sara's rescue comes about by an amazing coincidence, the book has the appeal of a Cinderella tale. While Miss Minchin's snobbery is condemned, the accepted class consciousness of Sara's patronizing attitude toward Becky may be offensive to modern readers. Lewis Carroll.

THE LITTLE SILVER HOUSE (Lindquist*, Jennie D., ill. Garth Williams, Harper, 1959), sequel to *The Golden Name Day** set in New England in the early twentieth century. During her year with her foster grandparents, the Bensons, Nancy Bruce, 9, meets the Bensons' childhood friends, Aunt Hanna and

Uncle George, when they visit. In talking over old times, Uncle George mentions a boarded-up house where they used to picnic, and takes Nancy, the three Carlson girls (the Bensons' grandchildren), and their crippled friend, Alex, on a wagon ride to see it in the moonlight, when it looks silver to the children. They learn that because of provisions of a will, it is maintained by a neighbor, Mr. Taylor, but it cannot be sold or rented except in the original owner's family. This happens at the first of the "topsy-turvy weeks," two weeks when a fire has closed the school and other events occur in unusual ways. They have a breakfast picnic at the farm, and they all go visiting different places: Alex to his grandmother's, Sigrid with Aunt Hanna to see Grandmother Carlson, Helga with her mother to visit an aunt, and Nancy and Elsa to spend a week on the farm with Aunt Martha. While there they hitch Whoa-Emma, the horse, to the buggy and drive to see the silver house again, catching a glimpse of a boy; another time they decide to plant bulbs near the house as the children do in Ewing's *Mary's Meadow*, and on this trip they meet the boy, Ben Emmons, who lives with the Taylors and is homesick for his old life in the city. Another day they are invited to see the inside of the house when Mr. Taylor airs it. They discover a portrait of a little girl which whets their interest. At the farm they make butternut fudge and are amazed when Cuckoo Clock, the kitten, learns to ring the doorbell to be let in. Most of the rest of the book is about preparations for and celebration of the Long Swedish Christmas: they each choose a special guest for one of the Sundays of Advent; they take Ben into their club, the Crimson Ramblers, and prepare gifts for his grandmother in a nursing home and for Ben's friend, a crippled boy in the city; they wrap "karamell," candies in fancy paper, for guests; they celebrate Lucia Day, with Grandma serving morning coffee as she wears a crown of candles. Mr. Sanborn, an educated neighbor who is Elsa's special guest, becomes interested in the silver house and learns that the owner had a daughter, Mariette, who died at ten, perhaps the child in the portrait. On Christmas Eve, Helga's special guest, the baby John August, leads the Long Dance, carried by his father. On *Annandag Jul*, the Second Christmas Day or the day after Christmas, they go in the sleigh to the little silver house where Ben and the Taylors have a surprise, a Christmas tree, and Grandpa has the news that Uncle George has bought the house, finding that it was no longer held by the will when all members of the original family are dead. Moreover, he has rented it to Nancy's parents so her mother can recuperate there when she leaves the hospital and Nancy can stay close to her friends. The plot has somewhat more unity than its predecessor, with the little house a stronger focus than the name-day issue, but the resolution is also more unlikely. Swedish customs are the most memorable parts of the story. Fanfare.

LITTLE TOWN ON THE PRAIRIE (Wilder*, Laura Ingalls, ill. Helen Sewell and Mildred Boyle, Harper, 1941), sixth in a series of seven autobiographical novels (*Little House in the Big Woods**; *Little House on the Prairie**; *On the Banks of Plum Creek**; *On the Shores of Silver Lake**; *The Long Winter**; *These*

*Happy Golden Years**), this one set in the frontier town of De Smet, S.Dak., in the years 1881-1882. Starting in the summer after the "long winter," Laura* Ingalls, now fourteen, takes a job sewing shirts at the dry goods store, though she dislikes sewing. She earns nine dollars to put with the savings for college for her blind sister, Mary*. She and her younger sister, Carrie*, go with Pa (Charles* Ingalls) to the Fourth of July celebration and see Almanzo* Wilder win the buggy race with his matched Morgan team, even pulling the heavy peddler's wagon. Although the black birds eat the oats and corn crops (and Ma, Caroline* Ingalls, makes blackbird pie), Pa sells a heifer so Mary can start college. While Pa and Ma take her to school in Iowa, Laura and Carrie take care of the youngest sister, Grace*, and do all the fall housecleaning. Back in town for the winter, they find problems and pleasures. School is taught by Eliza* Jane Wilder, bossy sister of Almanzo and Royal*, and Nellie* Oleson, whom Laura knew at Plum Creek, turns Miss Wilder against the Ingalls girls. When Carrie is punished for absentmindedly rocking the desk by having to continue rocking it, Laura jumps to assist her so vigorously that they are both sent home from school. The other pupils resent the unfairness and act up until Miss Wilder has no control. Pa and the other school board members visit, listen to her complaints which are mostly against Laura, then lay down the law to the students. Laura covets the pretty, flowered name cards that all the girls are getting to exchange, but she is surprised when Pa gives her twenty-five cents to get some. The day she picks them up Almanzo stops to give her a ride in his new buggy, and she shyly exchanges a name card with him, mostly thrilled because Nellie is so jealous that Laura has ridden behind the beautiful Morgans. Laura and Mary Power attend a church sociable, which they find dull, Ben Woodworth's birthday party, which is thrilling, a New England supper at Thanksgiving, where Laura and Ida Brown, the minister's adopted daughter, wash dishes all evening, and a whole series of "literaries," promoted mostly by Pa and the new schoolteacher, Mr. Clewett. These include a spelling bee, where Laura stands up to the end, a wax works imitation, charades, musical evenings, and end with a minstrel show in which Pa is the darky rattling the bones. After they move back to the claim in April, they have their first real blizzard of the winter. Laura studies all summer, determined to be ready by the next spring to get a teaching certificate so that she can help put Mary through college. Back in town in the fall, she is astonished when Almanzo sees her home every night from the week-long revival meeting. Before Christmas she takes the leading part in the School Exhibition, reciting from memory the first half of American history, with Ida taking the second half. Almanzo once again sees her home and asks if she would like to go sleigh riding if he makes a cutter for his horse to pull. Her performance impresses a Mr. Brewster, who has come to hire a teacher for his new little school twelve miles south of town. The county superintendent gives Laura an informal examination at home and a "third grade" certificate, and she is ready to teach school at fifteen. Though the book has less internal unity, it is a happier story than its immediate predecessor, with the good times that the townspeople make for themselves and the beginnings of a romance with Almanzo. With Mary gone, Carrie becomes a more important character, a frail child for whom Laura feels responsible and protective. A later edition is illustrated by Garth Williams. ChLA Touchstones; Choice; Newbery Honor.

LITTLE WOMEN (Alcott*, Louisa May, Roberts, 1868), warm family story, opening in the Boston area, presumably Concord, during the Civil War. The four March girls—Meg*, 16, Jo*, 15, Beth*, 13, and Amy*, 12—live with their mother, ''Marmee,'' in genteel poverty with only one servant, an old Irish retainer, Hannah, while their father serves as chaplain with the Union forces. Pretty Meg longs for nice clothes and the leisure wealth could give; tomboyish Jo wants to write and win fame; gentle Beth is musical and shy; artistic Amy is somewhat spoiled and wishes to be elegant. Part I starts with Christmas, for which all four girls spend their meager funds on presents for Marmee and take their breakfast to a poor immigrant family, the Hummels. Among the best-known episodes is the party Meg and Jo attend at which Jo must keep her back to the wall because she has scorched her only good dress by standing too close to the fire. Escaping a boy who is about to ask her to dance, she ducks into a curtained recess and finds a boy she already knows to be Theodore Laurence, ''Laurie*,'' the grandson of their wealthy next door neighbor, and they strike up a real friendship. Meg and Jo both work, Meg as a governess, Jo as a companion to crochety Aunt March. Beth stays home and helps Hannah. Amy goes to school until she is disciplined for having a treat of pickled limes in her desk, and then her mother allows her to study at home. Angry at Jo for not letting her go to the theater when Laurie is taking the older girls, Amy burns the manuscript of the book Jo has been writing. In retaliation Jo pays no attention to her little sister when she follows her and Laurie skating, and Jo is all contrition when Amy falls through thin ice and nearly drowns. When news comes that Father is ill, Marmee sets off, accompanied by John Brooke, Laurie's tutor, who is sent on ''business'' by old Mr. Laurence. Jo sells her one beauty, her long auburn hair, to provide money for Father's needs. While Marmee is gone, Beth visits the Hummels, is holding the Hummel baby when it dies of scarlet fever, and contracts the disease herself. Not wishing to worry Marmee, the girls and Hannah care for her, but as she gets worse they finally send for their mother. Before she arrives, Beth's fever breaks. On Christmas day, Father returns, accompanied by John. Having received her parents' permission to speak, he asks Meg to marry him. Although she intends to refuse, when they are interrupted by Aunt March who forbids Meg to become engaged to a poor man, she defends John and agrees to marry him after he has made a start in the world. Part II, known in England as *Good Wives*, starts three years later with Meg's wedding and details some of her difficulties as a young wife and, eventually, mother, for she has twins known as Daisy and Demi. Their aunt asks Amy to go to Europe instead of Jo, who had been promised the trip, and Amy thrives in the elegant and artistic atmosphere. Jo, having begun to sell some stories and thinking that Beth is in love with Laurie, gets out of the way by going to New York to write and to work as a governess for a rooming house proprietor's children. There she meets a poor but distinguished German professor, Frederick Bhaer, 40, who becomes much interested in her. When she goes home, Laurie proposes to Jo, she refuses, and, brokenhearted, he goes to Europe with his grandfather. Beth, who has never fully recovered her health, gradually loses strength and dies. Laurie, who has already seen something of Amy in Europe, goes to comfort her, falls in love with her, and they return together married. Professor Bhaer visits, Jo sees that they are ideally suited, they marry and, when Aunt March dies and leaves her large house, Plumfield, to Jo, they start a school for boys there. Although by modern standards there are many preachy passages and some sentimental touches, the book remains a favorite mainly because of its strong, natural characterization, particularly of Jo. Except for Beth's death, the most memorable scenes occur in Part I. Essentially plotless, the various episodes are held together by the girls' growing up and conquering their faults or ''burdens'' as they call them, referring to their early game of playing *Pilgrim's Progress*. Sequels. Books Too Good; Children's Classics; ChLA Top 10; ChLA Touchstones; Choice; Lewis Carroll.

LOFTING, HUGH (JOHN) (1886-1947), born in Maidenhead, Berkshire, England; creator of the remarkable Doctor Dolittle, who can understand and talk with animals. He attended St. Mary's College, Chesterfield, Derbyshire, and Massachusetts Institute of Technology, Cambridge, Mass., and London Polytechnic, studying engineering. He was a prospector and surveyor in Canada and a civil engineer on the Lagos Railway in West Africa, but he was not happy as an engineer and settled in the United States in 1912, working with the British Ministry of Information in New York City. In World War I he served with the Irish Guards in Flanders, and it was while in the trenches in France that he started the stories of Doctor Dolittle, illustrated with drawings, in letters to his children. Wounded and invalided out of the army, he returned to the United States and from 1923 on was a professional writer, publishing seventeen books of fiction, fourteen of them about Doctor Dolittle, and one book of verse, *Porridge Poetry: Cooked, Ornamented and Served by Hugh Lofting* (Stokes, 1924). His first book, *The Story of Doctor Dolittle** (Lippincott, 1920), tells how the gentle, matter-of-fact little doctor turns from human to animal practice, tutored by his parrot, Polynesia. *The Voyages of Doctor Dolittle** (Lippincott, 1922) intoduces Tommy Stubbins, the little boy who becomes his assistant and accompanies him on expeditions to outlandish and marvelous places, all told in the same straight-faced, unsensational style. Ten other Doctor Dolittle books followed. For the rest of his life, Lofting lived in the United States, and his books were all published first in this country.

LONDON, JACK (JOHN GRIFFITH) (1876-1916), born in San Francisco, originally named Chaney but took the name of his stepfather; novelist, short story writer, political essayist. He attended public school until he was fourteen, returned for a year at nineteen, entered the University of California but for financial reasons left after one semester. For several years he drifted, working at a variety of laboring jobs and as a seaman, until in 1897 he went to the Klondike with the gold seekers. After that experience he began writing seriously and during the Russo-Japanese War was a journalist and war reporter. He is credited with helping change American literary taste from Victorian propriety to a more rough and masculine style. For young people it is his dog stories that have been perennially popular, particularly *The Call of the Wild** (Macmillan, 1903) and *White Fang* (Macmillan, 1905).

THE LONE HUNT (Steele*, William O., ill. Paul Galdone, Harcourt, 1956), realistic novel set in the Cumberland Mountains of Tennessee about 1810. Yancy Caywood, 11, envies his brother Pleasant, 16, even though Pleas has worked hard for three years to take the place of their dead father on the frontier farm. When farm work is done, Pleasant can go hunting while Yancy must stay home to help his mother, doing what he considers girls' work since his sister Miriam has married and his grandfather is crippled with rheumatism. A quilting bee gives Yancy a chance to go off hunting with his dog, Blue, and they come upon some strange tracks and places where heavy, black hair has been rubbed off on trees. Although buffalo have been killed or driven west years before, he suspects that one is in the area. Yancy is determined to sneak off as soon as Pleasant returns from a hunting trip, but Pleas brings the news that someone else has spotted the buffalo and a group of men are setting off to hunt it. To Yancy's delight, Pleas persuades their mother to let the boy go along. The first night out Blue saves Yancy by attacking a bear wakened from hibernation. The next day the large group thins to nine men and Yance, and later, as it begins to snow, they decide to turn back. When Pleas turns off with one of them on a short cut to the man's cabin, where Pleas has some buisness, Yancy obediently goes off toward home with the other men, then makes an excuse to follow his brother, and with Blue turns back toward the buffalo tracks. The next day he continues to follow the beast, though he has nothing to eat. When he spots a deer, he thinks his problem is solved until he discovers he has lost all but two of his bullets. Torn between his hunger and his need to save his shot for the buffalo, he manages with Blue's help to kill the deer with his knife. He builds a shelter and is cooking the meat when an Indian appears, pointing a rifle at his chest. Though he fears this is a renegade one of the men mentioned is being hunted, Yancy offers him some meat, and they spend the night together. The next day Yancy continues after the buffalo, spots it, stalks it, and shoots. As the huge animal charges, Blue distracts it, and the two together crash onto thin ice of a stream. The buffalo scrambles out, and Yancy kills it with his last ball, then realizes that Blue has gone under the ice and drowned. Yancy's grief is interrupted by the Indian, who skins and butchers the buffalo and suggests that he sit with it while the boy goes for help to haul the meat home. A short distance away Yancy meets Pleasant and two other men on horseback, hunting for him. They find that the Indian, with a good deal of the buffalo meat, is gone, but there is plenty left for a big feast at home. Yancy's pleasure is tempered by his grief for Blue, but he finds a new, better relationship with his mother, and Pleas trades skins for a new puppy. Details of the tracking, the cold, the boy's longing to hunt, and his grief for his dog are convincing. The attack by the bear is an unnecessary addition, and the killing of the deer by knife strains credulity. Characters are adequate for their parts but not highly developed. Choice; Fanfare.

LONESOME TILLY (*Tree of Freedom**), generous, shy recluse who helps to drive Adam Frohawk from the Venable claim by frightening him with a copperhead snake.

THE LONG WINTER (Wilder*, Laura Ingalls, ill. Helen Sewell and Mildred Boyle, Harper, 1940), fifth in a series of seven autobiographical novels (*Little House in the Big Woods**; *Little House on the Prairie**; *On the Banks of Plum Creek**; *On the Shores of Silver Lake**; *Little Town on the Prairie**; *These Happy Golden Years**), this one set in De Smet, S.Dak., during the winter of 1880-1881. On the homestead about a mile from town, Laura* Ingalls, now 13 1/2, helps Pa (Charles* Ingalls) make hay and sees with him the first sign of the hard winter to come in the heavily built muskrat house. Other signs confirm Pa's suspicions, and as he hurries to cut more hay, Laura and Carrie*, her younger sister, go to town to get a replacement for a broken mower part, take a short cut through the long slough grass, get lost, and come out upon two young men cutting hay, the Wilder boys, Almanzo* and Royal*, who give them directions. As they hurry to get in their meagre crops off newly broken sod, Ma (Caroline* Ingalls) invents a green pumpkin pie. An October blizzard catches them in the thinly built shanty, a storm so bad that it freezes the cattle's heads to the ground with their own breath. In the store in town, an old Indian warns the settlers that there will be seven months of bad weather. Pa moves the family into his empty store building in town, and Laura, with Carrie, starts school where she meets Mary Power, who becomes her best friend, and lively, good-natured Cap Garland, as well as other young people. When the next blizzard hits, the teacher hesitates to dismiss school until a man comes from town to lead the children, and then, blinded by the whirling snow, they almost miss the town. That blizzard starts a series of storms that block the railroad, close the school, and isolate the family even from their neighbors across Main Street. Pa, with the other town men, takes a railroad handcar to Volga to help dig out the track at the cut, but the next blizzard blows the cut full again. Laura studies at home with Mary*, reading the lessons aloud to her blind sister. At Christmas Laura and Carrie buy Pa a pair of blue suspenders decorated with red flowers for twenty-five cents, and Pa has earlier bought and saved Christmas candy, but the rest of the gifts are homemade, since the trains have not been able to supply the stores. As winter continues, they run out of coal and burn slough hay, twisted onerously into sticks. Since there is no flour, they grind wheat in the coffee mill, a job that takes most of the day for enough to make one loaf. When the kerosene is gone, Ma makes a button-lamp in a saucer of axle grease. The town's one chance to get meat, when an antelope herd is sighted, is destroyed when one of the men gets excited and fires too soon. He is riding Almanzo Wilder's horse, Lady, which runs off with the antelope but Almanzo finds and retrieves her. When the family runs out of wheat, Pa takes a bucket to Royal Wilder's store, removes a plug from a knot hole, and lets the seed wheat that Almanzo has hidden in a bin between the walls run and fill the bucket, which he then insists on paying for. Alarmed to realize that people in town are that close to starvation, Almanzo and Cap decide to make a trip south of town where a homesteader is rumored to have harvested and stored a crop of wheat. Between blizzards, they start across the prairie swept clean of landmarks, a terrible trip as their horses keep plunging into hollows invisible from above and having to be unhitched, led out, and rehitched to their wagons. Almost by accident they sight smoke and find the homestead cabin, practically buried in the drifts. Then the homesteader refuses to sell until they offer him a price he can't pass up. On the way home, the boys run into another blizzard and almost miss the town. Ironically, the storekeeper who financed the purchase wants to more than double the price until Pa, leading the angry men of the town, points out that the store will depend on their good will later, and he gives in. The train comes through, finally, the first of May—with a load of telegraph poles and farm machinery! The station-master gives out some supplies from the emigrant car, however, and the next day the supply train comes in, bringing their Christmas barrel from the church congregation in the East, including a turkey frozen solid. The Boasts come in from their homestead to a Christmas dinner in May. More unified and dramatic than any other book in the series, this is dominated by descriptions of the cold weather, the howling winds and driving sleet, and the hunger and the fear that lurks in the back of all their minds, not to be dispelled by any attempt at cheerfulness. For the first time the point of view departs from being exclusively Laura's, skipping to Pa's and Almanzo's at various points. A later edition is illustrated by Garth Williams. ChLA Touchstones; Choice; Fanfare; Newbery Honor.

LORD TIMOTHY DEXTER (*Runaway Prentice**), wealthy eccentric who styles himself a lord. An influential shipbuilder, he lives on the large estate next door to the Arminters. It has deep orchards and broad lawns which he decorates with statues of figures important in early American history. He keeps a poet laureate, Jonathan Plummer, who accompanies him wherever he goes. It is on the Dexter estate that Jeff works as gardener's helper for a few days until Uncle* Hosy returns from his sailing trip. Because Lord Dexter mistakenly thinks Jeff is a thief and orders his men to fire upon him one night while Jeff is in the orchard, lawyer Minturn secures for Jeff a cash settlement, part of which Jeff uses to repay his sister, Mercy, for the loan of her butter money when he ran away from home. Lord Dexter was an actual historial figure, who seems interjected into the novel for effect.

LOST CORNER (Simon*, Charlie May, ill. Howard Simon, Dutton, 1935), realistic, mostly episodic story set in the Piney hills of the South in the 1930s. Melissa Jackson, about ten, lives in a remote area near Lost Corner with her parents, her slightly older brother, Jeb, and her younger brother, Chris. Twice a year her father takes the mule and wagon on the all-day trip to town, usually taking Jeb with him. Otherwise, their life is limited to the cabin and the nearby small fields and woods, and small events are major: a travelling photographer takes the family's picture; because the nearby school has lost its teacher, Pa gives lessons to the children and to their mother, too; they go berry-picking with Aunt Ella and her five teasing boys and make jam on the site; they pick cotton, and Jeb goes hunting. When Jeb has been exposed to measles, their mother sends Melissa and Chris to their aunt's, but they miss the bus and get lost on a short cut through the woods. They come upon Mr. Boggs, an old man living alone. He first takes them for his grandchildren, Martha and Lige, who left years before with their father. Delighted with his first company in years, he persuades them to stay instead of going on to try to find their aunt. After several days, he begins talking as if they will be with him permanently, but they see their cousin and father in the woods and discover that they are not far from their Aunt Ella's. The next trip to town, Papa punishes Jeb for disobedience by taking Melissa instead. She is amazed at the sights but passes the opportunity to see a moving picture show to go to the shooting gallery Jeb loves, where she wins a box of candy to take him. With the cotton picked, their mother sends Jeb and Melissa on the mule to take a cake to Mr. Boggs, and while they are visiting him a tornado comes and destroys his cabin, as they hide in a cave. The neighbors join together to build him a new house. On Christmas Eve the children sneak out to the barn to see the animals kneel, but Chris sneezes so they see only Sooky, the cow, on her knees. Mr. Boggs comes to spend Christmas day with them. In the spring all the Lost Creek families decide to contribute an animal each to raise money for a summer session of school. Melissa is full of guilt for not contributing her pet pig, Snoopy. When she finally decides to give up her pet, she finds that Snoopy has piglets, and she keeps one for a new pet. One day the children, hunting for the cow, are asked directions by a young couple in a car, and learn that they are Mr. Boggs's grandchildren grown up and returned. Since Papa has not been able to hire a teacher for the school, Marthy, who wants to stay with her grandfather, agrees to teach it. The mountain people are pictured almost as middle-class, suburban characters transplanted into a Southern hills setting, but there is an earnest effort at realism. If the events are not particularly exciting, neither do they greatly strain credulity. Fanfare.

LOTTIE'S VALENTINE (Eyre*, Katherine Wigmore, ill. Suzanne Suba, Oxford, 1941), brief novel set in New Orleans in the days of horse-drawn cabs, presumably in the late 1800s. Orphan Lottie, 8, has always lived at the Convent of the Good Shepherd and unlike the other girls has no relatives or friends to visit or take her into the city. One day she finds a banded pigeon injured, and, with permission of Sister Ursula she keeps it until it is well again. Jealous Terese, 10, takes an alley cat to Lottie's room, but the pigeon manages to escape to the curtain rod. Meanwhile, all is sad at the Cafe de Bon Gout, where Papa Michel Duval mourns his favorite pigeon, Coo-Coo, who has failed to return. On Valentine's Day, when Lottie makes a beautiful card and is taunted by Terese because she has no one to sent it to, she fastens it to the recovered pigeon's leg, writing on it her name, age, and address, and the request, "Please let me be your valentine." When Coo-Coo arrives home, Papa Duval is delighted, as is Mama Delphine Duval, the cook, and Jules, 12, the neighbor boy who works for them and who suggests that they should adopt Lottie. At first Papa is reluctant, but Mama Duval asserts herself and the next week, on her birthday, they take a cab to the convent and bring Lottie back to live with them. Terese gives Lottie her hat as a peace-making gift. The very simple story has many of the sentimental conventions of the late Victorian children's book—poor orphan, kindness to animals, unexpected adoption—but it also has a sort of charm that comes from its setting. Fanfare.

LOWNSBERY, ELOISE (ELLA LOUISE) (1888-), author of books for children, translator from the French, and social worker; born in Illinois, brought up in Iowa, educated at Wellesley. In 1911 she accompanied her family when they moved to California for her father's health. She was associated with the Camp Fire Girls in California and New York, went to France in 1917 with the Quakers to help with rehabilitation, and for ten years served with the Child Welfare Organization in New York. After she married Carl Stearns Clancy, who was with the Forestry Service, she made her home in Washington, D.C., but traveled extensively in Europe and the Middle East. She was a student of French history and architecture, interests which resulted in her first novel, *The Boy Knight of Reims* (Houghton, 1927), about a fourteenth-century apprentice goldsmith who works on a cathedral. She published seven more books for the young, among them the novels *Lighting the Torch* (Longmans, 1934), about Erasmus, *A Camel for a Throne* (Houghton, 1941), about a runaway Egyptian princess of about 2000 B.C., *Marta the Doll* (Longmans, 1946), a twice-reprinted book about a little Polish girl and her first doll, with a solid background in Polish farm life, and *Out of the Flame** (Longmans, 1931), about the experiences of a young page at the French court of the mid-1500s, which involves actual historical figures and events and is a Newbery honor book, and two books of biography. Critics of her time generally complained about her overplotting and praised her ability to depict setting vividly and to convey information pleasingly.

LOWREY, JANETTE SEBRING (1892-), born in Orange, Texas; teacher and author of books and short stories for children and young people. She grew up in Orange where her father was superintendent of schools. After she graduated from the University of Texas, she taught English in Texas high schools and was advertising manager of Houston Land and Trust Co. A free-lance writer after

1938, she published some dozen and a half books, among them several picture books, including the popular *The Poky Little Puppy* (Golden, 1942); novels for middle grade readers; a book of Bible stories; and a book of Greek myths retold, *In the Morning of the World* (Harper, 1944). Her first novel for older girls was *Margaret** (Harper, 1950), a Fanfare book about the experiences at home and at school of an orphaned girl who goes to live with her wealthy relatives in an East Texas town in the early 1900s. Its sequel, *Love, Bid Me Welcome* (Harper, 1964), tells how Margaret yearns to go to the University of Texas to be near her sweetheart, Michel Pujo. For younger readers are *Rings on Her Fingers* (Harper, 1941), and *Six Silver Spoons* (Harper, 1971), an I Can Read book of historical fiction.

LUCK OF THE "ROLL AND GO" (Carroll*, Ruth, and Latrobe Carroll*, ill. Ruth Carroll, Macmillan, 1935), realistic, episodic, animal novel set on the high seas and in the Antarctic in the early 1900s. A small tiger-striped kitten stows away aboard the *Roll and Go*, a ship in the harbor of Portland, Maine, loaded with a plane, various other equipment, sled dogs, and a crew bound for the South Pole. Dan, who handles the sled dogs, insists the kitten is useless and should be tossed overboard, but Terry O'Toole, kindly Irish cook, maintains he will bring good fortune and names him Luck. Except for Dan, who remains skeptical and disdainful toward him until the end of the trip, Luck becomes a shipboard favorite as he prowls the decks, adeptly scales the rigging, and suns himself on the lifeboats, growing stronger, braver, and more graceful as the ship follows its course down the Atlantic coast, through the Panama Canal, and across the Pacific to New Zealand. Although he never loses his fear of the rambunctious huskies, Luck has friendly romps with Big Boy, a mostly Newfoundland pup. He has a close call when a huge wave washes him overboard and then fortunately deposits him back on deck. In Antarctica, Luck sees killer whales and seals and has a tussle with a penguin. Although Colonel Gifford, the commander of the crew, says Luck should be left on the ship, the kitten steals a ride to Camp Challenge on Terry's shoulder. He settles in with the men for the long winter's night. In the spring he stows away again, this time on their plane, *Aurora*, for the flight over the pole to high peaks never before observed. When the motor temporarily dies and the men lighten the ship, Luck's sharp eye and flashing claws rescue valuable charts from being jettisoned along with the equipment. Luck, now a "pole cat," and the men happily break camp in the spring, return by sled to the *Roll and Go*, and head for home. On the ship, now full grown, courageous, and crafty, Luck has it out with the rats who have also stowed away on the *Roll and Go*, and with Big Boy's help chases their leader, vicious, old One Eye, overboard. Dan acknowledges he has been wrong about Luck, and both animals are honored at a farewell dinner. The Polar trip over, Luck goes to live with Terry at his cottage on Clam Cove in Maine not far from Dan's farm and Big Boy. Related in third person from the standpoint of Luck, this unsentimental story of no great moment about a kitten whose habit of stowing away brings him adventure reveals careful observation of cats and offers thrills and action in abundance for younger readers. Fanfare.

LUKE GREENMAN (*Homespun**), farm boy who longs to be a sailor. He is obligated to help his father on the family farm since he is the eldest son in the family. When Pepin Crandell moves in temporarily, Luke leaves with Dard* Rae, mixed breed, to trap west, hoping to earn enough in pelts to compensate his father for the loss of his labor. He and Dard are quite sure Catamount* has stolen Luke's pelts. Dard wishes to kill the renegade, lest he cause more trouble for them, but Luke, who is strongly ethical, cannot bring himself to sanction the act because they lack definite proof of Catamount's guilt. Later Catamount kills Luke just before he gets a glimpse of the sea for which he yearns.

LUPE ROMERO (*Blue Willow**), child of the Mexican migrants who live down the road from the Larkin family. She visits Janey* on the day the Larkins arrive, and the two girls soon become friends. She has long, dark, lustrous hair and expressive eyes. She enjoys having fun, but is also very dutiful, hardworking, and reliable about the house. She is very concerned about not hurting the feelings of others. She thinks Janey stays in the library tent at the fair because Janey does not want to admit she does not have enough money for the merry-go-round. Lupe offers Janey the brass ring she wins so Janey can ride, too. Lupe's family moves to town, at the end, where her mother opens an enchilada shop. Both Janey and Lupe now have permanent homes and can remain friends.

LYDIA GREEN (*Magic or Not?**), lively girl with long, light hair, about Laura's* age. On the train to Connecticut, she tells Laura and James* about the wishing well. Aloof and chippy, she has no friends, but Laura refuses to be put off and eventually she, James, and Lydia become fast friends. Lydia rides her horse day and night because she wants to master riding and is referred to in the community as the wild Green girl. Her grandmother, who Lydia says is a witch, is an accomplished if eccentric painter. Lydia wins a prize for the picture she enters in the local art contest, an event that moves her grandmother to pay more attention to her.

LYDIA NEWCOMER (*Rifles for Washington**), a Moravian orphan, with whom Davie McKail falls in love. Although she has always favored Davie, he thinks she and Peter Bricker are in love. She is pressured by her religious community fellows to marry a widower but holds out for Davie.

M

MAANA SHAH (*Bhimsa, the Dancing Bear**), uncle of the spoiled boy Prince*, wise, compassionate philosopher who alienated and then was deposed by his courtiers when, as previous Prince, he insisted either that everyone in his kingdom go barefoot, or that all, even peasants, be fitted with shoes so that everyone's feet would be equal. He gives Gopala and David refuge when they are pursued by the Prince and takes them to see the Haunted Village, the place destroyed by angry elephants.

MA BAXTER (*The Yearling**), Ora, large, humorless wife of little Penny* Baxter and mother of Jody*. Having lost all her children in infancy before Jody's birth, she seems to have no affection left for this late child, though sometimes her actions betray a fondness she usually hides. Her main concern is seeing that the family has enough to eat, no small task on their scrub pine farm, where mere existence requires back-breaking labor.

MACDONALD, FLORA (*Last Clash of the Claymores**; *Meggy MacIntosh**), historical Highland Scot girl who helped the Young Pretender, Bonnie Prince Charlie (Charles Stuart, grandson of James II of England) escape from Scotland after his disastrous attempt to regain the English throne in the mid-eighteenth century. Though imprisoned in England, she won the hearts of her captors as well as those of the Highland people. In later life, as wife of Kingsburgh MacDonald and mother of eight, she was, ironically, the leading figure in mustering a Highland army in North Carolina to support the British during the American Revolution, an army that failed because they were so poorly equipped and untrained to fight against the guerilla warfare of the frontier Revolutionists. A small woman with bright blue eyes, she had personal charisma as well as great bravery.

MACGREGOR, ELLEN (1906-1954), born in Baltimore, Md.; librarian and author best known for her humorous, exciting science fiction novels for later elementary readers featuring the intrepid, adventurous spinster, Miss Pickerell. The first of these, *Miss Pickerell Goes to Mars** (McGraw, 1951), a *Choice* selection, offers much the same sort of absurd logic as *The Peterkin Papers**, of which she was very fond. Based on careful research and including sound scientific information in simple, light, and easily understood language, this novel was followed by others in a similar vein, which take the dauntless lady of seven nieces and nephews into more escapades, with a Geiger counter (McGraw, 1953), undersea (McGraw, 1953), and to the Arctic (McGraw, 1954). The daughter of a physician and a librarian, whose careers influenced her own, she grew up in Wisconsin and the state of Washington. She earned her degree in library science from the University of Washington, majoring in science, and did further work in science at the University of California. She held positions as librarian in schools in Hawaii, for the Navy in Florida, and at the University of Chicago, was a researcher for Scott Foresman and Co., and at the time of her death, was research librarian for International Harvester in Chicago. Her writing career began in 1946 with a story turned in for a creative writing class at the Midwestern Writers Workshop, which was later published as a book, *Tommy and the Telephone* (Whitman, 1947). The character Miss Pickerell first appeared in a short story she published for *Liberty* magazine, ''Swept Her into Space,'' expanded later into *Miss Pickerell Goes to Mars*, one of the earliest books of science fiction for younger readers. She also published other short stories, and, after her death, her copious notes outlining further adventures for the popular character provided Dora Pantell with the material for continuing the series about the spirited lady who has attracted a wide following among middle and later elementary readers.

THE MACLAREN OF SPEY (*John Treegate's Musket**; *Peter Treegate's War†*), Scots Highlander who discovers Peter washed up on the shore of the Carolinas. He has been searching for salvage from shipwrecks when he comes upon the half-dead boy. He adopts Peter into his clan, teaches him to fight, and takes him on raids against the Indians. He is proud and stubborn and can be cruel. He hates the British to the point of foolhardiness. He feels no loyalty to the colonial cause but, rather, is motivated to fight on the side of the Continentals because he hates the British so much. His hatred goes back to the time when he lived in Scotland, where he was involved in the wars between the British and the clans. He represents an older ideology, that of loyalty to family and clan rather than country, which is presented in the novels as outmoded. He is a foil for John* Treegate, Peter's father.

MADAM (*A Lemon and a Star**; *Terrible, Horrible Edie†*; *Edie on the Warpath†*), stepmother of Ted*, Jane*, Hubert*, and Edie*, whose real name is Elsie Cares, in a series of turn-of-the-century setting, humorous family novels. Sprung on the children in the last episode of *A Lemon and a Star* with no warning (except some rumors overheard from the servants which they can scarcely believe), she wins them over with great tact and firm control of Father. Even Ted admits that she is good-looking and fashionable when she puts on a big hat, and Edie loves the way she smells of violets. Later she has two daughters, the Fair Christine (so named by Hubert when she is a squally, red infant) and Lou. In the last book she is suffering from asthma possibly brought on by nervous strain, and must spend winters in Florida.

MADAME CAPET (*The Happy Orpheline**), the eccentric old woman who almost adopts the happy orphan, Brigitte*. She believes she is rightful Queen of France because of her husband's name, and in her dilapidated apartment she sits in a gilt chair for a throne and curtseys to her confused husband. When she rides her motorized bicycle, she ignores the police and expects all other drivers to give way to her. Her only interest in adopting Brigitte is to get a girl to be maid-of-all-work.

MADAME FLATTOT (*The Happy Orpheline**, *A Brother for the Orphelines**, *A Pet for the Orphelines*†), the woman in charge of the twenty little orphan girls in a village near Paris. A maternal type, she has had no children of her own and treats the girls with affection and unconventional good sense. Her major concern is the decrepit state of their building. Although an honest person, she conspires in a little deception so that they can keep the baby boy they find in the bread basket.

MADAME MOREAU (*Heart of Danger**), owner of the Villa Rose in Nantes, the station known in the underground as Point 27, where Tod* Moran and Rudy* Behrens stay for several days on their way to Paris. She is a little old lady, aristocratic in manner, who dresses in black, uses an ebony cane, and wears jet earrings. Ostensibly a collaborator, she entertains German officers at pleasant dinners in order to pick up information for the Resistance. She helps Rudy and Tod escape from German captors in a Paris subway and later Rudy recuperates from Buchenwald at her family villa near Auvergne. She is a woman of intelligence, determination, and courage, one of the best-developed figures in the novel.

MADEMOISELLE MISFORTUNE (Brink*, Carol Ryrie, ill. Kate Seredy*, Macmillan, 1936), realistic novel of family life spiced with mild international intrigue and set in France in the 1920s in which a girl's skill at diplomacy restores the fallen fortunes of her family. In their Paris *pension*, the six Moreau girls are referred to as the six misfortunes*. Being girls, they are considered by his neighbors to be an unfortunate financial burden for their papa, a former ambassador to Peru, who has fallen on hard times. Alice*, at fourteen the eldest and a diplomat of some experience in mediating among her siblings, takes a position as traveling companion to an American woman, imperious, eccentric Miss* Hester Weatherwax, sister of a now-deceased archaeologist who made important discoveries among the Incas. During their trip to the south of France, Alice has many opportunities to exhibit her skill at resolving problems, particularly in smoothing out disagreements between Miss Weatherwax and Monsieur Huertelot, an artist whose itinerary coincides with theirs. Suspense is introduced into the story when Alice observes two dark-skinned men, possibly Peruvians, of dubious motives following Miss Weatherwax. After the travelers have settled into their apartment in Marseilles, Alice facilitates a friendship between Miss Weatherwax and Monsieur Huertelot and later secures for her brother, Edward, who has run away from home seeking independence, a position as gardener with the artist. When Papa Moreau falls ill of pneumonia, Alice returns to Paris to take charge temporarily. She learns from one of her father's visitors, a friend from better days and now Peruvian ambassador to France, that members of the notorious Peruvian Society of the Black Mask are known to be in the country. When Alice returns to Marseilles, she discovers the apartment ransacked and Miss Weatherwax missing. For complex reasons, Alice believes that Miss Weatherwax may be a prisoner in the villa next door. The police release her and apprehend her abductors, who are indeed members of the Society on a quest for information leading to the location of a long-lost Inca treasure. A careful search of a briefcase Miss Weatherwax inherited from her brother uncovers a map in his handwriting secreted in the lining, that indicates where a cache of gold lies hidden. The Peruvian ambassador puts Papa Moreau in charge of an expedition to recover the gold, and Alice effects a reconciliation between her father and Edward, who is delighted to travel to Peru as his father's assistant. Alice herself, now accustomed to independence, chooses to accompany Miss Weatherwax to the United States, pleased to have brought good, not ill, fortune to her family. Characters seem deliberately assembled, and the mystery seems melodramatic, artificial, and superfluous. Although her diplomacy is stretched to the point of tedium, Alice is likeable, staunchly independent, and ever resourceful. This chatty, lively story of virtue bringing financial reward projects an old-fashioned charm and appears intended to provide diverting and innocuous reading for girls. Fanfare.

MAGELLAN, FERDINAND (*Spice and the Devil's Cave**), historical figure presented as a bright-eyed, energetic youth fired with the zeal to explore, purely for the sake of discovering new lands. A page in service to King Manoel of Portugal, he brings news of happenings at court to his friends at Abel* Zakuto's house. He plans to go to sea as soon as his period of service is up.

MAGIC MAIZE (Buff*, Mary Marsh, and Conrad Buff*, Houghton, 1953), short, realistic novel of mid-twentieth-century rural life among the Maya Indians of Guatemala, for whom corn is the staff of life. Fabian, about twelve, is the second son in a large, poor family whose parents hold firmly to the old ways of their people. His older brother, Quin, 16, a peddler, gives Fabian twenty kernels of a new strain of corn he received from some foreign (gringo) archaeologists, which they say will produce larger, more regular, and hardier ears.

Quin advises Fabian to plant the corn secretly so that their father, who is suspicious of foreigners, will not destroy it. With the help of his friend Agustín, Fabian plants the kernels near an ancient, abandoned temple high on the mountain overlooking their village. While planting the corn, Fabian unearths an exquisitely carved ancient ear plug, an ornament worthy of a king. When Quin's archaeologist friends arrive to excavate the temple, Fabian's mother agrees to let the boy work for them because they have been kind to Quin. Happy days follow for Fabian as he learns English, samples foreign food, and delights in the stories the foreigners tell of what they have learned about the history of his Maya ancestors. After the two men discover another decorative ear plug, Fabian shows them the one he found. The silver pieces they give him in exchange for it help his family avert financial disaster when a sudden, violent rainstorm destroys Father's maize. Because the gringos have befriended both his sons, Fabian's father agrees to use the new corn and to allow Fabian to attend school as they suggest. The story appears intended to provide the writers with an excuse for teaching young readers about the life and problems of the modern Maya. The predictable plot lacks narrative tension and concludes abruptly and improbably. Characters are shallow types, and tone is condescending to both subject and audience. Numerous large, full-color paintings and some smudgy sketches illuminate some episodes and especially depict setting. Newbery Honor.

MAGIC MONEY (Clark*, Ann Nolan, ill, Leo Politi, Viking, 1950), realistic novel of family life set in Costa Rica near San José at an unspecified time but probably in the mid-1900s. Tony*, almost ten, lives with his loving Mama and Papa, his teasing older brother, Roberto, and his pretty older sister, Maria Rosita, in a pleasant, pink house with blue door and windows on the coffee plantation belonging to their Patron. Since they work hard, they make ends meet, but the family seldom has any money. When Papa sells the pig to buy new shoes for Rosita, who then leaves for San José to work for the Patron's sister, Tony naively concludes that with money things can be acquired like magic. He has a secret want that can only be satisfied by such money magic—a secret desire that he does not communicate to anyone until the end of the story, but which by Tony's actions, speech, and reported thoughts the reader soon understands. Tony wishes to buy oxen for his beloved Grandpapa*, whose animals have died, so that the old man can enter his beautiful, painted ox-cart in the big annual parade in San José. He consults Grandpapa about his problem, without telling him why he needs the money, and Grandpapa suggests that he earn the money by working for it. He persuades Tony's parents to let Tony help them pick coffee berries, but Tony finds the work too exhausting and falls asleep by mid-day. Then Grandpapa takes the boy to the sugar mill where he himself used to work. The manager hires Tony to shoo flies away, but the boy loses the job because he must care for Grandpapa who faints from overexertion while trying to show Tony how he used to cut cane. At first the boy takes all this in good part, but then becomes despondent over his problem. One by one the members of his very loving family offer to sell their personal possessions to get the money for him, but he steadfastly refuses their offers. Then Grandpapa has an inspiration; he and Tony can make a toy ox-cart and oxen to sell in the market in San José. Tony sells the toy to a North American woman for the equivalent of one U.S. dollar, and he joyfully rushes home to announce to Grandpapa that he can buy his oxen. The old man gently informs him that many more dollars are needed for oxen and points out that money is not magic in the way Tony thinks. He suggests that the two work together to make more carts for sale and that one day maybe they will have enough money for oxen. Tony is satisfied, and Grandpapa has renewed enthusiasm for life. The two main characters seem real, even if Tony is a trifle too babyish, but the rest of the famiy seems assembled for effect. There are good scenes of daily work (doing the washing, picking coffee berries, making sugar, going to market) and of pleasure (the peasants' picnic and the family party), but the way of life seems idealized, and the peasants are depicted as almost perpetually laughing in text and in illustrations, supporting the popular stereotype of Central Americans. Although contrived, the story is diverting, holds the interest, and moves to a satisfactory conclusion. The book seems intended to instruct young readers about peasant life in Costa Rica. Read today, it holds ironies, for example, that Costa Rica compares to the United States in opportunity for peasants to rise and that the Patron is considered a good man because he provides so well for his workers. Fanfare.

MAGIC OR NOT? (Eager*†, Edward, ill. N. M. Bodecker, Harcourt, 1959), realistic, episodic family novel set in the small town town of Cemetery, Conn., one summer in the mid-1900s. Serious James* and dreamy Laura*, twins about ten years old who believe firmly in magic, and their parents move from New York City to a big, old, red house where once George Washington had his headquarters and which promises excitement. In the yard the children discover an old well, which Laura is certain grants wishes. The children soon make friends with aloof Lydia* Green, who lives with her eccentric artist grandmother, who Lydia says is a witch, and who has a horse and is considered wild, and with easygoing, generous Kip*. The four children find excitement and make friends among the adults in town and countryside during the summer. After several dubious experiences with the well, Laura concludes that it works whenever requests made of it are unselfish, and thereafter the children allow the well to direct their activities. They persuade Hiram Bundy*, local banker, not to foreclose on the mortgage of pretty, elderly Miss Isabella King, long-time resident who has fallen on hard times and who has allowed them to play in her abandoned silver mine. In succeeding adventures they find a well-dressed little boy in the local drug store, who is really there with his nurse but whom they "rescue" because they conclude he is a lost heir. While exploring the river they happen upon his home, the lavish residence of a movie star, an actress, who has been frantically searching for him. They unite with the liberal forces in town to persuade the council to build a new school, an effort stalwartly opposed by outspoken dowager Mrs. Witherspoon, who sheepishly changes her mind when her own son, Gordy, a once flaccid, disruptive youth whose personality changes for the better through association with the four children, insists he will attend only the new school along with them. In their final and greatest adventure, they acquire the deed to a little house in the woods in which they find an old desk with a secret drawer containing enough money to pay off Miss Isabella's mortgage. Investigation leaves them uncertain about whether this stroke of good fortune resulted from magic or human intervention (perhaps from the movie star), but they are immensely satisfied with the outcome of their summer's experiences. The adults are types, but the four children are individualized and likeable, their conversations natural, and their plans typical of the kind of thing children might like to do if left on their own. The story is overextended, all on the surface, and of no great moment, offering light amusement for later elementary readers. Choice.

THE MAGIC SHOP (Dolbier*, Maurice, ill. Fritz Eichenberg, Random, 1946), short, spirited fantasy set in the mid-1900s in New York City about the attempts of two children to please their father. When Mr. Benton remarks that he wishes he had a magic wand to elevate the price of his stocks, young Denise and Dick naively set out to buy him one for his birthday. After trying all the best stores without success, they happen on a little Magic Shop on Ariel Street, in a part of New York they are unfamiliar with. Its proprietor is a friendly, tall, lean man, with flowing, white hair and a small, white beard, who informs them that every object in his shop is an original, the original magic carpet, the original cap of invisibility, the original seven-league boots, and so on. He even has the original Puck, whom the children have met riding on the magic carpet when they entered the shop. Mr. Oberon says he has been saving for the children a green and gold wand that will do just what they hope, provided that it does not fall into the hands of his unscrupulous rival who lives on Caliban Street and smells smoky. The children accept the wand gracefully and leave with their dog, Woofle*, who has accompanied them on this shopping trip and who has been fed magic talking biscuits by the mischievous Puck. On Mr. Benton's birthday, two mysterious workmen, who smell smoky, try unsuccessfully to get into the house. The party goes splendidly, and Mr. Benton accepts the wand with great pleasure, well aware of its power and of his responsibility, but the children forget to tell him about the rival on Caliban Street. That night after the children are in bed, Mr. Benton is interviewed by a reporter, who smells smoky. Woofle saves the day, chasing the intended thief from the house and through the street where Puck changes him into a lamp post. This amusing bit of fluff moves rapidly in improvising on obvious source material with tongue-in-cheek humor, high-sounding vocabulary, a few underlying shots, and lots of winks at the adult audience. Fanfare.

MALKUS, ALIDA (WRIGHT) SIMS (1895-), born in Genessee Valley, N.Y.; free-lance writer and occasional illustrator, remembered chiefly in children's literature for her novels of romance and adventure with historical settings. Although her family traveled extensively, in particular in the American West, she grew up in Bay City, Mich., the daughter of a lawyer, the eleventh of thirteen children, and an imaginative child with a bent for writing and drawing. She served in the censor's office in Puerto Rico during World War I and later joined the Albuquerque *Morning Journal* as editor of the woman's page and feature writer, then worked as editor and staff writer with *McClure's Magazine*, for which her husband, Hubert, also wrote. Her travels in the West and among the ruins of Mexico and the Yucatán Peninsula influenced her books. *The Dark Star of Itza** (Harcourt, 1930) is set among the Maya of 1250 A.D. A Newbery honor book, it was broadcast in both Spanish and English to open the Good Neighbor Program to Latin America after World War II. *The Citadel of A Hundred Stairways** (Winston, 1941), which appears on the *Horn Book* Fanfare list, reflects her travels among the Inca of Peru. Other titles from her some three dozen published books, many self-illustrated, include *Caravans to Santa Fe* (Harper, 1928), about the Santa Fe Trail, *A Fifth for the King* (Harper, 1931), about the conquest of Yucatán and the discovery of the Amazon, *Stone Knife Boy* (Harcourt, 1933), about Taos Indians, *Colt of Destiny* (Winston, 1950), about the California missions, *The Spindle Imp, a Book of Maya Myths* (Harcourt, 1931), and several books of biographical fiction on, among other subjects, Louis Pasteur, Winston Churchill, and Jacqueline Kennedy.

MAMINKA'S CHILDREN (Jones*, Elizabeth Orton, ill. author, Macmillan, 1940), episodic book for younger children set on a farm in the United States, presumably in the 1920s or 1930s. Maminka who has come as a girl from the Old Country, Bohemia, with her father, Old Grampa, has three children, a boy, Honzichek, and two girls, Marianka and Nanka, the youngest. In a series of very simple stories, Maminka makes brambory soup, Grampa plays the accordian, Marianka finds a fancy Easter egg under her favorite hen, and Maminka hurts her hand in the wringer as they are washing clothes. While she is gone to the doctor, Aunt Pantsy can persuade the cow to give milk only by giving her the red velvet rose from her hat, the girls make Christmas bread for Grampa, beautiful but too hard to cut, and Grampa puts Nanka to bed by pretending he is a goat who carries her on its back. Other highlights are the visit by Aunt Matylda, newly arrived from Bohemia with a feather bed complete with a Bohemian mouse, and the Christmas gifts the children make, a long, long, red, knit stocking for Grampa and a down pillow for Maminka for which they pluck the goose bare so that Aunt Matylda must knit it a jacket. There is also the Christmas time visit from Saint Mikulash, accompanied by the Devil and two angels, who surprise Nanka while she is wearing the big sheet of noodle that has been hung up to dry. All the episodes are brief and happy, even the crushed hand being no disaster because the children work hard and surprise their mother by finishing the washing. There are some nice touches, like Nanka's inability to understand Bohemian so the older children have to translate for her, but even young readers may want more action, real emotion, and tension in their stories today. Fanfare.

THE MARBLE FOUNTAIN (Angelo*, Valenti, ill. author, Viking, 1951), realistic novel of family and community life set just after World War II in a little village in Tuscany, Italy. The loose plot encompasses about a year and focuses mostly on red-haired, orphaned Piccolo*, 7. He and his brother, Andrea, make their way with their donkey, Cecco, to the village of Rosa to live with their Aunt Tina and Uncle* Gigi, a stonecutter and sculptor. They find their relatives living in an improvised house under the arch of the village bridge. The boys are welcomed and soon pick up their lives, going to school at the monastery on the hill, helping about the house, and playing with their new friends Corinna and Rita, the daughters of the Maletestas, who are close friends of the family and frequent guests. While playing around the abandoned Nazi army tank above the village, Piccolo discovers a half-buried statue of St. Francis of Assisi, done by an obviously skilled but anonymous artist. Father* Bellacosa's prediction that the statue heralds better times ahead comes true. The statue puts new heart into the villagers, inspiring a rebuilding and clean-up, fix-up campaign, which starts with the marble fountain in the town square where the statue is placed, and stimulates Mayor* Bruno Martini to take advantage of the newly instituted American European Recovery Act. The spirit of renewal culminates in a particularly joyous Easter, during which Grandfather is added to the household. A less important plot feature concerns the return of Piccolo's white dove, stolen from him en route to Rosa. While Piccolo is recovering from an illness diagnosed by the doctor as the result of the shock of war, the dove turns up. It perches on the shoulder of the statue of St. Francis, symbolizing to the lad peace, hope, and the promise of a good life ahead. Although dialogue seems made to order, many passages present anti-war sermons, and Americans are idealized, this warm account of simple people genuinely trying to get on with one another and better their lives after terrible destruction moves along and holds the interest. The story promotes faith in God and one's fellows, spirit of community, and a positive outlook on life, and an especially good feature is the depiction of Italian home and church life. (Gobo*) Fanfare.

MARGARET (Lowrey*, Janette Sebring, Harper, 1950), realistic novel of family, school, and community life set in an East Texas town in 1909-1910. The summer she is fourteen, shy, sensitive Margaret McLeod goes to Ashford to live with her wealthy Great-uncle* Archie McLeod, a scholar, and his sister, genteel Great-aunt Lila, relatives of whose existence she had previously been unaware. Since her parents died when she was a baby, Maggie has lived with gentle, caring Bonnie* Weems, former maid of Maggie's mother, and her husband, kind-hearted rover, Prince Albert, called P. A., in the village of Nichols Junction. Maggie leaves Bonnie's house with grave misgivings, impelled by a strong sense of duty and Bonnie's encouragement to take advantage of the opportunity for an education and an easier life. Although she excels in school and is soon elected to the school assembly committee in reward for her scholastic achievement and is regularly invited to parties by the young people of her relatives' social class, she feels ill at ease throughout the year. Singing "Barbary Allen," the only song she knows, when she must pay forfeit at a party, is a particularly humiliating experience that haunts her. The antagonism of Laura Rogan contributes most to her hesitation about remaining with the McLeods. Laura is a beautiful, sophisticated, young woman who comes to visit relatives and decides to stay the year. With unreasonable intensity but apparently to promote herself at the expense of easy prey, she verbally attacks Maggie on several occasions, hinting that Maggie has stolen her lavaliere, deriding her as "country," and calling into question Maggie's capability to serve on the committee. Although consistently encouraged by a small group of town youth, Moselle Corry, the most vocal on her behalf, Val Abernathy, and her brother, Stephen, a fair-minded youth who chairs the school committee, Maggie feels comfortable only with Jet Maypen, spunky farmer's daughter, who urges her to stand up to Laura and who actually gets into a fistfight with Laura at the annual syrup-making event. Realizing that Uncle Archie and Aunt Lila are ashamed of what is happening, Maggie decides to spare them further humiliation by leaving for Nichols Junction but on the way falls in with Miss Georgiana Wall, respected maiden lady of the town, who persuades her to remember her duty and not to run away, and who acts henceforth as her advisor and mentor. Disturbed by the tone of her letters, P. A. visits and urges her to "stick it out." In the spring Maggie stars in nervous, flighty Mrs. Preble's piano recital and celebrates her birthday with a cake Bonnie sends. Miss Georgiana gives her a locket that Bryce, Maggie's father, had once given Miss Georgiana, when apparently they were sweethearts, and the locket comforts her. Miss Georgiana also finds the lost lavaliere inside a piano. Near school's end, Laura objects to Maggie's naming Jet to succeed her on the school committee, but this time Maggie courageously stands up to the self-possessed, more self-confident girl. When news of P. A.'s death arrives, Maggie takes the train back to Nichols Junction, intending to stay there with Bonnie, but Bonnie insists that her duty lies in Ashford. A conversation with Michel Pujo, her ambitious young Cajun friend, who has left Nichols Junction to attend school in Houston, makes Maggie realize that there is no future for her in the village. This big book of many characters rambles along, weak in plot but vivid in its sense of small town life. The main characters are well realized, and hints of previous happenings and long-ago interpersonal relationships add depth and texture. The basic premise—that the McLeods have only just gotten around to tracing Maggie—strains belief, Laura is a phony character, and the reasons for Bryce McLeod's leaving Ashford remain mysterious. Interestingly, Maggie, who appears to be "country" to herself and others, including Jet, is never given ''country'' speech as is Jet. One wonders at the end whether Maggie will be more self-assured and less egocentric on her return to Ashford. Sequel is *Love, Bid Me Welcome*. Fanfare.

MARGARET STEVENSON (*Uncharted Ways**), a staunch young Quaker, in the novel presented as the niece of the actual historical figure, Marmaduke Stevenson, and the sweetheart of Jonathan* Coleman. She is orphaned as a child in England, when her father is killed in the wars with Scotland. In the New World, mysticism and determination unite in Margaret to make her an outspoken opponent of the Boston Puritans. After she participates in a Quaker meeting, she has a profound spiritual exprience which cleanses her of fear and hatred for the Whigpens, who have held her in virtual bondage for seven years. The next year sees her travel with Marmaduke and other Quakers testifying to her faith and meeting persecution in the form of jeers, scorn, a whipping, imprisonment, and finally a death sentence. She falls in love with Salisbury youth Jonathan Coleman, whose safety she at one point jeopardizes through sincere but ill-conceived efforts to proclaim her faith.

MARGUERITE (*Out of the Flame**), historical sister of Francois I of France and Queen of Navarre in Spain. She mothers the Royal Children of France, who love her very much. She encourages Pierre de Bayard to continue his studies, and he eventually goes to live at her court. While on a visit to Francois, she shows the children the ''Mona Lisa'' and Leonardo da Vinci's sketchbook. On an outing during a visit to her court in Navarre, Pierre and the two eldest boys, Francois and Henri*, are captured by a pirate, but Pierre manages to free them.

MARIA ROSALIA (*The Silver Fawn**), Chico's* mother and Señor* Bill's capable and solicitous housekeeper and cook. When Bill says he needs a cook, Chico asserts he will bring the Señor the best one in Taxco. At first skeptical, Bill soon is won over by Maria's culinary talents. She is a worrier and always sends them on trips with baskets bulging with food. Her kitchen is a colorful place, filled with the chattering of her two parrots, a gift from Chico.

MARK GREENMAN (*Homespun**), cool, level-headed, hardworking youth, a bit impetuous, who pledges his word to sell Mr. Rogers's calico in Sante Fe without first consulting his father. He is made of solid stuff, and, while he and his bride, Sukey*, are on the trail to Sante Fe, he helps Frazee, the stern, unyielding trail boss, keep the sometimes fractious travelers organized and safe. By the end of the novel, he and Sukey have completed two successful trading trips to Sante Fe and intend to settle there permanently.

MARSHALL, BERNARD G. (1875-   ), born in Massachusetts; writer and editor. He contributed short stories to the *St. Nicholas* and *American Boy*, wrote articles for technical magazines, and was editor for trade promotion magazines. His five action-filled, often melodramatic novels for older youth feature male protagonists in their late teens. The first of these, *Cedric the Forester** (Appleton, 1921), a romantic, historical novel of the rise to fortune and involvement in significant events of a worthy yeoman youth in thirteenth-century England, was a Newbery honor book. *Walter of Tiverton* (Appleton, 1923) is another historical romance set also at the time of Richard the Lion-Hearted and King John, while *The Torch Bearers* (Appleton, 1923) tells of the English Civil War. American in setting and less romantic are *Redcoat and Minuteman* (Appleton, 1924), about a youth who serves with Washington, and *Old Hickory's Prisoner* (Appleton, 1925), about the War of 1812.

MARTITIA HOWLAND (*They Loved to Laugh**), small, carefully protected girl, who is orphaned at sixteen and comes to live with the fun-loving Gardner family in North Carolina. Although she is delicately built and educated to paint, speak French, and play the spinet instead of to cook, churn, and weave, she has firm determination and works diligently to fit into the family farm life. At first she is frightened by the practical jokes of the country physician and his five big sons, but by the book's end she has learned to join in their laughter.

MARY CURTIS (*Bright Island**), staunch, hardworking, Scots-born mother of Thankful. Although sometimes indulgent of Thankful, particularly with respect to those daily tasks usually performed by women, she is often curt and caustic with her daughter and will tolerate no silliness from the girl. She has confidence that Thankful has good sense, and her careful tutoring (she is a former teacher), enables Thankful to excel in her classes at the Academy on the mainland. A round figure, she exhibits poor qualities, too; for example, she is swayed by her emotions when dealing with Robert. Thankful returns home early from her year at the Academy to nurse Mary when she has pneumonia.

MARY ELLEN WILLIAMS (*South Town**; *Whose Town?*†), mother of David* in a series about a southern black family that moves North. An ideal, hardworking black mother and wife, she wants to stay home and cook good Southern food for her family, but in the South she works for Mrs. Boyd when the white woman demands it and in the North she does day work in people's homes after her husband gets laid off. In both, she gets into some trouble by speaking her mind when pushed too far. After her husband's death, she sells their northern home to finance an office for David in the country near South Town. In *Whose Town?* she is inexplicably referred to as "Fannie."

MARY INGALLS (*Little House in the Big Woods**; *Little House on the Prairie**; *On the Banks of Plum Creek**; *On the Shores of Silver Lake**; *The Long Winter**; *Little Town on the Prairie**; *These Happy Golden Years**), beautiful, golden-haired older sister of Laura* in seven autobiographical novels. As a little girl,

Mary is always good and proper, a contrast and an irritation to rebellious Laura, and she is inclined to be bossy. After scarlet fever blinds her, their relationship changes, and she depends on Laura to "see out loud" for her. Always a quiet and nonadventurous type, she sits indoors, sews, and helps care for Grace, the youngest. When they live at Silver Lake, the Reverend Alden first mentions the college for the blind in Iowa, and for Mary, who has always liked to study, this becomes a goal. Eventually she is able to attend the school, partly because Laura works to help earn the money, and she returns more confident, an accomplished and lovely young lady.

MARY JANE (Sterling*, Dorothy, ill. Ernest Crichlow, Doubleday, 1959), problem novel set in the Southern town of High Ridge during the early years of school integration in the 1950s. Instead of going to black Douglass High School, as her older siblings did, Mary Jane Douglas, 12, has decided to start junior high at Woodrow Wilson High School, because it is a better school and will be integrated for the first time. Because she has spent the summer with her grandfather, a retired botany professor, on his farm, she has missed the controversy in the community, and she is uncomfortable at the encouragement and warnings well-meaning people give her as she gets ready. She is not prepared, however, for the mob of angry whites booing and shouting as she and Fred Jackson and four senior-high students are escorted into the school by their fathers and the police. The first days are confusing, frightening, and lonely. In French class, Darlene Duncan refuses to sit by her in alphabetical order. In the cafeteria, no one sits near Mary Jane and Fred. In the halls they are bumped and threatened. But phone calls and letters from all over the world praise her bravery. As time goes on the shouting crowd disappears, but the loneliness increases. Fred is on the basketball team and is beginning to be accepted. Mary Jane is told she "wouldn't fit in" as a cheerleader and, though she can't carry a tune, is asked by the music teacher to join the chorus because "all you people have such lovely voices." One day, walking home, she comes on a crowd of kids watching a cat attacking a squirrel. Fearlessly, she rushes in and rescues the squirrel,though she is badly scratched by the cat. Sally* Green, a girl who has previously made some friendly overtures, picks up her bookbag and follows her home, only to be coldly asked to leave when Mrs. Douglas is upset at Mary Jane's scratched face, thinking she has been attacked. With the squirrel, named Furry, as a common interest, Sally and Mary Jane become friends. When Mrs. Douglas refuses to have him in the house any longer, they take him to the science teacher, Mr. Stiller, who keeps him beside his white mice and turtles until a group led by Darlene's mother protests, pretending to be afraid of rabies. The girls then hide Furry in an empty dressing room behind the stage and eat lunch there, until one day the squirrel gets out and makes a mess in the cafeteria. The girls then confess, and Mr. Stiller suggests taking Furry to Mary Jane's grandfather's farm, and offers to drive the girls, their pet, and the French teacher, Miss Rousseau. At first Sally's parents agree, but when townspeople phone, alerting them that their daughter is friendly with "a little colored girl" and later threatening to boycott Dr. Green, they change their minds. The others take Furry anyway and have a fine day, but Mary Jane and Sally have no place to meet, since neither mother welcomes the other girl, downtown eating places won't allow Mary Jane to sit down, and even the parks are closed to blacks. Again Mr. Stiller solves their problem by getting them to start a junior high science club. As they start planning expeditions, Mary Jane bravely points out that she will not be admitted at many of the museums and laboratories, and the club votes to go only where she can go, too. Mary Jane realizes that she has been a successful ambassador. Although the theme is over-obvious, the situation stronger than the characters, and the solution forced, the book has merit in making not only Mary Jane's feelings believable, but also those of her parents and of Sally's parents. Historically, this is an interesting example of novels with upper middle-class protagonists that dominated books about blacks in the period between the condescending earlier stories and the later tough ghetto novels. Choice.

MARY LENNOX (*The Secret Garden**), unhappy, neglected child left orphaned in India and sent to the Yorkshire home of her uncle, Misslethwaite Manor. Sallow and disagreeable in expression, Mary is unattractive physically and unpleasant in personality when she arrives but is changed by her contact with nature and with the wholesome local Sowerby family.

MASSAROSA (*Nino**), the small, close-knit, Italian village in which Nino* and his family live before they emigrate to America. The place, the people, and the way of life reflect those of the childhood of the author, Valenti Angelo*, before he came to America from Tuscany with his family when he was eight years old.

MASSEY, JOHN (*The Windy Hill**), farmer who also makes beehives. The children meet him when they go there with the Beeman* to buy more beehives. He is Anthony Crawford's tenant. Because he is unable to pay the rent, Anthony puts him off the farm in spite of Anthony's niggardliness about providing him with essential materials and equipment. Anthony has refused to let John keep the dike in repair, and thus the dike is weakened and unable to retain the flood waters. John is an honest, hardworking man ill-treated by a grasping, miserly landlord.

THE MATCHLOCK GUN (Edmonds*, Walter D., ill. Paul Lantz, Dodd, 1941), brief historical novel in ten short chapters, which fictionalizes upon an actual happening, among Dutch settlers "in 1757, when New York State was still a British Colony, when the French were still leading Indians out of Canada against the settlers, and when the raid that came all the way to Guilderland, just outside of Albany, took place." Edward Van Alstyne, 10, greatly admires his father's handsome, Spanish matchlock gun, a family heirloom from Holland that hangs over the fireplace. When he leaves for the militia because Indians threaten, Captain Teunis Van Alstyne takes his musket instead of the matchlock, explaining to his son that the matchlock is too awkward and cumbersome because it must be primed with fire before it will discharge its shot. When their mother, Gertrude, tucks Edward and little Trudy, 6, into bed that night, Edward assures his mother that if Indians come he will help her drive them off, little realizing how soon he will do just that. After lunch the next day a neighbor rides by with the news that the Indians are attacking nearby settlements, and later in the day Gertrude sees their fires. With Edward's help, she props the heavy matchlock on the table, its barrel through the front window. She shows Edward how to fire it and tells him to shoot when he hears her call his name in Dutch, "Ateoord." Then she puts Trudy to bed and goes out to the bean patch, where she pretends to pick beans, all the while keeping her eye out for Indians. When she sees Indians on the road, she races for the house, calling out the names of family members as she goes. On the stoop, Indians at her heels, she shouts, "Ateoord," and Edward touches the candle flame to the gun, discharging it and killing three Indians. Gertrude drops from a tomahawk blow to the shoulder, and Edward and little Trudy drag her away from the burning cabin. Edward rescues the gun, and when the militia come by a while later, Teunis finds his family in the yard near the burned out cabin, Gertrude still unconscious, Trudy asleep, and Edward with the gun across his knees, guarding them. Characters are sketched in bold strokes, and it is easy to visualize the situations. The focus is on plot in this essentially single-incident story, an isolated happening that moves smoothly to its tense climax. The Indians are presented as fearsome savages; they run up the road "like dogs sifting up to the scent of food." Strongly executed, stiff color and black and white illustrations show setting and picture the action. Books Too Good; Choice; Fanfare; Lewis Carroll; Newbery Winner.

MATHILDE (*That Girl of Pierre's**), Danielle's grandmother. The problems that the family face after their return to Arsac-le-Petit prove too much for her to cope with, and Danielle must take the lead. She is a pleasant, comforting woman, who earns money through light laundry and is liked and respected in the village.

MATILDA SAWYER (*Rebecca of Sunnybrook Farm**), strict, old maid aunt of Rebecca* Randall, who takes in the child to relieve the problems of her widowed sister, Aurelia, mother of seven. She is irritated by Rebecca's talking, singing, whistling, by her carelessness in leaving doors ajar, forgetting to hang up the dipper, pinning flowers to her dress or hat—everything that goes against her inflexible and austere habits. She is particularly severe about anything that reminds her of Rebecca's handsome, feckless father, with whom she herself was in love, though she never admitted it. As she gets older, she becomes genuinely fond of Rebecca but continues to conceal it. She keeps from her niece the news that a business which has provided much of her income has failed, and although she pinches pennies tightly and refuses to dip into principal, she keeps Rebecca in school as she has promised.

MATTHEW STEELE (*Kaga's Brother**), fourteen-year-old son of an army officer whose father sends him on the McKenney-Cass expedition to Fond du Lac to make a treaty with the Indians in 1826. He feels it will be a good educational experience for the boy. At first Mat is highly impressionable and inclined to be silly in speech and behavior. But in time, his friendship with the Indian boy, Kaga*, and his experiences mature him, and by the end of the book he is ready to settle down to the useful and practical task of helping Captain Lewis start a school for whites and Indians at La Pointe. His letters to his father appear fairly reliable at reporting his experiences, but too full of data about the social and political affairs for a thrill-seeking, heroizing youth. Kaga gives him the Indian name, "Muskrat's Liver," an Indian term of affection which means something like "strawberry shortcake."

MATTHEW WOOD (*The Witch of Blackbird Pond**), Kit's uncle by marriage. A stern man, he represents rigid, traditional Puritanism. No flat figure, however, he speaks up for Kit when she is accused of being a witch. A fair, thoughtful man, he realizes that Kit is a good person who is the victim of circumstances and her own tempestuous nature.

MAUD VANDEVOORT (*Vinny Applegay**), youngest of Vinny's rather giddy Vandevoort cousins, the daughters of Vinny's proper and imperious Aunt Blanche. Maud is shy and frail, likes to play with dolls and to stay neat and clean. She enjoys outings and doing everything that Vinny does. She almost always lets Vinny take the lead, and occasionally she acts as Vinny's conscience. Now and then she shows unusual spunk, as when she gets up the courage to investigate the fiery face at the window.

MAUREEN BEEBE (*Misty of Chincoteague**; *Stormy, Misty's Foal†*), warm-hearted and emotional child, younger sister of Paul*. She is greatly moved by the beauty of the horses and works just as hard as Paul to accumulate enough money to buy the mare, Phantom, and her foal, Misty. When Paul wins the right to ride Phantom in the big race, she wills them to win, imagining herself flying with them along the track. In *Stormy*, she works just as hard as Paul to make Misty comfortable and to get the stall ready for Misty and Stormy. She often regrets being a girl and complains to Grandma* Beebe about it.

MAURICE PASCAL (*A Cat of Paris**), struggling, young, Parisian Left Bank artist, friend of the Belmonts, who purchase one of his paintings. Later he uses the last of the money to buy Thom* the cat from Charles*, the surly street urchin who has captured him. Maurice keeps Thom, since the Belmonts are on vacation, feeds him up, falls ill, and, when they return, is treated by Dr. Manning, uncle of Jane Manning, Polly's friend, who once lived in North Africa and buys some of Maurice's African paintings. Maurice is unselfish, kind, and gentle, a stereotyped character, who nevertheless works well in the story.

MAXWELL, WILLIAM (1908-), born in Lincoln, Ill.; educator, editor. At one time he taught at the University of Illinois and at another was associate editor of *New Yorker* magazine. His stories have appeared in *Harper's Bazaar* and the *Atlantic Monthly*. Memories of a period when, at seventeen, he worked on a farm in Wisconsin led to *The Heavenly Tenants** (Harper, 1946), a Newbery honor fantasy about the signs of the zodiac.

MAYOR BRUNO MARTINI (*The Marble Fountain**), pompous, officious mayor of Rosa. He complains a lot about his gout and about his responsibilities as mayor. After Piccolo* discovers the statue of St. Francis, he becomes so engrossed in ways of rehabilitating his village that he forgets his illness and becomes more cheerful and likeable. The villagers are inclined to humor him and let him think that their ideas about doing things are really his.

MCCLOSKEY, (JOHN) ROBERT (1914-), born in Hamilton, Ohio; artist, author and illustrator of books for children, best known for his Caldecott Award–winning picture books, *Make Way for Ducklings* (Viking, 1941) and *Time of Wonder* (Viking, 1957). His Ohio smalltown childhood provided the background and material for another picture book, *Lentil* (Viking, 1940) and for his only novel-length books, *Homer Price** (Viking, 1943), cited in *Children's Books Too Good to Miss* and *Choice*, and *Centerburg Tales** (Viking, 1951), a Fanfare book and also a *Choice* selection. Their tall-tale situation comedy episodes about Homer Price and his friends in the small town of Centerburg recapture and elaborate on many of his own youthful experiences. He studied art at Vesper George School in Boston on a scholarship and at the National Academy of Design in New York. He was a sergeant in the army in World War II, when he drew training pictures, and after the war studied art in Rome as a Fellow of the American Academy there. He has been a muralist, has done commercial art work, and has been an advertising consultant. He has won the Prix de Rome, and his fine art has often been exhibited in shows. In addition to illustrating his own books, he has illustrated books for many eminent writers, including Claire Huchet Bishop*, Ruth Sawyer*, and Keith Robertson*†, for whose Henry Reed books he drew the pictures. He married librarian Ruth Durand, the daughter of Ruth Sawyer, and had two daughters, who appear as characters in his illustrations in, among others, *One Morning in Maine* (Viking, 1952) and *Blueberries for Sal* (Viking, 1948). The McCloskeys have lived in Croton, N.Y., and on an island in Penobscot Bay off Maine.

MCCRACKEN, HAROLD (1894-), born in Colorado Springs, Colo.; explorer, pioneer radio commentator, naturalist, author of books about wild animals. He grew up on a ranch in Idaho and attended Drake University in Des Moines, Iowa, and Ohio State University. In 1912 he went to a relative's ranch in the Canadian Rockies of British Columbia, drove stage for the workers on the Canadian National Railway, and ran a fur trading post. He made airplane stunt films and later worked in aviation research in the Department of Physics at Columbia University, where he helped develop one of the forerunners of radar. A lover of the out-of-doors, he collected big game specimens for the Ohio State Museum and led the Stoll-McCracken Siberian Arctic Expedition of the American Museum of Natural History. Almost all of his books concern animals in their natural habitat, including *Biggest Bear on Earth** (Lippincott, 1943), *The Last of the Sea Otters** (Stokes, 1942), *Caribou Traveler* (Lippincott, 1949), and *Great White Buffalo* (Lippincott, 1946).

MCGINLEY, PHYLLIS (1905-1978), born in Ontario, Oreg.; poet, noted for both light and serious verse. She grew up on a ranch in eastern Colorado until her father died when she was about thirteen, after which she moved to Ogden, Utah. She was graduated from the University of Utah, taught school, and helped edit *Town and Country*. In 1961 she was awarded the Pulitzer Prize in Poetry for *Times Three* (Viking, 1960). Her first book for children, *The Horse Who Lived Upstairs* (Lippincott, 1944), was inspired by some drawings of city horses by Helen Stone. *The Plain Princess** (Lippincott, 1945) is a story on the folktale pattern. Of her ten books of verse for children, her volume of city poems, *All Around the Town* (Lippincott, 1948) is still the best known.

MCGRAW†, ELOISE JARVIS (1915-), born in Houston, Tex.; artist, novelist. She is a graduate of Principia College in Elsah, Ill., and studied at Museum Art School in Portland, Oreg. In 1942-1943, she taught painting at Oklahoma City University and has since taught at Lewis and Clark College in Portland and at Portland State University. With her husband, writer William Corbin*† McGraw, she has owned and farmed a filbert orchard in the Willamette Valley, Oreg. Her novels for young people mostly have historical settings, including *Moccasin Trail** (Coward, 1952), a story of the settlement of Oregon, and *The Golden Goblet†* (Coward, 1961), set in ancient Egypt, both Newbery honor books. More recently, she has turned to the contemporary period, as in *A Really Weird Summer†* (Atheneum, 1977), a mystery which won the Edgar Allan Poe Award. All her books are notable for well-developed characters and suspenseful action.

MCHE (*Lion Boy**), Simba's chubby, sometimes disobedient little sister, who is cherished and often indulged by the family. Although little, she is responsible for feeding her old grandmother, and the two are very close. After the grandmother dies, Mganga, the witch doctor, fashions for Mche a doll inside of which he has placed such items as her grandmother's hair and some toenail and fingernail clippings. He tells the little girl that the doll is the ghost of her grandmother. She carries the doll wherever she goes and is convinced that it protects her from a hyena.

MCKINLEY, CHARLES FREDERICK (1913-   ), born in Mansfield, Ohio; college professor whose brief, clever book for young children, *Harriett** (Viking, 1946), was illustrated by William Pène du Bois*† and was named on the *Horn Book* Fanfare list of the best books of the year. He is a graduate of Kenyon College and received his Ph.D. from Trinity College in Dublin. His teaching positions include Kenyon College, the State University of Iowa, Queen Aliyah College, Iraq, and Hiram College in Ohio. He also wrote *A Voyage to the British Isles* . . . (Kokosing Press, Mt. Vernon, Ohio, 1940).

MCNEELY, MARIAN HURD (1877-1930), newspaperwoman and author of novels and short stories for children and young people. She was born in Dubuque, Iowa, where her father, a lawyer, was a prominent citizen. She attended local schools and worked for several years on a newspaper. She published her first novel, *Miss Billy* (Lothrop, 1905), a joint effort, when she was twenty-seven. After her marriage to Lee McNeely, when she was thirty-three, the couple homesteaded on the Rosebud Indian reservation in South Dakota for two years. Their experiences in trying to make a living on the windswept prairies provided the material for what is still considered her best book, *The Jumping-Off Place** (Longmans, 1929), a Newbery honor book about the hardships of four orphans who try to establish their home on the South Dakota prairies. The couple later returned to Dubuque, where she continued her writing after her children were grown. *Winning Out* (Longmans, 1931), a novel about two sisters who pursue different careers, was published after her tragic death; she was struck and killed by a car in front of her own house. She also contributed many poems and stories to the *St. Nicholas*, *Youth's Companion*, and *John Martin's Book*, and a collection of her short stories was also published posthumously, *The Way to Glory* (Longmans, 1932). Another novel was *When She Came Home from College* (Houghton, 1909), about a Vassar girl who must assume the burden of running the family home.

MCSWIGAN, MARIE (1907-1962), born in Pittsburgh, Pa.; newspaper reporter and feature writer. She worked on Pittsburg newspapers for ten years, and became publicist for the Carnegie Institute Fine Arts Department and other organizations, including the University of Pittsburg. She wrote fourteen books, both fiction and non-fiction, but all based on real events, including *Snow Treasure** (Dutton, 1942), the story of how Norwegian children smuggled a fortune in gold bullion past Nazi soldiers on their sleds.

MEADER, STEPHEN (WARREN) (1892-), born in Providence, R.I.; editor, advertising copy writer, novelist. He grew up in New Hampshire, the setting for such books as *Red Horse Hill* (Harcourt, 1930), a story of harness racing, and was graduated from Haverford College, Pa., in 1913. He was a caseworker for the Children's Aid Society, Secretary of the Essex County Big Brother Movement, assistant editor of *Country Gentleman*, and advertising copy writer and director for publishing firms in Pennsylvania. His more than forty novels for young people include sea stories, like *The Black Buccaneer* (Harcourt, 1920), *Whaler Round the Horn* (Harcourt, 1950), and *The Cape May Packet* (Harcourt, 1969) and boyhood adventures, some with historical settings, like *Boy with a Pack** (Harcourt, 1939), a Newbery honor book which includes Erie Canal scenes, horse thieves, and Quakers who aid runaway slaves.

MEADOWCROFT, ENID LAMONTE (WRIGHT) (1898-1966), born in New York City; teacher, editor, author. She attended Lesley College in Cambridge, Mass., and taught school in Jersey City, N.J., Portland, Oreg., and New York City. From 1952 until her death she was writer and editor of Grosset "Signature Books," a biography series, and of Garrard's "How They Lived" series. She wrote about twenty-six books, half of them fiction, including *By Secret Railway** (Crowell, 1948), a story set in Chicago that includes a slave escape.

ME AND THE GENERAL (Wonsetler*, Adelaide H., and John C. Wonsetler*, ill. authors, Knopf, 1941), historical novel set in 1812 in the Lake Erie area, in what is now Pennsylvania, Ohio, Michigan, and southern Ontario. Lively, red-haired Powderhorn*, about twelve, is playing soldier near the cabin on the Little Muddy (Susquehanna) River, where he lives with old Biscuit, his foster father, when he is kidnapped by two Mohawks, fat, lazy Look-up-from-the-Ground, and tall Bite-the-Snake, both scouts for the British. They march Powderhorn across northern Ohio, saving the boy when they are ambushed as they cross a river, eventually arriving at the Indian village at Amherstburg, by Fort Malden, at the mouth of the Detroit River. Powderhorn has some conflicts with the Indian children, but he wins their respect by fighting, and he soon becomes part of the camp, the formally adopted son of both Look-up and Bite-the-Snake. He also visits the British general at Fort Malden, is tremendously impressed by the pomp of the military, and is soon jokingly known as the general's aide-de-camp or, to the men, "Me and the General." One evening, escaping well-deserved punishment at the Indian camp, he takes refuge in the fort where a dance is in progress, climbs up to look in a window, slips, and precipitates himself headfirst onto the dance floor, upsetting the table of refreshments and startling the general and his guests, who include Madame Marcella Bisquette Montreux, and her daughter Celeste. Madame Montreux insists that the boy should come to Montreux, the enterprise headquarters on the Thames River in Ontario, to be educated. With the Indian fathers' permission, Powderhorn is taken along with the chief's son, Hair-low, by Pere Dupre, resident priest, where he becomes part of the flourishing trading post, one of a mixture of races and nationalities, adults and children, who live in a house where manners, learning, and cleanliness are enforced by the martinet butler, Marcel. There he meets traveling British officers, one of whom brings him a cut-down uniform of the redcoats sent by the general, the Jewish post manager, French traders, and even the Indian chief, Tecumseh. Gradually he becomes aware that Madame Montreux and some of the men are sending information to the American army, and his quick thinking and action destroys evidence of this and protects Madame Montreux. As the war develops, however, Montreux is forced out of business; Madame and Celeste leave for Quebec, and Powderhorn goes back to Amherstville. There he finds the camp greatly enlarged with Indians assembled to fight. They demand a white prisoner to torture, and to Powderhorn's horror, the general gives them one, who turns out to be Biscuit. Powderhorn rescues him, arranges to meet him to go back to the United States, but first sneaks into a loft at the fort and overhears plans for a big British offensive. A storm prevents him from meeting Biscuit but he gets Bite-the-Snake and Look-up to take him on their scouting trip, wrecks their canoe at a critical juncture, and gives the information to the American troops following them. He is reunited with Biscuit, and both with Pere Dupre, who questions Biscuit, wishing that the old man will confirm Madame's hope that Powderhorn is really the son of her brother, lost at sea, a hope based on Powderhorn's age and appearance and the coincidence of the names Biscuit and Bisquette. The old man says that the boy is really son of his Revolutionary War officer. Madam, knowing her hopes might be groundless, has already said that she still wants Powderhorn to come and live with her and Celeste in New York. The book contains a good deal of historical information about the western campaigns of the War of 1812. Powderhorn is an active, unfrightened young hero, but events seem to fall his way unrealistically, particularly toward the end of the story, where his success becomes implausible. The patriotism that eventually draws him to the American side is also unlikely, considering the kindness and accepting attitude of his Indian fathers, the general (never named in the book), and his companions at Montreux, almost all of whom support the British. The characters generally take second place to the action. Fanfare.

MEANS, FLORENCE CRANNELL (1891-1980), born in Baldwinsville, N.Y.; author of more than forty books, most of them novels for young adults focused on minority groups and the disadvantaged. Her father was a Baptist minister who welcomed into his home people of all racial and ethnic backgrounds. When Florence was thirteen, the family moved to Denver, hoping the climate would be good for an older sister who was ill. There she attended the Henry Read School of Art, later studying at Kansas City Baptist Theological Seminary, McPherson College of Kansas, and the University of Denver. She is credited with being one of the first to write honest, realistic novels for the older child with minority group main characters. She spent much time in the Carolina low country and on its tidal islands, the setting for both *Shuttered Windows** (Houghton, 1938) and *Great Day in the Morning** (Houghton, 1946), both of which have black girls as protagonists. *The Moved-Outers** (Houghton, 1945), concerns the American Japanese forced into "relocation camps" during World War II. Although some of her books seem quaint and dated in their attitudes now, they are valuable as social history.

MEANS, PHILIP AINSWORTH (1892-1944), born in Boston, Mass.; educator, archaeologist specializing in the Inca culture. From 1921 to 1927 he was with the Anthropology Department of the Peabody Museum, Harvard University. Most of his books reflect his interest in ancient Peru, including *Tupak of the Incas** (Scribner's, 1942). Among his books for adults are *Ancient Civilizations of the Andes* (Scribner's, 1931), *Fall of the Inca Empire* (Scribner's, 1932), and *The Spanish Main: Focus of Envy, 1492-1700* (Scribner's, 1935).

MEGGY MACINTOSH (Vining*†, Elizabeth Janet Gray, ill. Marguerite de Angeli*, Doubleday, 1930), historical romance set in Edinburgh, Scotland, and North Carolina in 1775. Orphan Meggy MacIntosh, 15, of a good Highland family impoverished because her father supported Bonny Prince Charlie, has been taken in by her aunt and uncle, Sir Douglas and Lady Keith, who have provided her an old Highland minister, Mr. MacPherson, as a tutor, then ignored her. Meggy's only interest, besides Mr. MacPherson's tales and songs of the glories of Scotland, is in the social exploits which her beautiful cousin, Veronica, 18, confides to her. When Veronica agrees to elope romantically with Ewan* MacNeill, younger son in an acceptable Edinburgh family, and go with him to seek his fortune in North Carolina, Meggy knows her cousin will back out of the plan, so she takes the few jewels which are her inheritance and goes, secretly, in Veronica's place, making certain that no one who knows her sees her clearly until they are well out to sea. Ewan is furious, but when she offers a ruby to pay her way, the captain refuses to put back, and Miss Cameron, a woman traveling with her brother's two young sons, Willie, 12, and Alexander, 7, to his plantation, admires her spirit and befriends her. Meggy has determined to join Flora MacDonald*, the historical woman who, as a girl, helped Prince Charles escape from his disastrous campaign in Scotland and who now lives with her husband and large family in Wilmington. When the brigantine, *Bachelor of Leith*, docks, Meggy learns that Flora MacDonald has gone to "the back country," so Meggy stays restlessly with the Clayton family, whose daughters, Alice and Pherebee, welcome her. Here she begins to learn of the unrest in the colonies. The Claytons are Whigs or American patriots. Flora MacDonald leads the Scot settlers as Tories or English loyalists. Meggy meets David* Malcolm, an attractive cousin of the Claytons from Cross Creek, a settlement near Flora MacDonald's Killiegray, who promises to find a way to get her to Flora, though he is a Whig. Meggy goes for a while to Holy Quarter, the Cameron plantation, to be tutor to little Alexander and companion to Miss Cameron, but when a note comes from David she takes Tibbie* McNabb, a bound-out girl whose time she has bought with her last ruby, and goes back to Wilmington. There she gets Ewan, who has become friendlier as his hopes of fortune have decreased, to make the contacts David suggests with Capt. Alexander MacLeod, Flora's son-in-law, who is secretly in town. MacLeod agrees to let her and Tibbie ride with him, but the trip is too strenuous for Meggy, who collapses when they reach Cross Creek and is taken in by David's mother. In that Whig family she and Tibbie are both useful and happy, but she pushes on to stay with Flora MacDonald, who welcomes her but has plenty of bound-out servants and black slaves and no need for Meggy. After some time word comes that Mrs. Malcolm has been hurt, so Meggy takes Tibbie and they go back to Cross Creek, nurse her, and stay through the mustering of the Highland Army and its first disastrous encounter with the rebels, and there she waits with Mrs. Malcolm for David and his father, who have fought with the patriots, to return. After she arrives in America, the main plot question is whether Meggy will support her countrymen in the Highland army led by Flora and her husband and approved by Ewan or whether she will follow her instincts for freedom and independence to support the rebelling colonists, as exemplified by David. There is considerable interest in the little-known connection between the Jacobite pretender and the American Revolution in the Carolinas, and particularly in the ironical plight of those who had fought against the English at Culloden but were bound subsequently by an oath of loyalty taken under terms of surrender to fight for the British in the American colonies. Characters are underdeveloped, but Meggy's search for Flora and a political ideology with which she can be comfortable, though predictable in their outcome, sustain interest, and the occasional use of Scots brogue creates atmosphere and adds to the credibility. Meggy has lively adventures, but the emphasis remains on her emotional involvement with Ewan and David, and so, despite the action and history, the book is a ''girls' novel'' of romance. Newbery Honor.

MEG MARCH (*Little Women**), eldest of the four New England sisters who grow up during the 1860s. Pretty and slightly vain, Meg would love to have money for nice clothes but learns how false wealth can be when she visits a friend, allows her hostess to dress her in a borrowed gown and arrange her hair in a fancy style, and she realizes that Laurie* Laurence, the boy next door, is ashamed of her when they meet at the party. Meg, who always admonishes Jo*, her tomboyish sister, to be proper, herself turns into a proper young wife to John Brooke, but not without some problems. She overspends her small budget, is caught unprepared with a kitchen full of unjelling jelly when John brings a friend to dinner, and, after her twins are born, almost loses her husband by devoting all her attention to them.

MEIGS, CORNELIA LYNDE (1884-1973), born in Rock Island, Ill.; author of books and stories for children and young people and adult fiction and non-fiction. She grew up and attended private school in Keokuk, Iowa, where her father was an engineer engaged in government projects on the Mississippi. Her mother's family had been pioneers and her father's army and navy people, and, nourished on stories of what happened to them, she early developed a love for history. After graduating from Bryn Mawr, she taught English in Davenport, Iowa, and then at Bryn Mawr, where she became professor of English. Her first book, *The Kingdom of the Winding Road* (Macmillan, 1915), a fantasy, was published in 1915, and there followed over the next fifty years of her long and distinguished career some forty books, including thirty books of fiction, some written under the name Adair Aldon, two plays, and biographies for the young, as well as a novel and several books of non-fiction for adults. Three novels were Newbery honor books, *The Windy Hill** (Macmillan, 1921), a mystery set on the New England coast, *Clearing Weather** (Little, 1928), set in Massachusetts against the development of the China trade just after the American Revolution, and *Swift Rivers** (Little, 1932), set among the Swedish settlers of Minnesota and involving the logging industry, while *The Covered Bridge** (Macmillan, 1936), about the struggles of a Green Mountain farm family in 1788, and *Call of the Mountain** (Little, 1940), about a youth's efforts to establish himself on a Vermont mountain farm, were Fanfare books. Although their plots are uneven, conflicts are clear, and her books convey significant themes and a strong sense of time and place. Also well received was *Master Simon's Garden* (Macmillan, 1916), a novel set in Puritan Massachusetts, and her biography, *Invincible Louisa: The Story of the Author of "Little Women"* (Little, 1933) received the Newbery Award. Her highly regarded *A Critical History of Children's Literature* (Macmillan, 1953) remains a classic in the field.

MELINDY'S MEDAL (Faulkner*, Georgene, and John Becker*, ill. Elton C. Fax, Messner, 1945), realistic novel for early readers set in Boston in the 1940s. Melindy, 8, lives with her black father and grandmother and a canary named General Shaw in the Bethune Building of a federal housing project which is well cared for, with clean, neat apartments and attractive war-time vegetable gardens. Melindy's father, Joe, who won a medal for bravery in World War I, plays a saxophone at a night club. Melindy and her grandmother have been saving pennies and a few larger coins to buy him a new saxophone which they give him for his birthday. Grandmother tells Melindy stories of the bravery of her great-grandfather, a slave named Mo, who escaped and fought in the Civil War, and of her grandfather, who was in the Spanish American War. She regrets that Melindy, a girl, cannot win a medal as all the family men have. Melindy, who plays the piano well, gets her chance one day when she becomes sick at school. Her teacher tells her to go home instead of to assembly, but as she is getting her coat she sees smoke, rushes to the auditorium, and plays the fire drill music, clearing the whole school before the fire hurts anyone. She is ill for a long time and on recovering learns that she has been given a medal. This is one of the "good little colored girl" books of the 1940s, dated in its attitude toward blacks, girls, and war, but interesting as social history. The style is simple and the story slow-moving. Fanfare.

MEN OF IRON (Pyle*, Howard, ill. author, Harper, 1892), historical novel set in the early fifteenth century in England, during the reign of Henry IV. When he is only eight, Myles Falworth, standing with his blind father, Sir Gilbert Reginald Falworth, in the anteroom of their castle, sees the cold-blooded murder of Sir John Dale, his father's friend who has sought refuge there and has just yielded himself to protect his host. It is not until he is grown that he understands the political intrigue behind the scene, that his father and Sir John have been supporters of the late Richard II, and that Henry Bolingbroke, now Henry IV, and in particular some of his more unscrupulous advistors, are seeking out and killing the more influential and admired men who have opposed them. The next day Myles and his parents flee the castle, along with their loyal retainer, Diccon Bowman, and until Myles is sixteen live in seclusion in Crosbey-Dale, a simple farm owned by the priory which good Father Edward heads. There Diccon trains Myles in the use of arms and accompanies him to Delven Castle, with a letter to the great Earl* of Mackworth, Lord Falworth's kinsman, asking that he take Myles into service. The Earl appears reluctant but agrees and sends him for training to Sir James Lee, the grim, old, one-eyed knight who is Captain of Esquires. In his first days at the castle, Myles makes a good friend among the squires, Francis Gascoyne, and one enemy, Walter Blunt, the head squire. Blunt and the other older squires, who are called the bachelors, haze the younger boys. When Myles refuses to carry bath water for Blunt, it precipitates a rebellion which, with Myles at the head, succeeds in throwing off the oppression. Sir James, though hard and demanding, takes an interest in Myles and warns him that his father is outlawed and, should his place of residence become known, he would be in great danger. The next spring Myles, having struck a ball into the exclusive privy garden open only to the Duke and his family, climbs over the wall to retrieve it and falls through the lattice-topped arbor into the presence of Lady Anne, 20, the Earl's daughter, and Lady Alice, 14, his niece. Thereafter, Myles visits the forbidden garden to talk to the girls, particularly Lady Alice, for whom he has promised to be her true knight, until one day when Lord Mackworth discovers them. When Myles speaks boldly to him, he thinks better of having the boy publicly shamed, but after he intercepts a letter from Myles to Lady Alice, he sends for the boy, tells him that a powerful enemy at court caused his father's downfall and seeks to destroy him, and warns him not to think of Lady Alice until he has restored the Falworth fortunes. Shortly thereafter Myles is given a horse and begins three years of intense training at jousting. When King Henry visits Delven Castle, bringing with him a French count, the Earl arranges that the King will knight Myles so that he will be of a rank to challenge the French champion in the Count's entourage, the famous Sieur de la Montaigne. To the surprise of almost everyone, Myles unhorses the French knight. Then he serves six months fighting in France with Lord George Beaumont, the Earl's brother, before he is summoned back by the Earl, who has maneuvered for his own purposes to have Myles challenge his father's enemy, the Earl of Alban, the same man who treacherously blinded Lord Falworth and murdered Sir John Dale and has poisoned the king's mind against the good lord. The time is ripe, since Henry is ill and Prince Hal, his madcap son, has gathered a strong faction of which Mackworth is a behind-the-scenes leader. In the duel to the death, Myles is seriously wounded and his enemy, though he fought treacherously and Myles nobly, is killed. At the king's death, Lord Falworth's lands are restored to him, and Myles receives permission to woo Lady Alice. Myles is an impulsive but always honorable hero; his foil, Gascoyne, voices caution but follows Myles devotedly. The tale is romantic and swashbuckling, treating the late Middle Ages as a time of adventure and splendor, but it also gives a good idea of the life of noble-born boys of the day and of the intrigue practiced among the powerful and ambitious. Children's Classics; Choice.

MERCY WOOD (*The Witch of Blackbird Pond**), lame sister of Judith, who runs a dame school with which Kit helps. She is a peacemaker and a patient soul who brings joy to those around her. She marries John* Holbrook, whom she has secretly loved all along. She kept her feelings about him to herself because Judith was interested in him. She is Kit's steadfast friend.

MICHAEL O'SULLIVAN (*The Cottage at Bantry Bay**; *Francie on the Run**), oldest son in the close, loving family. A sturdy, responsible and enterprising youth, he soon outgrows the Bantry Bay schoolteacher, but the family does not have enough money to send him away to school. It is his idea to pick blackberries in the hills where he and Brigid* find the vellums which alter the family fortunes.

MICHAEL SLADE (*Clearing Weather**), tall, well-muscled, personable, red-haired youth from South Carolina, one-time companion of French adventurer Etienne Bardeau*, who becomes the close friend and assistant of Nicholas* Drury. Michael serves aboard the *Jocasta** as owner's representative, and for a brief time as captain when Captain Douglas falls ill, on the trading voyage around the world which brings financial solvency to the Drury shipyards and the prospect of prosperity to the people of the seaport of Branscomb, Mass., during the hard times just after the American Revolution.

MICHEL'S ISLAND (Hunt*, Mabel Leigh, ill. Kate Seredy*, Lippincott, 1940), historical novel set in 1800 on Mackinac Island off what is now the lower peninsula of the state of Michigan. The fictitious story and characters revolve around an incident in the lives of Joseph Bailly, a real Mackinac fur trader, and his five sons. High-spirited, mischievous, sometimes disobedient Michel Jarnac, 11, also called Loon Boy, loves Mackinac Island, where he has lived all his life. He cares deeply for his father, jovial Albert Jarnac*, a well-to-do French Canadian fur trader, his pretty, quiet Ottawa mother, Morning Star, and his four brothers. His older brothers, Louis, Dominique, and Jean, intend to become a fur trader, priest, and *voyageur*, respectively, and his younger brother, Joseph called Jacquence*, plans on being a sailor or soldier, all vocations that please their success-oriented father. But Michel feels caught between two worlds. He would like to become an herb doctor like the wise Ottawa Panace* and spend his life on Mackinac, an ambition of which his father makes light, calling Michel his *bois brulé* (burnt wood) son, because his skin is darker than his brothers' and because of his liking for the Indians. The summer passes quickly with games with young friends, parties on the shore when the trading canoes put in and at the Jarnac house for M. Jarnac's business friends, the arrival of La Rose, tall-tale telling *voyageur* who is a favorite of the children, and of the Indians for their annuity payments, a visit to his mother's family at Crooked Tree Village on the mainland, and herb gathering trips on the island and on the mainland with Panace. In October, M. Jarnac returns from his annual trading trip to Montreal with gifts for everyone. Not long after that he announces that he intends to send all five sons to Montreal to school the following summer, a decision about which Michel has mixed feelings. He longs for a dream or vision to show him how his life should go, like that his Ottawa cousin has had. While caught on an ice floe in early spring, he has a dream in which he sees himself as a loon returning to Mackinac from Montreal. Although Panace tells him to listen to his dream voice, he remains in doubt about whether or not he ever will come back to his beloved Mackinac. At departure time, Michel says his farewells and gets into the canoe, but when he sees his mother standing alone on the shore below the imposing Arched Rock, he jumps overboard and swims back to her, sure finally that his destiny lies on his cherished island. The author seems obligated to enliven the rather weak plot with the mysterious disappearance of M. Jarnac's standish (writing box) and the suspicious actions of the dour Indian medicine man, Zhikag*, but actually makes very little of these aspects, nor does she knit them well into Michel's problems. The uneven plot ambles along to its predictable and not well-exploited conclusion. The book is well researched, and its strength lies in its recreation of the times. Since Michel bridges the two worlds, the reader has splendid views of life among the French-Canadians and among the Indians as well. Stories from the history and folklore of Mackinac and the Indians give considerable depth. Michel is a sympathetic protagonist. The father, Panace, and Jacquence are other fleshed characters; Zhikag, the mother, and La Rose are stock; and most of the others are functionaries. Style is richly descriptive of setting and incident, there is some use of imagery, and action and dialogue abound. Fanfare.

MICKEY MCGUIRE (*The Iron Duke**), roommate of Jim Wellington and Fog* Smith at Harvard. A trim, tough, sturdy, likeable youth of Irish extraction, his reputation for stellar achievement on the football field precedes him to the university. Congenial and self-assured, he catches on to the ways of Harvard faster than Jim, exhorts Jim to "just get busy and work" when Jim is put on academic probation his first semester, and helps him with his classes and friendly advice. When McGuire stands up to the freshman coach on his first scrimmage, he is kicked off the team. Later the head coach reinstates him, and eventually the Harvard varsity elect him their captain.

THE MIDDLE MOFFAT (Estes*†, Eleanor, ill. Louis Slobodkin*, Harcourt, 1942), humorous, episodic family novel, second in the series about the close-knit family of Cranbury*, Conn., who have now moved to the little house on Ashbellows Place. The story is almost exclusively that of Jane*, now ten and still an earnest, energetic, imaginative little girl who likes to do things. Although the episodes are self-contained, Jane's concern that Mr.* Hannibal B. Buckle, at ninety-nine Cranbury's oldest inhabitant, reach his one hundredth birthday without mishap binds the vignettes together and gives them some cohesiveness. The year passes quickly as Jane establishes her identity as the middle Moffat, though to Mr. Buckle, who plays Hawkshaw the detective with her, she remains the "mysterious middle Moffat." Jane gives an organ recital for the neighbors, which is abruptly halted during her first number when the pedals break and hordes of moths fly out of the console. She stays for dinner at the house of Nancy* Stokes, her best friend, where she is confronted with the dilemma of whether she should take the last lamb chop or leave it for the maid. She spends an afternoon with Mr. Buckle admiring his chicken-bone furniture and playing solitaire, at which he solidly defeats her, starts a campaign to reclaim all the skates fixit genius Willie Bangs has promised to fix but hasn't, and writes a reply to Rufus's letter to Santa, explaining that all the ponies are needed in France for the war effort, because she knows he will be terribly disappointed at not getting one for Christmas. She plays Mama Bear in a play about Goldilocks to benefit the church and loses her bear's head, views a solar eclipse from Gooseneck Point with Nancy, and proves herself a star in her very first basketball game. The climax of the year for her comes at Mr. Buckle's one hundredth birthday celebration. After a big parade in his honor, Mr. Buckle acknowledges her concern for his well-being and invites her to ride home with him in his shiny black parade limousine. The simple charm that made *The Moffats** popular is also evident here, and the accumulation of detail makes the characters even more convincing and likeable. Sequel is *Rufus M.**. Books Too Good; ChLA Touchstones; Choice; Fanfare; Newbery Honor.

MIDGE GLASS (*Henry Reed, Inc.**; *Henry Reed's Journey†*; *Henry Reed's Baby-Sitting Service†*; *Henry Reed's Big Show†*), Margaret, slightly younger friend and partner of Henry Reed in a series of humorous, episodic novels. Although most of the ideas for projects are Henry's, Midge is not a passive partner. She dives into any undertaking with great energy and spirit. Somewhat more excitable than Henry, she is frequently responsible for complications and occasionally for solutions. Small and freckled, with her hair in a ponytail, she is a companion but not a romantic interest.

MIEP VAN OORDT (*The Level Land**), 18, eldest child in the close-knit Dutch family at the opening of World War II. Miep is a maternal type, trying to take her mother's place when Moeder is having a new baby. A realist, Miep foresees the German invasion, which her family refuses to believe is possible. She becomes engaged to Maarten, a young man she has met in Amsterdam where she is studying, and after he has been called into the army, she takes his car and finds her sister Ruth, who is recuperating from an illness at the seaside, and manages to get her home to the eastern Netherlands, driving through a hail of bullets on the way. Bandaged up, she turns back in an attempt to get the Jewish refugee boy, Werner, to Rotterdam, where he can get a ship for England or the Indies.

MIKE MACGREGOR (*Indian Brother**; *The Scalp Hunters**), Michael, red-haired Scotch-Irish boy who was captured by the Penobscot Indians at thirteen and adopted into the tribe, using the name Meguántep. Three years later he escapes with Martha Hilton when her brother Sam*, having escaped from the Norridgewock tribe, comes for her. During the winter when they live on the mountain feared by the Indians, Mike's skill with the bow and knowledge of Indian ways greatly help them. In the second book, Mike accompanies Sam to rescue his brother Billy, and eventually marries Martha.

MILES HENDON (*The Prince and the Pauper**), befriender of the true Prince of Wales, Edward* Tudor, after he has been mixed up with his look-alike, Tom* Canty. The middle of three sons of a country gentry family, Miles has been slandered by his wicked younger brother, Hugh, so that his father banished him for three years, which he served in continental wars, but was then captured and spent seven years in a dungeon. He is attracted to Edward because of the boy's spirit, is amused by what he deems his delusions of grandeur, and humors these pretentions thinking that kindness will mend the deranged mind. When they arrive at Hendon Hall and discover that, the older brother having died, Hugh has forged a letter telling of Miles's death and has taken over the title and property, Miles insists that his sweetheart, now Hugh's wife, will identify him. Lady Edith, having been warned by her husband that Miles will be killed if she recognizes him, denies that she knows him but tries to give him money and urges him to flee. He is arrested, whipped to save Edward from a beating, and placed in the stocks. Later he tests the young king by sitting in his presence, a right he has been granted by the boy whom he thought mad. He also regains his lands and is given the title of Earl, which the king as a pauper has granted him.

MILLER, ELIZABETH CLEVELAND (1889-1936), born in Seymour, Conn.; Red Cross child-welfare worker in the Balkan countries after World War I, author of novels about the area for children. Daughter of a clergyman, she lived as a child in Harlem, when it was still country and woods, in Ridgewood, N.J., and in New Bedford, Mass. In 1909 she studied kindergartening at the Ethical Culture School in New York City and taught at a settlement kindergarten and in private schools for seven years. Later she taught courses in geology at Columbia University. During World War I she enlisted in the YMCA as a canteen worker and served in Germany until the end of the occupation, then worked in Albania, in Rumania, and in France with the Red Cross until 1922. Her experience in Albania, where she started Children's House in Skodra to help mountain children forced into the city as refugees, gave her material for *Children of the Mountain Eagle* (Doubleday, 1927) and *Pran of Albania** (Doubleday, 1929), a Newbery honor book. *Young Trajan* (Doubleday, 1931) is set in Rumania.

MILLY PARKS (*Shadow across the Campus**), shy freshman girl who becomes Marjorie's closest friend among the pledges and who helps her write the history of the sorority. This project leads them to Julia Maude Crowder* and success in changing Zeta Nu policy toward admitting Jews. She represents the kind of girl who sees in what direction right action lies but who without the leadership of a more highly motivated person like Marjorie would merely go along with the crowd.

MILPA (*The Corn Grows Ripe**), a Maya cornfield, either planted or unplanted. The expression, "to make milpa," means to cut the trees, burn them off when dry, and to plant the corn in hills. After the *milpa* has been used for several years, it is allowed to revert to bush (forest), and the family clears a new area. Tigre makes *milpa* by himself after his father breaks his leg and as a result is regarded as a man in the village.

MIMI EDINGTON (*Sandy**), sister of Sandy Callam's deceased mother, who comes from Chicago along with her married daughter, Helen, and her two grandchildren, to summer in the New England resort village of Windrush. A frivolous, flippant, and changeable woman, Mimi is a revelation to Sandy, who has never known this side of her family. Mimi tactlessly points out that Wing, the young man Sandy covets, has eyes only for Helen. Thinking that Sandy needs to get away from the puritanical and high-principled influence of her other aunt, Kate* Callam, Mimi invites her to come and live with her in Chicago, meet some men, and have some fun.

MINGY (*The Gammage Cup**; *The Whisper of Glocken*†), town treasurer in the Minnipin village of Slipper-on-the-Water*, who speaks out against the villagers using their money to beautify the town to win the Gammage* Cup instead of keeping it to help the needy. For daring to question the wisdom of the Periods, the Minnipin leaders, he is outlawed along with four other nonconforming Minnipins. In the second book, he helps to rescue the New Heroes.

MIRACLES ON MAPLE HILL (Sorensen*†, Virginia, ill. Beth Krush and Joe Krush, Harcourt, 1956), realistic novel set in Pennsylvania during one year not long after the end of World War II. Because Dale has been a war prisoner and returned depressed and tense, his wife, Lee, has arranged that the family move to her grandmother's long-empty home on Maple Hill. Both Marly, 10, and

Joe*, 12, are hopeful but wary, afraid of their father's sudden angers and their mother's nervous worry. Even before they arrive, their car gets stuck in the snow and Marly, going for help, discovers the sugarhouse, where Mr.* Chris is boiling down the first-run maple sap into syrup. Not only does Mr. Chris pull the car with his tractor, his wife, Chrissie, gives them dinner. Soon they are discovering the wonders of nature in early spring, all of which seem like miracles to Marly. Not all the discoveries are happy. Marly is heartbroken when they destroy a nest of baby mice; she is frightened by a herd of calves; trying to be helpful and get breakfast, she produces only smoke until her father shows her how to use the damper; with Joe, she sees a family of foxes, bursts out with the news, and learns that Fritz, the Chrises' hired man, plans to shoot them for the bounty. This last incident works out well, however, after she and Joe sneak out at night and scare the animals away from their den. Exploring, she and Joe come upon the cabin of Harry* the hermit and are surprised and terrified when he discovers them in his springhouse. Harry, however, becomes a close friend, particularly of Joe, and when the family decides to live on Maple Hill all year round, he gives them two goats and eight chickens. Just before Christmas, Joe disappears and all the neighbors are out looking when Marly realizes he must have gone to see how Harry is getting along. They find him with the hermit, who has slipped and hurt his leg and would have frozen without Joe's help. Near the end of February, the maple sap begins to rise, and they all help Mr. Chris and then suddenly are in charge of the whole operation when he is taken to the hospital with a heart attack. The children stay out of school to help until the school nurse–truant officer makes a visit. She is so entranced with the sugaring process that she arranges for squads of high school students to help, so that they will learn about their heritage. Mr. Chris's crop is saved, he returns home, and Marly is ready for another year of miracles. Told almost entirely from Marly's point of view, the story has a tone of breathless wonder that could be cloying if she were not such a convincing character, bright, lively, and warm-hearted. The family tension is well presented as are Marly's slight sibling rivalry with Joe and Dale's gradual recovery. Descriptions of flowers and other growing things are frequent but well integrated into the story. Choice; Newbery Winner.

MIRSKY, REBA PAEFF (1902-1966), born in Boston, Mass.; musician, author. She was graduated from Radcliffe College and studied further at Harvard, at Basle's School Cantorum, and, on a Guggenheim fellowship, in Zululand, South Africa. This is the setting for *Thirty-one Brothers and Sisters** (Follett, 1952). She was a teacher and lecturer, a member of a concert ensemble, a harpsichordist and composer on the music faculty of New School, N.Y., and music director in New York Schools. Among her books for young people are biographies of Beethoven, Mozart, Haydn, Bach, and Brahms.

MISFORTUNES, SIX (*Mademoiselle Misfortune**), the six Moreau sisters, Alice*, Beatrice, Cecily, Drucilla, Estella, and Felicia, English names although they are French, because their papa went to school in England and was determined to be cosmopolitan. They are termed the Six Misfortunes by Madame Toussaint, the owner of the Paris *pension* where they live with their father, mother, and older brother, Edward, because according to French custom, their father will have to provide doweries for all of them and he has fallen on hard times. Alice is the diplomat of the six, Beatrice is the practical one, Cecily aspires to be an artist, and the little girls love fairy stories.

MISS HAVANA FISH (*The Sea Is All Around**), Mab's tiny, frail teacher before she goes to regular school on Pokenick*. Miss Fish's father was a ship's captain, and she was named for the harbor where her father's ship was moored while she was being born. She has a night-blooming cereus, which Mab goes late at night to watch open.

MISS HICKORY (Bailey*, Carolyn Sherwin, ill. Ruth Gannett, Viking, 1946), episodic fantasy about the adventures of an apple twig doll with a hickory nut head, whose stubbornness and inability to accept advice cause her to miss out on many of the pleasures and wonders of the farm on which she lives. When Ann, the little girl whose toy she is, goes to Boston for school and the big house is closed for the winter, Miss Hickory is left behind. She rejects the advice of Mr. T. Willard-Brown, the cat, to move to the barn, intending to continue to live in her corncob house under the lilac bush. When Chipmunk takes it over, Crow moves her to an abandoned robin's nest in an old McIntosh tree, where she remains until the robins return in the spring. Independent, stiff-minded, wrapped up in herself, she keeps largely aloof during the winter, knowing little of what goes on among her barnyard and woods friends. She misses the most important event of all—the Christmas procession of animals and the golden imprint of the Christ Child in the manger. But she does find the hen pheasants, deserted by their husbands, new homes in a patch of corn missed by the farmer, helps Bullfrog get a new coat, and observes Wild-Heifer, an adventurous calf, and Fawn share a supper of mash in the barn. Homeless again when Robin reclaims his nest in the spring, she has in mind to take over Squirrel's. But her acid tongue gets away from her, and, when she calls him witless, he retaliates by biting off her head. She scrambles up the McIntosh where she is later discovered by Ann and her friend, Timothy. She has become a scion, or new graft, of the apple tree and has a permanent home at last. The story is told with humor and affection for nature and its creatures, but the characters are overly anthropomorphized and one-dimensional. But the hardhearted Miss Hickory is a memorable and likeable character, if overdrawn. Choice; Fanfare; Newbery Winner.

MISS MINCHIN (*A Little Princess**), proprietress of the Select Seminary for Young Ladies where Sara Crewe is first pampered, then abused. A stereotypical, mean schoolmistress, she dominates her more humanitarian sister, Amelia, toadies to the parents with money, imposes unjust punishments, and saves pennies by starving and overworking her help. Her main distinguishing characteristic is her hypocrisy, shown in her flattering of Sara, whom she always dislikes, when the girl is rich, her bad treatment of the child when she is poor, and her attempt to curry favor again when Sara's fortune is restored.

MISS PETERSON (*Blue Willow**), Janey* Larkin's teacher at the camp school. Janey knows she is the right sort of teacher when she calls the horned toad a toad and not a lizard and recites Mother Goose verses. Miss Peterson brings gifts to the Larkin family at Christmas time.

MISS PICKERELL GOES TO MARS (MacGregor*, Ellen, ill. Paul Galdone, McGraw, 1951), amusing, short science fantasy set in the mid-1900s on a farm somewhere in the United States, on a voyage through space, and on Mars. Miss Pickerell returns from a visit to her seven nieces and nephews to discover a space ship trespassing on her cow's pasture. She angrily and intrepidly ascends the narrow ladder and climbs inside, determined to order the commander to remove it immediately from her premises. When he hears her arrive, Captain* Crandall mistakenly assumes she is his navigator, Mr.* Haggerty, and gives the order to take off. To her suprise and dismay, Miss Pickerell finds herself on a voyage to Mars. She soon settles in and does what she can to ensure the success of the venture. She learns how to walk, sit, and eat in space, enjoys looking at pictures of space and of Mars in particular, and even prepares meals for the three-man crew, using her apron as a tablecloth. Although the captain is very upset at finding that he lacks a navigator and has acquired a passenger, he, Mr. Killian, the executive officer, and Wilbur*, the crewman, manage to calibrate the instruments. Miss Pickerell keeps her eye on a certain star to help them stay on course and suggests the method by which they effect a safe landing. Captain Crandall refuses to let Miss Pickerell explore, telling her to stay on board and monitor their conversation by walkie-talkie. When Wilbur gets stuck between two rocks and is in danger of running out of oxygen but cannot communicate with his partners because the walkie-talkie system has broken down, Miss Pickerell puts on the extra pressure suit, grabs an oxygen tank, and climbs down from the space ship to rescue him. The four return triumphantly from their history-making voyage, and Miss Pickerell's collection of red rocks from Mars takes a gold medal for the outstanding exhibit at the state fair. The book is all plot, a fast-moving, predictable concoction of unlikely occurrences and amusing ironies intended as diverting reading for an elementary audience. Some vocabulary is quite mature, but sentences are short, and the meaning can easily be discerned from context. There is just enough elementary space science to make the preposterous plot believable, and bright-eyed, determined, articulate Miss Pickerell is a memorable heroine. One of a series about this energetic, undauntable, middle-aged lady. Choice.

MISS TERWILLIGER (*Homer Price**), one of the best-loved citizens in Centerburg. She runs knitting classes and has taught almost every woman in town to knit. All the women in town, Homer Price, and perhaps a few observant men know that she wins the ball of string contest by unraveling her knit dress. She chooses to marry Uncle Telemachus, and they go to Niagara Falls on their honeymoon. The sheriff*, Uncle Telly's unsuccessful rival, serves as best man.

MISS WEATHERWAX (*Mademoiselle Misfortune**), Hester Weatherwax, elderly American woman whose companion Alice* Moreau becomes on her tour to the south of France. An imperious, demanding, high-tempered sort, she is used to getting her way and often antagonizes people. Her brother was John Weatherwax, archaeologist to Peru and friend of Alice's father when Monsieur Moreau was ambassador to Peru. Bustle and bluster on top, she is really a kind and generous person. She takes Alice to the Paris opera and buys her clothes more suitable for traveling. At story's end, she plans to take Alice back to the United States with her, where Alice will continue to serve as her companion and will attend school at Miss Weatherwax's expense.

MISTI (*Secret of the Andes**), Cusi's beloved pet llama, a clever, black one, who often guides him when he is undecided or needs assistance. In a mystical scene, Misti leads the youth to a secluded spot on the mountain where he discovers an altar to the sun and a pair of small golden shoes, which he later learns were his mother's. They are a clue to his parentage and a link to his Inca heritage.

MISTRESS COCKBURN (*King of the Wind**), housekeeper for Jethro Coke. She becomes very fond of Agba*, mothering him and feeding him up with confections and rich foods. When she discovers quite by accident that he is in Newgate jail, she visits him there. Her chance encounter with the Duchess of Marlborough, who makes regular mercy visits to Newgate, leads to the youth's release and subsequent elevation in fortune.

MISTY OF CHINCOTEAGUE (Henry*†, Marguerite, ill. Wesley Dennis, Rand, 1947), realistic animal novel involving actual events set on the islands of Assateague and Chincoteague off the coast of Virginia, beginning in the days of the Spanish Main and then shifting to the mid-1900s. On Assateague live hundreds of wild ponies, the offspring of survivors of a wrecked Spanish galleon bound for Peru. Every July the islanders of Chincoteague go to Assateague and round up the colts to sell to buy firefighting equipment for their island. Paul* and Maureen* Beebe, a brother and sister about fourteen and twelve, are living with their Grandma* and Grandpa* Beebe while their parents are in China. They hope that this year the drovers will capture Phantom, the elusive, coppertoned mare with a map of the United States on her withers. By halterbreaking Grandpa's colts, digging for clams, doing odd jobs, and running errands, they earn one hundred dollars with which they hope to purchase Phantom. On Pony Penning

Day in late July, Paul proudly joins the roundup crew on Assateague. During the drive, he unexpectedly encounters Phantom and her foal and brings them in, to the astonishment of the other drovers. Although Paul is pleased with his feat, he feels a little dubious about depriving Phantom of her freedom. He names the silvery-gold colt, with a map like her mother's, Misty. On sale day, the children are disappointed to learn that someone else has spoken for Phantom and Misty. All day they struggle with their disappointment, when to their delight the man who had bought Phantom appears and announces that he has won a colt in the annual raffle and no longer wants Phantom and her foal. Misty takes to the children right away, and to the astonishment of the islanders, they soon succeed in taming Phantom. The following year the chief invites the children to race Phantom against the local champion, and with Paul on her back she wins easily. Shortly thereafter, Paul releases the mare, allowing her to return to the wild stallion, Pied Piper, and the free life she had so long enjoyed on Assateague. The children keep the colt, which is soon known as Misty of Chincoteague. The story is based on actual incidents involving real people. The colloquial dialogue contributes authenticity, and the two children and Grandpa Beebe are well realized if static. Although incidents sometimes seem unlikely and contrived, the story is often suspenseful and has a certain homely charm. The passages describing the wild horses and the drive are quite convincing, but, on the whole, style is pedestrian and movement uneven. The black and white illustrations picture incidents and contribute to setting. Choice; Fanfare; Lewis Carroll; Newbery Honor.

MOCCASIN TRAIL (McGraw*†, Eloise Jarvis, Coward, 1952), historical novel of the last of the fur trappers and the beginning of the settlers in the Willamette Valley, now in Oregon, in 1844. Jim* Keath, a Missouri farm boy, had run away at eleven to follow his trapper uncle, Adam, and, while still a greenhorn, had been attacked and badly wounded by a grizzly, which he managed to kill. Rescued by Crow Indians, he has been adopted and trained with the boys of the tribe in Absaroka. Later, he has left the Crows and joined an older trapper, Tom Rivers, and the story starts when he is nineteen and receives a letter delivered by Indians from his younger brother, Jonathan. Unable to read it, he parts company with Rivers and travels to the trading post at the Dalles, where Bob Rutledge, an older immigrant traveling with Jonnie, reads him the letter, which tells of the death of their father, the loss of their farm, and their mother's death on the trail west, and asks Jim to join him and their sister, Sally, 15, and Dan'l, 11, since only Jim is old enough to claim homestead land. Their reunion is full of mixed feelings. Jim looks and thinks like an Indian, and Sally, particularly, resents this. The other pioneers are suspicious, but Dan'l is fascinated and Jonnie genuinely is glad to see the brother he remembers. Jim gives them essential aid, then takes Dan'l on a harrowing trip driving the stock through the mountains while Jonnie and Sally, with the Rutledges, shoot the rapids of the Columbia Gorge on a raft. Although Jim and Dan'l all but starve, they meet as arranged and go on to the Willamette Valley, where Jim practices all night so he can sign the papers to take up the land. Their troubles of adjustment, however, are not over: Jim is unused to and scornful of the steady work of cabin building and clearing land; Sally is antagonistic to his Indian ways; steady, good-natured Jonnie is hurt when Dan'l abandons him in his hero-worship of Jim, and the other settlers are suspicious of Jim with his wolf-like dog, Moki, his beautiful wild horse, Buckskin, his long braids, and his Indian manners. When some nearby Indians steal horses and cattle from the settlers, Jim uses his trailing skill and knowledge of the natives to find and steal back the stock but creates a further misunderstanding when he steals one of the Indians' horses for Jonnie. In returning it to the Indians at Jonnie's insistence, Jim is wounded. Later, the new sheriff, Joe Meek, formerly a mountain man, drops by and in an agreeable conversation makes it clear that he admires Jim's skill but will tolerate no Indian ethics in the new settlement. When Tom Rivers shows up, Jim, discouraged over the failure of understanding with his own family, leaves with him but has second thoughts and returns, only to find that Dan'l has set out after him and been captured by slave-taking Indians. In an attempt to rescue Dan'l, Jim himself is taken and nearly killed, but both are rescued by Joe Meek and the settlers. Seeing Jonnie's concern and Sally's relief at his return, Jim realizes that he must make a choice of life styles, and symbolically cuts off his Crow braids. Although the scales at times seem weighted on the side of the settlers, the conflict of values is well drawn, and Jim's pride, hurt, and bafflement at his miscalculations are convincing and moving. The scenes of action, particularly the stock-drive over the mountains and Jim's escape after returning the stolen horse, are vivid. Choice; Lewis Carroll; Newbery Honor.

THE MOFFATS (Estes*†, Eleanor, ill. Louis Slobodkin*, Harcourt, 1941), humorous, realistic, episodic family novel, first in the series of three about the Moffat family, set in the small town of Cranbury*, Conn., at the beginning of World War I. The dozen, self-contained adventures revolve mostly around tomboyish Jane*, 9, and include artistic big sister, Sylvie*, 15; hardworking Joey*, 12; impulsive Rufus*, 5 1/2; and their patient, gentle, widowed Mama, the finest seamstress in Cranbury. Times are hard, and, when Dr. Witty decides to sell the run-down, yellow house the Moffats rent on New Dollar Street, the family must find another that suits their means, the problem which loosely ties together the various episodes. Mildly disconcerting happenings abound. Jane mimics the walk of the school superintendent, Mr. Pennypepper, and then fears Chief Mulligan will arrest her for disrespect. Told to look after recalcitrant Hughie Pudge on the first day of school, Rufus attaches himself to Hughie, and when Hughie runs away, joins him for an exciting train ride. Jane, Joey, and Rufus drive the Salvation Army man's wagon for him and lose him along the way. On Halloween, the children rig up Madame, Mama's sewing bust, and Catherine-the-Cat provides sound effects to give Peter Frost a good scare. Joey miserably substitutes for ill Chet Pudge to dance the sailors' hornpipe, the family is quarantined with scarlet fever, and later Joey fears he has lost the money Mama gave him to buy coal. Catherine-the-Cat has kittens in the spring, and the children have a wild trolley ride to Sandy Beach. The last episode sees the family move to another house a few blocks away on Ashbellows Place. The blow of moving is somewhat lessened for Jane by the discovery that a little girl just her age lives in the house behind, Nancy* Stokes. The episodes ring true to family life and the child's point of view. The style is simple, and the tone is warm and affectionate. Humor enlivens almost every episode, and characterization is rich and accurate. Slobodkin's whimsical, black and white line drawings add much to the entertainment value of the book. Sequels are *The Middle Moffat** and *Rufus M**. Children's Classics; ChLA Touchstones; Choice; Lewis Carroll.

MOLLY MATTERSON (*The Great Quest**), huge, dark-skinned adventurer who joins the brig *Adventure* in Cuba as mate. In a previous voyage he and Cornelius* Gleason, with two companions, have somehow come upon a treasure in jewels which two have stayed behind to mine, dig, or pan out while Gleason finds a vessel in which they can return. He has clearly been in the slave trade and is thoroughly ruthless, but he has coolness to whittle chess men and play a long game with Arnold* Lamont while they are held by siege in a jungle hut surrounded by hostile natives. Despite his great size, he has a soft, effeminate voice.

MONA MELENDY (*The Saturdays**), eldest of the four Melendy children. She has two long, thick, butter-colored braids that she does not like. She has them cut off on her first Saturday outing. She aspires to be an actress on the stage and often quotes from Shakespeare. In later adventures of the family, her performance in the Melendy variety show is admired by a New York producer, who auditions her and subsequently hires her for a radio serial. Her income adds appreciably to the Melendy resources. She is fifteen in the third book, more mature in attitude and behavior, and able to assume a good deal of responsibility about the house. She grows up convincingly for the period in which the series is set.

MONTGOMERY†, RUTHERFORD (GEORGE) (1894-   ), born in Straubville, N.Dak.; prolific writer of fiction mainly about wildlife and adventure in the out-of-doors. He grew up in the country near Velva, N.Dak., and on a Montana ranch. After attending Colorado Agricultural College, Western State College in Gunnison, Colo., and the University of Nebraska, he taught in public schools in Wyoming and was teacher and principal in elementary and high schools in Colorado. After that he managed a chamber of commerce, served as a judge, and was budget and efficiency commissioner for the state of Colorado in Denver. He moved to Los Gatos, Calif., where he became a free-lance writer and taught creative writing classes. He has published over ninety books, mostly of fiction for young readers, based on his own experiences in the outdoors through camping, ranching, and flying, including a Newbery honor book and Fanfare selection, *Kildee House** (Doubleday, 1949), about an elderly man whose friendship with wild animals enables him to make human friends for the first time in his life, and *The Stubborn One*† (Duell, 1965), a book of ranch life which won the Spur Award of the Western Writers of America. He writes fluently and manages to convey a good deal of information without sounding instructive, though his books tend to be formulaic in plot. His service in the Air Corps in World War I and time spent with the Strategic Air Command more recently provided material for his books on aviation. Later titles include *Big Red, A Wild Stallion* (Caxton, 1971), in which a forest ranger and his son seek to protect a herd of wild ponies from poachers and another of his books that deal with humans and animals together, and *Rufus* (Caxton, 1973), about a bobcat. He edited *A Saddlebag of Tales* (1972), a collection of stories for Western Writers of America, wrote a series of aviation novels for Grosset under the pseudonym Al Avery and several books under the name Everitt Proctor, wrote screen plays for Walt Disney Studios, ghostwrote the Dick Tracy series for five years, has written novels for adults, and has published over five hundred short stories for magazines.

MOON, GRACE (PURDIE) (1887? or 1883?-1947), born in Indianapolis, Ind.; artist and author of many books about Indians of the Southwest. She attended the University of Wisconsin and the Art Institute of Chicago, married Carl Moon, photographer and illustrator, and together they lived with various Indian tribes, painting, photographing, and writing about them. Her first book was published in 1917, and altogether she wrote nineteen, some of them in collaboration with her husband, among them *One Little Indian* (Whitman, 1950). Individually she wrote, among others, *The Runaway Papoose** (Doubleday, 1928), and *Daughter of Thunder* (Macmillan, 1942). Although they seem dated now, they were among the first books for younger children to present Indian life sympathetically and to treat their customs with respect.

MOORE, ANNE CARROLL (1871-1961), born in Limerick, Maine; librarian, editor, critic, and author of books for children. The daughter of a lawyer, she had aspirations toward law herself, but decided on librarianship after the death of her father. After graduating from Pratt Institute in 1896, she served there as children's librarian until 1906, when she became Supervisor of Work with Children at the New York Public Library until 1941. The only two positions she ever held, she initiated and shaped both of them. She pioneered in library work for children and became a noted authority and critic of children's literature. She was children's book critic for *The Bookman*, the New York *Herald Tribune Books*, and *Atlantic Monthly*, and was associate editor of *Horn Book* for over forty years. She lectured and served as consultant on children's books and librarianship for teachers, librarians, and publishers throughout the United States. Most of her books were for adults, including *Roads to Childhood: Views and Reviews for Children's Books* (Doran, 1920) and *The Three Owls: A Book about*

Children's Books, Their Authors, Artists, and Critics (Macmillan, 1925), and she contributed many articles to national magazines. For children she wrote *Nicholas: A Manhattan Christmas Story** (Putnam, 1924), a fantasy involving characters from children's books which was a Newbery honor book, and *Nicholas and the Golden Goose* (Putnam, 1932), and edited *Knickerbocker's History of New York* (Doran, 1928) and *Bold Dragon, and Other Ghostly Stories*, both by Washington Irving. Her numerous awards included the Diploma of Honor from Pratt Institute and a Doctor of Humane Letters from the University of Maine.

MORE ALL-OF-A-KIND FAMILY (Taylor*, Sydney, ill. Mary Stevens, Follett, 1954), realistic, episodic family novel, a continuation of *All-Of-A-Kind Family**. The year 1915-1916 finds the close-knit Jewish family still living on the Lower East Side, economically somewhat better off, still enjoying a warm relationship with one another and their relatives and friends, and still finding great pleasure in the ordinary, everyday things in life. Ella, now almost sixteen, acquires a boyfriend, Jules Roth, a wavy-haired, well-mannered youth she meets at the library. Eventually both win positions in the Rockaway Temple choir. Gertie struggles with conscience and clock after she thoughtlessly assures the teacher she can tell time. The irrepressible Henny stays out beyond her curfew and just misses a spanking when father mistakenly administers the blows to her friend Fanny in the dark. At Yom Kippur the girls buy mother a bouquet and try hard to fast, and Henny returns from their traditional family Hanukkah celebration at Aunt Rivka's with an umbrella laden with nuts. Little Charlie's perplexity about why Mama frowns so much (she's very busy, and he has been bothering her) results in several trips downstairs to Mr. Basch's bakery where he receives cookie consolation. The girls' May Day party, forced to the basement by rain, becomes complete when Uncle Hyman brings ice cream sandwiches. Linking together these and similar adventures is the romance between Uncle Hyman, Mama's younger brother, and jolly, fat, Lena Cohen, whom the family meets early in the book when she rescues Charlie, who has run into the street. The family happily helps to plan the wedding, when an epidemic of infantile paralysis strikes the city. Mama persuades Papa that the family should spend the summer at Rockaway beach, away from the city's heat and the threat of the disease. The wedding is postponed when Lena falls ill of the disease. She recovers, but her left leg is paralyzed. Fearing she will be burden to Uncle Hyman, she refuses to marry him, and he is brokenhearted. Mama intervenes; she invites Lena to recover at the cottage, where she chides her for selfishness and finally convinces her to change her mind. The book concludes with a grand wedding and with the family preparing to move to a new apartment uptown. Only bumptious, outspoken Henny and capable, motherly Ella have distinct personalities. The charm of the book lies in its warm and wholesome portrayal of Jewish family life and religious beliefs, its gentle humor, and the author's remarkable ability to make little things important. Choice.

MORGAN, JUSTIN (*Justin Morgan Had a Horse**), a Randolph, Vt., schoolmaster and singing teacher (1748-1798) who gave his name to a line of American horses. In the novel, although he is sympathetic to the wish of Joel* Goss to own Little Bub, a nondescript pony later to be known as "Morgan's horse," he is in debt and needs the income that renting out Little Bub can bring him. When he dies of lung fever, he leaves Little Bub to Sheriff Rice, who he knows will be good to the horse until Joel is freed of his apprenticeship and can take care of the animal, but Little Bub is sold and stolen, and disappears for years before Joel finds him and purchases him. Although the book is fiction, the basic facts are true.

MORRISON, ALBERT (*The Enormous Egg**), Canadian paleontologist who visits Freedom to see Nate* Twitchell's dinosaur and who emphasizes that the dinosaur is valuable because he is alive. He cautions Nate to do everything he can to keep Uncle Beazley that way, and Nate heeds him.

THE MOTHER THING (*Have Space Suit—Will Travel**), a loving space creature whose job is to patrol and bring in any beings whose existence threatens the Three Galaxies. She is described as having soft fur and being cat-like in her movements. She speaks by telepathic communication in a sort of music, and she survives being frozen stiff in the cold of Pluto. She represents the intelligence and good qualities possible in non-human beings of the higher orders.

MOUNTAIN BORN (Yates*, Elizabeth, ill. Nora S. Unwin, Coward, 1943), realistic, pastoral animal novel set somewhere in hills where sheep are raised, moving with the seasons and the lives of the sheep and focusing on the bond between Biddy, the black, ewe lamb who becomes the leader of the flock and Peter, the little boy who raises her. After a small, newborn lamb, given up for dead, is nursed to life by Benj*, the old shepherd, and Martha, Peter's mother, she is given to Peter to raise. The lamb, which he names Biddy, becomes his dear friend and companion, his "cosset," as the family calls her, and the means by which he is introduced to the work of the sheep farm owned by Andrew, his father. He gradually assumes more and more responsibility, helping with such tasks as tail-docking, shearing, and dipping, and notes with pride how, as Biddy grows, she shows signs of becoming the leader of the sheep. When she is sheared for the first time, her heavy, dark fleece is made into the coat which takes him to school for the first time and then serves him well when he is in the fields tending the flock. Five years pass with Biddy proving herself a discerning and capable leader by protecting her flock against predators and weather. After the sheep are sheared one spring and then taken again to the hills, Biddy brings them back to the barn safely during a terrible sleet storm. The effort proves too much for the aging ewe and she dies. Peter, who has learned to accept certain realities of life on a farm, takes comfort in the fine new coat made from her last fleece and in her energetic, assertive black ewe lamb, who shows signs of taking her place as leader of the sheep. This is a quiet story, emotionally moving but never sentimental, whose strength lies in its clear details of life on a sheep farm as the seasons change. It shows well the mutual dependence that binds farmers and their sheep. Characters are well-drawn, especially Benj, and Peter grows up believably. The setting is left open in time and place the better to point up the universality of experience of those whose lives depend upon nature and her creatures. Newbery Honor.

MOUNTAINS ARE FREE (Adams*, Julia Davis, ill. Theodore Nadejen, Dutton, 1930), historical novel set in the Swiss canton of Uri in the first two decades of the fourteenth century. Bruno, an orphan of about fourteen, has been taken in by the William Tell family, but knowing that his presence adds to their poverty, he takes the opportunity to join as a servant an Austrian, Sir Rupprecht von Lowenhohe, on his way to the castle of the Duke of Valberg on the Wulach River. There he meets Lady Zelina, 13, heir of Rathwyl, the richest fief in the Duke's domain and the object of Rupprecht's matrimonial intention. Miserable in the confined castle, Bruno attempts escape, fails but is befriended by the jester, Kyo, who is also friend and secret protector of Zelina. When war breaks out and Rupprecht insists on immediate betrothal and marriage to Zelina, Kyo and Bruno escape with her and eventually make their way to the mountains, where they find the Swiss suffering under the imperial bailiff, Gessler. The story skips forward several years, and Bruno is a witness to the scene in which Gessler forces William Tell to shoot the apple from the head of his younger son, Walter, then arrests him, and Bruno watches as the boat taking him across the lake to prison is swamped in a storm. He follows Tell, who escapes to shore, across the mountain and sees him shoot Gessler. Bruno is present at the other main events of the Swiss uprising and, when it is successful, finds Zelina wishing to marry him, even if it means giving up, or at least postponing, her claim to Rathwyl. The style is simple, and the fictional events are not entirely believable; Bruno's involvement in the William Tell episodes is awkwardly contrived. Characters are mostly stock figures, but the action is lively. Newbery Honor.

THE MOVED-OUTERS (Means*, Florence Crannell, ill. Helen Blair, Houghton, 1945), historical novel dealing with the internment of American Japanese during World War II. Sue* (Sumiko) Ohara, 18, and her brother, Kim* (Kimio), 17, are typical bright, popular high school seniors in Cordova, a small California town where their father, the only businessman of Japanese descent, owns a nursery and florist shop. Among their friends like Emily Andrews and Jimmy Boyd they are considered entirely American, but after the attack on Pearl Harbor in December, 1941, some of the townspeople become hostile. Almost immediately Mr. Ohara is taken by the FBI to an internment camp in North Dakota, and by March Sue and Kim, with their mother and other area Japanese, including Jiro* Ito, whom Sue has secretly loved for years, are sent to a temporary camp made from the stables at Santa Anita raceway. The Itos, Jiro, his timid sister,

Tomi, younger siblings and their parents, are camp neighbors of the Oharas, so Sue finds some excitement and pleasure in the experience, but her parents look down upon the Ito family and her mother frowns at their frequent association. Friends from Cordova, including Mr. Clemons, the minister, visit them at camp, and the young people help Sue and Kim slip through the barbed wire to go to a hamburger stand. At graduation time the principal at Cordova comes to award their diplomas and to announce that Kim is valedictorian and Sue salutatorian. Later the family is sent to Amache, Colo., a new, raw camp of barracks set in dusty flatland, and again Sue finds it bearable partly because Jiro Ito is nearby and is very helpful, building furniture for them and steadying Kim, whose volatile temperament becomes bitter and depressed after a local ''patriot'' shoots at a survey crew and wounds him. The happiness the family feels when Sue's father is allowed to join them at Amache is dimmed by news that an older brother Ted (Tadashi), who has been serving in the army, is killed in action. Kim seems attracted to the Yellow Shirts, young toughs of the camp, who break up a block party Sue has helped organize and are responsible for thefts in the co-op, but Jiro proves that at the time of the break-in, Kim was with him deciding to join the army. Jiro also enlists. Sue, who has a scholarship arranged by Mr. Clemons, gives it to Tomi but leaves camp to go to college at the University of Colorado. She and Jiro have an understanding; after the war, he plans to go to medical school. Although the book is obviously written to express a thesis and a great many speeches about democracy and rights of citizens and patriotic ideas are put in the mouths of the characters, the historical suffering and humiliation caused to the Japanese-Americans is not overdramatized. In working so hard to characterize the young people as typical, however, the author has not made them individually very interesting. Newbery Honor.

MOYI (*Flag of the Desert**), chief priest of the Jukon tribe of Nigeria, who has usurped power when the last Aku, local chief, died. Moyi has ruled by terror for three years, gradually arranging the murder of almost all the rightful claimants to the position. A sinister figure, he is large and soft of body, but alert and wary and very clever. He alone of the elders called together to choose the new Aku is unimpressed by the ''voice of the ancestor,'' rigged with a loud speaker by Bill and Terry, and suspects a trick.

MR. CHRIS (*Miracles on Maple Hill**), Maple Hill resident who helps Marly's family in many ways when they move to the country. A mine of information on plants and nature, he is also very understanding about humans, tactfully helping Dale recover from his experience as a war prisoner and saying just the right thing when Marly is feeling snubbed by her brother, Joe*. It is Mr. Chris who first mentions the ''miracles'' Marly finds in the country and who promises her a new one every week.

MR. DAKYNS (*Harry in England**), Harry's tutor while he lives at Silverthorne. A young man, Mr. Dakyns is tall, thin, gangly, and very energetic. He likes to go for strolls about the countryside and is a great talker. He has inventive and unconventional teaching methods. He helps Harry capture creatures for an aquarium to learn natural science, and he often dances and prances about and walks on his hands while reciting Latin phrases and stories from history. When Harry first meets him, he outwits a threatening bull by putting his head between his legs and running backwards towards it. He is more energetic and high-spirited than eccentric or comic.

MR. EDWARDS (*Little House on the Prairie**; *On the Shores of Silver Lake**; *The Long Winter**), the settler in Oklahoma territory who helps Pa (Charles*) Ingalls build the cabin and who walks forty miles to Independence and back and crosses the creek in flood at Christmas to bring Laura* and Mary* gifts that he says Santa Claus asked him to deliver. He describes himself as a "wild cat from Tennessee" and dances to Pa's fiddle music in a way that rather shocks Ma (Caroline* Ingalls). Pa runs into him again in Dakota territory at the Brookings homestead claim office where he helps Pa get into the office to file his claim by starting a fight among the men crowding to get in. Later, in De Smet, at the first of the long winter, Pa brings him home when the men have dug out the railroad tracks, and as he departs to go further west he secretly leaves a twenty-dollar bill in Mary's lap, a contribution to her fund to send her to college for the blind.

MR. HAGGERTY (*Miss Pickerell Goes to Mars**), young man to whom Miss Pickerell gives a ride on her way home from visiting relatives and who fixes her car. He tells her he is about to leave on an exciting, important trip. He has become a space scientist but really wants to be a veterinarian. At the end, he decides to go to vet school.

MR. HANNIBAL B. BUCKLE (*The Middle Moffat**), a veteran of the Civil War and, at ninety-nine, Cranbury's* oldest resident. He is good-natured and fun-loving and appreciates Jane* Moffat's concern for his welfare. He always has time for her and never patronizes her or is gruff with her. It is his prerogative to give out diplomas at graduation, and everyone in town knows and likes him. His daughter, Miss Buckle, gives the Moffats the organ.

MR. MURPHY (*Homer Price**), the bearded, Rip Van Winkle-like figure who comes to town with a musical mousetrap. He spent fifteen years in the hills developing this ingenious contraption for catching mice without hurting them. It is very elaborate and creates a sensation in Centerburg.

MR. NIGHT OWL (*Roller Skates**), Lucinda's friend; his real name is Hugh Marshall. He writes for the New York *Sun*. He takes Lucinda to the Barnum and Bailey parade on the first day of spring and to the circus later. She, Tony, and Mr. Night Owl get to don exotic costumes and help with the elephant act.

MR. PIERRE MINETTE (*Windfall Fiddle**), elderly florist who helps Bob Carson get the money he needs to buy a violin from Miss Adelaide, his neighbor and violin teacher. Mr. Minette is in his eighties, served as a flag bearer in the Civil War, sports a long, white beard, and speaks with a French accent which becomes more pronounced when he becomes excited. Mr. Minette also brings Miss Adelaide and Bob's Uncle David together by turning Miss Adelaide against her wealthy Rochester admirer. When the Rochester admirer orders a bouquet of fall flowers for her from Mr. Minette, he includes goldenrod, which aggravates her hayfever and drives her into Uncle David's sympathetic arms. Mr. Minette likes to entertain his friends with tales of his hair-raising exploits in the Civil War and as an Indian fighter.

MR. POPPER (*Mr. Popper's Penguins**), absent-minded, rather sloppy housepainter, who acquires a dozen penguins, trains them, and tours the theaters of the country with the act. Somewhat impractical, Mr. Popper has always dreamed of adventure and far-off places and finally achieves his desire when he goes as penguin keeper on an expedition to establish the birds in the North Polar region.

MR. POPPER'S PENGUINS (Atwater*, Richard, and Florence Atwater*, ill. Robert Lawson*, Little, 1938), light, amusing story set in Stillwater, a typical, small American city in the 1930s. After Mr. Popper, a housepainter who dreams of adventure, sees a movie of Admiral Drake's Antarctic expedition and writes a fan letter, the admiral sends him a gift of a penguin, to the delight of Mr. Popper and his children, Janie and Bill, and less enthusiastic reception from Mrs. Popper. The bird, which the Poppers name Captain Cook, necessitates some changes at the Popper home at 432 Proudfoot Ave.: holes must be bored in the refrigerator door and a handle installed inside, so that Captain* Cook can sleep there; the living room windows are left to open and the floor flooded to make an icy playground; eventually a large freezer plant must be installed in the basement. When Captain Cook's health seems to be on the decline, the curator at the aquarium in Mammoth City, whom Mr. Popper has consulted, diagnoses the illness as loneliness and sends a female penguin, Greta. Soon there are ten young penguins, and the Poppers, whose finances are strained by the feeding costs, train them for a stage act and go on tour to theaters owned by the entrepreneur, Mr. Greenbaum. All goes well until absent-minded Mr. Popper takes his act not to the Royal theater, as scheduled, but to the Regal, where a trained seal act is performing. The ensuing disturbance involves the fire and police departments and lands Mr. Popper and his penguins in jail, where he is visited first by Admiral Drake, back from Antarctica and planning an Arctic trip to establish penguins at the North Pole, and by Mr. Greenbaum, who brings a moviemaker with an offer of a Hollywood contract. Mr. Popper opts for the Arctic and goes along as penguin caretaker. Although there is little effort to make the episodes probable and the humor is obvious, the story has been a favorite for its good humor and undemanding comedy. Choice; Fanfare; Lewis Carroll; Newbery Honor.

MR. REVERE AND I (Lawson*, Robert, ill. author, Little, 1953), fantasy biography set in and near Boston in the period of the American Revolution, as is apparent from its long subtitle, "Being an Account of certain Episodes in the Career of Paul Revere, Esq. as recently revealed by his Horse, Scheherazade, late Pride of his Royal Majesty's 14th Regiment of Foot." Scheherazade arrives in Boston after a terrible sea journey as the mount of a foppish young officer, Leftenant Sir Cedric Noel Vivian Barnstable, Bart. She and her stablemate, Ajax, the handsome charger of Sir Dagmore Dalrymple, the colonel and commander, find the local people churlish and provincial. The stuttering Barnstable is given to gambling and his bets on races which fleet Scheherazade wins for him usually pay off his other gaming debts, but one unfortunate day a rowdy watching with Sam Adams* throws an oyster shell, causing Scheherazade to slip and fall. Trying to recoup his losses, Barnstable gambles away the horse to a glue factory owner. There she is hitched to a cart hauling offal, a humiliation so great that she bolts rather than meet Ajax again, wrecks the cart, and is commandeered by Sam Adams's Committee of Correspondence for Paul Revere*. At the Revere home she has a stall with a window looking into the kitchen and soon finds herself a part of the warm family and revolutionary political activity. She sees Revere providing clothes and jobs for deserters from the British army, men who were impressed into it; she carries him to nearby towns to inspect the Militia; she witnesses the action leading to the Boston Tea Party. In miserable December weather, Scheherazade carries Revere to New York to give the news of the tea party and, in May, to Philadelphia to enlist support if the British close the port of Boston, as they later do. Sherry, as Revere calls her, is part of the famous ride to warn the countryside of the British march on Lexington; she and Revere are captured by Colonel Dalrymple near Concord, and, as Sherry creates panic among the horses, Revere escapes. A short time later, Dalrymple and his men run into skunks and in the ensuing confusion Sherry flees, only to be shot in the left shoulder. Near Lexington, Sherry catches up with Revere, is given first aid and led slowly back, witnessing the rout of the British troops by the local militia. The famous revolutionary, Dr. Warren, removes the bullet and sews up Sherry's wound, a kindly farrier cares for her until she recovers, and she sees Ajax being loaded as the British evacuate Boston in March of 1776. Although a fantasy, the historical events are reported accurately for the most part, and the pictures of Revere, Adams, Washington, Warren, Hancock*, and other real people follow biographical facts. Much of the humor comes from the superior attitude and snobbish remarks of Ajax and, at first, of Sherry. Her gradual change to support of the Colonists reflects the grievances of the colonies and the ideals of the Revolution. The illustrations by the author add authentic details as well as humor. Choice; Fanfare.

MR. RICHARD HAGGIN (*Big Red**), wealthy businessman from New York on whose country estate in the Wintapi the Picket cabin stands. When he notices how much Danny likes Red and that Red takes to the boy, he hires Danny as Red's handler. On their trip to New York City and the dog show, Mr. Haggin explains the significance of shows and of the importance of selective breeding. Through him, Danny gets some sense of what the world outside the Wintapi offers.

MRS. KIRBY (*Jennifer**), one of Mrs. Martin's Alcoholics Anonymous friends who helps her to cope with her problem and to reach out to help others. Jennifer resents her because she reminds Jennifer of her mother's problem and the difficult times the family has had because of it. Jennifer comes to acknowledge that Mrs. Kirby has been a good influence. Mrs. Kirby's story about her experiences as an alcoholic reads like a classic textbook case.

MRS. OLIPHANT (*The Saturdays**), wealthy friend of the Melendys who appears occasionally in the three books to help out when the family needs a lift. In later adventures, she contributes Motor, her car, to them, gives them decorations for their fair, and brings with her to the variety show a New York friend of hers, who subsequently gives Mona a role in the radio serial he produces.

MRS. WEST (*Benjamin West and His Cat Grimalkin**), staunch Quaker woman, mother of Benjamin. Although horrified when she discovers that Benjamin has drawn a picture of baby Sally, she appreciates the aptness of the likeness, understands the boy's need to express himself artistically, and stands up for him against his father.

MR. TIDY PAWS (Sayers*, Frances Clark, ill. Zhenya Gay, Viking, 1935), cat story that hovers between realism and fantasy, set in an unspecified country in the deserted village of Beau Blossom, in a time that seems to be before automobiles. Christopher Tree, 9, and his grandmother, Betsy, are the only villagers who remain in Beau Blossom when a handsome, well-dressed, affable stranger named Mr. Jeremiad offers to build a town hall, a school, a church, and a library if the residents will all move twelve miles down the river and name the new town after him. As soon as the name is registered, he disappears, keeping none of his promises, but the villagers have neither money nor energy to return. When Christopher finds a black kitten, his grandmother hesitates to keep it, fearing an all-black cat is bad luck, until Christopher finds three white hairs on its shoulder. They name it Secret and are surprised that it acts so unlike other cats. One early spring night, Christopher follows the cat to a spot in the meadow where the grass grows in a circle of rich green and there sees him perform all sorts of tricks in the moonlight, accompanied by laughter from an invisible audience. Gran decides that he is a changeling, a fairy cat, and warns Christopher to pretend he doesn't know. Though they have a garden, a cow, and wild berries, they have no way to get money and fear that at summer's end they will have to move to Jeremiad. Instead, Christopher sets off to make his fortune, and Secret follows him. After some luckless days, they run into Monsieur Bo-Bo's Famous Dog and Pony Show, and just as Bo-Bo and his son, Joseph, are also turning down Christopher's request for work, Secret performs his many tricks in the middle of the road. Renamed Mr. Tidy Paws, he becomes the hit of the show. In the autumn, Christopher and Secret part company with the show and take home a bag of coins each for Gran. Since the cat never speaks and his thoughts are not recorded, the story could be interpreted realistically, with the fairy element just Gran's superstition, but the tone is more that of a literary fairy tale, pleasant but slight. Fanfare.

MR. WEST (*Benjamin West and His Cat Grimalkin**), pious, firm, loving father, a Quaker whose voice trembles and shakes the roof timbers of his inn when he prays. He is horrified when he discovers his son is sketching, scorning such activity as foolish and vain. But he is also an understanding man who loves his son, and, recognizing Benjamin's talent and need to express himself through drawing, he says the boy may continue to draw if the activity does not interfere with his chores about the house and yard.

MR. WOODLAWN (*Caddie Woodlawn**), clear-headed, principled father in the large, close Woodlawn family. After Caddie discovers some little, wooden-soled clogs in the attic, John Woodlawn tells his family the story of his childhood. His father, the son of an English lord, was disinherited for marrying the daughter of the village shoemaker. After his father's death, little John helped earn money by singing and dancing dressed in red breeches and wooden clogs.

MUCHERI (*Lion Boy**), brave warrior and hunter of the Wanyamlima. When the villagers cannot understand why the tall, strong fence they have erected around the *zizi* (corral) is not protecting their herd of buffalo, he offers to stand guard by himself. He climbs a tree, where he spends the night wrapped in a blanket. He discovers that a huge, clever, old lion has been organizing lion attacks against the fence to break it down and get at the animals.

MUGGLES (*The Gammage Cup**; *The Whisper of Glocken*†), disorganized, untidy collector of odds and ends, candymaker and curator of the museum in the Minnipin village of Slipper-on-the-Water*. Considered simple-minded and harmless, she is something of a trial to her fellow Minnipins because of her poor housekeeping. Since she is good-humored and obliging, she is tolerated until she becomes friends with "Them," the nonconformists who refuse to paint their doors green. All five are then outlawed from the village. Once on the mountain, Muggles becomes the leader of the group, and her foresight and decisiveness insure their survival. In the second book, she helps to rescue the New Heroes.

MUKERJI, DHAN GOPAL (1890-1936), lecturer and author for adults and children, best known in children's literature for his animal stories set mostly in the jungles of India. He was born near Calcutta, India, at the edge of the jungle he wrote about. He was raised on the stories and fables of old India, some of which made their way later into his children's books. Of a Brahmin (priestly caste) family, he was initiated into the priesthood and subsequently made a two-year begging pilgrimage through India. He studied in Calcutta and in Japan, and at twenty emigrated to the United States. He worked at odd jobs to finance his schooling at the University of California at Berkeley and at Stanford, from which he received his bachelor of philosophy degree. He married an American, lectured on comparative literature in England and the United States, and made his home in Connecticut. He wrote a novel, plays, verse, and books of personal experience and philosophy, translated the *Bhagavad-Gita* for adults, and published a dozen books, mostly novels, for young readers. Highly acclaimed were *Gay-Neck: The Story of a Pigeon** (Dutton, 1927), based on his own experiences in raising pigeons, which won the Newbery Award and is listed in *Choice*, and *Fierce-Face: The Story of a Tiger** (Dutton, 1936), a Fanfare book. Also episodic was his first novel, *Kari the Elephant* (Dutton, 1922), published when he was thirty-two, and *Ghond the Hunter* (Dutton, 1928) and *The Chief of the Herd* (Dutton, 1929) are in a similar vein. He also published a book of Hindu fables and a version of the *Ramayana* for young readers.

MULLER, MR. AND MRS. (*In a Mirror**), Bessie's* writer father, who churns out mystery novels for a more than adequate living and often goes off alone into his study to write, and Bessie's mother, who accommodates easily to his whims and needs. They exemplify a kind of one-sided marriage that contrasts with Donald* Dunn's.

MUSA (*Homespun**), son of an African chief, slave to Monsieur Foucher. Monsieur Foucher gives Musa to Stephen* in gratitude for Stephen's abrogating the Stillman-Foucher cotton contract after the Foucher gins are destroyed in a fire. Stephen abhors slavery, and with the first money he earns from the Stillman firm, he buys Musa's passage back to Africa and freedom.

MUSHROOM PEOPLE (*The Wonderful Flight to the Mushroom Planet**; *Stowaway to the Mushroom Planet**; *Time and Mr. Bass*†), the inhabitants of Basidium-X* and the humanoid race to which Mr. Tyco* Bass belongs. While primitive in many ways, they catch one another's thoughts instantly. They use the flesh of the bilba trees to make robes which they drape much like those of the ancient Greeks. They are smaller than people of Earth, are pale green in color when healthy, and have large, dome-like heads, small faces, and gentle, dark brown eyes. They are peaceful and kind by nature and live in igloo-shaped houses.

MY DOG RINTY (Tarry*, Ellen, and Marie Hall Ets*, ill. Alexander Alland and Alexandra Alland, Viking, 1946), very simple story set in Harlem in the 1940s and illustrated with photographs. David, a black boy about eight to ten, lives in an old building with his parents, his sister, and three brothers, and his dog, Rinty, who will not behave. Rinty chews through his rope and follows David to school; he bites at the edge of the nuns' habits; he chews holes in the carpet. When there are complaints, David's brothers offer to help make him a house with a lock out of an old box. When Rinty chews through the leather hinges on the door, David's father says he must go. David goes to put an ad in the paper, and a lady who sees Rinty adopts him. None of the diversions the family can think up—visits to friends who have an electric train, the library story hour—can keep David from being sad until one day Rinty shows up at the apartment door. David's father insists that he find the new owner and return the dog. The kind lady hires David to walk Rinty every day after school. When the dog chews her carpet, she takes him to obedience school, where the trainer points out that Rinty is merely showing the position of mouse and rat holes beneath the floor. When the apartment where the new owner, Mrs. Moseley, lives makes a no-pet rule, she gives the now well-behaved pet back to David, who earns money for dog food by renting Rinty out to show where there are mice and rat holes. Newspapers print pictures of David and Rinty calling them The Pied Pipers of Harlem. Like most stories illustrated with photographs, the plot seems contrived to fit the pictures. In addition, the clothes, cars, and situations belong to an earlier period and seem dated far more by the realism of the photographs than they might with some other sort of illustrations. Fanfare.

MY FATHER'S DRAGON (Gannett*, Ruth Stiles, ill. Ruth Chrisman Gannett, Random, 1948), talking animal fantasy set on the high seas. On the advice of a talking alley cat he has befriended, the narrator's father, Elmer Elevator, runs away from home and sails to Tangerina and Wild Islands. He hopes to rescue a baby flying dragon which has been enslaved by the animals there and forced to carry passengers across the river that runs through Wild Island. Elmer's equipment includes such assorted items as chewing gum, two dozen pink lollipops, rubber bands, and hair ribbons. With these items, quick thinking, trickery, and some luck, he pacifies tigers, lions, wild boars, a gorilla, and seventeen crocodiles to accomplish his objective. Although contrived, strained, and condescending, the story is not without suspense and absurd, comic logic. Numerous black and white drawings depict episodes, show locations, and add to the nonsense. The first of a series. Choice; Fanfare; Lewis Carroll; Newbery Honor.

MYRTLE SMITH (*Trigger John's Son**), wife of George* Smith, who adopts Trigger*. She is willing to take Trigger in because her own son has died, but she explains that she can't love him like her own because that would be wicked. She insists on calling Trigger "Robert," a more respectable name. Plagued by a strong conscience and an inflexible sense of duty, she is suspicious that enjoyment is sin. As Trigger explains to Dude* Quinlan, "She finds out what she wants to do just so she can stop herself from doing it." In the end, however, she stands up for Trigger even when she thinks he has misbehaved.

MY SIDE OF THE MOUNTAIN (George*†, Jean Craighead, ill. author, Dutton, 1959), Robinson Crusoe novel set in the Catskill Mountains near Delhi, N.Y., in the mid-twentieth century. Sam Gribley, a teenager tired of his New York apartment that houses a family of eleven, leaves home in May to live off nature on his great-grandfather's long-abandoned farm. He starts with only a flint and steel, a penknife, a ball of cord, an ax, and forty dollars. With the help of Miss Turner, the Delhi librarian, he locates the spot on an old map, but as they expect, the house has disappeared. The book recounts his year on the mountain where he builds a home inside an enormous hemlock tree, eats well on berries, roots, nuts, and other wild foods, skins and tans deer that hunters have lost to make clothes and blankets, and observes nature as one can only by living isolated and dependent upon it. He makes some animal friends, the most important being Frightful, a falcon he steals as a baby from a nest, raises, and trains to hunt for him. Others are a playful weasel, The Baron, and Jessie Coon James, a raccoon which plunders his supplies whenever possible. He is not completely isolated from humans. He skillfully hides from a fire warden, but an old woman, thinking he is a town boy, presses him into service picking all the wild strawberries he has hoped to use himself. A college English teacher whom he calls Bando, assuming he is an outlaw, wanders lost onto his campsite, stays several days, helps him make a raft to fish from the middle of the pond, and returns for Christmas vacation and again in the spring. Matt Spell, thirteen or fourteen, comes from Poughkeepsie hunting a story about the rumored "wild boy of the Catskills," hoping to sell it to the newspaper where he works part time, is fed by Sam, and agrees to keep him a secret if Sam will allow him to come back for spring vacation. Tom Sidler, a boy his own age, whom he refers to as Mr. Jacket when he meets him on a rare visit to Delhi, comes in the spring, stays over night, and returns frequently. A hiker named Aaron, a song writer from New York, meets him briefly one afternoon and returns for a week. Sam's father hunts him up at Christmas and stays until New Year's Day. In June he arrives with Sam's mother and eight siblings, planning to build a house and live on the mountain. By then Sam is ready for a return to family life and companionship. Like most Robinsonnades, the greatest fascination of the story is in the details of how things are done, the step-by-step preparation of shelter and food, the ingenious ways that natural materials may be substituted for those of civilized society, and the resulting communion with one's natural surroundings. In all these elements the author is explicit and convincing. In motivation and characterization, she is less successful. Sam's age, for example, is never clear; sometimes he seems about twelve or thirteen, at others at least seventeen. He is wise enough to take along an ax, but not a sleeping bag or even a blanket. He is determined to live off the land but uses the deer that a poacher shoots and later spots from a tree other deer shot by hunters and even conceals them with branches so they won't be found and claimed. All the clever ways he devises to get food and necessities are clearly possible, but the amount of time seems hardly sufficient for some, and his continual good luck is unlikely. Because he has no particular reason to be on his own and because he is continually near a town and road, the plot lacks tension, a weakness that has not, however, kept the book from being widely popular. Choice; Fanfare; Lewis Carroll; Newbery Honor; Stone.

N

NAH-TEE (*The Runaway Papoose**), a little Pueblo Indian girl, possibly five to seven years old, who is lost in the desert. She has fled when men attacked the group led by her father and has been unable to find them again. Too young to realize the dangers that she and the Navajo boy, Moyo, encounter, Nah-tee is generally happy and confident.

NANCY STOKES (*The Middle Moffat**; *Rufus M.**), Jane's* best friend after the Moffats move to Ashbellows Place. Jane describes her as brave, fearless, and kind to animals. She has golden curls, is an organizer, and has a hearty laugh which Jane envies. She and Jane have a falling out in *The Middle Moffat*, but Nancy comes to the conclusion that Jane was right and big-heartedly takes the initiative in making up. She lives in a house with floors so shiny and slick that Jane is afraid to walk on them lest she slip and fall, and Nancy's mother occasionally has a maid. Jane thinks the Stokes family is very well off. Nancy is the captain of the baseball team that Jane is on, the Fatal Four.

NAT EATON (*The Witch of Blackbird Pond**), son of the captain of the *Dolphin*, the ship on which Kit sails to Connecticut. He later has a ship of his own, the *Witch*, and marries Kit. He is a happy, life-loving youth, kind and generous, sometimes teasing and mischievous, who befriends Hannah* Tupper, because she once helped him. He rescues Hannah and takes her away on his ship when the townspeople burn her house because they think she is a witch.

NATE TWITCHELL (*The Enormous Egg**), son of the owner of the newspaper in Freedom, the *Freedom Sentinel*, who tells the story in breezy, intimate style. He is conscientious, really cares for Uncle Beazley, and refuses to let Uncle Beazley be exploited for commercial purposes even though he could make a lot of money doing so.

NATTY RINGO (*Whistlers' Van**), Nathaniel Ringo, intelligent, strong, well-built gypsy who instructs Gwilym in the ways and lore of the Rommanies. When he almost causes a riot by defeating a local hero in boxing at a fair, the Ringos meet Captain Lewis, Natty's old war friend. A horsemaster, Natty solves the problem of why Captain Lewis's fine new horse has gone mad and why Lewis's neighbor and horse have met mysterious deaths. When Thomas Anwyl refuses the kingship, Natty becomes the new king of the gypsies.

NECESSARY NELLIE (Baker*, Charlotte, ill. author, Coward, 1945), short, realistic novel set somewhere in the southwestern part of the United States at an unspecified time, but probably in the mid-1900s. The story revolves around the love of five Mexican-American children for their dog. Antonia, Leopoldo, Julio, Alberto, and Rosita live with their elderly grandfather. The little family is poor but happy, and, since the grandfather is often ill, the children must take care of one another. One day a nondescript, mongrel puppy, "a little slick white dog with one brown ear and one brown spot on her back" and big, brown eyes, appears at the door of their tiny house. The children fall in love with her and persuade their grandfather to let them keep her. Happy days follow as the children frolic with Nellie, often near the Old Mission by the creek. Their good friend, the jolly, kind priest, Father Lafferty, is engaged in restoring the Mission. One day when they cannot find Nellie, who has taken to wandering, the children are advised to try the dog pound. Since they do not have enough money to pay for a license, they persuade the dog catcher to take them to the judge. They impress him so much with their case for Nellie's necessity that he gives them the dollar to pay for the license. After a year passes without incident, Nellie presents the children with another major problem: how to get five dollars to license her five puppies. Nellie herself solves the problem by returning home from a day's jaunt with a five-dollar bill in her mouth. Julio deduces that she has discovered a buried treasure. When the children follow her on her travels the next day, she leads them to the Old Mission, where she digs furiously in an old well. The children dig, too, and unearth not a treasure in money, but the long-lost Mission bell, just what Father Lafferty needs to complete the restoration of the old Spanish-American church. The plot of this pleasant, fast-moving story is all on the surface, spun out with artificial incidents for the amusement of younger readers. Characters are undeveloped, and the children are virtuallly indistinguishable, except for Rosita, the youngest, who remains steadfast in her faith in Nellie's importance to the family. There is a fairy tale–like quality to events and little sense of how the family lives. Father Lafferty's description of the Old Mission and the Indians who once lived there has an instructive tone. Vocabulary is easy, sentences and chapters are short, and dialogue is abundant. Sketches in orange tones establish the setting on the outskirts of a big, Mediterranean-climate city. Fanfare.

NEJMI (*Spice and the Devil's Cave**), beautiful, shy, withdrawn, half-Arab daughter of a European spice trader in Aden, whose parents are slain by Arab pirates and who is sold into slavery. She is helped to escape by a sympathetic sailor, Scander, who later becomes fond of her and is pilot and friend of Nicolo* Conti, Venetian merchant who has established residence in Lisbon. Nejmi eventually makes her way ashore in Lisbon in a sugar barrel. She appears mysteriously one night in the courtyard of the house of Abel* and Ruth Zakuto who take her in and treat her like a daughter. She later marries Nicolo.

NELLIE OLESON (*On the Banks of Plum Creek**; *Little Town on the Prairie**; *These Happy Golden Years**), spoiled, disagreeable child who sneers at Laura* and Mary* Ingalls as "country girls" when they live in Minnesota and who reappears some years later in De Smet, S.Dak. At her party at the town near Plum Creek, she shows off her expensive toys but snatches them away before Laura can touch them. At the country party, Laura leads her into the muddy part of the creek where there are bloodsuckers. In De Smet, Nellie becomes intimate with the teacher, Miss Wilder, in an attempt to get to know her brother, Almanzo*, and to ride behind his beautiful horses, and she distorts things Laura has said to make Miss Wilder dislike the Ingalls girls. After Almanzo has begun to court Laura with weekly buggy rides, Nellie tries to cut in by coming along on the rides and flirting, but Laura wins by her honesty and her understanding of horses which she shares with Almanzo.

NEWELL, HOPE (HOCKENBERRY) (1896-1965), born in Bradford, Pa.; nurse and author. She was a graduate of Columbia University and studied nursing in Cincinnati, Ohio. During World War I, she served ten months in France with the U.S. Army Nurse Corps, then worked in public health nursing in New York City, and in World War II accepted a position with the National Nursing Council for War Service. Among her books are nursing stories, *A Cap for Mary Ellis* (Harper, 1953) and *Mary Ellis, Student Nurse* (Harper, 1958), and stories for young children based on the Dutch folk tales her father told her, including *The Little Old Woman Who Used Her Head** (Nelson, 1935) and *The Little Old Woman Carries On* (Nelson, 1947). *Steppin and Family** (Oxford, 1942), which grew out of her public health experience in Harlem, is an interesting example of the books with black characters published in the early 1940s, which now seem dated.

NEW LAND (Schmidt*, Sarah Lindsay, ill. Frank Dobias, McBride, 1933), realistic novel of the early 1930s. Arriving at the homestead of Sam Parsons near Upham, Wyo., with her feckless father, her little sister, Hitty, and her twin, Charley, 17, Sayre Morgan hopes that at last they will stop their wandering from failure to failure and will settle in a permanent home, even the "crate," as they call the shack Parsons has left them. Their discovery that they cannot have Parsons's claim transferred to them is the first of a series of disappointing discoveries. Later they find that Parsons intends to hang on to the claim with them doing the work and that he has sold all the alfalfa they raise to the town's big store owner, wheeler-dealer Franklin Hoskins. Sayre, determined not to give up, sees the high school coach-agriculture teacher, Kit Kitchell, and gets him to interest Charley in returning to school to play football and to let her enroll as the only girl in the part-time class in agriculture. Both she and Charley become much interested in "ag" projects, Charley rebuilding a manure spreader and planting field peas, Sayre raising chickens and turkeys. Charley also becomes involved in a rivalry with Frank Hoskins, sulky, handsome son of the store owner, both in football and in agriculture class. When the twins almost catch a thief stealing Sayre's turkey poults with a fishing rod and a grappling hook and the rod turns out to be Mr. Hoskins's, Charley and Frank have a fist fight which Charley wins and Frank resents. Later, when both are working on Hoskins's baler, the amount of hay on Parsons's place is mysteriously larger than calculated, and when it is shipped, it results in an embargo on all Wyoming hay because it contains alfalfa weevil, a fact that turns all the town against the Morgans. The reason is eventually revealed by Rene Osgood, Frank's girl, who confesses to Sayre that Frank has carted his own hay, which he knows to be buggy, to mix with the Morgans', and she also admits to being the turkey thief in an attempt to help Frank. By then both boys, returning from a stock-judging contest in Laramie, are caught in a terrible April blizzard and are believed dead. Kitchell tells Sayre that the embargo has been lifted after investigation reveals that the bugs are a harmless variety, and the boys are found in a shack still alive, with Frank having redeemed himself by saving Charley's life. Charley refuses Hoskins's offer to manage a dairy farm and proposes a partnership with Sayre to prove up on the Parsons land and claim it under the new, stricter rules. Sayre is determined, inclined to be bossy, and very hardworking; Charley, like his father, has been inclined to dream, then give up easily. Aside from this, characterization is minimal and minor figures are stereotypes. The strength of the book lies in its setting on the barren, western Wyoming plains and the earnest way it manages to make details of farming interesting. Although Sayre must influence Charley without his realizing it and is the family homemaker, she is also a feminist in joining the agriculture class and doing men's work on the farm. Fanfare; Newbery Honor.

NEYHART, LOUISE A(LBRIGHT), born in Amboy, Ill., she has lived since childhood in Freeport, Ill. After studying at Lake Forest College, she graduated from the National College of Education with a degree in teaching, and subsequently taught in the Freeport Public Schools. She has been very active in civic affairs, serving as trustee and on the citizens' committees for library and higher education boards. For exemplary public service, she received, among other honors, the Alumni Achievement Award of the National College of Education. Freeport, Ill., was the site of the most important of the Lincoln-Douglas debates. *Henry's Lincoln** (Holiday, 1945), intended for younger readers and a Fanfare book, resulted from her son's questions about that important historical event. It tells how a farm boy travels to Freeport to hear the debates, predisposed to favor

Douglas, and ends up supporting Lincoln. She has also written the biographies, *Henry Ford, Engineer* (Houghton, 1950) and *Giant of the Yards* (Houghton, 1952), about Gustavus Franklin Swift and the development of Swift and Company, for older youth.

NICHOLAS: A MANHATTAN CHRISTMAS STORY (Moore*, Anne Carroll, ill. Jay Van Everen, Putnam, 1924), episodic fantasy set in the heart of New York City some time after World War I. Nicholas, a tiny Dutch boy eight inches high, sails from Holland to Manhattan in search of Christmas, arriving on Christmas Eve. He goes straight to the public library, where he meets Brownie, who is planning a Christmas Eve party for all her storybook friends. Through Brownie he meets Ann Carraway, John Moon, a writer, Lucky, and Joe Star, adults who live nearby and with whom in the ensuing weeks he becomes close friends. He goes shopping with Ann and John, chats with such real-life people as Washington Irving and Mary Mapes Dodge, and, at Brownie's party in the library, he frolics with many such characters from children's books as the Peterkins, the Forty Thieves, Aladdin, Robinson Crusoe, Sinbad, and fairies and trolls. During the holiday season, his days are fun-filled, with sleighing, skating, tobogganing, rides on the Staten Island Ferry, the elevated and the subway, a trip to Portland, Maine, to visit friends of Ann's, plays, toy shops, and sporting with the animals in the zoo. Nicholas's newly made friends take him around the city, showing him the sights and telling him stories about the history and landmarks of New York, about such important national figures as George Washington, and about such seasonal features as "Little Town of Bethlehem" and "The Night before Christmas." He celebrates St. Valentine's Day and Washington's Birthday before sailing back to France just before Easter. Dated in language and approach, yet invested with an innocent charm, this frivolous romp is intended to instruct as it entertains. Extensive dialogue and numerous incidents move the story along rapidly, but, when considered by late twentieth-century standards for children's literature, it lacks substance and continuity, and is too obviously didactic and condescending toward its audience. Newbery Honor.

NICHOLAS DRURY (*Clearing Weather**), stalwart, impetuous youth whose vision and practicality save the once-thriving Branscomb, Mass., shipyards of his ill uncle, Thomas, from financial ruin during the hard times which afflict the United States after the Revolutionary War. He designs the sailing ship, *Jocasta**, and arranges to share its profits with the townspeople in return for their work in building the ship, earning their gratitude and loyalty for his generosity and public spirit. In spite of the obstructive efforts of greedy, scheming Darius Corland, his uncle's archenemy who wishes the shipyards for himself, Nicholas's courageous venture not only saves the family business but gives impetus to New England trade with China.

NICOLO CONTI (*Spice and the Devil's Cave**), young merchant from Venice who travels to Lisbon because he believes that Portugal will soon discover a sea route to India, opening up rich trade in spices and other exotic commodities. He discovers the Venetian plot to scuttle the voyage of Vasco da Gama around the Cape of Good Hope, also called the Devil's Cave, and to develop a system of forts and a water passageway near Egypt. He falls in love with and marries Nejmi*, the Arabian girl who fled from slavery and took refuge with Abel* and Ruth Zakuto, Nicolo's banker and his wife.

NIEHUIS, CHARLEY, born in Buck Grove, Iowa; outdoorsman, conservationist, author of stories on hunting and fishing. After a variety of jobs in Minnesota and Arizona, he began to photograph the out-of-doors, writing stories while he served as a stringer for the United Press. Since his first published story in *Sports Afield* in 1939, he has written many stories, articles, and books, including *Trapping the Silver Beaver** (Dodd, 1956), which won the Western Writers of America Spur Award. He set up the Division of Information and Education for the Arizona Game and Fish Commission and served as the executive secretary of the Arizona Game Protective Association, editing its magazine, the *Arizona Wildlife Sportsman*.

NINO (Angelo*, Valenti, ill. author, Viking, 1938), episodic family story set in the village of Massarosa*, Italy, just after the turn of the century, about the first eight years in a little boy's life, with emphasis on the last one. Nino*, his mother, Allinda*, and his grandfather* have lived by themselves since Nino was a baby and his father left for America. Conscientious and responsible, Nino grows up helping his grandfather and mother with their household and farm tasks and sharing their pleasures. Although the family is poor, they always have enough and are rich in love for one another and in the loyalty and respect of their friends. Nino's closest friend is Julio*, the son of Signor* and Signora Ditto, their nearest neighbors, and the exact same age as Nino. Although Julio is not always sensible and thinks mostly of filling his stomach, he and Nino get on very well, exchanging gifts and sharing confidences and play. Nino and his family have a jolly dinner with the Dittos and travel by Signor Ditto's donkey cart and then by rowboat on a canal to Viareggio to get Nino's picture taken to send to his father. Nino carries a candle in the procession to the little chapel on the Hill of Three Crosses, even though his feet, unaccustomed to shoes, pain him terribly. He acquires a pet pig, and on Easter, the mayor, the priest, the Dittos, and other villagers come for dinner, and later there is dancing. In the fall, Nino and Grandfather watch the miller press olives, and Signor Ditto makes the wine of which he is so proud. The family and the Dittos attend a fair where Signor Ditto wrestles the gypsies' bear. The new year brings a letter from Nino's father with money for passage to America, and the three leave joyfully for the new country which they regard as a glorious land of technical advancement and opportunity. Characters are likeable, if flat, and there is a comfortable charm about the everyday and festival activities in which they engage. The book presents a world of only minor complications and stresses such prudential virtues as love for family, loyalty for friends, hard work, and respect for God, adults, and the aged. Fanfare; Newbery Honor.

NINO (*The Boy Who Was**), honey-skinned, raven-haired, young goat boy of Ravello, Italy, who tells stories of events from Sorrento's past to an artist for whom he is posing. In some of these stories he participates as an actual character who shapes events and makes things go as they must to be historically accurate. In others he just relates what he observes is happening. Sometimes he is a humble goat boy, sometimes a servant or helper to someone of high position, but he always seems to know more than the other characters do. There is a sly, mysterious manner about him, but he is widely known and much liked for his friendly, helpful ways. He is always willing to share his rude cave and his goats' milk and cheeses with anyone who is in need.

NINO (*Nino**), young son of Allinda*, whose husband has emigrated to America from their small Italian farm. A steady, conscientious lad, he is respectful and obedient, eager to please his mother, grandfather*, and the village priest. Although he plays with Julio*, the son of Signor* and Signora Ditto who live near by, he does not share that boy's propensity for mischief.

NOAH LAWRENCE (*Great Day in the Morning**), wise though illiterate old grandfather of Lillybelle Lawrence. In her family, only Noah, who took her in when her parents died, appreciates that Lillybelle does most of the field work, and only Noah encourages her to get further education at Tuskegee Institute. In the end he deeds his home place to her because he knows she loves it and intends to return.

NOEL VENABLE (*Tree of Freedom**), eldest son of the pioneer Venables who migrate from North Carolina to Kentucky in 1780 to prove their claim. Influenced by the politics of his mother's Huguenot relatives who are Patriots, Noel would like to join General Francis Marion against the British. Intelligent and educated for the period, he is wise enough to realize that he might better serve the cause of freedom by fighting with Clark in the West. Although it is against their father's wishes, he is aided in joining Clark by his sister Stephanie*. When Clark sends him East on an errand to Governor Thomas Jefferson, Noel learns that the claim of another man to the Venable land is fraudulent.

NURSERY VALLEY (*The Biggest Bear on Earth**), the region in Alaska of mountain and tundra that Roughneck and his family and friends call home. It is called Nursery Valley by the author (who tells the story) because it holds the caves where Roughneck and many of the bears of the largest species of bear on earth have been born and is a naturally protective environment. Ironically, Nursery Valley is invaded by a prospector and his companion, who hunt bears for their hides as well as seek gold.

O

THE OAK TREE HOUSE (Gibson*, Katharine, ill. Vera Bock, Longmans, 1936), very simple story set in England in 1545. A Goodman and his Goodwife, having been evicted from their cottage for unpaid taxes, trade their goat for a hand cart, load their belongings into it, including their cat, Madame Pepper, and their dog, Mustard, and start up the king's highway. After a day of travel they come to a place where the road splits around a giant oak tree. They camp there for the night, and the Goodman gets an idea: he will build a house in its branches. This he does, with a rope ladder and a large kettle in which they can build a fire. One night a page boy named Jock, carrying a message to the king and being chased by bandits, seeks refuge in their tree house. Some time later he returns with a document signed by the boy king, Edward* Tudor (Edward VI), 8, giving them title to the oak tree and the green island in the highway on which it stands. Jock, now a squire, has told the young king about the tree house and has thereby persuaded him to agree to a necessary trip to Chester Town on the promise that he can visit the Goodman and his wife on the way. This he does, with Jock, now a knight, as his guide. The story has a bit of clever by-play between Madame Pepper and Mustard, both of whose thoughts are quoted, and between the king and Pepper, who spits at His Majesty as if he were a common boy. The story, however, seems outdated by its simplistic approach, even for young children. Historically, it is inaccurate, since Edward VI was not king until he was nearly ten years old. Fanfare.

OCEAN-BORN MARY (Lenski*, Lois, ill. author, Stokes, 1939), highly fictionalized story set in Strawberry Bank, N.H. (now Portsmouth), in 1732, based on the life of a real Mary Wilson of Londonderry, N.H. Mary, 11, comes from her inland town to help her ailing Cousin Jeanie, a fisherman's wife, and during her several months in the coastal town becomes known and loved by a wide variety of characters. Among them are Cousin Jock, Jeanie's son, Joey Mosely, the town cowherd who runs off to sea, Nathaniel Greenwood, artist who carves the figurehead for the *Golden Arrow*, Peggy Fayerweather, model for the figurehead and daughter of the captain, who eventually marries Nathaniel, Master Pecksniff, hunch-backed apothecary, Susannah Winslow, invalid daughter of the gaoler, and even Lieutenant-Governor Dunbar. Most notable is Philip Babb, the pirate who captured the emigrant ship on which Mary was born but, touched by the birth of the infant, released all the captives and allowed their vessel to continue. Although hated by Becky Armstrong, keeper of the almshouse, who was on the ship, he proves devoted to Mary when they meet again and gives her gold coins and eventually her first doll, a beautifully dressed "poppet" from Europe. In her several encounters with him she learns his hiding place at Goat Island, where his old mother, Goody Gregory, illegally weaves woolen cloth. After the *Golden Arrow* is sunk and Babb has been seen in town, Mary is forced to reveal his hiding place, but she contrives in his escape with the help of Susannah, to whom she gives the poppet in payment. The book is crowded with characters, including Indians, rope makers, loggers, the town crier, the woman who keeps the village store, inhabitants of the almshouse, the daughter of a wealthy merchant, the parson—all the types whom careful research would reveal as having lived in a New England port of that period. It therefore gives a thorough picture of the time and place but gives the impression of being over-researched and suffers from lack of probability and poor motivation in its plot elements, as well as a didactic tone and slow pace. Fanfare.

THE OFFICE (*The Saturdays**), the room in the attic which the Melendy children call their own, where they play, and where they have their I.S.A.A.C.* meetings. Later, when they move to the country, their office is an attic room on the third floor off which the cupola and the secret room with Clarinda's picture in it can be reached.

OLD HEROES (*The Gammage Cup**; *The Whisper of Glocken†*), the "outlaws" who save the Minnipins from the Mushrooms in the first book and who assist the New Heroes to triumph in the second. They are Walter* the Earl, Curley* Green, Muggles*, Gummy*, and Mingy*.

OLD RIT (*The Railroad to Freedom**), cook at Broadacres, a proud house slave, mother of Minty (Harriet Tubman). She is hardworking, proud, superstitious, aware, and respected by both whites and blacks. Although she loves her masters and serves them diligently, she yearns for freedom and is sorely disappointed when Master Carter dies without preparing her emancipation papers. She is hurt when Harriet delays freeing her and old Ben, not fully understanding the danger involved for her daughter.

OLD TIMOTHY (*The Enchanted Schoolhouse**), Brian Boru's old grandfather, who has raised the boy on tales of the little people, which gives the boy the idea of capturing the fairyman*, and who gives Brian Boru the brown earthenware teapot from the mantlepiece as a keepsake.

THE OLD TOBACCO SHOP (Bowen*, William, Macmillan, 1921), comic fantasy-adventure which begins and ends "in the city that lies on the river called Patapsco" which empties into Chesapeake Bay in the late nineteeth century. Little Freddie is sent by his father to the Old Tobacco Shop to buy a half-pound of Stage-Coach Mixture. At the door, his attention is caught by Mr. Punch, the wooden statue of a hunchback who holds in one hand a packet of black wooden cigars. He makes the acquaintance of garrulous Mr. Toby Littleback, the proprietor and the very twin of Mr. Punch in appearance, and his spinster aunt, Amanda, a plain and kindly seamstress. Mr. Toby sings Freddie a song about two old codgers, one with a wooden leg who "never bought tobacco when tobacco he could beg" and the other a sly old fox who "always had tobacco in his old tobacco box," warns him not to take tobacco from the Chinaman's head jar, and informs him that Mr. Punch's father lives in the clock tower and, when the hands of the clock meet, comes down from the tower and kidnaps little boys. For several months, Freddie returns periodically to the shop, finding it an intriguing, attractive old place and enjoying the company of the hunchback and his aunt, who yearns to be pretty and sometimes imagines she is married and has three children. When he is old enough to pronounce his name correctly, Mr. Toby takes Freddie to a performance of Hanlon's *Superba*, a play in which mute Mr. Hanlon survives many harrowing adventures. Later Freddie sneaks a pipeful of tobacco from the Chinaman's head and faints. When he awakens, he sees before him a sailorman with a green eye patch, Lemuel Mizzen, A.B., who gives him a map of Correction Island in the Spanish Main. Freddie, his Tobacco Shop friends, the two codgers, an obese Churchwarden, and Mr. Hanlon set sail in a leaky, old tub, the *Sieve*, to go to the island where each can be "corrected" and given the form or attribute he most desires and which is rightfully his. When the ship sinks, the little company is borne on mattress rafts to the island where they escape from pirates who are led by Capt. Lingo and live in a stronghold called High Dungeon. They are assisted by the Society for Piratical Research and the Churchwarden's Odour of Sanctity, against which no wicked spirit can stand. With the pirates' treasure, they travel to the City of Towers where they purchase from Shiraz the Persian rug merchant, a man so old he is almost a mummy, an hourglass through which each is disenchanted and given his "true" form, that is, the form he yearns to have: for example, Aunt Amanda becomes the beautiful Queen Miranda with a loving husband and three attractive children, Mr. Toby has a straight back, and Freddie is grown up. In attempting to help the Old Man of the Mountain, Freddie becomes so chilled he almost dies. His friends save him by taking their hourglasses and bearing him to the top of the King's Tower where they meet the Old Man, who informs them that they now only believe themselves disenchanted. He says that they actually have been enchanted by Shiraz and that their previous forms were their proper ones. He restores them all to their former condition, Freddie is cured, and all return to the Old Tobacco Shop and their former homes. The reader then learns that Freddie evidently has been ill for some time and that the trip, with its characters, incidents, and motifs from the Tobacco Shop and Hanlon's *Superba*, took place in a dream or hallucination he had while ill. His friends are delighted that he is well again. Episodes are too numerous, happen too rapidly, and are inadequately developed. Characters are the stock ones of comedy. Dialogue is extensive, self-conscious, and contrived. Moralistic passages are obviously intended to instruct. Nor is the nature of Freddie's illness ever made clear. As an artifact, the book projects a certain charm. It is typical of the kind of literary entertainment thought suitable for children of the period. Newbery Honor.

OLD YELLER (Gipson*, Fred, ill. Carl Burger, Harper, 1956), realistic dog story, set in the 1860s at Birdsong Creek, near Salt Licks, Tex. When a ''big, ugly, slick-haired yeller dog'' strays to the Coates log cabin and steals a side of meat, Travis, 14, who narrates the story, has no patience with the critter, but Little Arliss, 5, immediately adopts him. With his father gone for months driving cattle to market in Abilene, Travis has taken on the responsibilities of the farm work and hunting but is frustrated that his mother and Arliss don't show him enough respect. At first, Old Yeller is an added aggravation as he romps with Arliss in the pool of drinking water and fails to help when a couple of big, fighting range cattle knock down the fence and nearly wreck the cabin, but when the dog saves Arliss from a mother bear, Travis changes his opinion. Old Yeller becomes so much a part of the family that when Burn Sanderson, a young cattleman, comes to claim him and sees what he means to Arliss, he trades the dog for a home-cooked meal, but before he leaves he warns Travis that a plague of rabies, ''hydrophobia,'' is making the rounds. Soon after, Travis is wounded in the leg by a half-wild hog, and Old Yeller is badly injured saving him. With difficulty both get home but are too ill to help much when a bull and their milk cow both become rabid and, shot by Travis, must be burned. Mama and Lisbeth, a neighbor girl helping out, are attacked on their way home by a rabid wolf and saved only by Old Yeller's valiant defense. Since the dog has been bitten, however, Travis must shoot him. His gloom lifts a bit as he watches Old Yeller's puppy, given to Arliss by Lisbeth. Because Old Yeller is not a beautiful animal but tick-ridden, with one ear chewed off and thieving habits, the book escapes some of the sentimentality of many animal stories. The rigors of frontier life are well described, and the narrative voice of Travis is convincing. Newbery Honor.

OLD YELLER (*Old Yeller**), a big, ugly stray dog with one ear chewed off, who introduces himself to the Coates family by stealing a side of meat hanging in the dog run. His name comes partly from his color and partly from his noise, more a yelping than a bark. He raids neighboring smokehouses and hens' nests but proves a valiant protector until he tangles with a rabid wolf and must be shot.

OLIVER DAVENPORT (*Call of the Mountain**), brother of Tom* Davenport, a tinsmith and peddler of tin wares. Although he feels Tom may be foolish in pursuing his dream of inventing an electrical wheel, he loves his brother and loyally helps him along by selling all his stock at auction so that Tom can buy the electrical magnet he wants.

OLIVER MELENDY (*The Saturdays**), the youngest Melendy. A serious, persevering little fellow, he aspires to become an engineer until a mounted policeman brings him home when he is lost. Then he plans to become a policeman. He also likes to draw. In the country, he becomes an avid collector of butterflies and a very competent fisherman who regularly provides catches for Melendy meals. He is eight in the third book, *Then There Were Five*.

OL' PATCHES (*The Boy Who Had No Birthday**), a small, stooped man of about sixty, with a thin face and dark, haunted eyes, whose real name is Elijah Demdike. He looks poor and ragged because he has patches sewn all over his greasy clothes. He is the laughing stock of the region since he never wears anything but that ancient suit. He is stingy and spiteful and dislikes children, who very often make fun of him. At the end, David* Cring generously gives Ol' Patches the Bill Tweed (Boss Tweed) bank, that was bought for him in Indianapolis, because he is sorry for the sick, apparently poor, old man. His action pricks Ol' Patches's conscience and the old fellow owns up to finding the money that Davy's father had lost and tells the doctor that he has sewn it under the patches on his suit. His burdened conscience cleared, Ol' Patches becomes more agreeable and likeable.

ONE-EYED HANS (*Otto of the Silver Hand**), follower of the brutal robber Baron Conrad of Drachenhausen, who is father of frail Otto. A short, deep-chested, broad-shouldered man, Hans has extraordinary strength and is rumored to have drunk beer with the "Hill-man," who has given him the strength of ten. Hans is devoted to Conrad, and when his master is wounded has him brought to the Baroness, not suspecting that the sight will be too much for the pregnant young woman. When Otto is held by Baron Henry, it is Hans who effects his escape by posing as a peddler to get inside the castle's outer door, then squirming up a fireplace chimney and through the ducts until he can come down inside the kitchen, where he is taken for the devil and so terrifies the char-boy that he flees and Hans can hide in a bread chest. In the night, he is able to make his way to the dungeon where Otto is held and, using rope he has smuggled in, carries the boy down the castle wall to his waiting father. Hans is the stereotype of the utterly faithful retainer.

ONION JOHN (Krumgold*†, Joseph, ill. Symeon Shimin, Crowell, 1959), contemporary, realistic problem novel about the strained relationship between a boy and his father. Andy* Rusch, 12, son of the owner of the hardware store in the small town of Serenity, N.J., admires his father and enjoys helping out in the store. Although he is a town leader and successful in his business, Mr.

Rusch is determined that Andy attend engineering college, an opportunity that he never had. In spite of being well liked by the local boys, Andy develops a close friendship with Onion* John, town character who lives on Hessian* Hill in a house he made of piled up stones and who scrounges what he needs from the town dump. Andy's father, president of the Rotarys, decides that John is entitled to a better life and organizes the town in building a "proper" house for Onion John, with such modern conveniences as an electric stove. Unfamiliar with electricity, John sets fire to the place. When Onion John decides to leave Serenity for good to keep the townspeople from further trying to control his life, Andy wishes to go with him. A better understanding between father and son results as Andy's father accepts both Onion John's and his son's need for self-determination. Told by Andy in first person, this story tackles a common family problem with sympathy, humor, and occasional gentle satire and is rich in details of small town life. The main characters are warmly and distinctly drawn, and the plot, if improbably concluded, is mildly suspenseful and often amusing. The second in Krumgold's trio of books about modern American boys, it was preceded by *. . . And Now Miguel** and followed by *Henry 3†*. Choice; Fanfare; Lewis Carroll; Newbery Winner.

ONION JOHN (*Onion John**), eccentric, immigrant handyman from Eastern Europe who becomes best friend of twelve-year-old Andy* Rusch, Jr. Popular, congenial town character in Serenity, N.J., he gets his name because he eats "onions the way other people ate apples or pears." He lives on Hessian* Hill in a house built of piled up stones that has no running water and four bathtubs. He shops the local dump as other people do the supermarket and speaks such garbled English no one can understand him but Andy. Although wise in human nature, he is also superstitious and engages in such magical practices as making stews to get gold out of the moon, conducting rituals to bring rain, and exorcising evil spirits by burning oak. After he inadvertently sets fire to the modern house the Rotarys build for him, he leaves Serenity for good. Andy wants to leave with him but doesn't because he works things out with his father.

ON THE BANKS OF PLUM CREEK (Wilder*, Laura Ingalls, ill. Helen Sewell and Mildred Boyle, Harper, 1937), third in a series of autobiographical novels (*Little House in the Big Woods**; *Little House on the Prairie**; *On the Shores of Silver Lake**; *The Long Winter**; *Little Town on the Prairie**; *These Happy Golden Years**), this one set on Plum Creek in Minnesota and telling about two and a half years in the mid-1870s. It is a record of firsts: when the Ingalls family arrives from their year in Indian territory, they live for the first time in a dugout house, and later Pa (Charles* Ingalls) builds their first house of cut lumber; Laura*, 7 1/2, and Mary*, one year older, go to school for the first time, to church and Sunday school for the first time; they go to their first party at spoiled Nellie* Oleson's and give their first party, where Laura gets even with Nellie by leading her into the part of the stream where bloodsuckers lurk. In other ways

Laura's adventurous spirit contrasts with Mary's good behavior. Playing in the swimming hole, she strays into deep water against the orders of her mother, Caroline*, and Pa ducks her; she secretly sneaks off toward the forbidden hole another day and is scared back by a badger; when the creek is in flood, she swings off the footbridge into the water and is almost carried away; when Pa forbids the girls to slide down the straw stack, which they have scattered with their play, she entices Mary to climb up and roll down it instead. They also assume more responsibility. Laura helps Pa set his fish trap under the waterfall and care for the horses, and she helps Ma and their neighbor, Mr. Nelson, beat out a prairie fire; Laura and Mary meet the herdboy each evening and stable the oxen and their cow, called Spot or Wreath of Roses for her unusual ring of red spots on her side; when one steer runs loose and plunges a leg through the dugout roof, it is Laura who is trying to control him, and when the herd gets into the haystacks, she and Mary chase them away; they take care of their little sister, Carrie*, while their parents go to town and carry in most of the woodpile when a storm strikes. They have rather close neighbors for the first time, not always a good addition. Besides unpleasant Nellie, there is the Nelsons' little girl, to whom Ma insists Laura give her beloved rag doll, Charlotte. When Laura later finds Charlotte discarded and frozen in a mud puddle, Ma allows her to keep the old friend. Three Christmases occur during the book. For the first, the girls bravely say they want only horses, since Ma has told them that is what Pa needs, yet Laura is actually pleased with Sam and David. The second year, they attend a party at the church, where they see their first Christmas tree and are all given presents, Laura a fur cape and muff, prettier than Nellie's. The third year, Pa is caught in a blizzard as he returns from town, plunges into a snow-covered hollow, and stays there three days, eating all the oyster crackers and candy he is bringing for Christmas only to discover when the storm subsides that he is within sight of home. The great promise of their new home is destroyed for two years by grasshoppers that ruin the crops and make it necessary for Pa to walk three hundred miles east to get harvest work so he can pay for the house lumber and buy winter supplies. As in the other books of the series, the details of daily life are told with such clarity and precision that they make a fascinating picture of the pioneer struggles and joys. The description of the grasshopper plague is especially vivid. Ma's gentle propriety and Pa's fun-loving spirit are evident throughout. ChLA Touchstones; Choice; Newbery Honor.

ON THE SHORES OF SILVER LAKE (Wilder*, Laura Ingalls, ill. Helen Sewell and Mildred Boyle, Harper, 1939), fourth in a series of autobiographical novels (*Little House in the Big Woods**; *Little House on the Prairie**; *On the Banks of Plum Creek**; *The Long Winter**; *Little Town on the Prairie**; *These Happy Golden Years**), this one set mostly on Silver Lake, near De Smet, S.Dak., in the winter of 1879-1880. The two years since the end of *On the Banks of Plum Creek* have not been prosperous for the Ingalls family and, worst of all, they have suffered from scarlet fever, which has left Mary*, 13 1/2, blind.

Besides Laura*, now 12 1/2, Mary and Carrie*, about 8, there is a baby, Grace*. A sister of Pa (Charles* Ingalls), Aunt Docia, now married to a widower with two children, drives up in her buggy going west and offers Pa a job with the railroad where her husband, Uncle Hiram, is a contractor. Seeing a chance to get out of debt and get a homestead, Pa goes with her, leaving Ma (Caroline*) and the girls to come later by train. On that exciting first trip, Laura tries to "see out loud" for Mary, describing the train and the scenery, the first sign of a changed relationship, with Laura's jealousy of Mary's beauty and her resentment of Mary's goodness turning to responsibility for her older sister. At the railroad camp, Laura meets her new cousins, Lena, nearly 14, and Jean, a younger brother, and has a wonderful time driving and riding their black ponies. On their drive from there to Silver Lake, they are followed by a suspicious character but relieved when Big Jerry, a half-breed gambler and horse thief, rides up and protects them by his presence. At first they live in a shanty on the edge of the rough railroad camp, and Laura is fascinated by the work which Pa takes her to see. Two episodes of trouble are narrowly averted. When some horses have been stolen, men in the camp think Big Jerry is responsible and lie in ambush to shoot him, but Pa goes out to warn him and no more horses are missing after that. On payday, the men resent being paid for two weeks instead of a month and threaten to riot. Pa, as paymaster, is keeping them from looting the store when Big Jerry distracts them and leads them off to another camp. As the camp closes for winter, Pa gets permission to spend the season in the surveyor's house, the only real house on the lake shore, and to use the provisions stored there. One night, sliding on the ice of the lake in the moonlight, Laura and Carrie see a huge wolf. The next day, tracking it, Pa finds the spot where he wants to homestead. They have unexpected visitors on Christmas Eve: Mr. Boast and his new bride, Nell, coming to get an early start at their homestead. Later they are surprised by the Reverend Alden, the minister from Plum Creek, and another young minister, going west as missionaries. It is Alden who first tells them of a school for the blind in Iowa, news which makes Laura resolve that, no matter how much she hates the idea of teaching, she will become a teacher to earn money so that Mary can go to college. As spring approaches, a stream of settlers come and Ma and the girls charge them for meals and a place to sleep. Finally Pa gets away to Brookings to file on his homestead site and almost is beaten out of it. He builds a store building in the fast-booming town, and they live in it briefly, then move to a tiny shanty on their homestead to keep claim jumpers from stealing it. In spite of the scare they have when Grace toddles off and Laura finds her in the frantic search, happily playing among violets that cover an old buffalo wallow, Laura loves the homestead and is glad to be away from town. In some ways this is the least unified of the seven books of the series, but individual episodes are vivid and Laura's maturing personality is as appealing as ever. ChLA Touchstones; Choice; Fanfare; Newbery Honor.

OOD-LE-UK THE WANDERER (Lide*, Alice Alison, and Margaret Alison Johansen*, ill. Raymond Lufkin, Little, 1930), highly episodic boy's growing up story set in Alaska and nearby Asia among Stone Age tribes. Undersized, fearful Ood-le-uk, fifteen-year-old Eskimo youth, is a disappointment to his father, Kotuk, the chief of the village of Tekilerik on the west coast of Alaska where it juts out toward Siberia. One day Ood-le-uk discovers washed up on the shore a wooden case containing a piece of parchment folded around a bit of crossed metal. Certain that it is a good luck charm, he hangs it about his neck. On a hunt, Ood-le-uk is swept away on an ice floe to a peninsula far to the north of his village. During the long, dark winter, he laboriously fashions a kayak out of a walrus he kills, but the boat is swept westward to Siberia. Half-dead from exposure, he is discovered by the tribesmen of the village of Igirka, fisherfolk of the Tschuktschi tribe who have been partially converted to Christianity by the Russians. He is nursed to health in the hut of Valetka, the headman, who becomes fond of him and whose son, Etel, becomes his dear friend. The shaman, Ir-kaij, feels Ood-le-uk should be sacrificed to their old gods to avert a mysterious illness that is sweeping through the area. When the shaman is about to knife him, he sees the amulet with its Christian cross and spares Ood-le-uk's life. There follow happy, eventful years for Ood-le-uk, as Valetka and his wife and family come to think of him as one of their own. He and Etel follow the reindeer herds of Valetka's nomadic brother, Kotschal, try to capture a mysterious, white doe reindeer for him, and travel with him to the great fair at Ostrownoje, where they are pursued by gypsies and rescued by a priest who thinks they are Christian because of Ood-le-uk's cross. When famine strikes the Tschuktschi, Ood-le-uk feels the amulet is giving him the courage to go on a fearsome journey to the north where tradition holds there is a store of food. There the two boys discover mammoths whose bodies had been frozen in the ice hundreds of years before and return with a bountiful supply of food to save their people from starving. Two years later, a man grown, Ood-le-uk decides to try for home; he builds a sturdy sailing vessel and with the help of Etel and others sails back to his village. Too filled with wanderlust to settle down, he and Etel help others to build boats like theirs and initiate trade between Alaska and Siberia. The once fearful weakling has become a leader of men. The authors seem more concerned with acquainting the reader with the way of life of the Eskimo and their Siberian counterparts than in telling a good story well. The book is dated in style and tone. It is almost entirely narrative, with very little dialogue, and is too didactic and objectively related to grab the reader's sympathies. Incidents are not exploited for their dramatic potential, there is virtually no climax or suspense, and characters are conventional and shallow. Newbery Honor.

THE ORDEAL OF THE YOUNG HUNTER (Lauritzen*, Jonreed, ill. Hoke Denetsosie, Little, 1954), novel of family life with problem story aspects set among the Navajo of Arizona in the mid-1900s. In early spring, Old Two-Toes, a fearsome cougar, kills twenty-four of the sheep belonging to Jadih* Yazhi's family. Angry, Jadih, 12, vows he will never eat meat until he has hunted and killed the predator, mounted on Trader* Jim Whittaker's buckskin pony, Rawhide. A month later, while Jadih is herding, Two-Toes kills three more sheep that are eaten by a wily bear. Slim* Man, Jadih's father, summons relatives and friends to a Mountain Chant to drive away the bear spirit that he feels possesses his son, and still more sheep are killed to feed the guests. Now Slim Man cannot pay his bills to Jim and buy food for his family. Trader Jim suggests that Jadih might win the one thousand dollar first prize by performing his special animal dance for tourists in the annual inter-tribal powwow at Flagstaff. His parents endorse the idea, but Yellow* Nose, Jadih's uncle and a respected priest, staunchly opposes the plan. Confused and fearful, Jadih runs away on Rawhide into the mountains in search of Two-Toes and gets lost. When Rawhide breaks his tether and returns to the trading post, Jim tracks Jadih down and convinces him that dancing for the Bellicanos (Americans) will enrich their lives and is not disrespectful to Navajo traditions. In the arena, Jadih panics and runs. To rebuild the boy's self-respect, Jim takes him to the *chindi*, the Anasazi (ancient ones) ruins that the Navajo consider haunted and where Old Two-Toes has his den. The boy mounts Rawhide, seeks out the cougar, and slays him, keeping his vow. He returns with Jim to Flagstaff, faces his fears, and performs the dance so expressively and pierces Two-Toes's hide so accurately with his arrows to culminate the performance that he easily wins the prize. To cap his pleasure, Jim gives him Rawhide. Characterization is strong, and descriptions of the terrain, herding, ceremonies, modes of travel, food, clothing, and activity in the hogan, and the content of the dialogue produce a convincing picture of Navajo life and thought. Tone is often informative, sentences short and simple, vocabulary easy, and the plot, though appealing, is slow starting, unevenly paced, and improbable. Family relationships are warm and close, and scenes between Jadih and his little sister, Starflower, are very engaging. Child Study.

ORU AND MEBE (*The Wonderful Flight to the Mushroom Planet**; *Stowaway to the Mushroom Planet**; *Time and Mr. Bass*†), two men of the Mushroom People, the first of the race that David* Topman and Chuck* Masterson encounter on Basidium-X*. They are the Wise Men who serve as historians. Garrulous, easily flustered and often distracted, they provide comic relief.

OTHER PEOPLE'S HOUSES (Bianco*, Margery, Viking, 1939), adolescent "career" novel set in and near New York City in the depression of the 1930s. Her suburban home having been sold after the death of her father, and her mother and sister, Charlotte, 9, having moved in with relatives in Philadelphia, Dale Forrest, 17, goes to take her first job as a sort of companion-secretary to Mrs. Duchayne, a wealthy, eccentric writer. After several weeks with few duties except walking the dog, Dale is appalled to learn that her employer has suddenly left for California and that she must find a new job. Her strongest emotional support is her old friend, the boy next door named Dick Carter, now working as a mechanic in the city. With difficulty, since she has few skills, Dale gets one job after another: as maid for unpleasant, demanding Mrs. Heslop, as temporary lunchroom help for Miss Margaret Cole, who has an apartment in the house where Dick rooms, as all-round help to the ailing wife of a young artist, and as governess for nine-year-old Cornelia Carrington, a wealthy child, at their summer home near the beach. In this last job she is attracted to Barry, a cousin who visits, but is snubbed by Rosemary, Cornelia's sixteen-year-old sister. When Mrs. Oldham, the aunt who supervises the household, is gone, Dale learns that Rosemary is seizing the opportunity to go to a roadhouse. Dale accompanies Barry to save her from this den of iniquity, a rescue that Rosemary resents, and after an angry scene, Barry leaves and Dale is told that her services are no longer needed. Having learned something of life, Dale returns to help Miss Cole in the lunchroom and plans to learn the business, then start a small tea shop in Porter's Landing, a vacation town on the Jersey Shore where Dick and his friend have bought a garage. Dale and Dick will marry and bring Dale's mother and Charlotte to live with them. Today's readers will find the book dated not only by the wages and prices, detailed throughout, the attitudes toward girls' working, and the apparent safety of wandering through New York alone day or night, but also by the antiseptic romances with Barry and Dick, neither of which involves so much as the desire for a kiss. There is also an earnestness of tone typical of the period. The theme, that not money but independence and loving friends bring happiness, is stressed frequently. Fanfare.

OTIS, JAMES (*Johnny Tremain**), actual historical figure, presented in the novel as one of the revolutionary leaders who meet in the Lorne attic. He idealistically expresses the goals of the movement with the words, "That a man can stand up," himself standing straight and tall with his hands pushed up against the rafters over his head, a living symbol of his words.

OTTO OF THE SILVER HAND (Pyle*, Howard, ill. author, Scribner's, 1888), historical novel set in Germany in the latter half of the thirteenth century. Robber Baron Conrad Vuelphs of the grim castle Drachenhausen preys upon the merchant caravans that run between the rich towns along the road overlooked by the castle's Melchoir Tower. Although his young wife, the Baroness Matilda, begs him not to go on another raid, he disregards her pleas, is brought home seriously wounded, and the shock kills his wife, but not before she has given birth to a baby and named him Otto, after her uncle, the abbot of the monastery of St. Michaelsburg on the Rhine. As soon as he regains consciousness and learns of his wife's death, Baron Conrad, though still wounded, takes the infant to the monastery, gets the abbot's promise to raise and protect the child, and swears vengeance upon Baron Frederick Roderburg of the Castle Trutz-Drachen, who, having exacted protection payments from the merchants, led the attack against him. The delicate child grows to the age of ten in the monastery, cared for by the kindly abbot and the monks, particularly brain-damaged Brother* John, who sees visions of angels. Then Baron Conrad, having taken revenge by slaying Baron Frederick even as he knelt begging mercy, returns for the unworldly boy, who enters the brutal life with a naive piety and sense of wonder. Old Ursela, his mother's nurse, tells him of her death and his father's way of life, and he is profoundly shocked but uncondemning. The new Emperor, Rudolph of Hapsburg, summons Baron Conrad to his court to swear fealty and to promise to change his wicked ways, and while he is gone with most of his fighting men, Baron Henry, nephew and successor of Frederick, invades via the tower and burns Drachenhausen and seizes Otto. At Trutz-Drachen, Otto is thrown into a dungeon and, with Baron Henry looking on, his right hand is struck off so that he can never raise a sword against the Roderburgs. For some time Otto is so ill that his survival is doubtful. He gets visits from little Pauline, 8, Baron Henry's daughter, who becomes his friend and brings him word that his father, with six followers, has been seen in the vicinity of the castle. Through a swineherd, she sends word to Conrad of Otto's whereabouts, and Conrad's wily man, One-eyed* Hans, gets into the castle antechamber as a peddler, worms his way up a fireplace chimney, comes down soot-covered into the kitchen, and eventually gets to Otto's cell. There he cuts the bars, attaches a rope which he has smuggled in around his body, and with Otto clinging to his neck, slides down the rope to Conrad waiting below. They start off for the sanctuary of the monastery but are soon followed so closely that Conrad gives Otto to Hans to carry on, and he himself makes a last stand at a narrow bridge, where he and Henry kill each other. With his great-uncle, the abbot, Otto goes to the emperor's court to present his grievances to Rudolph, who offers to have all Henry's family killed to redress the wrongs, but Otto quietly informs him that he has promised to marry Pauline, so wishes no harm to her. Rudolph takes both children under his protection, has a silver hand made for Otto, and Otto grows up to be a peaceful advisor for the emperor. The story is unusual among the swashbuckling tales of medieval knights because its hero is such a mild child, who does no great or brave feats but is simply the victim of harsh times. Although the central action is the brutal mutilation, the tone is gentle. Pyle's illustrations add a feel of authenticity and excitement. Books Too Good; Children's Classics; Lewis Carroll.

OUT OF THE FLAME (Lownsbery*, Eloise, ill. Elizabeth Tyler Wolcott, Longmans, 1931), romantic historical novel set at the court of Francois I of France at the beginning of the Renaissance from 1529 to about 1535, concerning a boy's dilemma about what to do with his life. Young Pierre de Bayard, nephew and namesake of a great knight and ward of the king, has been raised along with the king's own five children as one of the Royal Children. Proud of his heritage, bright and enterprising, Pierre's ambition is to live up to the standard for knighthood set by his renowned uncle. A page at court, he is a pupil of Jacques Lefèvre d'Etaples (Master Fabri) and the king's sister, Marguerite*, Queen of Navarre, the only mother he has really known, who have taught him to respect life and value learning. After the return of the king's two older sons, Francois, 11, and Henri*, about ten, who have been held hostage and imprisoned in a dungeon by Charles V of Spain for three years, Pierre becomes increasingly confused about his relationship with the moody, haughty Henri, who often taunts and degrades him. While he is determined to cultivate the attitudes and skills which distinguish a fine knight and learns to control his temper when around Henri, Pierre questions the value of serving a king whose behavior and philosophy he cannot condone. He frequently confides his dilemma to Jac*, the dwarf whose life he saved. He grows and changes as he comes into contact with such thinkers and reformers as Erasmus, Rabelais, and Sir Thomas More, and hears about the demonstrations of students and movements like that of Luther, until finally he chooses the life of a scholar at the court of Marguerite. Pierre is a dynamic character, and, though his position parallels that of France at the time, he is real and convincing in his perplexity about serving the moody and psychologically scarred Henri. The Royal Children are individualized, an especially winning character being the sweet and vivacious Magdaleine, while among the other figures the dwarf, Jac, with his healing touch, and the maternal and learned Marguerite of Navarre stand out. The picture of the large and lavish French court, such historical events as the royal progress, the betrothal and marriage of Henri to Catherine de' Medici, the courtship of Magdaleine and James V of Scotland, and the voyage of Cartier and his return with Indians, and conversations about current events and thought lend strength and substance to this story of a boy's decision to be true to himself. Newbery Honor.

OWEN, RUTH BRYAN (1885-1954), born in Jacksonville, Ill.; politician, lecturer. The daughter of William Jennings Bryan, she was educated at the Monticello Seminary and the University of Nebraska and was politically active all her life. She was elected to the House of Representatives in 1928 from Florida, the first woman from any state of the old South, and was reelected in 1930. Later she became the United States Minister to Denmark. Her first brief marriage ended in divorce and her second with the death of Owen in 1927. She was married a third time in 1936 to a former captain in the Danish Royal Guards, a move which conferred automatic Danish citizenship upon her and forced her to give up her diplomatic career, even though her husband eventually became a naturalized citizen of the United States. Her books for young people include two collections of Scandinavian folk tales and *Denmark Caravan** (Dodd, 1936), a fictionalized record of a trailer trip she and her four children took through Denmark.

OZ (*The Wonderful Wizard of Oz**), fantasy land to which Dorothy* is blown by the cyclone and where she meets the Scarecrow*, the Tin* Woodman, and the Cowardly* Lion. Oz is a land in which there is pattern if no particular logic in events: The Munchkins of the East like blue, the Winkies of the West like yellow, the Quadlings of the South like red, and the central Ozians of the Emerald City like green. The ideal of each of the main characters, except Dorothy, is to be a king, and each gets his wish. All sorts of bizarre and incredible creatures occur in Oz, and magic of many different types happens with no relation to other occurrences in an unpredictable way. Oz is the setting for a long series of books, of which *The Wonderful Wizard of Oz* is the first.

P

PADDLE-TO-THE-SEA (Holling*, Holling Clancy, ill. author, Houghton, 1941), highly illustrated story set in the Great Lakes region during the mid-twentieth century. The hero is a one-foot-long canoe carved of wood with an Indian figure paddling, a tin rudder, and a lump of lead for ballast. Its maker, an Indian boy in Nipigon country north of Lake Superior, has carved on the bottom, "Please put me back in water. I am Paddle-to-the-Sea," then set the canoe on a snow bank because his teacher has explained about how their snow melt joins the river to Lake Superior and eventually to the Atlantic. As the weather warms, the little canoe is carried down stream, through a bursting beaver dam, then wedged into the bark of a log and carried to a sawmill. There a French lumberman rescues it from the saw, adds "from Nipigon Country, Canada," and returns it to the water. It starts a long journey around Lake Superior, being stuck for a while in a marsh, passing Duluth, being caught in a fishing net near the Apostle Islands, passing the copper country of the Keweenaw peninsula, and finally being washed up in a storm that wrecks a freighter near a lighthouse. There a Coast Guard man repairs it, replaces the tin rudder with copper, and adds a copper plate carrying a longer explanation and leaving room for the other cities where it is found to be scratched on the plate. He then sends it on to Mate Maloney, with instructions to get it through the locks at Sault Ste. Marie. Maloney means to put it into Lake Huron but carries it first to Gary, Ind., where it is accidentally dropped overboard in a bag of laundry. It takes three seasons to make its way back north through Lake Michigan, observing a forest fire from a small island near the Wisconsin coast on the way, then is washed through the Mackinac Straits and is picked up by a girl near Bay City, Mich. She and her father carry Paddle through Lake St. Clair and the Detroit River and set it off again in Lake Erie. Much later, Paddle is swept over Niagara Falls and travels through Lake Ontario. A little old lady who lives near the St. Lawrence River keeps it over the winter and sets it into the river in the spring high water. In the Gulf of St. Lawrence, it is washed by the Gulf Stream, then found by a fisherman's son on the Grand Banks of Newfoundland and carried by him to France. Back in Nipigon country, the lumberman who first returned it to the water reads about Paddle in a French newspaper and is overheard by the Indian who carved it, now a young man. Although in one sense a geography lesson, the story keeps interest in Paddle alive through its many adventures. It is difficult to consider the book apart from its illustrations, which surround the text with small drawings and diagrams and face each text page with a full-page painting. It has more words, however, than an average picture book and is intended for older readers as well as the little children who are attracted primarily to the pictures. Choice.

PADDY (*Farm Boy**), tobacco-chewing, Irish handyman of about seventy, whom John often helps with his chores. Paddy particularly enjoys gardening and teaches John much about the art of growing vegetables. While dumping the rubbish, the two get caught in a raging blizzard. Paddy is a talkative sort who likes to tell stories. Although he sometimes goes on drunks, he always returns to the goodwill of the Warners and the hands, who are all genuinely fond of the old man.

PADDY THE PIPER (*The Cottage at Bantry Bay**; *Francie on the Run**), wandering son of old Mrs. O'Flaherty, the neighbor of the O'Sullivans who owns the crotchety cow, Clementine. Paddy is a small man with twinkling eyes, ready grin, glib tongue, and generous heart. At the fair, he indulges Michael* and Brigid* with gifts of pennies, because he is genuinely fond of them, knows the family is poor, and wishes to make them happy. But he also often gives them fatherly advice about how to behave, and he shares with them his philosophy that love and friends are more to be valued than money. He is a good storyteller and knows many old and historical stories of Ireland. He is a memorable, if stock, character.

PAINTED SAINTS (Embury*, Lucy, ill. Guy Alexander, Viking, 1938), realistic novel set in Marseilles, France, at an unidentified time in the pre-industrial past. Old Father Serano, who works hard among the poor of the city, takes in an orphan boy, 12, known as Marcel of le Pont de l'Etoile, Marcel of the Bridge of the Star, so called because he sleeps beneath the bridge arches. He gently teaches the boy not to steal, to read, starting with "Assisi," the good priest's home, and to paint the Santibelli, the beautiful clay figurines of saints which he models and has fired in the kiln of the Friary of Francis run by his friend, the Abbe Perrato. When Father Serano needs money to save a starving woman, a mother of six, Marcel peddles the Santibelli for Christmas crèches, meeting on the way to market red-haired Sibilo, daughter of Poulet the Potter. Later Marcel visits Poulet and chops wood in exchange for a bag of clay, so the Father can teach him the art of modeling Santibelli. Friendship grows between the households, and after Father Serano has been ill, Poulet loans the priest his donkey, Bijou, and Marcel drives him in the donkey cart around Provencal, where they see various sights, including the gypsy fete at the fortress Church of Les Saintes Maries at the mouth of the Rhine River. When they return, Marcel shows the old priest the figures he has been modeling secretly—animals and people from the streets of Marseilles, which the old man praises for the life in them, though he is somewhat troubled that they are secular. When Marcel is sixteen, Father Serano dies. The Abbot offers him a place, but he chooses instead to go to Poulet to learn the art of pottery making and continue his modeling of figures. Eventually he marries Sibilo and has three children, the eldest named Serano. The story is a series of events without conflict or tension of plot. The gentle, idyllic tone is akin to the character of Father Serano; Marcel is a livelier, more worldly type and the theme is concerned with how these opposites complement each other, each gaining by their mutual love. The pace drags during their travels when too much information about Provencal is included, but generally it is a pleasant, slow-moving book. Fanfare.

PAJI (Kiviat*, Esther, ill. Harold Price, Whittlesey, 1946), short, realistic story in seven brief chapters set in Ceylon in the mid-1900s. Paji, a slim, brown Tamil boy of ten, lives in the village of Anapura. Every day he works in his uncle's Big Cheap Elephant Factory along with his grandfathers, uncles, and boy cousins, carving ebony elephants that will be taken to the city and sold to travelers from all over the world. Because he is tired of carving elephants that are always in the same poses, Paji gathers up his tools and four ebony logs, hitches up to his small cart Push-ba, his dish-faced water buffalo bullock, and runs away to the Hidden Temple deep in the cool, green jungle. There, day after day, he carves images he has longed to create: goddesses, the Buddha, a monkey, dwarfs, and Push-ba, until many shining black figures stand in rows inside the little temple and the logs are used up. While he searches in the jungle for more ebony, he comes upon a sign advertising the annual carving contest in Anapura. He rushes home in time to enter his carvings in the contest. Although his relatives ridicule his work, the judges award him the first prize of one thousand rupees for his originality and fine craftsmanship. His big uncle and other relatives are so impressed they urge him to return to the factory and teach them how to carve the figures. This entertaining, if unlikely, story is intended for younger readers. The plot is predictable, characters are undeveloped, and language is easy. The tone is light, and events move quickly. The writer describes the jungle quite credibly. The large poster-like illustrations, some in rich color, sometimes depict the Indians with features that appear more African than Asian. Fanfare.

PANACE (*Michel's Island**), wise, old, Ottawa herb doctor who is Michel's idol, dear friend, and advisor. He is a Christian and derides what he feels are old pagan superstitions but still holds to the old doctoring methods which he is convinced are proper and powerful. He takes Michel on herb-gathering trips on Mackinac Island and to the southern end of Lake Michigan. While they are together, he gives the boy kind, fatherly advice. He explains about the vision quest, and, when the half-Indian boy confides to him his perplexity about which world he really belongs to, white or red, tells him that what is important is not one's appearance or one's culture but doing what is right and letting the Master of Life be one's guide. Michel is very comfortable with him, and he has a great influence on the boy's thinking.

PANCAKES-PARIS (Bishop*, Claire Huchet, ill. Georges Schreiber, Viking, 1947), realistic problem novel set in Paris just after World War II. Two American soldiers reward a cold and hungry French schoolboy, Charles, 10, with a box of Aunt Jemima pancake mix for giving them street directions. Charles, however, cannot make the pancakes because he cannot read the instructions which are in English. Hoping to encounter someone who can help him with them, he takes the box to school, where his daydreaming about pancakes gets him into trouble. The teacher asks him a question concerning America, which gives Charles the idea of asking the American ambassador for help with the pancakes. At the American embassy, a kind secretary produces a recipe in French equivalents for him, and the two soldiers who gave him the mix take him home in their jeep. Then Charles discovers he has no grease to fry the pancakes in. Just as he is about to use water instead of fat, he hears a commotion in the hallway outside the kitchen door., The two soldiers have come with all the makings for a huge batch of pancakes, and Charles, the soldiers, Charles's family and friends enjoy the most marvelous Mardi Gras since before the war. Charles's misadventures in dealing with the soldiers' well-intentioned gift result in an amusing, if slight, story for younger readers. Charles is an unselfish, earnest lad, and the two soldiers are fun-loving and generous. Everyone behaves so well the book projects a feeling of the essential goodness of life. The soldiers are types; they reveal the spirit of friendliness and helpfulness for which American soldiers were known in World War II. The book shows in a limited way the hardships of the war and its effect on children. The sepia-toned illustrations in cartoon style play up the humor and irony of the situations and help to tell the story. Choice; Fanfare; Newbery Honor.

PAPA DUMARTIN (*That Girl of Pierre's**), vintner with whom Danielle gets a job. It is her responsibility to take care of the cart upon which the sprays are kept and to help the men who are spraying refill their sprayers. While working with Papa she learns about grape culture and also hears about the cooperatives that are springing up in France. He belongs to one in a nearby village and introduces her to people there who help her start the Arsac cooperative.

PAP FINN (*The Adventures of Huckleberry Finn**), brutish father of Huckleberry*, a man with no redeeming qualities who beats his son, keeps him prisoner, and tries to get the boy's treasure into his own hands. Dirty, ignorant, and bigoted, Pap thrashes his son for going to school and getting book learning, and he rails against a government that lets a free Negro vote. When he has drunk too much and suffers delirium tremens, he tries to kill Huck, thinking the boy is the Angel of Death. After Huck escapes from him and is with Jim* on Jackson's

Island, they explore a house washed down by the high water and see Pap's body shot in the back, but Jim keeps his identity secret from Huck until the end of the book.

PARISH, HELEN RAND, historian, author, specialist in the history of Latin America and the Spanish conquest of the New World. She has been a reporter, theater editor, and feature writer for newspapers in Atlanta and New York, and has lived in Mexico. Her earlier books for children, *At the Palace Gates** (Viking, 1949) and *Our Lady of Guadalupe* (Viking, 1955), are brief, highly illustrated stories, only a little longer and more complex than picture books. *Estebanico* (Viking, 1974) is a longer book based on her findings about the first black explorer in America, Esteban of Azamur, who was probably elected emperor of Mexico. A long and interesting note tells of her discovery of his life while she was pursuing her twenty-five-year study of the life of Fray Bartoleme de las Casa, defender of the Indians during the Spanish conquest.

PARRISH, ANNE (1888-1957), born in Colorado Springs, Colo.; illustrator, author. She attended private schools in Colorado and Delaware, then the Philadelphia School of Design for Women. Both her parents were artists, as well as her brother, Dillwyn Parrish*, and her cousin, the famous illustrator Maxfield Parrish. All the books she wrote were self-illustrated, some in collaboration with her brother. *Dream Coach** (Macmillan, 1924), *Floating Island** (Harper, 1930) and *The Story of Appleby Capple** (Harper, 1950) were all Newbery honor books, though the arch tone seems now to reflect a very dated attitude toward children.

PARRISH, (GEORGE) DILLWYN (1894-1941), painter, collaborator with his sister, Anne Parrish*, in both writing and illustrating two books for children. He began the first, *Knee-High to a Grasshopper* (Macmillan, 1923), a book of verses, from his sickbed in France during World War I, having left Harvard to drive an ambulance and become seriously ill. Later they wrote and illustrated together *The Dream Coach** (Macmillan, 1924). Although *The Story of Appleby Capple** (Harper, 1950) was inspired by an alphabet game he and his sister played as children, he was not directly involved in the writing or illustration, having turned to serious painting until his death by suicide, brought on by despondency over ill health.

PARTON, ETHEL (1862-1944), born Ethel Thomson in New York City. When she was very young her parents died, and she was brought up in Newburyport, Mass., first by her grandmother, then her aunt and her aunt's husband, James Parton, whose name she eventually took. After graduation from high school, she chose to become secretary, literary assistant, and occasional collaborator with her uncle, a biographer, essayist, and lecturer. She was an early suffragist. For more than forty years, she was a member of the editorial staff of *Youth's Companion*, a magazine to which she contributed stories and sketches, and her reviews appeared frequently in *Horn Book*, but she did not publish her first book, *Melissa Ann* (Doubleday, 1931), until she was sixty-nine. This and *Penelope Ellen and Her Friends: Three Little Girls of 1840** (Viking, 1936) are both based on stories told by her grandmother and other New England people she knew in her childhood. Both *Vinny Applegay** (Viking, 1937) and *Runaway Prentice** (Viking, 1939), set in Newburyport about 1800, feature orphans.

PASTOR NORELIUS (*They Came from Sweden**), Swedish circuit preacher, friend of the Larssons. He lives in Red Wing and travels by horseback to the Swedish settlements round about. He starts a school for Swedish immigrant children in Vasa, the town nearest the Larssons. A pleasant, warm, dedicated man, he convinces the settlers of the importance of education for their children's future. He maintains that a good education in Swedish first will make English school easier for them later. The Larsson children go to his school, and Gustaf*, who has more English than the others, is able soon to go to school in Red Wing and work for Judge* Turner there.

PATROLMAN M'GONEGAL (*Roller Skates**), Lucinda's good friend. He arranges for retribution against the toughs who raid Tony Coppino's family fruit and vegetable stand. He stands by Lucinda whenever she needs him.

PATSY'S PROGRESS (Knox*, Rose B., Dodd, 1935), realistic novel of school and family life set in Virginia and briefly in Chicago from May Day of 1896 to May Day of 1900. Fifteen-year-old Patsy Kirkland, orphaned in infancy, has been raised by her grandmother, Lysbeth Carter, matriarch of an old and respected family in the small town of Vine Hill. Proud, irrepressible Patsy dearly loves her large, gregarious clan, though their directiveness often irritates her, among them, sensible and loving Uncle Bathurst Lee, and her fussy, well-meaning aunts, Adora and Aurelia. After pampered Cousin Bob involves her in a minor gambling scrape, a family council sends her to Clement College for the finishing appropriate to a genteel, Southern lady, a move Patsy welcomes for the relative freedom and the prospect of parties, boys, and fashions. On the train to Clement, she meets John Day, the son of a wealthy, upland farmer and a University student known among his peers for his serious attitude. College proves all that Patsy dreams of, and much of the novel details girl-talk and antics about the school. Patsy quickly makes friends, her particular chum being her roommate, wealthy, generous, and lively Katrina ''Kitten'' Ray, with whom Patsy shares a variety of adventures. The two form the core of the K. K.'s, a socially active group. Patsy proves erratic in all courses but composition and also gains a reputation for mischief and daring. She encounters some thrills—the capture of a male intruder—and temptations—worldly Ethel White who steals smokes and reads questionable novels. A chance encounter with Ina Henley the night Ina steals away with her lover results in Patsy's expulsion. Her shocked family secures her a teaching position in the hills, where she rooms with the Perrys, who are neighbors of the Days. Eventually Patsy conquers self-pity and applies herself to her pupils. Encouraged by John, now a medical student in Chicago, who plans to practice among the poverty-stricken hill people, sobered Patsy enrolls at the University of Chicago where she does well in her courses, particularly in writing. May Day, 1900, finds her and John making plans for marriage. Scenes stand out—the Carter family council, the lively house party in Vine Hill for Patsy's school friends, Patsy and John caring for an ill baby in the mountains—while "school chatter," current fads and slang, references to such national events as the Cuban War and the speeches of William Jennings Byran, and Southern, smalltown life and attitudes toward women add texture to what would otherwise be merely another predictable and amusing girl's growing-up story with the stock characters and events of the school story. Fanfare.

PAUL BEEBE (*Misty of Chincoteague**; *Stormy, Misty's Foal*†), a practical and realistic youth of about fourteen, who with his sister, Maureen*, buys and tames Phantom. He is the planner of the two children, and most of their ideas originate with him. The story of Misty is told more from his point of view than from Maureen's. He wins the right to ride Phantom in the big race in a wishbone pull, Grandma* Beebe's idea. Similarly, he is more involved in what goes on in *Stormy* than is Maureen.

PAUL FAVOR (*To Tell Your Love**), nephew of Mr. Coombes, local banker who has raised him. He is serious but not stodgy. His mother wanted him to become a pianist, and he plays occasionally and well, but he decided to become a banker when he realized he was not good enough to make a career of music. His and Theo's* courtship has some comic aspects but seems quite credible, and their marriage appropriate.

PAUL TIBER, FORESTER (Gleit*, Maria, ill. Ralph Ray, Scribner's, 1949), realistic novel set in the coal mining town of Ashburn, Pa., mainly during the depression of the 1930s. Paul Tiber and his friend, Nicholas Dubinski, both sixteen, on a hike in the woods accidentally set a fire which burns a large area of the foothills of Black Dome mountain. Paul, already troubled by a remark he has overheard from a visitor to the town, "Imagine being stuck for life in a place like this," is consumed with guilt and a determination to make his town of bare yards and ugly slag heaps a better place to live. Shortly afterwards his father, who is determined that his sons will not work in the mines as he has, moves the family to Passaic, N.J., but though they are physically better off, they are homesick there and soon move back. Paul attempts to find work away from the mines but must take a job in the breaker house, first sweeping, then as a picker of slate from the coal. He is horrified when a boy named Whitey is crushed between the rollers of the ore breaker, and he is fired when he attacks a man who is endangering the life of another boy. His great desire to study forestry in college is transferred to his brother Dave, the only way he can foresee to keep the younger boy out of the mines, while Paul takes a job as mule driver in the mine to pay his brother's way. After several seasons there, he finally gets a job with the Forest Service fighting fires and manning the watchtower but in off seasons goes back to the mines. Finally, he sells the mine company superintendent the idea of replanting the burned-over areas with WPA workers and becomes the Colliery Forester. He takes his work with great seriousness, though he has to win over the skeptical adults, the children who often start the fires to get their parents extra income from fighting them, and the town drunk, who breaks the newly planted trees as a way to get back at the hated company. The children come over to his side when he gets them to plant the trees themselves in a Memorial School Forest. Eventually he finds a tree that will grow even on the slag heaps and changes the ugly town to a place of beauty. The story is based on the real life of a Stanley Mesauage and suffers from a florid style, a slow pace, and an awkward structure, which concentrates on the early years and leaves the years of accomplishment underdeveloped. It does have a couple of vivid scenes: the coping with the recalcitrant mules in the depths of the mine, and the climb up the ice-encrusted fire lookout tower in a storm, but the theme of how hard work and determination will win out and love of beauty will triumph is so often stated it becomes tedious. Child Study.

PAYNE, STEPHEN, writer of popular Western novels and stories, highly respected in his field. He was a Colorado cowhand and ranchman who made his home in Denver. He grew up in the world of hunters, miners, cowboys, trappers, sheepmen, cattlemen, and stagedrivers of which he wrote, riding the range and working in cow camps at the age of thirteen. He started writing in 1924, and for over thirty-five years his true-to-life stories of ranch and range life appeared in westerns and other magazines, including *Saturday Evening Post*, and in anthologies, such as those compiled by Western Writers of America. Although best known for his adventure stories and novels of the Old West for adults, he also wrote spirited and flavorful narratives for young people, including *Teenage Stories of the West* (Lantern, 1947), *Teenage Cowboy Stories* (Lantern, 1949), and *Young Readers' Stories of the West* (Lantern, 1951) and the novel *Young Hero of the Range** (Lantern, 1954), about the son of a homesteader who wants to become a cowboy, which received the Spur Award of Western Writers of America.

PEASE, HOWARD (1894-1974), born in Stockton, Calif.; author of adventure novels for young people, some with historical settings. He graduated from Stanford University after serving with the United States Army in World War I. Prior to teaching country school in California and English at Vassar, he was a merchant seaman for several years. His experience at sea provided the background for his several sea stories. He and his wife traveled extensively throughout the United States, once crossing the country in a trailer, and lived in various places, but they called California their home. In 1934, he gave up teaching for full-time writing. He won the Child Study Children's Book Award for *Heart of Danger** (Doubleday, 1946), a story of adventure and intrigue set mostly in France in World War II, his best-known novel and one in the popular Tod Moran fast-action series. He wrote a dozen other Tod Moran books of mystery, adventure, war, and danger, set variously, including *The Tattooed Man* (Doubleday, 1926), his first book; *The Ship without a Crew* (Doubleday, 1934), and *Mystery on Telegraph Hill* (Doubleday, 1961), his last one about this hero. Among his several other books are *Long Wharf* (Doubleday, 1939), about the San Francisco waterfront in 1850, and *Thunderbolt House* (Doubleday, 1944), about the San Francisco earthquake of 1906.

PEDRO CHAVEZ (*. . . And Now Miguel**), Miguel's younger brother, who, it seems to Miguel, has no wants and is always content, while life for Miguel is filled with unsatisfied yearnings and many perplexities. Although Pedro sometimes teases Miguel, he is mostly supportive of his older brother. When Miguel boasts that he has a plan which will insure his going to the mountains with the men this year, Pedro believes him and encourages Miguel in carrying it out. Since Miguel is a religious child with a strongly developed moral sense, his idle boast bothers his conscience.

PEEWEE REISFELD (*Have Space Suit—Will Travel**), Patricia Wynant, eleven-year-old genius who is captured by space pirates. Besides being highly intelligent, Peewee has an overdeveloped curiosity, a quality which is responsible for her original capture, since she was investigating things on the moon out-of-bounds for visitors. Although she has great courage and a scientific education beyond most professors, she occasionally dissolves in tears and carries with her constantly a rag doll called Madam Pompadour.

PEGEEN (Van Stockum*†, Hilda, ill. author, Viking, 1941), realistic novel of family life, the third in the series about the O'Sullivans. Michael* is now away at school, and the family takes in orphaned Pegeen Murphy, 7, until her Uncle Dan in America sends for her. Francie* and Liam are especially delighted to welcome her, and the children look forward to many happy times together. Pegeen is a gifted child, quick and intelligent. She speaks Gaelic fluently and can dance with astonishing grace and beauty. But her high spirits, sense of fun, and thoughtlessness soon get her into trouble. While fetching water, she loses the tea kettle in the pool. When she lets out Liam's pet rabbit, Brian, to feed him his cabbage, he hops away and feasts on the brussels sprouts. Told to stir the soup while Mother walks to town for salt, she gets bored and goes for a stroll with Patricia, Brigid's* cherished doll, which Pegeen knows she is not to touch. Bran, the dog, runs away with the doll, and the soup burns. Pegeen consistently disclaims responsibility for her misdeeds. Nourished on her grandmother's tales of giants and little people, she asserts that such mischievous spirits are to blame for her misbehavior. At school she insists she can read, although she has never before been to school, and must stand in the corner because she pulls Shamus McCormick's hair. Her most serious escapade occurs when she releases the pigs from their pen, with the well-meaning intention of giving them some freedom before they are led away to slaughter. When she realizes the seriousness of her act, Pegeen runs away to the hills. Francie and Liam rescue her when she is drowning in a mountain pool where the dread bull of the mountain has chased her. Her culminating escapade involves riding Mrs. O'Flaherty's surly, independent cow, Clementine, through the school grounds, into the schoolroom itself, and down the road into the O'Sullivan yard where Clementine breaks down the line upon which Brigid has hung Patricia's clothes to dry. Sobered by the seriousness of the trouble she has caused, Pegeen stays home to care for mother, whose rheumatism troubles her, while the rest of the family goes for a Sunday outing. A year after she has come to live with the O'Sullivans, Uncle Dan sends for her. The family have grown fond of her, in spite of her misdeeds, and offer her a permanent home, which she accepts. A good-natured book, the episodes are spaced well to hold the interest of later elementary readers, and there is plenty of action and excitement. Pegeen is a likeable scamp but changes too abruptly. The sense of Irish family life is strong. Fanfare.

PENELOPE ELLEN AND HER FRIENDS: THREE LITTLE GIRLS OF 1840 (Parton*, Ethel, ill. Margaret Platt, Viking, 1936), historical novel set in coastal Newburyport, Mass., in 1840. For a year, while her mother joins her sea-captain father on a voyage of the *Mercator*, Penelope Ellen Purvis, about ten or eleven, stays with relatives in the care of her lovely young aunt, Lucy Otway. Her friends are Cressy* (Lucretia) Pidgen, daughter of a widowed dressmaker, and Cressy's younger cousin, Thudy* (Arethusa Amelia) Thripp, whose father is a sailor on the *Mercator*. There are also two boys, polite, charming Ned Cherry, who lives with his doctor uncle across from Penny's Grandmother Purvis, and shy Zeph Ring, 12, Thudy's cousin with whom she lives. The plot ambles from one happening to another, loosely held together by the growing friendship and Penny's efforts to live up to her mother's injunction to be a good girl and cheer up Aunt Lucy, whose health is fragile. There is a series of terrible storms, in one of which the ship *Pocahantas* is wrecked with all hands lost within sight of town. Penny and Ned visit a black family where a woman is sick, and when she later dies of small pox and the children are ill, they are isolated, but their sickness turns out to be chicken pox. The political campaign of William Henry Harrison against Martin Van Buren excites the town and features a torch-light parade. The newly built railroad comes to Newburyport, and the three girls travel on it to a fair in Boston, accompanied by Cressy's Gran'ma* Pidgen and her lawyer uncle, Theophilus Powlett. Ned's dog, Tip (for Tippecanoe), is injured by the train when he has saved a colt from being killed, and after Penny helps bind his wounds, Ned arranges to give her a similar, black cocker puppy, which she names "Tyler Too." Aunt Lucy and Dr. Cherry are married, and Penny's parents arrive home just as the ceremony starts. Penelope Ellen is described as a lively child with coppery curls, and she does join in snowball fights and taffy pulls, but a great deal of her attention goes toward being good, and the story gives the impression of being written to tell how life was at the time rather than to develop character or plot. Fanfare.

PENNY BAXTER (*The Yearling**), small, wiry farmer and hunter in the Florida scrub, who imparts his honesty and love of nature to his son, Jody*. Having been worked too hard and too young by a stern father, he is inclined to let Jody off easily when the boy skips out on work, and he is compassionate with the son's love of his pet deer and the boy's terrible sense of loss when the animal must be destroyed. In a group of men, Penny is a fine storyteller, and glimpses given of him with Grandma* Hutto and Nellie Ginright, an old girlfriend, show he has been warm and fun-loving with women, but with his grim wife he is sober and mild, though when pushed too far he can lay down the law firmly. In Volusia he is respected for his integrity, and even the rough Forresters defer to him as the appropriate one to speak at Fodderwing's* funeral and admit he is the best tracker in the countryside.

PEPPERFOOT OF THURSDAY MARKET (Davis*, Robert, ill. Cyrus LeRoy Baldridge*, Holiday, 1941), realistic animal story set in the mid-1900s among the Berbers of the desert and mountains of North Africa. While walking home through the desert scrub from peddling charcoal in Thursday Market (the *souk*) with his grandfather, Hadj* Sidi Ahmed, the wise and respected headman (*Chirk*) of Ali Taza, ten-year-old Driss rescues from jackals a baby donkey which he raises on goat's milk. The lively-gaited, intelligent, little Egyptian donkey, his silvery-gray coat marked with a cross on his back, soon becomes a familiar sight, obediently trotting about the village like a dog at Driss's side. He earns the name "Pepperfoot" at Thursday Market when his flying hooves foil the skinny, sandy-haired dog that sly Dillal* Ben Abbes has trained to steal from the tradesmen's booths. Steady and sturdy, Pepperfoot helps Driss rescue his friend, Amroo, who has been wounded while the boys are collecting eagles' eggs, and he boldly kills a ferocious panther which has been raiding area flocks. During the barley harvest, Pepperfoot is stolen, and Driss, Amroo, and their chum, Omar, bravely search for him in the mountain villages. Driss discovers him far to the south among the Cheulas tribesmen, now the property of a merchant, who purchased him unsuspectingly from the thief, Dillal Ben Abbes. Driss demands a hearing at the court of justice, where he argues his case forcefully, proving that Pepperfoot is really silvery-gray beneath the brown stain and demonstrating the animal's obedience. When the French Legionnaires construct a road through the mountains, hostile tribesmen attack, bottling them up in the mountains. While Omar runs to inform the French command, under cover of darkness Driss and Amroo smuggle water to the soldiers in skins bound to Pepperfoot's back, Driss's way of repaying the French soldier-doctor who healed his infected foot. In a public ceremony the grateful soldiers proclaim Pepperfoot the official mascot of the legion. Characters are static, the most potentially interesting being the grandfather, and the plot is meager and contrived. While some incidents are well drawn and suspenseful and the matter of the thief contributes unity, accent falls upon recreating the history and geography of the region and the ways of the proud, enduring Berbers: their religious beliefs, educational system, marketplaces, decision-making processes, economy, courts, and daily life. Fanfare.

THE PERILOUS ROAD (Steele*, William O., ill. Paul Galdone, Harcourt, 1958), historical novel for middle readers set in 1863 on Signal Mountain near Chattanooga, Tenn. When Union soldiers raid his family's hill farm and take not only all their supplies for winter but even their only horse, Chris* Brabson, 11, is further convinced that Yankee soldiers are mean, inhuman monsters. He readily joins Silas* Agee, a middle-aged ne'er-do-well with whom he hunts, in an ambush but is discovered and chased before he can get off a shot. Just as Union soldiers are about to catch up to him, he squirms down a crack in the bluff, then slips and hangs precariously over a drop-off and is saved only by the arrival of his older brother, Jethro. Chris is further enraged and upset when he learns that Jethro plans to leave his wife and baby to join the Union army. To prove his loyalty to the Confederate cause to Lukie Trantham, whose father has become antagonistic because of Jethro's enlistment, Chris sneaks down to the Union mule corral on a stormy night, releases the mules, is almost caught, and is saved by Silas, who also is hanging around. This chance meeting convinces Chris that Silas is a spy for the Confederacy, a supposition Silas encourages, even after Chris has seen him with Trantham and some other men who burn Brabson's shed. While Jethro is hunting, he sees the Union supply train starting off across the Sequatchie Valley toward their supply depot at Bridgeport, Ala. He races to report this to Silas, then at home learns that Jethro has become a wagon driver and fears that he will be the cause of his brother's death. In remorse he goes down to the valley and through the evening stumbles from one campfire to another desperately hunting for his brother to warn him. The Yankee soldiers are kind to him, and when he falls asleep, exhausted, they put him to bed in one of the wagons. He wakes to find himself in the midst of a battle where he sees terrible slaughter on both sides. Finally he is able to escape back up the mountain, where he confesses all to an understanding father and, realizing that Jethro could not have been with the supply train and that Silas's spying was a fantasy, loses some of his sense of guilt. Complex issues are dealt with in terms that are not simplistic, unusual in a novel for this age level. The pace is rapid and the action, if a bit exaggerated, is plausible. Addams; Choice; Fanfare; Newbery Honor.

PERKIN (*Adam of the Road**), son of Wat the plowman, who with the help of the parish priest has become a student of St. Alban's Abbey School and there becomes a friend of Adam* Quartermayne, a minstrel's son. An intelligent and studious boy, Perkin goes on to Merton College at Oxford, hoping to become a lawyer. He represents the lowborn boy who, against great odds, could rise in station in the late Middle Ages through education.

PERTWOOD APP (*Sibby Botherbox**), twelve-year-old boy who lives next door to Hannah Poole and whom she considers too noisy and pushy to be a good playmate. He plans to be an auctioneer when he grows up and can often be heard practicing the auctioneer's sing-song jargon. He is fond of using current expressions, like "twenty-three skidoo." When the Apps move to Ottequoteky to live with his mother's brother who owns a potato chip business, Pertwood changes his mind and decides he will become a preacher, but his mother humorously observes that she will not be surprised if he ends up in potato chips.

PETER (*The Covered Bridge**), laconic, hardworking, resourceful youth, who becomes Connie's close friend. Grandson of the warm and loving Sarah, he decides to sell one of the calves, of which he is so proud, to ease her money problems. He changes his mind and offers the calf to Dick MacGowan who is running away to sea as an inducement to remain on the farm where he is so desperately needed by his mother. Ethan Allen* sells the calf anyway, but gives Dick a portion of the proceeds. A warmhearted youth, Peter forms emotional attachments quickly and chooses the orphaned lamb from Sam Breen's flock, even though it may not be as strong as another, because Sarah has nursed it to life. He willingly does a man's work in the novel.

PETER BRICKER (*Rifles for Washington**), a Moravian orphan who drives a wagon between the religious settlements. A beautiful boy with long eyelashes, he is dedicated to the Moravians' pattern of nonviolence, but he goes with Davie McKail to join Washington's army. He falls in love with the younger Sister Helena of the Dunkers, a community that doesn't believe in marriage, and finds that she, too, is an orphan, brought up in the community after being delivered there as a young child. When she turns out to be Davie's sister, Jennet, who was lost as an infant, she plans to leave the community to marry Peter.

THE PETERKIN PAPERS (Hale*, Lucretia P., Osgood, 1880), series of humorous episodes set in the last third of the nineteenth century about a family who live in a village near Boston and are greatly in want of common sense. Mrs. Peterkin is easily flustered and afraid of many things; her husband likes a little quiet time each day and is strikingly unable to see the obvious; Agamemnon, who has been to college (five different ones, none for a full term) is bookish and full of ridiculous suggestions; Solomon John is mechanically inclined; Elizabeth Eliza always wants to do the correct thing but has a terrible memory and a hard time making up her mind; the little boys, of whom there are two to four depending upon the story (Mrs. Peterkin, in one, cannot remember for sure), are mostly involved in running around, making noise, and putting on and pulling off their India-rubber boots. The lady from Philadelphia always offers aid or good advice to get them out of their predicaments. These include putting salt instead of sugar in the coffee, having too few cups for their tea party, being snowed in, and trying to hire foreigners to teach them languages. In one of the longer episodes, they celebrate the Centennial Fourth of July and are nearly blown up by Solomon John's homemade fireworks. The lady from Philadelphia appears in all but a few of the episodes, most of which first appeared in *St. Nicholas* magazine. In an 1889 edition an additional episode is included in which the family decides to go to the beach resort called Old Farm and go to the Poor Farm by mistake. The simple-mindedness of the Peterkins has a nonsensical charm, but the sameness of each episode makes sustained reading tedious. Children's Classics; Choice.

PETE THE SQUEAK (*The Bells of Bleecker Street**), Joey Enrico's best friend. Although his real name is Peter Ryan, he is called the Squeak because of his high-pitched voice. He plays the drums in the Bleecker* Street orchestra, which is directed by Professor* Dante. He always knows the news on the street and informs Joey that the old statute of St. John the Baptist in the Church of Our Lady of Pompeii is being replaced. Joey then takes the loose toe of the statue for a good luck charm. In an amusing scene, he and Joey fight over the toe. Later, Pete helps Joey glue it back on the statue. A foil for Joey, Pete is a brash, flighty, sometimes careless and thoughtless boy but still a thoroughly likeable one.

PHEBE FAIRCHILD: HER BOOK (Lenski*, Lois, ill. author, Stokes, 1936), novel of American life set in Connecticut in the 1830s. When her parents sail on her sea-captain father's vessel, the *Phebe Ann*, Phebe, 10, is sent to her paternal grandmother and her uncle Jothan's family in Winton, Conn. With her she carries her book, a Mother Goose, a treasured gift from her father. In the large family, she finds Aunt Betsy kind, but her grandmother and Aunt Hannah, her father's eldest sister who undertakes to tutor her, are puritanical and even the children disapprove of her pretty clothes and sashes. Only to Timothy, 15, does she dare show her book. Her high spirits keep getting her into trouble, as when Great-aunt Pettifer, a wealthy relative, calls and Phebe tries on her cloak and mimics her to the other children, and, carried away with daring, takes off down the road and even spends some coins from the reticule before she is apprehended and brought back. When she goes to apologize to the great-aunt, she unexpectedly finds an ally, a woman who also likes lively and pretty things and who tells her of her own father's rebelliousness and how he ran off to sea. A sub-plot concerns Uncle Benjamin's difficulties with Lucy Rogers, whom he loves but accuses of "outraging decorum." Together with Jeremiah, the peddler and clock maker, Phebe plays cupid and the book ends shortly after their marriage. Another friend is Christopher Ross, whom Phebe finds ill and brings home where Aunt Hannah nurses him to health. So much attention is paid to giving a well-researched picture of New England life of the period that the book has a stiff and didactic tone, and both the characters and incidents are predictable. Newbery Honor.

PHILBROOK, ELIZABETH, author of *Far from Marlborough Street** (Viking, 1944), a novel of a little girl's journey by stagecoach in 1793, and *Hobo Hill* (Viking, 1954), a story of a group of boys who band together to save a wooded hilltop from development.

PHILIP MARSHAM (*The Dark Frigate**), 19, son of a seagoing scrapegrace but grandson of the vicar of Little Grimsby, who ships aboard *The Rose of Devon**, in company with Martin Barwick, a chance acquaintance whom he has good reason to believe has piracy in his past. Phil is made boatswain by Captain Candle, but the ship is seized by Martin's old companion, Tom Jordan, and his crew of cutthroats, the captain murdered, and Phil pressed into becoming a priate against his will. When Jordan has Phil's admirable young friend, Will Canty, killed, Phil escapes, makes his way tormented by insect bites across the island, and swims out to a vessel he sights and hopes will rescue him. It turns out to be a man-of-war, where he is taken prisoner, returned to stand trial in England, and escapes hanging only through Jordan's testimony. Phil is a lively, naive young fellow, bright enough so one might expect him to go far despite his rough start.

PICCOLO (*The Marble Fountain**), younger brother of Andrea, an imaginative, very sensible boy who ponders the reasons for the bombings that have destroyed the Italian villages, killed his parents, and changed so drastically the way of life of the people he knows. While on the way to Rosa, he acquires a white dove, which to him epitomizes hope for peace and a better future.

PIERRE DUFOUR (*That Girl of Pierre's**), father of Danielle, husband of Jeanne. Jeanne finds him in a German hospital and takes him to a family nearby where she can care for him. Before they can leave for France after hostilities cease, they must pay for their expenses there. Danielle gives up her rights to the Dowry* Field in order to get the money. Pierre tends to be impulsive and hot-headed, and he worsens their case temporarily by confronting Porky* Guichard about the due bill and the Dowry Field. Later he cleverly sees the advantage of bringing pressure upon the lawyer who assisted Guichard in his scheme to get the land back.

PIERRE DUMENILLE (*Swift Rivers**), tall, dark, quick, proud, half-Chippewa, half-French Mississippi river pilot, deemed by many the best pilot on the river. He takes Chris's* raft of logs to Rock Island. He and Joe* Langford had been best friends prior to a falling-out some time before the story begins. Chris is instrumental in bringing the two back together. Pierre helps Chris get a good price for his logs.

PIERRE LAROCHE (*Calico Captive**), handsome and wealthy *coureur de bois* whom Felicité Du Quesne hopes to marry. Felicité becomes jealous when he pays attention to Miriam. He carries Miriam off to a ball at his rich grandfather's house one night when he is slightly drunk, shocking the guests. He admires Miriam's spirit.

PIETER PIM VAN OORDT (*The Level Land**), lively four-year-old, who innocently gets into many scrapes. Open-hearted and matter-of-fact, Pieter tries to share his sweet rusk with his newborn sister and is hurt when the nurse interferes. Seeing his friend the green grocer looking cold as he drives a market cart, Pieter generously gives the man his father's fur-lined jacket with a fur collar. When a new boy Pieter meets at the skating rink suggests that they have a treat at one of the refreshment booths, he readily agrees, only to find after he has eaten that the friend has spent all his money on himself. Pieter works off his debt shouting the wares for the booth owner, quite happily, until his father rescues him. When he starts kindergarten, he learns to read quickly and keeps the family informed about all the new wartime regulations posted in the village.

PLAIN GIRL (Sorensen*†, Virginia, ill. Charles Geer, Harcourt, 1955), realistic novel of an Amish girl in Pennsylvania in the mid-twentieth century. When men from the state come to the farm and tell Esther Lapp's father that she must by law attend school, she doesn't know whether to be scared or delighted. Although she is nearly ten, she has learned only at home, mostly from her Aunt Ruth, her mother's younger sister, because there are too few Amish in the neighborhood to have their own school. Esther's older brother, Daniel, had gone to school, though, and loved it, and her father believes that it was this which turned him to questioning and to worldly ways and made him leave home. For nearly a year he has been gone, and her father has forbidden the family to mention his name. Faced with heavy fines and possibly jail, her father starts Esther in school, but he drives her and picks her up in his buggy rather than let her ride the school bus, and he tells her not to look at any of the other children. At first she tries to obey him, though she knows the others think she acts strangely and laugh at her long dress and bonnet, but when Mary, the pretty blond girl in pink who sits in front of her, begins to talk to her and send her notes, she responds shyly. At a quilting party, Sarah Yoder, the girl Dan favored, tells Esther that he is back and that she has seen him at a farm auction. With his hair cut and wearing worldly clothes, Dan arrives at the schoolhouse and talks to Esther at noon, and together they make a plan for him to return at Christmas after his hair has regrown and Esther has smuggled to him the plain clothes he left behind. He tells her something of his adventures in the outside world but is shocked when she asks his advice about her big problem: dare she trade clothes for part of the day with Mary, as her friend wants her to? She decides she will trade but is relieved when Mary admits her mother objects. On Christmas Eve, when her father must welcome any visitor, Dan returns and becomes, again, part of the family, destined to marry Sarah, who has promised to see that Esther gets more fun and freedom at their house. Not only the restrictions of Amish life are shown but also the happy times, the courtship and wedding of Aunt Ruth and her Hans providing most of the occasions for merriment. Esther's struggles with her conscience and her disobedience to her stern father, though trivial by other standards, are developed as the major problems that they are to her, and she emerges as a real and interesting character. Child Study; Choice.

THE PLAIN PRINCESS (McGinley*, Phyllis, ill. Helen Stone, Lippincott, 1945), literary tale set in an imaginary kingdom at an unspecified time. Princess Esmeralda, the only child of the king and queen, is much loved and pampered, but she is clearly plain, with a nose that turns up, a mouth that turns down, and eyes that have no shine. At her eighth birthday party, Charles Michael, prince of a neighboring kingdom, who is destined to marry her, disappears and is found with the duck keeper's daughter, whom he prefers. The king offers a reward for anyone who can change Esmeralda from plain to beautiful, the penalty for failure being decapitation. Only one applicant applies, calm and confident Dame Goodwit, who proposes a magical cure with certain conditions: the Princess must come and live with her and her five daughters, Annabelle, Christobelle, Dulcibelle, Floribelle, and Echo; she must bring none of her many possessions except a few simple clothes and the pearl locket her godmother gave her; she must stay for nine months. The king agrees reluctantly, and Esmeralda starts a new life where she is not waited upon, spoiled, or petted. As she begins to notice how clever the other girls are at sewing and cooking, her nose no longer turns up. When she tries to make muffins by herself, with some success, she learns to smile, and when she gives her precious locket to Echo, her favorite, as a birthday gift, her eyes begin to glow. Her parents are delighted, the king insists that Dame Goodwit and the girls move close to the palace so that Esmeralda can continue to see them, and even Prince Charles Michael finds the Princess no longer plain but beautiful. The twist of making the "magic" a very practical change in lifestyle is clever, but otherwise the story is not particularly distinguished and depends on very obvious moralism for its point. Choice; Fanfare.

PLAYTIME IN CHERRY STREET (Bianco*, Pamela, Oxford, 1948), series of episodes featuring two children, Christine and her new neighbor, Martin, both almost five, in a typical mid-twentieth-century American town or suburb. They play with Christine's doll Nancy, her stuffed toys, Panda and Pandora and Teddy, and with Martin's stuffed Scottie and Easter Bunny, and with a real, neighboring toddler named Joseph. They buy piggy banks, draw a whole sheet of birds, make a tent with an old blanket, pick cherries, and in the end start their first day of school. Although their adventures have a Dick-and-Jane quality, the vocabulary is not controlled as in the "easy reader" books; sentence structure, however, is mostly simple. A large part of the book is in dialogue, much of which does not ring true for children of that age, not because of long words, which young children sometimes employ, but because of stilted adult phraseology: "How quickly the morning went." "I'll ask Mummie at once." "How nice!" "Draw it quickly." "Very well." Since both children talk this way, it does not seem to be an effort to characterize a particular child, and except for a few unlikely comments from Martin on how pretty Christine's dress or hat is, the speakers could be reversed in most situations. Fanfare.

POKENICK (*The Sea Is All Around**), a wind-blown, often fog-bound island consisting of just a few square miles located off Massachusetts, once a center of the whaling industry, where Mab goes to live. When she arrives, the island is not totally unfamiliar to her, because she learns something about it from an old woman with whom she shares a table in the dining car on the train.

POLYNESIA (*The Story of Doctor Dolittle**; *The Voyages of Doctor Dolittle**), wily, old parrot who first teaches Doctor* Dolittle the languages of animals. Being nearly two hundred years old, Polynesia has had many experiences—has sailed with pirates, has known people of many nations and degrees both high and low—and has acquired much wisdom and practical good sense. It is Polynesia who manages the escape of the doctor and his crew from imprisonment in Jolliginki, summons the Black Parrots to defeat the Bad-jagderags on Spider-monkey Island, and works out a way for the doctor to escape the job of being king. After the first voyage she remains in Africa but returns to England shortly after the doctor and Tommy Stubbins meet. It is she who first suggests that Tommy become the doctor's assistant. Somewhat cynical and scornful of many of the other animals and patronizing toward Tommy and Bumpo*, she is devoted to Doctor Dolittle and uses her considerable wits to protect his interests.

POPE†, ELIZABETH MARIE (1917-   ), born in Washington, D.C.; professor, novelist. She is a graduate of Bryn Mawr College, received her doctorate from Johns Hopkins University, and has been a professor at Mills College, Oakland, Calif. In addition to a scholarly book on *Paradise Regained* and articles in *Shakespeare Survey* and *Shakespeare Quarterly*, she has written novels, including *The Sherwood Ring** (Houghton, 1958), a fantasy, and *The Perilous Gard†* (Houghton, 1974), a historical romance set in the Elizabethan period.

THE POPPY SEED CAKES (Clark*, Margery, ill. Maud Petersham and Miska Petersham, Doubleday, 1924), highly illustrated episodic story for young children set in the United States in the early twentieth century. Although the various animals talk, there are no other fantasy elements. Three episodes feature Andrewshek, 4, and his aunt from the old country, Katushka; three feature Erminka,

4, and the red-topped boots brought from the old country by her Uncle Anton; two have both children. Auntie Katushka has brought with her five pounds of poppy seeds to make poppy seed cakes for Andrewshek. In each Andrewshek story, he has promised to watch something for her. but forgets; nevertheless, all comes out well in the end. While he is bouncing on the bed instead of watching the cakes, the Green Goose gets in and tries to take away the feather bed. Bribed with poppy seed cakes to stop, he overeats, bursts, and therefore provides feathers for pillows. The white goat gets in while Andrewshek is swinging on the gate and must be lured down with green vegetable tops. While Andrewshek is wading in the stream, a swan steals the picnic basket and sets it afloat. Auntie Katushka retrieves it with the handle of her green umbrella. Erminka is fascinated with the red-topped boots actually meant for her younger brother and too large even for her. She slips and crushes vegetables in the garden, lets live chickens loose in the market, and falls in the mud when the chicks chase her. Her father promises to get her boots that will fit her when he goes for a trip to the old country. In his absence, Erminka and her mother go to live with Uncle Anton next door to Auntie Katushka. The two children enlarge a hole in the fence so that they can get together for a play tea party, and all the animals follow. Andrewshek is put to bed, but the next day Auntie Katushka makes a real tea party to which all the animals come as guests. Although the "old country" is not specified, the illustrations and the names place it in Eastern Europe, probably the Ukraine. The stories are exceedingly simple, but pleasant, with some mild humor concerned mainly with Andrewshek's irresponsibility. Choice.

PORKY GUICHARD (*That Girl of Pierre's**), Armand Guichard, the greedy storekeeper who takes advantage of the people of Arsac-le-Petit and gouges them with his prices. After he is convicted of aiding the Germans during the War and is unable to hold a position elsewhere, he returns to the village in disgrace. When he tries to take his life, Marc stops him, and the village priest then appeals to the better nature of the villagers. They give him another chance by putting him in charge of the grocery section of the Cooperative. At first this is hard for Danielle to take, but she agrees that she does need help and this is work the man knows well.

PORTIA BLAKE (*Gone-Away Lake**), 11, responsible, feminine, brace-toothed, adventurous, but a little shy. She tends to follow her more assertive cousin, Julian*, as they explore about Gone-Away Lake and develop a friendship with Pindar Payton and Minniehaha Cheever, the elderly brother and sister who live there. Although she occasionally chafes at Julian's bossiness, Portia admires his quick mind and questing spirit and is usually ready to follow his lead. At the end, however, she and her new friend, Lucy, are pleased to play "dress-ups" with Minnie's old-fashioned clothes and leave the boys to their own pleasure.

POWDERHORN (*Me and the General**), a red-haired orphan and the "Me" of the title. A confident, unabashed youngster, he almost drowns on the journey with his two Indian captors because he assures them that he can swim well and is not prepared for the current in a river they must cross. At the Indian camp he fights the chief's son, and later, when the Indian children plan to make him run the gauntlet, he jumps the leader, seizes a club, and fights off the others, then throws the club at the retreating children and happens to hit the chief in the stomach. When his Indian fathers plan to dunk him in the icy lake for punishment, he slips on some fish heads and precipitates both of the braves into the water. His initial enthusiasm for the British general and the pomp of the army is at first reinforced by the small-sized red coat the general sends him but is destroyed when he learns that the general has allowed the Indians to torture and kill the captured Americans.

POWELL, MIRIAM, author of *Jareb** (Crowell, 1952), a novel of a poor family's struggle in the pine woods of South Georgia, widely praised by reviewers for its authentic dialect and picture of the locale. She also wrote, under the pseudonym of Mary Morgan, *Rainbow for Susan* (Abelard, 1962), a story of a twelve-year-old girl from Georgia who spends the summer with her Irish relatives on their goat farm inside the city limits of New York, an experience that at first humiliates her because it resembles a junk yard but which later enlists her sympathy and loyalty.

PRAN OF ALBANIA (Miller*, Elizabeth Cleveland, ill. Maud Petersham and Miska Petersham, Doubleday, 1929), realistic novel set in the mountains of Albania, presumably in the early part of the twentieth century. Pran, 14, lives with her mother, Lukia, her father Ndrek Palokit, and her twin brothers, Gjon and Nikola, 8, in the mountain village of Thethi, two days walk from Skodra. Two men and a woman, Giyl, brothers and widow of a man killed in a blood feud, visit Pran's home and there is talk of invasion of their territory by the southern Slavs, who already hold some land claimed by the mountain tribes. Later, in the woods, Pran and the twins meet a boy named Nush, who saves Nik's life when the more impulsive twin falls into a raging stream. When Pran is sent to take her ailing infant cousin to the doctor in Skodra, she again meets Nush, now dressed as a Moslem, who shows her the signal fires that presage the Slavic attack, and she is able to carry the warning to her village. The Maltsor tribe joins with others in a *bessa*, or truce, which puts aside the blood feuds for the common cause of resisting the Slavs. Pran, her mother, and the twins flee to Skodra, where they live in an abandoned Turkish barracks and take in Dil, a girl of Pran's age, and later find her younger brother and sister, Notz and Lul, who have been separated from her for some years since their village was attacked and their parents slain. Learning that the fighting men need food, Pran goes with some of their meager supplies to the front, finds her father, and delivers the food, but she gets turned around and hears voices talking in Slavic, a language she has learned slightly from Dil. She hides in a cave and overhears a traitor talking to two Slavs of the plan for the attack, news she reports to the mountain chief and so prevents a surprise. Waiting to see whether her father survives, she sees Nush, wounded, being carried away. After the Slavs are repulsed and the mountain family returns to their own village, Dil and her siblings with them, Lukja tells Pran that some time before Ndrek has betrothed her to a man named Prendnush in a distant village and that they will be married in the fall. Unable to bear the thought of marrying any man other than Nush, whose home and father's name she doesn't know, Pran takes a vow of virginity before twelve village men, a right granted to any girl who refuses her father's choice for a husband, after which she dresses and carries a rifle like a man and is let into men's councils. A year later she meets Nush, learns that he is Prendnush, son of Giyl, but has to go incognito because of the blood feud which killed his father. Since the *bessa* is about to be lifted, Pran goes to the council and speaks for a continued truce, her voice added to others tipping the scales in favor of peace. She then is allowed to renounce her vow, since she is willing to accept her father's choice, and is married happily to Nush. The detail of dress and customs of the Albanian mountain tribes, which often dominates the story, may still have some validity despite the present Communist government, since these are isolated peoples, and Pran makes a modern heroine, a strong woman despite her acceptance of a second-class place for females in tribal society, but the dependence upon coincidence, both in the finding of Dil's siblings and in the betrothal to Nush, as well as the lengthy descriptions, make the plot implausible and the style dated. Newbery Honor.

PRICE, OLIVE (M.) (1903-), born in Pittsburgh, Pa.; author of plays and books mainly of fiction for children and young people. She grew up in Pittsburgh and attended the University of Pennsylvania. In her teens she wrote plays for children which were produced locally, and when she was eighteen, she went to New York City and was successful in having her first book of plays published by Samuel French. Many published plays followed, and she was well known as a playwright for children, mostly on historical subjects, before she turned to writing books for the young. Several of her plays have been produced on radio and television. Her first novel, a book of historical fiction, *A Donkey for the King** (Whittlesey, 1945), is a short animal novel that fictionalizes upon Christ's triumphal entry into Jerusalem. It was selected for Fanfare by the editors of *Horn Book*. She has written some two dozen other books for young readers, including historical fiction, biographies, mysteries, animal stories, and picture book adaptations from the classics, among them, *Bob, Son of Battle* (1960) and *Five Little Peppers and How They Grew* (1963). Among her novels set in other times and places are *The Valley of the Dragon* (Bobbs, 1951) and *The Story of Marco Polo* (Grosset, 1953), both set in China, *Miracle by the Sea* (Whittlesey, 1947), also set in Biblical times, and *Kim Walk-in-My-Shoes* (Coward, 1968), set during the Korean War. She has also written under the names Anne Cherryholmes and Barbara West.

PRINCE (*Bhimsa, the Dancing Bear**), spoiled, arrogant, and haughty youth, manipulated by his courtiers, who insists that no peasant may wear shoes in his kingdom and that David remove the ones he is wearing. He wishes to have Bhimsa for his very own, but Bapu, a wise old dealer in skins, helps Gopala, David, and the bear escape by hiding them under the uncured skins of his bullock cart. When the Prince hotly pursues them in his big, American-made car, Bapu offends the boy's delicate nose by very slowly removing the uncured skins one by one from the cart. The Prince leaves when he can no longer stand the smell, certain that no one lies secreted under the malodorous skins.

THE PRINCE AND THE PAUPER (Twain*, Mark, Osgood, 1881), historical novel set in England in 1547. Tom* Canty of Offal Court off Pudding Lane in the most poverty-stricken and tough part of London was born on the same day as Edward* Tudor, Prince of Wales, soon to become Edward VI of England. Tom is forced by his brutal father, John* Canty, who is a thief, to be a beggar, as are his fifteen-year-old twin sisters, Nan and Bet. Their beggar grandmother is fiendish, but their mother is gentle though ignorant. Tom has been taught by Father Andrew and has read enough to be full of romantic notions, and he leads his ragged companions in imaginative games in which he is king, until one day he walks to Westminster Palace and catches a glimpse of Edward through the gate bars. A guard roughly pushes him away, an act seen by the young prince who intercedes and takes the poor boy to his own quarters. After he is fed and they talk a bit, the prince proposes that they trade clothes for fun, and when they look in the mirror, they are both astonished at how much they resemble each other. The prince notices that Tom's hand has been injured and impulsively rushes out to confront the guard, only to be seized and roughly thrown out. He is harried into Tom's slum neighborhood until John Canty finds him and drags him to the family's room, where they decide Tom has gone mad, though his mother has some doubts about his identity. In the meantime, Tom has been mistaken for Edward and has caused consternation to his cousin, Lady Jane Grey, his father, the ailing Henry VIII, his sister, the Princess Elizabeth, and the nobles, particularly his uncle and guardian, Lord Hertford, by his seeming madness. Hoping that it will pass, the king orders that none are to mention or seem to notice his strange lapses, and he is prompted and assisted by Hertford and others so that gradually he begins to fit and to enjoy his position. In the meantime, the real prince, beaten and hungry, wakes to be dragged off by Canty, who has killed Father Andrew in an earlier scuffle and is fleeing the city. Edward gets loose from him in the crowd, declares himself prince at the gates of Guildhall, is mocked and attacked by the mob, but defended by a former soldier, Miles* Hendon, who admires his spirit. As they make their way to Miles's lodging, the announcement comes that the king is dead. Miles tells his story, that he is of good country family but has been a prisoner in foreign wars for seven years, and, thinking the little prince is mad, determines to keep him and nurse him back to mental health. Asked what boon he wishes, Miles asks that he be allowed to sit in the presence of the king. The next morning, the prince is recaptured by Canty, who then joins a band of thieves and beggars led by the Ruffler. Tricked into seeming to be a thief by a jealous member of the band, the prince is arrested, rescued by Miles, who has been searching for him, and together they go to Hendon Hall, where instead of being welcomed, Miles and the king are thrown into prison by his brother, who has usurped his inheritance and his fiancée, Lady Edith. After serving in the stocks and being whipped to save Edward from stripes, Miles is released, determines to go to London to try to get help from a friend in high position, and gets separated from Edward in the coronation crowd. Tom Canty, meanwhile, has begun to enjoy the trappings of power until, in the coronation parade, he sees his own mother in the crowd, denies her, and then is filled with such shame that he hardly notices what is going on. At the ceremony, just as Tom is about to be crowned, Edward, who has sneaked into Westminster Abbey and hidden in the Confessor's tomb, appears and commands that the ceremony stop. Tom immediately falls on his knees and swears fealty, but the nobles are not easily convinced, and finally Edward proves his position by giving the place of hiding of the Great Seal, which Tom, not knowing what it is, has used to crack nuts. The next day Miles appears, tests the king by sitting in his presence, and gets his property and title back. Tom is made the king's ward, and Edward continues the reign of mercy Tom has begun. Using the old device of mistaken identity of look-alikes, the plot is plausible but makes no pretense of being completely historical. Most of the setting, the descriptions of inhumane laws, and the splendor of the court, are accurate, but the age of Edward (actually nine and a half when Henry VIII died) seems a little older in the book. Throughout there are satirical passages and a good deal of humor at Tom's mistakes. While not of the innovative caliber of *The Adventures of Tom Sawyer** or the depth of *The Adventures of Huckleberry Finn**, the novel is a thoroughly satisfying romance of a fascinating period. (Humphrey* Marlow) Children's Classics.

PROFESSOR BEHRENS (*Heart of Danger**), Rudy's* father who appears briefly late in the novel. He once taught German at the University of New Mexico in Albuquerque but at the beginning of the war returned to his native Germany. Rudy was led to believe that he had turned traitor to the United States. In reality, he went to Europe to set up a network by which Jews could be smuggled to safety. When Rudy discovers him in Paris, he runs a music studio which is a front for his underground operations.

PROFESSOR DANTE (*The Bells of Bleecker Street**), the music teacher of the children who live on Bleecker* Street. He occupies the upstairs of the Enrico house, where he has a garden of potted grape vines, tomatoes, and a fig tree. Although he is often exasperated with the children, he is good-natured and jolly and quickly forgives them. He helps with the VE Day parade, the celebration of Joey's father's return from the army, and the Christmas Eve puppet show and musical program.

PROFESSOR WILLIAM WATERMAN SHERMAN (*The 21 Balloons**), retired arithmetic teacher and honorary member of the Western American Explorers' Club of San Francisco, who in 1883 starts on a trip in a giant balloon, hoping to be the first man to fly across the Pacific Ocean. His attempt is thwarted when a sea gull dives into his balloon, puncturing it and bringing him down near the volcanic island of Krakatoa*, in the Sunda Straits between Java and Sumatra, where he finds a most elaborate and elegant society financed by the fantastically rich diamond mines of the island and kept secret to protect it against thieves and exploiters. Prof. Sherman is inventive and adaptable, but he is less interested in adventure than in the peaceful life promised by balloon travel. He has so wearied of schoolboy pranks in his forty years of teaching that he conceals his past from the inhabitants of Krakatoa, even though they need a teacher. When the island blows up and the populace escape on a balloon-borne platform, he is the only one lacking a parachute and so must ride the escape vehicle across Asia and Europe to crash it in the Atlantic. In telling his story to the explorers' club, he maintains dignity and a degree of formality, even though he reclines in a bed on the stage as he lectures.

THE PROMISED YEAR (Uchida*, Yoshiko, ill. William M. Hutchinson, Harcourt, 1959), realistic novel set on the Pacific and in California near San Francisco in the mid-twentieth century. Because her widowed mother is having trouble feeding her family in Tokyo, Keiko*, 10, accepts the invitation of her mother's older sister, Aunt Emi, and her husband, Uncle Henry, to spend a year with them in California. On board the freighter *Nikko Maru*, Keiko becomes very fond of her only fellow passenger, Mrs. Miyagawa, who wants to be called Auntie* Kobe, and soon shares her secret, that Auntie Kobe is keeping her cat, Tama, in her cabin. When there is a false alarm of a fire aboard ship, Keiko, in trying to rescue Tama, gives the cat's presence away to the purser; he calmly pretends he has not seen anything unusual. Faced with getting Tama ashore and through quarantine, Auntie Kobe solves the problem by giving the cat to Keiko. Aunt Emi is surprised and Uncle Henry less than pleased when Keiko arrives in San Francisco with a cat, which they fear will damage the carnations they raise for sale. They agree, however, to try to keep Tama. Keiko gets off on the wrong foot with Uncle Henry by helping Mike Michaelson, a boy about her age whose mother works in the flower business, debud carnations. Uncle Henry warns them not to touch the flowers without supervision. Her relationship with her uncle gets worse when Tama gives him severe allergic reactions, so he puts the cat out and it disappears. Mike goes to the Humane Society to try to find Tama and comes back with three wrong cats, which cause some havoc in the house before escaping. The children go to the newspaper, where Bob Fletcher, Mike's scoutmaster, works, to put in a lost ad, and Keiko thinks it will also be appropriate to include Auntie Kobe's son, Jiro, who came to America twenty years before and whom Auntie Kobe has come to seek. Mr. Fletcher suggests a feature story for Christmas, but that does not materialize and the ad does not produce Tama. Some nights later, however, the cat returns to Keiko's window, and she takes it secretly to Mike's house to be kept until Auntie Kobe returns. Aunt Emi becomes ill and is taken to the hospital; Keiko is sent to stay at Mike's house, where Tama sleeps in her room. When Tama wakes wheezing in the night, Keiko knows it means that smog is coming in and that smog can spoil the shipment of flowers Uncle Henry must send the next day. Alerted by Keiko, the family helps pick and pack flowers all night and saves Uncle Henry's shipment and future business. Auntie Kobe returns from Los Angeles, where she has been hunting for Jiro, in time to stay with Keiko and Uncle Henry for Christmas. Aunt Emi comes home in time for a New Year's celebration, made perfect when Mr. Fletcher arrives with Jiro, who has been working for his mother in Modesto. Uncle Henry, who has been taking allergy shots so they can keep Tama, honors Keiko with a special tea ceremony. Despite the dependence on coincidence to produce Jiro, this is a pleasant story with Keiko's adjustment to her new cultural and family environment as the main theme. She and Auntie Kobe are interesting characters; others are stock figures. Fanfare.

PRUDENCE CRUFF (*The Witch of Blackbird Pond**), fearful child whom Kit teaches to read. On the ship to Wethersfield, Kit jumps into the river to save the doll Prudence has accidentally dropped overboard, giving rise to the suspicion that Kit is a witch, because in Puritan belief, only witches can swim. It is on Prudence's testimony that Kit is freed from the charge of witchcraft.

PUMPKIN (*Johnny Tremain**), red-haired, insignificant little British soldier. A simple farmer back in England, he longs so much for life on the farm that he deserts the British Army. Johnny gives him work clothes and in exchange, receives the musket he passes along to Rab. Pumpkin is caught and executed. Perhaps the most heart-rending character in the book, he exemplifies the reluctance of the common British soldier to fight against his own kind and also the inhumanity of war.

PYLE, HOWARD (1853-1911), born in Wilmington, Del.; illustrator, author, art teacher, one of the strongest influences on American literature for children in both text and pictures. He attended schools in Wilmington and Mr. Van der Weiler's School, Philadelphia, and became a free-lance illustrator. He taught at Drexel Institute, Philadelphia, and later started his own school in Wilmington, where some of the most prominent illustrators of the early twentieth century were students. Besides illustrating many books written by others, he wrote and illustrated books of his own, including retellings of Robin Hood and a four-volume retelling of the King Arthur tales, collections of stories, and two novels, *Otto of the Silver Hand** (Scribner's, 1888), and *Men of Iron** (Harper, 1892), both set in the Middle Ages. He also wrote six novels for adults. He is credited with raising the standards of books published for young people, particularly in illustration, treating the books as serious literature and doing thorough research at a time when this was unusual in juvenile publishing.

Q

THE QUAINT AND CURIOUS QUEST OF JOHNNY LONGFOOT, THE SHOE KING'S SON (Besterman*, Catherine, ill. Warren Chappell, Bobbs, 1947), comic fantasy which plays with the familiar folk tale pattern of the virtuous human who is helped by talking animals. Peter Longfoot, a shoemaker so good he calls himself the Shoe King, sends his son, Johnny*, on a vacation visit to his Uncle* Lucas Longfoot. When Johnny finds that Uncle Lucas is a miser too stingy to keep him, Johnny leaves to look for food, taking with him Uncle Lucas's three guard dogs and bear, Fuzzy. He encounters Barnac* the Cat, Squire of Catnap, who offers Johnny gold if he obtains for him seven-league boots hidden in a cave on Coral Island. Assisted by eight large and brawny cats, the dogs, and Fuzzy, and accompanied by uncooperative Uncle Lucas, who wishes to keep an eye on the boy, Johnny builds a barge and sets sail for Coral Island, with one of the cats as Captain*. Morse code-reading sea creatures, among them sharks, whales, octopuses, and crabs, attack the ship but are mollified when Johnny agrees to stitch up their wounds, and Mr. Shark rewards Johnny with a special Sea* Passport. While Johnny is repairing the hide of a baby whale, a storm comes up, and he and the barge are borne in different directions, Johnny landing on an isolated desert bay and the barge on Coral Island. Uncle Lucas tricks Captain Cat into disclosing the location of the cave and sails away with the seven-league boots and other treasures. Invoking his Sea Passport, Johnny is pulled on a tortoise shell by various sea creatures and encounters Uncle Lucas, whose ship is disabled because sea gulls have made sieves of the sails. Tormented by thirst, he is now sorry for his misdeeds and miserliness, having come to the realization that money is not everything. The winds bear everyone home on a large kite, and Johnny presents Barnac with the boots which sea water has shrunk to the appropriate size. The story is overwritten, self-conscious, and patronizing, with too many underdeveloped incidents happening too fast and too much overly clever conversation. But then, the book has no serious purpose; it is intended as a romp, and to that extent it is successful. Fanfare; Newbery Honor.

QUEER PERSON (Hubbard*, Ralph, ill. Harold von Schmidt, Doubleday, 1930), novel set among the Indians in central Montana in the days of the earliest fur traders. One cold morning a young child clad only in a ragged remnant of a buffalo robe wanders into the village of the Pikuni, a Blackfoot Indian people. Unable to hear or speak, the boy is thought to be possessed by an evil spirit and is repeatedly turned away from the lodges until he settles among the dogs of an old woman, herself a near outcast. Granny discovers that he is not an idiot and raises him, teaches him to communicate by sign language, and he becomes a somewhat scorned member of the group, known as Queer Person. When Granny, skilled in folk medicine, saves the life of the chief's young brother-in-law, Middle Rider, the brave takes Queer Person under his wing and teaches him. His main friends are the chief's daughter, Singing Moon, and Twisted One, another of Granny's patients, a boy who is deformed after having been badly burned. Like the other adolescent boys, Queer Person goes off alone, fasting to seek his medicine dream, When he is sixteen, he begins to have violent headaches, shakes wax plugs, which he thinks are worms, from his ears, and begins to hear. Granny binds him to secrecy and teaches him to speak, but after four years he rebels, having fallen in love with Singing Moon, a lively girl who has defied custom by joining a war party against the Shoshone who have killed Middle Rider. Granny persuades Queer Person to wait until the chief's little son, Sun Pipe, 7, disappears, and Singing Moon is offered as bride to any who can return her brother, dead or alive. Queer Person reveals his abilities to astonished Singing Moon, then leaves alone, depending upon his "strong medicine" to lead him to the camp of the Absaroka, or Crows, where he enters disguised as an old person, unnoticed in the excitement of a ceremony, described in detail, in which the braves fasten skewers under their skin, attach them to thongs suspended from high poles, then dance until the skewers break the skin and pull loose. He later hears moans from the lodge and discovers Sun Pipe, unconscious but still alive, wrapped for a human sacrifice. In rescuing the child, he is apprehended and set to a trial by "porcupine dance," in which he must run with the child on his back across a course stepping only on newly skinned buffalo heads dipped in water to make them more slippery. Should he slip, the surrounding warriors are prepared to shoot him as full of arrows as a porcupine is of quills. He negotiates the course but is warned that Yellow Hand, a renegade Pikuni who abducted Sun Pipe, is waiting in ambush, and to escape is given a second trial, a chance to fight an old war chief with a weapon of his choosing. When he has killed the old chief and is given his horses and weapons, he is escorted from the village with Sun Pipe and told the reason the old chief chose to fight him: the old man was his father, who had married a woman stolen from the Pikunis. When Queer Person was an infant, the father had gambled away his wife, who, in despair, had killed herself. The child, deaf and dumb, was thought to contain an evil spirit and so was left near the village of his mother's people. With Sun Pipe, the old chief's possessions, and the knowledge of his own origins, Queer Person returns in honor to marry Singing Moon. Although the story contains some romantic ideas that may be imposed on the Indian culture, it is an authentic description of much of the life of the Blackfoot people before their contact with white men and does not avoid the less palatable elements of their culture. Highly intelligent, Queer Person is a believable character, able to overcome a handicap and win a place in his society. Newbery Honor.

R

RABBIT (*Seven Stars for Catfish Bend**), one of the seven animals awarded a silver star for heroism in ridding the bayou of hunters. Silly and giggly, he is a comic figure who makes ridiculous suggestions.

RABBIT HILL (Lawson*, Robert, ill. author, Viking, 1944), animal fantasy set in Connecticut in the mid-twentieth century. News spreads from animal to animal on the Hill: "New folks coming to the Big House." There is much speculation about whether they will be the right kind—Planting Folks! Mother Rabbit, a confirmed worrier, fears the worst, but Father, a gentleman from the Blue Grass region of Kentucky, given to long, pretentious speeches, is more optimistic. Little Georgie is wildly excited as are most of the residents: Willie* Fieldmouse, his friend Mole, Phewie the skunk, Porkey the woodchuck, Red Buck, Foxey, even the scatterbrained grey squirrels. Little Georgie is sent on a long trip up Danbury way to fetch his mother's Uncle* Analdas, who, being the eldest in the family, can give them valuable advice. On the way, preoccupied with the song he is composing ("New folks coming, oh my!"), Little Georgie is surprised by the Old Hound and chased into a position where his only hope is to leap Deadman's Brook, a marvelous soar of at least eighteen feet. Uncle Analdas, an irascible old fellow, watches suspiciously for traps, guns, poison, and dogs, as the New Folks move in, but finds they have only an elderly cat, Mr. Muldoon, who is no threat. Indications continue good. The Man puts up a sign in the driveway, "Please Drive Carefully on Account of Small Animals." Tim McGrath, the hired man, is told, "No traps. No poison. No guns," and concludes that the fault is with the many books in the house, since "reading rots the mind." When Willie Fieldmouse, climbing to the window sill to get news, falls into the rainwater barrel, he is rescued, placed in a box of cotton by the fire to dry out, then allowed to escape. On Dividing Night, by long custom the animals meet and select the portions of the garden each will claim, agreeing to hold off any harvesting until Midsummer's Eve. Then disaster comes. Little Georgie, everyone's favorite, is hit by a car, and the animals see the folks pick up his limp body and carry it into their house. There is great sadness until Willie sees him through the window, alive, his legs bound to sticks, sitting in the Lady's lap. Then there is great suspicion, led by Uncle Analdas, who suggests that the Folks are holding Georgie as hostage, to torture if the garden is damaged. When Tim McGrath delivers a large box, it is rumored to be traps and spring-guns, and when something is built, Analdas suggests it is a gallows. On Midsummer's Eve, the animals gather, fearing the worst, and suddenly Little Georgie appears, all well. The man takes the tarp off the construction and reveals a statute of St. Francis with the words, "There is enough for all." Around the base of the statue is set a feast for all the animals. The gentle story gets much of its humor from sticking to the viewpoint of the animals, interpreting each human action in relation to how it will affect them. Animals are anthropomorphized, Mother wearing an apron and cooking, Father walking with a cane, and each is individualized with a human personality. It is a light story, but warm and cleverly handled. Sequel. Choice; Fanfare; Lewis Carroll; Newbery Winner.

RAB SILSBEE (*Johnny Tremain**), enigmatic, self-contained apprentice for Mr. Lorne of the *Boston* Observer*, who becomes a great influence on Johnny's life. He gives Johnny a job delivering papers and helps him overcome his self-pity and self-centeredness. Johnny admires Rab very much and looks up to him.

RACHEL PYE (*Ginger Pye**), at nine, the younger child in the Pye family. She and Jerry*, her brother of ten, are very close and get on well together. She likes words, stories, doing the right thing, outings, and defending the underdog. She is an eager, skinny little girl with red-gold hair and an often-runny nose because she has hay fever. She is more imaginative than Jerry and comes up with more ideas than he.

RAGMAN OF PARIS AND HIS RAGAMUFFINS (Jones*, Elizabeth Orton, ill. author, Oxford, 1937), episodic story for young children, mostly realistic with occasional fantasy bits, set in Paris at an undetermined time period. Ragman, collecting rags on a spring day in his cart pulled by his horse, Mimi, finds a promising looking bundle which turns out to be two little boys, Mich, and his younger brother, Tobie. Ragman takes them home to where he lives with Madam Pouf, a jolly fat lady, and a cat named Poufon. The boys are made shirts of Madame Pouf's blue, checkered petticoat and told stories about a king and a cat with green whiskers by the cobbler, and they listen to Poufon, who has one green whisker, use up all but five of the words he is allotted each year. They talk to the man who feeds pigeons, fetch the prize loaf of bread, the longest made in a contest, from the bakery, and pause when they are fetching milk until a little frog jumps in and swims around in the can. When a neighbor's bird is stolen, they take Poufon to the bird market, and he rips the pants of a thief until the man gives up the bird. When they take over the job of street sweeper so he can go on a picnic with his children, they find a franc. First they decide to buy

Madom Pouf some flowers, then find their money is not enough, and agree to mind the cart; as a result they are given all the flowers they can carry. So they decide to have a picnic with their franc at the Luxembourg Garden. There an unusual old lady tells them the price of her cakes is "A wish, a whistle, and a whirl-around!" Tobie's wish, that she have a picnic herself, is rejected, but Mich's wish, that every time she gives away a cake two will replace it, pleases her so much that she gives him two cakes, which he shares. They spend a long day, have a ride in a goat cart, and build a sand castle. In the meantime, Madame Pouf and Ragman miss them and Poufon speaks her last words, "Locked in Luxembourg Garden!" They go in the cart drawn by Mimi and find the boys, who don't even know they've been locked in, and who still have their franc. They all go to the cathedral and use the money to light candles for each of them, including the animals. Poufon's last green whisker turns black, but Ragman buys him a silver bell to compensate. The style is one step above primer English and the stories are condescendingly clever in a very dated way. There is little motivation for actions, and the fantasy elements, like the talking cat, are fanciful rather than consistently developed. Fanfare.

THE RAILROAD TO FREEDOM (Swift*, Hildegarde Hoyt, ill. James Daugherty, Harcourt, 1932), biographical novel of the life of Harriet Tubman. In 1833, independent, high-spirited, quick-witted Minty (Araminta Harriet Greene), about thirteen, lives with her mother, Old* Rit, cook, father, Daddy Ben, sturdy farm worker, and older brother, good-natured Benjie*, on kindly Master Carter's plantation. Broadacres, near Cambridge, Md., where she was born. Her first real taste of the degradation of slavery occurs when arrogant, willful George, son of the master, who early takes a dislike to her, sells her without his father's knowledge to his cousin Susan, who abuses her. She runs home to Broadacres, where Master Carter takes her back and where she grows to adulthood, a sturdy, muscled woman who works beside her father in field and lumberyard. George arranges her marriage to John Tubman, a strong-bodied, weak-willed man whom she despises and who plays no part in the story. After Master Carter's sudden death of pneumonia, George drives the slaves, nor does he honor his father's pledge to free Old Rit and Ben and their family. When George sells the husband of Minty's best friend off the plantation, Harriet makes a break for freedom. Helped first by the sympathetic owner of the adjacent plantation, and then by Old Anne, his slave who knows the Underground Railway, Harriet makes her precarious way over countryside, through swamps, and over rivers to freedom in Wilmington. There Quaker Thomas Garrett assists her to Philadelphia where she lives with Emily Watson, Cousin Susan's anti-slavery sister, who actually first planted the notion of breaking for freedom in the girl's mind. Years pass, while Harriet makes her home in the North and embraces the cause of freedom. Against the background of increasingly heated debates in Congress over slavery and the Fugitive Slave Law, she earns the name of Moses as, a bounty on her head, she returns time and again to the South to lead to freedom over the

Underground Railway more than three hundred slaves, among them her mother, father, brother, and his family. She speaks at countless meetings in the North, testifying to her slave experiences. During the Civil War, she serves the cause of her people as nurse and scout, earning acclaim for her courage, fortitude, and good sense. As scout, she shoots a spy who turns out ironically to be her old master, George, and after the war ends, she returns to now-desolate Broadacres bearing the news of his death. Although melodramatic and sermonizing, this richly detailed book has great emotional appeal, and the author makes Harriet's experiences in slavery and her journeys adventurous and suspenseful with hair-breadth escapes and ticklish situations. The cast of characters is large, but only Harriet and her mother are fully developed. John Calhoun, Theodore Parker, and Thomas Garrett are among the figures of the period who appear, and issues of the day are presented with brevity and clarity. Curiously, the blacks speak in dialect, and the whites in Standard English. The author creates the moment well: Minty caring for Susan's baby, huddling in Old Anne's potato hole, making her terrified way through the streets of Wilmington, evading authorities hot on their trail after old Ben has innocently prattled on about making for Canada, among many other richly drawn scenes. Newbery Honor.

THE RAIN FOREST (Sperry*, Armstrong, ill. author, Macmillan, 1947), adventure story set in New Guinea in 1940. Chad Powell, 14, has arrived at Port Moresby to join his ornithologist father now in the upper Lakemanu district rain forest looking for the rare King of Saxony paradise bird. Since his father's supply plane has been damaged, Chad joins an expedition led by Patrol Officer Pat O'Malley to find and punish a tribe of pigmy Kuku-kukus, who have raided a supply station in an area not far from his father's camp. Also with the group is Natua, Papuan son of the chief native guard, Jigori. Chad and Natua become fast friends, learning enough of each other's language to converse and enjoying the exciting but grueling trip upriver and through the jungle and the camaraderie, which is marred only by the sullen hostility of Kaiva, one of the Papuan porters. After they reach the camp, O'Malley and Dr. Powell, neither of whom has been successful in finding what they want, set off to explore a new area, leaving Chad and Natua to care for the birds he has captured. A short distance from the camp they sight a King of Saxony, and in chasing it they start across a suspension bridge, which Kaiva slashes, causing them to fall into the river and be swept a long distance downstream. There they are captured by the Kuku-kukus, who are cannibals and head-hunters but are hesitant to kill the boys because of the "magic" of Chad's wrist watch, which ticks and glows in the dark. At the critical moment of the decision, thatch on one of the treehouses where the pigmies live catches fire and half the village burns, an occurrence attributed to Chad's magic. The next day the plane, now repaired, arrives, having spotted the fire, the pigmy leaders are arrested, and the boys are rescued. They take with them a pair of King of Saxony birds they have found in the village. Despite the interracial friendship of Chad and Natua, the book has the old "white hunter" tone that seems dated and perhaps offensive to modern readers. Action is fast, characterization is minimal, but illustrations by the author make the book stand out from stock adventure stories. Fanfare.

RANDOM JOTTINGS (*Stowaway to the Mushroom Planet**), Tyco* Bass's record of his scientific investigations. It is written in Basidiumite, the language of the Mushroom* People. Its full name is *Random Jottings on Some Inventions of Tyco M. Bass*. David* Topman and Chuck* Masterson guard it because the information it contains is very valuable.

RANDY (*The Saturdays**), Miranda Melendy, the third of the Melendy children. She is quick-witted and imaginative, and the Saturday Club (I.S.A.A.C.*) is her idea. She hopes to become a dancer or a painter. Although awkward at ordinary tasks and accident prone, she is light and quick on her feet while dancing. She is twelve in the third book in the series.

RANKIN, LOUISE S. (1897-1951), born in Baltimore, Md.; teacher, editor. She grew up in Maryland but lived in the West every summer, at Lake Tahoe or Carson City, Nev. After attending Goucher College, she went to Europe as research assistant to a professor, taught English in secondary school, and was on the editorial staff of *Reader's Digest*. Married to a Standard Oil man, she lived and traveled with him for nine years in India, the setting for her much-acclaimed *Daughter of the Mountains** (Viking, 1948). Her only other book for young people was *Gentling of Jonathan* (Viking, 1950).

RAWLINGS, MARJORIE KINNAN (1896-1953), born in Washington, D.C.; newspaperwoman, novelist, whose best books have immortalized characters from the Florida backwoods country. She was graduated from the University of Wisconsin, was a publicity writer for the YWCA and assistant service editor for *Home Sector* magazine, and from 1920-1928 was on the staff of the Louisville *Courier Journal* and the Rochester *Journal*. Her syndicated verse column, "Songs of a Housewife," ran from 1926 to 1928. With her first husband and brother-in-law she bought a seventy-two-acre orange grove in northern Florida in 1928, but the two men soon lost interest in the project, and she was left to operate it by herself. Four of her novels are set in northern Florida, which she came to know and love well: *South Moon Under* (Scribner's, 1933), *Golden Apples* (Scribner's, 1935), *The Yearling** (Scribner's, 1938), and *Jacob's Ladder* (University of Miami Press, 1950). *The Secret River*, published posthumously (Scribner's, 1955), is a brief story illustrated by Leonard Weisgard, the only one of her books originally published for children. For *The Yearling* she was awarded the Pulitzer Prize. Her home at Cross Creek near Jacksonville, which she kept even after her second marriage, to a Florida hotel man, is maintained by the University of Florida and is open to the public.

REBECCA OF SUNNYBROOK FARM (Wiggin*, Kate Douglas, Houghton, 1903), domestic novel set in Maine before the turn of the century. Little Rebecca* Rowena Randall, ten or eleven, but small for her age, comes by the mail coach from her home farm near Temperance to Riverboro to live with her two elderly Sawyer aunts and be educated. An unabashed and imaginative child, she tells Jeremiah Cobb, the stage driver, about the farm which she has named ''Sunnybrook,'' about her widowed mother and six siblings, about the mortgage that haunts them, and about how she is being sent instead of her sober, industrious older sister, Hannah, who is too useful at home to be spared. Her mother's oldest sister, Matilda* Sawyer, a severe spinster, is shocked to have Rebecca rather than Hannah and disapproves of almost everything about her. Timid Jane* Sawyer is confused but is kindly to the child. At school Rebecca makes a devoted friend of Emma* Jane Perkins, the lumpish daughter of the blacksmith, rejects the attentions of scraggy ''Seesaw'' Simpson, and generally fascinates the other children and her young teacher with her energy and imagination. Under Aunt Jane's direction she finally finishes making a dress of the brown gingham Aunt Matilda has provided, and, with Aunt Jane's support, persuades her no-nonsense aunt to let her next effort be pink. On Exhibition Day at school, finding both aunts out, she puts on the new dress and carries her pink sun shade, her only frivolous possession and, as she has told Mr. Cobb, ''the dearest thing in life'' to her. After a lovely, successful afternoon, she returns to her aunts' brick home to find Aunt Matilda furious; she has been ''crafty and underhanded,'' has used the forbidden front stairway, has left the screen open, has forgotten to clean up her lunch dishes, has left the side door unlocked (!), and has generally taken after her ''Miss-Nancy'' father. When she defends her father, she is sent to bed, and there decides to go back to the farm and let Hannah have the advantages of Riverboro. She climbs out the window and goes to the Cobbs to ask ''Uncle Jerry'' to take her home on the stage coach. He sympathetically and craftily leads her to see how many people that would disappoint, then helps her to sneak back to her room by distracting the aunts. She continues to get into trouble: she leans against the bridge rail without noticing the fresh paint sign and spoils her dress; she tries to punish herself by throwing her beloved sun shade into the well and manages to jam the chain gear. To help the poor younger Simpsons win a beautiful banquet lamp by selling the soap, she and Emma Jane take a supply, and she enchants a young man visiting his aunt who buys three hundred cakes, so startling Rebecca that she falls over backwards into the lilac bush. She calls him Mr. Alladin, though she soon learns that he is wealthy Adam* Ladd, who becomes a true, long-term friend. When both aunts have bad colds, they send Rebecca to represent them at the missionary meeting, where she is asked to play the hymn and, to her consternation, to lead in prayer, and she naively invites the missionary and his wife, and it turns out, his children, to stay at the brick house, all of which appalls Aunt Matilda but works out well. Having finished at Riverboro school, Rebecca and Emma Jane attend the seminary at Wareham, where Rebecca's writing ability and zest attract the attention of Miss

Emily Maxwell, a very superior young teacher. Adam Ladd, who is a trustee of the school and a friend of Miss Maxwell, sees her there at intervals and, mainly to help her, offers a prize of fifty dollars for the best essay which she wins and uses to pay off the interest on her mother's mortgage. When she graduates at seventeen in three years instead of four, she has two job possibilities and an invitation to spend a vacation with Miss Maxwell, but she learns that Aunt Matilda has had a stroke, brought on, one assumes, by money worries. No sooner is Rebecca's aunt somewhat better than her mother falls from the hay mow, and she must go back to the farm to care for her, Hannah having married by now. Her mother is still bedridden when Aunt Matilda dies, leaving Rebecca the brick house, where presumably she will move the family, their farm being in the path of the railway of which Adam Ladd is an executive and having been chosen as site for a station, all of which will bring enough money to pay off the mortgage and provide some income. Although she does not marry Adam Ladd in the book, the reader knows he is in love with her (though past thirty!) and that she is about to realize that she loves him. Rebecca is a lively and charmingly frank child, and the reader is told, rather too often, that she becomes a lovely young lady. There are many dryly humorous comments about small town life that counter-balance some sermonizing, a bit too much for modern taste. The early scenes of Rebecca's conflict with Aunt Matilda and her school days in Riverboro have kept this book a favorite for many years. Children's Classics.

REBECCA ROWENA RANDALL (*Rebecca of Sunnybrook Farm**), second of seven children whose widowed mother sends her from their poor farm to live with her spinster aunts in Riverboro. A bright and lively child, she is described as having unusual eyes: ''eyes . . . like faith'', ''eyes which glow like two stars'', her gaze ''eager and full of interest'' and ''brilliant and mysterious.'' Although she is somewhat tamed by the rigid life with her aunts, she is not cowed and does not lose her imagination or her dramatic and literary ability under their repressive rules.

RED PLANET: A COLONIAL BOY ON MARS (Heinlein*, Robert A., ill. Clifford Geary, Scribner's, 1949), science fiction novel set in the future on Mars, now colonized by Earth and under the control of the Mars Company, a monopoly whose franchise requires that certain services be supplied to colonists, including school and the annual migration to avoid the twelve-month sub-frigid winters in each hemisphere. Jim Marlowe and his friend Frank (Francis) Sutton set off for boarding school at Syrtis Minor, the company headquarters near the equator, the only place high school is provided. Jim insists on taking with him Willis*, a creature of Mars that he once saved from a vicious water-seeker and which has since that time lived with him, more as friend than as pet. Willis is ball-shaped, with retractable legs and eyes, and has the ability to initiate simple ideas and a remarkable skill to absorb conversations and repeat them in the original voices like a tape recorder. After a peaceful start, the school year is plunged into chaos when the headmaster retires and is replaced by Marquis Howe, a relative of a company bigwig, who starts a tyrannical regime and confiscates Willis. Retrieving Willis, the boys leave the school by the garbage chute and catch an ice-craft called a scooter, determined to return to their homes at the South Colony, but are put off at a way station where word has come that they are to return to face arrest. Instead they start out skating, spend one night in an empty shelter built along the canal, another in a huge, cabbage-like plant, which folds up (with them inside) to survive the sub-zero Martian nights, eventually reach a Martian ''ghost-city,'' where they run into a native Martian, a fourteen-foot tall, three-legged creature who exudes good feeling and who takes them through tunnels in some extremely fast vehicles, eventually to South Colony. Word that they are wanted by the law has preceded them, but they are able to tell Jim's father what they have learned from Willis, via a conversation he has repeated between Howe and the Resident Agent General, Beecher, that the Company plans to discontinue the annual migration which makes life bearable for the colonists. After a town meeting, the colonists decide to force the issue, start the migration, are trapped and imprisoned in the school, eventually break out and stage a revolution which they win, with some help by the Martians. They establish self-rule. Although the human characters are stock types, the action is fast and the Martian creatures ingeniously conceived. Since the book is fantasy, it is dated less in relation to recent scientific learning about Mars than by its sexist attitude toward women, who are pictured as silly, domestic creatures, capable of cooking but taking no effective part in the action. (Doctor* MacRae) Choice.

RED SAILS TO CAPRI (Weil*, Ann, ill. C. B. Falls, Viking, 1952), mystery-adventure set on the island of Capri off Naples, Italy, in November of 1826, fictionalizing on the discovery of the now-famous Blue Grotto. Michele Pagano, 14, helps his father and mother run their inn for tourists on Capri. When three tourists arrive in a boat with red sails, the fisherman, Angelo*, considered a garrulous, ne'er-do-well by the villagers, contrives that they stay at the Pagano Inn. Monsieur Jacques, a writer, Lord Derby, a painter, and Herr Nordstrom, a student of philosophy, have come in search of adventure, beauty, and truth, respectively. While guiding Monsieur Jacques about in the red-sailed boat one day, Michele steers a wide course about a certain cove, refusing to enter and insisting that the villagers regard it as too dangerous to approach. When they discover that no one knows just why the cove is regarded as dangerous, the three men insist on being taken to the place. An expedition of three small fishing boats is organized, with Angelo in charge, and Michele and his best friend, Pietro, the island donkey boy, accompany the three tourists, Angelo, and Signor Pagano. Behind a narrow entryway they discover a beautiful, small cave infused with a marvelous, ethereal blue light, called henceforth the Blue Grotto. The visitors have gained what each sought from his trip to Capri, the superstitious villagers have new perspectives on the nature of truth, and Michele and Pietro have enjoyed adventures. This book is marred by the defects typical of the genre. The plot, while interesting and plausible, is thin and spun out by extensive, occasionally witty, but often contrived, dialogue and attempts to amuse. Angelo is the best-drawn figure, but on the whole characterization is shallow, and the boys, both of whom seem immature for fourteen, are unconvincing. The story exudes local color, however, and tone is warm and affectionate. Newbery Honor.

REUBEN SPARKS (*Far from Marlborough Street**), the old gentleman with gout whom Nancy meets on the stagecoach. In his younger days he was instrumental in financing essential supplies for Washington's army, selling part of his own land and stumping the countryside to get contributions. During Nancy's trip he rescues Dave* Tolliver from a life of crime and rides some distance beyond his own town just to keep the little girl from being lonesome.

REUNION IN POLAND (Karsavina*, Jean, ill. Lynd Ward, International, 1945), historical novel about the reconstruction of Poland after its liberation from the Nazis near the end of World War II. The story starts at New Year's in Moscow in 1945, when the Polish Committee of National Liberation announces that a provisional government has been set up in Lublin and encourages Poles in exile to return home to rebuild their nation. Among the refugees are Wanda Gorska, 16, who has been attending a Polish school near Moscow, her father, Adam* Gorski, a civil engineer, and close friends, Dr. Stefan and Dr. Helena Zaleski, Maciej Biruta*, who will oversee land distribution, and Wanda's favorites, Stella and Alfred Rosenthal, another engineer, who are Jewish. Wanda, from whose point of view the story is told, yearns to go home. A happy, sensible girl, however, she has adjusted well to the inevitable and has made friends at school. She bids a sad farewell to her best friend there, Ania, likening herself to the earliest of the swallows to return in the spring, those who pave the way for the remainder of the flock. The refugees collect their few possessions and travel by train and military convoy to Lublin, where the Gorskis take a tiny apartment in an overcrowded building. All soon become involved in the work of reconstruction except Wanda, who is too young to be assigned a specific task. Since Adam is often away with Alfred directing the rebuilding of roads and bridges, Wanda becomes lonely. She finds pleasure, however, in anticipating the birth of Stella's baby, and at Stella's suggestion and with Dr. Helena's help she opens a nursery school for the children in the apartment house. She gains a roommate, ex-partisan Janka Haracz, also sixteen, a stern, resolute, self-contained girl, with whose help Wanda searches for information about her mother and Bolek* Piotrowski, her foster brother of twenty, both partisans who were lost when the family fled from Warsaw. Janka discovers an elderly woman artist, Jadwiga Zaruba, who reports that she saw Bolek near Warsaw and who draws his picture for Wanda. Trouble arises briefly when traitors, in the service of the government in exile, which wishes to perpetuate the old authoritarian regime based on wealth, try to dynamite the car Adam and Alfred are using and distribute anti-Jewish leaflets.

In the spring, Wanda and Adam travel to Warsaw where they find their home in ruins. In the countryside, they encounter peasants who lead them to Bolek, still a partisan in the underground. He informs Wanda and Adam that their mother is dead, shot while on an errand for the underground. In spite of this not-unexpected bad news, the family is joyfully reunited, and in the final scene, Bolek urges Wanda to grow up quickly so that he and she can be married. The artlessly constructed plot proceeds through a series of artificial, underdeveloped episodes without much tension to the overforeshadowed reunion with Bolek. Short flashbacks provide texture and information, but characterization is shallow, and even Wanda, who is a round character, changes little as a result of her experiences. The final scene, in which Bolek more or less proposes, seems incongruously romantic. The novel is intended to be instructive, and it is best for the clear, if limited, view it gives of the camaraderie, problems, and aspirations of the exiles. Their high expectations seem very ironic in view of subsequent historical developments in that part of the world. Fanfare.

REVERE, PAUL (*Johnny Tremain**), historical figure, presented in *Johnny Tremain* as one of the revolutionary leaders who meet in the Lorne attic. He is also shown as a skillful, respected silversmith and loving family man. He gives Johnny advice about how to make the silver piece for John Hancock*. In *Mr. Revere and I** his involvement with the Revolution is described in detail in a manner which is both whimsical and tongue-in-cheek, as told by his horse.

RHOADS, DOROTHY (MARY) (1895-   ), born in Pekin, Ill.; free-lance writer. She graduated from Wellesley College and held positions as a translator for the United States Government in French and Spanish and as reporter and society editor for the Rock Island *Argus*, and later lived in Sante Fe, N.Mex. Her books for children grew out of her many trips to Central America, where she lived and worked with her sister and her sister's archaeologist husband in the 1930s and the 1940s. She also traveled extensively in the American Southwest and was in Italy when Mussolini assumed power in 1922. Her books for children include *The Corn Grows Ripe** (Viking, 1956), about a Maya farm family in eastern Yucatán, which was a Newbery honor book and was listed in Fanfare. *The Story of Chan Yuc** (Doubleday, 1941), a short story about a brocket deer brought from the Maya jungle to the Washington Zoo, was also a Fanfare book. She also published for children *The Bright Feather and Other Maya Tales* (Doubleday, 1932) and contributed many stories and articles to magazines.

RICCO SANTO (*Hill of Little Miracles**), second son in the large, gregarious Santo family, Italian Americans who live on Telegraph Hill overlooking San Francisco Bay. Ricco's father is a fisherman, and after he helps his father and Uncle Luigi scrape, calk, and paint the hull of the *Piccola Nina*, Ricco accompanies them on an ocean fishing trip during which they lose their way in a heavy fog. Ricco is physically handicapped; his left leg is shorter than his right. He likes to draw, and Uncle Tito, an artist, says that he shows promise. Ricco paints the sign for the Hill-Billies' clubhouse, calling it so because all the members live on Telegraph Hill. He believes strongly in prayer and in miracles.

RICHARDS, LAURA E(LIZABETH HOWE) (1850-1943), born in Boston, Mass., the daughter of the poet Julia Ward Howe, who wrote "The Battle Hymn of the Republic," and for whose biography for adults she received the Pulitzer Prize in 1917, and Samuel Gridley Howe, who founded the Perkins Institution for the Blind. She was a prolific and highly successful writer of prose and poetry during the late nineteenth and early twentieth centuries, publishing over five dozen books for the young, largely of fiction but including plays, verse, and non-fiction, and almost two dozen books for adults of different genres. Today she is remembered mainly for her often-reprinted book of verse, *Tirra Lirra* (Little, 1921), whose "Eletelephony" and "The Monkeys and the Crocodile" are considered classic nonsense. Her prose works seem quaint and contrived when read today and can be found on few bookshelves, though when written they were more realistic and better crafted than much literature of the period for the young. Her last novel for children, *Harry in England** (Appleton, 1937), an episodic family novel about a small boy's adventures at the countryside estate of his wealthy grandmother set in the mid-1800s, was chosen for the *Horn Book* Fanfare list. Probably her best-known novel is *Captain January* (Estes, 1891), which sold over 300,000 copies and was twice filmed, the second time starring Shirley Temple. She did not write seriously for the young until after her marriage, when she began making up jingles for her own seven children. Her husband encouraged her to submit them to the *St. Nicholas* magazine, which accepted them, and her career was launched. She made her home in Maine with her architect husband, where she was friendly with New England literary figures of the time and also assisted philanthropic causes.

RIFLES FOR WASHINGTON (Singmaster*, Elsie, ill. Frank E. Schoonover, Houghton, 1938), historical novel set in the period of the American Revolution, 1775-1781, starting in York County, Pa., and following the campaigns from Cambridge, Mass., to Yorktown, Va. When Uncle* Jehoida Proudfoot, veteran of the French-Indian Wars and an old Indian fighter, sets out to join Washington's army early in the war, his nephew, red-haired Davie McKail, 16, an orphan whose parents were killed and his infant sister carried off by Indians, rides from McCesson Town to Getty's Tavern (Gettysburg) and then to York to see him off. There they stay in the home of a Moravian minister and Davie meets Lydia* Newcomer, 15, an orphan raised by the religious community. Instead of going home to German-born Widow Bets Cruncleton, their housekeeper, Davie stows away in the covered wagon driven between Moravian settlements by orphan Peter* Bricker. He is taken in overnight by the Brethren of the Dunkers, a Seventh Day Baptist celibate group, where he briefly sees a red-haired girl, Sister Helena. He meets up with Uncle at Bethlehem and persuades him to allow him to go along. At Cambridge, they meet Washington, take part in a foray, and Davie is wounded in the arm. At home again he escapes the wiles of Eliza Scammel, regains the use of his arm, and becomes godfather to the baby of Andy* Westbrook, whose father is with Uncle and whose mother has died in childbirth. Davie returns to the front, now in New York, this time with Peter, who puts aside his religious scruples to fight. Although both boys are dismissed at Perth Amboy, they stay, cross to Staten Island, talk to Hessian soldiers, report to American officers what they have heard, and Peter starts for home, but Davie stays to hunt for Uncle, who has been wounded on Staten Island. David finds him ill with smallpox, nurses him in a hut in the woods, gets him home to the Widow Cruncleton, and returns to the front. The story follows Davie and Peter through winters at Lowantica Valley and Valley Forge and a battle at Brandywine Creek where Peter is wounded. Nursed by the Dunkers, Peter recovers and declares his love to Sister Helena; Davie, wounded and nursed at Bethlehem, talks again to Lydia. Uncle Proudfoot, physically well but somewhat confused, goes on an Indian fighting expedition to the head of the Finger Lakes. Returning, he meets Davie at Dunkertown and, with Sam Gettys to vouch for it, insists that Sister Helena is Davie's sister Jennet, taken then abandoned by Indians. This releases her from her vows to the community and makes her free to marry Peter when he returns. Davie learns that Lydia has gone to Salem to marry a widower and is disconsolate. All the main male characters are together at the surrender of Cornwallis at Yorktown, then march south, expecting the war to wind up soon. Near Salem, Davie comes upon a schoolhouse where Lydia is teaching children to sing, sees that she wears a pink ribbon which indicates she is still single, and they pledge to marry. The novel has such a crowded canvas and the point of view shifts so rapidly from one character to another that it is confusing to follow. The style is full of strange skips, and scenes are often more suggested than developed. If the effort is to show the confusion of war, it succeeds, but if it is to include all the major events of the war, it is too ambitious. There are many interesting characters and happenings, however. The descriptions of the religious communities are memorable. Fanfare.

RIFLES FOR WATIE (Keith*†, Harold, Crowell, 1957), historical novel set in Kansas, Missouri, Arkansas, and the territory of the Cherokee, Creek, and Choctaw Indian nations in what is now Oklahoma during the American Civil War from April, 1861, to May, 1865. The novel is built around the involvement of the Indians in the western sector of the war and the smuggling of repeating rifles, at that time a military innovation, from the North to the South. Both Union and Rebel viewpoints are presented through the experiences of Jeff* (Jefferson Davis) Bussey, a sixteen-year-old Kansas farmboy, who fights for the North and also serves as a scout behind the Southern lines. Jeff's unit must restore to their homes refugee, Northern-sympathizing Indians, a duty which brings Jeff into contact with the Washbournes, well-to-do, highly respected, "civilized," Rebel Cherokees, through whose daughter, Lucy, Jeff learns how the Indians have rebuilt their lives after being removed from their homes east of the Mississippi. When a scout, Jeff falls in with the forces of the Rebel Cherokee general, Stand Watie*, where he learns that the captain of his own unit, Asa Clardy, has been smuggling guns to Watie. Although the plot and most of the characters are fictitious, the story is based on extensive research into the war in the West and includes such battles as those at Wilson Creek and Prairie Grove and such real historical figures as generals Watie, Blunt, and Adair, while Jeff's flight back to his unit with his important information has a historical counterpart in the escape to freedom of a slave. This richly conceived book offers a keen sense of the problems, ways, and thinking of the times, and a fine picture of the Indians of the area. Although over-foreshadowed, the plot is often suspenseful, and scenes stand out vividly: Jeff's terror under fire; the execution of Lee Washbourne, Lucy's brother and a Rebel scout; death of Jimmy Lear, the boy drummer; tending the wounded in the military hospitals; and Jeff's tramping along the dusty military road with the Indian youth, who tells of the Cherokee Trail of Tears. Of the many minor characters, some, like Noah Babbitt, the itinerant printer who is Jeff's valued comrade-in-arms, and Heifer, the ugly, kindhearted, Rebel cook who takes care of Jeff when he has malaria, are very deftly drawn, the hot-tempered, sadistic Captain Clardy is over-villainized from his first encounters with Jeff, but Jeff himself and Lucy, who develop a romantic attachment, are dynamic and sympathetic figures. Even though the research is not always skillfully integrated with the plot, this story of a boy's maturing and developing independence of judgment is convincing and memorable. Books Too Good; Choice; Fanfare; Lewis Carroll; Newbery Winner.

RIP VAN WINKLE (Irving*, Washington, Lippincott, 1863, originally in *The Sketchbook of Geoffrey Crayon, Gent.*, C. S. Van Winkle, 1819-20), fantasy set in the Kaatskill (Catskill) Mountains of New York in the last half of the eighteenth century. In a village founded by Dutch settlers lives a genial, lazy fellow named Rip Van Winkle, much henpecked by his termagant wife. To escape her constant criticism and efforts to get him to work, he often takes his gun and his dog, Wolf, and goes squirrel hunting in the mountains. On one such trip, toward evening, he is surprised to hear his name called and then to see a short, square-built old fellow dressed in the antique Dutch fashion and carrying a stout keg. He makes signs for Rip to help him and leads him through a cleft in the cliffs to a small natural amphitheater where a company of similarly dressed little men are playing at ninepins. By signs Rip is told to serve the beverage round, and he soon begins to taste it himself until he falls into a deep sleep. When he awakens, stiff and sore, he finds his gun replaced with a rusted fire-lock, its stock worm-eaten, and Wolf gone. Suspecting theft, he retraces his steps to try to find the scene of the party, but a stream is running through the cleft in the cliff, and he can find no amphitheater. He makes his bewildered way to the village, where he sees strangers and strange houses. He is ridiculed for his appearance, which he discovers includes a long beard, and is almost attacked when he says he is "a loyal subject of the King, God bless him!" When he names his old friends, he learns they are dead or gone, and when he asks of Rip Van Winkle, they point to a man, his son, lounging against a tree, and when, recognizing a young woman with a child as his daughter, he asks, "Does nobody know poor Rip Van Winkle?" an old woman in the crowd peers at him closely, then welcomes him home and asks, "Where have you been all these twenty long years?" Rip finds that many changes have occurred, including the American Revolution and the death of his wife. One old resident recalls the tradition that every twenty years Hendrick Hudson, with his crew, comes back to keep a guardian eye on the river and the city and is said to play ninepins in the mountains, though most people think it is thunder. The story, originally published for adults, is told in a leisurely, artistic, humorous style, cleverly leaving open the possibility for disbelievers to scoff. It was based partially on a German folk tale, "Karl Katz," but has become so well known that Rip Van Winkle is an almost universally recognized character. Children's Classics.

ROBERT (*Bright Island**), spoiled, rich youth, unreliable, willful, and opportunistic, who becomes interested in Thankful while they are at the Academy and visits her family at Christmas time so that Mary* Curtis can tutor him for his Harvard entrance exams. His brashness and exhibitionism alienate the men of the family, though not Mary, whose motherly instincts he arouses. Finding the Curtises' life too slow and restrictive, he leaves right after Christmas dinner. When his sailboat capsizes because he is a poor sailor, Thankful rescues him and Selina*. He is a foil to Dave* Allen.

ROBERTSON, FRANK C(HESTER) (1890-1969), born in Moscow, Idaho; prolific author of many books, mostly Western novels. His formal education ended with grade school, and he worked as ranchhand, sheepherder, construction worker, and homesteader, settling in Utah, where he wrote an award-winning column, "The Chopping Block," for the Provo *Daily Herald*. Among his many novels, some written under the pseudonyms of Robert Crane, Frank Chester Field, and King Hill, is *Sagebrush Sorrel** (Nelson, 1953), winner of the Western Writers for America Spur Award.

ROBERTSON†, KEITH (CARLTON) (1914-   ), born in Dows, Iowa; free-lance writer since 1947. He lived in Wisconsin, Minnesota, Oklahoma, Missouri, and Kansas as a boy, attended the U.S. Naval Academy at Annapolis, Md., and served in the navy from 1930 to 1945. For two years he worked for a publisher but started writing full time and has published more than twenty-five books for young people. A number of them star the youthful Carson St. Detectives, as in *Three Stuffed Owls** (Viking, 1954). His most popular books have been his four episodic, humorous novels of Henry Reed: *Henry Reed, Inc.** (Viking, 1958), *Henry Reed's Journey†* (Viking, 1963), *Henry Reed's Baby-Sitting Service†* (Viking, 1966), and *Henry Reed's Big Show†* (Viking, 1970).

ROBINSON, MABEL L(OUISE) (-1962), educator and author. She was born and grew up in Waltham, Mass., of an old New England family that spent their summer vacations at Point Allerton on the Atlantic coast near Boston. Previous to receiving her master's and doctorate from Columbia University, she attended normal school, taught in public school, and went to Radcliffe College. She became professor of English at Columbia, where she taught creative writing and conducted workshops for writers. Prior to that, she taught at Wellesley and Constantinople Colleges. She wrote over a dozen books for children of all ages on various subjects and themes. Some were serious books for younger readers, like *Little Lucia* (Dutton, 1922), *Little Lucia and Her Puppy* (Dutton, 1923), *Robin and Tito* (Macmillan, 1930), and *Robin and Heather* (Macmillan, 1932), while others were for older girls, like *Island Noon* (Random, 1942), her first novel and a love story set on an island off Maine, *Bitter Forfeit* (Bobbs, 1947), a novel of marriage that was serialized in *Saturday Evening Post*, and what was regarded as her best novel, *Bright Island** (Random, 1937), a convincing and well-characterized girl's school story set in Maine in the early thirties that was a Newbery honor book. Her books of non-fiction include *Runner of the Mountain Tops* (Random, 1939), a biography of Louis Agassiz, also a Newbery honor book, and *King Arthur and His Knights* (Random, 1953), a retelling of the stories of the legendary English king. She also wrote many short stories, contributing frequently to *St. Nicholas* and *Youth's Companion* and other periodicals, and wrote textbooks and books about writing. She made her home in New York and spent her summers on the Maine coast. She was in her eighties when she died.

ROBINSON, TOM (THOMAS PENDLETON) (1878-1954), born in Calais, Maine; architect, author, playwright. He grew up in Pennsylvania, in lumber towns and camps, then attended Boston schools and studied architecture at Massachusetts Institute of Technology. Best known as a playwright, he won the Drama League-Longmans Green Prize and the Morosco Prize for dramas. His book for children, *Trigger John's Son** (Viking, 1934), is a twist on the usual orphan story, this being about an independent boy who makes sure he gets a good look at his prosepctive parents before he decides to let himself be adopted.

ROGER (*Knight's Castle**), the first of the four children to enter the fantasy world of Scott's romance, *Ivanhoe*, where he becomes a legendary figure, the hero to whom the fantasy characters look to solve their problems. He has a strong personality, likes to be the leader and do things, but he also likes to read, and when lonely or bored, he plays with his toy soldiers. In the course of the story, he grows less self-assured and more humble.

ROGER QUARTERMAYNE (*Adam of the Road**), father of Adam, a talented court minstrel in the late thirteenth century. At the book's opening, Roger has been at the minstrels' school held each Lent at Cambrai, France, to learn new romances to tell the lords and ladies of England. Richly rewarded for his entertainment at the wedding of his patron's daughter, Roger gambles away both his money and his horse. Though irresponsible, he is a fond father and, when he and Adam are separated, hunts for his son and leaves word which helps the boy eventually find him.

ROLLER SKATES (Sawyer*, Ruth, ill. Valenti Angelo*, Viking, 1936), realistic, episodic period novel of family and neighborhood life, set in New York City one year in the 1890s and loosely based on the author's own childhood. While her parents are in Italy for her mother's health, energetic, imaginative, strong-minded Lucinda Wyman, 10, moves in with family friends, the genteel Misses Peters, one a robust schoolteacher, the other a sweet, plump seamstress. The book tells of the people she meets, the friends she makes, and the things she does at home in the pleasingly informal Peterses' apartment, at Miss Brackett's school, and on her skates whizzing around the neighborhood of Bryant Park, Eighth Avenue, and Broadway. She makes friends with Patrick Gilligan, the warm, Irish hansom cab driver who helps her move her things and whose home she visits for tea and griddlecakes. She enjoys the Browdowskis*, the struggling young couple who live upstairs with their little golden-haired, four-year-old daughter, Trinket, and the roomers next door at Miss Lucy's, among them, Mr.* Night Owl, a reporter for the New York *Sun*. On a Saturday duty visit to her domineering, proper Aunt* Emily, perceptive, kindhearted Uncle* Earle rescues her from a scolding and introduces her to Shakespeare. Other friends include Patrolman* M'Gonegal and Tony Coppino, who runs his father's fruitstand and with whom she has picnics in a vacant lot, attended also by Old Rags and Bottles, the rag picker, and who helps her put on a production of *The Tempest* for Twelfth Night, an enterprise sparked by Uncle Earle's reading of the play. Thanksgiving brings her many invitations to share dinner, and the need for money for Christmas presents leads to her taking jobs as walker for Pygmalion, a dog, and tutor in English to an elderly woman, whom she dubs Princess Zayda because of her exotic dress and unusual apartment. She attends a circus and views a murder. The saddest thing that happens to her during the year is the death of Trinket, whom not even skillful Dr.* Hitchcock can save. Spring finds Lucinda back on her skates again, on picnics with Tony, on a visit to a real Shakespearean play, *As You Like It*, with Uncle Earle, and serving as bridesmaid in a teacher's wedding. She is happy when her parents return and claim her, but she is sure she'll never again be as happy as she was the year she was ten and spent her "orphanage" with the Misses Peters and her sidewalk and apartment house friends. She has learned to reach out to people and now has a broad circle of acquaintances of her own making, has gained some control over her restlessness and impulsiveness, and rejoins her family with vistas broadened and self-image heightened. This highly entertaining, somewhat contrived, occasionally melodramatic novel comes alive with the sights, smells, and sounds of the city and its vividly drawn, thoroughly engaging heroine. The cast of characters is large and assorted but sketched skillfully, dialogue carries conviction, and episodes move in rapid succession, exuding a joy of living that builds as the book moves along. Many references to familiar classics and cultural functions add a strong literary note, and there is a good sense of the period. Sequel is *The Year of Jubilo**. Fanfare; Lewis Carroll; Newbery Winner.

ROMAN EAGLE (Godwin*, Stephani, and Edward Godwin*, Oxford, 1951), historical romance set in ancient Palestine, in Rome, and in several other parts of the Roman empire during the last two years of Jesus' life, in which the Apostle Peter helps to reunite two estranged lovers. The story begins in Galilee where Marcus Decius, 15, the handsome and proud son of a Roman noble falls in love with Damaris, the Hebrew daughter of the owner of the neighboring villa. Though both know that their families would disapprove, the two young people secretly marry. When Marcus's father is recalled to Rome, Marcus bids Damaris a tearful farewell, vowing to love her always and to return to her as soon as he can. When Damaris's proud, widowed, Greek-born mother, Althea, learns of their relationship, she beats Damaris and confines her. In attempting to escape, Damaris hurts her ankle and becomes crippled. Later she gives birth to Marcus's son, a handsome baby whom Althea rejects but whom Damaris's grandfather, the wise and kindly scholar, Lemuel, learns to cherish. Lemuel strikes up an acquaintance with Andrew and Peter, two followers of Jesus, who has gained some renown as a teacher and healer. Lemuel's hopes that they will be able to heal Damaris are disappointed, and Damaris becomes self-pitying and skeptical that God exists. Later the two travel to Jerusalem at Passover, but Jesus is crucified before they can contact him. In Rome, Marcus falls in with a crowd of highborn youths who indulge in riotous living. He fully expects to wed Aquilla, the haughty and beautiful daughter of a socially prominent and politically powerful family. His hopes come to nothing when his father incurs the disapproval of Sejanus, the deputy of Tiberius, the emperor, and commits suicide. Marcus joins the Roman army, serving with little distinction in Gaul, where he is captured and almost sacrificed to the Gallic gods before escaping. Awakened to the error of his ways, he decides to return to Galilee and find Damaris. He takes a position as clerk in his uncle's shipyards by the Sea of Galilee, where he applies himself diligently. He chances to meet Peter, to whom he confides his story and who encourages him to persist in finding Damaris. The two are accordingly reconciled, and, recognizing that Marcus is no longer the "conceited puppy" he once was and has developed integrity and good sense, Lemuel accepts him into the family and later puts him in charge of his estate. Peter heals Damaris, whose faith has grown strong, blesses the young people, and predicts that the future holds both dire trials and deep joys for them as Christians before he departs for Rome. This sentimental, quite predictable story holds the interest chiefly for its revelation of ancient life and thought. Obviously didactic in intent, it reads in many places like a travelogue of the ancient world, handbook of ancient customs, book of profiles, and retelling of the story of Jesus' last days and the early Church. Fanfare.

THE ROSE OF DEVON (*The Dark Frigate**), the frigate bound for Newfoundland out of Bideford on which Philip* Marsham sails under Captain Candle. It is seized by pirates which it has rescued from their sinking ship and turned toward the Caribbean. After a series of misadventures, the *Rose* is taken by the British man-of-war *Sybil* and sailed in custody back to England where its pirate crew is put on trial. The *Rose of Devon* is a dark ship, both realistically and symbolically.

ROSS, M(ARGARET) I(SABEL) (1897-), author of some dozen novels of historical fiction and adventure for young people. *Kaga's Brother** (Harper, 1936), chosen for Fanfare by the editors of *Horn Book*, tells of a boy's adventure among the Chippewa in the Upper Peninsula of Michigan and in Wisconsin while with the Cass expedition in the early 1800s. Other novels set against the background of a scientific expedition include *Green Treasure* (Harper, 1948), in which a youth accompanies an expedition to the Dutch West Indies, and *Back of Time* (Harper, 1932), which deals with scientific investigations in Australia. *Greentree Downs* (Houghton, 1937), and *The Dawn Hill Brand* (Houghton, 1939) are adventure novels also set in Australia, while *Land of Williwaws* (Houghton, 1934) is a Robinson Crusoe-like tale of shipwreck in the Falklands. *South of Zero* (Harper, 1931) and *White Wind* (Harper, 1937) are ostensibly diaries of youth on expeditions to the Antarctic. Critics have noted that her books are uniformly interesting, offering plenty of fast-paced action and thrills and a good deal of information besides. They praise her ability to create a strong sense of place and her witty, lively style, but have found her characters wooden, her plots sometimes quite far fetched, and the occasional touches of romance extraneous.

ROSS PICKETT (*Big Red**), Danny's father and staunchest supporter. Although he feels Danny should let Red hunt ''varmints'' and especially should use Red to bay Old Majesty, he never goes beyond suggestion to get his way. A hound man, he comes to appreciate setters by the end of the book, when he loses his heart to the sleek, patrician Sheilah MacGuire. An uneducated man with simple wants, he is satisfied with his life in the Wintapi, but he hopes that Danny's connections with Mr.* Haggin will open doors to broader horizons for his son.

ROUNDS, GLEN (HAROLD) (1906-), prolific author and illustrator of books for children. The son of a rancher, he was born in a two-room shack near Wall, S.Dak., in the Badlands where many of his stories are set. After growing up on ranches in South Dakota and Montana, he drifted for a while, holding jobs as a sign painter, sawmill hand, cowpuncher, railroad hand, mule-skinner, and side-show medicine man, collecting information and impressions that would later appear in his many books and give them the authenticity and atmosphere that critics have praised and have made them popular. He attended the Kansas City Art Institute and the Art Students' League in New York and was a sergeant in the army in World War II. Since the appearance in 1936 of his first book, the classic *Ol' Paul, the Mighty Logger* (Holiday, 1936), the story of the tall-tale hero Paul Bunyan, he has published some two dozen books of fiction, many of them picture books, and a dozen and a half other books of non-fiction or editions, in addition to writing radio scripts for "School of the Air," contributing to magazines for children, and illustrating dozens of books for such authors as Jim Kjelgaard*, Richard Chase, Wilson Gage, Rebecca Caudill*, and Robbie Branscum. Two novels have been elected to the Lewis Carroll Shelf, *The Blind Colt** (Holiday, 1941), which introduced the popular young cowboy, Whitey, is also a *Choice* book, and is considered a classic novel of the West, and *Stolen Pony** (Holiday, 1948), its sequel. These stories are marked by vernacular speech, a succinct style, and a strong sense of setting. Also acclaimed have been *Wild Horses of the Red Desert* (Holiday, 1969), a non-fiction book which traces the season to season activities of a band of wild horses and which was a Lewis Carroll Shelf book, and *The Day the Circus Came to Lone Tree* (Holiday, 1973) and *Mr. Yowder and the Giant Bull Snake* (Holiday, 1978), both tall tale picture books. Other books about Whitey, which also recall Rounds's own life on the ranch, include *Whitey's First Round-up* (Grosset, 1942), *Whitey's Sunday Horse* (Grosset, 1943), and *Whitey's New Saddle* (Holiday, 1963), and others about Mr. Yowder include *Mr. Yowder and the Lion Roar Capsules* (Holiday, 1976) and *Mr. Yowder and the Steamboat* (Holiday, 1977). He lives in Southern Pines, N.C., which has also provided settings for some of his books.

ROWLIE PALMER (*Lassie Come-Home**), traveling potter with whom Lassie journeys southward in part of her trek from Scotland back to the Yorkshire village of her birth. A little, cheery, red-faced man, he sings as he goes, jokes with the women on his route, and puts on a little show with his small trick dog, Toots. He is grateful that Lassie saves him from thugs, but he willingly lets her go when he turns north and she wants to continue traveling south.

ROYAL WILDER (*Farmer Boy**; *On the Shores of Silver Lake**; *The Long Winter**; *Little Town on the Prairie**), older brother of Almanzo*, who shares chores with him on the big, family farm in New York State and later lives with him and runs a feed store in De Smet, S.Dak., where they homestead. Early in his life, Royal decides that the life of a storekeeper is preferable to that of a farmer, and while he is shown working on the homestead in Dakota, he returns to Minnesota where his parents are now farming before Almanzo and Laura* Ingalls marry.

RUDY BEHRENS (*Heart of Danger**), nineteen-year-old musician and composer, who is so disillusioned by his German-born father's defection to the Nazis at the beginning of World War II that he drops out of music school to enlist. His mother is Jewish, and as the war wears on Rudy comes to identify with the Jews. He is described as sensitive, moody, and often abstracted as melodies for compositions run through his head. After he sees a cattle car loaded with Jews bound for Buchenwald while he and Tod* are on their way to Paris, he composes ''The Prisoners' Song,'' a musical piece which serves to give some unity to the novel. A rather passive figure, he mostly reacts to situations, only occasionally taking the initiative in influencing his destiny. Two of the most significant of these are when he creates a diversion to enable his father to escape and is thus himself captured and when during imprisonment at Buchenwald he offers to orchestrate for the guards' band. Although he loses an arm at Buchenwald, he regards himself as lucky compared to what happened to other prisoners. Through flashbacks, the reader learns about his family background. Rudy is particularly ashamed of his father's defection to the Nazis, and he agrees to undertake the spying mission to compensate for his father's action. Those around him usually ascribe his introversion to his being a musician. He is a sympathetic, not altogether convincing protagonist.

RUFUS M. (Estes*†, Eleanor, ill. Louis Slobodkin*, Harcourt, 1943), humorous, episodic family novel, which follows *The Moffats** and *The Middle Moffat**, and continues the adventures of the lovable Cranbury*, Conn., family. The action covers roughly a year in their lives and deals mostly with their involvement in World War I on the home front. The focus is on Rufus*, who learns to write his name because he wants a library card and who knits washcloths for soldiers. He plants a Victory garden of beans and sells popcorn to become a Victory boy. In other episodes of the total thirteen, Rufus proves extremely adept as a left-handed backstop and saves the game with his home run for Jane's* baseball team, the Fatal Four. He learns how player pianos work in an especially funny episode, discovers the ''eyes'' in the sewer pipe are really those of Catherine-the-Cat, and is sent to the school superintendent for practicing ventriloquism in school. He finds some money under a patch of ice, chips it out, and hires Spec Collum to fix the frozen pipes in the basement, thus saving the day for the Moffats, spends fourth of July with Jane and Joey* at the beach, and rides his tricycle to the circus, where he gets a free ride on Jimmy the merry-go-round horse. Another very amusing episode revolves around Joey, who with Jane visits Miss Myles, Joey's first grade teacher. Joey suffers so severe an attack of self-consciousness while they are at her house that he contributes only two words to the entire conversation. At the very end, the family rejoices at the armistice in Europe and looks ahead to better times for all people everywhere. These appealing situation comedies are related, as are the other Moffat books, in direct, uncomplicated, easy-going language and a good deal of natural dialogue. Characters and situations are created with warmth, sympathy, and insight. The Moffats have become some of the most beloved figures in literature for children and young people, and their books are considered classics among family stories. ChLA Touchstones; Choice; Newbery Honor.

RUFUS MOFFAT (*The Moffats**; *The Middle Moffat**; *Rufus M.**), 6, younger brother in the Moffat family. An impulsive, energetic, earnest little boy, his adventures are mainly told in *Rufus M.**, but he also appears in the other two books.

RUGH, BELLE DORMAN (1908-   ), born in Beirut, Lebanon; teacher, writer. The daughter of an American missionary doctor, she was educated in this country at Vassar College and Columbia University, but returned to Lebanon to teach English at Women's College in Beirut and at Ahliah School. She married a man who had grown up in China and lived there for some years, teaching at Yenching University in Peking. She also has taught at Connecticut State College and has made her home in Wethersfield, Conn. *Crystal Mountain** (Houghton, 1955) is set in Lebanon as she knew it in her childhood. Two of her other books, *The Path Above the Pines* (Houghton, 1962) and *The Lost Waters* (Houghton, 1967), are also set in Lebanon.

THE RUNAWAY APPRENTICE (Evernden*, Margery, ill. Jeanyee Wong, Random, 1949), realistic adventure story set in Peking and the countryside in the Middle Kingdom of ancient China. When his stepmother and then the Old, Old One, his much-loved and greatly respected grandmother, scold him for telling tales and playing pranks, mischievous, fun-loving Chao Ho, the fourth son of a wealthy merchant, runs away to the hills. He falls in with a trio of itinerant shadow players. The shadow master, poor, honorable, talented Wang Fu, takes the boy at his word that he is motherless, penniless, and unwanted and makes him his apprentice. Fat, kindly, old Wu, who fashions the figures, readily accepts and instructs the boy, but Kung, Wang Fu's disagreeable nephew, resents Ho from the start and makes him look bad before the master whenever he can. Months pass as the little party travels by foot through the countryside, carrying the shadow figures and stage equipment in an ornately decorated box. They eke out the barest of livings by performing occasionally for the wealthy and influential, but mostly for the common people, because Wang Fu feels a duty to lighten the hard lives of the peasants through performing for them whenever he can. In the West, they observe roving bands of soldiers beat and harass the villagers and farmers. A merchant, Lord Lei, observing Wang Fu's integrity, commissions him to perform the story of the Stone Monkey for the emperor in Peking as a message about the political unrest in the provinces. Back in Peking, Ho, who has by this time revealed his identity to Wang Fu, discovers that his father's enemies have discredited him with the emperor, who has imprisoned the merchant and confiscated his property. The treacherous Kung runs away at the critical moment, leaving only Wu and Ho to help Wang Fu put on the most important performance of their lives. The play is well received, and the emperor gets the intended message. In reward for Ho's help, the emperor restores Ho's father to his former position. Ho now can return to his family, but much sobered, he chooses to remain with the master and make the shadows his life. This is a simple, rather sketchily developed adventure story that gives some sense of the political and economic realities of old China. The myths and tales that Ho recalls and that others tell add color and interest. The author deals superficially with the artistic medium of the shadows, and how they are made and used is never really clear. Fanfare.

THE RUNAWAY PAPOOSE (Moon*, Grace, ill. Carl Moon, Doubleday, 1928), realistic novel set in southwestern United States in the first third of the twentieth century. Nah-tee*, a small girl of a Pueblo Indian tribe, becomes separated from her parents when the group they are with is attacked as they travel through the desert. Lost and frightened, Nah-tee finds a Navajo boy, Moyo, herding his sheep, and he agrees to take her to a big festival at a mesa some distance away, reasoning that they must have been heading for that place. On the way, they run into various difficulties, including a storm and flash flood which makes it impossible for them to leave the canyon where they are sheltering. They are aided by a mysterious old man, Naybi, whom they follow to a deserted Pueblo city, where they fall into a kiva and discover a treasure in turquoise. Naybi, who is the watchman over the deserted cliff dwellings, tells them to take it to the chief of the festival mesa, Lampayo, whose people once lived in this cliff city but left and split into two groups. Naybi retrieves their straying pony and sets them on their way again to the mesa where they are aided by another pair of youngsters, Chi-wee*, a Pueblo girl, and Loki, a Navajo boy, who turns out to be a friend of Moyo. Before they can deliver the stones to the chief, however, the man who is next in line, evil Su-hu-bi, kidnaps Nah-tee, Moyo, and Loki, shuts them in a hogan, then pays a trader to take them far away. Chi-wee, learning of this, recruits some helpful grown-ups and gives chase. The three are brought back to the mesa where they expose the evilness of Su-hu-bi and Nah-tee is reunited with her mother and father, who is of the other branch of the tribe that used to live in the deserted cliff city and has been summoned to be successor to Lampayo. Although there is no condescension in the attitude toward the Indian people or culture, there is toward the children, and this tone dates the book. There is also a curious element introduced but never developed about a notice brought that all children will have to leave their families to attend a school far away where they will learn to be like white men, a prospect that seems to be treated as a good thing. The trip by Moyo and Nah-tee gives a good feel for the country, and their adventure in the canyons is vivid. Newbery Honor.

RUNAWAY PRENTICE (Parton*, Ethel, ill. Margaret Platt, Viking, 1939), historical novel set in Newburyport, Mass., in 1800, in which the subplot grows out of the strife between the United States and the Barbary Coast pirates. With the help of his sister, Mercy, young orphan Jeffrey Datcham runs away from the cruel leathermaker in Vermont to whom he is apprenticed to their Uncle* Hosy Datcham in Newburyport. Lighthearted Uncle Hosy and his sharp-tongued, hardworking wife, Lury (Philura), operate a bakeshop and eating house, the Bell and Fiddle. Coincidentally, Mercy has just discovered from a passing sailor, Tom Harnage, that their brother, Nolly (Oliver), a sailor, may not have been drowned at sea, as commony believed, but may be a prisoner of the Barbary pirates. Jeff is to ask Uncle Hosy to investigate the story and arrange for ransoming Nolly. Uncle Hosy takes off for a sailing trip before Jeff can tell his story, and in desperation Jeff confides in his cousin, imperious, sensible, resourceful Susan, who promptly enlists the aid of school friends, Tibby* Arminter and her older brother, Tris*, the youngest members of a large and wealthy merchant family. The Arminter children are convinced that their lost brother, Will, may also be a prisoner. With Susan's consent, the Arminters hide Jeff in their dovecot and then get him a job as handyboy to Bartholomew Bargle, the gardener of their wealthy and eccentric neighbor, Lord* Timothy Dexter. When Jeff rescues Mary Arminter, whose horse is threatening to bolt, the children share Jeff's secret with this older sister, who had been Nolly's sweetheart. A little tension arises when Batty* Bargle, the disagreeable, stubborn, obese son of the gardener, and then Batty's mother discover Jeff's identity. Uncle Hosy returns before they turn Jeff in, and the children learn to their surprise that Aunt Lury has suspected all along that they have been harboring the youth who has been advertised as a runaway. Uncle Hosy promptly consults lawyer Matthew Minturn about Jeff's problem, and soon Uncle Hosy is Jeff's legal guardian. Jeff enrolls at Tris's school and with the weight of the apprenticeship off his mind becomes more lively and outgoing and dares to dream of becoming a doctor, a long-held ambition. Minturn interviews the sailor Mercy had seen and takes steps to locate the lost sailors. Disaster strikes when Aunt Lury and Susan are burned in a bakeshop accident, and Jeff drops out of school temporarily to keep the business going. The doctor commends Jeff for the skill with which he tended their burns and for his presence of mind. Shortly thereafter, Uncle Hosy gives the boy the mortar and pestle that had belonged to his great-grandfather, Dr. Hezikiah Datcham, and informs him that he can look forward to attending medical school. Attention now focuses on the subplot. In the summer, a beau of one of the Arminter sisters has a water party. When their sailboat becomes stranded on a reef, the group is rescued by sailors from a passing ship, who turn out to be Nolly and Will, ransomed and newly arrived home. Nolly and Mary resume their relationship, and the book ends on a patriotic note with Nolly expressing joy at being home in a land where people can enjoy "life, liberty, and the pursuit of happiness." Chance plays a strong part in what happens in this long, fast-moving, action-filled, "talky" story of many characters, which knits plot and subplot quite clumsily. There is little tension, and the reader never doubts that things will turn out all right for Jeff and Nolly. Many incidents border on slapstick, and the novel has an incongruously comic tone that is considered patronizing to the audience, judged by late twentieth century critical standards. Scenes set at home, in church, at school, and in garden, restaurant, and bakeshop, during the week and on Sunday, at work and at social events give a child's-eye view of what it might have been like to live in a medium-sized port at the time. Characters are shallow, the principals are obvious foils, and the most interesting figure is Lord Dexter, who really existed. Fanfare.

RUSH MELENDY (*The Saturdays**), thoughtful, serious-minded second eldest of the Melendy children. He aspires to be a pianist or a construction engineer, but as time passes he concentrates more on his music. His earnings as a piano teacher and church organist add to the family income. He rescues Isaac, the stray dog, on his way home from his Saturday adventure. He smuggles Isaac into his room, a matter of good fortune for the family, because Isaac rouses Rush when the house fills with coal gas, saving the lives of the Melendy family. Rush has neglected to close the furnace door after stoking it with coal as Willy* Sloper, the Melendy furnace man, has instructed him to do. After the Melendys move to the country, he spends a lot of time by himself and with Mark Meeker, just exploring. He is fourteen in the third book of the series.

RUTH VAN OORDT (*The Level Land**), intense, serious eleven-year-old sister in a close-knit Dutch family. Her fierce love for her brother, Jan, 13, makes her intercede with his principal to gain him another chance to improve his grades enough to be recommended for high school. Then she feels duty-bound to keep Jan at his studying, even when he resents her nagging. At her own school she knows she could do better than the best student, Elly Verschuren, if she didn't daydream, and is surprised to discover that Elly is jealous of her ability to write well. In her delirium when she is ill, she keeps referring to the hair ribbons she bought specifically to wear to Elly's party, knowing the other girls will admire them and Elly will be annoyed. Ruth is at the seaside recuperating when the war breaks out and is rescued and brought home by her older sister, Miep.

S

SAGEBRUSH SORREL (Robertson*, Frank C., ill. Lee Townsend, Nelson, 1953), horse story set in western ranching country in the pre-automobile era. Orphan Ollie Bentley, 14, suffers from the harsh treatment and sarcastic jibes of Mel Tidwell, who is paid by the county to care for the boy, though Ollie works hard enough to earn his keep. Ollie loves kindly Martha, Mel's wife, however. Tidwell's place is a run-down, shoestring operation in contrast to the prosperous Worth ranch across the road, but Helen Worth, about Ollie's age, is friendly, and Ollie, though shy, secretly admires her. When they are riding up Picabo Mountain on one of Ollie's rare free days, they see a thoroughbred mare and her colt, obviously of a quarter-horse sire. The horses disappear in a thicket, but the youngsters have named the colt Rowdy and determine to get him eventually. The mare has been stolen by a horse thief named Red Antler, ridden in a getaway to Beaver Creek meadow, where he has left a relay, and abandoned exhausted, has found a cave with a brush-covered entrance where she has had her colt. Later in the summer Antler comes back, brands Rowdy with his outlaw "37," and some time later, again fleeing from the law, picks up the mare, and, to keep her from slowing up for the colt, shoots him, creasing the top of his head to knock him out but not kill him. So Rowdy spends his first winter in the creek valley, surviving only because he has the cave for shelter, but emerging so gaunt that Mel tries to shoot him when he and Ollie see him in the spring and is prevented only by Ollie deliberately getting in the way of the shot. Several times in the next two years Ollie and Helen see Rowdy, but he eludes any attempt to capture him and spends his second winter with wild horses, particularly a pinto mare. Mel takes every opportunity to harass and humiliate Ollie, but the boy's love for Martha keeps him from running away. In the colt's third summer Ollie manages to rope Rowdy and lead him in, and even though Mel claims the horse is his if it eats his hay, Ollie insists on breaking the colt himself and is backed by Martha. With kindness and patience, he trains Rowdy, and even though Mel scares him into bucking Ollie off once, he is shaping up to be a good horse when Mel decides to ride him. Rowdy bucks him off and gets away, and Mel is so furious he takes off on another horse to shoot Rowdy. Ollie follows and sees Mel trail Rowdy to the cave and shoot. Having missed, Mel is kicked by the colt, which then heads for the high mountains. Mel admits it was his own fault and dies. Rowdy, still saddled, fights the stallion of the wild band and gets the pinto to follow him. The next summer Ollie joins the roundup of the wild horses and manages to catch Rowdy, still wearing the remnants of the saddle, but just then Red Antler reappears and claims him. One of the other men bets Antler he can't ride Rowdy. He tries, is bucked off, and with a broken thigh, is identified by way of his horse as a wanted thief, and he admits he stole Rowdy's mother. Ollie, now the adopted son of Martha, gives the pinto to Helen and determines to gentle Rowdy again. Much of the story is told from the point of view of Rowdy, with good detail of the natural setting and without anthropomorphizing the horse. The conflict between Mel and Ollie gives interest to the human characters, but neither Mel's dying admission of fault nor Antler's admission of horse theft is convincing. Spur.

SALLY GREEN (*Mary Jane**), unusually small, blond girl who befriends black Mary Jane when she enters newly integrated Woodrow Wilson High School. Because of her size, Sally is often left out and ridiculed, and she chooses to be friends with the black girl partly because she has no popularity to lose. Although her lack of prejudice is explained partly by her parents' attitude, their hasty capitulation to pressure from their bigoted neighbors and friends exposes their commitment to racial harmony as shallow. Sally's efforts to get to know Mary Jane even though rebuffed are not entirely plausible in a character not herself socially secure.

SALLY SMITH (*Away Goes Sally**; *Five Bushel Farm**; *The ''Fair American''**), niece of Uncle* Joseph, Aunt Nannie, and others. She is a spunky little girl of about ten in the stories. She makes friends easily on the road to Maine and after they arrive, and it is her resourcefulness and ingenuity that sometimes save the day. She and Andrew make friends with Indian children while out berrying near Five Bushel Farm in the book of that name. Later during a tense scene between Uncle Joseph and the Indians, the friendships she made among the children help to reconcile the distrustful adults. When in *The ''Fair American''**, the ship is boarded by a Frenchman searching for Royalist refugees, Sally boldly asserts that Pierre is her elder brother and then appeals to the Frenchman's love of children by giving her beloved doll, Eunice, to him as a gift for his own daughter.

SAM CARRACLOUGH (*Lassie Come-Home**), original owner of Lassie and father of twelve-year-old Joe. A Yorkshire man, slow of thought and speech, Sam has a strong sense of honesty and three times insists that the dog must be returned when she breaks out of the Duke's kennel and comes home. After she has made her way from Scotland back to their Yorkshire village, he practices the skills of a dog ''coper,'' usually employed to make a poor dog temporarily look good but this time in reverse to make Lassie look like an undesirable mutt that the Duke will not know or want. Even then, he cannot bring himself to lie but asks, ''Does it look like any dog that belongs to thee?''

SAM HILTON (*Indian Brother**; *The Scalp Hunters**), impulsive but brave and resourceful British boy who is captured by Indians in his effort to rescue his twin sister, Martha, and his younger brother, Billy. Although he becomes a blood brother to Sosepsis*, a Penobscot Indian, and cannot bring himself to take a scalp for bounty, he kills the brutal Indian who expects to marry Martha, and later, in his rescue of Billy, kills a number of Indians, whom he refers to as savages and whose cruelties he details frequently.

SANCTIFY (*Great Day in the Morning**), five-year-old cousin of Lillybelle Lawrence. A scamp, the little boy rides the cow despite Lillybelle's scolding and is at least partly responsible for the poor creature's demise. Out of her small school savings, Lillybelle buys a new cow and makes Sanctify promise to drink the milk, which he dislikes. His illness after he falls in the fire and develops complications from the burns that will require long hospitalization helps to make Lillybelle decide on a career in nursing.

SANDOZ†, MARI (SUSETTE) (MARI MACUMBER) (1901-1966), teacher, editor, lecturer, regional novelist, historian and biographer, noted in children's literature for her books of fiction and non-fiction about Indians for children and young people. She was born in Sheridan County, Nebr., the eldest of the six children of a hard-bitten Swiss immigrant for whose biography for adults, *Old Jules* (Atlantic, 1935), her first book, she received the *Atlantic Monthly* fiction prize of five thousand dollars. She grew up in the Sand Hills cattle country of northwest Nebraska, early working as a hand about the ranch. Beginning when she was nine, she attended rural school for four and a half years. She took the examination for a teacher's certificate and taught country school for five years, while attending the University of Nebraska. The college refused her a degree because she had never been to high school but later awarded her an honorary doctor of letters. She was a proofreader and researcher for the Nebraska State Historical Society, associate editor of *The School Executive* in Lincoln, proofreader for the Lincoln *Star* and *Nebraska State Journal*, and associate editor of *Nebraska History* magazine. She was staff leader for writers' conferences and director of courses in writing, and lectured, taught, and wrote for over thirty years until her death, receiving many awards and honors for her work. She published over a dozen and a half critically acclaimed books of fiction and non-fiction and a collection of short stories, and she was frequent contributor to magazines. For young people she wrote *The Horsecatcher** (Westminster, 1957), a Newbery honor book and a Fanfare book, about a Cheyenne youth who does not wish to become a warrior and who has a remarkable talent for taming and training horses. *The Story Catcher*† (Westminster, 1963), winner of the Spur Award of Western Writers of America, is another novel about an Indian youth seeking to identify his role in their rapidly changing society. She also wrote for young readers *Winter Thunder* (Westminster, 1954), a short novel recently reissued along with some of her short stories in an edition for young adults, *The Battle of the Little Bighorn* (Lippincott, 1966), and *These Were the Sioux* (Hastings, 1961), a book of non-fiction. She was noted for her crisp style, her careful attention to detail, and her authentic portrayals of the Old West.

SANDY (Vining*†, Elizabeth Janet Gray, Viking, 1945), novel for teenaged girls set in a New Hampshire resort town during the last years of World War II. Motherless Sandy (Alexandra) Callam, 17, and her Aunt Kate*, headmistress of Miss Callam's School for Girls, arrive for their annual summer vacation in the resort village of Windrush, with a new housekeeper, Mrs. Terminia* Sparhawk, and Sandy's west highland white terrier, The Laird of Cockpen, usually called Cocky. The war has taken all the older boys of the "gang," and Sandy, who had to give up a job as cashier in a food store because of the protests of her aunt and father (a naval officer on sea duty), anticipates a dull summer until she learns that Wing Garrison, 23, a distant cousin, is in Windrush for the summer. Wing, an engineer in a deferred occupation, is recovering from an operation for a ruptured appendix. He tells Sandy that her other aunt, her mother's sister, Mimi*, now Mrs. Eddington from Chicago, whom Sandy scarcely knows, is also summering in Windrush with her married daughter, Helen, and Helen's two uncontrolled children, little Helen and Jackie. When Miss Sophie Skilton, who runs the inn, complains that she needs another waitress, Sandy impulsively volunteers, and after some initial difficulties, is soon waiting on the summer guests with two village girls, Martha Shillingford and Myrtle Champillion. Most of the novel is concerned with Sandy's efforts to capture Wing's attention and to bridge the gap between the permanent residents and the summer people. Many of the villagers, though dependent on the summer business, resent the butterfly existence of the summer people, both those who own cottages and those who stay at the inn. Led by Sandy, the gang organizes weekly square dances. At first the blundering summer folk are scorned by the experienced dancers among the permanent residents, but after two practice groups, made up of Sandy's friends and a number of inn guests, bone up, the dances succeed in mixing the two levels of society. Though Myrtle is friendly, work at the inn is made difficult by resentful Martha. When another college girl, Isabel, joins the staff, Sandy stands up to Martha, who has been taking Isabel's tips, and Sandy gets fired. Her conquest of Wing goes no more smoothly. Though he takes her to the square dance, he becomes ill, and she has to drive the caller home in Wing's car, which has a flat in a deserted road, and she has to change the tire. Wing prefers the company of Helen, whose husband is overseas, and treats Sandy as casually as she treats devoted Charlie Smith, 16. Mimi proposes that Sandy give up the exclusive college which she has been attending as Kate did before her, come to

Chicago, get a job in her uncle's office, and meet some men. Sandy is torn, but eventually decides to let neither aunt plan her life, but to go to the University and take courses that will fit her to work in postwar reconstruction in Europe, as Isabel is planning to do. It is difficult to imagine girls of the 1980s or boys at any period finding this novel interesting. Not only do Sandy's naive problems and worries seem foreign, the elitist assumptions of the story are antiquated even for the 1940s. As a picture of a social situation that is now mostly a thing of the past and of the attitudes of and toward "well bred" girls of the period, it should be of interest to social historians. Fanfare.

SANGRE DE CRISTO MOUNTAINS (. . . *And Now Miguel**), the mountain range in eastern New Mexico to which the Chavez family take their sheep for summer pasture. These mountains symbolize maturity and acceptance as an adult to Miguel.

SANTIAGO (Clark*, Ann Nolan, ill. Lynd Ward, Viking, 1955), realistic novel of the problems of the modern Maya in finding their role in Guatemala society as seen through the experiences of an educated Maya youth. Santiago, an orphaned Maya boy, has been raised as her son by Tía Alicia, a proud Guatemalan lady of good Spanish family, who runs a tourist home in Guatemala City. Frequent guests in her house are a family from the United States, whose father manages a banana plantation and with whose son, Jim, Santiago becomes close friends. Santiago hopes, by attending college in the United States, eventually to carry out the wishes of his parents to be a good Indian in the modern world. On Santiago's twelfth birthday, a Maya clansman claims him and takes the boy back with him to his mountain village to live the life of a burden bearer. Although Santiago tries with heart and body, he cannot learn to carry the burdens as do his people in their centuries old manner, and he is horrified by some of the ways and beliefs of his proud and complex tribespeople. Released by his clansman, having failed as an Indian, and feeling unworthy of living again on Tía Alicia's generosity, Santiago embarks on a search, which lasts for several years, to discover his identity and his purpose in life. He works for some months on a coffee plantation, where he makes friends with Eduardo, a Latino youth with a strikingly beautiful singing voice; gets caught up in a demonstration against the dictator, during which Eduardo is wounded; resorts to thievery; and cuts chicle in the jungle before he is discovered by Jim's father. He works for a while on the banana plantation for Jim's father who plans to send him to Honduras where he will receive managerial training. Santiago elects to remain in Guatemala and work among the illiterate mountain people like his new friend, Luis, a teacher. He feels that in this way he can best accomplish his parents' wishes. Although sentences are short and vocabulary easy enough for younger readers, the earnest, even urgent, tone and the underlying concepts require a more mature audience. Descriptive passages are alive with imagery, but characterization is minimal. After a gripping start filled with human interest, the novel degenerates into a fictionalized social science text about the Guatemala of the mid-twentieth century. Santiago's experiences seem intended to show the life choices open to modern youth there and move predictably to an instructive conclusion. Fanfare.

SARA CREWE (*A Little Princess**), wealthy child who, when her father dies and his fortune seems lost, shifts from being a privileged parlor boarder to a drudge in her school, teaching the younger children, running errands, fetching and carrying for the cook, and living in a rat-infested attic. Throughout, Sara retains her good nature and dignity because, in her imagination, she is a princess and she is determined to act the role. She endures her hardship and comforts her fellow-sufferer, the servant girl Becky, with tales spun by her lively fancy. At one point, almost starving, she finds four-pence, buys six buns, and gives five of them to a hungry beggar child. Her final act, when she regains her fortune and status, is to arrange with the bakery woman to give free buns to hungry children on cold days and to send her the bill. Although her goodness is rather unbelievable at times, she is no Pollyanna, but a spirited child who controls her temper by feeling superior to her tormentors.

SARAH'S IDEA (Gates*†, Doris, ill. Marjorie Torrey, Viking, 1938), realistic novel of family life with animal story aspects, which takes place at an unspecified time that sounds like the 1930s. In March, Sarah's father, a doctor, gives up his practice and moves the family to a prune ranch in the Santa Clara Valley of California, because he hopes that farm living will improve Sarah's delicate health. Pig-tailed, lean, little Sarah, 9, is delighted with the move, and when they arrive, is overjoyed to discover that there is a barn on the place, for she has a secret wish to own a burro. She longs to be a tomboy and maybe some day to become a cowgirl on the range. When she investigates the barn, she finds an empty stall, a perfect place to keep her longed-for pet. Days pass before she communicates her wish to anyone. In the meantime, she and her younger sister, Linda*, 7, explore the farm. They discover that a mother cat has made her home in the stall, and later the same day Sarah falls into the creek while she and Linda are sailing leaf boats on the water. While on a picnic in the poppy hills with Mother, the girls encounter a flock of sheep, whose old herder has a little, gray-brown burro, Jinny, which captures Sarah's heart. Impulsively reacting against what she regards as the patronizing attitude of Mr. Thomas, the prune buyer, Sarah blurts out her secret desire. Since she is a persistent child, her spirits are only slightly dampened when Father speaks discouragingly about it. Prune harvest finds Sarah in far better health and brings the arrival of the pickers, a migrant Italian family, the Rizzos, who have four children. The eldest, Johnny, Sarah's age, warns the girls about Nanny, the family goat. Determined to prove that she can handle Nanny and be a real "tomboy," Sarah persuades Linda to help her hitch the goat to a wagon. The result is a wild ride through the barn and yard. By hanging on, Sarah demonstrates that she can cope with rough situations. After the Rizzos leave, Sarah gets the best idea of all—to earn money for the burro by picking the late-ripening fruit. Linda generously helps her, and the two industriously gather eleven boxes of prunes, which Father sells to Mr. Thomas, who says they have enough money to buy a burro. Mr. Thomas takes the family for a ride into the Santa Cruz mountains to visit a burrokeeper. To Sarah's immense delight, she discovers Jinny there and immediately buys her. In the fall, the girls ride Jinny to school to show her off to their schoolmates. Always inventive, Sarah then decides to enter Jinny in the San José rodeo. When Jinny proves balky, Sarah resourcefully entices her to continue in the parade by dangling before her nose hay attached to a long prune switch. The two win the hearts of the crowd and the twenty-five dollar first prize for the most humorous entry. The story ends abruptly with Sarah dreaming of adding to her funds until she can buy a cattle ranch. Parents are types, and the plot lacks tension. The jovial, pigtail-pulling Mr. Thomas is a potentially interesting, undeveloped character, about whom Sarah suddenly changes her mind. The premise that farm life can solve health problems seems dated. The two sisters are characterized quickly and richly. Sarah is a winsome heroine, whose growing appreciation of her sister is an especially noteworthy aspect of the book. Because the author focuses on Sarah's attempts to achieve her aims, tells the story without sentimentality from Sarah's point of view, and depicts Sarah with attitudes and behavior typical of a girl of her age who longs to be active, the story has a universality and conviction that transcends most such stories intended for little girls. Fanfare.

SARANGA THE PYGMY (Gatti*, Attilio, ill. Kurt Wiese, Scribner's 1939), realistic novel set presumably in the early twentieth century in the jungle of equatorial Africa. Since he is already three feet tall and has had his teeth filed to points to show he is no longer a child, Saranga, 12, wants to learn first hand of the greatest jungle animals, so he watches from a tree the elephant herd led by Great Maama, a herd that no Mambuti pygmy will molest since Great Maama saved the Old One, Saranga's grandfather, from a leopard when he was an infant. On his return trip to the village, Saranga sees the tracks of a bongo, a great antelope with sharp horns and a belligerent nature, and when the men of the meat-needy village hunt it the next day, Saranga joins the hunt, unasked, and gives warning that saves his older brother, Taroo, from being gored to death. Thrown by the horns, Taroo receives broken ribs and a broken arm and in his delirium talks of the goods he means to get when he trades his elephant tusks to the Arabs who come to the village of the huge plains-dwelling blacks at the jungle's edge. Believing that it is Taroo's *lodi* or soul giving him directions, Saranga takes the tusks and secretly sets out for the trading village where he is well received but tricked by the Arabs, who put a white powder in his tobacco, steal back the goods they have traded him, and throw him and his dog, Boo-a, out of the hut. Dazed and hallucinating from the strong drugs, Saranga wanders through the great river into the taboo land, avoided by all the pygmies because it once was filled with evil spirits that made animals foam at the mouth and bite madly, presumably rabies. After seven days of wandering, he finally regains his senses and with the help of Boo-a and his own sharp jungle skills, survives in this country now full of game and prepares his homeward journey. After several days he comes to an area deserted by animals but dotted with elephant skulls, including the tusks, and realizes that he has come to the secret place where the great beasts go to die. There he comes upon Great Maama, her trunk swollen shut by the egg sac of the dread *makula* fly, which can kill an elephant by suffocation. With Great Maama too weak to attack him, Saranga cuts out the egg sac, then bandages the trunk with healing leaves and clay, and brings food and water to the huge beast until she is well enough to find her way back to her own country. Following her, Saranga notes a great wealth of tusks about which he will tell Taroo and, after crossing the Great River at the elephant's secret bridge of rocks, is reunited with his family. Not only does the book tell an absorbing and convincing adventure, it also gives a great deal of information about the jungle skills and beliefs of the pygmies and, more important, a feeling for the loving and gentle nature of the small but hardy and happy people. Saranga is a staunch and self-reliant hero, and his skills, his fears, his close relationship with his brother, and his belief in Muungu, god of the jungle, are treated with respect. Fanfare.

SAREY SUE TRIVETT (*Blue Ridge Billy**), 12, mountain girl who, with her grandmother, makes a living by digging herbs. A tough and quick-thinking youngster, she is worried when Billy is fighting two rough Buckwheat Holler boys at the mill, and to distract their attention she swipes the horse belonging to one of them to carry her ground corn home. She plays the accordion that once belonged to her father and generally acts like a tomboy, but her great desire is for a pretty calico dress instead of the brown homespun Granny makes her. When Pappy gets Christmas things from the mail-order house in Chicago, Billy begs a piece of figured lawn to give to Sarey Sue for a new dress.

SASSOONAN (*Benjamin West and His Cat Grimalkin**), Indian chief and friend of the West family. He and his Indian friends show Benjamin how to make paints of various colors. Previously the boy has had only charcoal to work with. The boy and the Indians paint together in the forest. This is Benjamin's first art class, and he admires the Indians' talent with bark and pigments.

SATTLEY, HELEN R(OWLAND), born in St. Paul, Minn., but spent much of her early life in the area of Chicago; librarian and author of novels for teenaged girls. After receiving her bachelor's and master's degrees from Northwestern University in psychology, she took a degree in library science from Western Reserve in Cleveland. After serving as a public librarian in St. Louis and a school librarian in Evanston, Ill., and teaching at Columbia University and then at Western Reserve, she became director of School Library Services for the New York City Board of Education. Widely recognized as a consultant in library services, she has specialized in books for children and young adults for school library collections and in particular books on India, Japan, and Russia. She has held many offices in professional organizations, among others, serving as chair of the Newbery-Caldecott Committee in 1963-1964 and as president of the Children's Services Division of the American Library Association from 1964-1965. She has written many articles for library and education journals and has published a bibliography of children's books about foreign countries. Of her three novels for older girls, *Shadow across the Campus** (Dodd, 1957), about a girl's attempt to combat prejudice in her sorority, received the Child Study Association Award. Her other novels are *Young Barbarians* (Morrow, 1947), about a girl's junior year in high school when she acquires a stepmother, and *Annie* (Dodd, 1961), which fictionalizes on the history of the author's own family while emigrating from London to Chicago, focusing on her Aunt Annie. She also published *The Day the Empire State Went Visiting* (Dodd, 1958), a picture book. She has made her home in New York City.

THE SATURDAYS (Enright*†, Elizabeth, ill. author, Farrar, 1941), realistic, episodic family novel, set in New York City about 1940, the first in a series of three books about the Melendys, including *The Four-Story Mistake* and *Then There Were Five*. The four motherless Melendy children, Mona*, 13, Rush*, 12, Randy*, 10, and Oliver*, 6, live with their father and elderly housekeeper, Cuffy*, in a rambling, old house, the top floor of which forms the Office*, the children's own special area. One boring, rainy Saturday while in the Office, the four form a club, I.S.A.A.C.* (Independent Saturday Afternoon Adventure Club), and decide to pool their allowances each week so that each child, in turn, can have a Saturday to do what he or she most desires. Since the idea is Randy's, her turn comes first. An aspiring painter, she takes in the French exhibit at the Art Institute, where she encounters wealthy dowager, Mrs.* Oliphant. Over tea, Mrs. Oliphant tells Randy the story of how she was kidnapped by gypsies when she was a child in France. Rush, the music lover, attends the opera *Siegfried*. On the way home, he rescues a stray dog which he names Isaac in memory of the club and his first Saturday. Mona goes to a fashionable downtown shop and has her braids bobbed and her nails manicured a bright red, creating quite a stir in the household. On his day, Oliver goes off to the circus without informing the family, gets lost on the way home, and is assisted by a friendly, mounted policeman. Because Oliver's adventure upset the family so much, the children decide to spend future Saturdays together, still pooling their allowances. When they go for a rowboat ride on Central Park Lake, Randy falls in. Later Isaac awakens Rush when the house fills with coal gas, saving their lives. Because father decides they need to install a gas furnace, the family cannot afford a summer vacation in the country as usual. Happily, Mrs. Oliphant invites the children to spend the summer with her at her lighthouse by the sea. The Melendys are a warm, happy family with an optimistic outlook on life. The children's adventures reflect their individual personalities and tend to be intellectual. Distinctively drawn characters, extensive, unforced dialogue, some humor, a light and affectionate tone, and a polished narrative style rich with concrete details make for lively, now somewhat dated diverting reading. Books Too Good; Choice.

SAUER, JULIA L. (1891-1983), born in Rochester, N.Y.; librarian, author. She attended the University of Rochester and New York State Library School and worked all her career at the Rochester Public Library. A vacation home in Nova Scotia gave her the setting for both *Fog Magic** (Viking, 1943), a time fantasy, and *The Light at Tern Rock** (Viking, 1951), a realistic Christmas story, both Newbery honor books.

SAWYER, RUTH (1880-1970), born in Boston, Mass.; storyteller and author best known for her work for children. She grew up on New York's Upper East Side, spending summers with the family in Maine and cared for by an Irish nurse whose stories awakened in her a love for traditional storytelling. She attended Garland Kindergarten Training School in Boston, graduated from Columbia University, where she studied folklore and storytelling, was a reporter for the New York *Sun*, started the first storytelling program in the New York Public Library, told stories in missions and schools, and lectured in storytelling throughout the United States. She first collected stories in Cuba, and later on trips to Ireland, Europe, and Mexico. She published over thirty-five books of fiction and non-fiction for children and adults and collections of traditional stories, and many short stories, articles, plays, and poems as well. Among the most highly acclaimed of her books are her two autobiographical novels, *Roller Skates** (Viking, 1936) and its sequel, *The Year of Jubilo** (Viking, 1940). The former, which won the Newbery Medal, was a *Horn Book* Fanfare book, and was chosen for the Lewis Carroll Bookshelf, tells of free-spirited Lucinda Wyman's year in New York with the Misses Peters in the nineties, while *Jubilo*, a Fanfare book, takes Lucinda to Maine after the death of her father. Also Fanfare books are *The Least One** (Viking, 1941), a realistic story about the close bond between a small Mexican boy and his burro, and *The Christmas Anna Angel** (Viking, 1944), a short story of family life set in Hungary in World War I and illustrated by Kate Seredy*. *The Enchanted Schoolhouse** (Viking, 1956), cited in *Choice*, combines modern American school life and Irish folklore. Although most of her fiction seems contrived and sentimental to late twentieth century audiences, her writing reveals a good sense of the storytelling situation, a sharp eye for ethnic detail, and a keen ear for the rhythms of common speech. She also published *Joy to the World* (Little, 1961), a book of tales and carols that was chosen for Fanfare, *Picture Tales from Spain* (Stokes, 1936), a collection that contains her best-loved Spanish story, "The Flea," and *The Way of the Storyteller* (Viking, 1942), a book of traditional stories and philosophy about storytelling for adults. The acknowledged great lady of American storytelling, she received the Laura Ingalls Wilder Award for her many books, tales, and work as a storyteller. She married Albert Durand, an opthalmologist, and lived in New York state and

Maine. Her daughter, Margaret, became the wife of illustrator Robert McCloskey*, with whom Sawyer collaborated on her lively version of the pancake story, *Journey Cake, Ho!* (Viking, 1953).

SAYERS, FRANCES CLARKE (1897-   ), born in Topeka, Kans.; librarian, editor, author. She attended the University of Texas and Carnegie Institute of Technology, then was employed at the New York Public Library as superintendent of work with children. At the University of California at Los Angeles she has been a lecturer in children's literature and is well known for her works on the subject, including *Anthology of Children's Literature* (Houghton, with Edna Johnson and Evelyn R. Sickels, 3rd edition, 1959, on) and *Summoned by Books* (Viking, 1965) for which she won the Clarence Day Award. Among her other awards are the Joseph W. Lippincott Award for distinguished service in the profession of librarianship in 1965 and the Southern California Children's Literature Award in 1969. Among her books for children is *Mr. Tidy Paws** (Viking, 1935), a story of a most unusual cat.

SAYYAD KHAN (*Little Boat Boy**), moneylender in the village in the Kashmiri valley where Hafiz and his family live. Hafiz's father borrows money from him to send Abdullah* to school. A one-dimensional figure, Sayyad is a fat, pretentious man, greedy and grasping. He presses Hafiz's father for his money, would like to lure the Sahib away from Hafiz's houseboat to his own, and even claims the red ball Hafiz finds under the floor of the houseboat belongs to him. In the end, Hafiz's father is able to pay him off with money from the English Sahib.

THE SCALP HUNTERS (Coryell*, Hubert V., ill. Wilfred Jones, Harcourt, 1936), historical novel, sequel to *Indian Brother**, detailing the events in 1725 after Sam* Hilton and his twin sister return from capture by the Indians in Maine. Mike* MacGregor and Sam, hunting together, kill an Indian scout, but Sam, remembering his father's mutilated body, refuses to take the scalp even though the British have begun offering bounties of one hundred pounds per scalp. Martha goes to help out Mike's old aunt, and Sam, with his younger brother, Billy, works aboard their Aunt Margaret's sloop trading along the coastal waters. When Billy, fishing ashore, is attacked by Indians and captured, Sam and Mike set off to find him at Pegwocket, an Indian village where they believe he has been taken. On reaching the village, they find it temporarily deserted and leave messages written in English, which the Indians cannot read, telling Billy to escape and where to meet them. Knowing that Captain Lovewell is leading a scalp-hunting expedition on the village, Sam intercepts him to try to persuade him to hold off the attack until Billy has escaped. Lovewell and his men will not agree and, expecting to attack the village, are ambushed. Except for the expert direction of the scout, Seth Wyman, none would have escaped, and even so, many are killed or badly wounded. When they leave under cover of darkness, Sam parts with them, knowing that Mike has met with Sosepsis*, Sam's Indian "brother," who has been on a peace-making mission, and that Sosepsis has been wounded. Sam has kept this knowledge from Lovewell, because his men, eager to take scalps for bounty, are not particular about whether the Indians killed are friendly or not. Billy manages to escape, but he and Mike, who comes to meet him, are both nearly sucked under by quicksand, and the group is saved by the wounded Sosepsis who comes in the nick of time. They return to Brunswick, where Martha and Mike expect to marry. As in the earlier book, most of the incidents and many of the characters are historical, as a postscript tells us, and in this novel the ambivalent attitude is even more pronounced, since Sam, the narrator, is unable to make himself take an Indian scalp, but Lovewell's men, particularly Seth Wyman, are depicted as courageous on their bounty hunt and the Indians, except Sosepsis, are referred to as savages. Mike is able to marry Martha with the money that comes from scalps he has taken. Fanfare.

SCARECROW (*The Wonderful Wizard of Oz**), cheerful character who joins Dorothy* and Toto* on their trip to the Emerald City and in further adventures. The Scarecrow wants the Wizard* to give him brains. After the Wizard has been revealed as a humbug, he takes the sawdust from the Scarecrow's head and refills it with bran mixed with needles and pins, proof that the Scarecrow is sharp. He becomes the king in Emerald City after the departure of the Wizard.

SCHMIDT, SARAH L(INDSAY), mystery novelist and author of stories with a western setting, including *New Land** (McBride, 1933), a novel of homesteading in northern Wyoming in the 1930s which was a Newbery honor book. Among her other books are *Ranching on Eagle Eye* (McBride, 1936), *The Secret of Silver Peak* (Random, 1938), *Shadow Over Winding Ranch* (Random, 1940), and *The Hurricane Mystery* (Random, 1943).

SEABIRD (Holling*, Holling Clancy, ill. author, Houghton, 1948), highly illustrated, realistic story of several generations of seamen, telling the history of shipping from about 1830 to the mid-twentieth century. At fourteen, Erza Brown of New Bedford, ship's boy on a whaler, noticing in a snowstorm the sudden shift in the flight of an ivory gull, realizes that they are bearing down on an iceberg and cries warning in time to save the ship. Afterwards, he carves a gull from two walrus tusks, joined cunningly together, with an amber beak and coral eyes. This Seabird stays with him on many voyages, overlooking his rise to be captain and, finally, skipper of a clipper ship. On his first clipper trip he takes his son, Nate, 10, as cabin boy in a journey around Cape Horn. The Bosun resents the agile, fearless boy and makes life hard for him, and in San Francisco, where he leaves the ship, he throws Seabird overboard. Nate, an excellent swimmer, dives for the bird, and, unable to get down far enough, goes hand-over-hand down the anchor chain, recovers Seabird, and is pulled out of the water unconscious. The ship goes on to Hawaii, where Nate swims with the native youngsters, and on to China, Siam, Burma, Ceylon, and India. As he grows up, Nate turns to steamers, but is still happiest on ships that carry sail. Nate's son, James, fascinated with machinery, is not himself a sailor but a ship designer, the one who develops the first oil burner. In 1923, Ezra, still alert at 105, visits James's newest liner with his great-grandson, James's boy, five-year-old Ken, who has inherited Seabird. Ken is destined to sail the skies as a flyer, still taking Seabird with him. As with other Holling books, the simple but interesting story is overshadowed by illustration which consists of both full-page paintings and small, detailed drawings bordering the text that show how ships are rigged, the anatomy of whales, techniques of ship building, and other information pertinent to the story. This combination makes a book with a wide age appeal, one that conveys a great deal of information in a nonpedantic way. Newbery Honor.

THE SEA IS ALL AROUND (Enright*†, Elizabeth, ill. author, Farrar, 1940), realistic novel of family and neighborhood life set about 1940 mostly on the often fog-bound, windblown island of Pokenick*, a close-knit community off New Bedford, Mass. Mab (Maybeth) Kendall, 10, an independent, spirited little orphan, has been living with her Aunt Sarah in Golden Creek, Iowa. With a little apprehension but mostly pleasant anticipation, in November Mab makes the long journey by train and boat from Iowa to the island and into the welcoming arms of warm Aunt* Belinda Prior, and many new friends, exciting times, and ultimately the decision to remain with this new-found, loving aunt. At first, the two just get acquainted. Mab investigates the house and gets a little sense of family history, they go to the movies together, and they visit Aunt Belinda's adult friends, among them one who becomes a great favorite with Mab, Yancey Bates*, who runs the local curiosity shop and gives her little items that he knows will delight her heart and please her eye but "that don't amount to much." She catches up on her schoolwork in private lessons with Miss* Havana Fish, a frail woman but an exacting teacher. Restless and bored after the holidays, she goes for a walk on the moors, gets lost in a fog, and spends the night in a hut by the shore, pleased to discover that she can keep her head and take care of herself under even life-threatening conditions for the book's most exciting adventure. Aunt Belinda introduces her to lively, red-haired Candy* Crocker, also ten, and her three spirited brothers, and at the beginning of February, Mab starts regular school, where she makes still more friends, none of whom ever supplants Candy in her affections. In the spring, she, Candy, and Chan and Casper Crocker explore the Crocker children's Secret Place in the marsh and eat a picnic lunch on the gravestone of a local resident, as it happens, on his birthday. The last Saturday in May, while picking a bouquet of flags in the meadow just beyond Aunt Belinda's house, Mab discovers the decorative knife her mother lost here when she was a child and then Cato the parrot finally speaks her name, both signs, she thinks, that she really belongs to the island. Although the plot moves unevenly and pacing is off, this story of a girl's growing into self-confidence as she settles into a new home situation offers a spirited heroine and convincing adult and child characters and remains lively and interesting even though there is no strong plot problem, probably because of the author's graceful, winning style and exceptional ability to capture the sights, sounds, and smells of the seaside region and the thoughts and feelings typical of children. Fanfare.

SEA PASSPORT (*The Quaint and Curious Quest of Johnny Longfoot, the Shoe King's Son**), given to Johnny* Longfoot by a grateful shark because Johnny has patched his hide. It guarantees safe passage and is "valid for shallow, medium and deep waters."

SEA PUP (Binns*, Archie, ill. Robert Candy, Duell, 1954), realistic animal novel set on Puget Sound in the mid-1900s. Clint Barlow, 13, whose father's logging camp touches the Sound, loves the sea and has been studying its creatures so long he is considered somewhat of an authority by his parents and neighbors. While on a sailboat outing on Pirate Bay, he discovers a baby seal, whose mother has been shot by hunters, brings it home, and persuades his parents to let him keep it. He raises Buster on the bottle, and, when it is time, teaches him to swim. Soon winsome, mischievous, clownish Buster has become a member of the family, lying by the hearth, swaying to music, and toddling around after his human friends. When Buster receives a gunshot wound and a broken flipper after a night alone on the Sound, Clint and his parents splint the flipper, stitch up the head wound, and nurse him back to health. The year continues with the two pals going sailing together, on swims, oyster and clam hunts, and on outings with Clint's school chums. But true to Mr. Barlow's predictions, Buster gets into trouble. He milks cows, steals fish, and delights in mischievously frightening the neighbors. When Mr. Barlow reminds Clint that he has agreed to keep Buster only as long as he stays out of trouble, Clint reluctantly agrees for Buster's good to allow Capt. Johanson to carry the year-old seal up the coast to British Columbia and release him on some appropriate inland cove. Within a week after relocation, the seal is back with the Barlows, his homing instinct unerringly restoring him to what he obviously considers his proper home. Although Clint builds a sturdy pen, the seal soon squeezes out and returns to his former ways. Buster staves off the inevitable when he becomes a hero by rescuing from drowning Clint's friend, little Harry Dexter, but, while on an end-of-the-summer outing at Pirate Bay, where he had found Buster, Clint faces up to the truth that life on the Sound is too dangerous for the seal. Story's end finds Buster safely in an aquarium in Oregon happily entertaining schoolchildren. An essay Clint wrote about geoducks has attracted the attention of biologist Professor Willis in Seattle. He offers Clint, now high school age, a home while the youth attends school in Seattle. Clint looks forward to reading his paper to Prof. Willis's students and to studying marine biology and oceanography. The plot seems tailormade and moves as expected, characters are conventional, and conversation is unnatural. The story is unsentimental, however, and gives much clear and easy-to-understand information about seals and shoreside creatures. Books Too Good.

THE SECRET GARDEN (Burnett*, Frances Hodgson, Stokes, 1911), story set in Yorkshire in Edwardian England. Mary* Lennox, 10, a sallow, disagreeable orphan, arrives from India to live at Misselthwaite Manor, an isolated mansion on the moors owned by her uncle, Archibald Craven. Having been both spoiled and neglected, she is considered an unpleasant child by the housekeeper, Mrs. Medlock, is ignored by her unhappy uncle, and is befriended only by Martha Sowerby, the housemaid, a cheerful, naive local girl, who tells her about the family where she is one of twelve children, particularly about her nature-loving brother, Dickon*, 12. With no companions and nothing to do, Mary becomes fascinated with Martha's story of a garden locked up for ten years because it belonged to her uncle's wife, who was killed by an accident there. Mary follows the crusty old gardener, Ben Weatherstaff, who introduces her to a robin which lives in the secret garden. When the robin pecks up a rusty key and the wind blows back a curtain of ivy to reveal a door, Mary finds her way into the garden, which looks all dead in the late winter. She finds some shoots of early flowers, digs away the grass around them, and is ready with a request when her uncle finally sends for her, at the suggestion of Martha's mother: "Might I have a bit of earth?" Permission granted, she works in the garden with Dickon, who has brought her garden tools and has been let into the secret. One night, following a sound of crying she has heard before, Mary goes down an unfamiliar hallway and through a door and finds her invalid cousin, Colin*, 10, who has been pampered but kept a secret because he is not expected to live. Mary tells him about the garden, and he soon agrees to go outside, then, with the servants commanded to stay away, to have Dickon push his wheelchair into the garden. There he gradually recovers his strength by what the children call Magic, but the reader is told is fresh air and exercise. Only Ben Weatherstaff, who climbs over the wall to tend his beloved roses, knows of the activity in the garden, and he keeps the secret. Mary, under the wholesome influence of Dickon and the garden, becomes much more healthy, pleasant, and physically attractive. Dickon's mother, Susan* Sowerby, supplies them hearty food, comes to visit the garden, and eventually writes to Colin's father, who is traveling on the continent, urging him to come home. Her letter coincides with a sort of vision he has had of his wife calling him back to the garden, so he hurries home and arrives to hear voices inside the garden. The door bursts open and Colin, now healthy and self-confident, runs into his arms. The explicit theme, that nature has regenerative powers for humans, is too frequently mentioned for modern narrative technique, and assumptions about class differences may seem unfortunate to readers today, but the basic story of two unpleasant, misunderstood children saved by their common interest in growing things has a timeless appeal. Children's Classics; Choice.

SECRET OF THE ANDES (Clark*, Ann Nolan, ill. Jean Charlot, Viking, 1952), novel set in the mid-1900s among the Indians of the Peruvian mountains, which combines realism, legend, and here and there a touch of fantasy. Cusi, about twelve, the last of the royal line, has been chosen to preserve the secret store of gold and the llama herds of the ancient Incas. He has grown up in remote Hidden Valley, high in the Andes, unaware of his parentage or destiny, as herdboy to old Chuto*, his wise teacher and the present guardian of the herds. Never having had contact with outsiders, Cusi becomes curious about the family who have moved into the valley below, and Chuto decides it is time to introduce the boy to the outer world. In poetic, deceptively simple language, the novel describes the coming of a laughing minstrel to whose songs of ancient legend Cusi thrills; Cusi's first trip out of the valley with Chuto over treacherous terrain to the salt flats below, where the boy sees oxen, burros, and an hacienda and gets some idea of what the coming of the Spaniards meant for the Indians; and the arrival of Amauta, the stern, somber teacher, who instructs the boy in the ancient lore. Through all this Cusi increasingly feels the need for family love and companionship. When Chuto thinks Cusi ready to venture out by himself, the llamas are loaded with wool, and Cusi makes his way down the mountain to the market at Cuzco, stopping along the way at the ancient ruin of Ayllu. The boy thrills to the sights of the city but feels unwanted and alien in a place where his llamas, even his cherished pet, Misti*, may not enter. His trading finished, he returns joyfully to Chuto. He has seen enough of the outside world to realize that Chuto, his llamas, and his dog, Suncca, are family enough for him. He takes the sacred oath to follow in Chuto's footsteps and preserve the holy herds. The pace is slow, the plot seems contrived, Cusi changes predictably, the atmosphere is overly mystical, and the mystery of Cusi's background, while it adds some suspense, seems an unnecessary complication. The best part of this novel lies in its rythmical prose, in its descriptions of the hill Indians' way of life, in the sense it conveys of their respect for nature and pride in their ancient culture so drastically altered by the coming of the Spaniards. Choice; Newbery Winner.

THE SECRET OF THE PORCELAIN FISH (Evernden*, Margery, ill. Thomas Handforth, Random, 1947), realistic novel of adventure and suspense set in China in the city of King-te-chen during the Ming dynasty. Homeless, orphaned, young Fu, with only a jade amulet to remind him of his family, accidentally destroys porcelains belonging to renowned potter, Shen Ki, and becomes the master's apprentice to pay for them. Shen Ki treats the boy kindly, and he makes friends with Ki's lively, pretty daughter, Lotus, who shows him a special porcelain dish bearing the design of a fish, which appears only when the dish has water in it and of which the family is very proud. Fu rejoices with the family when Ki receives a commission from the emperor for porcelains. He works hard to help make them and is pleased when the master shares with him the secret of making the fish. Even so, he longs to be wealthy and to travel to far and exotic places. When Ki sets him free because he has been so hardworking and loyal, he accepts the offer of the rich and haughty porcelain merchant, Wang, with whom the Ki family is on poor terms, to sail to Ceylon on one of the merchant's ships. On board, he discovers that Wang Lin, the merchant's proud, deceitful, and often mischievous son, has stolen the procelain dish. Wang Lin imprisons Fu for many days hoping to starve him into revealing the secret of making the fish. Released by the captain when the ship catches fire, Fu flees to Nanking where a restaurant owner seizes his amulet when he cannot pay for his meal. He is befriended by a monk, who has a similar amulet. It comes out that the amulets are proof of service to the rightful heir to the Chinese throne. The monk informs Fu that the heir has entered a monastery and no longer wishes to be emperor. Fu returns to Ki's house where he is forgiven and warmly welcomed as a son of the house. Conventional characters and incidents and a limping, underdeveloped, poorly paced and motivated plot, that sometimes violates logic, are relieved by a style richly descriptive of street scenes, life on the river, and the making of pottery. The book is obviously intended to give middle and later elementary readers an idea of what life was like in ancient China. Slightly comic black and white illustrations contribute to setting but interject a note of humor that seems inappropriate. Fanfare.

SELINA (*Bright Island**), Thankful's roommate at the Academy. Selina's main object in life is to have a good time. An open, charming girl, at first she resents having to share her quarters with gauche, poorly dressed Thankful but comes to appreciate Thankful's steadiness and quick mind. After she visits Thankful's home at Thanksgiving, she helps Thankful buy appropriate clothes, and later she warns her about Robert's unreliability and opportunistic attitude.

SENATOR GRANDERSON (*The Enormous Egg**), United States Senator, a pompous, posturing blow-hard, who seeks to make political hay out of Uncle Beazley, by insisting that keeping him is a waste of taxpayers' money. He makes speeches in the Senate against Uncle Beazley and introduces a bill prohibiting dinosaurs in the United States. He is Nate's* chief adversary.

SEÑOR BILL (*The Silver Fawn**), Chico's* employer in Taxco. A typically good-hearted, somewhat naive American, he is kind to Chico and his mother. He owns the shop in which Chico rises to become an artist in silver.

SEREDY, KATE (1896-1975), born in Budapest, Hungary; artist and author and illustrator of children's books. The daughter of a well-known Hungarian teacher and storyteller, she attended the Academy of Art in Budapest for six years, receiving an art teacher's diploma. During World War I, she served for two years as a nurse in war hospitals, an experience which left her a confirmed pacifist. In 1922, she emigrated to the United States, and for years she made her living by illustrating lampshades, greeting cards, and sheet music covers. She was well known as an illustrator before she began writing books for children. She illustrated books for other writers, among them the Newbery Award winning *Caddie Woodlawn** by Carol Ryrie Brink*, as well as her own. *The Good*

*Master** (Viking, 1935), her first and most popular book, tells the humorous, episodic adventures of spoiled Cousin Kate (the author herself) with her uncle, the Good Master, and his son on their Hungarian horse ranch. It was a Newbery honor book, a Fanfare book, and is cited in *Choice* and *Children's Books Too Good to Miss*. Its more serious sequel, *The Singing Tree** (Viking, 1939), also a Newbery honor book and Fanfare book, takes the family through World War I, while the grim, didactic *The Chestry Oak** (Viking, 1948), a Fanfare book set in Hungary during World War II, conveys a strong anti-war theme. Her novels with American settings are less substantial, among them, the Fanfare book *A Tree for Peter** (Viking, 1941), the sentimental story of how a simple tramp brings joy to a small boy's life and transforms a shantytown. Her other books include *The White Stag* (Viking, 1937), a non-fiction retelling of the legend of the founding of Hungary that won the Newbery Medal, *Listening* (Viking, 1936), *The Open Gate* (Viking, 1943), *The Tenement Tree* (Viking, 1959), and *A Brand-New Uncle* (Viking, 1961), all with American settings, and *Gypsy* (Viking, 1952) and *Lazy Tinka* (Viking, 1962), both picture books. Her novels reflect love of family, respect for authority and the aged, satisfaction in hard work, perseverance, and the evil of war. Characters in the early books are more strongly drawn, her plots, though thin, generally sustain the interest, and her descriptive passages are written with an artist's eye for visual detail.

SETH UPHAM (*The Great Quest**), abrupt, proud storekeeper uncle of Joe Woods, who sells all to go on a treasure-seeking expedition promoted by Cornelius* Gleason, a con artist who was his friend in their younger days. Although the picture of respectability now, Seth obviously fears the knowledge Cornelius has that a murder for which Cornelius was blamed was really Seth's unwitting fault. As he grows aware that he is being used and will be defrauded, he alternates between being imperious and humble and, finally, in Africa, completely loses his mind, believing he is in his store in Massachusetts. In this irrational state, he walks out toward the hostile natives, singing a hymn, and is killed.

SEVEN STARS FOR CATFISH BEND (Burman*, Ben Lucien, ill. Alice Caddy, Funk, 1956), talking animal fantasy set deep in the bayou near Catfish Bend on the Mississippi River somewhere north of New Orleans at an indefinite time in the recent past. "I," a human narrator, probably the author, reports the story told him by his old acquaintance, Doc Raccoon, of the terrible year in which the animals of the Pact (who have agreed not to fight among themselves and whose code word is "Ararat") contend with hunters both human and animal. The animals, among them, J. C. Fox*, an old frog*, a rabbit*, a beaver, and a goose*, foil their enemies largely through the cleverness of Doc Raccoon, their acknowledged leader, and Judge* Black, a big blacksnake. They dispose of Old Joe, the voracious alligator, by sentencing him, after a trial *in absentia*, to swallow a jug. They tip off the sheriff to the illegal activities of a poacher and then persuade bees to sting the poacher's fearsome bloodhound. Then they learn to their dismay that the state has rented their swamp to a hunting club. So many hunters swarm in that the seven friends pack up and trek northward to safety. Along the way Judge Black is shot in the back by some boys with an air rifle, outlaw rats capture the rabbit, and a prowling panther with an inferiority complex, named Perceval, becomes friendly when Doc suggests they build up his ego by calling him Scarface. They are almost to St. Louis when they decide to stop running from their problem and return to have it out with the hunters. Back in the Bayou, they discover that the hunters have planned a big shoot with prizes for animal calling, snaring, and shooting. Old Doc mobilizes the animals to confuse the hunters with hoots and howls and to stampede a farmer's cows through the hunters' camp. The animals give the hunters a taste of their own medicine by driving them into pools and bogs where mosquitoes and leeches attack them. The hunters resolve to give up hunting for good, and the state turns the area into a game refuge. The seven animals are awarded silver stars for bravery. The use of the human narrator in the frame story, careful attention to details of plot and character, lots of humor, a chatty, matter-of-fact, playful tone, and strong local color combine to make plausible the symbolic triumph of the animals against tremendous odds and keep the story from degenerating into an ecological message. Though humanized and obviously representative of human types, and animals never lose their reality as animals and happily engage the reader's emotions. One of a series. Fanfare.

SEVENTEENTH SUMMER (Daly*, Maureen, Dodd, 1942), realistic novel of romance in a family and small town setting, which takes place in Fond du Lac, Wis., on the shores of Lake Winnebago in the mid-1900s. Pretty, protected Angie (Angeline) Morrow, 17, the third of four girls, is very close to her sisters, mother, and father, a traveling salesman. She has attended the local girls' academy and has never had a "proper date." Angie describes the summer in which she meets and falls in love with Jack Duluth, basketball star and son of the owner of the town bakery. Jack first invites her to go sailing with him on Lake Winnebago. Parties, dances, outings, and rides in his family bakery truck follow, and Angie becomes known as "Jack's girl." A brief interruption in their relationship occurs when Angie accepts a date with Tony Becker, who unknown to her is considered "fast." To her bewilderment, Jack drops her and dates Jane Rady, until a chance encounter in McKnight's Drug Store results in reconciliation. Thereafter, Angie dates only Jack, steady dating being considered proper procedure in their town, and the course of their romance runs smoothly with a middle-class, "respectable" boy-girl relationship. Jack declares his love for her, and summer's end finds him giving her his class ring and seeing her off on the train to college, while he makes plans to move to Oklahoma with his parents. Angie's final romantic reflection is that "never again would there be anything as wonderful as that seventeenth summer." Paralleling and contrasting with Angie's romance are those of her sisters. Margaret, the eldest, is engaged to Art, the "right sort" of boy, pleasant, reliable, respectful, home-oriented, and hardworking, while Lorraine, who has felt left out because she does not have a boyfriend, becomes infatuated with Martin (Marty) Keefe, a smooth-talking, flashy, university man, who "drinks Scotch and things" and who eventually dumps her. Most of the book presents Angie's adolescent, romantically idealized reactions to people and situations and "girl talk" about dresses and boys. Angie often expresses herself in figures drawn from the natural world. Characters are mostly types, but Angie herself is a sympathetic figure who changes believably during the summer, becoming less shy and more sure of herself socially. Both she and Jack reflect middle-class values of the period, though Jack, who appears to be content to continue working in a bakery, is perhaps not quite the "proper match" for an intelligent girl of Angie's social level. The book is true to the spirit of adolescence but projects an air of innocence and wholesomeness that dates it when compared to the more frank and earthy romances of the late twentieth century. Lewis Carroll.

SHADOW ACROSS THE CAMPUS (Sattley*, Helen R., Dodd, 1957), realistic novel for girls, a school story, set at an indeterminate time but perhaps in the 1930s or 1940s. When they arrive at Northwestern University in Evanston, Ill., high school chums Marjorie Howard, Kate Stewart, and Cecilia (Cele) Engle confidently look forward to pledging Zeta Nu social sorority, for them the highlight of their freshman year. When Cecilia fails to receive a bid from the Zetas because she is Jewish, Kate protests by refusing her pin. Kate soon loses herself in writing for the school paper and in activities with her roommate, athlete Joan* Lockhardt, who feels she cannot afford to join a sorority, while sociology subsumes much of serious Cele's time. Margie, however, decides to join the Zetas because she very much wishes to be a part of the group and because she believes she can best attack the problem of religious intolerance from within the system. She tries hard to live up to the expectations of her future sisters, enjoys the support she receives from them, in particular, from pledge mother, junior Stan* Fredericks, and is to her delight elected freshman president. Although she grows increasingly involved in house affairs, she continues to reach out to her dorm friends, the author's way of keeping the reader apprised of how the "other half" lives. Margie and pledge sister Milly* Parks are assigned the task of writing a history of the Zetas. This project not only results in their learning about the history of their dormitory, Willard* Hall (an actual building), but also leads ironically to the Zetas admitting Jews to membership. After Hell Week (a vividly described series of episodes) in the spring, Marjorie realizes that she endured the hazing primarily for herself, and, conscience-stricken, strengthens her resolve to change Zeta policy. On the upper floor of Willard, she finds old Zeta records that describe the furor that resulted when an early twentieth century member, Julia Maude Crowder*, championed social causes. Margie consults her, and the patrician old woman visits the campus. She encourages Margie to continue her fight and eventually persuades National to change its policy. Margie organizes the freshman pledges to petition the local Zetas to admit Jews. After stormy sessions, the Zetas do so and elect Cele to membership. With encouragement from Miss Crowder, who decries this ''shadow'' of prejudice across the campus, Cele accepts. Kate and Joan, who is offered but refuses a Zeta scholarship, decline membership since they have developed so many interests on campus that they see no advantage to membership. At the end of the year, Margie and Joan are elected to the Sophomore Squad. Don* Becker, now Margie's steady, who has encouraged her to fight for her convictions, declares he loves her. Marjorie is an interesting character, and most of the leading figures are well drawn, but they all obviously represent campus types. The book is heavy with message; one hears the author's voice in speeches about the advantages, disadvantages, and possible future of the Greek system and about the history of the Jews, but the book never really comes to grips with the problem. Studying is occasionally alluded to, ''girl talk'' abounds, and the emphasis focuses on social activities. The reader receives clear views of what campus social life was like during that period, particularly for those girls from upper middle-class families. Looked at from a late twentieth-century standpoint, the romantic aspects seem amazingly innocent. Child Study.

SHADRACH (DeJong*†, Meindert, ill. Maurice Sendak, Harper, 1953), very simple, warm story of a little boy's first pet, set in a village of the Netherlands, presumably in the first part of the twentieth century. Having been very ill, Davie, 6, is sent not to school but to Grandma's house to rest each afternoon. Grandpa has promised to buy him a little, black rabbit when Maartens, the china peddler, comes next Saturday. While Grandma dozes, Davie slips out of bed one day to sit in the barn and admire the hutch Father has built and another day to fill three bags of clover at the edge of the dangerous canal. His feelings for his older brother, Rem, vacillate from gratitude, when Rem lies about how he got his feet wet, to fury when Rem breaks the hutch and laughs at his gathering clover so far ahead that it will spoil. When Saturday comes, Davie follows Maartens's wagon in the rain to make sure the peddler has the rabbit. At first the pet, whom Davie has named Shadrach, is everything he has hoped for, but when the rabbit, despite his care, stays skinny, he worries, and when it squeezes out between the bars of the hutch and disappears, he spends hours searching the barn. Seeing a dark object behind a post, he creeps up and grabs it, to find that he has not Shadrach but a barn rat which, in his terror, he cannot turn loose. After he has been comforted and put to bed, he overhears the family planning that Father will ride his bicycle through the rain to get a new rabbit to replace Shadrach. Unable to explain that he doesn't want a different rabbit, Davie creeps out to search the barn once more and finds Shadrach eating oats in Grandfather's ''secret'' room, an old one-room school built into the barn. When Father returns empty-handed, Davie has Shadrach back in the hutch. Very little happens in the story, yet it captures and keeps the attention by its point of view, which is consistently and sensitively that of a young child, so that events like Grandma's helping in burying the spoiled clover in the compost pile and Davie's worry over whether it is wicked to think of Shadrach as ''Fairest of ten thousand to my soul'' assume major importance. The adults are all warm-hearted, and their approval floods Davie with joy but their misunderstanding fills him with despair. Even Rem, a rough-and-tumble boy, is well characterized. Choice; Newbery Honor.

SHANNON, MONICA (-1965), born in Ontario, Canada; librarian, author. She received her B.L.S. degree from a school in California and served in the Los Angeles Public Library from 1916 to 1925. She spent her childhood partially on a ranch in the Bitterroot Valley of Montana, where the immigrant Bulgarian ranch workers told her stories of their homeland, material she incorporated into her best-known book, *Dobry** (Viking, 1934), a Newbery Medal winner. Many of the incidents in the book are from the life of the illustrator, Atanas Katchamakoff. Her other four books for children include one of verse, two of artistic fairy tales, and one other novel, *Tawnymore* (Doubleday, 1931), a pirate story of a half-breed boy.

SHERBURNE, ZOA (MORIN) (1912-), born in Seattle, Wash.; author of contemporary problem novels for adolescents. She attended schools in Seattle and worked at various jobs before marrying Herbert Sherburne, settling in Seattle, and raising eight children. She began writing while her family was still small and first wrote stories for magazines. Bryna Ivens of *Seventeen* magazine urged her to write a novel, and the result was *Almost April* (Morrow, 1956), about a girl who goes to live with her father and his new wife after her divorced mother dies. This book launched a twenty-year career that has seen her publish a dozen novels about youth in family situations exploring such concerns as alcoholism, divorce, death of a parent, mental illness, and drug addiction. She has also been a prolific publisher of short stories and verses for magazines. She received the Child Study Award in 1959 for *Jennifer** (Morrow, 1959), a message novel about a girl whose mother has alcoholism. Her recent books also with girl protagonists include *Too Bad about the Haines Girl* (Morrow, 1967), about premarital pregnancy, *The Girl Who Knew Tomorrow* (Morrow, 1970), about extra-sensory perception, *Leslie* (Morrow, 1972), about drugs, and *Why Have the Birds Stopped Singing?* (Morrow, 1974), about epilepsy.

SHERIFF OF CENTERBURG (*Homer Price**; *Centerburg Tales**), Homer Price's friend. He spends a lot of time playing checkers and talking politics with his friends and frequents Uncle* Ulysses' lunchroom and the barbershop. He gets his words mixed up when he gets excited. He competes with Homer's Uncle Telemachus in a contest to determine who has the biggest ball of string in Centerburg, the reward to be Miss* Terwilliger's hand in marriage, and loses.

THE SHERWOOD RING (Pope*†, Elizabeth Marie, ill. Evaline Ness, Houghton, 1958), romantic fantasy set in New York state in the mid-twentieth century but with characters who emerge from the American Revolutionary period. Peggy Grahame, 17, at her father's death goes from Scotland to her family's ancestral home, Rest-and-be-thankful, now owned by her uncle, Enos Grahame, a fanatic for family history and tradition. Arriving on foot, she encounters a lovely girl in a red cape riding a black horse, who directs her to a young man repairing a car just up the road. This proves to be Pat Thorne, a graduate history student from England, who gives her a lift but is inexplicably and rudely commanded to leave by Uncle Enos. In a portrait in the house, Peggy recognizes the young woman as Barbara Grahame, sixteen in 1773, and soon meets her brother Dick (Richard Grahame II), a dashing young officer of Washington's army, who starts telling her the story of his efforts to capture a British officer, Peaceable Drummond Sherwood, who is organizing guerilla action in Orange County, N.Y. In subsequent scenes, Peggy meets Eleanor Shipley, a neighbor of the early Grahames, a lively and independent girl who eventually marries Dick, and Sherwood himself, who falls in love with Barbara. Through what these "ghosts" tell her, we follow the romantic tale of captures and escapes during the Revolution. At the same time, Peggy is unraveling the mysteries of why Uncle Enos forbids her to see Pat and what happened to the documents from the Revolutionary period which he once found in his Aunt Mildred's house in England and of which she now denies any knowledge. Predictably, it turns out that they are the journals and letters of Peaceable Sherwood, which the aunt has sold to Uncle Enos (though they really belong to Pat, the present day Earl of Thorne, whose real name turns out to be Peaceable Sherwood). The lively plot skips from past to present with alacrity, but the characters are poorly developed, particularly the three girls, who are scarcely distinguishable except that the twentieth century Peggy is less competent than her predecessors. Placing a seventeen-year-old in a sheltered position with neither a job nor school dates the story, as does the resolution, her engagement to Pat. The eighteenth-century characters are more interesting but seem more like twentieth-century people in costume than authentic figures of a historical period. Fanfare.

SHORA (*The Wheel on the School**), fishing village in the Netherlands, in which the school children decide to attract storks by making a nesting place. In the childhood of the oldest village woman, Shora had trees and storks, but a great storm ruined the trees and the position of the village on the sea, subject to salt spray in every storm, has kept trees from growing again.

SHUTTERED WINDOWS (Means*, Florence Crannell, Houghton, 1938), realistic novel of a black girl from Minneapolis who goes in the 1930s to live in the sea islands of South Carolina, where her only living relative, her great-grandmother, lives. After her mother's death, bright, attractive, musically talented high school senior Harriet Freeman has great curiosity about her ancestor, great-great-great-grandfather, Black* Moses, a slave at Taliaferro Plantation, and Lucy Mary Freeman, her great-grandmother, still living on Gentlemen's

Island, where freed slaves settled after the Civil War. Planning to visit her great-grandmother and possibly enroll in Landers School for girls at nearby Bosquet, Harriet is taken by her foster parents, the Rev. and Mrs. Trindle, to South Carolina. Her first view of the school shocks Harriet. Its buildings seem dilapidated, its rules antiquated, its students ignorant and crude. Granny, though she lives in a shack and speaks a dialect strange to Harriet, is another story. She looks like an Ethiopian princess, has great dignity and commands the respect of her neighbors. Living with Granny is the ''drift,'' Lily, a child she has taken in. Living in the nearest house is Richard Corwin, a boy Harriet's age, who helps Granny out, goes to school on a nearby island, and aspires to become an agricultural teacher to help his people make a better living from their meager farms. Feeling at first that she must return to Minnesota where she can get good musical training and there are no Jim Crow laws, Harriet changes her mind when she learns that Granny's farm has been bought for taxes by a white northerner, some years before, and decides to stay where she can investigate and perhaps help. Her first experiences at Landers are negative. The only girl with whom she has much in common is a faculty member's daughter, Jamaican-born Johnnie La Rocque. Her roommate, Mossie Clapp, is a frightened child from a primitive, backwoods community unreached by even a road. Despite a number of blunders, Harriet gradually is accepted by the other girls, even Willie Lou, the militant activist, and is invited to play on the basketball team and voted vice-president. After a happy Christmas break with Granny, she decides on the advice of Mrs. Trindle, to take her annuity money and transfer to a school in Charleston. Before semester's end, she is taken to visit country schools, where conditions appall her, and to Taliaferro Plantation, where she finds the white descendants of the slaveholders living in decayed splendor without education, energy, or adequate nourishment. As she is preparing for exams, Richard comes to fetch her to care for Granny, who is very ill with flu, as also is Lily. Harriet nurses them both. When she realizes that Granny is frantically worried about losing her home and that the white owner, having lost his money in the Depression, has not paid the taxes, she sends Richard to buy it back with her annuity, saving it from being sold to a market gardener. Having persuaded Richard to stay with his dream rather than to join a popular music group, she decides to return to Landers, then become a teacher in the islands. Although set long before the civil rights movement, the story of the cultural shock a middle-class northern black encounters when she is placed in an isolated southern black area is probably still valid. The attitudes expressed at the school are dated, particularly the disapproval of Willie Lou's militancy, as are references to clothes and forms of address (''Miss Harriet''), but the appreciation of the natural area is strong, and the characterizations are skilled. Fanfare.

SIBBY BOTHERBOX (*Sibby Botherbox**), Hannah Poole's imaginary playmate. A little younger than Hannah, who is nine, Sibby is a cheeky, lively, teasing child, who sometimes annoys Hannah with her chatting and occasionally proposes mischief, but whose energy and daring complement Hannah's own tendency to be retiring. Sibby is the alter ego created by Hannah's imagination to satisfy her need for companionship. Activities with Uncle* Willie Axelrod lessen Hannah's need for Sibby, and when Celia moves in next door, Hannah bids Sibby goodbye.

SIBBY BOTHERBOX (Hunt*, Mabel Leigh, ill. Marjory Collison, Lippincott, 1945), realistic episodic novel of family life set in the small town of Gladbrook, probably in New England, one summer while Theodore Roosevelt is president. The summer in which she is nine brings adventures and a new outlook on life for Hannah Poole, who lives with her respected dentist father, her solicitous and loving mother, and Mattibelle, the doting black housekeeper. Hannah considers Pertwood* App, 12, the boy next door and the only other child in the neighborhood, a rowdy showoff, and she yearns for a girl her own age to play with. She finds companionship in an invented friend, Sibby* Botherbox, a small alter ego who complements Hannah's own, somewhat shy, personality and who appears whenever Hannah needs someone to talk to. Although Hannah's mother disapproves of Sibby and urges Hannah to put Sibby out of her mind, visiting Uncle* Willie Axelrod, a Harvard Professor of English, accepts Sibby as a normal part of childhood. He recognizes in her the epitomy of the imaginative process and even incorporates her into his book of essays on the English Romantics. As the summer passes and Hannah and Uncle Willie have fun together, Hannah finds less and less time for Sibby. When the Apps move away, the Pooles buy their house. Mother takes her time renting it, hoping that a family with a girl Hannah's age will move in. To everyone's delight, the new school principal rents it. He has a daughter, Celia, who is lame, in need of a playmate, and just Hannah's age. With Celia's friendship, Hannah is able to relinquish Sibby and that part of her childhood and sentimentally bids Sibby farewell among the daisies on Tumbledown Hill. Although predictable, peopled with conventional characters, and dated in tone and concept, this pleasant story projects a tranquil, occasionally humorous, picture of warm family life in a close-knit community. All problems are small and easily solved, adults are presented positively, and visits from uncles and ministers, church functions like Children's Day, birthday parties, and trips to ice cream parlors are great events. Fanfare.

SID SAWYER (*The Adventures of Tom Sawyer**; *The Adventures of Huckleberry Finn**), Tom's tattle-tale, younger half brother, a well-behaved, quiet boy who learns his Bible lessons and keeps his clothes clean. It is Sid who points out to Aunt Polly that Tom's shirt collar is sewn with black rather than white thread, a sure sign that Tom has played hookey and gone swimming. Although Sid serves as a foil for Tom's character, he does not play a prominent part in the novel. In *The Adventures of Huckleberry Finn* he is referred to when Tom takes his name while visiting his Aunt Sally Phelps, since Huck* has already claimed to be Tom, but Sid does not actually appear in the book.

SIGNOR AND SIGNORA DITTO (*Nino**), parents of the mischievous, gluttonous Julio*, near neighbors and good friends of Nino's* family. Signor Ditto is very proud of the wine he makes. At the fair, he tries to wrestle a bear and fails. Signora Ditto is fat and middle-aged, proper, well mannered, and very polite. Neither is quite able to cope with Julio's whims and willfulness.

SILAS AGEE (*The Perilous Road**), middle-aged friend of Chris* Brabson, who hunts with him and has helped him cure deer skins and cut out a leather shirt. Although the adults consider Silas a lightheaded wastrel, Chris believes Silas's boast that he is a spy for the Confederate Army and his explanation that he helped burn the Brabson's shed in order to keep the angry neighbors from doing worse damage.

THE SILVER FAWN (Weil*, Ann, ill. E. Leon, Bobbs, 1939), realistic problem novel of family and town life set in the mid-1900s in the central part of Mexico. Chico*, 13, lives with his widowed mother, María* Rosalia, in a hut in Taxco. He works as guide and errand boy for American tourists who visit the popular silver center. Chico's greatest wish is to become an artist in silver like his father. When Señor* Bill, an American writer, hires Chico as houseboy and María as cook, the little family's fortune changes dramatically for the better and excitement enters Chico's life. Señor Bill takes Chico with him on a business trip to Mexico City. While the two are admiring Aztec art in the National Museum, Chico confides his ambition to Bill, who gets the idea of opening a small silver shop where reproductions of ancient Aztec jewelry can be sold. For several days he sketches the ancient designs, and once back in Taxco, he and Chico fix up a rickety, old store and hire silversmiths. The little shop soon becomes a popular tourist stop and does very well financially. To diversify for a more stable income Bill hires Indian weavers whose serapes soon are much in demand among Mexicans as well as tourists. During this time, Chico practices hard with silver, becoming good enough to serve as assistant to their chief artisan and designer, Alfonso, the leading silversmith in Taxco. A famous Mexican artist, Donna Gamanio, hears about their fine work and orders four pitchers. Alfonso finishes three of them with splendid success but burns his hand before completing the fourth one. Chico works on it secretly at night, decorating it with an exquisite fawn design, drawn from the appearance and behavior of his pet deer. Donna Gamanio is very pleased with the piece, which is much admired in Mexico City, and Bill makes Chico, now sixteen, a designer. The other workers decide to call the shop "The Silver Fawn" in honor of Chico's talent and rise to fame. This pleasant, predictable success story seems designed to promote the virtue of hard work and introduce the reader to different facets of Mexican life and culture during the early to mid-twentieth century from the standpoint of a youth with whom children can identify. Chico changes from a scatterbrained youngster whose mother upbraids him for laziness to a responsible young man, respected in his chosen profession. The few other characters are types. Language and style are undemanding, straightforward, and rather pedestrian. The activities and travels of Bill and Chico give readers views of life in a Mexican home, in a silver shop, about Taxco, in the big city, in busy marketplaces, on the road, and even among the Indians who live in the mountains. The plot is interesting, but many things that happen seem unlikely or highly coincidental or contrived for the amusement or edification of young readers. Fanfare.

THE SILVER PENCIL (Dalgliesh*, Alice, ill. Katherine Milhous, Scribner's, 1944), largely autobiographical novel of an Edwardian girl's growing up and finding her way into the profession of teaching and writing. The book starts on the tropical island of Trinidad, where Janet Laidlaw at nine lives with her English mother, who enjoys being an invalid, her Scottish father, a houseful of native servants, and, eventually, her older brother, Lawrence, 19, whom she has never met because he had first been away at school and then had run off to sea. When Janet's father dies suddenly, Mrs. Laidlaw pulls herself together and decides energetically that she should take her daughter to England to be educated. There Janet meets Scottish cousins, makes a close friend of another colonial girl, Moira Somerville, from India, attends Wimbledon Hill School, watches the coronation procession of George V, and generally fits into English life. Always interested in writing and early encouraged by her father, who gave her a silver pencil, she enters stories in a contest run by the magazine *Throne and Country*, and wins three times until disqualified by becoming sixteen, and then collaborates with Moira to win another under her name. Looking forward to winning a scholarship to Girton, the girls' college at Cambridge, she is shocked to learn that for reasons of both finances and her mother's health, they must return to Trinidad. Although she is bored and feels useless, she finds Lawrence a kindred spirit and through him meets Mary Shoreham, a Canadian, who encourages her to go into kindergarten teaching. She attends Clark Training School in Brooklyn, which teaches the rigid system of Friedrich Froebel, and lives at the home of family friends, the Monroes. There, although warned by his brother Tom, she falls in love with handsome Stephen Monroe, who predictably encourages her, then drops her when she visits a school friend, sensible Helen Chapman, at vacation time. In her experience with children, she finds she can charm them by storytelling but is insecure in discipline. Her first job in the Normal School demonstration kindergarten at Geneseo is not entirely successful because she is unprepared for the freer system, but she makes two good friends, Martha Dunn, a librarian, and a young physics teacher from the high school, Hank, who starts her telling stories at the settlement house. Deciding she needs more training, she enrolls at Columbia Teachers' College, where Helen is a student. The first World War ends, but Janet finds herself teaching in Philadelphia and very ill with arthritis. During her months in the hospital, she rediscovers the silver pencil and when she goes to Nova Scotia to recuperate, she starts to write stories of the village, which are eventually published as her first book. Janet returns to Columbia, where Hank is now a student, resists his attempts to propose to her, meets Stephen at graduation and resists his invitation to become reinvolved with him, teaches for a summer at Valley City, N.Dak., returns to New York where she finds success in teaching, returns to Nova Scotia where she buys and fixes up a beach cottage and meets Perry Arnold, from Cornwall, who helps her forget Stephen and encourages her to become an American citizen. The book is crammed with events and characters, few of them developed fully, and while it has many interesting anecdotes, particularly about teaching, the style and structure are more suited to memoir or autobiography than to fiction. Newbery Honor.

SIMON, CHARLIE MAY (CHARLIE MAY HOGUE FLETCHER) (1897-), born in Monticello, Ark.; author of many regional stories and biographies for young people. She attended Memphis State University, the Chicago Art Institute, and Le Grande Chaumiere, Paris, and married the poet, John Gould Fletcher. Among her biographies are those of Albert Schweitzer, Andrew Carnegie, Dag Hammarskjold, and Martin Buber. Typical of her earlier regional stories is *Lost Corner** (Dutton, 1935), a story set in the southern mountains where she grew up, and *Teeny Gay** (Dutton, 1936), about people who live on the river in the Arkansas Ozarks in the 1930s.

SIMON HARDING (*Call of the Mountain**), nearby farmer whom Nathan assists when high waters threaten his house. He helps Nathan burn off excess timber and get the oaks down the mountain and to the sawmill. He represents the spirit of Vermont neighborliness.

SIMON PERKINS (*By Secret Railway**), Mississippi-born abolitionist who helps Jim escape after he has lost his freedom papers, been stolen, and been sold to a Missouri tobacco farmer. Having become aware of the cruelty of slavery when his father sold his boyhood slave companion, Perkins has dedicated his life to helping blacks escape and to getting them in touch with Underground Railway stations. A man of many disguises, he most often travels as a minister or a peddler, and he carries with him a supply of compasses and clothes to help runaways.

SINGER, CAROLINE (1888-), born in Colfax, Wash.; journalist, specialist on Africa and the Middle East. She attended Mills College preparatory school and worked as reporter and feature writer for the San Francisco newspapers, the *Bulletin*, *Daily News*, *Examiner*, and *Call*. During World War I she was in government press and publicity work in Washington, D.C., and in Paris, France. In 1921 she married Cyrus Baldridge*, an illustrator who had been a war correspondent; he collaborated with her on *Ali Lives in Iran** (Holiday, 1937), and *Boomba Lives in Africa* (Holiday, 1935). For children she published a number of other books and for adults many magazine articles and books, including *White Africans and Black* (Norton, 1929) and *Half the World Is Isfahan* (Oxford, 1936). She and her husband led a most adventurous, globe-trotting life, being guests of the Ethiopian emperor, three times under attack when cities in China in which they were living changed hands in wars, stranded in the Syrian desert when their guide abandoned them, and having many other exciting experiences in their travels.

THE SINGING BOONES (White*, Dale, ill. Dorothy Bayley Morse, Viking, 1957), historical novel that sees an Independence, Mo., farm family travel west in 1852 to seek their fortunes in the California gold fields, told mostly from the point of view of sixteen-year-old Ellen, the eldest child. After spending a year carefully building and outfitting their covered wagon, the entire Boone family, mother, Molly, father, Aram, and eight children, their spirits high, join Captain Jack's Blue Elephant Company of wagons. The author describes in some detail the rigorous, exhausting, and often debilitating passage on the Overland Trail over rivers, through deserts, and up and down treacherous passes. Since the Boones have prepared so diligently, they have far fewer problems maintaining a supply of food and clothing, caring for their animals, and meeting their problems generally than most of their fellow travelers. Their greatest difficulty arises from the frail health of the parents, and for much of the journey Ellen and Matt, 15, must assume the responsibility for the family's well-being. They keep things going and care for their ill parents, while Luke, 10, looks after the oxen, Mark, 12, hunts, and Mary, Mark's twin, helps Ellen with housework and meals. Cooperation and spirits are high throughout the train, and the travelers quickly provide moral and physical support to one another. Good times include chats around fires in the evening, lively square dances, songs provided by the Boone family chorus, side trips to visit landmarks along the Trail, a wedding, and the christening of the Boones' youngest child. Additional unity in the narrative arises from the growing romance between Ellen and Jed* Green, the young scout, a relationship that culminates in their betrothal at the end of the trip. Once in the gold fields, Aram, increasingly despondent over his lack of success, moves the family from camp to camp seeking a claim, while Molly and the children make a meager living by baking for the miners. Finally, the eldest five children, fearful for their father's health, leave their parents and younger brothers in Grass Valley and try for a claim on their own. When luck eludes them and their food runs out, they get the idea of singing for money. The entertainment-starved prospectors eagerly compensate them for the pleasure of their music, and they return to the family with a substantial supply of gold. Aram immediately capitalizes on their growing reputation as singers to organize the whole family into a traveling road show which performs throughout the winter so successfully that they earn enough money for the family to buy land, build a house, and settle down. Though the Boones are a bit too cooperative and loving and their wholesomeness sometimes cloys, they are a likeable and attractive family. The conflict for Ellen and Matt between responsibility to their family and their desire to pursue their own lives, Ellen with Jed and Matt with the study of law, seems quite reasonable. The plot moves evenly and plausibly, and family members are well individualized, but

Jed is too much a paragon of all manly virtues, the perfect young man for a nice young girl. The picture of the Overland Trail is superficial but does serve as an introduction to what the trip must have cost the gold seekers in material, human, and animal resources and how disillusioned many of them must have been upon their arrival. (The Van* Ruyksdaels) Fanfare.

THE SINGING TREE (Seredy*, Kate, ill. author, Viking, 1939), realistic novel of family life which takes the Nagy family of *The Good Master** through World War I and in which historical events shape the story. Jancsi and Kate, now thirteen, enjoy life on their Hungarian sheep and horse ranch. Kate is proud of her chickens, and Jancsi is pleased when Márton gives him his own small herd of horses. During the wedding of their neighbors, Mari Vidor and Peter Hódi, the news arrives that Francis Ferdinand, heir to the throne of Austria-Hungary, has been assassinated. His murder plunges Hungary into the conflict that soon engulfs the world. At first the war means little to the children, involved as they are in daily chores, animals, and seasonal activities, as well as in helping young Lily* Kormos, spoiled and willful daughter of the local judge, adjust to living on the ranch and develop a better attitude toward life. Before long, they see how war affects lives as the shepherds, herdsmen, villagers, and ranchers of military age are gradually called up into the army. Among them is Kate's father, Sándor, who is soon taken prisoner by the Russians, and Peter, the recent bridegroom. Later, Peter deserts because he yearns for his home and new wife, and the children help to hide him until he returns to his unit. In mid-1915, Márton is called up, leaving young Jancsi to run the ranch with the help of wise, old Moses Mandelbaum, the beloved Jewish storekeeper in the village. Because he needs workers, Jancsi applies for and receives six Russian prisoners of war. Peasants and workingmen, they soon fit in and become family favorites, especially burly, bearish, lighthearted Grigori, to whom eventually Kate even entrusts her precious chickens. Later Jancsi's grandparents, Mari Vidor and her new baby, and six half-starved German children also find a haven on the ranch. When Márton's letters cease, the family worries about him, but a miracle brings him home. The children come upon him in a military hospital, a victim of amnesia. Seeing them restores his memory. The end of the war brings home many of their friends, the sad realization that the conflict has been costly in lives, among them old Uncle Moses's son, and the hope that in the future nations will be able to solve their problems without force and live together as brothers. The highly episodic story is more unified than its predecessor, similarly combines humor, action, and much conversation, is constructed upon the same themes and gives clear views of Hungarian village and ranch life during the war. It is more sentimental and contrived, and its anti-war message is so obvious that the book seems very didactic. Lily is a duplication of Kate herself but is not as well developed, and the character Moses Mandelbaum is clearly intended to combat anti-Semitism. Choice; Fanfare; Newbery Honor.

SINGMASTER, ELSIE (1879–1958), born in Schuylkill Haven, Pa.; author of historical novels. She grew up in Brooklyn, N.Y., Allentown, Pa., and Gettysburg, Pa., where a number of her novels are set, including *Swords of Steel** (Houghton, 1933), a Newbery honor book, about the Civil War. She attended normal school, then Cornell, then Radcliffe College. Among her other books is *Rifles for Washington** (Houghton, 1938), a story of the Pennsylvania men who fought in the Revolutionary War.

SKIPPACK SCHOOL (De Angeli*, Marguerite, ill. author, Doubleday, 1939), highly illustrated historical novel for younger children set in 1750 near Germantown, Pa. The family of Eli Shrawder, probably eight to ten, Mennonites from Germany, arrive in America and settle on Skippack Creek on land purchased from Uncle Jacob in German Town. Neighbors gather to help them erect a house, and Eli helps his father clear the land around the cabin and starts to build a carved bench for his mother, but his parents insist that he attend school. Although he finds the master, Christopher Dock, firm and kindly, Eli is frequently in trouble for letting his attention wander and one day breaks one of the glass windows with a ball, damage his father must pay for by selling Eli's curved bench. One day when he returns to school for a forgotten lunch basket, he hears Dock praying for him and resolves to reform. As a reward for his improvement, he is allowed to read the Scriptures the next morning, but his mother, who knows something of medicine, is called out to help an ailing neighbor while his father is away, so Eli must miss school to care for his four-year-old sister, Sibilla. He manages to milk the cow and do the other chores, and even feeds an Indian, White Eagle, who stops and asks for food. Later Dock takes him to German Town, where he teaches three days a week, and Eli visits the school there as well as a paper mill and a printing shop, sees Indians feasting in the Market Square, and stays with his father's cousins, Hannah and Jacob. He determines to use the paper given to him to make a little book relating his experiences and carves a printing block to make a picture for the cover, decorated with colored ink. He reads it to the school, then gives the book to Dock. While the story itself is not compelling, the book is pleasant in a mild way and contains a great deal of information, both in text and pictures, about life in the area in the mid-eighteenth century. The dialogue is in the speech patterns of the Pennsylvania Dutch. Fanfare.

SKOOKUM AND SANDY (Bennett*, Richard, ill. author, Doubleday, 1935), realistic short story set in the mid-1900s in an Indian village in the Pacific Northwest. Skookum, which means "very big," is a tiny, mischievous goat. The old Indian to whom he belongs gives him to a young white boy, Sandy McNab, because he eats so much. Sandy's parents are displeased at having Skookum join the family, and in particular Grandma McNab warns the family not to trust the animal. Skookum has been bored living with the Indian, and the next day his active curiosity gets him into trouble. After he explores the McNab farmyard, he leaps over the enclosing stone wall into the McNab yard. When the family returns from market, they find their yard and garden in a shambles. Grandma insists that Sandy return the goat the very next day. Sandy sets out to pick berries near the logging camp in the hills, fully intending to return Skookum to his former master on the way. But Skookum so antagonizes the Indians they meet, by, among other misdeeds, stealing an Indian woman's basket, that Sandy decides he had better keep Skookum. In the woods, Skookum breaks his tether, runs off, and encounters a bear cub and its mother. Terrified he flees full tilt back to Sandy. He runs so fast he bumps into the boy, knocking him over and out of the way of a falling tree and saving the boy's life. Skookum is hailed as a hero and earns a permanent place in the McNab establishment. This is an action-filled, entertaining story for younger readers. Skookum's antics are amusing, and one never fears that things will not turn out all right for the naughty little goat. There is a short fantasy sequence in which Skookum converses with the other animals. The author also reports Skookum's thoughts and motives. The Indians are stereotypes. Numerous, realistic black and white line drawings add to setting and point up incidents. Fanfare.

SLIM MAN (*The Ordeal of the Young Hunter**), Jadih's* father, who keeps to the old ways of the Navajo, but who believes that for survival the Navajo must adapt to changing circumstances. Unless the family can get money to buy more sheep and pay their bills, he will have to leave home and take a job in the beetfields of Idaho. He encourages Jadih to perform for the tourists.

SLIPPER-ON-THE-WATER (*The Gammage Cup**), the Minnipin village from which Muggles* and four others are outlawed. It received its name, according to Minnipin legend, when the Minnipins first encountered their valley, the Land-Between-the-Mountains. Their leader, Gammage, lost his left slipper in the water, and it floated three days and three nights in the same spot. Ten Minnipins decided to found a village there and name it for the observed phenomenon. Over the years the village grew to some size. The people decided to erect a museum for the slipper. There it is displayed on a pedestal, in the company of other articles of historical importance to the Minnipins. Muggles is curator of the museum.

SLOBODKIN, LOUIS (1903–1975), born in Albany, N.Y.; sculptor, illustrator, author. He attended the Beaux Arts Institute of Design in New York, worked as assistant in sculpture studios in the United States and France, taught sculpture at the Master Institute of United Arts, Roersch Museum, New York, and at the Art League, and was head of the sculpture division of the New York City Art Project. Statues by him are in buildings in New York, Washington, D.C., Johnstown, Pa., and North Adams, Mass. His first venture into books for children was as illustrator for the Moffat books by Eleanor Estes*†. His illustrations for James Thurber's* *Many Moons* (Harcourt, 1943), won the Caldecott Medal.

Eventually, he started writing his own books and produced more than forty, all self-illustrated, seven of them verse and many of them picture books. Among his longer stories are a number in a humorous science fiction series for younger readers, the first being *The Space Ship Under the Apple Tree** (Macmillan, 1952).

SMALL DEN (*Young Fu of the Upper Yangtze**), unfriendly apprentice who makes Young Fu's life at the coppersmith shop miserable on his arrival and later shows his jealousy in a variety of ways. Clever with the abacus, Den is not an imaginative designer, and when he goes to work for Wu, a rival coppersmith, he makes a deal with the accountant to "borrow" a vase and tray so that he might copy the designs and pass them off as his own.

SMITH, AGNES (1906–), born in Clarksburg, W.Va. She married Richard Parrish, editor of the *West Virginian*, published in Fairmont, and has lived on a farm near Fairmont. Her fantasy, *An Edge of the Forest** (Viking, 1959) is a strange story of a friendship between a leopard and a lamb, described by critics as subtle and poetic. She also wrote *The Bluegreen Tree* (Westwind, 1977).

SMOKY, THE COWHORSE (James*, Will, ill. author, Scribner's, 1926), realistic horse story set in the American West of the early twentieth century. Told in colloquial cowhand diction, the story chronicles the birth, early life on the range, eventual rounding up, and training of an intelligent horse. Clint, a cowboy specializing in breaking new mounts, spots him and takes special pains to train him, and Smoky becomes a one-man horse, the envy of every other cowboy and even the boss, who tries to fire Clint to get possession of the pony but can't ride him. Smoky becomes a top-grade working horse but one winter is stolen with a group of other horses by a sadistic half-breed Mexican who beats him until Smoky has an opportunity to kill his tormentor. Found running wild with an empty saddle, Smoky is captured for a rodeo horse, renamed The Cougar, and becomes famous for his killer instincts. Eventually wearing down, he loses his value to the rodeo and is sold to a riding stable, where he is over ridden, until he is resold for chicken feed. Before he is shot, however, he is traded to a brutal drayman, and there Clint sees him being abused, saves him, and realizes it is Smoky. Well fed and turned out on the range of the small ranch Clint has acquired on Smoky's home range, the horse begins to recover his health and his spirit. Although the plot is virtually a retelling of Black Beauty, and slow moving at that, the book has great appeal for its fine authentic detail of life on a working ranch and for its conversational tone: "And like I was saying with Smoky, he remembered how that rope had upset him that first day he was picketed to that log outside the corral, and he wasn't hankering to be 'busted' that way again. That little horse had brains." Although it tells of a strong attachment between a man and horse, it avoids sentimentality and doesn't ascribe human feelings to an animal. It may be considered offensive to some because of its references to the thief as a dark-skinned breed, but it is careful to distinguish that this particular man has inherited the worst of both sides of his ancestry. Newbery Winner.

SNEDEKER, CAROLINE DALE (PARKE) (1871–1956), born in New Harmony, Ind.; author noted in children's literature for her historical novels for older children and young adults. She was the great-granddaughter of Robert Owen, the Welsh social reformer who brought together scientists and educators in the effort to found a ''village of cooperation'' in New Harmony in 1825. She grew up in nearby Mt. Vernon and early developed a keen interest in history, literature, and classical music. She studied piano and composition at the College of Music in Cincinnati, and after the death of their father, she and her three sisters gave concerts to support the family. She was also an instructor of music before her marriage to a clergyman, who was Dean of the Cathedral of Cincinnati. The couple moved to Hempstead, Long Island, where she began to write with his advice and encouragement. She wrote thirteen juvenile novels, two novels for adults, and some articles, stories, and poems. Her novels drew upon Greek, Roman, and American history. With Roman settings are *The Forgotten Daughter** (Doubleday, 1933), a Newbery honor book, and *The White Isle** (Doubleday, 1940), a Fanfare book. The first of these tales tells of the romance of a Greek slave girl and a Roman aristocrat during the time of Tiberius Gracchus, while the second takes place in Britain during the reign of Emperor Hadrian. Her novels based upon American history include *Downright Dencey** (Doubleday, 1927), also a Newbery honor book, and *Uncharted Ways** (Doubleday, 1935), Fanfare books both about Quakers. The latter tells how the Quakers persecuted in Massachusetts establish a new home in Nantucket, while *Dencey* concerns the friendship between a little Quaker girl and a waif after the Quakers are well established on the island. *The Beckoning Road* (Doubleday, 1929) takes Dencey's family west to New Harmony, Ind., while *The Town of the Fearless* (Doubleday, 1931) fictionalizes upon Snedeker's own family's connection with the New Harmony project. Well-received when published, her books show conscientious research but are too labored, romanticized, stiff in dialogue, and moralistically didactic to appeal much to modern audiences. She also wrote under the names Caroline Dale and Caroline Dale Owen.

THE SNOW TREASURE (McSwigan*, Marie, ill. Mary Reardon, Dutton, 1942), realistic novel based on a real occurrence in Norway in the winter of 1940, when the Germans invaded the country in World War II. Peter Lundstrom, Michael Berg, Helga Thomsel, all about twelve, and Peter's younger sister, Louisa, 10, are playing with their sleds when they see Peter's Uncle Victor heading to his fishing boat, *The Cleng Peerson*, which he keeps in the almost hidden fiord called the Snake. Surprised that he is north so early, before the ice is gone, they know something unusual is happening and are further alerted when they see air-raid shelters being built in the town square. Uncle Victor visits school and organizes a Defense Club, appointing Peter the head. Shortly afterwards, Peter's father wakes him at night and takes him up the mountain into the forest and shows him a "cave" the men are building out of blocks of snow against a cliff, where they are hiding thirteen tons of gold bullion from his bank, worth about nine million dollars, that must be kept out of German hands. Then he leaves to join the army. Uncle Victor organizes the children from the school into four teams led by Peter, Michael, Helga, and Louisa. After the Nazis come, two teams of children go out each day, carrying the paper-wrapped bars of gold which an old servant, Per Garson, helps load and tie onto their sleds, and sliding with them, up and down hills, the twelve miles to the Snake. There they bury the bars in the snow and build a snowman over each cache so that Victor can find it and take it to his boat. They then drag their sleds to a nearby Holms farmhouse where they can stay the night. The next day the other two teams repeat the trip, always travelling in groups of two or three so they will not look suspicious. Though they never see *The Cleng Peerson*, they know it is waiting camouflaged until they get all the gold to it and Victor can get a map of the mines along the coast. Though they never speak to the Germans, they recognize some of them, the friendly captain who orders his troupe aside so the children can slide past, a blue-eyed private who seems to want to join their fun, and the fierce new commandant, who refers to Norwegians as cattle. The trips to the Snake are exhausting and many, for the gold is heavy and the younger children cannot carry much, and before they get it all to the ship there are scares. The weather warms and it seems the snow may disappear, but a late cold spell sets in. The commandant declares that the children must go to school again, but the doctor conveniently discovers an epidemic of a strange malady among the younger children, and orders the others to stay away from school and play in the open air. Just as they have most of the gold aboard, the blue-eyed private skiing near the Snake discovers them burying their load. Victor and one of the crew capture the soldier and learn that he is Jan Lasek, a Pole impressed into the German army, and that he wants to go to America with the boat. The next day, as Helga and Louisa are burying the very last of the bullion, the commandant leads a squad to the Snake, hunting for Jan. Infuriated because the children will not answer him, he starts to kick down Louisa's snowman, and Peter, to distract him before he discovers the gold, throws a snowball at him and runs. He is caught and imprisoned in the barracks. That night Jan risks going back and helping him to a daring escape in which they must swim the icy water to *The Cleng Peerson*. Since he cannot safely return, Peter heads for America with Victor, Jan, and the gold. The story gets most of its impact from being, in essence, true. The style is stiff, the children not much individualized, and the plot almost too implausible for fiction. Choice.

SONG OF THE PINES (Havighurst*, Walter, and Marion Havighurst, ill. Richard Floethe, Winston, 1949), historical novel of Norwegian lumbering in Wisconsin in the mid-nineteenth century. When Nils Thorson, 15, hears the enthusiastic accounts of opportunities in America which Cleng Peerson tells villagers in the mountains of Norway, he determines to reach the new world and gathers as a talisman a pocketful of the soil Cleng has brought with him. Trained as a knife-grinder by his father (now deceased), Nils gets aboard the New York bound ship to sharpen knives for the crew and stows away, but he is discovered and thrown off. An old sailor tells him another ship is leaving from Bergen, so he heads over the mountains hoping to board it. While he is waiting for a chance to stow aboard this ship, he observes a fishing boat just where the ship will crash into it at the wharf and, thinking quickly, dashes over and cuts the boat's hawser so it can escape. For preventing this accident, Capt. Frykman of the *Lyngen* lets him work his passage. Aboard he meets the Svendsen family from the fishing boat, Kristen, 14, Helvor, 11, and Lisa, 5, traveling with their parents to Koshkonong country in Wisconsin. He joins with them and helps them put up their cabin on their claim, where they are threatened by an unfriendly Irish neighbor, Aaron Finch, but welcomed by Norwegian neighbors. With his grindstone in a sack over his shoulder, Nils then sets off to make his fortune but has, at first, poor luck in a country where there is little cash money. Finally, he gets a job sharpening rusty knives that a peddler has sold to a storekeeper cheap and returns to the Svendsen family in time to prove their claim against that of Aaron Finch by showing that the stakes were whittled with a knicked knife, one that Helvor had nearly ruined earlier on the trip. Thinking that lumberjacks will need sharp axes, Nils heads for lumbering country as winter comes, only to learn that they use huge grindstones and have no use for his services until he sees men trying to load logs with crow bars and fashions a cant hook for them to make the job easier and safer. In partnership with Luke Sampson, a blacksmith, he spends the winter making cant hooks, now in large demand. When spring comes, he hears that Cleng Peerson is in Indian Lake and heads off to meet him, coming there to find that Cleng has with him Lisa, who had wandered away from a family gathering, been picked up by traveling Indians, recognized and turned over to Cleng by Red Otter, an Indian whose hand her mother bandaged during the winter. They all return to the Svendsen cabin to be met with great rejoicing, and when Cleng plans to return to do more recruiting in Norway, Nils sends with him the soil he has always carried in a little canvas bag made by Kristen. The book shows considerable research and has interesting events, but the characterization is minimal, and the blatant patriotism expressed dates it. Newbery Honor.

SOPHRONIA HALLET (*Away Goes Sally**; *Five Bushel Farm**), Sally* Smith's cousin, whom Andrew regards as a magpie because she chatters so much. She is spoiled and willful. She has no duties about the house because her mother, Jennie, wants to raise her as a lady. She teases Andrew, calling him a charity boy in imitation of her mother. Sally does not care much for her.

SORENSEN†, VIRGINIA (1912–   ), born in Provo, Utah; novelist for both adults and children. She grew up in Utah's Sanpete Valley, received her A.B.

from Brigham Young University, and did graduate work at Stanford University. She was awarded two Guggenheim fellowships for work in Mexico and in Denmark, which is the setting for *Lotte's Locket*† (Harcourt, 1964). In addition to novels for adults, she has written a number of books for young people, including *Plain Girl** (Harcourt, 1955), which received the Child Study Award, and *Miracles on Maple Hill** (Harcourt, 1956), a Newbery Medal winner. She and her writer husband have lived in Tangiers, Morocco.

SOSEPSIS (*Indian Brother**; *The Scalp Hunters**), blue-eyed, brown-haired Penobscot Indian, who becomes blood brother to Sam* Hilton and is instrumental in his helping his twin sister, Martha, escape from captivity and in rescuing their younger brother, Billy. Although Sosepsis is three-quarters white, he is regarded as an Indian and is so loyal to his people that he cannot betray them even to help Sam escape, but he does buy Sam's freedom from death by torture. In later life Sosepsis became the historical figure known as Joseph Orono, who figured in the American Revolution.

SOUTH TOWN (Graham*†, Lorenz, Follett, 1958), realistic novel set in a southern state in the 1950s. David* Williams, 16, is an earnest rural black, who hopes to become a doctor. The Williams land, too small for a farm, has a garden, a cow, and a few chickens, but Ed* Williams works as a mechanic in the city, coming home when possible on weekends, while David, his mother, Mary* Ellen, and his sister, Betty Jane, 9, take care of things at home. Ed's former employer, Mr. Boyd, owns the Ford agency, the bank and much of the land in the county. Mrs. Boyd thinks she can summon Mrs. Williams to do her housework whenever her own maid is away, and their son, Harold*, tries to scare David and Betty Jane off the road with his expensive car. When David and his friend, Ben Crawford, are swimming at the old mill, Harold Boyd and his young cousin, Red, show up. Harold orders the black boys out of the water; they dawdle but comply. When David sees Red about to be carried over the dam, however, he dives in and saves the boy. Mr. Boyd gives David a summer job at the Ford agency and pressures him to get his father to come back to work for him. After Ed is laid off, he hesitates for a while, then goes to Boyd, but when he insists on the mechanic's pay for doing a mechanic's work, Boyd has him arrested and fires David. The sheriff calls at the house and confiscates their shotgun and .22 rifle. Their desperate efforts to get Ed out are futile. The lawyer is conveniently out of town, and the judge says there is nothing he can do. That night, in response to rumors of impending trouble, friends with guns gather at the house and wait in the dark as a parade of cars goes restlessly along the road, slowing down as they pass the front gate. Among the friends is Ben's older brother, Israel, a one-armed veteran, Solomon Travis, a white veteran with an artificial leg, and Sam McGavock, also white, the oldest mechanic from Boyd's agency. McGavock, "Mr. Mack," insists on sitting on the porch where the state trooper leading the procession can see him in the spotlight, and his scornful words turn the mob away. The blacks, led by the Reverend Arrington, are giving thanks when the cars speed back, wild shots ring out, and Travis is killed. The sheriff arrests everyone in the house, including Betty Jane, but none of the night riders. They are released after two days in jail with no charges, and Ed is released, but he has already been badly beaten. Harold and Little Red come to the house to say they are sorry; at first David tells them to get out but eventually thanks them for coming. Ed decides his children will never get a chance for a good education in the South. He sells his house to Israel Crawford and heads north. Details of the country life and people in the South are the book's strongest point. Events are predictable, however, and characters seem assembled to prove a thesis about racial oppression. Too many ideas are told in the dialogue rather than shown in action. Child Study; Choice.

SPACE CAT (Todd*, Ruthven, ill. Paul Galdone, Scribner's, 1952), short talking animal and science fantasy set during the mid-1900s somewhere in the desert of the American southwest and then in space and on the moon. A nondescript, adventurous, gray kitten sneaks aboard a plane and is adopted by a passenger, Capt. Stone, another free spirit, an airman who admires the cat's spunky charm, dubs him Flyball, and takes him back with him to his desert space station where he is training for a moon shot. Flyball makes himself at home right away, in his view overseeing the various tasks of the humans and skillfully organizing the dogs and cats of the place to his satisfaction. He goes for jet flights with Capt. Stone, whose lucky mascot he becomes, and stows away on the captain's trial rocket flight, where, minus pressure suit, Flyball is amazed to find himself become thin as a waffle though he still feels the flight is a thrilling experience. Pleased with the cat's daring and obvious enjoyment, Capt. Stone orders a pressure suit for him, and over the objections of the general, who fears complaints from animal protection societies, takes Flyball with him on the moon shot. Flyball again enjoys himself thoroughly, learns to cope with the bulky suit and weightlessness, remains alert to all the action, and on arrival bounds joyously to the moon's surface, eager to explore this new environment, too. He soon discovers a cave with exotic vegetation, strange yellow orchids, and floating blue balloons. When Capt. Stone slips and falls, knocking himself out and puncturing his helmet on a sharp rock, Flyball comes to the rescue. The hovering balloons draw his attention to the sticky growths, which he manages to pluck and plaster over the puncture, thus saving Capt. Stone's life and insuring the success of the voyage. Capt. Stone congratulates him on making a very significant scientific discovery—that there is *thinking* life on the moon. The two return safely to earth where they are acclaimed heroes. Capt. Stone is hustled to Washington to be honored by the president and Congress, while Flyball calmly assembles the base cats and dogs, and under the light of what he now considers to be *his Moon* basks in their admiring glances and looks forward to further adventures. Low-key tongue-in-cheek humor, plenty of action, and careful attention to details of situation and episode combine for an exciting story for younger readers which now seems dated and bland but which was a forerunner in its genre. Choice.

THE SPACE SHIP UNDER THE APPLE TREE (Slobodkin*, Louis, ill. author, Macmillan, 1952), science fiction novel for younger children set on a farm near Albany, N.Y., in the mid-twentieth century. Eddie Blow, 11½, visiting his grandmother for the summer, sees what appears to be a meteor fall in the apple orchard just over the hill. Grandma is worried that it might have damaged the tree they call Grandfather's apple tree, because it was planted by her grandfather, so Eddie promises to go look in the morning. Without waiting, he goes out the window and up to the orchard, where he finds a strange, little man walking head down along a branch of a tree. The little man, using a "Dictionary Box" to find the right English words, explains that he is a Scientist Explorer from the planet Martinea. He shows Eddie his Astral Rocket Disk, a small flying saucer. Eddie takes him back to sleep in his room but the next morning finds that he has returned to his ship. There he shows Eddie his Radio Heliocopter Miniature, a pin-wheel which he can fly by holding in one hand over his head, and other wonderful features of his vehicle, including the source of the Secret Power Z, a small spool of Zurianomatichrome wire, which he removes from the ship and carries with him. At Grandma's, Eddie introduces him, and his grandmother thinks that he has said Martin E. Ann, so she calls the little man Marty, and, thinking he is a new boy in the neighborhood, provides him with a pair of Eddie's old blue jeans so he won't get his green suit dirty. At first Marty is suspicious, but he goes with Eddie to the store and is calmly accepted by the storekeeper and the scoutmaster, who happens in. Then Marty realizes he has lost his spool of wire. They find that Grandma has cut off a piece to patch the screen door and either the gander or the goat has picked up the spool and carried it off. Marty cannot leave or even contact Martinea without the power. He hunts all week and finally finds it in the pond, ruined by the water. He is despondent but agrees to go with Eddie to the Boy Scout Jamboree, where, with his Non-Gravity shoes, which he can set for any speed, he easily wins. Eddie tries to explain to him that it is not fair to win by using special equipment. Some time later, a strange, sudden storm hits the area, and shortly afterward Marty appears in his own clothes to say goodbye. He explains that a message from Martinea has come through on an outmoded gadget he carries called a Willen Wingulagulin telling him that a new supply of Secret Power Z is being sent, and he is now ready to return. He confesses, however, that he is really only a Junior Scientist Explorer and has failed in his mission to explore Earth. Eddie gives him school books on history and geography so he will go back loaded with information. The science fiction is unsophisticated even for very young readers, but there is a good deal of light humor in the way adults never seem to notice Marty's strange speech or appearance. This is followed by several other books in a series. Choice.

SPEARE†, ELIZABETH GEORGE (1908–   ), born in Melrose, Mass.; author most noted for her two Newbery Award–winning historical novels, *The Witch of Blackbird Pond** (Houghton, 1958), set among the Puritans of Connecticut Colony in the late 1600s, and *The Bronze Bow†* (Houghton, 1961), set in Palestine in the first century after Christ. The former was also a Fanfare book and cited in *Choice* and *Children's Books Too Good to Miss*. She has lived all her life in New England, attending Smith College and receiving her bachelor's and master's degrees from Boston University. Before marrying Alden Speare, an industrial engineer, and settling in Wethersfield, Conn., the locale of *The Witch of Blackbird Pond*, she taught English in Massachusetts high schools for several years. *Witch* grew out of her interest in the history of Wethersfield and tells of the problems that confront a young, free-spirited, Anglican woman when she goes to live with Puritan relatives in Wethersfield. Before that, she published the absorbing but less well crafted *Calico Captive** (Houghton, 1957), also a Fanfare book. It fictionalizes upon the journal of a real pioneer woman who was captured by Indians and sold to the French in Montreal during the French and Indian War. Although their plots lack conviction, these books present serious, well-researched, vivid pictures of their times, which blend skillfully the protagonists' personal problems and those of their periods. Her most recent juvenile novel, intended for younger readers, is *The Sign of the Beaver*† (Houghton, 1983), a Newbery honor book set in the wilds of Maine in the late 1700s that is less original in conception than her Newbery winners but also melds research and plot well. She also wrote a book of non-fiction for children, *Life in Colonial America* (Random, 1963) and a novel for adults, *The Prospering* (Houghton, 1967), about the Stockbridge experiment in western Massachusetts. She has published articles and stories for women's magazines and plays and currently lives in Easton, Conn.

SPERRY, ARMSTRONG (1897–1976), born in New Haven, Conn.; illustrator, author. He attended the Yale School of Fine Arts, the Art Students League in New York and Academic Colarossis, Paris, and served in the U.S. Navy in 1917. For ten years before he tried writing, he was a commercial artist and illustrator. In 1925–1926 he was assistant ethnologist for the Kaimiloa expedition to the South Pacific for the Bishop Museum in Honolulu, where he learned to speak Tahitian and fulfilled a desire planted by his sailor great-grandfather's stories about the South Seas. A number of his twenty novels for young people are set in this region, including *The Rain Forest** (Macmillan, 1947), the best known being the legend-like *Call It Courage** (Macmillan, 1940), a Newbery Medal winner. Many of his others concern the sea, including *All Sail Set** (Winston, 1935), a story of a voyage on a clipper ship, which was named a Newbery honor book. His illustrations add greatly to the novels.

SPICE AND THE DEVIL'S CAVE (Hewes*, Agnes Danforth, ill. Lynd Ward, Knopf, 1930), historical mystery adventure set in Lisbon, Portugal, from about 1497–1499, focusing on the role of Jewish bankers in opening sea trade routes and the Portuguese effort to wrest control of trade with the Far East from Venice and the Arabs. The house of Abel* Zakuto, respected Jewish banker and noted mapmaker, and his wife, kind and matronly Ruth, is the center of a group of enthusiasts who are determined to prove the existence of an all-sea route to India around the Cape of Good Hope at the tip of Africa, popularly called the Devil's Cave from its treacherous winds. Spirited and adventurous, they include Bartholomew Diaz, Vasco da Gama, Ferdinand Magellan*, and Nicolo* Conti, a young Venetian merchant who envisions great prosperity for Portugal once the Way of the Spices is established. Abel and Ruth befriend a mysterious, young Arab girl, Nejmi*, a fugitive, whose father had traded with the cape. Since her information verifies the actuality of a sea passage to India from the cape, King Manoel is persuaded to commission an expedition under Vasco da Gama. At about the same time, responding to pressure from Spain, Manoel issues an edict expelling the Jews from Portugal, and Abel and Ruth sadly prepare to leave their home. Abel invests his banking resources in a trading and warehousing venture begun by Nicolo on the strength of da Gama's success. The edict is rescinded before they depart, and Abel continues making maps in his small workshop. Nicolo discovers that the Venetians are plotting to steal Abel's maps and have commissioned pirates to interrupt da Gama's voyage. Da Gama by chance alters his route and returns to a jubilant court. Abel and Ruth leave Lisbon anyway, while they are still in control of their destiny, and Nicolo and Nejmi marry and go to live in Abel's house. This is a book of depth and substance, one that gives a good sense of the times from the standpoint of those whose struggles, hopes, and aspirations opened the East for sea trade. The Jewish edict and the escape of Nejmi, if replete with stereotypical episodes, speeches and characters, are well integrated with the plot, and Nejmi provides the occasion for romance as well as mystery. The characters while likeable are not wholly convincing, and dialogue is often trite, but the suspense is skillfully sustained, and the reader gets a good sense of the period. Newbery Honor.

SPYKMAN†, E(LIZABETH) C(HOATE) (1896–1965), born in Southboro, Mass.; author of four humorous and genuine episodic family novels set in the first decade of the twentieth century. She had a childhood much like that of Jane* Cares in her novels, living on an estate-like farm surrounded by those of her relatives, with an autocratic father and numerous servants. She traveled widely and wrote articles published in the *Atlantic Monthly*, but her contribution to children's literature consists of four books with memorable characters about a life now departed, seen not with nostalgia but through the matter-of-fact perception of a child: *A Lemon and a Star** (Harcourt, 1955), *The Wild Angel* (Harcourt, 1957), *Terrible, Horrible Edie†* (Harcourt, 1960), and *Edie on the Warpath†* (Harcourt, 1966).

STAN FREDERICKS (*Shadow across the Campus**), Marjorie's pledge mother. A pretty blonde girl, she is warm and supportive, and Marjorie thinks she is one of the nicest girls in the Zeta Nu house. She encourages Margie to stand up for her convictions and work to get Jews admitted to the sorority. By doing so, she makes herself vulnerable to attack from the upper-class Zeta Nus. When the upper-class girls call a sorority meeting for the purpose ostensibly of protesting the impropriety of freshmen challenging the rules of the house, Stan speaks out and forces them to address the issue at hand—prejudice against Jews. When later the girls discuss letting Joan* into the sorority, Stan reminds them that there is a Zeta scholarship fund which allows girls who do not have money to join, too. She tells them that she herself is at Northwestern on a scholarship. The girls then realize how much Stan stood to lose by not opposing Margie's efforts to force the Zetas to examine their policies towards minorities. Stan is one of the author's mouthpieces for examining the sorority system.

STEAMBOAT UP THE MISSOURI (White*, Dale, ill. Charles H. Geer, Viking, 1958), historical novel set on the Missouri River during the summer of 1863. Red-haired Dave MacLaren, 15, who has been apprentice pilot on the Osage Queen, a passenger packet from St. Louis to Kansas City, wants more than anything to join the navy, or failing that, the army. His master, pilot Joshua Barnard, and his father, Douglas, a partner in the Western Department of the American Fur Company, both refuse permission, and he is despondent until his father reveals that he is needed for a more important fight. Confederate sympathizers within the fur company have been rousing the Sioux to an Indian war, knowing that the Union forces will be weakened if they have to fight on two fronts at once, and other tribes, many of whom have been cheated on their government-supplied annuities by corrupt company agents, are about to join the uprising. Having resigned from the company, Douglas outfits a boat, the *Eagle*, loads high-class merchandise bought at his own expense for the annuities, and with Barnard as pilot, Dave as cub, and Black Jim, former MacLaren slave and boyhood friend of Dave, as steward, they start up river, hoping to beat the company boat, the *Beaver*, to the various rendezvous points with the Indians and dissuade them from joining the Sioux. The company does not hesitate at violent and underhanded tricks: the *Eagle* crew is waylaid and attacked on their way to the *Eagle*; the notations of channel changes left by downriver pilots at regular call boxes have been tampered with; the woodyards have been bribed to refuse to sell to them; they are fired on from the *Beaver*; they are almost rammed by a barge loaded with explosives. In the last, final race, lightened because, at Dave's suggestion, they have temporarily put ashore the passengers or "stampeders" headed for the gold strike at Alder Gulch, Montana, with their gear and the stock, the *Eagle* reaches the mouth of the Platte, where the *Beaver* grounds herself trying to cut ahead. The Pawnees there, the first test of their ability to woo Indians from the Sioux cause, are impressed by the superior trade goods in the "nooties" and delighted with the cake-walk Jim performs for them. Douglas, however, finds that he will have to go overland to deal with some tribes, taking Jim along to entertain, while he sends the *Eagle* on to Fort Benton, with Dave empowered to deal with the Indians. The rest of the trip north is full of hazards, an attack by the Sioux and low water that keeps threatening to ground them or rip the bottom out of the boat. They finally make it, partly because

Barnard rises to the challenge and partly because one stampeder, a merchant who owns much of the cargo, allows them to unload and hide it on an island to make the boat ride higher. All the way, Dave deals with the Indians, who accept his authority because he has his father's red hair and wears his father's bear-claw necklace. When they return and rendezvous with his father, they find that a major Indian war has been averted and that they have laid the groundwork for a future lucrative trade system with both the Indians and the prospectors. Just how much of this is fiction is not clear, but the research on early Missouri river travel is obviously sound and dominates the interest, despite an effort to make Dave's patriotic desire to join the Union forces of some concern. Dave is mostly characterized by his big appetite, Barnard by his autocratic ways. Jim is a dancing, singing, minstrel-show darky, a characterization that even his friendship with Dave does not make more palatable. Spur.

STEELE, WILLIAM O(WEN) (1917–1979), born in Franklin, Tenn.; author of about forty books for children, many of them about pioneering adventure. He received his B.A. degree from Cumberland University in Lebanon, Tenn., and did graduate work at the University of Chattanooga, after serving in the U.S. Air Force in World War II. The majority of his fiction is for the eight-to-twelve-year-old reader, vigorous novels of wilderness travel and pioneer life, like *Winter Danger** (Harcourt, 1954) and *The Lone Hunt** (Harcourt, 1956). In his early books the point of view is that of the white settlers, as in *Flaming Arrows** (Harcourt, 1957), but he turned to the point of view of the Indian in some of his later books. A departure from his pioneer books is *The Perilous Road** (Harcourt, 1958), a Civil War story which was a Newbery honor book and won the Jane Addams Award. With his wife, writer Mary Q. Steele†, he lived in Tennessee.

STEPHANIE VENABLE (*Tree of Freedom**), eldest daughter of the pioneer Venables who migrate from North Carolina to Kentucky in 1780 to prove their claim there. Sturdy, practical, and visionary, she plants the apple sapling, "Tree of Freedom," and helps her brother Noel* leave home to join Colonel George Rogers Clark's forces. When both her father and brother are gone, she provides moral support for her worried mother as well as doing the major share of work about the cabin and supervising the younger children. Her quick thinking in sending her younger brother, Rob, for hermit Lonesome* Tilly saves their claim when Adam Frohawk arrives to take it for its West Indian claimant.

STEPHEN (*Homespun**), third son of John Greenman. He accepts the invitation of his Uncle Nathan Stillman, who has no heir, to join his New Orleans firm which trades in cotton and indigo. Stephen conscientiously follows his uncle's advice and sets out to learn the speech and ways of the Creoles. A warm-hearted, decent sort, he wins the respect of the slaves and of his uncle's business associates, particularly Monsieur Foucher, a large planter, by his generosity and fair-mindedness. He becomes his uncle's heir and marries Alexandrine* Foucher. The end of the book sees them leaving on their honeymoon to Paris. Stephen is the most fun-loving and lighthearted of the three Greenman sons.

STEPPIN AND FAMILY (Newell*, Hope, ill. Anne Merriman Peck, Oxford, 1942), realistic novel set in Harlem in the 1930s. Steppin (Stephen) Stebbins, about thirteen, who lives with his widowed mother and his younger sister, Mary Ellis, wants to be a dancer and saves his hard-earned money for a course at the Elite Dancing School. His initial call at the school ends in disaster when his dog, Pedigree, chases his newly purchased white rat all over the school, creating havoc. While he is sitting on the curb depressed, a man in a fancy car gets him to do an errand, then takes him for a ride and, hearing his story, gives him a note to a school run by Dad Kirby, a crippled former dancer. At first Steppin is disgusted with the exercises when he wants routines, but when his friend, who turns out to be the famous dancer, Bob Williams, gives him a pass for ''Steppin and family'' to his new show, he realizes that real dancing takes that kind of preparation. With great determination he devotes himself to learning and to the clean-up duties that pay his way. When Dad asks him to look out for a new boy, Pierre Bergeret, from Haiti, he foresees trouble with the toughs of Harlem's Dread Avengers, a gang he once hoped to join. Pierre, however, is the son of a lightweight champion boxer, and he flattens the bully, Butch Weldon, earning himself the friendship of all Butch's former victims. Taking the name of Pete, he becomes Steppin's best friend, and when school is on a two-week vacation they go to camp together at Lake Oneishta, a camp that takes some boys free because of contributions of the well-to-do blacks, including Pete's father. They even arrange for Slakey Lewis, one of the former Avengers, to go to camp with them. Pete's mother agrees to give Mary Ellis piano lessons, and the boys find a wealthy family giving away a piano and manage to roll it to their apartment. But bad luck strikes when Steppin's mother is found to have heart trouble and must give up her job as superintendent of their building. At Steppin's request, Bob Williams finds him a job, a small part in a review he is to be in. Roddy, a boy from Dad Kirby's school, has a major dancing part. On the last day before the show is to go on the road, Roddy and his understudy both get measles, and Steppin steps into the part. Unlike many earlier books about blacks, the dialogue is not in ''mammy'' dialect, but neither is it in black English. In fact, except for the Harlem setting and the frequent mention of brown skin, the book could be about white characters. While its period may explain its upward-striving, crimeless Harlem, it is not realistic, even for the 1930s. Much of the plot is based on coincidence, and the ending is too easy, though there are interesting passages about dancing. Fanfare.

STERLING, DOROTHY (DANNENBERG) (1913–), born in New York City; civil rights worker and free-lance writer. She attended Wellesley College and received her B.A. degree from Barnard College. After working for the

Federal Writers' Project and as a secretary for *Architectural Forum*, she became a researcher for *Life* magazine from 1941 to 1949. Investigating the first school integration, she was very impressed by the black children who entered white schools despite community resistance and wrote a non-fiction account, *Tender Warriors* (Hill & Wang, 1958), for adults. From the same experience she wrote a novel, *Mary Jane** (Doubleday, 1959), for children, a story which honestly explores the problem although she admitted later that the happy ending was too hopeful. For both *Mary Jane* and for *Captain of the Planter* (Doubleday, 1958), she was given Bloch Awards for the book which best fosters intercultural understanding. She has also written books to stimulate an interest in biology and other science among elementary age children.

STEVE (*The Black Symbol**), also known as Samson. Silent, angry, blind man with Doc* Cathcart's traveling medicine show. A young man, he has long hair and is billed as the strongest man in the world. His act is the climax of the "bally." He lost his sight when he was a small boy, and his father then sold him to Cathcart for fifty dollars. Cathcart has held him in virtual slavery since then. Alone of all the people in the show, Steve is kind and gentle with Barney, because Barney respects him and neither pities nor fears him. The two become very good friends, and Steve urges Barney to use his head and think situations and problems through carefully, advice which the boy heeds.

STEVE DOAK (*"Hello, the Boat!"**), reliable, sensible elder son in the Doak family. He pitches in with a will along the way to Cincinnati to do whatever needs to be done, from hunting (during which he often teases his younger brother, Davie, who is quite awkward and overly imaginative) and fishing to manning the sweeps. He learns early in the trip not to take chances and to obey his father's instructions. He knows a great deal about boats and particularly likes steamboats, which he sees as the coming mode of transportation in the West. He talks to people about the boats as often as he can. He has red hair, and his father, Charles* Doak, calls him Red.

STEVENS, ALDEN GIFFORD (1886–), graduate of Yale; writer of novels and non-fiction for children. After graduating from high school, he worked in New Mexico and Texas and served a term in the army of Honduras. He then returned to the United States and attended Yale and later lived for six years in Africa. His experiences there resulted in three novels about Africa, *Lion Boy: A Story of East Africa** (Stokes, 1938), episodic story of the adventures and daily life of Simba, the lion boy, and his fellow tribesmen which projects a vivid sense of setting and was selected for Fanfare, and its sequels, *Mark of the Leopard* (Lippincott, 1947) and *Lion Boy's White Brother* (Lippincott, 1951). He also wrote *The Way of a Lion* (Stokes, 1939), a non-fiction account for young readers of the life of an African lion.

STOCKTON, FRANK R(ICHARD) (1834–1902), born in Philadelphia, Pa.; editor, writer. He attended Philadelphia schools and worked as a wood engraver for nearly twenty years. In 1868 he became assistant editor of *Hearth and Home* magazine and in 1873 moved to *St. Nicholas*, where he was assistant editor for five years and frequent contributor for the next ten years. He wrote realistic stories, histories, and travel sketches, sometimes under the pseudonyms of Paul Fort or John Lewees, but he is best known in children's literature for his fanciful tales like *The Griffin and the Minor Canon** (originally part of a collection, *The Bee Man of Orn and Other Fanciful Tales*, Scribner's, 1887; later republished as a book illustrated by Maurice Sendak, Holt, 1963). This shows his typical gentle humor and use of realism to make fantasy convincing. After 1887 he wrote mostly for adults, though some of his novels published for adults, like *The Casting away of Mrs. Lecks and Mrs. Aleshine* (Century, 1886) are often read by children.

STOLEN PONY (Rounds*, Glen, ill. author, Holiday, 1948), short animal novel set in the Badlands somewhere on the American plains in modern times, exact time unspecified. Thieves rustle a high-spirited gray, spotted pony from his home ranch. The shaggy ranch dog slips into the thieves' truck with his friend. When the thieves discover that the pony is blind, they turn the two out in the Badlands at the edge of the range, many miles from their home. The lost animals wander for days searching without success for a break in the fence that borders the rimrock, as the dog loyally remains with his handicapped friend. They descend to the floor of the canyons for water, the pony picking his way cautiously behind his canine protector on the slippery, treacherous, rocky trails. Old instincts help the pony find pasture, and the dog learns to flush mice and gophers, suck eggs, and otherwise live off the land. The pony falls into a washout during a storm, and the dog gets caught in a coyote trap. They are driven off by wild mustangs and attacked by wild cows. They come upon a remote ranch where the dog raids the domestic dogs' food, until both are gently hazed away by the kindly rancher. When a prairie fire sweeps through the area, panic-stricken wild cows trample down the fence, enabling the two friends to cross into territory familiar to the dog. The dog follows the state road back to their ranch, where after enduring weeks of storms, winds, heat, thirst, and hunger, the emaciated wanderers are welcomed home by the old cowpuncher and the boy to whom they belong. The story is intended for young readers. Language is easy, and events move directly and with some suspense, a little humor, and some pathos. The narrative gives some sense of what the range is like and how wild and domestic animals behave. The animals are not sentimentalized, but the thieves are incongruously comic. Numerous black and white sketches picture the setting and situations. Sequel to *The Blind Colt**. Lewis Carroll.

STOLZ†, MARY SLATTERY (1920–), born in Boston, Mass.; for over a quarter of a century a prolific author of popular novels of romance and growing up for older girls and of children in family and neighborhood situations for younger girls. Her more than forty published books include picture books, easy-to-reads, as well as novels of fantasy and realistic fiction. She attended Birch Walthen School, Columbia University, and Katharine Gibbs School, sold books at Macy's and worked as a secretary at Columbia Teachers' College. She married Thomas Jaleski, a doctor and amateur painter, and has lived in New York and in Connecticut. She began writing her first novel, *To Tell Your Love** (Harper, 1950), while she was recovering from a long illness. A Fanfare book, it tells the lesson-oriented story of an adolescent girl's ill-fated summer romance. Also a Fanfare book is *Because of Madeline** (Harper, 1957), which tells of changes that occur in the lives of some wealthy New Yorkers when a scholarship girl enrolls in their private school, while *In a Mirror** (Harper, 1953), in which an overweight aspiring writer tells of her three years in an exclusive girls' school as roommate of a lively dance major popular with the boys, won the Child Study Award. She has published two Newbery honor books, *Belling the Tiger*† (Harper, 1961) and *The Noonday Friends*† (Harper, 1965), and *The Edge of Next Year*† (Harper, 1974) was a finalist for the National Book Award. *Cat in the Mirror*† (Harper, 1975) and *A Dog on Barkham Street*† (Harper, 1960), both Fanfare books, *The Bully of Barkham Street*† (Harper, 1963), and *A Wonderful, Terrible Time*† (Harper, 1967) are all named in *Choice*. Slipshod in plotting and often carelessly assembled, her novels are perceptive and compassionate records of human emotions and desires. *Emmet's Pig* (Harper, 1959), an I Can Read Book and *Frédou* (Harper, 1962) are among her popular books for younger readers. Her recent novels include *Go and Catch a Flying Fish* (Harper, 1979) and *What Time of Night Is It?* (Harper, 1981), in which children must cope with disintegrating family circumstances. She received the Recognition of Merit Award from the George G. Stone Center for Children's Books in honor of her body of work for the young. She has also been a frequent contributor to such popular magazines as *Seventeen* and *Ladies' Home Journal* and has written books and short stories for adults as well as children. Some of her books have been translated into foreign languages and issued in Braille.

STONE OF ODIN (*Wind of the Vikings**), an ancient stone of Stromness, in the Orkney Islands, which is rediscovered by two young people. It was associated with a ring of Standing Stones known as the Ring of Stenness and was equally large but had a rough hole in the center through which a man and woman joined hands to plight their troth. Sir Walter Scott visited it and wrote about it in *The Pirates*, but shortly afterward it was stolen by a farmer for a building stone.

STONG, PHIL(IP DUFFELD) (1899–1957), born in Keosauqua, Iowa; journalist, writer. He was a graduate of Drake University and also attended Columbia University and the University of Kansas. For four years he was a high school athletic director and journalism teacher, then worked in an editoral capacity for the Des Moines *Register*, the Associated Press, and the North American Newspaper Alliance. He later was associated with *Liberty* magazine, *Editor and Publisher*, and the New York *World*. He wrote eighteen books for children, all illustrated by Kurt Wiese, the most popular being *Honk: The Moose** (Dodd, 1935), a lighthearted story set among the Finnish of the Minnesota Iron Range. For adults, he wrote one book of verse, six of non-fiction, and seventeen novels, among them *State Fair* (Century, 1932), which was twice made into moving pictures.

STOR THE STRONG (*And the Waters Prevailed**), Andor's chief antagonist. Tall and strong, he is a bully who from their youth teases and persecutes Andor whenever he can. His voice carries weight at tribal councils because he is so physically strong and aggressive. When he sees the flood coming, true to form, he blames Andor for not having specified the exact time that the waters would arrive. The two men, now old, achieve a kind of reconciliation as they attempt to escape the rising flood together. Stor is a one-sided character, who provides tension for the story. A foil to Andor, he represents rigid adherence to the established way of life and total inability to imagine any other one.

THE STORY OF A BAD BOY (Aldrich*, Thomas Bailey, Fields Osgood, 1869), autobiographical novel set in New England, in the mid-nineteenth century. At the age of about ten, Tom Bailey is sent from New Orleans, where his father is in the banking business, to Rivermouth (Portsmouth, N.H.), to live with his maternal grandfather, Captain Nutter, and go to school. On the trip on the *Typhoon*, he is seasick most of the time, but he makes one important acquaintance, Benjamin Watson, "Sailor Ben," a marvelously tattooed seaman. The Nutter household consists of the Captain, his unmarried sister, Miss Abigail, the maid-of-all-work, Kitty Collins, and the little mustang pony, Gypsy, which Tom's father has sent for him. Tom starts at the Temple Grammar School, taught by strict but fair Mr. Grimshaw, where he makes an enemy the first day, a boy named Conway, and several good friends, among them Pepper Whitcomb, a plump, cheerful boy with freckles, and golden-haired Binny Wallace, a younger boy. Tom gets into a good deal of mostly harmless mischief. As William Tell in an amateur theatrical in the barn, he misses the apple and shoots Pepper in the mouth. He sneaks out the window to the Fourth of July bonfire and helps drag an old stage coach to heap on the flames, is arrested, escapes, and gives up the pocket money from his father to help pay for the damage. He fights and thrashes Conway, who has been harassing Binny. He is initiated into the secret club, the Rivermouth Centipedes, and takes part, as a North Ender, in the great snowball fight against the South Enders on Slater's Hill. A sadder end comes to a picnic to Sandpeep Island with Tom and three other boys, joint owners of a row boat named the *Dolphin*. When a storm comes up, Binny is in the boat without oars, and is swept out to sea and drowned. Not long after that, watching a rare ship put in at Rivermouth, Tom recognizes Sailor Ben in the long boat and takes him to his house, where the seaman is astonished to see Kitty Collins, the girl he married and lost track of when he was shanghaied onto a whaler ten years before. After a happy reunion, he stays in Rivermouth. Sailor Ben (or "The Admiral" as the boys often call him) helps with their most spectacular prank by fixing the fuses when they decide to fire the dozen old cannons from the War of 1812 rusting abandoned on an old wharf. Timed to go off every few minutes after Tom lights the main fuse at midnight, the guns wake the town, blow themselves to ruins and provide a very satisfactory sense of achievement for the Centipedes, who are never suspected. Tom has his share of flirtations, all carried on with great secrecy, with girls from Primrose Hall, dormitory for Miss Gibb's Female Institute, but falls really in love, at fourteen, with a nineteen-year-old niece of the Captain, Nelly Glentworth, who comes to visit, and he is crushed when the young man who comes for her is revealed to be her fiancé. News comes that his parents, whom he has not seen since his arrival in Rivermouth, cannot visit as planned because his father's bank has failed, and he must remain in cholera-stricken New Orleans to clear up his affairs. Tom determines to go as a cabin boy on a ship to New Orleans, runs away on a train to Boston, but fails in his endeavor because he is trailed by Sailor Ben. When they return it is to the sad news that his father died. Because the Captain has lost money in the bank failure, Tom has to give up hope of going to Harvard and instead leaves for New York to enter an uncle's counting house. Although the names and the town are changed slightly, the incidents are told in first person and appear to be largely autobiographical, and the tone is one of vigorous nostalgia, with frequent intrusions of adult author comment, though very little sermonizing. Tom is a lively character, stout-hearted and honest in the manner of Tom Brown (a work Aldrich quotes) and, as the author says at beginning and end, "not such a very bad boy." Children's Classics.

THE STORY OF APPLEBY CAPPLE (Parrish*, Anne, ill. author, Harper, 1950), alphabet book which carries on a continuous story while introducing a set of characters to illustrate the various letters. Appleby Capple, on his way to Aunt Bella's party for Cousin Clement's ninety-ninth birthday, is searching for a zebra butterfly, the only type that Cousin Clement has never seen. He is chased by a crocodile, saves a caterpillar who then spins a cocoon on his coat, runs into an elephant let loose from a zoo, an Indian, and a monkey named Jocko. He is searched for by Mr. Perkins, a patient postman, and by a birdwatcher named Mr. Rollo Roberts, who eventually is joined to Cousin Lucy in a wedding ceremony while both Cousin Clement and Appleby are still lost. In a grand finale, Cousin Clement returns, muddy and disheveled from following butterflies, then Appleby arrives riding on the elephant, and out of the cocoon hatches a Zebra butterfly. The story is told with frequent "cute" asides from the author to the child reader (speaking of Sir Droppit, Deerfoot's dog: "I know what I hope. I hope he is behaving more like a bloodhound than Quentin is, and has caught scent of Apple . . . It's time someone found Apple.") The cleverness which works the letters into the story is strained, and the story itself is not in any way plausible or interesting enough to hold attention. If the purpose is to teach the alphabet, the text is too long and confusing; if it is a story book, the action and characterization are not sufficient for the length of the book. The illustrations, in black and white, are cartoon-like, frequently full page, with the letters which are represented by the people and things in the drawings superimposed upon the figures. Fanfare; Newbery Honor.

THE STORY OF CHAN YUC (Rhoads*, Dorothy, ill. Jean Charlot, Doubleday, 1941), short animal story which takes a brocket deer about twenty inches high at maturity from her birthplace in the jungles of Yucatán to the Washington Zoo in the mid-1900s. Indian hunters take Chan Yuc, whose name means "Little-Deer-Who-Never-Grows-Up" and whose mother they have killed, to a clearing in the jungle where American archaeologists are excavating. They give the tiny creature, about the size of a baby rabbit, to a woman they call Señorita, who feeds her milk with a medicine syringe and makes her a bed of excelsior in a small basket. Indians and scientists despair that the baby will live, but, although at first she is very lonely and misses her mother greatly, she begins gradually to take an interest in the world about her. Her first ventures from her basket provoke expressions of encouragement and optimism that she will live. As she grows steadier and stronger, she trots behind the American woman and learns to drink from a bowl and to eat grass and weeds, though she prefers rose pedals, orchids, and hibiscus flowers. Happy in her small but expanding world, she explores the clearing and makes friends with a turkey gobbler. She becomes a great favorite with the scientists and the Indians who indulge her, as does even the cook whose special flowers she eats. When the scientists have finished their work, Chan Yuc poses a problem for them: they cannot return her to the jungle because she has never learned how to live in the wild, nor can they take her into the United States because of laws against hoof-and-mouth disease. Their problem is solved when they secure a special permit allowing her to be placed in the Washington Zoo. Soon, along with another of her kind, a tiny male, she makes the long journey by car, ship and train to Washington, where she becomes a great favorite of zoo-goers. This is a true story, told here a little condescendingly in third person by an omniscient narrator, who mostly sees things from the deer's point of view. Occasionally the animals speak to one another, but they never have conversations with the humans. The simple, descriptive text gains believability and depth from the accompanying mural-like, two-dimensional paintings in soft jungly greens, tans, and browns which suggest ancient Maya sculptures. Fanfare.

THE STORY OF DOCTOR DOLITTLE (Lofting*, Hugh, ill. author, Lippincott, 1920), fantasy starting in the town of Puddleby-on-the-Marsh in England but largely concerned with a voyage to Africa "when our grandfathers were little children," presumably in the first third of the nineteenth century. Doctor* John Dolittle, though a clever doctor, has gradually lost his practice because he cares more for animals than humans. When, at the suggestion of the Cats'-Meat-Man, he becomes an animal doctor instead, he does well for a while, mostly because his parrot, Polynesia*, a wise, old bird, teaches him to speak the language of the animals. After he allows a crocodile from a circus to live in his garden pool, however, humans are afraid to send their animals to him, and his sister, Sarah, who has been keeping house for him, leaves in a huff to get married. His animals take over the housekeeping duties, but money for food becomes critically short. Then Chee-Chee*, the monkey, gets a message via swallow from his cousin in Africa that a terrible sickness is killing the monkeys there. Although the doctor has no money, he is able to borrow a boat from a seaman and get supplies on credit. He sends most of his animals back to their old homes and sets off with the crocodile, Polynesia, Chee-Chee, Jip, his dog, Dab-Dab*, a duck, and Gub-Gub, a pig, led by the swallow who brought the news. They reach the coast of Africa in a storm that wrecks their boat, but they are able to get ashore, only to be captured and taken to the King of Jolliginki, who imprisons them because a white man once cheated him and despoiled his land. Polynesia is able to fly through the prison bars, hide under the king's bed, and, disguising her voice as the doctor's, scare the king into thinking he is invisible and able to make the king and his people ill. The doctor and his animals are released and flee before the king realizes he has been tricked. Then he sends all his men and even his Queen Ermintrude to chase them. Led by Chee-Chee, they escape to the edge of Jolliginki, where the monkeys make a "Bridge of Apes" by holding hands, and the others walk across the deep gorge on them. In the land of the monkeys, Doctor Dolittle vaccinates all the healthy monkeys and cures the others with the help of the lions, the leopards, and the antelopes, which he presses into service as nurses. To reward him, the monkeys capture the rarest animal of all, the two-headed pushmi-pullyu and persuade it to go home with him to help him earn money to pay for the voyage. On the return trek across Africa, they are again captured by the Jolliginkis and escape only because the king's son, Prince Bumpo*, reads romantic fairy tales and thinks he could marry the sleeping beauty if he were only white. Polynesia tricks him into thinking the doctor can bring this about, and when he has a ship ready for them, the doctor concocts a basin of medicine that temporarily removes the pigmentation from his face. With the help of thousands of swallows pulling the ship, the doctor and his animals get away, only to find at their first stop that the rats are leaving because their ship is unseaworthy and will sink. While they are on the island, pirates board their ship, so they take the pirate ship and get away when the rats' prophecy comes true. On the pirates' ship they find an eight-year-old boy in a room where he was locked after the pirates captured him and his uncle. They then set about finding the uncle with the help of the porpoises, who know he has not been drowned, the eagles, who cannot spot his red hair anywhere on land, and finally Jip, who directs the ship to the cave where the man is hiding by scenting the smell of the man's Black Rappee snuff. At home again, the doctor shows the pushmi-pullyu for sixpence admission and earns enough to pay his debts and have lots of money left over. The story is written with a matter-of-fact simplicity that has charmed generations of readers. Doctor Dolittle himself is wise but unpretentious and unworldy, a genuinely good man who treats other living creatures with respect, and his main animals have well-defined characters. Unfortunately, the book employs terms for blacks used at the time of its writing that are now recognized as offensive and, a more serious fault, treats the Jolliginki royal family as comic characters, Prince Bumpo's gullible desire to be white being questionable to modern tastes. Later books in this series are less subject to these criticisms. Lewis Carroll.

THE STORY OF SERAPINA (White*, Anne H., ill. Tony Palazzo, Viking, 1951), cat fantasy set in a typical suburban area in the mid-twentieth century. One day Mrs. Salinus notices a large cat with one blue eye and one green eye sitting on the hearth rug. Before she has time to shoo it out, she notices that it *is* out, and then without anyone opening the door, it is back inside. Soon the family, Mr. and Mrs. Salinus, Sally, 12, Peter, 10, and Bobby, 4½, learn that this cat is named Serapina and that it is a most unusual cat. She not only has a ringed prehensile tail, with which she can open doors, carry milk-bottles, bat balls, and suspend herself from tree branches, she is able to read minds and has a highly developed sense of responsibility. Soon she is waking the parents in the morning, seeing that the children wash and dress properly, and reminding Sally to practice her piano lesson. The children are delighted, Mr. Salinus perfectly accepting, but Mrs. Salinus is uncomfortable with a cat "that doesn't make sense." Neighbor children and workmen who come to the house begin reporting on the strange animal, and the neighbor adults become upset, particularly Mrs. Polly Potts, who knows all about cats, Mrs. Amanda MacPherson, a dog lover, and Mrs. Fanny Fowler, who loves birds. They resent the stories, which they consider lies and exaggerations, about Serapina's accomplishments, and since she refuses to perform for the curious and skeptical, the Salinus family soon is shunned and isolated. Seeing that she has made them unhappy, Serapina makes enough noise to attract the whole neighborhood, goes through all her tricks for her astonished audience, and then disappears. When she fails to reappear for several days, the Salinus family gives a party in her memory, and in the midst of the festivities, she appears pulling a wagon full of kittens. She distributes them among the neighbors and retires from managing the Salinus household, becoming quite an ordinary cat thenceforth. The story has some of the fun of a tall tale told with a straight face, but it is slow paced and the Dick-and-Jane picture of suburbia dates it. Fanfare.

STOWAWAY TO THE MUSHROOM PLANET (Cameron*†, Eleanor, ill. Robert Henneberger, Little, 1956), science fantasy set in the mid-1900s in Pacific Grove, Calif., and Basidium, sequel to *The Wonderful Flight to the Mushroom Planet**. With the help of Theodosius* Bass, Tyco's* cousin, David* Topman and Chuck* Masterson build another space ship and rocket to Basidium*. Stowed away on board is Horatio Quimby Peabody, secretary to Dr. Frobisher of the St. Julian Observatory and a scientist who hopes to become famous by telling the world about the Mushroom* People. Horatio soon antagonizes the shy, private Basidiumites by his aggressive and callous attempts to learn about their planet and their customs. He hurries off for the Great Hall in the mountains hoping to get precious stones like those in Ta's necklace. Ta, the boys, and Theo follow him to the Hall where they encounter Oru* and Mebe, Ta's Wise Men who have withdrawn from society in despair because they feel they have not served Ta well, and Tyco Bass, who has arrived on Basidium for a short visit before leaving on an errand for the Ancient Ones in another part of the Galaxy. Tyco reasons with Horatio, reminding him that his behavior violates the ancient Laws of Order by which everything in the universe happens in its own good time. Suddenly the mountain crashes in, destroying the entranceway and trapping the party in the Hall, but Tyco leads them out through a secret passage, and they arrive safely back at the space ship. Chuck, David, and Horatio set out for home, but Theo elects to stay with his countrymen on Basidium. Just before departure Horatio quaffs a cup Ta gives him, not realizing it contains a Drink of Forgetfulness. By the time they arrive in Pacific Grove, he has forgotten most of what happened on Basidium. He soon embarks on a return flight, but the ship orbits into a hole in space. A month later, the boys are amazed to see the ship plummet into the ocean near 5* Thallo St. Horatio is washed up on shore, once again a humble secretary whose pride has dissipated in the fall. As in its predecessor, the accent is on adventure, and even though the plot is deliberately extended and motivations are flimsy, something interesting or amusing is always going on. Theodosius is a likeable fellow, bouncy and inventive, fatherly at times like Tyco, but at other times displaying the candor and enthusiasm of a child. Horatio is a comic villain. Overdrawn and exaggerated, he epitomizes the shallow, stupid men of science who proceed without regard for possible social consequences of their investigations. Careful attention to details of the flight and information about the solar system create credibility. Language is easy, and the themes of courage, optimism, pride, and greed are repeatedly reinforced. Choice.

STRAWBERRY GIRL (Lenski*, Lois, ill. author, Lippincott, 1945), realistic novel set in Florida about 1900. Birdie (Berthenia Lou) Boyer, about eleven or twelve, and her family have just moved into the previously deserted old Roddenberry house and intend to raise crops for sale, particularly strawberries. Their nearest neighbors are the shiftless, slovenly Slater family, who have used the land as open range for their scrawny cattle and resent both the fencing and what they call the Boyers' "airs." Shoestring (Jefferson Davis) Slater, 12, particularly annoys Birdie, though he seems somehow different from his hard-drinking, mean father, Sam, his slovenly mother, his tough older brothers, and his raggedy little sisters. The Slaters' animals trample Boyer crops and strip leaves from the young orange trees, and when Boyer fences off the right-away to the water, Slater cuts his fences. Slater hogs continue to break through the repaired fences. When

Birdie and her father rescue a Slater cow stuck in the swamp and Shoestring refuses to care for it, Pa Boyer whips him with a stick. The Slaters steal the spotted calf that has been given to the youngest Boyer, ''Bunny'' (Robert). In retaliation, Pa Boyer kills three Slater hogs and the Slaters poison the Boyer mule, Semina, and start a grass fire that burns down the schoolhouse, threatens the Boyer home, and nearly traps Dovey Boyer, Birdie's younger sister, and the two little Slater girls, Essie and Zephy, playing together in the palmetto grove. A beginning of peace comes when Mrs. Slater invites the Boyers and others to a ''Chicken Perloo'' made with the chickens whose heads her husband had shot off while drunk. A little later, Shoestring appears at the Boyer house late at night, seeking help for his mother and younger siblings who are very ill while his father and older brothers are away. Mrs. Boyer and Birdie nurse them back to health. A visiting preacher, having been fed at Slaters' by the Boyers, holds a camp meeting and converts Sam Slater, who abruptly reforms and becomes a good neighbor. Shoestring decides to attend the rebuilt school, and the Boyers buy an organ for Birdie. Written in a simple style, this book gives a good picture of backwoods life still prevalent in Florida at the turn of the century, and it contains enough dramatic happenings to keep the interest, but the characters are mostly stereotypes and the sudden conversion at the ending is not convincing. Newbery Honor.

STREET, JAMES HOWELL (1903–1954), born in Lumberton, Miss.; journalist, novelist, author of non-fiction books on both the Civil and Revolutionary Wars. He grew up in Laurel, Miss., and started early on a journalistic career, being a part-time reporter for the Laurel *Daily Leader* at fourteen and a full-time reporter for the Hattiesburg *American* at eighteen. For a brief time in the 1920s he became a Baptist minister but gave it up to work for the Pensacola, Fla., *Journal*, then the Arkansas *Gazette* in Little Rock, then joined the Associated Press, working in all the southern states. He went to New York, became a reporter for the World Telegram and, in 1938, a free-lance writer, living in Old Lyme, Conn. Among his novels are *Oh Promised Land* (Dial, 1940), *The Biscuit Eater* (Dial, 1941), which was made into a movie, *In My Father's House* (Dial, 1941), and *Good-bye, My Lady** (Lippincott, 1954), a dog story set in Mississippi. He collapsed and died after addressing a meeting of the North Carolina Associated Press Broadcasters in Chapel Hill in 1954.

STREET FAIR (Fischer* Marjorie, ill. Richard Floethe, Smith, 1935), light-hearted realistic novel set in France in the late 1920s or early 1930s. After touring museums and art galleries and being ordered sensible meals, Anna, 9, and John, 11, are thoroughly bored by their European tour with their mother and Aunt Margaret, who insist that they must learn to appreciate good things. When the adults go out, the children elude the maid, enjoy a street fair, where they discover newly invented yo-yos, and get themselves back to their hotel beds with no one suspecting. They visit the chateau of the Countess de Beaumont, whose daughter-in-law was a school friend of Mother, and John gets into a fist fight with the proper Andre but likes the old countess, who advises him to see a street fair and to have fun. When Mother and Aunt Margaret are invited to accompany the de Beaumonts to Cannes, Anna and John persuade Marie, the maid, to visit her sick mother and get her cousin to replace her, but before they meet the cousin, they are put aboard a train for the Riviera by accident and start a long, marvelous adventure on their own. Having very limited spending money or knowledge of French, they elude the conductor until the train has passed Cannes. They escape at Beaulieu, where they spend a day at the beach, find a small, white dog, which they adopt and name Bouilliabaisse or Bou for short, sleep on a fishing boat which takes them to sea, work their passage as stowaways, help villagers salt away the catch when fishing boats come in, find themselves at Monte Carlo where a gambler doubles their remaining ten francs for them and use it to bribe a soldier to get Bou back when he scares the octopus in the aquarium. At one point they eat at Hotel Splendid and, caught in a terrible storm, spend the night in an attic room where they see a painting of a jungle which they later buy from the proprietor for all the money father has given them for "something special." Unable to afford the telegram they planned to send Mother, they hitchhike towards Cannes, only to be arrested when Bou eats a basketful of rolls they cannot pay for. At this point, the Countess de Beaumont comes along, having received their telegram which the operator sends collect, rescues them, takes them back to her Cannes chateau, and turns aside the wrath of Mother and Aunt Margaret. She also discovers that the painting, which they have repeatedly misplaced and retrieved, is by Henri Rousseau, who had painted it to pay a bill when he was an impoverished customs official. The story moves from one rollicking adventure to another, all plausible if unusual, and seems completely logical through the point of view of the two matter-of-fact youngsters. Fanfare.

STROBOSCOPIC POLAROID FILTER (*The Wonderful Flight to the Mushroom Planet**), a special device invented by Mr. Tyco* Bass that fits over a standard telescope. It not only makes certain heavenly bodies visible in the daytime even though they have never been seen before but also penetrates heavy vapors that may envelope them. With it Basidium-X* is visible.

STUART HALE (*Swift Rivers**), adventurous youth of a well-off Pennsylvania family who grew weary of Princeton and left to seek his fortune in the West. He falls afoul of thieves who pursue him through most of the story, clearly a sub-plot interjected by the author to create some suspense and which seems extraneous in context. Stuart has a quick mind and is a leader. He learns to put his native intelligence to positive purpose and to control his temper and recklessness. At the end, he decides to return to Pennsylvania and complete his schooling.

STUART LITTLE (White*†, E. B., ill. Garth Williams, Harper, 1945), episodic fantasy set in New York City in the mid-twentieth century. Stuart, the second son of Mr. and Mrs. Frederick C. Little, looks "very much like a mouse in every way." He adjusts handily to an environment in which everything is scaled for human beings, helpfully retrieving his mother's diamond ring from the drain, unsticking piano keys for his brother, George, and racing a toy sailboat in Central Park pond. To escape from a dog, he takes refuge in a garbage can and is rescued by his friend, a bird named Margalo. When she is threatened by Snowbell, the cat, Margalo flies way, and Stuart sets out to find her. On the way, he acquires a tiny car, discusses the world's problems as a substitute teacher, and meets a young woman his own size, Harriet Ames, but that romance never blossoms, and Stuart leaves to continue his search for Margalo. Although people find him unusual, they greet him without astonishment or disbelief. Plucky and resourceful, he meets his problems with *savoir-faire* and overcomes them readily. A matter-of-fact and objective tone and careful attention to detail, combined with wry humor and tongue-in-cheek comments on contemporary life, make implausible situations thoroughly convincing. Choice.

SUE OHARA (*The Moved-Outers**), Sumiko, American of Japanese descent, whose senior year in high school is interrupted by the evacuation of the family to an internment camp after the attack on Pearl Harbor. Sue is bright but not studious, a typical, spirited teenager, interested in clothes and sports and the boy on whom she has long had a crush, Jiro* Ito. She experiences her first discrimination, the hardship of camp, and the loss of an older brother killed in action, but she rallies her spirits, teaches in the camp kindergarten and resists the bitterness others feel in the experience.

SUKEY CRAY GREENMAN (*Homespun**), quick-witted, hardworking young woman, bride of Mark* Greenman. Never garrulous or gossipy, she uncomplainingly accepts the hardships of the trip overland to Santa Fe by ox-drawn wagon, lashing down the canvas during the storm and conserving precious water and other necessities. Her most valuable possessions are the two white Plymouth Rock hens, Prissy and Perry, that she received as a wedding present from Jerusha. When they are stolen in Santa Fe, she pursues the thief all the way to the governor's palace, where he works in the kitchens. This gives her the opportunity to meet the governor, to whom she communicates Mark's problems with the customs officials. The governor orders Mark's impounded calico to be released. Mark then sells the cloth for a good price to Henry Babcock, the son of the Mr. and Mrs. Babcock* who befriended Mark and Sukey while they were in Independence awaiting a wagon train west.

SUSAN DOAK (*"Hello, the Boat!"**), eldest child in the Doak family and the only daughter. She longs to do the things the boys do and often is allowed to frolic with them. In particular, however, she would like to go for swims in the river, but her mother, a former school teacher, though rather relaxed for the period in what she requires of her daughter, feels that would not be at all seemly. Susan meets and immediately falls in love with a young law student. Their romance is not very convincingly handled in the context of the story, nor is Susan herself a very believable figure.

SUSANNA JOHNSON (*Calico Captive**), historical elder sister of Miriam Willard, a warm-hearted, practical, and enduring woman, whose loyalty and love for her husband never waver. She gives birth to her third daughter, Captive, while on the march to St. Francis. She keeps her head and courage, even when her children are taken from her. Polly, 2, is adopted temporarily by the wife of the mayor of Montreal but is returned before Susanna leaves Montreal. Susanna, 4, becomes the ward of two French-Canadian women. She is ransomed after the family returns to Massachusetts. Sylvanus, 6, grows up as an Indian, eventually returning to white society a youth who can no longer speak English and is Indian in his ways and attitudes. Susanna is presented as a type figure, who serves as a steadying influence on Miriam.

SUSAN SOWERBY (*The Secret Garden**), mother of Martha and Dickon, the wholesome Yorkshire children who get to know Mary* Lennox. Although her own twelve children never have quite enough to eat, she buys a skipping rope for Mary, knowing that her health and spirits will improve with the exercise, and later supplies food to the three children working in the garden so that they can keep the secret of Colin's returning health until his father returns. Although uneducated, she is a wise, all-good woman, who keeps her home clean and raises healthy, respectful children, an idealization of the peasant mother.

SUSAN'S SAFE HARBOR (Eyre*, Katherine Wigmore, ill. Decie Merwin, Oxford, 1942), story for girls set in San Francisco in the early 1940s. Susan Hill, 9, is unhappy but brave about her family's move to a Russian Hill apartment on Firenze St. overlooking San Francisco Bay, Columbus Square, and Telegraph Hill. The neighbors of mixed nationalities and races seem strange to her but she soon makes friends with Franchesca Pezzola, also nine, one of a large family who live below their studio apartment, where Susan's artist father paints. With Franchesca's brother, Giuseppe, Susan helps repaint the apartment, and with Franchesca she visits the Pezzola fishing boat, the *Stella Maris*, and experiences her first freedom from constant parental observation. When baby Vincent Pezzola has convulsions, presumably caused by the old-country way Grandmother Pezzola has fed him, Susan's mother, a newspaper writer, saves him, and when the *Stella Maris* is caught with a broken engine in a storm, Susan's father, though given to seasickness, goes out in the rescue boat which saves Papa Pezzola and older brother Joe. At Susan's suggestion, Papa Pezzola hires Mr. Hill to paint pictures for his new Fisherman's Wharf restaurant, where Mama Pezzola is cook and Franchesca dances. Mr. Hill's paintings are so much admired that Mrs. Hill will be able to stop work, and Susan is given the cocker spaniel puppy she desires. The main attraction of the book is its San Francisco setting. The attitude deploring mother's working and determinedly tolerant toward ''foreigners'' is very dated, and good, brave, little Susan, so concerned about her dresses and birthday party, is not an interesting protagonist. Fanfare.

SWIFT, HILDEGARDE (HOYT) (1890–1977), born in Clinton, N.Y.; author and teacher. Her father was a professor of English at Hamilton College, and after a private education, she graduated from Auburn High School and Smith College. After studying further at the New York School of Social Work, she lived at a settlement house and worked with children. She married Arthur Swift, Jr., a minister who became a member of the faculty at Union Theological Seminary, and the couple made their home in New York City. She lectured at home and abroad, taught children's literature at the New York School for Social Research, and conducted workshops in writing for young people. In 1929, she began writing children's books. Of her several books of fiction, two were Newbery honor books, *Little Blacknose** (Harcourt, 1929), a fantasy about one of the first ''iron horses'' in the United States, and *Railroad to Freedom** (Harcourt, 1932), a biographical novel about the life of Harriet Tubman. Her highly regarded book, *The Little Red Lighthouse and the Great Gray Bridge* (Harcourt, 1942) was an American Library Association Notable Book, as were her two biographies, *The Edge of April* (Morrow, 1957), about John Burroughs, and *From the Eagle's Wing* (Morrow, 1962), about John Muir. In another novel, *House by the Sea* (Harcourt, 1938), an old house tells the story of its life beginning with Indian days, and *North Star Shining* (Morrow, 1947), is a pictorial history of the black people.

SWIFT RIVERS (Meigs*, Cornelia, Little, 1932), period novel set in the early 1830s among the Swedish settlers of the forests of the northernmost, virtually unexplored reaches of the Louisiana Purchase and then upon the Mississippi River down to St. Louis. The story follows the varying fortunes of shy, earnest, responsible young Chris* Dahlberg, 17, orphan, beginning in early winter when he is turned out by his hard-fisted, sour-tempered Uncle Nels Anderson, a prosperous farmer in Goose Wing Valley. Chris goes to live with his grandfather, respected old Alexis* Dahlberg, who occupies a rude cabin up the valley overlooking the river and who needs money to provide for his old age. A chance remark of adventurer Stuart* Hale, 20, about floating logs down the Goose Wing River to market them in far-off St. Louis, motivates Chris to cut some of his grandfather's imposing stands of virgin forest and to try to sell them as Stuart suggested, a feat no man in the region has ever attempted, let alone a stripling youth. With the help of neighbor Eric Knudson, Chris readies the logs, along with the mighty walnut his grandfather cuts from in front of the cabin, and in the spring he and Eric work the logs down the swollen stream, overcoming Uncle Nels's efforts to stay their progress and making the confluence of the Mississippi, where Eric turns back and Chris joins his logs to the raft of French-Indian Pierre* Dumenille, most respected pilot on the great river. A large cast of characters figures in Chris's story. In addition to Pierre, they include Stuart Hale, Joe* Langford, pilot whose enmity with Pierre Chris heals, and Barton Howland*, elderly settler on the Mississippi who is instrumental in influencing Chris to continue his education. The hazardous undertaking is fraught with dangers and disappointments, all of which Chris and his friends eventually surmount. The worst difficulty occurs when the entire raft breaks up on the terrible shoal at Lone Tree Crossing above St. Louis, where Joe Langford falls ill and is unable to control the logs. After backbreaking labor, most of the logs are recovered, and Chris and Stuart even venture into a village of unfriendly Indians to bring back some logs, including the much prized walnut. The logs bring a fine price in St. Louis, the walnut from a New Orleans businessman who buys it for a figurehead for his ship. Chris shares his profit appropriately with Stuart and returns to his native valley a hero who has opened new economic opportunities for the region. He intends to cut more timber for another trip the following spring and then to pursue his schooling in St. Louis. This ambitious, curiously static book never lives up to its potential for emotional impact because the author spends too much time telling the reader and fails to get around to showing. Dialogue is stilted, plot uneven, and characters are conventional figures who change predictably or not at all. The enmity of Joe and Pierre and Stuart's problems with thieves are obviously intended to contribute suspense and human interest but seem gratuitous and melodramatic. Indians are traditional stereotypes. The best part of the book is the clear sense the author conveys of the forest area and of the way the logs were transported to market. (King* of Spain's Daughter) Newbery Honor.

THE SWORD AND THE SCYTHE (Williams*, Jay, ill. Edouard Sandoz, Oxford, 1946), historical novel which fictionalizes upon the peasants' revolt in Swabia in southern Germany in 1524. Sixteen-year-old peasant youth, Martin Biemler, has been taught to read and write by the parish priest, Pastor Knelle. Lured by the prospect of romantic storybook scenes, he spies on a gathering of lords in the castle of Baron Hugo* of nearby Ritterswald and overhears the impoverished knights hatching a plot to take over the towns of Memmingen and Kempton. Caught and cast into Hugo's dungeon, he escapes with the help of the castle magician and alchemist, Johannes Thrice-Magister, and sets in motion a chain of events that leads to a peasant uprising throughout southern Germany. Encouraged by Konrad, a one-eyed itinerant who calls himself King of the Beggars of Saxony and who travels about bearing news of the peasants' attempts to achieve freedom and justice, Dietrich* the smith, Martin, and some other villagers form a local Union Boot, an organization of peasants determined to resist Hugo's oppressive demands. After Hugo kills Martin's father to enforce payment of a new tax, the peasants seize his castle, free the prisoners, and set the place afire. They help the people of Memmingen defeat the knights, who then join forces with the peasants to combat their common foe, the princes of the Swabian League. Revolt spreads rapidly but almost as rapidly dissipates as conspiracy and treachery divide the ranks. Just before the showdown battle between the forces of the peasants and knights and those of the princes, Martin learns that Hugo, their commander, has turned traitor and kills him. The battle goes against the peasants, but Martin, Johannes, and Pastor Knelle escape to Switzerland. Although the revolt has failed, they are optimistic that the future will bring eventual freedom to the oppressed. This adventurous rather than suspenseful story of a troubled period ends on an upbeat note that seems incongruous in view of Martin's increasing cynicism as the story progresses and obviously reflects the author's personal philosophy and post-World War II vantage point. Martin's painful experiences during the year's conflict mature him believably, as he discovers that the knights of the storybooks and of reality are two different kinds of creatures. A vigorous style, now satiric, now playful, now matter-of-fact, and a convoluted plot filled with action, intrigue, and ironies compensate for the one-dimensional characters who are too numerous and flat to keep straight. (Kilian*) Fanfare.

THE SWORD IN THE TREE (Bulla*†, Clyde Robert, ill. Paul Galdone, Crowell, 1956), novel for beginning readers set in Britain in the days of King Arthur. When a wounded knight arrives at Weldon castle, Lord Weldon takes him in and the old deaf and dumb servant, Nappus, treats his injuries, but they are surprised to learn that he is Lionel, Lord Weldon's scapegrace brother, returned from overseas. Shan, the Lord's young son, and Lady Marian, Shan's mother, are not happy with the rough friends of Lionel who gather as he convalesces. When Lionel and a group of his friends return from hunting and report that Shan's father has been killed in quicksand, Lady Marian retreats to her room, but Shan confronts his uncle and protests the replacing of the faithful servants with strangers and his use of Lord Weldon's sword. That night, he quietly takes the sword from the great hall and hides it in the hollow oak in the courtyard. Shortly afterward, being warned by Nappus's message written in hearth ashes, Shan and his mother flee to the forest, where they are robbed by bandits but eventually come upon a herd boy, Magnus, and are taken in by his parents, Adam and Phebe. After some months, Shan and Magnus travel to Camelot, where Shan puts his grievances before King Arthur and is assigned Sir Gareth as his champion. The boys and Sir Gareth return to Weldon Castle, where Shan proves his identity by retrieving the sword from the tree. Sir Gareth fights Lionel, defeats him, and sends him and his men off to Camelot. Nappus leads Shan to the dungeons where they find Lord Weldon still alive. While the vocabulary is not controlled, the style is extremely simple, with short, almost primer sentences: "Sir Gareth led the way on his black horse. Shan rode behind him on a brown pony from the king's stables. He carried Sir Gareth's shield. Magnus rode his donkey behind Shan. He carried Sir Gareth's lance." The characterization and plot are also simple but provide believable persons and interesting action for children just starting to read independently. Choice.

SWORDS OF STEEL (Singmaster*, Elsie, ill. David Hendrickson, Houghton, 1933), historical novel set during the Civil War and subtitled, "The Story of a Gettysburg Boy," following the life of John Deane from twelve to eighteen and a half. With his father, David, his grandfather, "Gran'sir," and his two sisters, Sue and Sallie, 16, John lives at Wildwood, not far from the edge of Gettysburg, Pa. His main interest is the colt, Lady Gay, which Black Nicolas, servant to the Swifts who live on March Creek Road, is training, though he is not immune to the charms of Maggie Swift, red-haired granddaughter about his age. When Nicolas, though free, is captured by the slave-catching Finnegan gang and rushed south to be sold, John is heartbroken and Gran'sir breathes fiery pro-war sentiment. Father, who solicits orders for the Acme Carriage Factory, takes John with him to Harper's Ferry, where they meet John Brown, under the name of Smith, witness the attack by the abolitionists, and help a black man escape north. Gettysburg celebrates Lincoln's election, the local militia leaves after war breaks out, and eventually Father joins the cavalry. When fighting nears the town, Gran'sir and John set off with an express wagon of supplies for the wounded only to run into the southern troops and have their wagon, horses, and supplies confiscated. On the way home afoot, they discover that Lady Gay, hidden at the Swifts, has also been taken. When the Union forces charge past Wildwood, Gran'sir chops the fences down so they can march through the crops unimpeded, but soon they are pushed back and the Confederates take over the house, shutting John, who is home alone, in the cellar. To his astonishment, their cook, who takes over the kitchen, is Nicholas; secretly, Nicholas slips him food and a coat for the several days he is held there while the house is battered by shellfire, the animals butchered, and the crops ruined, before the troops move on. Sallie marries her young teacher from the seminary, Mr. Thatcher, who eventually returns minus his left arm. They hear Lincoln give the Gettysburg Address. Word comes that Father has been captured and is held in Andersonville. When he is freed by exchange and returns, very ill, he finally allows John to join the Amantine Guards in his place. John sees service through the last phases of the war and then for several months in the clean-up operations. When he returns in July of his nineteenth year, Sue is about to marry her local boyfriend, Sam Dannehower, and Maggie, now a schoolteacher, promises to wait for John while he finishes his education. The book makes a valiant attempt to combine history and fiction, but history wins out. The amount of information included is impressive, and the scenes of the Gettysburg countryside are vivid and those of battle are exciting, but it is too much to allow adequate character development. John mostly observes the events of the six and a half years, and as a little boy is more interesting and individual than as a young man. Newbery Honor.

SYLVIE MOFFAT (*The Moffats**; *The Middle Moffat**; *Rufus M.**), 15, the very active, elder sister in the warm and loving Moffat family. The artistic member of the four children, she dances and sings and acts in school plays. She graduates from high school at the end of *The Middle Moffat** and plans to marry Jack Abbott. She seldom affects the action of the episodes.

T

TALKING DRUMS: A BOY'S STORY OF THE AFRICAN GOLD COAST (Fleming*, Waldo, ill. Frank Dobias, Doubleday, 1936), realistic mystery-adventure novel set in the early 1900s in Africa among the Ashanti of the Gold Coast, at that time a British colony, in which an English youth's musical talent and his understanding of African ways enable him to avert a war between the Ashanti and the British. Philip Baring, 18, is the son of the superintendent of a construction company responsible for building a railroad through the Ashanti savannah and jungle. Philip returns from a year in England studying music to find his father tense and upset because native drums have been stirring up his laborers. Timothy O'Hara, Irish construction boss, is convinced the natives are merely lazy and are using the drums as an excuse to play off, while Philip's father is certain that Jumumu, an Ashanti chief once jailed for anti-British activity, is behind the drumming. After a worker falls ill of what is eventually diagnosed as sleeping sickness, Philip's sharp ear for tone and sense of rhythm enable him to detect the Ashanti word for sleeping sickness in the drumming. His close friend and body-servant, the Ashanti youth Utassi*, at first evasive when queried about the drum language, confirms that the messages are indeed about the disease, which soon threatens to reach epidemic proportions. Jumumu sends four ill men to the camp for treatment and accuses the English of spreading the disease, a contention surprisingly supported by British Dr.* Edgerton, who asserts that in advancing the railroad the British are indeed inadvertently spreading its carrier, the tsetse fly. Determined to get the British out of his country, Jumumu drums a message ordering the workers to strike and then prepares to attack the camp. As they attack, Philip, who with Utassi's help has mastered Ashanti drumming, drums a message purporting to come from the Ashanti god, the Pale Ghost, advising friendship with the British. The Ashanti capitulate, the railroad is completed, the British send medical teams to combat the plague, and Philip is rewarded with an Oxford scholarship to continue his musical studies. Witchcraft and treachery offer further complications for a novel unusually rich for its genre. Characters are sharply delineated, if static and occasionally stock, and the mild conflict between the idealistic and aesthetically inclined Philip and his pragmatic father adds texture to the narrative. The skillfully motivated, evenly paced plot, in which the story and the protagonist's character are well integrated, grips immediately with an atmosphere of impending trouble and builds evenly and surely to a tense and believable climax. Descriptions of jungle and savannah, dress, customs, religious beliefs, and particularly the drumming and the use of many Ashanti proverbial expressions recreate the setting and provide a sympathetic view of the Ashanti, while at the same time the writer conveys a clear sense of British chauvinism without being judgmental. Fanfare.

TAMNA (*Flag of the Desert**), rightful heir to become chief or Aku of the Jukon tribe of Nigeria. Knowing that the high priest, Moyi, has arranged for the murder of the other heirs and that his life has been spared because he is only a boy, he keeps a low profile, acting like a lowborn village boy, until Bill and Terry ask that he be made their guide because he speaks a language they know as well as his native tongue. When he is arrested and imprisoned in a hut by Moyi, he gives himself up for dead, but when the white boys rescue him, he quickly falls in with their scheme to impersonate the voice of the ancestors over a loud speaker rigged in the sacred grove. Only Tamna has the presence of mind to realize that he must return to the prison hut so he will have a clear alibi.

TANG THE COOPERSMITH (*Young Fu of the Upper Yangtze**), owner of the shop and master of the apprentice, Young Fu. Though blunt and sharp-tongued to his workmen and frequently ironic, he is a kindly master who feeds his apprentices sufficiently, doesn't beat them, and takes an interest in their personal problems. An expert craftsman, he is also skilled at handling people and at bargaining. Having lost his wife and children to illness, he is attracted to Young Fu's intelligence and enterprise and decides to adopt the boy as his heir.

TARRY, ELLEN (1906–), born in Birmingham, Ala.; teacher, newspaperwoman, and social worker. She attended Alabama State University, Fordham University, and Bank Street Writers' Laboratory, New York City. At one time she was Story Lady in the Harlem Community Center and worked for equal housing opportunities for blacks for the federal government. One of the first writers to use blacks as protagonists in nonhumorous stories, she is known for such books as *Janie Bell* (Garden City Press, 1940), a story of a foundling, and *My Dog Rinty** (Viking, 1946), a realistic story written with Marie Hall Ets* and illustrated with photographs shot in Harlem.

TAYLOR, SYDNEY (BRENNER) (1904?–1978), born in New York City; actress, dancer, teacher of dance and dramatics, and author of books for children. She studied dramatics at New York University and attended Martha Graham Dance Studio. She was an actress with the Lenox Hill Players and a dancer with the Martha Graham Company before in 1942 joining Cejwin Camps, where for thirty years she taught dance and dramatics to girls from seven to eleven years of age. She wrote, directed, and choreographed many plays for the campers. She married Ralph Taylor, president of Caswell-Massey Co., chemists and perfumers, who was responsible for the publication of her first, best-known, and most highly regarded book, *All-of-a-Kind Family** (Follett, 1951), a Fanfare book also listed in *Choice*. The couple had one child, a daughter, for whom Taylor told and then wrote down stories of her own life as middle daughter growing up in a large Jewish family in New York's Lower East Side. During the summer of 1950, while she was away at camp, her husband submitted the manuscript to Follett without her knowledge. The book subsequently won the annual Charles W. Follett Award and the Isaac Siegel Memorial Award of the Jewish Council of America, in addition to its Fanfare citation. *More All-of-a-Kind Family** (Follett, 1954), *All-of-a-Kind Family Uptown** (Follett, 1958), *All-of-a-Kind Family Downtown* (Follett, 1972), and *Ella of All-of-a-Kind Family* (Follett, 1978) continue in similar episodic fashion the warm, affectionately detailed account of the close-knit family and their friends, but the first book, gently amusing and very strong in sense of place and Jewish ethnic customs, remains the favorite. She also wrote *Mr. Barney's Beard* (Follett, 1961) and *The Dog Who Came to Dinner* (Follett, 1966), both beginning-to-read books, and *Now That You Are Eight* (Association Press, 1963) and *A Papa Like Everyone Else* (Follett, 1966), and contributed short stories to publications for children.

TED CARES (*A Lemon and a Star**; *Terrible, Horrible Edie†*; *Edie on the Warpath†*), Theodore, imperious eldest son in the wealthy, turn-of-the-century family of Summerton, Mass. To his three younger siblings, Ted is a power to be placated and avoided most of the time, though Jane* and Hubert* rebel occasionally, and he is the main object of Edie's* war against men. When his stepmother arrives, only Ted holds out against her, and she wins him over by defending him firmly when Father blows up and by even arranging that Ted, then thirteen, learn to drive the Ford. In *The Wild Angel*, second book of the series and the only book with some episodes from Ted's point of view, he is revealed as having heroic, if misguided, impulses.

TEENY GAY (*Teeny Gay**), a warm-hearted child who believes that wishes can come true. She is very obedient and has a strong sense of right and wrong. She very much wants to be a good girl. She has a warm and generous nature and invites Dallas* and Larry* Bill to live on the houseboat with the Gays. Although not completely convincing, she is far more believable than her parents.

TEENY GAY (Simon*, Charlie May, ill. Howard Simon, Dutton, 1936), realistic novel of family life set on the White River in the Arkansas Ozarks at an unspecified time but probably in the 1930s. On New Year's day, lonely, only child Teeny (Cyrilda Caldonia) Gay wishes for a brother or sister to play with. While she is exploring the levee, she discovers in a run-down houseboat orphaned, young Dallas* Tyler, ailing and alone, and brings him home to the Gay houseboat. Both Mr. and Mrs. Gay take to the high-spirited, earnest youth, who plays both harmonica and violin, and plan to adopt him. Later, in the spring, Teeny and Dallas invite Larry* Bill, a kind, jolly, ex-circus clown, who had been living in a shack on a nearby island, to live on the houseboat, too, and now Teeny has two brothers. Teeny acquires a sister during the great flood that comes with the spring rains. With Mr. Gay's fishing motorboat, the *Tiddleywinks*, Larry Bill and Mr. Gay rescue the pretty Susan Smith, whose farmhouse is floating down the river. After the flood subsides, Larry Bill departs on a mysterious errand (to search for Susan's lost parents), leaving Susan with a note that brings a deep blush to her cheeks. Then a townsman in Big Fork, noting Dallas's bravery in plugging a hole in the levee, like the Dutch boy of legend, and appreciating the boy's musical talents, offers to pay for his education. After some soul searching, Dallas decides to accept and leaves for Little Rock. Teeny now has only a sister. She gains a best friend, however, Gladys of Big Fork, when Mr. and Mrs. Gay decide it is time she attended a real school, and they moor the houseboat near town. Then Susan leaves the Gays to marry Larry Bill and settle in a houseboat he has built not far away. At Christmas, Teeny asks for a doll and receives six of them from friends, but the best doll of all is a brand-new baby brother. This is a pleasant, rather condescending story for young girls. The author describes in moderate detail the worklife, pleasures, and hardships of the river people. The flood is a major disaster but never seems really threatening. Characters are stock, and the plot moves evenly through some conventional scenes, for example, a circus and a shopping trip, to an abrupt and contrived conclusion. Mrs. Gay is the stereotypical nurturing mother and supportive housewife. She defers to her husband but tries to influence his decisions by serving him his favorite foods. Mr. Gay is the kind-hearted, protective patriarch who always knows best. Language is easy and there is a lot of dialogue. In its warm picture of family life, the book recalls the Little House books, but it is far less skillfully written than they. The numerous, stiff black and white sketches depict situations and help with setting. Fanfare.

TERMINIA SPARHAWK (*Sandy**), housekeeper who accompanies Sandy Callam and her aunt to their summer cottage in Windrush. A small woman who rushes about, she is an excellent cook but a complainer, who finds the three-story cottage too small, too inconvenient, too antiquated. Because she doesn't have a private bathroom, she insists she needs a washstand and ''ewer'' set, the search for which provides much of the humor in the novel. Before the summer is over, but just after the ewer set has been acquired at auction, Terminia decamps, leaving behind a note telling where to send her wages.

TERRENCE O'HARA (Burns*, Thomas, ill. Reginald Birch, Harcourt, 1939), light fantasy set in Ireland near the headlands of Ballycushen. Terrence O'Hara, worrying about how to help his parents so that his fisherman father will not have to go to sea in stormy weather, suddenly finds himself surrounded by fairies, tiny people whose queen complains that someone is knocking down all the toadstools. When Terrence tells her it is Mickey Malone's cow, she sends wasps to drive the creature home but rewards Terrence by telling him to get the job of cowherd. In order to soothe the cow and the fairies, he learns to play the pipe. One day, while herding and piping, he is joined by an old gentleman with a fiddle and his golden-haired daughter, Molly, and together they play and dance all the way to Malone's, and soon have the cow, pigs, rooster, hens, Malone, and the Widow O'Connor and her donkey dancing, too. The widow stops for a cup of tea with Malone, while the fiddler and his daughter spend the night at O'Hara's. That night the fairies come for Terrence, make him small as they are, and have him pipe for an all-night dance. Back to his normal size in the morning, he bids the fiddler and Molly goodbye, but his sadness is soon interrupted by Malone, riding the widow's donkey and insisting that they find the old gentleman to play at his wedding to the widow. Remembering the fairy queen's advice that he will find good fortune if he takes the road south to Ballysmore, Terrence knows where to find them. They return, and Terrence and the fiddler play for the wild wedding party, which ends with the old gentleman telling a story within the story about Flanagan and the Fairies. The local folk all offer to contribute something to the fiddler if he will stay and entertain them for the winter, and Terrence and Molly end with their arms around each other. Narrated in a broad, Irish pattern of speech in storytelling style, the book keeps open the possibility that Terrence's encounters with the fairies are dreams. It pleasantly combines something of the tone of a tall tale with that of legend. Fanfare.

THAT GIRL OF PIERRE'S (Davis*, Robert, ill. Lloyd Lózes Goff, Holiday, 1948), realistic novel telling of the struggles of a French family to re-establish themselves after World War II. The first year home sees stalwart, dependable, courageous Danielle Dufour, 16, surmount personal and community difficulties and earn acclaim from her fellow villagers for her dedication, cleverness, and hard work. After three years as homeless refugees, she, her grandmother, Mathilde*, and little brother, Jeannot, 7, return tired but joyful to their village of Arsac-le-Petit, looking forward to a good life with parents and friends. But their house is empty, no one knows the whereabouts of the parents, Pierre*, a soldier, and Jeanne, a labor conscript, nor has anyone heard news of Marc Bracessac, her fiancé, also a soldier. Then Porky* Guichard, the unscrupulous, grasping grocer, refuses to honor the due bill Pierre had left at the store, and in addition he has conspired to defraud Danielle of the Dowry* Field, the property that comes down through the women of the family, now belongs to Mathilde, and is to come to Danielle when she marries. Undaunted, Danielle digs in and with pluck, resource, and luck not only provides for her little family but also eventually squares things with Porky. At the suggestion of Father* Ambrose, the village priest, she takes a job in the vineyard of Papa* Dumartin and gets Mathilde a position as light laundress for the Chateau nearby, and Jeannot watches cows for a neighbor. She cleverly trades off unneeded items for repairs to the house and sells off some timber for a little nest egg. Soon people are remarking about the industry and resource of ''that girl of Pierre's.'' She remains patient, understanding, and hopeful during Marc's long convalescence after his return and even gives up with good will her last remaining claim to the Dowry Field to pay the expenses of bringing home Pierre, also wounded, and Jeanne, and then capitalizes on overheard conversation to initiate with the help of Marc and Papa Dumartin an Agricultural Cooperative in Arsac. This results in a revival of community spirit and cohesiveness as well as the promise of economic stability for the village with the redevelopment of the vineyards and leads also to the establishment of a Health Cooperative. Authorities arrest Porky for complicity with the Germans during the war, and his property is confiscated. Pierre uses the scandal advantageously to pressure Guichard's accomplice, a lawyer, to return the Dowry Field. The marriage banns are posted for Marc and Danielle, and with paying supervisory positions at the cooperative and the Dowry Field for food crops, the two young people look forward to a bright future together. The story makes few demands on the reader, but the style is pleasing, characters attractive, if types, incidents carefully arranged for mild suspense, and the picture of French village life vivid and alive, if rather rose-colored. The passages about how Danielle and Marc get the Cooperative organized are particularly interesting. Fanfare.

THEE, HANNAH! (De Angeli*, Marguerite, ill. author, Doubleday, 1940), realistic story of a little Quaker girl in Philadelphia before the Civil War. Youngest of six children, Hannah, 9, is impatient with serious Quaker ways and longs for fancier and brighter-colored clothes than the staid garments she must wear. The household is not poor, since they have two Irish servants and Granny Welsh, who comes every day to help, but they live simply with high thoughts. When Hannah's non-Quaker friend, Cecily, lends her a pink silk sash, she is almost caught trying it on before her older sister's mirror, and stuffs it into a drawer where it is stained by her sisters' pomade (hand lotion). Appalled, Hannah hides it in the bedding closet in the attic and decides to save enough money to buy a replacement. Her guilty conscience is relieved, however, when her mother finds it and is understanding but firm that she must forego her allowance until the new sash is paid for. On other occasions, as on this one, she listens to ''Old Spotty,'' Satan, instead of acting like a good Quaker: she shows off when they are skating, almost falls into a hole in the river ice, and spoils the day for the others by having to be taken home; she dresses up in Cecily's new dress and bonnet, goes with her on an errand, and runs into her father; she decorates her new scoop bonnet with real flowers which stain it, and then must wear the stained bonnet to remind her of the folly of worldy display; during ''Quaker Week,'' when the house is full of guests, she finds an old, lacy petticoat and cuts it up to make pantalettes like Cecily's, which she much admires, but trips over them, falls downstairs, and must endure her mother's shame and sorrow, increased because the petticoat was an heirloom from her grandmother's trousseau. When she and her sister, Sally, 11, are invited to visit friends for several weeks, her father says that Hannah is not old enough, that she doesn't seem able to remember that she is a Friend. She is lonely but keeps busy helping at home and starting a quilt for her sister Rebecca's wedding gift. When she is on an errand one day, a black woman hiding in a passageway between two houses calls to her. She discovers it is a runaway slave with a sick child and, knowing that Quakers are committed to helping, she summons her father, who brings food and water and that evening brings the woman a Quaker bonnet, which will hide her face, and, carrying the child, escorts her to his house. There they are kept until the little boy is well and until passage can be arranged to Canada with a sympathetic ship captain. The woman explains that she knew she could trust Hannah because of her Quaker bonnet, and this makes Hannah see the true meaning of being a Friend. Although the attitudes expressed are historically correct, the sins that Hannah commits are tame by modern standards. Facts about life of the times—street cries of vendors, descriptions of the market, scenes in Quaker meetings—are described and depicted in illustrations and are rather heavily didactic for the slight story. Fanfare.

THEO ARMACOST (*To Tell Your Love**), Anne's elder sister, a nurse at the local hospital. Well-read, she is the one whom Mr. Coombes, wealthy local banker and philanthropist hurt in a fall from a ladder, chooses to write letters for him. She meets through him his nephew, Paul* Favor, of whom he is very fond, who returns his affection, and who is an officer in the bank. Theo is sturdy, decisive, warm-hearted, a very likeable person. She provides some ballast for Anne. Though she has some reservations about marrying into such wealth, she accepts Paul's proposal, but the two have scheduled the wedding for December to allow themselves time for second thoughts.

THEODOSIUS BASS (*Stowaway to the Mushroom Planet**), Mr. Tyco* Bass's wandering cousin, who settles on Basidium*. He turns up at 5* Thallo Street, after Mr. Bass has blown away, intending to settle down and devote himself to science there. When he learns that Tyco has gone and hears about Basidium, he decides to go there to live. He is a bouncy, energetic, genial little man, with a large, round head, small face and gentle eyes, who wears an aging and weathered, greenish opera hat and a tight, old-fashioned suit with a black cape flung over his shoulders and carries an ancient auto robe and an old carpet bag. He helps the boys rebuild the space ship which has been smashed to smithereens in a storm after the boys returned from the first flight to Basidium. He signals messages to them from Basidium by special lantern.

THESE HAPPY GOLDEN YEARS (Wilder*, Laura Ingalls, ill. Helen Sewell and Mildred Boyle, Harper, 1943), last in a series of seven autobiographical novels (*Little House in the Big Woods**; *Little House on the Prairie**; *On the Banks of Plum Creek**; *On the Shores of Silver Lake**; *The Long Winter**; *Little Town on the Prairie**), this set in and near De Smet, S.Dak., in the years 1882–1884. Laura* Ingalls, not yet sixteen, sets off to teach her first two-month term of the Brewster school, twelve miles south of town. She has to live at the Brewsters' shanty, where the unhappy, quarrelsome wife seldom speaks to her, the neglected little boy cries, and the morose husband spends most of his time in the stable. Of her five students, three are older than Laura. One of these, Clarence Brewster, is saucy and gives her some trouble until she follows the advice of Ma (Caroline* Ingalls) and learns to manage him. To her surprise, Almanzo* Wilder comes to get her on Friday and after that takes her home every weekend, even though she tells him candidly that she doesn't intend to go with him when the term is over. One night Mrs. Brewster's screaming wakes Laura, who sees her standing with an upraised knife. It is not clear whether she intends to stab herself, her husband, or Laura, but it so frightens Laura that she hardly dares to sleep in the house again. The bitter cold makes teaching in the shanty-built schoolhouse difficult, and on one trip to town, when the temperature is well below forty degrees below zero, Laura and Almanzo nearly freeze, but she finishes the term successfully, without complaining. Since she has studied in the evenings, she finds when she returns to school that she has kept up with her class. After she sees the other young couples riding up and down the main street in their cutters, she regrets her dismissal of Almanzo, and when he stops to ask if she'd like a sleigh ride, she is quick to accept. Saturdays she sews for Mrs. McKee, the dressmaker, to earn more money for her sister Mary's* college expenses. When Mary comes home for the summer visit, Laura finds her blind sister much improved in abilities and confidence and as beautiful as ever. After some time, Laura takes a job with Miss Bell, the milliner and dressmaker, earning fifty cents a day. One late Sunday, after snowfall, Almanzo takes her sleigh riding behind a pair of colts he is breaking, and, after that, every winter Sunday they ride behind the wild colts. At Christmas, Laura receives a case with ivory-backed comb and hairbrush at the church celebration; there is no giver's name, but Pa has seen Almanzo buying it at the drugstore. In the spring a new schoolhouse, the Perry school, is built near the Ingallses' homestead, and Laura teaches a happy three-month term to the three little children attending. With her earnings they buy an organ to surprise Mary, who has learned to play at school, but Mary decides to visit her roommate's family in Iowa instead of coming home, a big disappointment to them all. Almanzo, who has purchased a new buggy, starts taking Laura riding again, but one Sunday he has with him Nellie* Oleson, who flirts with him and dominates the conversation. The next Sunday, Laura deliberately lets a dust robe flap to scare the horses and make them run to frighten Nellie, and when they get home she tells Almanzo not to come for her the next week if he has Nellie, then wonders if he'll ever come again. He does, and soon they are breaking a team, Barnam and Skip, runaways that respond to Laura's gentle touch even better than Almanzo's. In the fall, Almanzo takes her to the new singing school and later gives her an engagement ring, then goes back to Minnesota with his brother, Royal*, intending to return in the spring. At Christmas, the first they spend on the claim, Almanzo unexpectedly returns. Laura takes the teachers' examination, passes with a second-grade certificate, and leaves school for the last time to teach a three-month term at the Wilkins school, a post she gets partly because she has befriended Florence Wilkins. The wedding she and Almanzo plan for the fall they move up because his sister, Eliza* Jane, and his mother decide to come to De Smet to run a big wedding, which neither of the young people wants. They go alone to the Reverend Brown's, Laura wearing black cashmere, have a family dinner at the Ingallses' and then go to the new little house Almanzo has made on his claim. The most memorable part of the book is Laura's first teaching experience, but the quiet, understated romance has an old-fashioned charm. Books Too Good; ChLA Touchstones; Choice; Newbery Honor.

THEY CAME FROM SWEDEN (Judson*, Clara Ingram, ill. Edward C. Caswell, Follett, 1942), historical novel about Swedish immigrants to farms in Wisconsin and Minnesota from February, 1856, to December, 1857. Sturdy, industrious, independent Carl* Larsson, a cotter (tenant farmer) in his native Sweden, emigrates to America with his family, his wife, motherly, hardworking Anna Marie, his brother, Ernst, 17, also a farmer, and his three children, Gustaf*, 12, Elna, 8, and Hans, 5, determined to make a good life for his family in the land of opportunity where he can own his own farm. In Milwaukee, he buys a ten-acre farm with cabin near Watertown, Wis. The family trudges west and soon settles into the little log cabin and puts in crops. Gus hires out to a blacksmith, who encourages him to learn to read and write English as does a friendly stage driver, Elna works as a hired girl for a farm woman nearby, and Ernst hires out to a nearby farmer. Things go well, they make friends, and Christmas is joyful. When Carl hears that homestead land is going for $1.25 an acre in Minnesota, he sells the little farm at a tidy profit and heads west with the family. There are a few problems along the way, most of them small and easily overcome by ingenuity or effort, except for the loss of their cow, Blossom, on the Mississippi crossing. Ashore at Red Wing, Minnesota Territory, the mother takes a job temporarily as a cook in a hotel and the boys run errands, while Carl goes west to stake their claim near Vasa. By spring they are on the land, breaking ground with rented oxen and starting their sod house. They receive help from Big* Whistle, a Dakota Indian, and from other Swedes who settle in the area. They put in long, hard hours, but the sense of achievement is high and the grain yield exceptional. With the help of Pastor* Norelius of Red Wing, the children are able to go to school, and Gustaf, who wants to become a lawyer, gets a job helping Judge* Turner in Red Wing to earn board and room while going to school and learning the law business. In Red Wing, Gustaf gains renown, the reward of an Indian pony, and Judge Turner's praise for heroism during a barn fire. The family's second Christmas finds them prospering and happy in what for them is truly the land of opportunity. Characters are wooden, and they and the plot are obvious vehicles for the author to inform a young audience about Swedish homesteading in the upper Midwest. The story moves fast, and the style is descriptive but never heavy with details of everyday life, and language is easy but not stilted. The book exalts the virtues of hard work, education, family spirit, teamwork, neighborliness, and respect for authority. Altogether, the author paints a rosy picture of life for the immigrants. Fanfare.

THEY LOVED TO LAUGH (Worth*, Kathryn, ill. Marguerite de Angeli*, Doubleday, 1942), realistic novel set in 1831 in Guilford County, N.C., based on the life of an actual girl, family memories, old correspondence, and records. When Martitia* Howland, 16, her parents having died of typhoid fever, is brought to his home by Doctor David Gardner, she is at first frightened by his five tall, boisterous, fun-loving sons, Jonathan, 21, Milton, 20, Clarkson, 18, Barzillai, 17, and Addison, 15, and by their grim Quaker grandfather, Daniel, and their critical sister, Ruth, 14. She is soon made to feel at home by their gentle Quaker mother, Eunice, who begins to teach her cooking, cleaning, and other practical skills, since her education has been limited to such things as speaking French and playing the spinet. Though the boys play tricks on her, like pretending to be poisoned by her first attempt at bread making, and Ruth is scornful, Martitia persists, particularly developing skill at weaving, a family chore formerly done by an older sister now married. Her letter from her aunt in Richmond agrees, with poor grace, to take her in but is so insulting to her dead father and to the Gardners that she realizes how attached she has become to the merry family and even to Grandfather Daniel, who likes her gentle ways. At first she is afraid of Jonathan, handsome and serious law student, but she is always most attracted to him; kindly Clarkson is nicest to her. When she tells her aunt that she prefers to stay with the Gardners, her Uncle James writes, accusing Dr. David of having designs on her inheritance, small though it is, and insisting that she come to Richmond, not because they want her but because his pride is hurt; since roads are by now impassable until spring, however, Martitia stays. During the winter Grandfather Daniel dies. In the spring, Uncle James, on business in the area, arrives to demand that Martitia accompany him to Richmond, but Dr. David replies that when his son Jonathan, who is studying law, returns he will enter a plea for guardianship, since Martitia has become like a daughter to him. Uncle James vows to contest it. Clarkson, who is clearly in love with Martitia, and Barzillai go to Wilmington to learn the export trade, and Jonathan comes home for the summer. Martitia helps him overcome his fear of public speaking by being his audience as he practices in the mulberry orchard. During the summer, they visit a Gardner cousin, Sarah Gardner Mendenhall, a formidably educated woman whom Jonathan, it is assumed, will marry, and Martitia feels overwhelmed until they call on a French woman who raises silk worms and weaves silk, and Martitia is able to display her ability at French and to play the spinet. In the court, Jonathan's well-prepared case wins Martitia's guardianship for Dr.

David. A letter from Brazillai brings the news that Clarkson died of yellow fever. This calamity is added to poor crops and high cost of farm labor, and Dr. David fears that Jonathan will have to give up his law studies, but Martitia gets silkworm eggs from her French friend, and with the help of Addison and, finally, Ruth, she raises the worms and earns enough to keep him studying. When Martitia falls and gets shut by accident in the icehouse, Jonathan saves her, but in her confusion she thinks it is Clarkson come to greet her in death, and Jonathan assumes that her heart is given to his dead brother. In November, Jonathan, traveling with a judge in the area, comes home for a night, and together he and Martitia witness a great display of falling stars on Nov. 13, 1833, thinking perhaps the world is coming to an end. This shared experience makes Jonathan realize Martitia's love, and they agree to marry. The novel is more domestic romance than historical fiction, since emphasis throughout is on Martitia's adjustment to the family and her choice of a Gardner son for a husband. The details of her learning practical skills and, more important, to join in the laughter of the family, are interesting though never highly compelling or dramatic. Fanfare.

THIMBLE SUMMER (Enright*†, Elizabeth, ill. author, Farrar, 1938), episodic family novel set in Wisconsin one hot summer during the Great Depression. Tomboy, mischievous Garnet Linden, 9½, lives with her father, mother, older brother, Jay, and younger brother, Donald, on a grain and hog farm. Times are hard, and drought threatens the crops. While swimming with Jay in the river, Garnet finds a silver thimble which she thinks is magic. That night rain comes, and shortly thereafter her father gets a government loan to build a badly needed new barn. Eventful days follow for Garnet as she visits her friend Citronella Hauser, 11, whose great-grandmother tells the children a story about when she was a little girl and acquired a coral bracelet. On the night Garnet stays at the lime kiln with her father and Jay, an orphaned boy, Eric*, 13, appears, attracted by the fire. Destitute and homeless, he is taken in by the Lindens and becomes one of the family. Garnet and Citronella become so absorbed in their reading at the Blaiseville library that they are locked in when the librarian leaves for the night. On threshing day, Garnet feels unappreciated and unwanted and runs away, hitchhiking eighteen miles to New Conniston, where she spends most of the afternoon shopping for presents for her family. When she returns she finds that everyone has been too busy with threshing to miss her, except for Mr. Freebody, a kindly neighbor and special friend of Garnet's, who scolds her for being naughty. In September, Garnet enters her pet pig, Timmy, in the county fair at New Conniston. She and Citronella view the exhibits, ride the merry-go-round, take in some sideshows, and eat lots of ice cream. Although Timmy takes first prize for the best young boar, Garnet misses the judging because at the time she is on the Ferris wheel, which has gotten stuck. When she later reflects upon the happenings of the summer, Garnet attributes her good times and adventures to the thimble she found and decides to call this her "thimble summer." A pleasant story more concerned with a little girl's everyday activities than with farm or Depression problems, style is crisp and descriptive with interesting details about threshing and the fair. Except for Garnet, who appears as lively and fun-loving, characterization is shallow, and the little mystery introduced with Eric never comes to anything. Choice; Fanfare; Newbery Winner.

THE 13 CLOCKS (Thurber*, James, ill. Marc Simont, Simon, 1950), literary fairy tale told with puns, plays on words, inventive reversals of cliches, and other witty use of language. In Coffin Castle are thirteen clocks that have frozen at ten minutes to five, murdered by the cold Duke, who slew Time with his sword, wiped his bloody blade on its beard, and left it bleeding hours and minutes. The only warm hand in the castle belongs to the lovely Saralinda, supposedly the Duke's niece, but actually daughter of good King Gawain of Yarrow, stolen by the Duke in her infancy. Her nurse placed a spell on the Duke, preventing him from marrying Saralinda until she is twenty-one, and forcing him to allow other suitors to try for her hand. For these rash young men he thinks up impossible tasks, and when they fail he slits them from the guggle to the zatch and feeds them to the geese. Then a wandering minstrel arrives, a thing of rags and patches, calling himself Xingu, but really Prince Zorn of Zorna. He is advised by a little man who appears, calling himself a Golux, a creature of good will but flawed magic, who is never sure of his own statements because he makes things up and then forgets that they are not true. The Duke gives him only ninety-nine hours for a task that Zorn estimates will take ninety-nine days, to get one thousand jewels and to return when all the thirteen clocks are striking five. After several worthless suggestions, the Golux thinks of Hagga, a woman given the power of crying jewels after she frees King Gawain from a bear trap. Because she cried too much and made jewels too common, the gift had been amended to say that she will no longer be moved to tears and that if she laughs jewels, they will turn to tears in a fortnight. The Golux tries to make her laugh, finally succeeding. They collect one thousand jewels, hurry back just within the time limit, and the Golux shows Saralinda how she can start the clocks by holding her warm hand near them. The Duke's spy, Hark, reveals himself as an agent of King Gawain, also under a spell. Prince Zorn and Saralinda leave, after a fortnight the jewels turn to tears, and the Duke is eaten by the repulsive Todal, which looks like a blob of glup. In plot, the story is almost a parody of the traditional fairy tale. The clever language, particularly the use of alliteration and onomatopoeia, makes it fun to read aloud. Choice.

THIRTY-ONE BROTHERS AND SISTERS (Mirsky*, Reba Paeff, ill. W. T. Mars, Follett, 1952), realistic story set in the South African veld in an undetermined time. Warm-hearted and affectionate, Nomusa, 10, is the daughter of the Zulu Chief Zitu and the fourth of his six wives. Although she loves playing with her little brother, Themba, and caring for her baby sister, Bala, she would rather do the things that boys do and envies her brothers, Mdingi and Kangata, who take the cows to pasture and do not have to weed the garden or do household work. When the boys come into the kraal, the group of huts of Zitu and his wives, with one cow missing, Nomusa willingly goes to hunt for it, knowing its loss will be important in a culture which judges women by the number of cows they will merit for a bride price and will bring shame and trouble to Mdingi if it is not found. She must go deep into the woods before she finds it, its foot entangled in a vine. All the older boys and girls of their kraal, her half-brothers and sisters, go to a party at a neighboring kraal for Damasi, a boy to whom Nomusa is especially attracted, where she wins a prize for the best body paint, a pet monkey named Dube. Late in the evening of the party (which lasts all night), Nomusa sees a wild boar entering the kraal and manages to kill it with a spear. Because she found the cow and killed the boar, Zitu takes her on an elephant hunt, an unprecedented privilege for a girl, instead of Mdingi, who is older. The hunters walk for five days, see lions, kill two elephants, and encounter a band of pygmies. Nearly home, weary Nomusa falls into a pit trap, which contains a dead leopard. Damasi comes back to find her and pulls her out. She gives the leopard skin to Mdingi and tells him about the elephant kill, a dramatic episode that he recites at a celebration in a song composed with his special skill, thereby redeeming himself in his father's eye. The main interest in the book is in the country and customs of the Zulu people and the pygmies they meet on the hunt. Nomusa is a pleasant heroine, but it seems unlikely that in a culture where sex roles are so strictly differentiated she would have been allowed to accompany the men on the elephant hunt. This, like many of the minor episodes, seems contrived to introduce an activity typical of the tribe. The illustrations show the huts, clothes, weapons, animals, etc. But the faces are not African, more like American whites painted darker. Choice.

THIS BOY CODY (Wilson*, Leon, ill. Ursula Koering, Watts, 1950), amusing, realistic, episodic novel of family life set among the farm people of Cumberland Mountain in Tennessee in the mid-1900s. The five self-contained adventures revolve around impulsive, self-assured, active Cody Capshaw, 10, and his relations with his inventive father, Milt, his capable mother, Callie, and his sometimes annoying sister, Omalia, and their helpful and friendly neighbors. The family is poor, but they make the most of what they have and find happiness and excitement in small, everyday things. In the spring, on Cody's tenth birthday, the Capshaws build a new cabin with the help of their farming neighbors, Uncle Jeff Applegate, a thin husk of a man who works in wood, Amos Clodfelter, who is also a barber and stonemason, and Orvel Swinney, who assures Cody that the sourwood leaf he catches on that day will bring him good luck. With everyone pitching in, the house goes up in one day, and Callie and Omalia's fine dinner caps the houseraising event. Some weeks later, Milt and the two children trace some bees to their bee tree, and Mr. Swinney helps them saw down the tree and move the trunk to their yard, so that the Swinneys and the Capshaws will have a convenient hive of their own. On the longest day of the summer, Cody has a fantastic adventure in the hills after a long afternoon of huckleberrying. He loses track of time and is forced to spend the night in an abandoned cabin. During the night several talking domestic and wild animals arrive and settle in to await the appearance of a mysterious friend known to them as Martin. Cody takes to his heels at dawn, without waiting for Martin to show up. Being unable to solve the riddles Callie and his neighbors pose shakes Cody's self-confidence briefly, until he gets the hang of using his head and applying common sense to the puzzlers. The book ends with a rousing housewarming at Christmas time. Santa Claus comes with gifts for the Capshaws and their friends, everyone square dances to Milt's banjo and Uncle Jeff's fiddle, and Callie's sumptuous cooking satisfies everyone's appetite. Cody reflects that the sourwood leaf has brought him a year filled with good fortune. Loquacious, tall tale style, dialogue enlivened with picturesque hill expressions, a good sense of mountain life, some pleasing characters, and plenty of action and humor combine for light reading for those who are just mastering the printed word. Sequel is *This Boy Cody and His Friends*. Fanfare; Lewis Carroll.

THOM (*A Cat of Paris**), self-centered, vain, disobedient Siamese kitten, who ignores his mother's admonitions to behave and is sold in the Paris Bird Market and carried home in a bird cage for his mischievous ways. Luckily, he is bought by an American family, whose father is an artist. Through various misadventures he learns to control his mischievous inclinations and his pride and to appreciate his comfortable and loving home. He also gets his portrait painted, a long-held desire, by the struggling young artist, Maurice* Pascal.

THOMAS COFFYN (*Downright Dencey**), ship captain and loving father of Dencey. He likes to have fun and appreciates beautiful things. He brings home to Dencey and the family strange and exotic gifts which stir Dencey's soul and foster her love of beauty. These are not always welcomed by the strict Quaker family he has married into. Life is more pleasant for Dencey when he is at home because he is relaxed and easy-going and Dencey's mother, Lydia Severance Coffyn, seems less tense and abstracted. He is a sympathetic character and foil for Dencey's mother.

THOMAS TEENEY (*The Enchanted Schoolhouse**), Brian Boru's helpful school teacher in Ireland, who tells him how to catch the fairyman*: by the scruff of the neck while you snatch the red cap from his head. He also persuades Brian Boru that it would be fair and just to release the little man after he has done his enchantments, explaining to the boy that nothing likes to be imprisoned forever.

THREE SIDES OF AGIOCHOOK: A TALE OF THE NEW ENGLAND FRONTIER IN 1775 (Kelly*, Eric P., ill. LeRoy Appleton, Macmillan, 1935), historical novel set in New Hampshire in the early days of the American Revolution. Some sixteen years earlier, Ayonba*, a Wabanaki Indian scout, coming upon the massacre of the Indians at St. Francis on the St. Lawrence river, has saved the infant son of Louise Gill, a French-Indian girl married to an English soldier held prisoner. The child, blond, blue-eyed Philip Brewster, has been raised by a minister in Montreal but has always spent summers with his Indian Gill cousins. At the book's opening, he is a student at Moor's Charity School, a prep school for Indians associated with Dartmouth College in Hanover, N.H., a settlement on the edge of the frontier. Because it seems his Tory sentiments will not be questioned, Philip is chosen by the founder of the college, Eleazar Wheelock*, to take a message to Joseph* Brant, a Mohawk Indian and former student of the school, asking him to get his Mohawks, who side with the British, to spare the school, which supports the revolutionaries. Unfortunately, word of Philip's mission gets out and he is ambushed, injured, and captured by Mohawk Indians, traditional enemies of the Wabanaki, who have been alerted by the British, but he is rescued by Ayonba, who has secretly kept track of the boy. Together they travel north, hiding out on one stormy night on Mt. Washington, where Philip has a vision of the three sides of the mountain, known as Agiochook by the Indians: the British and revolutionists on one side, the Indians on another, and the French on the third, all three being parts of Philip's own ancestry. Philip is ill and mentally confused after his head injury and collapses. As his canoe is about to be smashed, it is pulled from the rapids by Antoinette Raoul, daughter of a French trapper. She takes Philip and Ayonba in, and Philip's mind gradually clears, but the Mohawks surround and fire the cabin, and they are able to escape only when the attacking Indians are scared off by the cry of the Chibal, the ghost. This turns out to be Thomas Sargent, father of Philip, who has lived as a hermit since the death of his Indian wife. Antoinette stays with Sargent, and Philip and Ayonba continue, but, nearly to St. Francis, they are captured by hired thugs under a British army captain. Fortunately, the cook is Antoinette's father, conscripted against his will, and he releases Ayonba, who alerts Joseph Brant. Brant rescues Philip and promises to spare Dartmouth from Indian raids. Despite the historical basis for most of the story, the plot is so dependent upon coincidence as to be often implausible, and the characters are mostly stock figures: Ayonba, the noble savage; Antoinette, the beautiful rose of the wilderness; Philip, the visionary hero of mixed ancestry, etc. The action, however, is fast paced and the story gives an idea of some little-known history of the American Revolution. Fanfare.

THREE STUFFED OWLS (Robertson*†, Keith, ill. Jack Weaver, Viking, 1954), mystery story set in Belleville, N.J., in the 1950s. The co-owners of the Carson St. Detective Agency, Sweed (Stephen) Larson and Neil Lambert, both 16, become involved in solving a diamond-smuggling case when a young neighbor, Ginny Haggard, 10, hires them to find her brother's bicycle which was stolen from the rack at the drug store after she had taken it without permission. While hunting for it, they win a piglet, which they name Mildred, at the Grange carnival. By chance, they go to nearby Princeton Junction, find the bike, and get a description of the man who left it when he boarded a train there several days before. Later they learn that a Carl Nystrom, who worked for a German-born taxidermist, Von Brugge, has disappeared suddenly, leaving his clothes and even money behind. By the description, which includes a missing right index finger, they deduce that Nystrom is the bike thief and at night they visit Von Brugge's shop, a lonely place that used to be a diner on the highway. There they are startled by the unearthly screech of a barn owl, though the three owls in the window are clearly stuffed. A couple of days later, the boys, trying to train Mildred like a hunting dog, see Von Brugge carrying a gun and follow him to an old barn. They rescue him from an abandoned manure pit where he has fallen and become good friends. He gives them the stuffed owls, one of which, he explains, is fitted with a small speaker that emits shrieks and which he has used to scare off prowlers. The boys set two of the owls in a tree in the Lambert yard with wires to the old carriage house which contains their agency, in order to scare a fussy neighbor. Both boys are shocked when they hear that Von Brugge has been arrested for a diamond smuggling scheme, in which the jewels are shipped in stuffed birds which he imports from Antwerp. They persuade Mr. Lambert to get an attorney friend, Dave Robbins, to defend the taxidermist, and the boys set out to solve the mystery, which they are convinced involves Nystrom. Events follow fast: they discover Nystrom in a lakeside cottage and overhear an argument between him and his brother, Dan, whose voice they recognize as belonging to the man who picked up an imported owl identical to theirs from Von Brugge's shop; they are battered in a storm as they return on their bikes and find the police too busy to be interested in their news; at Robbins's suggestion, they visit the old barn and find a diary that dropped from Von Brugge's pocket in the manure pit but are themselves trapped there by the Nystrom's brother, who has overheard them speculate that one of their owls, because of a mix-up, is really the imported owl; to get him to leave, they tell him that the owl is in the tree, figuring he will have to wait until dark to retrieve it, then they build a platform on which Steve can stand and Neil, climbing on his shoulders, can clamber out; they arrive in Lambert's yard just as the villain runs off with the owl, but Mildred, who has often joined in their football games, dashes up and blocks him. When it is discovered that Nystrom is dead, his brother confesses to the smuggling to prove an alibi. It is later discovered that Nystrom's death was an accident. Although the plot moves fast, at many crucial points it depends on unlikely coincidence. The attempt to make the boys seem real by having them ride bikes around town and enjoy malts and banana splits at the drug store succeeds in dating the story and making them seem about three years younger than the sixteen they are said to be. Choice.

THUDY THRIPP (*Penelope Ellen**), Arethusa Amelia, friend of Penelope Ellen and cousin of Cressy Pidgeon, who is a year and a half older. Motherless Thudy lives with the large Ring family, her cousins, while her father is at sea, and she tags along after Cressy and Zeph Ring, 12, feeling sorry for herself and sniffing mournfully. Friendship with lively Penny rehabilitates her and raises her self-image.

THURBER, JAMES (GROVER) (1894–1961), born in Columbus, Ohio; editor, cartoonist, writer of some of the most original books of his period. He attended Ohio State University, then served as a code clerk in the American Embassy in Paris in 1918–1920. Later he worked as a reporter for the Columbus *Dispatch*, for the Chicago *Tribune* in Paris, and for the New York *Evening Post*, and in 1927 he joined the *New Yorker* as an editor and writer, continuing to contribute to the magazine until his death, although blindness caused him to discontinue his drawing in his later years. His first book published for children was *Many Moons* (Harcourt, 1943), a clever picture book whose illustrator Louis Slobodkin*, was awarded the Caldecott Medal. This was followed by *The Great Quillow** (Harcourt, 1944), a humorous story of how a toymaker defeats a voracious giant, *The White Deer* (Harcourt, 1946), *The 13 Clocks** (Simon, 1950), and *The Wonderful O* (Simon, 1955), all stories that employ reversals of typical folktale patterns and exuberant word play.

TIBBIE MCNABB (*Meggy MacIntosh**), tall, gangling Highland girl who travels in steerage on the *Bachelor of Leith* and is ridiculed for saying frankly that she is going to America to find a husband. Because she spent her passage money wildly on inappropriate clothes, Tibbie has paid her fare by becoming a bound-out girl to neighbors of the Claytons in North Carolina. When her employers decide to return to Scotland, they plan to sell her time to a brutal-looking man who almost bought her earlier, but Meggy trades a ruby for Tibbie's time, plus a riding outfit and an old white horse. Tibbie is delighted and grateful and becomes a devoted companion to Meggy.

TIBBY ARMINTER (*Runaway Prentice**), Isabella, sister of Tris*, youngest of the Arminter children, who helps Jeff hide after he runs away from his master. In a comic scene she smuggles food to him from the Arminter pantry. She insists the children tell Mary that Nolly may have been seen by the sailor, and her left-handedness convinces lawyer Minturn that the second sailor was really Will Arminter. Nolly had previously been identified by the tune he whistled, "Over the Hills and Far Away." Tibby is much like Susan (Sukey) in her tastes and behavior.

TIEN PAO (*The House of Sixty Fathers**), the young Chinese boy who, when swept downriver into Japanese-held territory, bravely makes his way back to Hengyang through many dangers, accompanied by his pig, Glory* of the Republic. Naive and frightened, Tien Pao is nonetheless a child of determination and courage. His warning shout saves the American airman he sees crash, and his stubborn conviction that he will find his parents eventually brings about their reunion, with the help of the "sixty fathers," the American flyers who have taken him in.

TIETJENS, EUNICE (HAND HAMMOND) (1884–1944), born in Chicago, Ill.; widely traveled author of books set in exotic countries. When she was thirteen her father died and her mother took her to live in Europe. She later lived in China, Japan, North Africa, and the South Pacific. During World War I she was an overseas correspondent for the Chicago *Daily News*. A poet herself, she was for many years on the staff of *Poetry* magazine and taught at the University of Miami in Florida. Among her books for young people are *Boy of the Desert* (Coward, 1928) and *Boy of the South Seas** (Coward, 1931), a Newbery honor book.

TIL CAREY (*In a Mirror**), Mathilda, college roommate of Bessie* Muller, dance major, focus of the reader's interest. Graceful, beautiful, proud, loyal, she accumulates boys with ease, each of whom she casts off when the passion to perform dominates her. Her infatuation with literature professor Donald* Dunn seems contrived and not in keeping with her character as presented. Child of divorce, Til spends holidays with Bessie's family, enjoying a home life with Mr. and Mrs. Muller* and Bessie that she has never known. She captivates Rab Corn, Bessie's father's young cousin, who writes gushy poems to her.

TIN WOODMAN (*The Wonderful Wizard of Oz**), character whom Dorothy*, Toto*, and the Scarecrow* find rusted stiff in the woods on their way to the Emerald City and who joins them in order to ask the Wizard* for a heart. Though he exhibits kindness and sentiment during all their adventures, he still thinks he needs a heart, so the Wizard gives him one made of silk and stuffed with straw. The Tin Woodman becomes the king of the Winkies.

TODD, RUTHVEN (1914–   ), born in Edinburgh, Scotland, a descendant of Sir Walter Scott and other eminent Scottish literary figures; poet, novelist, essayist, biographer for adults, and writer of a once-popular series of science fiction stories for children. The eldest of the ten children of an architect, his early ambition was to become an artist. He attended Edinburgh College of Art and won some prizes for his paintings. Times being hard, he worked for two years as a shepherd and farm laborer on the island of Mull, where he began writing poems in his spare moments. Returning to Edinburgh, he assisted in an art gallery, worked at a literary agency, and became assistant editor for the *Scottish Bookman* and *Horizon*; then he moved to London where he held a variety of positions, teaching, operating a pottery gallery, copywriting, selling books, and working for Civil Defense in World War II. After emigrating to the United States in 1948, he operated the Weekend Press in New York and taught creative writing at Iowa State University and at the State University of New York at Buffalo. He began writing professionally during World War II, and some thirty books, from thrillers to scholarly works, followed, the novels for adults mostly under the pseudonym R. T. Campbell. The writer William Lipkind suggested that he write a space novel for children, and the result was *Space Cat** (Scribner's,

1952), about spirited Flyball's trip to the moon, which is listed in *Choice*. Other adventures of the intrepid gray cat appear in *Space Cat Visits Venus* (Scribner's, 1955), *Space Cat Meets Mars* (Scribner's, 1957), and *Space Cat and the Kittens* (Scribner's, 1958), more spoofs on the science fiction genre. His other books for young readers are *First Animal Book* (Lunn, 1946), *Trucks, Tractors, and Trailers* (Putnam, 1954), and *Tan's Fish* (Little, 1958), about a Chinese boy who finds a new species of fish in a mountain stream. He has received many honors for his writing, including a citation from the National Institute of Arts and Letters. He became a citizen of the United States in 1959 and has made his home in Martha's Vineyard.

TOD MORAN (*Heart of Danger**), young third mate on the freighter *Araby*. At first he opposes Rudy's* accompanying him on the spying mission to Paris because he feels the younger man lacks courage and endurance. Tod is a realist; he is more assertive than Rudy and is a bit of a rogue. He is a foil for Rudy and is much less well developed as a character. He is the central character of a series of adventure novels.

TOD OF THE FENS (Whitney*, Elinor, Macmillan, 1928), mystery-farce with historical novel aspects set against the development of England's merchant fleet and its trade in wool with the continent in the early fifteenth century. A bluff and brawny man, with an infectious laugh and a great shock of unkempt hair, Tod of the Fens leads a band of merry rogues and adventurers who live in rude huts in the fens near the port of Boston. Of obscure and shadowy background, they prey on travelers to make sport of them. Tod takes into his band Dismas, who is really Henry, the Prince of Wales. For a lark, he wagers Tod's men that in a week and a day he will make fools out of all the townsfolk in Boston. Assuming various disguises, he steals one-by-one the five keys to the town strong box. He leaves the contents untouched and deposits the keys at the foot of the steeple of St. Botolph's church. The townspeople assume their treasure has been stolen and are in great dismay. Suspicion soon falls on Sir Frederick Tilney, councilman, overseer of the wool trade in Boston, and newly become a Merchant-Adventurer. He had begun building his own fleet to trade in wool on the continent in opposition to the powerful Hanseatic League. Two nefarious councilmen, suspecting that the treasure is intact, plan to break open the coffer, steal the money, and put the blame on Tilney. Ranolf, a Hanseatic trader, kidnaps Sir Frederick's daughter, pretty, lively Johanna, newly betrothed to Gilbert Branche, son of another Merchant-Adventurer. On the pretense of giving her information, he lures her to a midnight tryst at the church, where she happens to find the keys. A series of amusing misadventures ensues involving a large number of people until finally Tod of the Fens takes possession of the treasure. He enlists the aid of Prince Henry (Dismas) to straighten things out and put the town back to rights again. Henry does this with the help of Tod and his men at the festival on Corpus Christi Day. Tod and his men become sailors for Sir Frederick, Tod commanding Tilney's first vessel, and all have a good future in store for them as England assumes mastery of the seas. Once this mixture of high-jinks and coincidence gets going, it becomes very entertaining and suspenseful, and conveys as well a limited sense of the problems, customs, and the daily life of the period. The cast is large, though easy to keep track of, but there is little attempt at character development. Dialogue, if spiced with "thee's" and "thou's," is lively and quite apprehensible, and the faulty pacing is forgivable in this rollicking comedy of errors. Newbery Honor.

TOM CANTY (*The Prince and the Pauper**), London slum boy who, through an odd chance, changes places with Edward* Tudor, later Edward VI of England. Because a kind priest has taught him to read, Tom's lively imagination has been fueled by ideas far from his beggar status, and he had developed lordly manners in play with his ragged friends. These manners and his learning, as well as the real prince's clothes, make the courtiers believe that he is the real prince, touched by madness. Terrified at first, Tom adjusts to his situation and cleverly pumps those around him for information that helps cover up his ignorance. Though he has a brutal father and a fiendish grandmother, he has been influenced by his kindly mother, and as king he shows an unprecedentedly merciful nature.

TOM DAVENPORT (*Call of the Mountain**), blacksmith of Forestdale, who is an inventor on the side. A real historical figure, he buys an electric contrivance with which he invents an electric wheel that he hopes to patent and sell, providing a revolutionary new source of energy. Most villagers think he is foolish, a dreamer who wastes his time when he should be building up his blacksmith business. Among these is Rufus Goss, the father of Emily, whom he marries and who remains loyal and supportive. When he needs silk cloth for his invention, Emily tears up her wedding gown into the necessary strips. Tom is a good friend of Nathan, whose story somewhat parallels his own.

TOM SAWYER (*The Adventures of Tom Sawyer**; *The Adventures of Huckleberry Finn**), epitome of happy, carefree boyhood in the book that bears his name but petty tyrant in its sequel. Although Tom is a leader of the other boys in their play battles and "pirate" adventures, and he enjoys acting the character of Robin Hood, he is clearly indulging in romantic make-believe in the first book, but in *The Adventures of Huckleberry Finn* he is obsessive in his insistence on the "right" (literary) way that Jim's* escape must be engineered. His unkindness in prolonging his aunt's grief in *Tom Sawyer* is forgivable as boyish delight at the prospect of appearing at his own funeral. His cruelty to Jim in prolonging his fear and slavery and adding to it torments of rats, spiders, and hard labor has no purpose beyond a compulsive insistence on his ideas from romantic literature.

TOM WHIPPLE (Edmonds*†, Walter D., ill. Paul Lantz, Dodd, 1942), short historical novel set mostly in Russia in 1837, which retells a true story of how a persistent, practical Yankee farm boy, who thinks he is as good as any man alive, gains an audience with the emperor of Russia. While on a trip to Washington with his mother to collect her widow's pension, Tom Whipple develops a yearning "to see something of the world." Over his mother's objections, he signs on the sailing ship *Flora Bascom*; then he later learns the ship is bound for Russia. Tom thinks he would like to talk things over with the ruler of the country that licked Napoleon Bonaparte. He recalls the words of his mother's neighbor, Supervisor Utley, whose homespun philosophy often comes to Tom's mind, that, when you want to find out about something, you go to see the top man. Mr. Dallas, the American minister in St. Petersburg, informs Tom that it is customary to give the emperor a present and helps him contact the Chamberlain. When Tom appears confidently at the palace in dusty peajacket and clicking sea boots, he is informed that the emperor's day is too full to allow an unscheduled appointment. Tom insists on giving the emperor his present in person, and the Chamberlain, baffled by Tom's calm persistence, relents. The emperor introduces himself simply as "Nicholas" and ushers Tom into his office, to Tom's mind, behaving in quite a neighborly fashion. Tom's present, an acorn from Mt. Vernon, delights the emperor, who says he greatly admires George Washington. Tom and Nicholas have a long chat about various state affairs, and Tom stays for lunch with the empress and the children. One of the emperor's daughters shyly gives Tom a crochet for his mother, and the emperor gives him a gold watch with a chain and ruby and gratifies his wish to see the city of Moscow. At the end of the afternoon, Tom politely takes his leave. He enjoys the sights of Moscow, escorted about the city by Nicholas's Cossacks, and then works his way back home on the *Francis I*. He hurries to Westernville, where, his wanderlust satisfied, he shares his Russian experience with his mother and her neighbors, Supervisor Utley and his wife. The story, if slight, exhibits a distinct flair for storytelling that is reinforced by understatement, droll humor, and savory dialect. Numerous full-page, realistic, black and white drawings and a few full-color paintings point up scenes, show character, create setting, and add credibility to a real life tall tale. This telling of Tom's story may have been inspired by World War II, when efforts to promote patriotism and convince Americans of their potential for success were in vogue. Fanfare.

TONY (*Magic Money**), Manuel Antonio, called Tony, a little Costa Rican boy of almost ten who lives with his parents and brother and sister on the estate of a coffee-growing Patron. Tony has a secret yearning to buy his Grandpapa* a new pair of oxen. Tony is naive and tends to bite off more than he can chew. He is quite emotional and easily moved to tears. He learns to look at things more realistically and to listen more carefully to advice. He is not as convincing a character as is his Grandpapa.

TONY SANTO (*Hill of Little Miracles**), restless elder son in the Santo family, Ricco's* older brother. He keeps things lively around the house. He and a pal, Danny* O'Reilly, are caught by Danny's father, Policeman O'Reilly, helping themselves to bags of peanuts they think have been abandoned and are arrested for theft. Policeman O'Reilly arranges for a judge to give the two a good scare in the courtroom the next day. They get two months' probation and whippings from their fathers.

TOO MANY CHERRIES (Carmer*, Carl, ill. Jay Hyde Barnum, Viking, 1949), short realistic novel set about 1945, which starts and ends on a cherry farm in New York State. Cherries are so abundant this year that prices have fallen to the point where Bill Bailey's father feels he must let the cherries rot. He cannot afford to hire pickers. Aunt Betty's chance remark that her relatives in New Orleans would gladly pay double to get them gives Bill, 10, an idea. He suggests that the family load the pickup truck with cherries and peddle them in the cities themselves, rather than work through a middleman. In the middle of the night, he and George, the hired man, head for Pittsburgh with five hundred boxes of cherries. Before dawn, they stop for breakfast at Miss Maggie's truck stop restaurant, where they have chocolate cream pie and enjoy the banter of the truckers gathered there. Two semi-drivers, Fax, who is transporting chickens cross country, and a milk truck driver, put on a Road-e-o, a parking contest, which Bill helps time. On the way into Lancaster, Pa., in Amish country, the pickup develops engine trouble, and they just make it into the city. While George arranges for a mechanic, Bill makes friends with Conrad Weisenberger, an Amish youth, and his father, who have come to sell produce at the market. Bill sells the cherries to the Weisenburgers, saving the cost and inconvenience of securing a sales license. The cherries sell quickly, and after a hearty noon meal of ''plain'' food with the Weisenburgers, Bill and George head home. They stop again at Miss Maggie's, where Slim, another semi-driver, offers Bill a ride back to the family farm in his ''suicide'' box, the cot in the rear of his cab. Bill greets his family with the cheerful news that the people of Lancaster want more cherries. Incidents and characters seem artificial, deliberately assembled to give young readers views of three different economic and social groups. The book consists mostly of dialogue, and there are a few exciting scenes. The result is an amusing, innocuous, somewhat instructive story for young readers. Fanfare.

TO TELL YOUR LOVE (Stolz*†, Mary, Harper, 1950), realistic novel of an adolescent girl's love affair set for a few days one summer in the mid-1900s in a small city not far from New York City. Attractive, literary, voluble Anne Armacost, 17, just graduated from high school and planning on college, lives in a middle-class community with her loving and supportive family, her father, a high school English teacher, her mother, her older sister, Theo*, 23, a nurse, and her brother, Johnny*, 14. In flashbacks and linear narrative, the book tells of her romance with handsome, polite Douglas Eamons, a college freshman, about how he first notices her at Christmastime and how she falls ecstatically in love, about their dates and her growing jealousy for pretty, fun-loving, boy-chasing Dody Colman, whom Doug also sees, and about how she tries desperately to cling to him when he fails to call and becomes moody and even sharp with her family. A subplot involves another, contrasting love affair, that of practical, sensible, aphoristic-speaking Theo, who meets, is courted by, and falls in love with wealthy Paul* Favor, serious-minded, life-loving nephew of one of her patients. Contrasting with both these love stories is that of Nora Chapin, Anne's high school chum and wife of Sam, a friend of Doug. Nora marries at seventeen, and at eighteen has a baby whom she loves but considers an encumbrance. Both she and her young husband, now a college student by night and a mechanic by day, love and enjoy each other but have many money worries. Lightening the tone and adding depth are Johnny's teenaged escapades with his school friends and incidents of ordinary everyday family life at the Armacost* house and with some neighbors. At the end of the story, Anne visits Nora and sees how she has changed. On a family picnic the following Sunday she sees Doug with Dody, reads the plea for understanding in his eyes, and realizes that Doug feels college is best for him now. Anne's hurt is not gone, but she sees that overpossessiveness and love are incompatible. This blend of rich characterizations, sensitively drawn family relationships, some humor, witty dialogue, and a style too florid with adjectives but still pleasingly and appropriately literary remains interesting to the end. Although obviously lesson-oriented, the book never lapses into tract, sentiment, melodrama, or ''girlishness,'' but the hospital scenes strike a false note. (Mrs. and Mrs. Armacost*) Fanfare.

TOTO (*The Wonderful Wizard of Oz**), little, black dog belonging to Dorothy*. Because Dorothy is chasing Toto, they fail to get into the cyclone cellar in time, and so are blown to the land of Oz*. Because Dorothy is chasing Toto in the Emerald City, she fails to get into the Wizard's* balloon before it rises on what they hope will be a return trip to Kansas. Unlike some of the animals in Oz (the Cowardly* Lion, for instance), Toto cannot talk.

THE TOUGH WINTER (Lawson*, Robert, ill. author, Viking, 1954), sequel to *Rabbit Hill**, also set in Connecticut, probably a couple of years later. The animals on The Hill, having become accustomed to generous handouts, are appalled to learn that the Folks are leaving to spend the winter in the Bluegrass country of Kentucky. Uncle* Analdas predicts a tough winter, and Little Georgie has to help him and Father collect, dry, and store bundles of clover all through the beautiful autumn. After the first snow and ice storm, just as the Folks are about to leave, their cat, Mr. Muldoon, is missing. Willie* Fieldmouse, who tunnels under the snow, knows that the cat is iced into a hole near the wall. At Little Georgie's suggestion, the mice steal some of the meat from the Thanksgiving turkey carcass that Foxy has taken and give it to the cat, but the rabbits cannot break the ice and must enlist the help of the Buck to free the cat. The caretakers bring with them a city dog, a mongrel who knows none of the accepted rules of the chase and almost catches Uncle Analdas. When the dog almost digs Porkey, the woodchuck, out of his den, Little Georgie saves the day by enlisting the help of Phewie, the skunk. Tim McGrath, the neighboring farmer who does odd jobs for the Folks, having been converted by them to be a friend of the animals, confiscates the Caretaker's gun after a couple of blasts at Little Georgie and Father. A fire, started by the Caretaker's cigarette, sweeps over the hill and most of the animals are forced to move to find food. The firetruck crushes the Rabbit family's store room, destroying most of their provender. They have a respite from short rations at Christmas, when Tim McGrath spreads a feast of hay, grain, and nuts, but their supplies are gone by Groundhog Day, and they wait anxiously through the grey morning for Porkey to emerge. When he does, Father engages him in a long conversation, much to the consternation of Uncle Analdas, until a glimmer of sunshine breaks through and he sees his shadow, insuring six more weeks of winter. Mother goes to stay with a married daughter, so Georgie, Father, Uncle Analdas, and Willie, who has moved in with them, live on what little they can scavenge. The old uncle starts asking questions about the Bluegrass region and finally sets off alone, determined to find the Folks and bring them back. Half dead, he stumbles into Tim McGrath's barn, half a mile from The Hill, sure that he has reached his destination. Hunting for him, Father becomes ill. Finally, the six weeks past, spring comes. The Caretakers leave; the Folks return. Mother comes back and is grieving for Uncle Analdas when the old rabbit turns up, fat and sleek, having spent the last of the winter in Tim McGrath's "bluegrass region." As in the first book, the events are seen through the eyes of small animals, with considerable warmth and humor. The desperate situation of animals in a bitter winter is the focal point, so the story is not as lighthearted as its predecessor. Choice; Fanfare.

THE TOWER BY THE SEA (DeJong*†, Meindert, ill. Barbara Comfort, Harper, 1950), story based on a legend set in the village of Katverloren, Holland, some time after the year 1000. A wise old woman living alone in a cottage by the graveyard saves a fledgling magpie and a kitten, which has survived an attempt to drown it because it has one blue eye, an evil sign. A slightly crazed, lonely wife of the lighthouse keeper, a young childless woman named Alice, haunts the graveyard at night, believing that she has had a child buried there. When a fever strikes the children, the villagers think it is caused by the old woman, who must be a witch, and when Alice, hearing that all the babies are dying, steals the burgomaster's baby to take it to her island for safety, the villagers blame the witch for the baby's absence and set out to burn her. The old woman's cat, which has been tortured by the village boys by having a pot tied to its tail, is rescued by Alice and taken with the baby in her boat. In the storm, the boat overturns, but the cradle stays right side up and, with the cat jumping back and forth to balance it, washes in toward shore. It is spotted in time so that the old woman, the baby, and the cat are all saved. While the story has some qualities of legend (only Alice, for instance, has a name), it also has a realistic explanation for all the phenomena, and it gives an understanding of the feelings of the animals without attributing human qualities to them. Its theme is a strong indictment of superstition. Fanfare.

TRADER JIM WHITTAKER (*The Ordeal of the Young Hunter**), the Bellicano (American) who runs the Navajo trading post near which Jadih* lives. He is a polite, unassuming young man, who respects Navajo ways and beliefs. He has a great influence on Jadih's life. He suggests the boy enter the dance contest in Flagstaff and that he make an animal dance more dramatic by giving it a storyline and concluding it with an exhibition of his expert marksmanship with bow and arrow. He is also called Mr. Jim.

TRAPPING THE SILVER BEAVER (Niehuis*, Charley, ill. Chris Kenyon, Dodd, 1956), realistic adventure novel set in the mid-twentieth century in western Arizona along the Colorado River, which forms a border with California. Orphan Webb Dodge, 17, has landed in jail for killing and butchering a calf whose mother bogged down in marshy ground and died, a killing that has sent his Uncle Jake to prison and, on top of a record of poaching and truancy, seems destined to put Webb in reform school. When Judge Schaulkler puts him on probation in the care of the game warden, Brant Murphy, Webb is surprised and suspicious but grateful to Brant for keeping his beautiful Labrador, Champ, while he's locked up and for letting him live in a shack near his cabin and trap muskrats. Knowing the Slough, the swampy area east of the river, better even than the warden, he is well suited until one day he runs into Bango, the tough who was tank boss while he was in jail, and another man, poaching beaver. With their bigger boat they run him down, wreck his boat, and finally leave, thinking he has been killed by their propeller. The next day Brant, having hired Webb to guide him to do a beaver study, gets the whole story out of the boy but doesn't know whether to believe it. When they return, Webb sees that his cabin has been searched. Since the river for some miles is going to be flooded by a dam, Brant gets permission to run controlled trapping in that area and hires Webb and an older trapper, Tom Jesson, a one-eyed, nature-wise outdoorsman whom Webb likes immediately, to handle the operation. Still, signs of trouble appear. Tom finds a couple of beavers that have each lost a foot recently in another trap, a sign that poachers are busy. On an evening in town, Webb is offered a deal for hiding some of the pelts and selling them to the poachers. After he refuses, their island camp is set afire, and he and Tom narrowly escape with their stock of pelts. Webb takes Judge Schaulkler goose hunting and shows how beautifully trained is Champ, the dog he found as a pup and schooled himself. Soon after, Webb is hired to take a stranger named Savote hunting. In the blind, Savote explains the big deal he has in beaver fur and offers to cut Webb in. Webb refuses and discovers that Bango is part of Savote's group. Bango beats him up and dumps him in the river for dead. Webb is able to get to land only with

Champ's help. He has scarcely recovered when Tom is injured as they try to shoot a rapids, and Webb is left to carry on alone. He does well with the trapping but discovers that he is being watched from a point across the river, and, as the pelts pile up and Brant doesn't come to collect them, he worries. When he returns to camp one day to find the bales of pelts gone, he chases the poachers' boat, maneuvering in the rapids by his superior skill so that their attempt to wreck his boat backfires and they crash. Bango is killed. Webb saves the other poacher and recovers the floating bales of pelts. Judge Schaulkler wipes out Webb's court record, and Brant, who knows that Champ is a valuable animal, hunts up the original owner, buys the dog, and gives Webb legal ownership. The story of the trapping and poaching is based on a good situation, and the details of beaver operation and of the setting are interesting. The story of Webb's reformation, however, is predictable, and the narrow escapes from the vicious poachers are too numerous to be believable. Characters are types. Spur.

TRAVIS COATES (*Old Yeller**), narrator who has been left in charge of the Texas homestead by his father. Travis shows a mixture of sound judgment and childish resentment at the trouble caused him by his brother, Little Arliss, and the big, yellow, stray dog. At the crucial moment he forces himself to shoot the dog, which has been bitten by a rabid wolf, an action that demonstrates maturity.

A TREE FOR PETER (Seredy*, Kate, ill. author, Viking, 1941), realistic novel of family and community life set in Shantytown on the outskirts of a large American city in what appears to be the mid-1900s. Small, lame Peter, 6, is lonely and afraid of many things. He lives with his widowed mother in a one-room tumbledown shack, staying by himself every day while she works in the city. He gradually outgrows his fears and shyness with the help of a kindly, bearded, elderly tramp, Peter King, whom Peter calls King Peter (King Peter calls him Prince Peter) for his gentle ways and regal manner. The tramp encourages the boy to be friendly to a stray dog, who becomes his companion, Pal, and with the local policeman, Irish Pat, who becomes the staunch friend of both Peter and his mother. The tramp gives Peter a little, red shovel, with which the boy and Pat make a tiny bit of lawn edged with flower bulbs in the rubbish-strewn yard. At Christmas time the tramp leaves a small tree covered with glowing Christmas lights in a hole Peter has painstakingly dug with the red shovel. The warmth and beauty of the cheerful, little tree lures residents from the ramshackle dwellings, and soon the previously anti-social inhabitants of Shantytown begin to enjoy one another's company. In the spring, Peter's bit of lawn glows green with new life, and the bulbs he and Pat planted bloom. The occupants of Shantytown are inspired to a clean-up and fix-up campaign, for which Pat secures funds from city hall. Soon the depressing huts have become snow white houses of which the people are justly proud, and all that is left of Shantytown is the name. The third person narrative about Peter Marsh is enclosed within a frame story, in which Peter Marsh, a famous builder, whom another builder, Thomas Crandon, consults about restoring Shantytown, reflects on his life. Crandon decided to become a builder because, ironically, he had seen from a train window, when he was a boy, little, lame Peter (now Marsh) gazing desolate and wistful through the Shantytown iron fence. The frame story seems an unnecessary complication. It overforeshadows events and underscores the sentimentality of the main story. Style is very descriptive, dialogue is cliched, and characters are types. Numerous romantic, brown-toned, strongly composed, representational illustrations help ground the story in reality. Fanfare.

TREE OF FREEDOM (Caudill*†, Rebecca, ill. Dorothy Bayley Morse, Viking, 1949), historical novel about the land rush into Kentucky in 1780, told from the point of view of thirteen-year-old Stephanie* Venable. Descendants of Huguenots, her family, hardworking Jonathan, staunch Bertha, and their five children, the eldest of whom are practical Stephanie and idealistic Noel*, about fifteen, travel on foot from North Carolina to Jonathan's claim of four hundred acres four miles from Harrod's Fort in Kentucky, still part of Virginia colony and not yet a state. Plucky and confident, they have only such essentials with which to start their new life as a cow, a few pigs, and some chickens, axes, and hoes. Stephanie plants an apple seed carefully in a sheltered spot at the edge of their clearing. Calling it her "Tree of Freedom," she tends it carefully, regarding it as the symbol of their hopes and dreams in this sometimes frightening but usually promising land of opportunity. The family toils to raise a log house and clear ground for crops to meet the coming winter, to insure their survival in this densely forested area in which their nearest neighbor is a recluse, Lonesome* Tilly, and hostile Indians may lurk behind any tree. When they are informed that their land is claimed by a wealthy British-sympathizing gentleman from the West Indies, they realize how important for them will be the outcome of the war between Britain and the colonies. Jonathan takes a job as a courier, and shortly after his departure, instigated by the British, Indians attack a nearby settlement. Noel leaves to join Colonel George Rogers Clark whose detachment defeats the Indians at Chillicothe. While Jonathan and Noel are away, much of the responsibility for keeping the place going and for the safety of the family falls on Stephanie. When Jonathan returns with money to buy an additional thousand acres and Noel with information that the West Indies claim is fraudulent, the future looks bright for the Venables. Substantial and convincing characterization, a colloquial, homespun style with lots of dialogue, and many details about the thinking, ways, and problems of the pioneers combine to produce an interesting story which conveys a good sense of what it must have been like in frontier Kentucky during the Revolutionary War. (Lonesome* Tilly) Choice; Fanfare; Newbery Honor.

TREFFINGER, CAROLYN ELIZABETH (1891–   ), born on a farm near Seville, Medina County, Ohio; educator who wrote several books for children, the best known being *Li Lun, Lad of Courage** (Abingdon, 1947), which was named to the *Horn Book* Fanfare list, the Lewis Carroll Bookshelf, and a Newbery honor book. She attended Wittenberg College and taught in Ohio schools, her last position before retirement being elementary school principal in Wadsworth. After retirement she moved to Hastings, Nebr. Her other books include *Jimmy's Shoes* (Penn, 1934), and *Rag-doll Jane* (Saalfield, 1935).

TRIGGER (*Trigger John's Son**), 12, red-haired orphan who comes to Beechwood, Pa., to be adopted by Mr. and Mrs. George* Smith. Wary from his experience in a series of foster homes in Maine, Trigger comes the last portion of his trip in a boxcar so he will have a chance to look over the Smiths before he agrees to live with them. A bright boy, full of ideas, he quickly takes the lead in any activity he is in. He also has an earnestness that finally wins even Myrtle* Smith to his side.

TRIGGER JOHN'S SON (Robinson*, Tom, Viking, 1934), gently realistic novel set in Beechwood, Pa., in the first third of the twentieth century. Trigger* John's son, 12, a red-haired orphan from Maine, skips train near Williamsport and arrives in Beechwood via boxcar freight so that he can get a first look at Deacon and Mrs. George* Smith, who plan to adopt him, before he agrees to the arrangement. He falls in with the Goosetown Gang, who hide him out with an old Englishman in his shack up a ravine north of town. There George Smith, a quiet, humorous, understanding man, lets himself be looked over, and Trigger agrees to go live with him. Myrtle* Smith is a less flexible type, well meaning but stiff with propriety. George gets Trigger a suit and a dog, to both of which Myrtle at first objects but reluctantly agrees. Trigger suffers through being looked over by the town at church and challenged by the nicer element in town at Kate Kerby's party for him. In the meantime, he has become the unacknowledged leader of the Goosetown Gang, though Dude* Quinlan is still president, and has persuaded them to commit themselves to raising the one hundred dollars necessary to send the old Englishman to Baltimore for a cataract operation. Their first project is to run a fried cheese sandwich booth at the circus in DuBois. George Smith, who is chief clerk at the general store, gets them the cheese and arranges that they take the delivery wagon, obstensibly to pick up some furniture for Mr. Woodruff, the stuffy store owner. Their sandwiches are not a success, but their mascot, a rattlesnake, attracts attention, and they make $25.75 selling the snake rattles that they all carry for luck. To get more money, Trigger persuades the others to expand the gang to include three of the "nice" boys on the condition that they raise half the remaining $74.25. They do this by sponsoring the appearance of a traveling minstrel show, but the real work is done by tomboy Kate Kerby, who also wants to get into the gang. They elect her a Western Star, a sort of ladies' auxiliary. Townspeople have offered to take in all the actors except the end man, the only real Negro. The gang put him up in their lodge and persuade him to act as an Indian for a patent medicine sale to earn the rest of the money. The old Englishman leaves for Baltimore, and the gang gets around to its long-postponed baseball game with the Castle Garden Gang. The game ends with a score of forty-six to thirty-seven in favor of Goosetown, but before the mitt and facemask, for which they are playing, can be presented, they are confiscated by Mr. Woodruff, who has been tipped off by the high school principal, Herbie Lord, that the boys are gambling for stakes. After a summer of planning, the boys get revenge on Herbie, who is quite a ladies' man, by suggesting that some of the older boys, including one who hates Herbie for alienating the affections of his girlfriend, come to the first day of school. Challenged, Herbie refuses to fight and leaves town. Mr. Woodruff investigates, much to the discomfiture of the School Committee, and calls a public meeting where he accuses Dude Quinlan of being the ring leader and demands that he be sent to reform school. To save Dude, Trigger takes the blame and is expelled from school, though a hero to the town. Myrtle sends for Aunt Clarissa, who sensibly suggests that Trigger will have more scope for his considerable abilities with her in Boston. George Smith gets a petition signed calling a meeting to force the school board to rescind its decision. When Mr. Woodruff finds out and tries to fire him, he resigns; Woodruff, brought to his senses, backs down on both issues. The old Englishman returns with his sight and plans a party for the boys. Life as reflected in the story has a Norman Rockwell quality. The Goosetown Gang gets skinned knees and an occasional black eye, but they are a far cry from the tough urban gangs of modern novels. George Smith's engaging personality and wry comments add genuine humor. If the small town atmosphere of Beechwood is a little too folksy and the boys' escapades a little too imaginative to be entirely believable, the many small, realistic details make it seem as if life might actually have been that way at that time. A reissue in 1949 is illustrated by Robert McCloskey*. Fanfare.

TRIS ARMINTER (*Runaway Prentice**), Tristram, tall, slender, energetic, inventive youth with an audacious, merry nature, a foil for Jeff. He helps hide Jeff in the family dovecot, gets him the job as gardener's helper, and gives him the fictitious name of Peter Pickles. He becomes Jeff's good friend and confidant.

THE TRUMPETER OF KRAKOW (Kelly*, Eric P., ill. Angela Pruszynska, Macmillan, 1928), historical novel set in Krakow, Poland, in 1461. The story harks back to a legendary trumpeter in the Church of Our Lady Mary, who died at his post in an attack on the city and whose hymn, the "Heynal," was always played thereafter ending on his broken note. The family of Joseph Charnetski, 15, traveling from the Ukraine is set upon by a brigand known as Peter Button-face, who tries to take by force a pumpkin which Joseph's father, Andrew, guards with his life. Finding the cousin they hope to stay with has fled the city, the family is at a loss, but Joseph saves a girl, Elzbietka Kreutz, from a frenzied dog, and her uncle, the alchemist Nicholas Kreutz, offers them lodgings. Their enemies stir the crowd against them, but the good priest, Jan Kanty, intervenes and, learning that they are bringing to the king the great Tarnov crystal, which has been in their family for generations, he helps them hide their identity and gets Andrew a job as night trumpeter in the Church of Our Lady Mary. Joseph learns to be a substitute trumpeter and becomes close friends with Elzbietka, whose uncle is becoming obsessed with experiments done in the company of the sinister student, Johann Tring. In an attack one night Peter's men are scared off by the alchemist, who uses chemicals to make a weird fiery appearance, and the crystal disappears from the Charnetskis' lodging. Although they believe Peter has made off with it, actually the alchemist has rescued it and begins to seek its reputed magic properties to find the secret of turning base metal into gold, prodded on by Tring, who hypnotizes him. Elzbietka, more alone and frightened than ever, makes a pact with Joseph that should she ever hear him, on her sleepless nights, play the ''Heynal'' straight through without the stop at the broken note, she will know he is in danger. When Peter makes a second attack and overcomes Andrew in the church tower, Joseph plays the ''Heynal'' using their signal, and Elzbietka sneaks out and reaches Jan Kanty, who sends the guard. Shortly thereafter, Tring and Kreutz in their experiments start a fire which rages through the city. The family escapes, and Kreutz is found wandering in a daze with the crystal under his robe. The king having returned to the city, Jan Kanty takes the men and Joseph to present the great jewel, only to find that it has been sought for political reasons to rouse the Tartars against the Poles. In the middle of the audience, Kreutz, half crazed, seizes the crystal and throws it into the Vistula river. Although the story contains longer passages of description of the scenery, dress, and customs of fifteenth century Poland than would be likely in a more modern story, the romantic action and the complicated plot retain the interest. Newbery Winner.

TUNIS†, JOHN R(OBERTS) (1889–1975), born in Boston, Mass.; sportswriter, sportscaster, and author noted for his authentic fast-action sports stories for older children and teenagers. He was born in Boston and graduated from Harvard University where he played tennis and ran distance track. After service in France in World War I, he became a sportswriter for the New York *Evening Post* and Universal Service and a sportscaster for NBC, covering major sports events at home and abroad for many years. He was himself a title-winning tennis player, and in 1932 he had the distinction of announcing the first broadcast by short wave from Europe of a Davis Cup match. He was forty-nine when he published his first novel for young people, the Fanfare selection *Iron Duke** (Harcourt, 1938), about a Harvard athlete in football and track. Twenty other novels for young readers followed over the next thirty years, including the sequel *The Duke Decides* (Harcourt, 1939), *Keystone Kids** (Harcourt, 1943), a baseball story which received the Child Study Award and is cited in *Choice*, *Highpockets* (Morrow, 1948), which received the junior book award of the Boys' Clubs of America, *All-American* (Harcourt, 1942), and *Grand National* (Morrow, 1973), about horse racing and his last book. His firsthand experience as an athlete combined with his expert knowledge of the sports world gained as an announcer gave his books their authenticity, and his plots, though formulaic and didactic with social values and lessons in sportsmanship, are exciting and peopled by very human protagonists to whom it is easy to relate. Two late books take their readers into World War II, *Silence over Dunkerque*† (Morrow, 1962), and *His Enemy, His Friend*† (Morrow, 1967). He also wrote a novel for adults, *American Girl* (Brewer, 1930), loosely based on the life of Helen Wills Moody, ten books of non-fiction, and hundreds of articles for national magazines like *Collier's*, *Esquire*, and *New Yorker*.

TUPAK OF THE INCAS (Means*, Philip Ainsworth, ill. H. M. Herget, Scribner's, 1942), novel set in Peru in the time of the Inca empire, before the coming of the Spaniards. Tupak, 14, the great-grandson of Sapa Inca Pachacutec, greatest ruler of the empire and descended from Inti, the Sun, should be a prince, but because his father, in a fit of rage, has killed his mother, the boy has been stripped of his royal rights and raised with the women of the palace, while his father dies slowly in prison. With the coming of Cusi Coyllur, daughter of the prince who is governor of Quintu, he finds his first friend, since he has been shunned by all others in the palace, and he gains self-esteem. When she must return to Quintu, he runs away to follow, knowing that his father has died and his uncle, the present ruler, is indifferent to his plight. He meets up with a soldier named Ucumari, who has greatly admired his father and who takes Tupak under his wing. Through the post runners, who call out messages for the next runner to carry, like a verbal relay, along the Imperial highway, Ucumari learns that there are orders to allow Tupak to continue and if he should reach Quintu, to test him to see whether he is worthy to be a prince. Through the long and difficult trip, Tupak proves his mettle and is assigned in Quintu to the Yacha Huasi, the Teaching House for boys. Ucumari is assigned to be his personal attendant and teacher. Tupak learns that Cusi Coyllur is in the House of the Chosen Women, the nearby training school for highborn girls. At the Yacha Huasi he learns manly arts and fights the bully, Huaraca. At the end of his training, he is given a seemingly impossible task, to run, after six days of fasting, a race with nine other youths, in which he will be handicapped by carrying a heavy jug of water on his back and a lighted brand in his hand. When he succeeds at this ordeal, he is taken into the presence of his uncle, who restores his title of Prince and arranges a marriage for him with Cusi Coyllur. While the adventures Tupak encounters should be exciting, the book gives the impression of having been written to acquaint the young reader with the Inca empire. Despite this didactic purpose, there is no indication of how much is based on archeological research and how much is speculation. The characters are stock figures, and the theme of self-realization through persistence and noble thoughts is obvious. Fanfare.

TWAIN, MARK (SAMUEL LANGHORNE CLEMENS) (1835–1910), born in Florida, Mo.; one of the top few all-time novelists in American literature.

Twain started as a printer's apprentice at twelve and worked on newspapers in a number of towns and in 1857 became a riverboat pilot's apprentice and in 1859 a pilot, an experience immortalized in *Life on the Mississippi* (Osgood, 1883). During the rest of his life, he was a miner, newspaperman, lecturer, editor, and publisher, but always a writer, publishing literally hundreds of stories, articles, novels and books of non-fiction. Ironically, his most famous book for children, *The Adventures of Tom Sawyer** (American, 1876) was written for adults, and *The Adventures of Huckleberry Finn** (Webster, 1885) usually thought to be his deepest work, he considered a boys' book. Both are based on experiences of his childhood and youth on the Mississippi River. His excursions into historical fiction were mostly not as successful, but *The Prince and the Pauper** (Osgood, 1881) is an appealing story set in sixteenth-century London.

TWENTY AND TEN (Bishop*, Claire Huchet as told by Janet Joly, ill. William Pène du Bois*†, Viking, 1952), short historical novel set in the French mountains for about a week just after Christmas vacation, at the beginning of 1944, during World War II. The Germans occupy France, and twenty French fifth-graders, and Louis, the little brother of one of them, have been taken for safety to Beauvallon, a big house in the country. One of the children, Janet*, 13, tells the story. She and the others are playing at the Flight into Egypt, a game based on the Biblical story about Jesus, when Sister Gabriel interrupts them. She hurries them into the schoolroom, where a young man enlists their aid in sheltering ten Jewish refugee children. The French children immediately see the parallel between their situation and the ancient story and enter wholeheartedly and high-spiritedly into what at first appears to be just another game. Their shortened rations, however, at lunchtime sober them, and they realize that the situation is very serious. Several days later, while Sister Gabriel goes to town for the mail, the children resume their game, in which Louis, the youngest, plays Jesus. When the children spy two Nazi soldiers coming down the road, they quickly hide the refugees in a cave they have discovered. They agree that when they are questioned, they will pretend to be mute. In spite of threats, and even though Henry is imprisoned in a coal shed, the children maintain silence. During the night Janet and Philip smuggle food and blankets to the refugees. The next day the Nazis leave, but the children rightly suspect trickery. The soldiers return with candy and fruit and try to bribe the childen into disclosing information. To the children's horror and the Nazis' delight, Little Louis breaks silence. He asserts that there are indeed Jews present. He points to the children standing about him, and when asked his name, he responds "Jesus." The children burst into laughter, and the Nazis leave in humiliation and disgust when Sister Gabriel informs them that Louis is referring to a game that the children often play. This amusing, very suspenseful story reflects actual incidents in France during the war. It moves with little decoration to its humorously ironic conclusion. The Nazis are stock characters, but the French children are credible, and dialogue and behavior are convincingly childlike. Janet's often naive observations and romantic attachment to Henry add some interest, and the plot and the game are skillfully integrated. Du Bois's black and white illustrations contribute to setting and illuminate incidents. Child Study; Choice.

THE 21 BALLOONS (Du Bois*†, William Pène, ill author, Viking, 1947), humorous fantasy concerning balloon travel and the Pacific island of Krakatoa*, which was actually destroyed by a volcanic eruption in 1883. Within a third-person frame story, the main part of the book is a recital by Professor* William Waterman Sherman, a retired arithmetic teacher, to the American Explorers Club of San Francisco about his balloon trip across the Pacific, of his wreck near Krakatoa, an island in the Sunda Strait between Java and Sumatra, of his discovery of the elaborate and sophisticated but secret social group occupying the island, and of the explosion which destroys that society. Since the island contains fabulous diamond mines, the inhabitants are able to live in great luxury by traveling each year to a different port and trading a few small diamonds for all their material needs, being careful not to bring down prices by flooding the diamond market or to leave a trail that will attract suspicious followers. They have worked out an unusual system in which each of the twenty families is known by a different letter, each lives in a house built in a style of a different culture, and each entertains the others, in turn, in a restaurant serving food of a different nationality. Since all have been chosen for their artistic and scientific interests, the community is a marvel of ingenuity, and except for the frequent quaking of the ground, Professor Sherman anticipates a happy life there for the remainder of his life. The fateful eruption of Aug. 27, 1883, however, destroys the island, and the inhabitants escape with difficulty on a platform attached to twenty-one balloons. All parachute to safety, except Prof. Sherman, who wrecks in the Atlantic near Ireland and is picked up by the SS *Cunningham*. We leave him, lionized by an adoring public, making plans for a new balloon trip. The story is told, tongue-in-cheek, in a documentary style. While there is little characterization, the factual tone of a report helps a reader accept the outlandish exaggeration, and detailed illustrations by the author add greatly to the humor of the novel. Newbery Winner.

TWIG (Jones*, Elizabeth Orton, ill. author, Macmillan, 1942), fantasy for young children set in a city in an unspecified time, though the illustrations imply the mid-twentieth century. A little girl, Twig, who lives on the fourth floor, finds an old tomato can and places it beside a dandelion in the bare square of a backyard, making, she thinks, an ideal house for a fairy. To her surprise, the house soon has an occupant, Elf, a tiny boy brought there by Mrs. Sparrow, who has found him coming out of the public library with a book under his arm. Using the book, which tells how to work magic, Elf changes Twig into his size. Together they help hatch Mrs. Sparrow's eggs and start out to look for the missing father but get no further than climbing Old Boy, a sleepy ice-wagon horse, and falling asleep in his ears. Sparrow turns up with the Fairy Queen, having gone to fairyland to find an occupant for Twig's house. The Queen is soon followed by the befuddled Royal Magician, Lord Buzzle Cobb-Webb, who is the author of Elf's book. They agree to take the children to fairyland, but Twig changes her mind at the last minute, remembering that her mother and father would miss her, and as they fly out of sight on the magic kerchief, she finds herself a normal-sized girl again. She half realizes that each of the characters in her adventure resembles a person in her apartment house. The story has a rather coy cuteness with arch references to imagination being the true magic and seems over-long for the limited action. Choice.

THE TWO UNCLES OF PABLO (Behn*†, Harry, ill. Mel Silverman, Harcourt, 1959), brief, realistic novel set in Mexico in contemporary times. The tranquil life of Pablo Pico Ruiz, 9, is changed when his mother's Uncle Silvan comes to their isolated mountain farm with a letter for his mother, Maria, which none of them can read. Expansively, he gives Pablo the burro, Angelito, that he has ridden and predicts that the news of the letter will make Maria and her husband, Felipe, wealthy. Pablo accompanies him to San Miguel to learn to read and finds that Angelito did not belong to Silvan, who is an unemployed moocher. To earn money for food, Pablo carries groceries for Miss Iris, who, on learning his name, sends him to Don Francisco Pico, a reclusive poet, who turns out to be Pablo's father's uncle. The two very different uncles spar for Pablo's favor, Don Francisco offering to send the boy to school and Uncle Silvan offering to work and buy the burro back from its owner. Although Uncle Silvan spends the money advanced by Miss Iris for Angelito, Pablo manages, with great tact, to make both uncles happy and goes home on Angelito, with presents for the whole family, to help his father plant the corn, promising to come back to learn to read. The contents of the letter will have to wait. This very simple story is memorable for the characterization of Silvan, a likable ne'er-do-well, and of Pablo, who is resourceful and dignified in his adventures. Fanfare.

TYCO BASS (*The Wonderful Flight to the Mushroom Planet**; *Stowaway to the Mushroom Planet**; *Time and Mr. Bass†*), born at 11:00 P.M., June 28, 1580, he has always had second sight. A rare Mycetian, he has a life expectancy of four or five hundred years on Earth and received from the Ancient Ones the gift of travel by thought. A wispy-haired, dome-headed, perky little man, he arrived on Earth as a spore. He is a scientist and inventor who wills his house and observatory to David* Topman and Chuck* Masterson as headquarters for their Society of Young Astronomers and Students of Space Travel.

U

UCHIDA, YOSHIKO (1921–   ), born in Alameda, Calif.; writer about Japanese folklore and culture. She is a graduate of the University of California in Berkeley, and after experiencing relocation to Utah in World War II, received her master's degree in education from Smith College. During her career she has been a teacher in Philadelphia and has worked for the Institute of Pacific Relations in New York, the United Student Christian Council, and Lawrence Radiation Laboratory at the University of California. In 1952 a Ford Foundation Fellowship took her to Japan, and subsequently she wrote articles on folk art for the *Nippon Times*, Tokyo, and for *Craft Horizons*. Her more than twenty books for young people are all about Japanese culture or Japanese Americans. *The Promised Year** (Harcourt, 1959), is about a girl from Japan who spends a year with relatives in California.

ULLMAN, JAMES RAMSEY (1907–1971), born in New York City; newspaperman, playwright, producer, and writer of fiction and non-fiction books of adventure for adults and young people. After studying at Phillips Academy in Andover, Mass., he graduated from Princeton University. Before becoming a free-lance writer in 1939, he was feature writer and reporter for newpapers and produced plays in New York City, among them the Pulitzer Prize–winning "Men in White" of 1934, and for two years was an executive with the Works in Progress Administration Federal Theater Project in New York and California. He won the British Star of Africa for distinguished service during World War II with the British Army in Africa as a member of the American Volunteer Ambulance Corps. A world traveler and avid mountain climber, he was a member of the first American expedition to Mount Everest in 1963 and belonged to the select American Alpine Society. Several of his some twenty books have been made into motion pictures, among them, the much acclaimed *Banner in the Sky** (Lippincott, 1954), which was a Newbery honor book, a Fanfare Book, a Lewis Carroll Shelf selection, a *Choice* book, and a selection of *Children's Books Too Good to Miss*. An outgrowth of his own mountaineering adventures, it fictionalizes on the true story of the first scaling of the Matterhorn in 1865. For young readers he also wrote *Down the Colorado with Major Powell* (Houghton, 1960), a real-life story of adventure. He contributed many short stories and essays to nationally circulated magazines.

UNCHARTED WAYS (Snedeker*, Caroline Dale, ill. Manning DeV. Lee, Doubleday, 1935), historical novel set mostly in Massachusetts Bay Colony from about 1652–1660, concerning the persecution of the Quakers and making use of actual historical figures and events. Orphaned, ten-year-old Yorkshire girl, Margaret* Stevenson, proud and determined to make her own way in life, attaches herself to the family of Roger Whigpen, offering to work for them if they will take her with them when they emigrate to the New World. Whigpen is agent for the London-based ironmaking firm, the Beex Co., which uses captured Scottish soldiers as laborers. The Whigpens treat Margaret cruelly and make her work very hard. During the year the family lives in Boston, Margaret is befriended by the family of John Cotton, and she grows especially fond of the noted Puritan divine, who senses her growing spirituality. To escape persecution for embezzlement, Whigpen moves the family to the forest near Dover, where they settle on a small farm in Indian territory. After six more bitter years of unappreciated labor, blows, and verbal abuse, Margaret runs away. In despair, she stumbles upon a tiny Quaker meeting in a grove outside Dover Point. The leader of the group is, coincidentally, Marmaduke Stevenson, her own uncle whom she tried unsuccessfully to contact while she was still in England. In the months that follow she flourishes under his love and kindness. She adopts his faith and soon moves hearts with her ability to cure and her sincere and eloquent religious testimonials. As hatred and suspicion toward the Quakers increases in the colony, Uncle Marmaduke, his companion, William Robinson, and Margaret intensify their efforts to witness to their faith. They are imprisoned and whipped publicly at Dover. When Marmaduke learns that Boston has passed the sentence of death against those who profess to be Quakers, he takes Robinson and Margaret there with him to witness to their faith. The three are arrested, tried, and sentenced to death. Although Marmaduke and William are hanged, Margaret is reprieved at the very last moment. Governor Endicott has been swayed by the persistent efforts of her sweetheart, Jonathan* Coleman of Salisbury, to save her. Jonathan and Margaret sail to Nantucket where, along with Jonathan's Aunt and Uncle Macey and several other Salisbury families, they found a settlement. This is a big book, a moving, richly detailed account of a dark period of persecution and bigotry. It sets in ironic relief the greater political freedom and more intense religious beliefs of the New World as compared with religion and politics in northern England at the time of Cromwell. Margaret is a dynamic character, embodying the fearless faith and undaunted courage of her historical counterpart, the Quaker martyr, Mary Dyer. Uncle Marmaduke, William Robinson, and others of the story's many characters also actually lived. Margaret's romance with Jonathan provides a narrative frame for her life with the Whigpens, her spiritual experiences, and her work with Marmaduke, adding a superfluous and awkward element to the plot. The novel is stylistically pleasing, but the author often interrupts the action with brief information essays, and sometimes she judges past practices by the standards of her own time. An author's note at the end gives historical background. More about the Quakers of Nantucket appears in *Downright Dencey**. Fanfare.

UNCLE ANALDAS (*Rabbit Hill**; *The Tough Winter**, irascible old rabbit, uncle of Little Georgie's mother. Although he resents Father's polished manners and long-winded conversation, he stays with the family through the Folks' arrival and tenure on The Hill, and during the tough winter sets off for the Bluegrass region which Father loves to describe. When he comes to Tim McGrath's barn and finds ''grass of a blue-green hue'' near a house with ''neat white fences'' and ''contented cattle of every description,'' he is sure he has reached his destination, his half-mile trek through a blizzard seeming the long, long journey Father has said it would be to get to Kentucky.

UNCLE ARCHIE MCLEOD (*Margaret**), Maggie's uncle, scholar, head and last, with his sister, Lila, of the McLeods, except for Margaret. He is kind, loving, and accepting, shares his books and house freely with Maggie, and enjoys her company, especially on outings to the country. Like proper Aunt Lila, he lives in the past. Having Maggie gives point to their lives and helps them re-enter community life.

UNCLE DRUM (*Vinny Applegay**), Stephen Drummond, ex–Civil War cavalry major who lives with Vinny's Uncle* Lamb and who meets Vinny when her ship comes in from Boston. He is gentle, good-humored, proud of his Scottish heritage, and likes dogs. He reads to Uncle Lamb, whose eyes are very sensitive and easily strained. On the day he and Kate MacQuarrie get married, he sends the children off under Wattie's* care for a delightful outing in Central Park. He is a more vividly realized character than Uncle Lamb.

UNCLE EARLE (*Roller Skates**), Lucinda's congenial uncle, who stands up for her against her commanding Aunt* Emily, who is a stickler for propriety. He introduces her to Shakespeare, takes her to her first Shakespearean play and to Sherry's for dinner, and encourages her to be gregarious and eclectic in her friendships. He calls her Snoodie, from the *Peterkin Papers**. The two get on famously.

UNCLE EBEN SMITH (*Away Goes Sally**; *Five Bushel Farm**; *The Fair American**), Sally* Smith's jolly, fat, lazy uncle, who likes to talk, joke, and eat. He helps Uncle* Joseph build the little house on runners. On the way to Maine he rides behind the horse in a sleigh which he shares with Hannibal, the bear cub. Sally loves him very much.

UNCLE EDMUND (*Caddie Woodlawn**), Caddie's fun-loving, mischievous uncle, her mother's younger brother, who visits the Woodlawns during the story. He takes Caddie hunting with him, because she has a keen eye for game, and tricks her by loosening the pins on her raft, so that the logs come apart while she poles it, dumping her into the river. As a peace offering he gives her a silver dollar which she prizes highly.

UNCLE GENE WARNER (*Farm Boy**), John's great-uncle, owner of O-at-ka farm, where John gains self-respect and self-discipline through hard work from March through September. "One of the old school," Uncle Gene is around seventy, a heavy, quiet man of great strength of character. He is one of the most respected farmers in the area, who combines up-to-date farming methods with old-fashioned virtues. He believes in firmness without rigidity and talks out problems with John and the men who work for him. As a character he is well revealed, if a recognizable type.

UNCLE GIGI (*The Marble Fountain**), jolly, big man, family-loving, resourceful, and respected in the village. He fashions bunk beds for the boys in their home under the bridge and has sculpted a statue of the Virgin Mary and Child for his yard, beside which the statue of St. Francis is placed for cleaning before it is taken to the marble fountain in the village. He supervises the work of excavating the statue and moving it to the town square.

UNCLE HOSY DATCHAM (*Runaway Prentice**), Hosea Datcham, Jeff's merry, fiddle-playing uncle, who arranges for his release from his apprenticeship in Vermont. Uncle Hosy seems ineffectual, but he easily takes command of situations when he has a mind to. Jeff likes him and has confidence in him.

UNCLE JEHOIDA PROUDFOOT (*Rifles for Washington**), York County sharpshooter and veteran of the French-Indian Wars, who joins his old commander, George Washington, with his nephew Davie McKail. Described as looking like Don Quixote, Uncle Proudfoot is tall and gaunt and has a bare spot on his head where an Indian scalped him. He talks continually, sings, quotes from the Bible, and launches into memories of his Indian fighting days. Since his sister, her husband, and son were all killed by Indians and their young daughter, Jennet, carried off, he has sworn to kill two hundred Indians and gets past one hundred in the story. After he has been wounded and has smallpox, his mind is confused so that he keeps forgetting the important plan he has and tells his fellow soldier, young Henry Donelson, to remind him, "Take Sam Gettys along." When he gets back from the expedition that destroyed Seneca Town, he is able to remember, gets Sam Gettys to Dunkertown as his witness, and insists on seeing Sister Helena, whom Sam Gettys recognizes as the image of Jehoida's sister and proves she is the lost Jennet.

UNCLE JIMMY OWEN (*Brighty of the Grand Canyon**), the most important human character in the novel, Brighty's loyal friend. He is a small, wiry, elderly man with sandy hair and mustache and an "old timey" way of speaking. He treats the wounds Brighty receives in the fight with the mountain lion with pine resin and uses his own cut-off trousers and suspenders to make protective leggings for Brighty. He later makes a kind of capsule out of a carrot in order to administer cough syrup to the balky burro. He is a very likeable, if stock, character.

UNCLE JOSEPH SMITH (*Away Goes Sally**; *Five Bushel Farm**; *The Fair American**), staunch, hardworking brother of Nannie, Deborah, and Esther, brother of Eben, and uncle of Sally* Smith. He is quick to recognize the economic possibilities of emigrating to Maine and cleverly comes up with the idea for the house on runners. He is a peacemaker also with the Indians. He respects the Indians who live in the area of Five Bushel Farm and agrees to give them five bushels of cornmeal every year for the right to use their land. He plans carefully and works very hard to make the house on Five Bushel Farm a fine one for Aunt Nannie.

UNCLE LAMB (*Vinny Applegay**), Lambert Applegay, Vinny's beloved uncle, a writer, scholar, and professor of history, who is somewhat shy and mousey and a little impractical. He welcomes Vinny to his house and soon introduces her to the city, showing her the sights appropriate for a child, and takes her shopping and for outings. They have a thoroughly satisfying relationship. He never scolds, always expects good behavior and gets it, and is never grumpy or waspish. He is an ideal uncle and guardian because he tries to see things from the child's point of view.

UNCLE LUCAS LONGFOOT (*The Quaint and Curious Quest of Johnny Longfoot, the Shoe King's Son**), Johnny* Longfoot's uncle, who lives at Shoestring Manor and is stingy, selfish, sober, and cowardly. Although uncooperative, he accompanies Johnny on his quest for the seven-league boots. After he has stolen the boots and the treasure and his ship has been disabled by sea gulls, he sees the error of his ways and reforms.

UNCLE PHINEAS PENNINGTON (*Benjamin West and His Cat Grimalkin**), kindly merchant from Philadelphia, who tells Benjamin about painters' brushes made of camel hair. This gives the boy the idea of making brushes out of Grimalkin's* fur. Since the brushes wear out quickly, Grimalkin soon looks as patchy as a rag bag from all the snippets of fur Benjamin has taken from his coat, causing the family to think that he may be suffering from the mange. Uncle Phineas also sends Benjamin boxes of paints from Philadelphia. It is through him that Benjamin leaves to live in Philadelphia and study there. Uncle Phineas has a great influence on Benjamin's life.

UNCLE THIRSTY (*Jareb**), Thurston Andrews, old man thought to be crazy and suspected of being an arsonist. Seemingly driven out of his mind by the sight of fire, he wraps burlap around his feet and dances around, stamping out the flames. In reality he is an educated man whose home was burned and family killed many years before and who suspects the Slatterys of setting the recent fires just as he is sure their father set the fire which destroyed his house. Knowing that Gabe Judson is sure to face a fight with one of the Slattery gang, he teaches Gabe boxing techniques he learned in college.

UNCLE ULYSSES (*Homer Price**; *Centerburg Tales**), Homer Price's uncle. He owns the Centerburg lunchroom, a popular gathering place for the townspeople. He has a weakness for gadgets and laborsaving devices.

UNCLE WILLIE AXELROD (*Sibby Botherbox**), fun-loving brother of Hannah's mother, an absent-minded Harvard Professor of English, who spends the summer in Gladbrook with the Pooles. He teaches Hannah to ride a bicycle and takes her on outings, among them to Tumbledown Hill where they gather daisies for Children's Day at church. They go to Goodyjohn's dry goods store where he buys a Teddy Roosevelt ten-gallon hat, to Hannah's mother's consternation, since she considers such headgear inappropriate for one of his position. They travel by train to Ottequokety, where Uncle Willie almost forgets the surprise birthday party for Minerva Martin, the pretty Sunday School teacher Hannah privately calls Miss Amber Necklace, has planned for her. He and Miss Amber Necklace fall in love and the end of the book sees them making plans for their wedding. The family fashions a makeshift office for him under the grape arbor in the yard, where he works sporadically on his book on the English Romantics.

UP THE HILL (De Angeli*, Marguerite, ill. author, Doubleday, 1942), realistic story of a Polish-American family set in a Pennsylvania mining town in an unspecified time, probably the 1920s or 1930s. Aniela, 10, wants to help her brother, Tadek, 14, get paints and training to develop his talent for drawing although their father, a musician, thinks Tad should stick to his job of driving the mules in the mine. Their mother works in a shirt factory, partly to help her younger brother, Stanislaw, who is in medical school. Aniela's chance comes with her school project, at which she is to represent Poland in costume. A visitor proves to be an artist come to paint a mural in the church, who happens to be from the same district as her mother, whose dress she is wearing. When she shows him the map Tadek decorated for her, he expresses interest and agrees to talk to her father. With the artist's encouragement, Tadek wins his father's approval for further study and, since Stan is now able to support himself, the efforts of the women can turn to helping Tadek. Included are descriptions of ethnic customs, Christmas, Easter, and Saturday school, where the children learn Polish language and history. Also, Aniela goes to the next valley to visit the small farm of her *Dziadek*, her grandfather, where her *Babcia*, her grandmother, contracts with her to sell eggs for a commission of three cents a dozen. She contributes her whole savings of sixty cents for her brother's education, though she has been hoping to use it to help pay for a new straw hat for Easter. Her mother gets her the hat anyway. Information about Eastern Europe is included rather heavy-handedly through the school project, and in the story, pleasant though it is, the appropriateness of the family's efforts to be concentrated on educating the men is not questioned. Illustrations by the author show all rosy-faced, smiling women and girls. Fanfare.

UTASSI (*Talking Drums**), Ashanti youth, very close friend from boyhood and servant of Philip Baring. His conscience forces him to admit that he understands the language of the drums. Although he hesitates to betray his people, he comes to see that he can best help them by helping Philip learn drumming. Although occasionally obsequious and emotional, the stereotyped native, he has a strong sense of propriety and is genuinely fond of Philip. He realizes Philip feels deep respect and affection for the Ashanti. He contracts sleeping sickness but recovers.

V

VAINO, A BOY OF NEW FINLAND (Adams*, Julia Davis, Dutton, 1929), historical novel of the Finnish revolution during World War I, which freed the country from Russian domination. Vaino Lundborg, a young Finnish boy, lives near Helsingfors with his widowed mother, his sister Anniki, 18, a student at the University, and their brother, Sven, 20, both of whom are involved in revolutionary activity. Early in the story, Vaino is frightened by an imperious Russian officer, but after the revolution of 1916, led by Kerensky, when the same officer comes to their door fleeing the Reds, Vaino and his mother hide him. With Anniki, Vaino helps smugglers bring in guns and a wireless set and later takes supplies to Sven, who is hiding out with other supporters of the Whites. There he finds the same Russian, whom he now knows as Vladimir, and joins the young men in scaring off a party of Reds and obtaining their weapons. Word comes from Anniki that she has joined and married her revolutionary friend, Scarelius, but things go badly for the Whites, and Sven and his companions must escape in a terrible journey across the ice to Estonia. Vaino and his mother are under suspicion and must leave their home and move to two different places in Helsingfors. They suffer as the city becomes a battleground, then rejoice as Mannerheim takes the city and liberates Finland. The history is confusing to a modern reader, with the relationship of the White Russians, the Reds, and the Germans never explained, and the war which involves France, England and the United States ignored. There is some exciting action, but the story is interrupted at high points by long tales from the *Kalevala* told by Vaino's mother, interesting in themselves but in no way integrated into the plot. Except for Vaino, dependable and brave for his age, there is almost no attempt at characterization, and the total effect is one of a laudatory and didactic evocation of the Finnish national spirit. Newbery Honor.

THE VAN RUYKSDAELS (*The Singing Boones**), the Dutch family whose wagon is the largest and most elaborately decorated and outfitted in Captain Jack's Blue Elephant Company. Mr. Van Ruyksdael's arrogant disregard for the rights and needs of others and his insistence that the other men exert special effort to protect his property cause so many problems for the travelers that he and his wagon are finally left behind at a good stopping-off place. He is also cruel to his wife and daughter, who are much afraid of him. They leave him and continue with the wagon train to California where they make good lives for themselves. The Van Ruyksdaels are very fat and overdressed. They epitomize foolish, improvident pioneers and gold seekers.

VAN STOCKUM†, HILDA (1908–), born in Rotterdam, Netherlands; painter and translator, author, and illustrator of books for children. Because her father was a naval officer, the family traveled extensively in Europe and the Far East while she was growing up. She attended art schools in the Netherlands, France, and Ireland, where she met the family about whom she later wrote in the novels about the close and loving O'Sullivans, the peasant family who live in a peat-burning cottage on the shores of Bantry Bay, and their friends and neighbors: *The Cottage at Bantry Bay** (Viking, 1938), a Fanfare book which is also cited in *Children's Books Too Good to Miss*; *Francie on the Run** (Viking, 1939); and *Pegeen** (Viking, 1941), both Fanfare books. The first book mostly concerns the O'Sullivans' need for money so that lame Francie's leg can be repaired, the second tells about Francie's flight from the Dublin hospital, and the third describes the misadventures of orphaned, willful Pegeen Murphy while she lives with the O'Sullivans. Van Stockum married an American who was studying at Trinity College in Dublin, came to the United States, and lived in New York, Washington, and Montreal, all places to which his work took the family. She also studied art at the Corcoran School of Art in Washington and Thomas More Institute in Montreal. She specialized in portraits and still life, and her work has been exhibited in numerous shows and galleries. She speaks Dutch, German, and French and has translated books for children by such writers as Siny R. van Iterson and Achim Bröger, and has illustrated editions of *Little Women*, *Hans Brinker*, and many books by other writers. She has published two dozen books for older and younger readers, mostly self-illustrated, among them, the acclaimed *The Winged Watchman†* (Farrar, 1962), about a Dutch family's problems during the German occupation of World War II. Her first novel was a Newbery honor book, *A Day on Skates** (Harper, 1934), an amusing story about the adventures of some Dutch children while skating on a canal on the first day of winter. Her novels have been praised for their humor, liveliness, and understanding of the ways and needs of children. They carry the conviction of personal experience gained with her own six children and the young people she has met in her travels and the places she has lived. Her family provided the models for *The Mitchells* (Viking, 1945), a novel about five lively children in Washington, whose father is away in World War II. She has also published several picture books.

VINING†, ELIZABETH JANET GRAY (1902–), born in Philadelphia, Pa.; educator, novelist, librarian. She is a graduate of Bryn Mawr College and studied library science at Drexel Institute of Technology. At one time she taught high school in a New Jersey resort town, a setting used for her novel *Sandy** (Viking, 1945). She was married and lived in North Carolina, but after only a few years of married life her husband was killed in an automobile accident. During World War II, she joined the American Friends Service Committee in Philadelphia, writing reports, appeals, and articles, and was recommended by the Friends' Society to become tutor to the Crown Prince of Japan, a position she held for four years and which is the subject of her autobiographical book, *Windows for the Crown Prince* (Lippincott, 1952). Her Japanese experience is also used in her novel, *The Cheerful Heart** (Viking, 1959). She has also written biographies for young people of Walter Scott, William Penn, and John Greenleaf Whittier, but her most successful books are historical fiction, like *Meggy MacIntosh** (Doubleday, 1930), set mostly in North Carolina during the American Revolution, *I Will Adventure*† (Viking, 1962), set in Shakespearian England, and *Adam of the Road** (Viking, 1942), a Newbery Medal winner, set in England in the medieval period.

VINNY APPLEGAY (Parton*, Ethel, Viking, 1937), realistic episodic novel of family life set in 1870 mostly in New York City. Little Vinny (Venetia) Applegay, an orphan, travels by train and boat from South Amesbury, Mass., to Boston, and then to New York to live with her Uncle* Lambert Applegay in his comfortable brownstone near Stuyvesant Square and Central Park. Self-assured, spunky, outspoken Vinny gets on well immediately with Uncle Lamb, a scholar and writer, and his good friend and live-in companion, Stephen Drummond, an ex–Civil War cavalry officer, whom Vinny immediately likes and dubs Uncle* Drum. Before long, her cousin, Maud* Vandevoort, a sweet but mouseish child, too frail for regular school, joins her for daily lessons with Uncle Lamb, and a year of good times follows for the two girls. Every chapter of this big book relates at least one adventure at home or in the neighborhood, with friends or relatives, as Vinny becomes acquainted with her new surroundings and acts as Uncle Lamb's "lady of the house." She helps deal with the tempermental, superstitious black cook, Zenobia, and thrills to the stories about Ireland told by the new cook, Maggie. She and Maud regularly pick up flowers from Frazier's greenhouse, where they play dolls in an Enchanted Forest and make friends with the handyboy, Wattie* MacQuarrie, whom Uncle Lamb takes on as a special pupil and loans books to. Uncle Lamb takes the girls to a china shop to buy the tiny five-cent dolls they are partial to and shopping for a wedding present for Linda, Vinnie's elder sister. He thinks Vinnie's choice of a group by the eminent contemporary artist, John Rogers, most appropriate. While they are in the store, Vinny attracts attention when she tells about John Greenleaf Whittier, the New England poet, with whom she is acquainted. The girls get caught in a storm on the way to the florist, go for outings in Central Park, acquire a kitten, Lady Jane Grey, which forms a particular attachment to Uncle Lamb, and eventually also a dog, get their picture taken by a studio photographer, and investigate a peculiar, night-time, fiery face at the window, which turns out to be the reflection of a gas lamp, left burning because Maud is afraid to sleep in the dark. When the family is invited to view the St. Patrick's Day parade from the office window of a friend of Uncle Lamb's, Vinny shows herself a perfect lady, particularly in comparison to another horrid, complaining little girl there, when Vinny forces herself to eat raw oysters during lunch. The most exciting episode occurs when Vinny and neighbor boy George Nandle discover burglars in the house of friends who are away and are instrumental in their capture. To climax the book, Uncle Drum and Wattie's mother get married, a romance that the children have been unaware of. Vinny welcomes Wattie as a kind of cousin and is pleased to turn over her position of lady of the house to this warm-hearted, new, very ''aunty aunt.'' This amusing story for young girls is filled with the kind of detail about clothes, everyday life, and social and recreational activities that writers of the time felt would, or should, appeal to them. Almost everyone behaves very well, and those that don't are obviously engaging in behavior that should be avoided. Some adults, among them disapproving, self-engrossed Mrs. Beadle and eccentric Zenobia, who believes in ''gobbleums,'' are too grossly comic for credibility, and the children are a little too wise on occasion to be convincing. Vinny is appealing, while Maud is a shadowy figure and a too-obvious foil, as are her social climbing sisters on the other extreme. Scenes are well done, and there is some humor, but episodes rather ramble on, and some dialogue seems almost pointless. The author manages to give some sense of the times. The many characters are mostly stock or types, but the principals seem real. (Joey* Nandle) Fanfare.

THE VOYAGES OF DOCTOR DOLITTLE (Lofting*, Hugh, ill. author, Lippincott, 1922), second in a series of fantasies with a home base at the town of Puddleby-on-the-Marsh in England, this one set in 1839. Told in the first person by Tommy Stubbins, the cobbler's son, 9½, this introduces Doctor* John Dolittle, the physician who can talk with animals, five years later than the first book, after he has had many voyages and has become a famous, though not wealthy, naturalist. Tommy, who has always been interested in animals, wishes to get the doctor to treat a squirrel with a broken leg and finds him by accident, bumping into him in the rain, then going to his comfortable but unconventional house to get his clothes dried. Fascinated by the cheerful, unpretentious doctor and his household of animals, Tommy soon becomes his assistant, is taught animals' language by the parrot, Polynesia*, and is with the doctor when he saves Luke the Hermit by translating at the trial the evidence of Bob, Luke's bulldog, the only eye-witness to a murder of which Luke is wrongly accused. When the doctor plans a voyage, Tommy, of course, is part of the crew which includes Polynesia, Jip, the dog, and Chee-Chee*, the monkey. They start for Spidermonkey Island off the coast of South America, the place where the world's other great naturalist, Long Arrow, son of Golden Arrow, was last seen, according to Miranda, the Purple Bird-of-Paradise, who brought the news. Before they start, they receive a visit from Bumpo* Kahbooboo, Crown Prince of Jolliginki, now attending Oxford, who decides to take a holiday and go with them. Hardly are they on their way than three stowaways are discovered: Matthew Mugg, the Cats'-Meat-Man, and Luke and his newly rediscovered wife, all by this time willing to be put ashore. Another stowaway, Ben Butcher, able seaman, they discover later and, fearing he may mutiny, lock him up until they can put in to the Capa Blancas, on the advice of Polynesia. At Monteverde, where they need supplies because Butcher has eaten so much but have no money because the doctor has given all he has to Luke, Doctor Dolittle makes a wager with the chief promoter of the bullfights that if he can outperform the chief matador, all bullfights will be discontinued. He then, with the help of the bulls with whom he has conferred in their language, puts on a marvelous show, while Bumpo, who has learned about side bets at Oxford, replenishes their fortunes. Further on the trip they catch a small fish, a Silver Fidget, which speaks some English, having once been in an aquarium. The fidget advises the doctor that he may be able to learn the language of the shell fish, as he wishes, from the Great Glass Sea Snail, if he can find the creature. Later their ship is wrecked, a circumstance that worries the doctor very little, and the pieces of wreckage are pushed together and then on to Spidermonkey Island by helpful porpoises. There Doctor Dolittle discovers a very rare Jabizri beetle, with a picture message written in blood on a dried leaf tied to its leg. He rightly interprets it as from Long Arrow saying that he and companions are trapped in a cave by a landslide. Led by the beetle, they find the cave, dig under the slab of rock which blocks the opening, and release the Indians. At the Popsipetel Indian village, they learn that the humans and vegetation are all suffering because the island, which is floating, is drifting too far south into Antarctic regions, and the people have never known fire. Doctor Dolittle makes fire with a bow and drill, teaches the Indians to use it, and gets whales to push the island back to tropic regions. Then the other tribe on the island, the Bag-jagderags, attack and though Bumpo and Long Arrow fight side-by-side with the doctor, they are almost overcome until Polynesia recruits millions of Black Parrots from the main land, who fight by grasping the hair and ripping bits from the edges of the ears. The Indians of both tribes are so impressed that they join forces and insist that Doctor Dolittle become their king. At his coronation, the great shouts and cheers dislodge the hanging stone at the edge of an old volcano so it crashes through the hollow air-space in the island's center and causes it to settle, fortunately in water not deep enough to cover the island. At the secret suggestion of Polynesia, the Great Glass Sea Snail, which the doctor is treating because the island came to rest on its tail, offers to carry them back to England. The story, though told by Tommy, has the same matter-of-fact simplicity of the first book (*The Story of Doctor Dolittle**), with the added advantage of a young protagonist. The treatment of Bumpo, while amusing because the black prince uses long words, often malapropisms, is not offensive, more affectionate than ridiculing. The wildly imaginative adventures always have a seeming logic. (Dab-Dab*) Children's Classics; Newbery Winner.

VULPES THE RED FOX (George*, John, and Jean George*†, ill. Jean George, Dutton, 1948), realistic animal story set in rural Maryland in the mid-twentieth century. Born one of seven pups in a den near the abandoned Chesapeake and Ohio canal and not far from the Potomac River, Vulpes is protected in his early life by both his parents. A brother is taken by Bubo, the great horned owl, but Vulpes escapes and learns, from watching three hunters, about his greatest enemy, man. He learns to outrun and outwit the hounds trained by Buck Queen, the wily fox hunter, even his experienced red bone hound, Brownie. He even learns in a near-miss in which he loses a few hairs from his foot, to avoid the traps cleverly set by Will Stacks. During the winter after his bachelor year, he travels some distance seeking a mate and finally, on an island not far from his home, finds Fulva, a vixen to suit him. For a while they stay on her home island, then cross on the thin ice to the area near where Vulpes was born. They dig their den and in late March, Fulva gives birth to nine puppies. Through the summer both parents watch and teach their offspring. In September a flood threatens them; they escape but the family scatters. In November Vulpes gets involved with a Hunt Club of Maryland chase but easily escapes. In a much more serious hunt by Buck and Will and a couple of their friends, Vulpes shows his real abilities, leading the hounds from early morning through all the day, all the following night, and through most of the next day. He loses Joe, the blue tick hound, when they cross the thin ice and the exhausted dog crashes through and sinks. Old Brownie keeps chasing but finally gives up when Buck's young dogs are loosed to the hunt. Vulpes fools the inexperienced dogs, and that hunt is finished. Years later, Vulpes, after many other hunts, is brought down by a shot from Buck. Although the human characters are little more than types, Vulpes is developed in great detail and with very little anthropomorphizing. Occasionally a human emotion is attributed to an animal—"the old fox was watching him in amusement"—and Vulpes is shown as actually enjoying the sport of outwitting the dogs and the long runs ahead of the pack. The book's strength is in the way it presents a great deal of natural history in an authentic and interesting way. Fanfare.

W

THE WAHOO BOBCAT (Lippincott*, Joseph Wharton, ill. Paul Bransom, Lippincott, 1950), realistic animal novel set in central Florida in the early decades of the twentieth century. With no anthropomorphizing, the story follows the adventures of a bobcat or catamount for a couple of years in the water prairies and scrub pine woods in the thinly settled area at a time when teachers still "boarded around" with their pupils' families. The main humans in the story are the family of Bill Henry, whose son, Sammy, 9, is saved by the bobcat from the attack of a half-wild sow that he is trying to chase from the strawberry patch, and the neighbors, Andy Rogers and his two nearly grown sons, George and Lem, who hunt the bobcat with their black hound and a pack of scraggly mongrels. The story follows The Tiger, as this large bobcat of the Wahoo swamp is called, through his escapes from the dogs and his gradual acceptance of Sammy as a friend, his being marooned on an island with his mate during flood season, his encounter with a panther, his fights with rivals, and his adopting as a companion one of his own kittens when his mate flees the panther with the other. Man's destruction of the environment is chronicled when they drain the swamp to make more farmland, and nature's destruction, in the form of fire, follows, but The Tiger escapes both. He does not escape the trap set by the Rogers boys, though he manages to break the wire and drag the trap with one front paw caught. When the boys bring their dogs, the hampered Tiger is almost caught but pulls his paw loose, pulling off two toes as he does, and fleeing finally to the schoolhouse, where the dogs chase him round among the pupils in a wild scene. The teacher manages to clear the room of children and dogs and orders George and Lem, who have followed with girls, to get out. After they all leave, she calmly lets the bobcat rest, then opens the door so it can escape. Later, when Sammy and the teacher come face to face with the panther, Andy Rogers finally admits that it is the predator killing the pigs, not The Tiger, whom he has blamed. After he has killed the panther, he takes Sammy fishing to make amends for hunting the boy's friend, and they witness the near death of The Tiger, who swims to escape the dogs and is nearly caught by an alligator. Andy beats off the alligator and jumps in to help the drowning bobcat, although he knows the gator has gone for his black hound. At first it seems that The Tiger has drowned, but Andy and Sammy see him regain consciousness in the boat and leap to the shore. The human characters are adequate but relatively undeveloped; the main character is The Tiger, and his actions, thoughts, and way of life are made very real and believable. The setting of the swampland is vivid and sensitively drawn. Fanfare.

WALTER THE EARL (*The Gammage Cup**; *The Whisper of Glocken*†), courageous, persevering Minnipin, lover of antiquities, one of "Them," those considered not quite respectable for their non-conforming ways and outlawed from the village of Slipper-on-the-Water*. He discovers the ancient treasure of armor and swords that enable the Minnipins to defeat their traditional enemies, the Mushrooms, who have made their way into the Minnipin valley through an ancient gold mine. In the second book, he helps to rescue the New Heroes.

WAR PAINT, AN INDIAN PONY (Brown*, Paul, ill. author, Scribner's, 1936), realistic horse story set in the western United States, probably in the early nineteenth century. Born a wild range colt, War Paint narrowly escapes the many hazards presented by nature including wolves, prairie fire, a puma, famine, cold, and a bear. He also escapes from a Kiowa Indian wild horse drive but is later captured by Grey Eagle, a Cheyenne. He then becomes a much-admired pony and is employed when Grey Eagle and his young friend, Whistling Arrow, attempt to steal horses from the Comanches and narrowly escape capture. In a cloudburst he leads the other horses across a surging river to safety, and in a buffalo hunt he helps Grey Eagle save Whistling Arrow from being trampled. When news of an impending Comanche attack comes to the village, Grey Eagle rides him on the war path, and by pretending to be seriously wounded with an injured horse, he leads the Comanches into a Cheyenne ambush. Essentially plotless, the book is a series of episodes told without ascribing thoughts or emotions to the horses or the Indians beyond those that might be noticed by an observer. The language is fairly simple and the tone objective. Although the text is much longer than a picture book, the illustrations are an intrinsic part, each page containing ink drawings placed around the printed words, all in black on a sepia background with a white border. The pictures are realistic and full of action. Fanfare.

WATERLESS MOUNTAIN (Armer*, Laura Adams, ill. Sidney Armer and author, Longmans, 1931), realistic family novel set in the late 1920s in the arid, rugged Navajo country of Arizona about a boy who feels called to become a medicine man like his mother's brother, Uncle. This episodic personal quest story covers several years in the life of Younger Brother, 8, who, while he herds his mother's sheep, senses that he is being helped and guided by such creatures of nature as Pack Rat and Yellow Beak, the eagle. Instructed by Uncle, he learns the songs and stories of his people and participates in such ceremonies as the wedding of his older brother and the Night Chant, all of which brings him closer in spirit to the gods, called Yays, and the powers of nature. Like Uncle, Mother, Father, and Elder Brother recognize the boy's growing spirituality and encourage him in his attempts to walk the path of beauty with the gods. Among his friends are two "Pelicanos," Big Man, the trader who feels a special affection for the boy and his family and who helps him reach the western ocean when he is searching for the goddess Turquoise Woman, and the curator of a museum in Santa Barbara for whom his mother demonstrates her skill at weaving rugs and his father his talent at silverwork. Navajo myths, legends, and poems contribute to the mystical atmosphere and add depth to this slow moving and unpretentious story. The impact of the book lies neither in plot nor characterization but in the vivid sense it conveys of the everyday life, customs, and beliefs of devout Navajos. Choice; Newbery Winner.

WATIE, STAND (*Rifles for Watie**), actual Cherokee general during the American Civil War who led a detachment of Rebel Indians against northern troops in the area of the Indian Nations. He appears as a small, long-haired, dark-skinned, quiet, elderly man, much loved by his troops, who arranges to buy repeating rifles from Captain Asa Clardy, the Union officer who commands the unit to which Jeff* Bussey has been assigned, and for whom he is a foil character. Jeff develops respect and admiration for his ability as an officer and affection for many of the men whom he commands.

WATTIE MACQUARRIE (*Vinny Applegay**), fun-loving, earnest youth who works for the Frazier greenhouse and who becomes Uncle* Lamb's special pupil. He and his mother are immigrants from Scotland, and he yearns for an education. He is particularly kind to Vinny and Maud* and gives them choice flowers. He reads to Uncle Lamb occasionally, when Uncle Lamb's eyes are tired. He is the link by which his mother, Kate, meets Uncle* Drum.

WEIL, ANN (YEZNER) (1908–1969), born in Harrisburg, Ill.; educator and author of fiction and non-fiction for children. She attended the University of Illinois, Southern Illinois University, and Evansville College, and taught in elementary schools in Illinois and in Evansville, Ind., before becoming a full-time writer of books for children. She was a member of the children's literature staff to instruct in writing for children at the University of Indiana and lectured in English for Evansville College. Of her several novels, one was a Fanfare book, *The Silver Fawn** (Bobbs, 1939), a novel strong in local color about a little Mexican boy who helps an American open a silver store in Taxco; and one was a Newbery honor book, *Red Sails to Capri** (Viking, 1952), a fictionalization of the discovery of the Blue Grotto near Naples, Italy. Though considered shallow in characterization and weak in plot, her fiction has been praised for its lively incident, warmth of tone, and convincing re-creation of place. She also wrote *My Dear Patsy* (Bobbs, 1941), a novel about Thomas Jefferson's daughter,

Patsy; some picture books; and several biographies for the Bobbs-Merrill Childhood of Famous Americans series. She traveled extensively, particularly in southeast Asia, Russia, and its satellite countries, and made her home in Evansville, Ind.

THE WELPS (*The Jumping-Off Place**), surly, disreputable claim-jumpers who seek to drive the Linville children from their Rosebud Reservation claim by such acts of harassment as breaking windows, tearing out the pump at the well, damaging crops, driving away their cow, and refusing to share the water at the nearby spring. The Welp boys, Pete and Bill, are particularly rowdy at school where they create discipline problems for Becky* Linville, the teacher. The Welps are eventually run out of the area by angry neighbors, fed up with their shiftlessness and troublemaking.

WESTON, CHRISTINE (GOUTIERE) (1904–   ), born in India; novelist and short story writer for adults. She grew up in India, the daughter of a barrister who was a naturalized Englishman. World War I prevented her from receiving the typical English education of the day, but she early enjoyed books and reading, interests her father encouraged. Later she helped him with his law work, coming into contact with clients of every nature and class. In 1923, she married an American, came to the United States, and made her home in Maine. India provided the setting and subjects of her writings, and critics praised her for her authentic and sensitive portrayal of the people and problems of her native subcontinent. Her short stories appeared in the *New Yorker* and other magazines, and in 1940 she received a Guggenheim fellowship. She wrote for adults six novels, a book of short stories, and a book of travel and personal experience in Ceylon, and for children one novel, *Bhimsa: The Dancing Bear** (Scribner's, 1945), an adventure story set in Northern India with a strong sense of place. A Newbery honor book, it was also selected for Fanfare by the editors of *Horn Book*.

WHEELOCK, ELEAZAR (*Three Sides of Agiochook**), historical founder and president of Dartmouth College. Described as portly and pompous, he gives directions with a touch of arrogance, but his determination to bring learning to the Indians has prompted him to found his school in the wilds of New Hampshire. His liberal spirit leads not only the college but also Moor's Charity School, where Indian boys can work to support themselves while they prepare for Dartmouth. In the early days of the American Revolution, he prevailed upon his former student Joseph* Brant, a Mohawk in the service of the British, to spare the school and the Connecticut Valley.

THE WHEEL ON THE SCHOOL (DeJong*†, Meindert, ill. Maurice Sendak, Harper, 1954), realistic novel set in the Netherlands, probably in the early years of the twentieth century. When Lina*, the only schoolgirl in Shora*, writes an essay wondering why the village has no storks, she and the other five pupils and then most of the town become involved in an effort to put a wheel on the schoolhouse roof so that storks will nest there. Slow, clumsy Eelka, the smartest boy, finds an ancient wheel in the loft of a high barn, smashes it in getting it down, and in retrieving the parts, loses the rim in the canal. Big husky Jella takes a farmer's wheel and is apprehended. Auka, a "nice, everyday boy" almost gets the decrepit wheel from the tin peddler's cart, trades it for a brightly painted wheel on a roof in a nearby town, but ends with no wheel for the school. The twins, Pier and Dirk, dare to enter the yard of the bad-tempered Janus*, an ex-fisherman whose legs have been amputated, and find a friend in him. Lina sees a wheel through a hole in an overturned boat beyond the dike and learns from old Douwa that as a child he saved his fisherman father by cutting that hole and pulling him out. When Lina and Douwa are stranded on the boat with the tide coming in, the tin man and his horse, directed by Janus, rescue them and pull out the wheel. In the storm that follows, the children and then the wives pester the fishermen fathers to put the wheel on the school, a difficult and dangerous feat directed by Janus, but they all fear that the young storks, who would be looking for new nesting sites, have been killed in the bad weather. When two younger children are accidentally locked in the clock tower, they spot a pair of exhausted storks stuck on a sandbar and, with Janus and Jella rowing, Lina and Pier go out to rescue them. At last there are storks in Shora, just as there were in the childhood of the town's oldest woman, Grandmother Sibble III. In a simple style, DeJong draws sharp characterizations and, by a point of view inside the head of each child in turn, makes the problem of the wheel of primary importance and even such unlikely episodes as the fishermen braving the storm to install the wheel convincing. The theme that much can be accomplished by determined effort and cooperation is clear but not didactically expressed, and the subtheme of the importance of communication is well illustrated in Lina's discovery of common interests with Janus, Grandmother Sibble, and Douwa, all of whom she feared before. Newbery Winner.

WHERE THE WINDS NEVER BLEW AND THE COCKS NEVER CREW (Colum*, Padriac, ill. Richard Bennett*, Macmillan, 1940), talking animal fantasy set in a never-never-land at a time indefinite. After they have been abandoned by the Old Woman with whom they have been living, her creatures, Gruff, the laconic dog; Old Mother Gabble, the sensible goose; Tibbie, the bossy cat; Droileen, the flighty wren; Croodie, the lone pigeon; Speckie, the timid guinea hen; Krak-krak, the cricket on the hearth; and the goat without a name at all, leave home, too. They travel up hill and down dale until they come to the house of another Old Woman in the land Where the Winds Never Blew and the Cocks Never Crew, "not different, as far as any person or creature can see, from any other place in the wide world" except that "no one is ever born there, and no one ever dies there." After their arrival, the virtually plotless story ambles along, offering simple complications and mildly suspenseful adventures of the animals singly or in small groups. The creatures add to their number the lame black crow, Hoodie, who becomes their watchman, are visited by a flock of starlings who sing a strangely haunting, repetitive song, and enlist the aid of a crane in dealing with a stubborn and somewhat troublesome scarecrow. After the goat, who decides she wants to "go somewhere," reaches the top of the mountain where she sees the water horse rise from the moonlit lake, most of the creatures succumb to the lure of parts unknown or the mysterious pull of heredity. After joining the starlings for a time, Droileen leaves for the hills, Old Mother Gabble goes to the place the visiting swans sang about, Hoodie departs for the woods where he knows his kind resides, and Gruff goes to seek tall, white stags and tall, white hounds—one by one the animals leave home until only the cricket and the cat remain in the house to keep the Old Woman company. Most of the interest in this slow-moving, seemingly purposeless story comes from the interplay of character, the extensive homely dialogue about mostly ordinary things, the comfortable, homey atmosphere with its keen sense of Irish whimsey and mystery, and the strongly rhythmic, very musical, storytelling style. Fanfare.

WHISTLERS' VAN (Jones*, Idwal, ill. Zhenya Gay, Viking, 1936), boy's adventure story set among the gypsies (Rommanies) of Wales after World War I. Every spring a horsedrawn gypsy van pauses near Moor House, the farm on which Gwilym and his sister, Myfi, live with Taid, their grandfather, Thomas Anwyl. Gwilym notices that when the gypsies whistle a certain tune, Taid behaves strangely. This spring Taid mysteriously goes off in the dead of night just before the whistlers appear. Gwilym joins them, hoping to discover the secret of the melody and to locate Taid. The whistling gypsies are twins Natty* (Nathaniel) Ringo, bold, decisive horsemaster; Jubal*, taciturn craftsman; and their grandmother, Gammer. The Ringos' jaunts through the villages and country roads lead them to a variety of happenings and people, among them, a fair at which Natty is the star boxer and to Natty's war friend, Captain Lewis, a Georgio (house folk), whose horse Natty cured of madness. In spite of occasional homesickness, Gwilym comes to enjoy life close to nature and the camaraderie of the wanderers, even as he is disturbed by what appears to be an unending conflict between the gypsies and the people who live under roofs. At the annual gathering of the gypsies, the Sirnihatch, Gwilym learns that his grandfather was a Ringo, who had adopted the settled life when he married a landed Welsh lady. When at the Sirnihatch Taid is made king of the gypsies, he declines the honor, turning the royal ring and leadership over to Natty. Gwilym, now the last of the Ringos, will henceforth spend half of the year with the roving side of the family and half with Taid. This pleasing story of an exotic people idealizes life in the open without responsibilities and mechanical innovations. While the plot problem is not strong and things turn out as any thinking reader would expect, little mysteries, active episodes, and hints about Taid's background engage the emotions and hold the interest. The gypsy principals are well drawn, although Gwilym seems a plaster figure intended to unify the story, and many Welsh and gypsy words add spice to the dialogue and create setting. Fanfare; Newbery Honor.

WHITE, ANNE H(ITCHCOCK) (1902–1970), born in St. Louis, Mo.; actress, writer. She attended Milton Academy and Vassar College and acted and directed at the Neighborhood Playhouse and the American Laboratory Theater. During World War II she served as instructor at the Air Force Training School in Boston. Later she joined her husband in Madrid, where he was with the United States Embassy, and then in London, where she worked as a member of Reports Board for the Office of Strategic Services. Among her writings are one novel for adults and several animal stories for children, including *The Story of Serapina** (Viking, 1951) and *Junket** (Viking, 1955).

WHITE, DALE (MARION TEMPLETON PLACE) (1910–), born in Gary, Ind.; Montana author of many books, both fiction and non-fiction, mostly about the history of the frontier. She received her B.S. in library science from the University of Minnesota and her B.A. degree from Rollins College. With a passion for research, she has produced novels with sound factual background, among them *Steamboat up the Missouri** (Viking, 1958), about riverboats during the Civil War, *Hold Back the Hunter** (Day, 1959), a story based on the Washburn-Langford-Doane expedition to explore the area which became Yellowstone Park, both of which won Spur Awards from Western Writers of America, and *The Singing Boones** (Viking, 1957), a historical novel of a family who go overland from Missouri to California to find gold but make their living instead by singing to entertain on the frontier. In the 1970s she wrote a series of books on the legendary Bigfoot, starting with *On the Track of Bigfoot* (Dodd, 1974).

WHITE†, E(LWYN) B(ROOKS) (1899–1985), born in Mount Vernon, N.Y.; journalist, humorist, author for adults and children. Although he is best known for his essays for adults, he became noted in children's literature for the three fantasies for which he received the Laura Ingalls Wilder Award in 1970: *Stuart Little** (Harper, 1945), about the second son of Mr. and Mrs. Frederick C. Little, who looks "very much like a mouse in every way," listed in *Choice*; *Charlotte's Web** (Harper, 1952), about the spider who spins words in her web to save the life of a runt pig; and *The Trumpet of the Swan†* (Harper, 1970), about Louis, the trumpeter swan, who was born mute and who learns to play the trumpet, listed in *Choice* and a National Book Award finalist. Among the most popular stories ever written for children, these are landmark books, particularly *Charlotte's Web*, whose numerous honors include the George G. Stone Award, election to the Lewis Carroll Shelf, and selection for the Children's Literature Association Touchstones and Top Ten, Children's Classics, and *Children's Books Too Good to Miss*. Deceptively easy in style and language, these books have strong characterization and deep themes, and appeal to readers of all ages. White was educated at Cornell University, served in the United States Army in World War I, and worked as a reporter for the Seattle *Times* and as a production assistant in an advertising agency in New York. He was associated with the *New Yorker* magazine for many years as a writer and editor, doing the "Talk of the Town" column, and also wrote "One Man's Meat" for *Harper's* magazine. He has made his home in North Brooklin, Maine.

THE WHITE ISLE (Snedeker*, Caroline Dale, ill. Fritz Kredel, Doubleday, 1940), historical novel set in Rome, on the overland route to Britain, and in Britain in the first part of the second century A.D., about ninety years after the death of Christ, early in the reign of Emperor Hadrian. Plain, warm-hearted Lavinia, 13, lives with her proud, patrician father, Publius Favonius Claudius, her loving, dutiful mother, beautiful Aurelia, and her companionable brother, Marcus, 15, in a comfortable, modest villa on the Palatine Hill in Rome. Favonius incurs the displeasure of Hadrian and is dispatched to a post in Britain. Although the parents deplore leaving Rome, Marcus and Lavinia look forward to the excitement of the journey and a new house on the distant island. Lavinia especially longs for adventure and new faces away from the city where she recently suffered the embarrassment of being jilted by a youth who rejected her as ugly and beneath him. Along the way she acquires a Celtic pony, thrills to the beauties of the countryside, and enjoys hospitality at country villas of ex-patriots and locals of Greek extraction. Although the journey has inconveniences, the family has few real difficulties. The road is well contructed and safe, and the local people are eager to entertain them and to learn the news from Rome. Marcus falls in love with Neraea, a wealthy Gallic girl, but ironically Favonius regards the match as unsuitable because the father is a Greek freedman. Once in Britain, the family soon settles in a villa outside of London. Favonius serves as circuit judge and then takes command of the Second Augustan Legion, while Marcus joins the Ninth, both of which are soon mobilized against the Celts in the North. At this time, the great fortification known as Hadrian's Wall is being constructed to contain the restive tribesmen. While taking the waters at Aqua Sulis, Aurelia encounters old friends from Rome, who invite her and Lavinia to visit them in their home in the west. On the way, they are captured by marauding tribesmen. They are soon rescued by a party led by a British-born Roman named Govan, who has adopted Christianity. Lavinia and Govan fall in love, and he converts her to his beliefs. Marcus dies when Celts defeat the Ninth, but Favonius returns safely. Aurelia persuades him to accept Govan, and the two young people marry. Lavinia's quick conversion and her father's acceptance of her conversion and of Govan are not convincing. Characters are mostly types or functionaries, including Lavinia, who matures predictably. The plot lacks urgency and pacing, and the conclusion is abrupt. Most dialogue is natural, but the brogue of the slaves interjects an incongruously comic note. The author seems concerned with contrasting pagan and Christian values. Although plot and picture of period mesh well, period overshadows story. The strength of this pleasant, romantic novel lies in the good sense it conveys of the everyday life, recreation, religious beliefs, attitudes toward Christians, roles of women and men, treatment of slaves, and values systems of the upper classes in Rome and in Britain in those days. Fanfare.

WHITNEY, ELINOR (1889–1980), born in Dorchester, Mass.; librarian, teacher, editor, and author of books for children. She grew up in Milton, Mass., in the family mansion next door to the little house of her grandmother, a well-known author of stories of New England life. After graduating from Milton Academy and from the Library School of Simmons College, she became assistant to the librarian of Boston Museum of Fine Arts, then taught English at Milton Academy for several years. In 1919 she took a position with the Bookshop for Boys and Girls in Boston. This led to her association with Bertha Mahoney and the founding in 1924 of *Horn Book* and her long connection with that publication. *Tod of the Fens** (Macmillan, 1928), a lively romp set in England in the fifteenth century, was a Newbery honor book. She also wrote *Tyke-y—His Book and His Mark* (Macmillan, 1925), a dog story, *Try All Ports* (Longmans, 1931), set in Boston in 1850, *Timothy and the Blue Cart* (Stokes, 1930), a story of New England country life, and *The Mystery Club* (Stokes, 1933), as well as several significant critical works about children's books, among them, *Contemporary Illustrators of Children's Books* (Bookshop for Boys and Girls, 1930). She married William Field, headmaster of Milton Academy.

WIBBERLEY†, LEONARD (1915–1983), born in Dublin, Ireland; reporter, editor, and author of books of fiction and non-fiction for adults and young people, best known in children's literature for his ambitious series of historical adventure novels that span the American Revolutionary period and involve the Treegate father and son and their associates. One of these was a Fanfare book, *John Treegate's Musket** (Farrar, 1959), which begins the not too skillful blend of research and story with Peter's estrangement from his father, John, an official of the Colonial government, and his growing up as the ward of the dour Scot, the Maclaren of Spey. It and its three successors have all been *Choice* books, *Peter Treegate's War†* (Farrar, 1960), *Sea Captain from Salem†* (Farrar, 1961), and *Treegate's Raiders†* (Farrar, 1962). Wibberley was educated in schools in Ireland and in England. After serving as apprentice to a London publisher, working for London newspapers as a copy boy, reporter, and editor, and becoming editor of the *Chronicle* in Trinidad, where he also worked briefly for an oil company, he came to the United States in 1943 as a foreign correspondent. He later served as editor of the *Independent Journal* in San Rafael, Calif., and then took a position as columnist with the Los Angeles *Times*. He made his home in California. After 1947, under his own name and also under the pseudonyms Patrick O'Connor, Leonard Holton, and Christopher Webb, he published for young people over forty books of fiction, chiefly romantic novels in the vein of *Treasure Island*, his favorite book from childhood, as well as two books of verse and several books of non-fiction, including *The Epics of Everest* (Farrar, 1954) and the highly regarded four-part biography, *Man of Liberty: A Life of Thomas Jefferson* (Farrar, 1963–1966). Regarded as a good storyteller, he also published the novels *Attar of Ice Valley* (Farrar, 1968), about a Stone Age youth who seeks new hunting grounds for his tribe, *Leopard's Prey* (Farrar, 1971) and

The Last Battle (Farrar, 1976), both in the Treegate series, *Flint's Island* (Farrar, 1972), his sequel to *Treasure Island*, and *The Crime of Martin Coverly* (Farrar, 1980), about pirates in the 1700s. He also wrote over forty novels, plays, and books of non-fiction and personal experience for adults, and several of his novels have been made into motion pictures.

WIGGIN, KATE DOUGLAS (SMITH) (1856–1923), born in Philadelphia, Pa.; kindergarten organizer, anthologist, novelist. She was educated in private schools in New England and at Mrs. Severance's Kindergarten Training School, Los Angeles. In 1877 she became head of a private kindergarten in Santa Barbara and the next year founded, with Felix Adler, Silver Street Free Kindergarten, San Francisco, about which she wrote *The Story of Patsy* (Murdock, 1883). In 1880 she founded, with her sister Nora A. Smith, the California Kindergarten Training School in San Francisco. Altogether, she wrote eleven novels, three plays, one book of short stories, one of verse, and several of non-fiction for adults and four plays, many anthologies, and nineteen books of fiction for children, among them *The Bird's Christmas Carol* (Murdock, 1887) and her best-loved book, *Rebecca of Sunnybrook Farm** (Houghton, 1903).

WILBUR (*Charlotte's Web**), naive, emotional runt pig belonging to Fern* Arable, raised on the Zuckerman* farm. When he is to be slaughtered for Christmas, his friend, Charlotte*, the spider, saves his life by spinning words into a web. At first unable to cope with the idea of death, he matures until, in the end, he is able to accept Charlotte's inevitable death and recognize death as a natural part of life.

WILBUR (*Miss Pickerell Goes to Mars**), the pleasant young man who first tells Miss Pickerell about the trip to Mars and who on the way teaches her some of the elemetary principles of space travel. She rescues him when he gets into trouble while trying to get rocks for her collection.

WILDCAT FURS TO CHINA: THE CRUISE OF THE SLOOP "EXPERIMENT" (Carmer*, Carl, ill. Elizabeth Black Carmer, Knopf, 1945), short historical novel which fictionalizes on the true story of the voyage of the *Experiment* to China in 1785, the first single-sticker and the second American ship ever to sail to China and return successfully. Tired of running errands up and down the Hudson River—all his sixty foot sloop is good for, people say—tall and likeable Captain Stewart Dean, formerly an American officer in the Revolutionary War, decides to "sail by the stars" and "plow some surfaces" where he is not "likely to run aground." He lays in a cargo of ginseng, furs, tobacco, rum, and other American products known to be popular in the East, installs weapons in anticipation of attack by pirates, and engages a crew, among them two lively and mischievous cabin boys, Billy de Wever, a Dutch-American boy, and Blackboy Prince, whose Daddy was a King in Africa, through whose experiences the story is told. They set sail from Albany in high spirits to a small but rousing farewell from friends and relatives and pursue a southeasterly course past the West Indies, by West Africa, and around the Cape of Good Hope to Macao at the entrance of the Pearl River in China. Off Africa, Blackboy's ability to speak the language proves advantageous in communicating with a native pilot, who later presents them with a monkey they name Yankee Doodle, and when they cross the equator a seaman garbed as King Neptune installs them as his subjects. At Macao, Captain Dean orders everyone to be on his most polite behavior, especially when they entertain the great Hoppo, the customs inspector, and later he takes the two boys with him when he dines at the house of the Houqua, the greatest merchant in Canton. The boys introduce the merchant's son to the game of Stump the Leader, during which they all three get dunked in the pool on the grounds of the merchant's magnificent estate. After a year of highly profitable trading, the *Experiment* returns to a jubilant reception in New York harbor. Captain Dean has proved his worth as a merchant sailor and the prowess of his sloop, and the two boys proudly share their portion of the voyage's profits with their families. All characters are real, and all events actually happened. The author has chosen those incidents and written from the point of view of those characters and in language that would appeal to middle graders. Brief but clear descriptions vitalize the river life on the Hudson and on the Pearl, and vigorous dialogue carries the burden of the story. There is little attempt at character development. The accent is on action, and the result is a superficial but interesting look at the hazards and rewards of early China trade. Fanfare.

WILDER, LAURA INGALLS (1867–1957), born near Pepin, Wis.; author of a series of books about her childhood that have become classics of the American pioneering experience. She attended school in De Smet, S.Dak., became a teacher before she was sixteen, and taught for seven years in Dakota Territory schools. For about nine years she and her husband farmed near De Smet, then moved to Mansfield, Mo., where they farmed for the rest of their lives. At the urging of her daughter, novelist Rose Wilder Lane, she wrote her first book, *Little House in the Big Woods** (Harper, 1932), telling of her early childhood in Wisconsin, published when she was sixty-five, followed by *Farmer Boy** (Harper, 1933), about her husband's childhood in northern New York State. The other books record the moves of the Ingalls family to Kansas in *Little House on the Prairie** (Harper, 1935), to Minnesota in *On the Banks of Plum Creek** (Harper, 1937), to what is now South Dakota in *By the Shores of Silver Lake** (Harper, 1939), *The Long Winter** (Harper, 1940), *Little Town on the Prairie** (Harper, 1941), and *These Happy Golden Years** (Harper, 1943), which ends with her marriage to Almanzo* Wilder. Three books were published posthumously, *On the Way Home* (Harper, 1962), her diary of the trip to Mansfield, *The First Four Years* (Harper, 1973), an unfinished book of the early years of her marriage, and *West from Home* (Harper, 1974), letters she wrote on a visit to her daughter in San Francisco, all interesting to Wilder devotees but none with the quality of her original books, which are distinguished for their clear, simple style, their wealth of detail, and their picture of a warm family quietly accepting hardship and enduring. The American Library Association award for "substantial and lasting contribution to literature for children" was named for her, and she was the first recipient.

WILLARD HALL (*Shadow across the Campus**), actual dormitory on the Northwestern University campus, scene in the novel of much of the action. On its sixth floor are locked, unused rooms where once the Zeta Nu sorority sisters held their meetings and in which Marjorie finds the documents that leads to a change in current Zeta Nu policy toward admitting Jews to membership. The public rooms of the dormitory are described in detail that makes it easy to visualize what they were like.

WILLIAM ASHBY (*The Witch of Blackbird Pond**), most eligible young bachelor in Wethersfield who soon pays court to Kit. He is a well-to-do young farmer who builds her a fine house, an enterprise which occupies most of his thinking while he is courting her. Kit breaks off with him when he does not come to her defense, and he informs her that he expects her to be more conscious of the effects of her behavior. He marries Judith.

WILLIAMS†, JAY (1914–1978), born in Buffalo, N.Y.; actor and entertainer, prolific writer for both adults and children. He attended the University of Pennsylvania in Philadelphia and Columbia University and served in the U.S. Army during World War II. For some years before the war he was a nightclub entertainer and film and stage actor. For adults he wrote some fourteen novels and several books of non-fiction. For children he wrote thirteen books of non-fiction, one of verse, and thirty-three books of fiction, besides the thirteen Danny Dunn science fiction books written in collaboration with Raymond Abrashkin*, of which *Danny Dunn and the Homework Machine** (McGraw, 1958) is typical. Among his other books for young people are *The Hawkstone†* (Walck, 1971), a time fantasy set in Connecticut, and *The Sword and the Scythe** (Oxford, 1946), historical fiction set in southern Germany in the sixteenth century.

WILLIE FIELDMOUSE (*Rabbit Hill**; *The Tough Winter**), friend of the young rabbit, Little Georgie, who provides information about the Folks by climbing to the windowsill and peering in, and who moves into the Rabbit family's burrow during the bitter winter. Willie is a particular friend of Mole, who often says, "Willie, be eyes for me," and he is able to keep the animals in touch with each other during the winter by making tunnels under the snow. He serves as a sensitive, friendly, younger-brother figure to Little Georgie.

WILLIE SLOPER (*The Saturdays**), the Melendy handyman who takes care of their furnace in the city. He helps with various chores after the family moves to the country in the later books.

WILLIS (*The Red Planet**), a Martian roundhead shaped like a fuzzy ball, a little bigger than a basketball. More a friend than a pet of Jim Marlowe, the little creature has an amazing ability to absorb and repeat any music or conversation and to repeat it like a tape recording, a skill that is crucial to the plot when he overhears a plan by the Resident Agent General of the Mars Company to impose inhumane conditions on the colonists in order to increase his own profit. Somewhat scatterbrained, the irrepressible Willis is a difficult responsibility for Jim but shows unexpected abilities, for instance to extend a saw-tooth arm, somewhat like his retractable eyes and legs, with which he saws through the desk-back and wall to escape imprisonment by the headmaster. For a reason unknown to the colonists, the native Martians cherish Willis and decide not to wipe out the Earth people mostly because of the evident love between Jim and Willis. Doctor* MacRae, who knows most about the natives, speculates that roundheads may be an embryo stage in Martian development.

WILSON, LEON, regional author of novels for children, son of writer Harry Leon Wilson, who wrote *Ruggles of Red Gap*. He has been a sardine canner in Monterey, Calif., and a story researcher in Hollywood, and worked as a record clerk and medical secretary in a hospital in Washington, D.C., among other jobs. For three years he served on the staff of a Cumberland mountain school in Tennessee. His amusing, bouncy homespun novels for middle and later elementary readers, *This Boy Cody** (Watts, 1950) and its sequel, *This Boy Cody and His Friends* (Watts, 1952), in which Cody's Uncle Jeff teaches him to make and play a fiddle, exude local color and show that the author is familiar with the ways, pleasures, and problems of the hill people among whom he worked. *This Boy Cody** appeared on the Fanfare list and was elected to the Lewis Carroll Shelf.

WINDFALL FIDDLE (Carmer*, Carl, ill. Arthur Conrad, Knopf, 1950), realistic novel of family and neighborhood life set in the small town of White Springs in western New York State in the 1920s. Twelve-year-old Bob Carson yearns to play the violin like his father, the local superintendent of schools, and his Uncle David. When the violin he earns by saving soap wrappers proves a dud, Miss Adelaide, a family friend, violin teacher, and Uncle David's sweetheart, offers to sell him hers for twenty dollars, provided he earns the money himself and pays her by October 1. The ensuing six months find David tackling various jobs in his efforts to meet the deadline. Although willing, he proves shy and unimaginative about getting work, and most of his jobs come from the suggestions of interested adults. Dr. Norton suggests Bob hire himself and his red cart to local artist, Mr. Hayslip, who needs someone to pull him alongside the circus parade as it winds through town so that he can sketch the lion. Bob mows a few yards for neighbors and sells lemonade during the lumberyard fire. He delivers flowers for Mr.* Minette, the elderly florist, who takes a particular interest in his project. Mr. Minette also suggests he apply for a job weeding lettuce beds on Mr. Dimella's truck farm. His father suggests he gather and sell windfall apples to the local cider mill (apparently the episode that gives the book its title). Bob suffers a severe setback when he is bilked of five dollars by Red Eagle, a cure seller who claims to be both gypsy and Onondaga Indian. When it seems that Bob cannot possibly achieve his objective, Mr. Linville, President of the County Agricultural Society, makes him chairman of the art department for the county fair. A last-minute complication arises when Bob generously pays the entry fee for Marie Dimella, for whom he has developed a fondness, leaving him two dollars short of his goal. When Marie's painting happily takes first prize, Bob is able to pay for his violin. A subplot involves the slowly advancing romance between Uncle David and Miss Adelaide, who are brought together at the end of the book by Mr. Minette. Extended descriptions of such local events as the fire, the circus, and the fair and Mr. Minette's several tall tales spin out the predictable plot. Stock adults dominate the action in this morally didactic, momentarily diverting story which recalls the Andy Hardy films of about the same era. Fanfare.

WIND ISLAND (Collin*, Hedvig, Viking, 1945), realistic family novel set shortly before World War II among the fisherfolk of the island of Fanoe (Wind Island) off Jutland, Denmark. The tiny island, carpeted with flowers in the summer, during the other seasons suffers the buffets of mighty winds that make the fisherman's trade precarious. The greatest wish of the Andersen children, Kristian, 9, Peter, 6, and little Hanne, 2½, is to present their mother with an amber necklace for her birthday. Secretly, in their tiny hideaway under the sand dune near their house, they busily prepare the golden beads with saw, grindstone, and pumice. To their dismay they discover they do not have enough amber to make an appropriate centerpeice. They know that only another storm can bring them a piece the size they need. But a storm will also endanger the lives of the island's fisherman, now out on the water with the fleet, their father among them. Hanna, the aged doll maker, assures them that a three-day storm will bring amber the size they need, and she instructs them to get to the shore very early in the morning before Coast-Madsen, the beachcomber, does. Days pass while the children wait for a storm. They sport among the dunes, rejoice with a neighbor who receives a gift from San Francisco, bathe in the surf, and take in the sights of Riga on the mainland with Mother. In spite of their mixed feeling about it, they find the first storm exhilarating. During the three days it lasts, they rescue a baby seal, which they name See-See, help Leen, the painter, about her house, and have a pleasant chat with the famous writer, Isak Dinesen. The storm over, Kristian hurries to the beach at daybreak, where he finds a hunk of amber as big as two fists, and, to his relief, observes the fishing fleet returning, all boats intact. Mother celebrates her birthday in bed with breakfast prepared by her three children, her gift a stunning amber necklace with a beautifully carved cross (the carving the contribution of Amber Signe, the village amber worker), a party made even more joyful by the knowledge that her fisherman husband is safe. Numerous full and partial-page realistic black and white drawings and muted watercolors follow the story and clarify incidents. Short chapters, extensive dialogue, homely details, and a cozy atmosphere create a pleasant, warm, somewhat suspenseful story for young readers. Fanfare.

WIND OF THE VIKINGS: A TALE OF THE ORKNEY ISLES (Cormack*, Maribelle, ill. Robert Lawson*, Appleton, 1937), realistic novel for teenagers set in the Orkney Islands in the early 1930s. When her father's business fails, Karin Kincaid, 17, goes from her New York home to live with her grandmother and her Uncle Garnock in the old house, Quoybanks, on the island of Eday. There by her willingness to work and her natural charm, she wins the hearts of her stern uncle and of the other residents, particularly young Ian Balfour, neighbor and mate of Garnock's fishing boat, *Island Belle*. Ian confesses that his great ambition is to study ship design and to make boats especially suited to the treacherous tides of the Orkneys. Karin and Ian, exploring the Hiding Hole, a cave cut off at high tide where Eday men hid from press gangs in the Napoleonic wars, find both a Bible left by Karin's great-great-grandfather and, more importantly, a rune stone of which they make a rubbing. In a fog, Karin stumbles upon a demented old woman, who, taking her for a Hill One, or fairy, shows her a hill dwelling of the ancient Picts. When Professor Thompson, an archeologist from Edinburgh University, charters *Island Belle*, Garnock takes Karin as cook and extra crew. They run into a terrible storm, save a Shetland yawl in distress, and reach Sule Skerry Light safely. At Stromness, they look for the Stone* of Odin, which was stolen from the Ring of Stenness more than one hundred years before. By reasoning, they find the broken and buried stone nearby and the local people arrange to have it reset. After hard work at kelp-burning, Karin and Ian take a sail in the boat Ian has built, the *Eday Scarf*, are caught by a sudden wind, and blown for four days to Norway, where Karin's great uncle, a ship builder, hears of their exploit and comes to see them. When they return, they find an excited letter from Prof. Karl Stromberg of Oslo, who has translated and wants to examine the rune stone. Ian and Karin revisit the Hiding Hole and this time discover an inner chamber which contains a true Viking ship burial, which they believe to be of Frithjof, saga hero. Stromberg comes with Karin's great-uncle Gosta, and soon afterwards Karin's father, Alec, comes. With a prize for the best find in Northern antiquities, both Karin and Ian can go to college, and Uncle Gosta is prepared to set Ian up in a shipbuilding firm with Alec as business manager. While the book gives an interesting picture of life in the Orkney Islands, and the storm scenes, particularly, are vivid, the multiplicity of ancient treasures found by the young people strains credulity. Characters are standard types, though Garnock, stout sailor and fond but stern uncle, who in the end marries Ian's widowed mother, is more memorable than the others. Fanfare.

THE WINDY HILL (Meigs*, Cornelia, Macmillan, 1921), realistic novel of family life with mystery story aspects set about 1920. Oliver Peyton, 15, and his sister, Janet*, 13, have looked forward to spending the summer with their mother's cousin, Jasper Peyton, in his well-appointed mansion overlooking the farming community of Medford Valley somewhere along the coast of New England. Both are disappointed to find their usually congenial cousin moody and aloof and soon connect his odd behavior to the coming and goings of an ill-mannered, hard-eyed man, who drives a rattletrap wagon. Oliver encounters on Windy Hill nearby the confidence-inspiring Beeman* and his daughter, sensible, friendly Polly, who he later discovers are also cousins, Thomas and Eleanor Brighton. Through stories that Beeman tells, advice he gives them, and their own ingenuity, Oliver and Janet discover that the source of their kindly cousin's distraction lies with still another cousin, Anthony Crawford, of whose existence they had also been unaware and who is the hard-eyed man they dislike so much. Anthony, Jasper, and Thomas were once law partners. After they quarrelled over a questionable scheme of Anthony's, through which he fell afoul of the law, Anthony went West, to return years later and force Cousin Jasper to deed to him certain family property. Anthony now threatens to besmirch the family name unless Cousin Jasper gives him the remaining property. Events come to a head when a storm causes the river to flood. The waters breach the dike in the part of the valley which Anthony owns and has neglected, and threaten to inundate the farms in the valley. Anthony admits the error of his grasping ways and labors all night with his cousins and the farmers in a successful effort to contain the flood. He attests that a remark of Oliver's opened his eyes to his evil ways and leaves with his family to make his home elsewhere. The events of this romanticized, mildly Gothic, uplifting and dated story, in which the children accomplish what adults cannot, strain credulity but remain entertaining to the quite satisfying, anticipatory ending. The stories which the Beeman tells and that comprise a good portion of the book are in themselves entertaining and serve to build suspense. They give a capsule summary of the history of New England as well as provide necessary background for solving the mystery. The style is descriptive and the pace leisurely. Characters are stock but suit the story. Virtues acclaimed are honesty, integrity, generosity, and standing up for what is right, while greed, selfishness, and moral ambivalence are shown to result in disaster and unhappiness. (John Massey*) Newbery Honor.

THE WINGED GIRL OF KNOSSOS (Berry*, Erick, Appleton, 1933), historical novel set in Bronze Age Crete which improvises upon the stories of Daidalos and Theseus from Greek mythology and upon the discoveries of Arthur Evans at Knossos. Inas, the impetuous, fun-loving, teenaged daughter of Daidalos, famed architect and clever inventor who built the Labyrinth, the palace of Minos, King of Crete, is an accomplished bull-vaulter and close friend of Ariadne, the king's daughter. She helps Ariadne contact Theseus, the tall, blond Athenian slave sent as tribute to Minos, with whom Ariadne has fallen in love. On orders from Ariadne, Inas helps Theseus escape from his gloomy palace prison by stringing a black thread from his cell to the prison door. Daidalos, who has been trying to fashion a glider of sticks and canvas, has aroused the enmity of the common people of Crete who believe he is dealing in black magic. When Kres, the goldsmith, jealous of Daidalos's skill and position with Minos, incites the people against the inventor, Daidalos and Inas flee to Siceli, an island in the west. There Minos is slain and his fleet destroyed when he tries to bring Daidalos back to Crete. Although her father remains in Siceli, Inas is rescued by Kadmos, the serious-minded son of the commander of Minos's fleet, and brought back to Crete. Later both escape on Daidalos's wings from Crete to a small boat and head for Greece where Ariadne and Theseus are now living. Although Inas changes convincingly as she is forced to assume responsibility for the well-being of her vague and abstracted father, characterization on the whole is superficial. Tone is romantic, pacing uneven, and potential for suspense unrealized, but the novel does give some sense of what life must have been like in ancient Crete when the empire of that advanced, powerful sea-going people was at its height. Newbery Honor.

WINTERBOUND (Bianco*, Margery, Viking, 1936), domestic novel set on a Connecticut farm in the 1930s. With Father away on a two-year scientific expedition and family finances low, the Ellis family rents an old farm house and learns to cope with country life. Kay, 19, who wants to go to art school and misses concerts, is unhappy, but Garry (Margaret) loves the outdoor life, and the younger children, Martin, 12, and Caroline, somewhat younger, make the change easily. When Penny, the mother, must accompany a tubercular niece to New Mexico, she arranges that a widow, Mrs. Cummings, will come to "supervise" the household, but the newcomer is critical, demanding, and unpleasant, and Kay, driven to an uncharacteristic assertiveness, fires her and pays the forty dollar advance she demands. Helped by the rural taxi-driver, Edna, and the good neighbors, Neal and Mary Rowe, the girls learn to cope with wood stoves, bitter weather, illness, and shortage of funds. Garry takes a job helping a nursery-owning couple who have just had a baby, and Kay sells a picture book she has written and illustrated. Garry answers an advertisement seeking a quiet country place for a writer, and they soon are providing room and board for Miss Emily Humbold and her dog, Arabella. Garry loses her way while walking and comes upon Jane Bassett, a girl about her age, who has been thrown from her horse, and together they find their way home. Jane turns out to be the sister of their landlord, Charles, who is starting to fix up the big house on the hill, and niece of Emily. At the book's end, Penny returns, having driven alone across the country, Garry is likely to get a job with the nursery, and a romance between

Kay and Charles seems about to blossom. Characters are well differentiated, and there are some amusing moments, but the novelty of two young women coping alone seems so dated that the novel is of interest mostly as social history. Fanfare; Newbery Honor.

WINTER DANGER (Steele*, William O., ill. Paul Galdone, Harcourt, 1954), realistic novel for middle readers set in frontier Tennessee in the late eighteenth century. With his woodsy father, Jared*, Caje (Micajah) Amis, 11, has been living in the open, sleeping in hollow logs, eating game when they can get it, parched corn (and little enough of it) when game is scarce. As December approaches, Caje expects his father to turn north toward settlements where they can find a deserted cabin to winter in, as they did when his mother was alive, and he is dismayed to learn that Jared plans to stay in Indian country, living in a cave. They spot buffalo, stalk them, but find Indians instead. After a series of hair-raising escapes, they kill some of the Chickamungas and lose the rest, and Jared thinks it a fine adventure, but when he sees thousands of squirrels moving through the trees like a fur blanket, migrating south, he knows it will be a hard winter with game scarce, so he heads back toward the Holston River where Caje's uncle, Adam Tadlock, lives. At the Tadlock cabin, Jared is uncomfortable and irritable, but Caje likes the warmth and the food, and even the company of his cousins, Burd, 13, Dorcas, almost a young lady, and little Marthy, though Sam, 10, a hare-brained braggart, resents his presence. Caje tries to help with the farm chores, though they are unfamiliar, while Jared, who fiercely hates to be beholden to anyone, hunts to pay their keep with game. Caje is not really surprised when Jared disappears, leaving him behind. As bitter weather sets in, he worries about Jared and about the burden that feeding him is to the Tadlocks. When a neighbor comes collecting food for an unfortunate family, he is surprised to see Aunt Jess contribute generously from their scanty supplies. In the record cold winter wolves come right into the barn, and a panther gets the cow, and, worse, Uncle Adam falls on the ice and breaks his leg. Burd has already gone to stay with his grandparents to help them, little Marthy is sickly, there's no game, and Uncle Adam gets a fever. Sam and Caje hike through the snow to the neighbors to beg some milk, and Caje is again surprised as they give willingly from the little they have. Deciding to ease the burden of his presence, at least, Caje sets off alone and soon sees that he has little chance of surviving in the deep snow and cold. As he hunts for shelter, he sees the white puff of breath that indicates a bear's hibernating cave. He rouses the bear, kills, skins, and butchers it, makes a crude sled of poles to load it on, and starts back. Wolves follow and begin to close in at twilight, so he makes a fire and sings and shouts all night to keep them off. The next day he gets back just before the Tadlocks have to kill the old horse for food and is welcomed as much for his own presence as for the meat. He learns that neighborly sharing and mutual help are not matters of debt and payment. The action against the Indians in the early part of the book is exciting but less believable than the details of Caje's misery and of the hard winter on the farm. Caje's preference for a settled life instead of the freedom of wilderness roaming is an interesting twist, unusual in a book for children. Books Too Good; Lewis Carroll.

THE WITCH OF BLACKBIRD POND (Speare*†, Elizabeth George, Houghton, 1958), historical novel set in Wethersfield, Conn., in 1687. Orphaned Kit (Katherine) Tyler, 16, raised in luxury in Barbados, comes to America to live with her Uncle Matthew* and Aunt Rachel Wood and their two daughters, proud, tart-tongued Judith, and patient, lame Mercy*. Kit assumes responsibility about the house and especially finds satisfaction in assisting Mercy with her dame school. But her high spirits and precipitous nature soon bring her into conflict with the duty-ridden, rigid Puritans. She unthinkingly playacts Bible stories, angering the stern Puritan authorities. In despair, she flees to the meadow near Blackbird Pond, where the gentle, old Quaker woman, Hannah* Tupper, a social outcast some call a witch, consoles her. Her friendship with Hannah not only sustains her through troubled months but also makes her the object of suspicion in the community. A mysterious illness strikes, and then Kit's efforts to teach lonely and frightened little Prudence* Cruff to read come to light, and Kit is arrested and tried for witchcraft. Nat* Eaton, young ship's captain and friend of Hannah, persuades Prudence to testify on Kit's behalf. Kit is exonerated when Prudence states that Kit has been teaching her to read the Bible. Kit breaks off with William* Ashby, well-off young farmer who has been courting her, and is preparing to return to Barbados, when Nat proposes marriage. The end of her first year in Connecticut finds Kit a more sober, less rash young woman, who looks forward to happier days in the colony. The novel's three romances seem contrived to please a teen audience. Judith marries William, while Mercy pairs off with John* Holbrook, a young divinity student. Most characters are types or functionaries, but Kit is a strong protagonist. Kit's rigidly principled Uncle Matthew is an especially well-drawn figure; Hannah is sentimentalized. This rich, substantial book excels in its depiction of setting. The author recreates well Puritan superstitions, intolerance, and daily life. Some minor historical figures and events appear in the novel. The controversy over the colony's charter took place as described. (Goodwife* Cruff) Books Too Good; Choice; Fanfare; Newbery Winner.

WIZARD OF OZ (*The Wonderful Wizard of Oz**), ventriloquist who has been blown to Oz in a balloon from a fair and who has by trickery and showmanship convinced the people there that he is a wizard. He has commanded that everyone entering the Emerald City wear green-tinted glasses, so that everything appears green, and he manages by tricks to appear as a disembodied head, a beautiful woman, a horrible beast, and a ball of fire. After he has been revealed as a humbug, he proposes that he and Dorothy try to return to Kansas in his balloon, but he takes off before she can get aboard.

WOLF BROTHER (Kjelgaard*, Jim, Holiday, 1957), historical novel set in the southwestern United States in the 1880s, when the Apaches are first confined to reservations. The story is fiction but is based on actual events in Apache history. After six years in white schools, Jonathan, 16, Apache, returns to his reservation at Quartz Flat. He rashly assaults an army officer and flees for his life. He joins the band of outlaws led by Cross* Face, the leader of the free Apaches, whom the Apaches regard as a valiant symbol of their traditional unrestrained way of life and whom the whites consider a notorious renegade. For months Cross Face's little band hunts, raids, and fights, eluding capture countless times. Jonathan earns the name of Wolf Brother when he finds and tames a wolf cub, Hallee, which serves the group well as watchdog. The inscrutable, wise old chieftain deploys his diminishing forces with skill and wit. They are harried and hounded, forced farther and farther back into the canyons and hills, until finally without food and virtually weaponless, reduced to nine men, they are captured. Cross Face tells Wolf Brother that it is hopeless to continue to resist the whites and instructs him to lead the Indians in a newer, better way of life. The fugitives are tried and sentenced to imprisonment in Florida. On the way there by train, Cross Face creates a diversion, enabling Wolf Brother to escape. The youth works his way back over fifteen hundred miles to Apache territory, arriving two years later at the remote, grassy canyon that Cross Face once used as a hideout and which he himself found particularly appealing. He finds there a young half-breed, Pete Whitman, rounding up cattle left from Cross Face's raids. The two young men become partners in ranching, and with the help of Jack Morton, the new agent at Quartz Flat, who is sympathetic to the Indians, enlist other Apaches in their venture, one that can result in improved conditions for the Apaches. Characters are cardboard, dialogue is stiff, and, although there are some exciting moments, the plot moves quickly over the years without much suspense or a proper climax. The author's purpose appears to be to inform young readers of what it was like for the Apaches during the time they lost their free, independent way of life and were moved onto reservations. The point of view is sympathetic to the Indians and shows the material and spiritual poverty of those on the reservation and the anger, resentment, and hopelessness of the resisters. The only memorable character is Cross Face, and Jonathan is merely a literary device, never emerging as a truly flesh and blood being. Spur.

THE WONDERFUL FLIGHT TO THE MUSHROOM PLANET (Cameron*†, Eleanor, ill. Robert Henneberger, Little, 1954), science fantasy set in Pacific Grove, California, and on the planet Basidium-X* in the mid-1900s. In response to an ad in the paper, David* Topman and Chuck* Masterson design and build a cigar-shaped ship of spare parts and junk material. They haul it six blocks to 5* Thallo St., where Mr. Tyco* Bass lives. Mr. Bass is a wispy-haired, perky, dome-headed little man who says he is a member of the Mushroom* People who live on the planet Basidium-X and that he arrived on earth as a spore. He wishes the boys to rocket to Basidium because he is certain that his people are in trouble and because he wants a canning jar of Basidium air with which he hopes to determine why the atmosphere there is green. After the boys observe Basidium through a telescope outfitted with the Stroboscopic* Polaroid Filter that Mr. Bass has developed in his expertly equipped observatory, the boys depart, taking Mrs. Pennyfeather, the Topman hen, as mascot, and travel uneventfully to Basidium. They discover two Mushroom Men, the Wise Men, Oru* and Mebe, in despair because their leader, the Great Ta, has condemned them to death for failing to maintain the plant that is the source of the Mushroom People's special green color. The boys soon identify as sulfur the strange odor that permeates the place where the plants have been growing. They give to Ta Mrs. Pennyfeather, whose eggs will provide the sulfur necessary for keeping the people green. As reward, Ta spares the lives of Mebe and Oru and gives the boys his necklace of large, richly colored stones. After filling the canning jar with air, the boys return through a ticklish rainstorm to a welcoming Mr. Bass. Later they are informed by a neighbor boy that Mr. Bass has been blown away by a blast of wind, like a spore. In his home, they discover a letter in which Mr. Bass leaves his house and observatory to them as headquarters for the Society of Young Astronomers and Students of Space Travel. Although the conclusion is flat, and motivations are sometimes not clear, the details of the flight are carefully worked out, and the problems keep the reader involved. There is some humor, and vocabulary is easy enough for later elementary readers. Tone is good-natured, if occasionally condescending, and David and Chuck are enterprising, courageous youths with whom young readers can easily identify. Conventions of science fiction appear: characterization is shallow, futuristic technology (outmoded by late twentieth century standards) provides much of the interest, and events move fast, but there is less emphasis upon social and political issues than is normal for the genre. Choice.

THE WONDERFUL WINTER (Chute*, Marchette, ill. Grace Golden, Dutton, 1954), historical novel set in Shakespearean England during the winter of 1596–1597. In Suffolk, young Sir Robin (Robert) Wakefield, an orphan probably in his early teens, lives with his three cheerless aunts until one day when two new elements enter his life—a pleasure-hating tutor and a loving spaniel puppy. At his aunt's order to have the dog disposed of in the morning, Robin sneaks out, releases the dog which he named Ruff, and together they set out for London. Near starvation, he finds himself close to the theaters and, to escape a thug trying to steal Ruff, he enters the playhouse, sees a play which delights him, and, seeing the thug waiting outside, sneaks into the prop room and hides with Ruff in a bed. There he is discovered by two players, afterwards identified as Shakespeare and John Heminges. The latter takes him home, where his wife, Rebecca, feeds him and puts him to bed with their apprentice, Sandy (Alexander) Cooke. He stays at the Heminges home, helping with the chores, playing with the three young daughters, and enjoying his first experience of loving family life. Known by the name he has given, Robin Johnson, he eventually gets to know such real life members of the acting group besides Shakespeare, Heminges and Cooke as Richard and Cuthbert Burbage and Thomas Pope. As spring approaches, it appears likely that the playhouse, The Theater, will lose its lease, and Robin decides to return to Suffolk. He tells his friends his real name, exchanges gifts with them, and with Ruff travels home, where he is greeted with love by his aunts. The adventure is pleasant and generally plausible, though Robin's entrance into the actors' world is rather too easy and his escape from the dangers of London too fortuitous to be entirely convincing. Details of the life of the playhouse are more interesting than the plot, which, after the initial escape from Suffolk, has little tension. Books Too Good.

THE WONDERFUL WIZARD OF OZ (Baum*, L. Frank, George M. Hall, 1900), first of fourteen fantasies Baum wrote about the imaginary land of Oz* (the series was continued by Ruth Plumly Thompson after his death). This book starts in the 1890s on "the great gray prairie" of Kansas, where Dorothy* lives in a one-room gray house with unsmiling Aunt Em and Uncle Henry and her little black dog, Toto*. One day a cyclone picks up the house, with Dorothy, who did not get to the cyclone cellar in time because she was chasing Toto, and carries it for some time, setting it down suddenly in a "country of marvellous beauty." A little old woman introduces herself as the good Witch of the North and tells Dorothy that she is in the Land of the Munchkins, little people who inhabit the eastern portion of Oz, and that her house has landed on the Wicked Witch of the East, who has kept the Munchkins in bondage. To get back to Kansas, they can only suggest that Dorothy follow the yellow brick road to the Emerald City in the center of Oz and consult the great Wizard* of Oz who rules there. With Toto she starts off, wearing the silver shoes that belonged to the Witch of the East and bearing on her forehead the mark of the kiss of the Witch of the North, which will keep anyone from injuring her. On the way she meets and is joined by a Scarecrow*, who wants brains, a Tin* Woodman, who wants a heart, and a Cowardly* Lion, who wants courage. They run into various dangers: the Kalidahs, fierce creatures with bodies of bears and heads of tigers, a ditch which they must be carried across, one at a time, by the lion, another ditch too broad for the lion to leap that they cross on a tree chopped down by the Woodman, a river that they raft across, temporarily losing the Scarecrow, and a field of deadly poppies, whose scent anesthetizes the living creatures but has no effect on the Woodman or the Scarecrow. At the Emerald City, where green-tinted glasses are locked on each of them so that everything appears green, the great Oz sees them one at a time, appearing to Dorothy as a disembodied head, to the Scarecrow as a beautiful woman, to the Woodman as a horrible beast, and to the Lion as a ball of fire. Of each he demands that they kill the Wicked Witch of the West, who has enslaved the Winkies, before he will help them. The Witch of the West, who can see a great distance, sends against them her wolves, which are killed by the Woodman, her crows, which are scared by the Scarecrow, her slave Winkies, who are scared by the Lion, her bees, which die after trying to sting the Woodman, and finally the winged monkeys, who carry Dorothy, the Lion, and Toto to her castle and try to destroy the others. There Dorothy is enslaved until she becomes so angry that she throws water at the witch, who shrivels up to nothing. Dorothy then releases the Lion and with the help of the grateful Winkies, they repair the Woodman and the Scarecrow, and the winged monkeys carry them back to the Emerald City. There they discover that Oz is a humbug, actually not a wizard but a ventriloquist who has fooled the people for years. He gives the Scarecrow, the Woodman, and the Lion tokens of brains, heart, and courage, virtues they have exhibited all along, and proposes to try to get Dorothy back to Kansas in a balloon, since he first arrived in Oz accidentally in one. Just as preparations are ready, Dorothy rushes off to catch Toto, and the wizard leaves without her. The companions set off to try what seems to be their only remaining hope, Glinda, the good Witch of the South, who lives in the land of the Quadlings. On their way they encounter difficulties: trees whose branches reach out and throw them back, a wall of china they must scale and a country peopled by little china men and animals which they must pass through with care, a monster shaped like a spider, and the armless Hammerheads, who batter them when they try to climb a hill. They appeal to the flying monkeys, who must obey three requests of the owner of a crown Dorothy got in the West, and are carried into the land of the Quadlings. Glinda, the beautiful Witch, takes the crown and uses her three requests to get each character to the place he wishes to stay, the Scarecrow to Emerald City, where he will be king, the Woodman to the Winkies, who make him their king, and the Lion to the forest, where the animals make him their king. To Dorothy, she points out that the silver shoes will take her back to Kansas if she clicks her heels together three times. She does, and they do. The book, unquestionably the most successful of the series, has long been a favorite despite its flat, often tedious style. Those familiar with the extremely popular movie version will note that in the film Dorothy is older, Kansas, Aunt Em and Uncle Henry are less grim, there are farm hands and a traveling showman who reappear as characters in Oz, and the story has been simplified by the elimination of various events, usually to its benefit. Choice; ChLA Top 10; Lewis Carroll.

THE WONDERFUL YEAR (Barnes*, Nancy, ill. Kate Seredy*, Messner, 1946), realistic novel set apparently in the first decade of the twentieth century in Colorado. When Ellen Martin, 11, learns that she and her parents are leaving Norton, Kans., to start a fruit ranch in Colorado in hope of aiding her lawyer father's health, she takes the news apprehensively, as she and her father, Will, both take life in general. Her stylish, vivacious mother, Jo, welcomes the adventure and organizes the expedition, with Father riding in the baggage car with the horse, Billy, and the fox terrier, Bobby, and Ellen in charge of the canary. At first they live in a tent, then in a cabin, which Jo decorates with portieres, velvet carpet covered with pale roses, and grandmother's carved ebony piano. Ellen begins to love the new life and makes a friend, Ronald Errington, 15, youngest in a family of Englishmen batching on the next ranch. She also gets the only thing she has ever asked for, a bicycle, and to her dismay and her father's, she can't learn to ride around the smooth little track he has made for her. When finally she tries it out on the rut-filled road, she masters the technique. Most of her summer centers on Ronnie, who treats her quite differently from the way American boys would treat a girl four years younger, as a friend, though with some male condescension. He gets lost with her, comforts her when she is alone during a storm, buys her a boy's hat for her birthday, and tells her judiciously, "Someday you'll be a beauty." When he flirts with other girls at a dance in Fruitvale, she is crushed, and later when they move for the winter to Mesa, Colo., instead of back to Kansas, she feels out of place, homely, and disliked. Her conversion to a pretty, popular schoolgirl and Ronnie's sudden re-emergence in her life when he comes to live in their house and go to agricultural school are not very believable and too pat, but the characterization, particularly of Ellen's parents, is sharp and often witty. Ellen's inclination to cover up her ability to shoot better than Ronnie and to let him lord it over her would not suit modern feminists, but in the context of the period and their age difference it makes sense. As a picture of life where "roughing it" includes deep, leather lounge chairs and ecru, net curtains, the book provides a fine and humorous contrast to many stories of frontier hardship. Newbery Honor.

WONSETLER, ADELAIDE H. , wife of John Charles Wonsetler*, who collaborated with him in the writing of *Me and the General** (Knopf, 1941).

WONSETLER, JOHN CHARLES (1900–   ), born in Camden, N.J.; painter and illustrator of textbooks on history, social studies, and languages. He studied at the Philadelphia Museum School of Industrial Art, where he was influenced by the Howard Pyle tradition, and worked as a mural painter. In 1939 he turned to book illustration, and with his wife, Adelaide Wonsetler*, wrote and illustrated *Me and the General** (Knopf, 1941), a novel of the War of 1812 in the Lake Erie area.

WOODEN SADDLES (Lay*, Marion, ill. Addison Burbank, Morrow, 1939), novel of adventure set in Mexico south of Mexico City during the civil strife of the mid-twentieth century, intended to inform young readers about customs and problems of Mexico and to focus attention on Mexico's Indian heritage. Young Chucho, a lazy, blond boy of twelve, and his friend, lame Luis of Indian descent, were captured by gypsies when they were infants. Badly treated by their captors, except for the old woman, Zoira, who encourages Chucho to practice rope tricks, the boys plan to run away. Chucho manages to do so, taking with him a fawn that he has found by a spring during a drought. Adventures follow in rapid succession after a knife-sharpener, with whom Chucho leaves his fawn for safe-keeping, sells the animal. Leaving hastily with the money, Chucho seeks, first, the lost fawn, which he never recovers, and second, a place to live permanently.

He falls in with the traveling variety circus owned by Señor Gallardo. When Gallardo's daughter, pretty Lilia, encourages Chucho to demonstrate his skill at rope tricks, he wins the prize, a *riata* (rope). He flees the circus when the gypsies appear, joining an itinerant peddler, Paco, who is really running guns for insurgents. Captured by police and put on a train for the capital for questioning, he is helped to escape by a friendly brakeman when he falls ill of a fever. A poor charcoal maker, Tamian, and his kindhearted wife, Elota, who live in the Street of the Weavers in the village of Chirimoya, take him in and nurse him back to health. He stays for some time with these generous and happy descendants of the Zapotec Indians, enjoying their hospitality and helping them with their work, even contributing the remainder of the money he received for his fawn toward the purchase of a much-needed cow. When the circus comes through, Lilia invites him to rejoin the show. Happy days follow as Chucho is accepted as a full member of the circus family of acrobats, dancers, and riders. He acquires a cowboy suit and a wooden Indian saddle and stars in a roping act with Lilia. Just before she elopes with an army officer, Lilia gives Chucho her prize pony, Hummingbird. Remembering that she told him to take good care of the little horse, Chucho flees the circus when Gallardo orders the players to ride their mounts through shark-infested waters. He encounters the gypsies again, and this time he helps Luis to escape. The two decide to travel northward to the Hacienda Laguna de Ora, whose cowboys had previously befriended Chucho and offered him a home. The superficial plot moves feverishly fast through a series of underdeveloped, fabricated, fortuitous incidents and a profusion of stock and undeveloped characters to an abrupt, coincidental ending. Chucho plunges from one tense situation to another, escaping from pitfalls by wit and luck. Spanish terms support setting and build authenticity, and there are many descriptions of dress and customs. Fanfare.

WOODS HOLE, MASS. (*Jane's Island**), site of the marine biology laboratory which figures as setting. The spot is at the end of a narrow neck of land between Nantucket Sound and Buzzard's Bay.

WOODWARD, HILDEGARD (1898–), born in Worcester, Mass.; artist, teacher of design. She studied at the School of the Museum of Fine Arts in Boston and later taught design there and also at the School of Fine Arts and Crafts in Boston. She also has taught art in private schools in New York and has been a portrait painter, specializing in pictures of children. Her home has been in Connecticut, the setting for *Jared's Blessing** (Scribner's, 1942), a story of colonial times which she wrote and illustrated.

WOOFLE (*The Magic Shop**), the dog of Dick and Denise Benton. He is called Woofle because he says, "Woof!," and is the color of a well-done waffle. Puck feeds him magic biscuits that temporarily give him the power to speak. He is instrumental in saving the magic wand.

WORTH, KATHRYN (1898–   ), born in Wilmington, N.C.; poet and author. She attended boarding school in Switzerland, Radcliffe College, and the Columbia University Pulitzer School of Journalism. Her novels are mostly based on stories of her ancestors, among them *They Loved to Laugh** (Doubleday, 1942), about an orphan taken in by a Quaker doctor's family in early nineteenth-century North Carolina. Her first published work was a book of poems for adults, *Sign of Capricorns* (Knopf, 1937). This was followed by a book of poems written for her daughter, *Poems for Josephine* (Doubleday, 1943). Among her other works for children are *New Worlds for Josie* (Doubleday, 1944), a boarding school story, *Middle Button* (Doubleday, 1941), a novel of a middle girl in a family of eleven in 1880 who aspires to become a doctor, and *Sea Change* (Doubleday, 1948), set in the late nineteenth century involving religious prejudice in an ultra-conservative family.

X 31 (*Heart of Danger**), German officer who calls himself Major Braun, who is passing secrets to the Allies via the French Underground and whom Rudy* Behrens and Tod* Moran meet in Paris at the Café d'Auvergne. He helps the Allies to avenge the death of his foster mother, a Jew who was sent to Belsen. From him Rudy learns that his father is not a traitor to the United States.

Y

YATES, ELIZABETH (1905–), born in Buffalo, N.Y.; lecturer and writer for adults and children, most noted in children's literature for her Newbery Award–winning biography *Amos Fortune, Free Man* (Aladdin, 1950), about the struggles of a black man to buy his own freedom and that of several other slaves as well. Of a well-to-do family, she attended schools in Buffalo and Mamaroneck, N.Y., and spent summers on her father's farm south of Buffalo. She went to New York City to satisfy a long-held ambition to become a writer, at twenty-three married William McGreal, a businessman, and for several years lived in London, where she continued to write reviews, articles, and short stories, edit, and do research. She traveled extensively in Europe, and published her first novel in 1938. In 1939, after her husband's sight failed, the couple returned to the United States, settling in the New Hampshire countryside, where they bought and restored an old farmhouse and she built her life around her writing and he around work with the blind. Her writing career of over forty years has been distinguished, prolific, and varied, seeing the publication of many different kinds of books. She has published over a dozen and a half books of biography, legends, Bible stories, and other non-fiction, many novels and books of non-fiction for adults, and numerous articles, essays, and reviews for periodicals. The most highly acclaimed of her novels for the young are the Newbery honor book *Mountain Born** (Coward, 1943), which depicts life on a sheep farm, *A Place for Peter* (Coward, 1952), its sequel, and *Carolina's Courage* (Dutton, 1964), which describes a family's journey overland from New Hampshire to Nebraska during which little Carolina gives her doll to an Indian girl, insuring a friendly welcome to the territory. Of her non-fiction, her biography *Prudence Crandall, Woman of Courage* (Aladdin, 1955) has received praise, and *Rainbow Round the World* (Bobbs, 1954), which explains the work of UNICEF, won the Jane Addams Award. More recently she has published *The Seventh One* (Walker, 1978), a novel about the seven dogs a man acquires during his lifetime, and *My Diary—My World* (Westminster, 1981), her own story about her youth and her determination to become a writer over her father's objections. She has taught at writer's conferences at the University of New Hampshire, the University of Connecticut, and Indiana University, among others, and has lectured widely on books and writing.

THE YEARLING (Rawlings*, Marjorie Kinnan, ill. Edward Shenton, Scribner's, 1938), realistic novel set in Northern Florida a few years after the Civil War, about 1870. With hard work and skill, wiry little Penny* (Ezra) Baxter scrapes a living from a "pine island" in the arid scrub for his large, humorless wife, Ma*, and his one son to survive beyond infancy, Jody*, 11. Their only neighbors, four miles away, are the Forresters, an aging couple with six huge, black-bearded grown sons and one crippled boy Jody's age, Fodderwing*, whose "wits are addled," but who has a great understanding of wild animals. Penny, a gentle, sensitive man, teaches Jody his hunting skills and his love of nature as they track game or try to get Old Slewfoot, the bear that has killed their brood sow. At the Forresters, Jody sees a different sort of life in the loud, boisterous family. In one memorable scene, the six big men, roused stark naked from their beds by a varmint chase in the night, turn to making music and drinking their homemade whiskey while the old parents join in and Jody and Fodderwing watch, delighted. Jody and his father make an occasional trip to Volusia, on the river, the nearest trading town, where they stay with pretty, feminine Grandma* Hutto and sometimes see her sailor son, Oliver. On one trip, when Oliver is being beaten by the Forresters in a quarrel over yellow-haired Twink Weatherby, whom both Oliver and Lem* Forrester claim, both Penny and Jody jump into the fight on Oliver's side, thereby winning the enmity of the Forrester clan. Later, hunting their hogs that have been baited and penned by their neighbors, Penny is bitten by a rattlesnake. He kills a doe, uses the liver to draw out the poison, and sends Jody on to the Forresters for help. Though mean Lem would send Jody away, Mill Wheel rides for the doctor and Buck* rides to pick up Penny, then stays at the Baxters to do the farm work until he recovers. Jody, who has always longed for a pet, persuades his father to let him find the doe's fawn, though his mother grudges it the food. When Jody goes to show Fodderwing his pet, he finds the family in shocked grief over the crippled boy's death. He stays for the burying and gives his fawn the name Fodderwing had chosen for it, Flag. His companionship with the deer makes Jody happy, although the family suffers setbacks: a flood kills most of the game; wolves kill the heifer calf; Old Slewfoot kills the new calf just before Christmas. Penny and Jody track the bear a great distance and finally kill it, then head for the Christmas doings at Volusia, where Ma will meet them, but first they run into the Forresters, riding drunk to Fort Gates. News of the bear changes their plans; they quarter it, take it to Baxter's Island, and all go to Volusia, where Buck dresses in the bear skin to scare the congregation and is almost shot. In their wild carousing, the Forresters burn Grandma Hutto's house, but to keep Oliver from getting killed in a feud, she says she left a lamp where a curtain blew into it, and insists on starting immediately for Boston with Oliver and Twink, now married. As spring arrives, Flag becomes a real problem, eating the new corn shoots. Since Penny is ill, Ma helps Jody build a fence, and when that doesn't keep the deer out, shoots and wounds him. Jody must finish him off, and then, heartbroken and feeling that Penny has betrayed him, he leaves, planning to go to Boston and off to sea with Oliver. In a leaky dugout, he gets out on Lake George. Lost, sick, and starving, he is picked up by the mailboat, fed, and deposited in Volusia. He walks home, fearing rejection, and finds Ma gone to trade for seed corn to the Forresters, Penny ill but thankful for his return and compassionate about his loss. Having matured, Jody faces the prospect of being the main worker to support his aging parents. Though the relationship of the lonely boy and the deer is central to the plot, it is Jody's relationship to Penny that gives the book a pervasive sense of love despite hardships, and the sensitively evoked appreciation of nature makes the scrub forest a place of beauty. Even minor characters are strongly individualized, and the dialect has a convincing rhythm and vocabulary. Originally published for adults, this is long in comparison to most children's books, but not too difficult for good readers. Books Too Good; Choice; Lewis Carroll.

THE YEAR OF JUBILO (Sawyer*, Ruth, ill. Edward Shenton, Viking, 1940), realistic family novel set in the mid-1890s, which follows *Roller Skates**. After Mr. Wyman's business fails and he dies, the Wymans, Lucinda, now almost fourteen, her three older brothers, Duncan, David, and Carter, and their mother, whom they call Grasshopper, their father's affectionate name for her, move to their cottage on Penobscot Bay in Maine. With only seventy-five dollars in the bank, their main problem is survival. As they learn to live off the land and the sea and become a part of the rural community, they grow closer as a family, develop new spiritual and economic resources, and have some lively adventures as well, for what they come to call their Year of Jubilo, a term from the old song they often sing to signify a time of joy after a trying period. David becomes their fisherman and Carter their woodsman, while Duncan tends their garden plot. Lucinda takes over the kitchen, and Mrs. Wyman provides encouragement and ballast. Later they are joined by Peter Blakely, a youth whose family sends him to the country for his health. The story is told from Lucinda's point of view, and, while it describes the family's efforts to make a good life without Father, it also shows Lucinda slowly growing out of being ''Wymans' Tag'' and gaining acceptance as a Wyman in her own right. She pluckily applies herself to learning to cook, picks berries for jam and for sale in the village, makes friends with wise-beyond-her-years, ambitious, hardworking Gladiola Murphy, a haunting if stock figure, the eldest daughter of the village ne'er-do-wells, helps the boys with the mackerel run and winterizing the house, and realizes she is now considered a real Wyman when the boys take her camping with them on an island in the bay. Sturdy Maine natives parade through the book: Ben Butler, who takes Lucinda to a circus on July 4; hearty Ellis Freeman, a local mailman whom Lucinda sometimes accompanies on his rounds; supportive Captain Calderwood, who teaches her to make chowder and takes her sailing with him on their shared birthday; and slightly mad Adolphus Higgins, itinerant teacher of Spencerian hand. The Wyman youths earn a five hundred dollar reward for capturing thieves in the act of ransacking the local inn for an exciting if unlikely adventure, and scenes in which the Wymans help Gladiola Murphy bury her baby sister exude sentimentality. The book concludes with Lucinda coping with her crush on Peter Blakely and in an improbably romantic episode arranging Duncan's marriage to his sweetheart Maggie Campbell, by way of cheering him up because he blames himself for Mrs. Wyman's very serious illness. The author evokes well the sights, sounds, and smells of the Bay and countryside. Lucinda's letters to old friends, which appear at the ends of chapters, present her feelings about the most important events in the chapters and reveal a more polished use of language and sense of structure than might be expected in even as bright a girl as Lucinda. Life for the Wymans never seems quite as hard as it must have been, and events seem deliberately concocted for a wholesome, uplifting book for girls, to provide innocuous entertainment for them, and to illustrate such virtues as obedience, hard work, cooperation, self-control, family loyalty, and faith in the future. Compared to the inventive *Roller Skates**, this is a humdrum book, if true to this stage in Lucinda's life. Fanfare.

YELLOW NOSE (*The Ordeal of the Young Hunter**), priest of the Navajo and Jadih's* uncle, his mother's brother, and a respected leader of the people. He opposes Jadih's dancing for the tourists in Flagstaff, because he feels that it would be using the traditions of the Indians for selfish ends (to win the prize money to pay off debts and buy more sheep) and would poke fun at the Indians' animal friends. He conducts the Mountain Chant ceremony, after which he and Jadih make up the animal dance for the entertainment of the guests. Trader* Jim Whittaker is present, sees the dance, and gets the idea for entering the contest. Yellow Nose would like Jadih to become a priest like himself. He represents the Navajos who hold to the old ways.

YONIE WONDERNOSE (De Angeli*, Marguerite, ill. author, Doubleday, 1944), brief, realistic story set in the Pennsylvania Dutch Amish community of Lancaster County, Pa., at an unspecified time, presumably mid-twentieth century. Yonie (Jonathan), 7, is called a "Wondernose" by his father because he is so often diverted from his duties by his curiosity. When his parents and two older sisters go visiting overnight, leaving Yonie and his little sister, Nancy, in the care of their Granny, Yonie promises to keep his mind on his work. He tries, but has some mishaps: he takes time out to go swimming in the brook, then, hurrying to catch up with his chores, shuts Granny in the chickenhouse by accident and lets the dinner burn while he hunts her. That night, lightning sets the barn afire and Yonie, with Granny's help, gets the horses out, then the chickens, the cows and the calves. While Granny goes for apple butter to soothe the burn on one cow, Yonie runs to get Dunder, the bull, but hesitates and stops to see where a big timber falls near the pig pen and to let out the pigs. He stops to look at the fire engine arriving before he remembers Dunder, now raging mad from a burn on his back. Yonie is able to lead him off. When his father returns, he gives Yonie one of the ten piglets born to the sow Yonie saved and the little black calf and promises to let him ride the big work horse when they harrow the field for winter wheat. The style and the plot are simple, but the Pennsylvania Dutch dialect gives the story some distinction, as do de Angeli's illustrations. Choice.

YOUNG FU OF THE UPPER YANGTZE (Lewis*, Elizabeth Foreman, ill. Kurt Wiese, Winston, 1932), realistic novel set in Chungking, China, during five years of the 1920s. Fu Yuin-Fah, 13, comes to the city with his widowed mother, Fu* Be Be, to begin an apprenticeship arranged by his village Headman with the coppersmith Tang*. Everything about the city fascinates him, even their cramped room on Chair-Makers' Way with a pigpen at the rear, and he is especially pleased when the scholar, Wang, who lives upstairs, speaks to him in a kindly way. At first he suffers at the coppersmith's by being taunted as a "countryman," particularly by Small* Den, an apprentice, but another apprentice, Young* Li, becomes his friend. Wang Scholar, seeing him intelligent and interested, begins to teach him reading and the wisdom of the ancients. Several months later, after he feels confident in the city, he comes upon a group of soldiers insisting that a coolie abandon his load of rice and carry their bedding. When the coolie refuses, one of the soldiers calmly shoots him and impresses Young Fu into carrying the load. Later, almost dead with fatigue, he is rescued by another soldier, who urges him to run. The city poses other hazards to him: beggars near the gate, angry that he interferes to bring justice to a leper, trip him and ruin a brazier he is delivering; an unscrupulous shopkeeper sells him a cheap watch with flourescent hands, then hounds him for payment; plague invades the city and Young Li becomes ill; a flooding river catches him outside the city walls after the gates are shut, and he narrowly escapes drowning with two old people who have befriended him and whom he leads to safety; a disgruntled workman, Wei, returns with his Communist friends to raid the shop while Young Fu is left in charge, and he is saved from death only by the early return of Tang; tricked into gambling, he loses the money Fu Be Be has entrusted to him; as he returns with Tang from a river journey to deliver valuable brasses, their boat is attacked by bandits and Young Fu saves the money by hiding in a pile of rags; when certain beautiful pieces disappear from the shop, he is suspected of theft but discovers that Small Den, now working for another coppersmith, has taken them to copy; Lu, a steady, honest journeyman, is arrested when opium is found in the shed behind his house. In each instance, Young Fu either distinguishes himself or learns a valuable lesson. He leaves the city on the night of the new year, when the shopkeeper can demand payment, and visits a cousin in the mountains where a rare snow falls—"dragon's breath"—thought to be great good luck. Borrowing two buckets, he fills them, hurries to the city, and sells enough to pay his debt and to give Fu Be Be forty coppers. When the foreign hospital catches fire, he alone of the watching crowd dares to climb to the roof of the house in the compound to throw off a burning brand, and as a reward the foreign woman sends five dollars. For a return gift, he asks his master to sell him a small kettle, and shrewd Tang lets him buy a beautiful specimen for only fifty cents, knowing that the advertisement among the foreigners will be worth more. Through his knowledge of the hospital, Young Fu persuades the foreign doctor to see Young Li when he is ill, and he is saved from acute appendicitis. Young Fu wins Tang's respect in various ways, chief among them by confessing his gambling to Fu Be Be, though he could have kept quiet since Tang has loaned him money to cover the loss. Tang himself asks Young Fu to spy on the household of Lu, to solve the mystery of the opium, and the boy discovers that regular drug smugglers have been using the shed for a cache and that Lu and his sons are innocent. During the five years, Young Fu becomes a skilled journeyman coppersmith, and Tang promises to adopt him as a son to inherit the business. Although Young Fu's good fortune is almost too much to believe, it is balanced by hardships and difficulties, many of them of his own making. Most of his good luck comes from questioning the old superstitions and trying new ideas, and the theme clearly is that fortune comes to one who thinks for himself. Young Fu is a lively hero, and the plot moves through a series of interesting complications. The picture of China in transition, contemporary when the book was written, is now of historical interest. Choice; Lewis Carroll; Newbery Winner.

YOUNG HERO OF THE RANGE (Payne*, Stephen, ill. Charles H. Geer, Lantern, 1954), boy's growing up novel set in the western plains in the foothills of the Rocky Mts. about three hundred miles west of Kansas at the end of the open-range era. Resourceful, self-reliant Stan Adams, 12, the son of a nester (homesteader), would like to become a cowboy. His family is poor, and he lacks a cowhorse. When he offers to take care of an abused buckskin, X O, for the V 9 outfit, the wrangler loans him the horse for a year. For the horse's keep and ten dollars a month, most of which he dutifully turns over to his family, Stan takes a job as handyboy during the fall and winter months for Mr. Shell's Pothook ranch. Although kindly, businesslike Mr. Shell keeps the boy busy chopping wood, milking, and feeding the domestic animals, Stan has time to make friends. He especially likes elderly, rangewise Jake Hornsby, who treats him like his nephew, and Ham, the accommodating black cook. Jake helps Stan make a saddle, bridle, blanket, and other items in a cowboy's rig, and often gives him practical advice about everyday life and getting on with people. Although there is friction between Stan and surly Nate Grimshaw, a cowboy no one likes, and his own disobedience and fractious X O sometimes get him into trouble, two main problems confront Stan: hostile Floyd Betcher, the rancher who threatens to drive the Adamses from their farm, and keeping X O at the end of the year. Off and on, Stan has trouble with the Betchers, father and son, who are bullies, and twice X O comes to Stan's rescue by driving them off with flying hooves. During spring roundup Stan and some friends find Mr. Betcher in danger of being swallowed up in a bog. In spite of a strong inclination to let the rancher sink, Stan risks his own life to rescue the man. Mr. Betcher then has a change of heart about the Adams family and compensates Mr. Adams for the damage done the farm by his cattle. About the same time, Mr. Fulton, the owner of the V 9, visits the Pothook to buy some bulls and reclaim X O. Although Stan has won the pony's confidence, the buckskin has a reputation for bucking, and the rancher hopes to train him for rodeos. When a bull goes berserk and charges Mr. Fulton, Stan and X O courageously rescue the rancher. Mr. Fulton offers to give the boy the pony in appreciation. Mr. Adams, however, a fiercely independent man, refuses to let Stan accept the pony. He gives him fifty dollars of the Betcher money with which to buy his cherished pony. Mr. Fulton offers Stan a job as a wrangler for the next fall, and Stan accepts. With a good horse and a good job on a ranch, Stan is much closer to achieving his objective of becoming a cowboy. Except for Stan, who grows in understanding of himself and human nature, characters are stock and flat. The plot is contrived and predictable. Events move fast, dialogue, forced and overly explicit at times, is extensive, tone is often moralistic, and style is pedestrian. The book introduces later elementary and early teen readers to life on a well-run ranch from a young boy's point of view. Spur.

YOUNG LI (*Young Fu of the Upper Yangtze**), apprentice friend of Young Fu, who with his caution and acceptance of tradition acts as a foil for the more adventurous hero. When Li is ill, his parents argue about whether to call in the priests or the doctors, and agree to let the foreign doctor operate only when the coppersmith Tang* intercedes. Later Young Li is worried because his mother insists on arranging a marriage for him, but is relieved when his wife is docile and causes no dissension in the household.

YOUNG MAC OF FORT VANCOUVER (Carr*, Mary Jane, ill. Richard Holberg, Crowell, 1940), historical novel of the year 1832 in the life of a young Scot-Indian boy at Fort Vancouver, on the Columbia River in what is now Washington State. Donald MacDermott, 13, known as Young Mac to distinguish him from his deceased trader father, Big Mac, has left his part-Cree, part-French mother in the Red River settlement of Prince Rupert's Land and traveled with the voyageurs of the York Factory Express who are coming from Hudson Bay to the Pacific, it having been his father's wish that he be sent to Dr. McLoughlin, head of the Fort Vancouver trading post, for schooling. Finding that there is no school at the fort, he hopes to travel on with the voyageurs, especially Henri LeGrand, who has been like a foster father to him, but he learns that his father expected him to spend a year at the fort. He meets the other boys of the fort, all part Indian, including McLoughlin's son, and makes an enemy of Antoine, the bully, by fighting him and getting his job of exercising the fine mare, Bluebelle, and of the old medicine man, Three Gulls, who fears loss of his power over the Indians. When a group of American traders are stranded at the fort, one of them starts a school, and Young Mac shows great promise as a scholar. When Bluebelle trips and throws him, he is almost attacked by wolves, which the horse fights off, and is rescued by an Indian who takes the unconscious boy to Three Gull's medicine lodge. The old man thinks he is the prophesied boy sent to learn his medicine lore, dyes his hair and face dark, but succumbs to the plague that has been killing the Indians, and Young Mac is bound and taken by other Indians who blame him for Three Gull's death. He is rescued by Yellow Bird, a squaw he has befriended, and returns to the fort to find it has been assumed that he ran away because of a story Antoine has concocted, hoping to ride Bluebelle in a big race instead of Young Mac. Struck by the plague, Young Mac is unable to ride and, having made friends with Antoine, gets the other boy permission to ride the race, which he wins. Young Mac decides to opt for the white man's life and is given a letter written by his father, which tells of an estranged grandfather living in Quebec. In a brief coda he comes to Quebec after ten years of study in Edinburgh to meet his grandfather and finds there Mia, a girl he rescued when she was a slave of some Pacific Coast Indians, who has been studying in a convent in Quebec and has effected the reunion. Although Young Mac chooses the white man's life, the book shows considerable respect for the Indian culture; the less palatable elements of Indian life—ignorance, slavery, lack of sanitation—are not overlooked, however. Such actual characters as McLoughlin are introduced throughout, but while Young Mac is a believable boy, characterization is not as strong as action and setting. Newbery Honor.

Z

ZHIKAG (*Michel's Island**). Ottawa medicine man shunned by everyone. He has been a bitter, frightened man since an old sorceress pronounced a doom upon him. He lives in a cave on Mackinac near the great chasm called the Crack. He is bound by old beliefs and serves as a foil for Panace*, the herb doctor who is Christian. Panace tells Michel that the spell will be lifted when Zhikag brings himself to perform an unselfish act. Zhikag steals the standish (writing box) belonging to M. Jarnac* in order to place a spell on Jarnac and runs off with Rufin, one of the Jarnac slaves. Michel finds the box in Zhikag's cave, and later M. Jarnac forgives Rufin and frees him. After Zhikag rescues Jacquence*, who falls from the Arch while the boys are playing their Gitche Manitou game there, the old medicine man becomes a different person, because he feels the curse has been lifted.

ZUCKERMAN'S FARM (*Charlotte's Web**), the place where Wilbur*, the runt pig, grows up. He lives in the basement of the barn, described by E. B. White* in vivid, sensory detail: "It smelled of hay and it smelled of manure. It smelled of the perspiration of tired horses and the wonderful sweet breath of patient cows. It often has a sort of peaceful smell—as though nothing bad could happen ever again in the world." Lurvy, the hired man, slops him here, his young mistress, Fern*, visits him, and his friend, Charlotte*, the spider, saves his life by spinning words in her web.

INDEX

Names and titles in ALL CAPITAL LETTERS refer to the actual entries of the dictionary, and page numbers in *italics* refer to the location of the actual entries of the dictionary.

About the Authors

Alethea K. Helbig is Professor of English Language and Literature at Eastern Michigan University. She has published articles in *Children's Literature, Children's Literature Association Quarterly, The Alan Review, American Women Writers*, and *Writers for Children*. She has compiled *Straight on Till Morning: Poems of the Imaginary World* and *Dusk to Dawn: Poems of Night* (with Agnes Perkins). She is Past-President of the Children's Literature Association (International).

Agnes Regan Perkins is Professor of English Language and Literature at Eastern Michigan University. Her articles have appeared in *A Tolkien Compass, Unicorn, Children's Literature, Children's Literature Association Quarterly*, and *Writers for Children*. In addition she is co-compiler of *New Coasts and Strange Harbors: Discovering Poems*.